WORSHIP MUSIC: A CONCISE DICTIONARY

Worship Music

A Concise Dictionary

Edward Foley, Capuchin

Editor

Mark Bangert
Melva Wilson Costen
Carol Doran
Mark Kligman
David Petras
Rebecca Slough

Consultants

A Michael Glazier Book
THE LITURGICAL PRESS
Collegeville, Minnesota

A Michael Glazier book published by The Liturgical Press

Cover design by Ann Blattner

| 1 | 2 | 3 | 4 | 5 | 6 | 7 | 8 |

Library of Congress Cataloging-in-Publication Data

Worship music : a concise dictionary / Edward Foley, editor ; Mark Bangert . . . [et al.], consultants.
    p. cm.
    Includes bibliographical references.
    ISBN 0-8146-5889-X
    1. Church music—Dictionaries. 2. Synagogue music—Dictionaries. I. Foley, Edward. II. Bangert, Mark Paul.

ML102.C5 W67 2000
781.7'003—dc21
99-054363

To the memory of
S. Theophane Hytrek, S.S.S.F.

mentor
artist
and pastoral musician *par excellence*

Magnificat anima mea Domine!

Contents

Introduction

This dictionary has been produced through the combined effort of many people from diverse faith traditions who practice, teach and study the music of worship. It is designed for those who wish to understand and appreciate something of the breadth and richness of this music, especially in its North American context. While there is care for and attention to the broad musical and liturgical traditions which have shaped contemporary practice, the special focus of this dictionary is the worship music of English-speaking North America, which is often under emphasized or ignored in other musical reference works.

Worship Music pays particular attention to the religious and ritual aspects of music. This is not a general music dictionary, and thus many common musical terms which do not have an explicit religious or ritual reference (e.g., pitch) are not included. Instead, this volume provides entries on various musical topics which are important to the worship of one or more of the faith traditions represented here (e.g., hymnody). It also provides entries on other aspects of worship which have some musical reference or implication (e.g., the *bimah*). The dictionary further contains an ample number of articles on influential composers, performers and scholars who have shaped the music of various faith traditions. Many historical figures are included, but with particular emphasis on their liturgical, religious or sacred works. Thus, while there is an entry on Beethoven, this monumental figure in Western music has been assigned a relatively short article, given that only a small amount of his work was overtly liturgical, religious or sacred. Isaac Watts, on the other hand, who is often omitted from other musical reference works, has been assigned a major entry.

From the outset, this project has been an ecumenical and interfaith venture. Jewish and Christian authors from Canada and the United States have together shaped the dictionary, first by suggesting what entries should be included and how extensive those entries should be, and then by providing the articles. Some readers will undoubtedly be surprised by the results of this "bottom-up" approach and by what the various collaborators have underscored as more or less significant from the viewpoint of their faith traditions. This distinctiveness in perspective and emphasis has been a rich part of the collaboration which has shaped this project, and is a singular contribution of *Worship Music*.

The project was first suggested by Virgil Funk, whose interest and support has not waned over the eight years it has taken to bring this book to press. The Music Study Group of the North American Academy of Liturgy has served in an advisory role on the project since its inception. Besides their many useful suggestions, this group was especially helpful in generating the word list and many members of that group became contributors to the dictionary. Special thanks are in order for the area consultants: Mark Bangert, Melva Costen, Carol Doran, Mark Kligman, David Petras and Rebecca Slough. Their wisdom and enormous productivity permeate virtually every page of this work. Finally, I wish to thank the staff of The Liturgical Press for their support of this project through its various stages of development and production.

In spite of the inspiring collaboration which has marked this venture, omissions and errors undoubtedly remain. It is my hope that as this dictionary is used and critiqued, these will be brought to the attention of the editor, so that they may be corrected in future editions. Providing a reference work on worship music across a broad ecumenical and interfaith spectrum that respects the polyphonic voices emanating from each tradition is a precarious undertaking. It also has been an enlightening and inspiring one. It is hoped that the energy, respect and profound commitment to the music of worship which produced this volume will translate into a faithful guide for those who open these pages.

Edward Foley, Capuchin

General Abbreviations

<>	alternate spelling of a word or alternate name	CA	California
		CE	Common Era
()	seldom used portion of a name	chp, chps	chapter, chapters
		Chr	Book of Chronicles
[]	linguistic information or editorial addition	Co	County
		CO	Colorado
		CT	Connecticut
adj	adjective	*d*	died
AK	Alaska	D	*Deutsch*
AL	Alabama	Dan	Book of Daniel
AME	African Methodist Episcopal	DC	District of Columbia
AMEC	African Methodist Episcopal Church	DE	Delaware
		Deut	Book of Deuteronomy
AMEZ	African Methodist Episcopal Zion	DMA	doctor of musical arts
		E	East, Eastern
AR	Arkansas	ed., eds.	editor, editors
AZ	Arizona	*EJ*	*Encyclopaedia Judaica,* Ed. Cecil Roth and Geoffrey Wigoder. 16 vols. Jerusalem: Keter Publishing House, 1972
b	born		
bapt	baptized		
BBC	British Broadcasting Company		
BCE	before the Common Era	Ex	Book of Exodus
BCP	Book of Common Prayer	Ez	Book of Ezekiel
Bibl	Bibliography	*fl*	flourished
BVM	Blessed Virgin Mary	FL	Florida
BWV	*Bach-Werke-Verzeichnis* [German, "Catalog of Bach's Works"]	GA	Georgia
		Gen	Book of Genesis
		Heb	Book of Hebrews
c	*circa* [Latin, "about"]	Hob	Anthony Hoboken (*d* 1983), compiler of authoritative
C	central		

	catalogue of the works by J. Haydn		Ed. Stanley Sadie. 20 vols. New York: W. W. Norton, 1980.
HI	Hawaii		
IA	Iowa	NH	New Hampshire
ID	Idaho	NJ	New Jersey
IL	Illinois	NM	New Mexico
IN	Indiana	Num	Book of Numbers
Is	Book of Isaiah	NV	Nevada
JAMS	*Journal of the American Musicological Society*	NY	New York
		OCP	*Orientalia Christiana Periodica*
K	Ludwig von Köchel (*d* 1877), cataloguer of Mozart's music, whose listing has been updated several times.	OH	Ohio
		OK	Oklahoma
		ON	Ontario
		op.	opus
KS	Kansas	OR	Oregon
KY	Kentucky	PA	Pennsylvania
LA	Louisiana	Ph.D.	doctor of philosophy
Lev	Book of Leviticus	pl.	plural
LXX	Greek Septuagint	Ps, Pss	psalm, psalms
MA	Massachusetts	RC	Roman Catholic, Roman Catholicism
Macc	Book of Maccabees		
Matt	gospel of Matthew	rev.	revised
MD	Maryland	RI	Rhode Island
ME	Maine	sing.	singular
MI	Michigan	S	South, Southern
Mk	gospel of Mark	Sam	book of Samuel
MN	Minnesota	SC	South Carolina
MO	Missouri	SD	South Dakota
MQ	*Musical Quarterly*	TN	Tennessee
MS	Mississippi	TX	Texas
MT	Montana	UMC	United Methodist Church
N	North, Northern	US	United States of America
n., nn.	number, numbers	UT	Utah
NC	North Carolina	VA	Virginia
ND	North Dakota	VI	Virgin Islands
NE	Nebraska	vol., vols.	volume, volumes
NGDAM	*The New Grove Dictionary of American Music.* Ed. H. Wiley Hitchcock and Stanley Sadie. 4 vols. London: Macmillan Press, 1986.	VT	Vermont
		W	West, Western
		WA	Washington
		WI	Wisconsin
		WV	West Virginia
NGDMM	*The New Grove Dictionary of Music and Musicians.*	WY	Wyoming

Abbreviations of Contributors

ACL	Austin C. Lovelace	JKW	J. Kevin Waters
ADC	Andrew D. Ciferni	JLB	James L. Brauer
AJB	Andrew J. Bernard	JMH	Joan M. Halmo
AJL	Alan J. Lewis	JMJ	J. Michael Joncas
AWR	Anthony W. Ruff	JMT	J. Michael Thompson
BES	Benjie Ellen Schiller	JPM	Joseph P. Metzinger
BEW	Benedict Weisser	JWK	James W. Kosnik
CAD	Carol A. Doran	KRH	Kenneth R. Hull
CFS	Carl F. Schalk	LFH	Lawrence F. Heiman
CJK	Columba J. Kelly	LJC	Linda J. Clark
CLV	Catherine L. Vincie	LMT	Lynn M. Trapp
CRY	Carlton R. Young	MAK	Martha Ann Kirk
CSP	Charles S. Pottie	MDJ	Martin D. Jean
DCI	David Clark Isele	MEC	Michael E. Connolly
DMP	David M. Petras	MEM	Mary E. McGann
DMR	Daniel M. Rosenfeld	MFM	Michael F. Moody
DWM	David W. Music	MFR	Mary Frances Reza
EBF	Edward B. Foley	MJG	Michael J. Gilligan
FCQ	Frank C. Quinn	MJK	Marie J. Kremer
FJM	Fred J. Moleck	MLK	Mark L. Kligman
FKG	Fred K. Graham	MPB	Mark P. Bangert
GET	Gordon E. Truitt	MSD	Michael S. Driscoll
HCB	Horace Clarence Boyer	MWC	Melva Wilson Costen
IAG	Israel A. Goldstein	NDM	Nathan D. Mitchell
ISK	Ilene S. Keys	PAB	P. Alan Barthel
JBF	John B. Foley	PAJ	Paul A. Jacobson
JBW	John B. Weaver	PHW	Paul H. Westermeyer
JDW	John D. Witvliet	PKG	Philip K. Gehring
JKL	John K. Leonard	RAD	Regis A. Duffy

RAL	Robin A. Leaver	SDC	Sheila D. Case
RDH	Robert D. Hawkins	SIW	Steven I. Weiss
RGD	Rosemary G. Dubowchik	SJW	Steven and Jennifer Weiss
RJB	Robert J. Batastini	VAC	Virginia A. Cross
RJS	Rebecca J. Slough	VAL	Vincent A. Lenti
RKW	Robin Knowles Wallace	VCF	Virgil C. Funk
RTR	R. Todd Ridder	VEG	Victor E. Gebauer

Contributors

Bangert, Mark P.   Lutheran School of Theology at Chicago, Chicago, IL

Barthel, P. Alan.   Emmanuel College, Toronto School of Theology, Toronto, ON

Batastini, Robert J.   GIA Publications, Chicago, IL

Bernard, Andrew.   Temple Beth El, Charlotte, NC

Boyer, Horace Clarence.   University of Massachusetts at Amherst, Amherst, MA

Brauer, James L.   Concordia Seminary, St. Louis, MO

Case, Sheila.   The Suburban Temple, Wantagh, NY

Ciferni, Andrew D.   Daylesford Abbey, Paoli, PA

Clark, Linda.   Boston University, Boston, MA

Connolly, Michael.   The University of Portland, Portland, OR

Costen, Melva Wilson.   Interdenominational Theological Center, Atlanta, GA

Cross, Virginia A.   Western Baptist College, Salem, OR

Doran, Carol A.   Bexley Hall Seminary, Rochester, NY

Driscoll, Michael S.   The University of Notre Dame, Notre Dame, IN

Dubowchik, Rosemary G.   Southern Connecticut State University, New Haven, CT

Duffy, Regis A.   St. Bonaventure University, St. Bonaventure, NY

Foley, Edward.   Catholic Theological Union, Chicago, IL

Foley, John B.   St. Louis University, St. Louis, MO

Funk, Virgil C.   National Association of Pastoral Musicians, Washington, DC

Gebauer, Victor E.   Lutheran Music Program, Minneapolis, MN

Gehring, Philip K.   Valparaiso University (Emeritus), Valparaiso, IN

Gilligan, Michael J.   American Catholic Press, South Holland, IL

Goldstein, Israel.   Hebrew Union College-Jewish Institute of Religion, New York, NY

Graham, Fred Kimball.   United Church of Canada, Etobicoke, ON

Halmo, Joan M.   University of Saskatchewan, Saskatoon, SK

Hawkins, Robert D.   Lutheran Theological Southern Seminary, Columbia, SC

Heiman, Lawrence.   St. Joseph's College, Rensselaer, IN

Hull, Kenneth R.   Conrad Grebel College, Waterloo, ON

Isele, David Clark.   The University of Tampa, Tampa, FL

Jacobson, Paul A.   Episcopal Church of St. John the Evangelist, San Francisco, CA

Jean, Martin D.   Yale University, New Haven, CT

Joncas, J. Michael.   University of St. Thomas, St. Paul, MN

Kelly, Columba J.   St. Meinrad Archabbey, St. Meinrad, IN

Keys, Ilene.   Temple Sinai, Oakland, CA

Kirk, Martha Ann.   University of the Incarnate Word, San Antonio, TX

Kligman, Mark L.   Hebrew Union College-Jewish Institute of Religion, New York, NY

Kosnik, James W.   Old Dominion University, Norfolk, VA

Kremer, Marie J.   St. Monica Church, St. Louis, MO

Leaver, Robin A.   Westminster Choir College, Princeton, NJ

Lenti, Vincent A.   Eastman School of Music, Rochester, NY

Leonard, John K.   Edgewood College, Madison, WI

Lewis, Alan J.   Calvary Episcopal Church, Pittsburgh, PA

Lovelace, Austin C.   Wellshire Presbyterian Church (Emeritus), Denver, CO

McGann, Mary E.   The Franciscan School of Theology, Berkeley, CA

Metzinger, Joseph P.   Gesu Church, University Heights, OH

Mitchell, Nathan D.   The University of Notre Dame, Notre Dame, IN

Moleck, Fred.   Mount St. Peter's Church, New Kensington, PA

Moody, Michael F.   The Church of Jesus Christ of Latter-Day Saints, Salt Lake City, UT

Music, David W.   Southwestern Baptist Theological Seminary, Fort Worth, TX

Petras, David M.   Byzantine Catholic Seminary, Pittsburgh, PA

Pottie, Charles S.   Gregorian University, Rome, Italy

Quinn, Frank.   Aquinas Institute, St. Louis, MO

Reza, Mary Frances.   Archdiocese of Santa Fe, Albuquerque, NM

Ridder, R. Todd.   The University of Dayton, Dayton, OH

Rosenfeld, Daniel.   Monmouth Reform Temple, Tinton Falls, NJ

Ruff, Anthony.   St. John's University, Collegeville, MN

Schalk, Carl.   Concordia University, River Forest, IL

Schiller, Benjie.   Hebrew Union College-Jewish Institute of Religion, New York, NY

Slough, Rebecca.   Associated Mennonite Biblical Seminary, Elkart, IN

Thompson, J. Michael.   Schola Cantorum of St. Peter the Apostle, Chicago, IL

Trapp, Lynn M.   St. Olaf's Church, Minneapolis, MN

Truitt, Gordon E.   National Association of Pastoral Musicians, Washington, DC

Vincie, Catherine L.   Aquinas Institute, St. Louis, MO

Wallace, Robin Knowles.   Methodist Theological School in Ohio, Delaware, OH

Waters, J. Kevin.   Gonzaga University, Spokane, WA

Weaver, John B.   Madison Avenue Presbyterian Church, New York, NY

Weiss, Jennifer.   Temple Kol Emeth, Marietta, GA

Weiss, Steven.   Temple Kol Emeth, Marietta, GA

Westermeyer, Paul.   Luther Seminary, St. Paul, MN

Witvliet, John D.   Calvin College, Grand Rapids, MI

Young, Carlton R.   Emory University, Atlanta, GA

Guide to the Edition

Bibliography: From 1 to 3 bibliographic references are provided for what were deemed to be the more important entries. These references ordinarily cite the best available reference(s) in English.

Capitalization: Words are capitalized if they refer to some faith tradition's understanding of God (e.g., Trinity), a proper name (e.g., Notre Dame Cathedral), a proper title (e.g., the *B-minor Mass* by J. S. Bach), or the opening word of a proper text or prayer (e.g., *Ledor vador*). Common liturgical terms which do not fall under these categories are not capitalized, e.g., benediction, mass or *seder*.

Cross-references: Extensive cross-referencing has been employed to keep the articles as concise as possible. Cross-references are noted by an asterisk before the cross-reference entry, e.g., *Chapel Royal. Asterisks are placed before that part of a name under which the entry is to be found alphabetically, e.g., liturgical *year indicates that the entry is found under "year." A term is cross-referenced only once an article, no matter how many times it may be further repeated in that entry.

Foreign words: Foreign words are ordinarily italicized, including elements of worship, e.g., *Magnificat*. One exception to this rule is the proper name of an institution, e.g., Hochschule für Musik. English translations are usually provided either within the article in which the term occurs, or in a cross-referenced article on the term itself.

Names: Entries on individuals are ordinarily listed according to the surname, followed by the first and middle names. An individual with no surname is listed according to the first name, often followed by the place with which one is associated, e.g., Thomas Aquinas. Seldom used names for an individual are placed in parentheses, e.g., Ellington, Duke (Edward Kennedy). Titles are placed after a name, e.g., Augustine of Hippo, St. Alternate spellings are included in angled brackets, e.g., Pérotin <Perotinus Magnus, Magister Perotinus>.

Place-names: Where possible, city names are provided to designate a place. Where the location of the city could be in doubt, a state, region or country is added, e.g., Lechner, Leonhard (*b* Adige Valley, S Tyrol 1553?; *d* Stuttgart 1606).

Psalmody: Psalms are numbered according to the Hebrew, not the Greek or Vulgate versions of the Bible, i.e., Pss 1–9 and 149–150 are the same for all; from Pss 10–148 the numbering of the Hebrew Bible is one ahead of the Greek and Vulgate, which join Pss 9 and 10, and Pss 114 and 115, but divide both Ps 116 and Ps 147 into 2.

A

AAM. See *Association of Anglican Musicians.

Abbatini, Antonio Maria (*b* Città di Castello 1609–10; *d* there *c* 1679). Composer. *Maestro di cappella* St. John Lateran (1626–28), St. Mary Major (1640–46, 49–57, 72–77) and elsewhere. His works (some in *polychoral style) include *masses, *psalms, *antiphons and *motets. MJK

Abelard <Abaelardus, Abailard>, **Peter** (*b* Le Pallet 1079; *d* St-Marcel 1142). Philosopher and theologian. He wrote six biblical *planctus* (Latin, "lament") in lai form and compiled a collection of over 140 *hymns for the nuns of Le Paraclet. JMJ

Abendmusik [German]. "Evening music." Popular concerts (1646–1810) on the 5 Sundays between mid-November and *Christmas of mostly dramatic religious music at St. Mary's (Lutheran) Church in Lübeck. They were organized and conducted by *Buxtehude from at least 1673 until his death. MPB

Abraham and Isaac. (1) *Britten's Canticle II (op. 51, 1952), scored for male alto (Isaac), *tenor (Abraham) and piano. The text is from a medieval (Chester) *miracle play based on Gen 22.

(2) A sacred ballad by *Stravinsky (1962–63) for baritone and chamber orchestra, with a Hebrew text, dedicated to the people of Israel. AJL

Abyssinian Baptist Church worship music. An historic, Harlem based congregation founded in 1808 with a nationally recognized music program. With seven *choirs, its music ranges from *Handel's *Messiah* to *Crouch's *gospel music. Featuring paid section leaders, the choirs have performed with the New York Philharmonic. The congregation, accompanied by pipe *organ, sings from the *New National Baptist Hymnal* (1977). HCB

A cappella [Italian]. "In the chapel style." Choral music sung unaccompanied. The term often refers to music in the style of *Palestrina. During the *Renaissance, however, *instruments were commonly employed in church to double vocal parts. EBF

ACC. See *American Conference of Cantors.

Accentus [Latin]. "Accent." A term used since the 16th century to refer to the simple *plainsong recitation of a text in the *liturgy (ordinarily by a priest) on very few notes; as opposed to *concentus. LJC

Acclamation. A brief formula shouted or sung by a group. Common to many rituals across a broad range of traditions, acclamations frequently occurred in ancient Jewish (*amen, *halleluyah) and Christian (*hosanna, maranatha) worship. Currently in Christian *liturgy the term refers to particular congregational responses such as the *alleluia before the *gospel (*gospel acclamation) or the response after the *institution narrative (*memorial acclamation). EBF

Actus tragicus [Latin]. "Tragic act, death." A designation given to J. S. *Bach's *cantata *Gottes Zeit ist die allerbeste Zeit* (BWV 106, *c* 1707), likely a musical setting of a 17th-century manual on the art of dying. MPB

Adam de la Halle <Adan le Bossu, "Hunchback"> (*b* Arras 1245–50; *d* Naples 1285–88). The last and most advanced trouvère poet and composer. He was active in Paris and Italy, composing works, both *monophonic and *polyphonic, in virtually all genres, especially *chansons, rondeaux* and *motets. LFH

Adam of St. Victor (*b* Britain? *c* 1110; *d* Paris 1180). *Precentor of Notre Dame in Paris, he held a prebend at St. Victor in

Paris from 1133. He authored *c* 45 *sequences characterized by varying meters, extensive word-play, alliteration and allegorical use of the Hebrew Bible. JMJ

Addir Bimluchah <*Bimlukkah*> [Hebrew]. "Mighty in Kingship." A *hymn sung at the end of the *Pesach *seder*. The text consists of 8 *verses and a *chorus; each verse enumerates various attributes of God. It was first incorporated into the *haggadah* in the German tradition in the 13th century. MLK

Addir Hu [Hebrew]. "Mighty is He." A *hymn sung at the end of the *Pesach *seder*. The text implores God to rebuild the Temple. It has appeared in printed texts of the *haggadah* since the 16th century. It is more prominent in *Ashkenazic communities than *Sephardic. The popular Ashkenazic melody is incorporated into the singing of the *Hallel and *Mi Chamochah* on *Pesach*. MLK

Adeste fideles [Latin]. "[O] Come [all you] faithful." *Christmas *hymn. The tune and Latin text are probably by John Francis Wade (*d* 1786). It became popular when it was sung in the RC chapel of the Portuguese embassy in London. AWR

Adler, Samuel (Hans) (*b* Mannheim 1928). Teacher, composer and arranger of Jewish *liturgical music specifically for *Reform Judaism. He served on music faculties at Eastman and Juilliard. Adler edited a celebrated 2-volume collection of music for the *High Holidays, *Yamim Noraim* (1972). DMR

Adonai malach [Hebrew] "God reigns." (1) The *incipit* of Pss 93 and 97, which are recited on Friday evenings as part of *kabbalat Shabbat* in the *Adonai malach* *mode (though many Ashkenazic congregations chant Ps 93 in the *magein avot* mode). Ps 93 is also part of the preliminary section of *Sabbath *shacharit,* and is the special Friday psalm recited near the conclusion of Friday evening *kabbalat Shabbat.*

(2) A family of *Jewish prayer modes that takes its name from the opening phrase of Ps 93. This mode is used on Sabbath evening and morning, and on the *High Holidays. The pitches of this mode are derived from conjunct tetrachords, each containing identical intervals of a whole step + a whole step + a half step. This produces a major-sounding scale with flatted 7th and 10th scale degrees.

Bibl: G. Ephros, *The Cantorial Anthology,* vol. 4: *Shabbat* (New York, 1976) 71–6.   AJB-IAG

Adon olam [Hebrew.]. "Lord of the world." A popular liturgical poem often sung to conclude *Sabbath and festival *services. This *hymn praises the one eternal God in whose sovereignty all may trust and lack fear. Of unknown authorship it is sometimes attributed to the 11th-century poet Simon Ibn Gabirol; it first appeared in the 14th-century German *liturgy, spreading to Jewish communities worldwide. Though many composers (e.g., *Gerovitch) have set the text for congregational singing, others (e.g., *Rossi, *Bloch, *Milhaud) composed more elaborate choral settings.   BES

Adoro te devote [Latin]. "I adore you devoutly." A eucharistic *hymn in *mode 5. The text is ascribed to *Thomas Aquinas, and is often associated with *benediction.   MSD

Advent. The opening season of the Christian liturgical *year (approximately 4 weeks in the W, longer in the E) preceding *Christmas; characterized as a period of joyful expectation. It was established in the W by the 6th century. Advent acquired an increased eschatological and penitential focus in the *Middle Ages. Musically it is marked by the elimination of the *Gloria in excelsis* and the inclusion of proper *antiphons (e.g., *O antiphons, *Alma Redemptoris), and traditional *hymns or *chorales (e.g., C. *Wesley's "Come thou long-expected Jesus" and *WACHET AUF).   MJG

Aeolian-Skinner Organ Co. See *Skinner, E. M.

Aeoline [from Greek *Aiolus,* the Greek god of the winds]. (1) A small-scaled open metal pipe of 8-foot pitch providing the softest pipe *organ string tone, supposedly imitating the Aeolian harp.

(2) A reed *keyboard *instrument of the early 19th century, antecedent of the *harmonium.   ACL

Aevia <aeuia>. An abbreviation for *alleluia (composed of its vowels) found in *chant manuscripts and books. The placement of the vowels under the music indicate where the syllables of alleluia are to be sung.   JPM

African American Baptist worship music. The worship music of African American Baptists is foundational to the birth and perpetuation of African American music traditions. The repertoire parallels that of white Baptists, except in the frequent use of *spirituals, African American *gospel music, innovative reshaping of *hymns to meet the needs of oppressed people, a continuation of the *lining out tradition, and spontaneous outbursts of corporate singing during worship. A "devotional period," filled with *a cappella* singing and testimonies by the congregation was created historically out of the need to wait for people to gather. This continues in some churches as a time for spiritual renewal and praise. The spectrum of worship and music styles is extensive, ranging from congregational involvement in oral music traditions to multiple *choir leadership with intricate choral repertories. *Instruments include piano, *organ (pipe and *electronic) and, in some settings, percussion, strings and brass instruments. See *Baptist worship music.   MWC

African drums. The most widely used sub-Saharan percussive *instruments, employed for the production of simple to intricate *polyphonic sounds and rhythms. They are also used to transmit verbal messages, create atmosphere for religious and civic ceremonies, and accompany the movement of people. They vary in structure, shape, size and manner of sound production. Geographical locations and environments are determinative in drum production. The 2 main styles are 1) membranophones, which produce sound through a vibrating membrane, and 2) idiophones, which use the instrument's own body to produce sound.   MWC

A(frican) M(ethodist) E(piscopal) <AME> Publishing House. Incorporated in 1818, this Nashville firm prepares and supplies the eight million members of the *AME Church with *tracts, disciplines, Sunday school materials and *hymnals, including the *AME Church Bicentennial Hymnal* (1984).   HCB

A(frican) M(ethodist) E(piscopal) <AME> worship music. The AME Church, founded in 1787 and incorporated in 1816, has the longest published hymnological history of any African American Protestant denomination. R. *Allen published its first *hymnal, *A Collection of Spiritual Songs and Hymns, Selected From Various Authors* (1801), containing 54 *hymn texts; a revised, enlarged edition (1801) had 64 texts. An official hymnal (1818) of the newly incorporated denomination, compiled by Allen, D. Coker and J. Champion, contained 314 hymns. Other editions appeared in 1837, 1876, 1892, 1898 (the first denominational hymnal in the US with music), 1941, 1954 and 1984.

The *AMEC Bicentennial Hymnal* (1984) includes a variety of AME worship music. It attends to African, African American and Afro-Caribbean songs in general and AME worship music in particular, issues of ecumenism, provides texts by AME bishops, arrangements by African American musicians, and hymns of C. *Wesley. It embodies the AMEC reputation as "singing African American Methodists." This worship book with alternative Sunday *services also includes optional services of *holy communion (with service music), other rituals of the church, and a 3-year *lectionary. Performance practices are marked by largely congregational singing, the use of multiple *choirs with varied repertoires of hymns, *anthems, *gospel songs and *spirituals. Accompaniment is with *organ and piano, with the recent addition of percussion.

Bibl: J. Spencer, *Black Hymnody* (Knoxville, 1992), 3–24.   MWC

A(frican) M(ethodist) E(piscopal) Zion <AME Zion, AMEZ> Publishing House.

A denominational press, established in 1896, which publishes Sunday school materials, Bible study guides, tracts and supplemental religious material for teenagers. *Hymnals that incorporate Wesleyan *hymns, Negro *spirituals and *gospel music account for most sales. The present hymnal is the *AMEZ Bicentennial Hymnal* (1996).   HCB

A(frican) M(ethodist) E(piscopal) Zion <AME Zion, AMEZ> worship music. The AMEZ Church had its origins in the late 18th-century discriminatory practices of members of the Euro-American controlled John Street Methodist Episcopal Church in New York. Separate worship was held from 1795; the 1st new church was built in 1800; the church was officially organized in 1820. AMEZ hymnological history extends from the publication of *Hymns for the use of the African Methodist Episcopal Zion Church* (1839) to *The AME Zion Hymnal* (1996). Five publications between these *hymnals (1858, 1872, 1892, 1909 and 1957) were similar to those of the Methodist Episcopal Church, though the 1892 *hymnal included hymns by AMEZ ministers. The 1996 hymnal addresses themes of adoration and praise, the Trinity, church and Christian life, with additional sections on the Christian *year, African American and Zion Methodist heritage, ancient *canticles and hymns and rituals of the church. Performance practices are marked by largely congregational singing, the use of multiple *choirs with varied repertoires of hymns, *anthems, *gospel songs and *spirituals. Accompaniment is with *organ and piano, with the recent addition of percussion.
   Bibl: J. Spencer, *Black Hymnody* (Knoxville, 1992), 25–43.   MWC

Agende [German]. A liturgical *book containing the outlines, formularies and rubrics for public worship in the German Protestant (Evangelical) Church, primarily for use by the clergy. Many of these contain music.   JDW

Agnus Dei [Latin]. "Lamb of God." The fifth element in the *ordinary of the mass; now considered the *fraction litany accompanying the fraction rite of the *mass. The text is derived from John 1:29. It was introduced into the Roman rite in the late 7th century. Originally it was repeated until all the bread was broken and wine poured for *communion, with the congregation singing at least the final phrase of each petition, *miserere nobis* ("have mercy on us"). Later it was sung by the *schola with only 3 petitions: the final phrase of the third petition changed to *dona nobis pacem* ("grant us peace"). In a *Requiem,* the first 2 petitions are *dona eis requiem* ("grant them rest"); the final petition is *dona eis requiem sempiternam* ("grant them rest everlasting"). In RC reforms after *Vatican II, the *Agnus Dei* was reinstated as an expandable *litany to cover the fraction rite.
   Bibl: R. Crocker, "Agnus Dei," *NGDMM* I:157–58.   GET

AGO. See *American Guild of Organists.

Agostini, Paolo (*b* Vallerano *c* 1583; *d* Rome 1629). Composer and organist. He studied with *Nanino. He served as organist and *maestro di cappella* in Vallerano, then Rome at S. Maria in Trastevere and St. Peter's (from 1626). His *psalms, *Magnificats*, *antiphons, *masses and other works display contrapuntal ingenuity; some were written for as many as 48 voices.   MJK

Agricola, Alexander (*b* Flanders *c* 1446; *d* Valladolid 1506). Composer and singer. He served extensively in Italy, Burgundy and Spain. His compositions in complex, contrapuntal style include *chansons*, 8 *masses, *c* 25 *motets, *hymns and *Magnificat*s.   LFH

Ahavah rabbah [Hebrew]. "With great love." A family of *Jewish prayer modes that takes its name from the first words of the *blessing immediately before the *Shema* in *shacharit*. Commonly considered the most "Jewish sounding" modal family, its salient musical feature is an augmented 2nd between the 2nd and 3rd scale degrees. It is used on *Sabbath morning, for weekday *shacharit* and *ma'ariv*.   AJB

Ahavat olam [Hebrew]. "Everlasting love." The prayer preceding the *Shema* in all *ma'ariv* *services, recalling that God gave the Torah because of the love between God and the Jewish people. A popular *folk melody sung at *Sabbath services and an elaborate setting for *cantor, *choir and *organ by *Helfman are among this text's many settings.   BES

Ahle, Johann Rudolf (*b* Mühlhausen 1625; *d* there 1673). Organist and prolific composer of *sacred music in a popular style, especially *arias and *hymn tunes, notably LIEBSTER JESU, WIR SIND HIER. RAL

Aichinger, Gregor (*b* Regensburg 1564–65; *d* Augsburg 1628). Composer, organist and RC priest. He ranks with *Hassler among the most important, prolific 17th-century *sacred music composers in S Germany with *c* 30 published collections, mostly Latin vocal works. He maintained a lifelong association with the prominent Fugger family, who sponsored his early study with G. *Gabrieli.   RJB

Ainoi [Greek; Slavonic *chvalitny*]. "The Praises." A series of 8, 6 or 4 *stichera* intercalated between the last 6 or 4 *verses of the Psalms of Praise (Pss 148–50) sung towards the end of Byzantine *orthros*. For 8 *ainoi*, extra *psalm verses are added to the Psalms of Praise (e.g., for Sunday, Pss 10:12 and 9:2). *Ainoi* only appear on Sundays and feasts, not in daily *orthros*.   DMP

Ainsworth Psalter. Published in Amsterdam in 1612 by Henry Ainsworth (*d c* 1623), *The Book of Psalmes: Englished both in Prose and Metre* contained 39 tunes. Brought by the Pilgrims in 1620, it was the principal *psalter in America prior to publication of the *Bay Psalm Book*.   PAB

Aitesis [Greek; Slavonic *ekteniya*]. "Request." A *litany in the Byzantine *divine office consisting of 2 petitions with the *response "Lord, have mercy," 6 petitions with the response "Grant it, O Lord," and a commendation to Christ with the Mother of God and all the saints. It was the concluding litany for the *office. Also called the "Angel of Peace" litany from its characteristic fourth petition, it was usually sung by the deacon.   DMP

Akathistos [Greek; Slavonic *akathist*]. "[Hymn sung] standing." A poetic, devotional Byzantine *office during which the congregation was expected to stand. Though its origins are earlier, the genre was particularly developed by St. *Romanos. It ordinarily consists of 24 *kontakia and *oikoi, the original melodies of which are lost and are now sung according to the system of *octoechos. The final lines of the kontakia and oikoi are sung by the congregation as a *refrain. Included in the office are *hymns to the Lord, the Mother of God, the saints and even hymns for particular occasions, e.g., penance or *communion. The most well known akathistos is to the Mother of God, sung during *orthros of the Fifth Saturday of *Lent (thus, called "Akathistos Saturday").

Bibl: E. Wellesz, "The 'Akathistos'," Dumbarton Oaks Papers 9–10 (1956) 141–74; English trans. by Mother Mary and K. Ware in The Lenten Triodion (London-Boston, 1978) 422–37. DMP

Akdamut [Hebrew]. "In introduction." A double alphabetical acrostic 92-line *piyyut. In the *Ashkenazic tradition, it is chanted on *Shavuot morning preceding the *Torah reading. The author's name is indicated halfway through the *hymn by a second acrostic, spelling out "Rabbi Meir the Son of Isaac" (11th century). The text promises Israel's ultimate bliss because of its love for God and Torah. A notable poetic device is each line ending with the syllable "-ta". In contemporary practice, leader and congregation sing 2-line *stanzas responsively to a popular melody in the *Adonai malach *mode. This melody is the leit-motif for Shavuot and the identifying musical theme in the evening *Kiddush *blessing. SDC

Akers, Doris (b Brookfield MO 1923; d Minneapolis 1995). Singer, pianist, composer of African American *gospel music, publisher and recording artist. Her best known composition is "Lead Me, Guide Me" (1953), from which an African American RC *hymnal (1987) took its name. MEM

Akoluthia [Greek; Slavonic chin]. "Order." A general name for a *service in the Byzantine rite, in the sense of the sequence of *hymns, prayers and rubrics to be done. Thus, the akoluthia of baptism. DMP

Akrostichis [from Greek akros, "pointed, first" and stichos, "row"; Slavonic akrostich]. The first letters of a series of *hymns which, in the Byzantine tradition, often spell out the name of the hymn's author or the feast for which it is intended. For example, the first letters of the *Theotokia of the Sunday *aposticha spell IOANNOU A ("by John, Amen," probably referring to John of Damascus). DMP

Alabado [Spanish]. "Praised." A religious *hymn related to a Spanish form of poetry of the same name. In the New World the term referred to a form of *hymnody that developed and spread under the influence of early Franciscan missionaries. Sung as a profession of faith at the end of a day's work, it is also considered a "worker's song." Retaining the free rhythm of *plainsong, Alabados are sung today at *velorios, processions, and the way of the cross. MFR

Alabanza [Spanish]. "Song of praise." A 17th-century term for a particular form of religious *hymnody sung in the New World, modeled on the Spanish romance, often on the theme of Christ's passion. Today it has become a general term for all religious hymnody. MFR

Alain, Jehan (*b* St-Germain-en-Laye 1911; *d* Petit-Puy near Saumur 1940). Composer and organist; the brother of M.-C. *Alain. A student of *Dupré, Alain's music is known for its pictorial impressions and religious fervor. He was killed in World War II.   MSD

Alain, Marie-Claire (*b* St-Germain-en-Laye 1926). Organist; the sister of J. *Alain. A student of *Duruflé at the Paris Conservatory (1944) she was the winner of the Bach *Prix des Amis de l'orgue* (1951). She is renowned for her interpretation of *Baroque *organ music. MSD

Alborado [Spanish]. "Dawn." Morning music (as opposed to evening music or "serenade"), which is often performed on festive occasions for royal or other persons especially honored (e.g., a bride on her wedding day).   LJC

Albrechtsberger, Johann Georg (*b* Klosterneuburg 1736; *d* Vienna 1809). Theoretician and composer. He was court organist in Vienna (1772), and *Kapellmeister* at St. Stephen's Cathedral (1792). He taught *Beethoven *counterpoint. Only 27 of his 224 works were printed, including some *organ *preludes. In manuscript are 26 *masses, 43 *graduals, 34 *offertories, 6 *oratorios and other *church music.   JLB

Albright, William (*b* Gary 1944; *d* Ann Arbor 1998). Composer, organist and pianist. He was a student, then music professor at the University of Michigan. A leader in the creation of modern American organ music, he also has written some choral works including 2 *masses and an *oratorio.   VAC

Al chet [Hebrew]. "For the sin." A prayer consisting of a long list of transgressions; also called the "Confession of Sins." It is recited twice at each *Yom Kippur *service, serving to remind one of every possible act or thought of wrongdoing. The shorter form is *Ashamnu.   SJW

ALCM. See *Association for Lutheran Church Musicians.

Aldrich, Henry (*b* Westminster 1648; *d* Oxford 1710). Music scholar, architect and theologian. As dean of Christ Church, Oxford (from 1689), he significantly influenced the teaching of music. He wrote *Theory of Organ Building*. His compositions include *anthems and *services. MJK

Aleatory music [from Latin *alea,* "game with dice"]. Chance music. Music in which each performance is distinguished from another in overlap of lines, rhythms, pitches or dynamics. Changes may occur in more than one of these elements. *Liturgical music, attentive to the dynamics of the rite, may display such characteristics.   JKW

Aleinu <*Alenu*> [Hebrew]. "It is our duty." A prayer recited at the end of *ma'ariv, *shacharit and *minchah. By the 3rd-century CE it is found in *High Holiday *musaf, where it introduces the *Malchuyot* section of the *shofar service; it became part of daily prayer in *c* 1300 CE when it was joined with a second paragraph (*Al kayn nekaveh,* "We therefore hope") and became the closing prayer. As a declaration of faith it is said standing. On High Holidays its opening lines are sung to a traditional solemn

Ashkenazic melody, one of the *Misinnai melodies. SIW

Alexander, Charles (*b* Meadow TN 1867; *d* Birmingham, England 1920). Revival music leader for R. A. Torrey and J. W. Chapman and publisher of *gospel hymns. Alexander was known for his flamboyant song leading style, vivacious personality and extensive use of piano in revival music. DWM

Alexander Balus. An *oratorio by *Handel (1747) to a libretto by Thomas Morell, based on the story of Alexander Balus, king of Syria, as found in 1 Macc. DWM

Alexander's Feast. An *ode in praise of music, set by *Handel (1736); the text is from Dryden's *Ode for St. Cecelia's Day* (1697) with additions from N. Hamilton's *The Power of Music;* it was reorchestrated by *Mozart. AJL

Aliquotstimmen [German] <mutations>. "Partial voices." *Organ stops which sound at pitches higher than the fundamental, corresponding in pitch to certain harmonics of the fundamental. PKG

Aliyah [Hebrew]. "Ascent." In Jewish worship, a member of the congregation called up to the *bimah* to bless the Torah in preparation for its reading on any day there is a *Torah reading (*Sabbath, Monday, Thursday, *Rosh Chodesh, *Rosh Hashanah, *Yom Kippur* and the *Three Festivals). During *Bar* or *Bat Mitzvah* ceremonies it marks the celebrant's official status as a full member of the congregation. DMR

Allegri, Gregorio (*b* Rome 1582; *d* there 1652). Composer of a celebrated

setting of Ps 51 (*Miserere*). Its use outside the papal chapel was prohibited; nevertheless it was disseminated from 1730 and published in 1771. *Mozart wrote out the work from memory when he was 14. AWR

Allelouiarion [Greek]. 1) A series of *psalm *verses in the Byzantine rite sung with a triple *alleluia as a *refrain. An *allelouiarion* is sung between the *epistle and *gospel at the *divine liturgy. At *orthros* on days of fasting, variable *psalmody begins with an *allelouarion* with verses from the Canticle of Isaiah (Is 26); thus penitential days are called "days of alleluia."
2) A triple alleluia together with the exclamation "Glory be to you, O God," concluding a section of *psalmody in the Byzantine rite. DMP

Alleluia [Latin form of Hebrew]. "Praise God." A *refrain or *acclamation appearing in the *psalms, employed frequently in Jewish (see *halleluyah*) and Christian worship. Possibly an independent chant before the *gospel (*Easter day only) in Rome by the 4th century; there is an established pattern for always singing an alleluia before the gospel in E and W by the 7th century. It became part of the *proper of the mass with a tripartite form: alleluia-scripture verse-alleluia; replaced by the *tract during *Lent. Melodies are *melismatic, often marked by a *jubilus. The alleluia is also added to other texts of Christian *liturgy during the Easter season. Alleluia before the gospel in some Christian denominations today is considered a *gospel acclamation.
Bibl: D. Hiley, *Western Plainchant* (Oxford, 1993), 130–39, 500–5. GET

Alleluia Symphony. F. J. *Haydn's Symphony n. 30 in C (Hob I:30). The 1st movement of this early 3-movement work is based on the *incipit of the *Gregorian chant *alleluia for *lauds of *Easter. Composed in 1765, perhaps for Eastertide.   RTR

Alleluiatic <alleluyatic> **sequence.** A Latin *sequence *(Cantemus cuncti melodum)* ascribed to *Notker Balbulus. In medieval English monastic usage it replaces the *office *hymn for first *vespers of Septuagesima Sunday. Translated into English by J. M. *Neale ("The strain upraise of joy and praise"), it was set to *Anglican chant by A. H. Dyke Troytte for the *English Hymnal.   JMT

Allen, Richard (*b* Philadelphia, 1760; *d* there 1831). Minister, bishop, founder of the AME Church and *hymnal editor. Born a slave, he purchased his freedom and began preaching in 1780. Allen led a movement in Philadelphia (1787) for separate worship for African Americans experiencing exclusion and oppression in Euro-American congregations. When denied an opportunity to kneel and pray during worship at St. George's Methodist Episcopal Church, Allen and other African Americans withdrew. They utilized the location of their recently incorporated "Free African Society" (a mutual aid and benevolent society for African Americans) as a place of worship. This was the beginning of the AME Church, formally established in 1816, the same year Allen was consecrated its first bishop.

Allen published the *hymnal *A Collection of Spiritual Songs and Hymns Selected From Various Authors* (1801). This is the first anthology of *hymns collected and published for African American Protestant worship. It serves as an index to some of the music used in African American congregations at this time, particularly in the Philadelphia area.

Bibl: R. Allen, *The Life and Experience and Gospel Labor of the Rt. Rev. Richard Allen* (Philadelphia, 1887); C. Wesley, *Richard Allen* (Washington DC, 1935).   MWC

Allerseelen [German]. "All Souls Day." A song for voice and piano by R. Strauss (op. 10, n. 8, 1882/3) on a poem by von Gilm. It was orchestrated by others in 1930 and 1933.   AWR

Alma Redemptoris Mater [Latin]. "Nourishing Mother of the Redeemer." An *antiphon of the BVM sung at the conclusion of *compline between the First Sunday of *Advent and the Feast of the Presentation of the Lord (February 2). A *chant version is in existence by the 9th century; later it is set *polyphonically, e.g., *Dufay, *Josquin, *Palestrina. NDM

Alphabetos [Greek]. "Alphabet." A series of 24 *hymns in the Byzantine *office, each beginning with a consecutive letter of the Greek alphabet. The *akathistoi or *kontakia with their *oikoi are often alphabetical.   DMP

Alter, Israel (*b* Lemberg, Galicia 1901; *d* Brooklyn 1979). *Cantor and teacher. He held cantorial positions in Vienna (1921–25), Hanover (1925–35) and Johannesburg (1935–61); from 1961 he was on the faculty of NY's Hebrew Union College-Jewish Institute of Religion. Alter achieved great success as a singer and interpreter of the *liturgy, which probably explains why he was among the most admired and widely published of composers. His prolific output includes 4 volumes of accompanied *recitatives (*Shirei Yisroel,* 1952; *Malchuyos Zichronos Shofaros,* 1961; *Hallel, Tal* and *Geshem,* 1962) and music for the entire liturgical *year (except weekdays). He also wrote Yiddish songs, including the popular "*Moishelach Shloimelech.*" IAG

Alternatim [Latin]. "Alternately." A manner of performing sections of *liturgical music alternately between dissimilar forces, e.g., between soloist and *choir, or *organ and choir (see *organ mass). The practice is rooted in the *antiphonal psalmody of the early Church. *Polyphony in *alternatim* with *plainsong was common in the *Renaissance.   LMT

Alternating. The practice of dividing the singing of some musical element between 2 *choirs of the same rank. In alternating *psalmody, the *verses are sung to the same musical formula; this practice is often extended to texts other than the *psalms.   FCQ

Ambo [Latin from Greek *ambon*]. "Pulpit." A raised platform in a church, clearly in evidence by the 4th century. It is used for chanting scriptural parts of the *mass, preaching, announcements, lessons of the *divine office and chanting the *Exultet.*   GET

Ambrose of Milan, St. (*b* Trier *c* 339; *d* Milan 397). Bishop. Born into an aristocratic family, educated at Rome in law and the liberal arts, he entered civil service becoming provincial governor of Liguria and Aemilia (*c* 370) with his residence at Milan. There he was elected bishop (374), although still an unbaptized catechumen. He gained widespread recognition for his orthodox stand against Arianism and his defense of ecclesiastical rights against imperial encroachments. His pastoral skills are revealed in letters, treatises, biblical commentaries and sacramental catecheses. He is credited with writing metrical *hymns and with introducing his flock to *antiphonal singing. The rite of Milan and its *chant are named after him (*Ambrosian chant) although there is no definite evidence of his connection with either.

Bibl: N. B. McLynn, *Ambrose of Milan* (Berkeley, 1994).   NDM

Ambrosian chant. *Chant for the rite of Milan. It is preserved in *c* 300 N Italian manuscripts; some 11th, most 12th century. The chant is named for *Ambrose of Milan, although the repertoire developed after his time. Chants may be very simple or very ornate; specific genres lack a single definable style. Characteristic features include: prevalence of conjunct movement in melodies; repetition of motifs or phrases, often within long melismas; *antiphons sung surrounding the gospel and during the fraction rite (see *confractorium*) at *mass; and numerous *psalm tones in the *office, as distinct from the 8-*mode system. After the Council of *Trent, this Milanese rite was revised; following *Vatican II, it was renewed and translated into Italian. Today the use of the traditional Latin chants in the Milanese rite is no longer uniform.

Bibl: T. Bailey, *The Ambrosian Cantus* (Ottawa, 1987); T. Bailey and P. Merkley, *The Melodic Tradition of the Ambrosian Office Antiphons* (Ottawa, 1990).   JMH

Ambrosian hymns. *Strophic *hymns ascribed to *Ambrose of Milan. They are written in iambic dimeter, a popular *meter characteristic of Latin hymns intended for the congregation rather than for the *choir. Usually in 8 4-line *stanzas. According to *Augustine such hymns were used to combat heresy and to give heart in times of conflict. They are typically filled with themes of praise, ending in a trinitarian *doxology, e.g., *Veni redemptor gentium* ("Savior of the Nations, Come") or *Splendor paternae gloriae* ("O Splendor of God's Glory Bright"). Hymns in this style supplanted the parallelism of the *psalms and the syllabic meter of Greek hymns.

Bibl: H. Leeb, *Die Psalmodie bei Ambrosius* (Vienna, 1967), especially chp 3.   VEG

Ameln, Konrad (*b* Neuss, Rhineland 1899; *d* Lüdenscheid 1994). Musicologist, editor and *choir director who worked at Kassel, Leipzig and Hanover. He authored numerous articles on *hymnody, *Bach, *Handel and *Lechner, many of which appeared in *Jahrbuch für Liturgie und Hymnologie* which he coedited for a time.   MPB

Amen [Hebrew, Greek]. "Certainly." A word of affirmation which appears in the Hebrew Bible (e.g., Deut 5.22) and New Testament (e.g., 1 Cor 14.16), often as an expression of assent at the end of a prayer, *hymn or *creed. This practice continued in Judaism and Christianity. Sometimes amen is the congregation's spoken or sung response to a liturgical formula offered by the prayer leader; often it is the final word of a communally offered *doxology or hymn.   EBF

Amen cadence. A musical setting of *amen attached to *hymn tunes using a IV-I progression, often immediately following an authentic (V-I) cadence. First used extensively in *Hymns Ancient and Modern*. See *church cadence.   RJS

American Baptist Publication Society. Founded as the Baptist General Tract Society (1824), it published the first important American Baptist denominational *hymnal (text only), *The Psalmist* (1843). In 1944 it merged with the Northern Baptist Board of Education; in 1972 it became the Board of Educational Ministries of the American Baptist Church of the USA.   VAC

The American Conference of Cantors. The professional cantorial organization of *Reform Judaism, founded (1953) by alumni of Hebrew Union College-Jewish Institute of Religion School of Sacred Music. It provides placement, pensions, continuing education and counseling for its members, as well as referrals and information for the Jewish community.   BES

American Guild of Organists <AGO>. A national professional association of 21,000 members in 350 chapters throughout the US and in Europe, Korea and Argentina. Organized in 1896 (*Foote serving as the first president) the Guild seeks to maintain high musical standards and promote understanding and appreciation of all aspects of *organ and choral music.   CAD

American organ. The earliest American-made *organ was built in 1737. Important 19th-century builders included *Roosevelt, W. *Johnson, *Hook and Hastings. The pervasive use of electric action in the first half of the 20th century enabled the creation of gigantic *instruments with unique tonal qualities. Since then there has been a return to historic European principles of tone and construction, often blended with American innovations.   JBW

American Society of Jewish Music. A professional society dedicated to advancing Jewish music through concerts, publications and education. Members include musicians, *cantors and scholars. Founded (1962) as the Jewish Liturgical Music Society of America, it assumed the present name in 1974. This society publishes *Musica Judaica* (from 1975).   MLK

Amidah [Hebrew]. "Standing." The central prayer and main element in the Jewish *service on all occasions. Traditionally recited standing, facing Jerusalem. Also known as *Ha-Tefillah* ("the prayer"), *Avodah* ("service") or, in the *Ashkenazic tradition, *Shemoneh Esrei* ("18") after the original number of *blessings employed for its weekday recitation.

Though there are variations, the basic structure can be reduced to two forms: 19 blessings on weekdays, or 7 blessings on *Sabbath and *Three Festivals (with certain insertions for various other holidays and events). All forms include the same opening blessings: *Avot* invokes the names of Abraham, Isaac and Jacob, reminding God to send a redeemer (Reform, Reconstructionist, and some Conservative congregations include the names of Sarah, Rebecca, Rachel and Leah); *Gevurot* praises God for being powerful, sustaining the living, freeing the captive and keeping faith with those who sleep in the dust.

Major differences occur in the middle section, specifically the *Kedushah and intermediate blessings. On weekdays the *Kedushah* is a short paragraph including a pledge to sanctify God's holiness and name from generation to generation; the middle blessings are petitions for understanding, forgiveness, redemption, healing, and the ingathering of exiles; the final 3 blessings (used in all forms of the prayer) mention the rebuilding of Jerusalem (*Velirushalayim Ir'cha), request that God hear our prayers, and ask for thanks (*Modim) and peace (*Sim Shalom on mornings, *Shalom Rav on afternoons and evenings). On *Sabbath the petitionary prayers are replaced with a longer, more elaborate version of the *Kedushah* that celebrates the Sabbath; this includes *Veshamru and *Yismechu in the *musaf. Special sections (e.g., *Ya'aleh Veyavo, *Tal, *Geshem) are inserted for festivals and holidays.

Traditionally the *Amidah* was recited individually, then repeated by the *chazzan;* to recite aloud required a quorum of 10 men; at *ma'ariv it was not said out loud. Today's practice varies regarding the gender of the quorum and portions that are said individually and publicly in non-Orthodox synagogues. On Friday night *Me'ain Sheva is recited after the *Amidah*.

A special melody is used for reciting the *Amidah* in the Ashkenazic tradition. The cantorial settings by *Alter are standard. More recent, well-known settings of sections of the *Amidah* include: *Veshomru* by Rothblum and Weiner; *Yishmechu* by *Freed and *Steinberg; *Reitsei* by S. Richards; *Sim Shalom* by *Janowski; *Shalom Rav* by Steinberg and J. Klepper. Numerous popular folk settings of these also exist.

Bibl: 19th-century musical settings are found in A. Baer *Baal T'fillah* (New York, 1953 [1883]; J. Heinemann, "Amidah,"

EJ 2:838–46; I. Elbogen, *Jewish Liturgy,* trans. R. Scheindlin (Philadelphia, 1993 [1913]).   DMR

AMM. See *Association of Methodist Musicians.

Anabaptist Hymns. *Hymns created by Anabaptists (rebaptizers) of the left wing of the 16th-century *Reformation. Anabaptists, whose beliefs regarding baptism and nonviolence were thought to threaten the stability of the countries in which they lived, were persecuted and executed in all parts of Europe for nearly a century beginning in 1527. Frequently their hymns were personal testimonies of martyrdom, laments of their suffering, expressions of assurance in Christ's ultimate victory over evil and exhortations to other believers to remain faithful. Many texts were long, cumbersome and not of high poetic quality. The tunes used by the early Anabaptists were drawn from *folk, *Meistersinger,* Bohemian Brethren and RC sources. The primary collections of early Anabaptist hymns are *Ausbund etlicher schöner Christlicher Geseng. . .* (1564, 1583), *Die Lieder der Hutterischen Brüder* (gathered from 1527–1725), *Het Offer des Herren* (1563–99) and *Ein schön Gesangbüchlein Geistlicher Lieder. . .* (1565, 1569). Hymn writing flourished during the years of severe persecutions, but never again reached the productivity of the early years of the movement.
Bibl: H. S. Bender, "Hymnology," *The Mennonite Encyclopedia* 2 (1955–59) 869–86.   RJS

Anabathmoi [Greek; Slavonic *stepenny*]. "Flight of steps." *Gradual psalms in the Byzantine rite, sung at *orthros* on Sundays and feast days following the variable *psalmody and before the *gospel. They are sung in 3 sections together with 3 *antiphons consisting of 3 *troparia* each, though often the *psalms are omitted and only the *troparia* are sung. There are 8 sets of *anabathmoi* for each of the *octoechos.*   DMP

Anagnostes [Greek from *anágnōsis,* "reading"; Slavonic *chtets*]. The reader in the Byzantine rite who has received first of the minor orders (Greek *cheirothesia*). He is to chant the lessons from the Hebrew Bible, Acts of the Apostles and *epistles in the *divine liturgy and *office. Often only given as a step to priesthood, the office is being revived in many Byzantine churches.   DMP

Anamnesis. See *anaphora* and *eucharistic prayer.

Anaphora [Greek; Slavonic *anafora*]. "[Prayer of] offering." Already a technical term at the time of St. John Chrysostom (*d* 407) for the central prayer of the *divine liturgy. In the E church it usually consists of a narration of God's saving work culminating in the institution narrative from the Last Supper, an *anamnesis* (commemoration), *epiclesis* (invocation of the Holy Spirit) and intercessions for the living and dead. The congregation takes an active part, responding to various exclamations of the presider with *hymns or *amens. Each E church has varying numbers of anaphoras, usually attributed to an apostle or saint. The Byzantine Church uses 2, attributed to Sts. John Chrysostom and Basil the Great. See *eucharistic prayer.
Bibl: J. R. K. Fenwick, *The Anaphoras of St. Basil and St. James* (Rome, 1992).   DMP

Anastasima [Greek; Slavonic *stikhiry voskresny*]. "Resurrection [hymns]." *Stichera* for the Byzantine Sunday *office. Four *stichera* exist for *hesperinos (3 intercalated with *verses from Ps 141; 1 at the beginning of the *aposticha) and 4 for *orthros (intercalated with verses from Pss 148–150). Eight sets of these hymns exist, 1 for each of the *octoechos. DMP

Anastasima eulogetaria [Greek; Slavonic *anhel'skij sobor, neporochyni*]. "Resurrection praises." Six *stichera* sung at the end of Ps 119 at Sunday *orthros in the Byzantine rite. The theme of the *stichera* is the visit of the myrrh-bearers to Christ's tomb on *Easter. There is an alternate set for Saturday morning, for *orthros for the deceased and for funerals (*nekrosima eulogetaria*, "Praises for the deceased"). DMP

Anatolika [Greek; Slavonic *stikhiry vostochny*]. "Eastern [hymns]." Eight *stichera*, erroneously attributed to Patriarch Anatolius (*d* 458), first appearing in the Byzantine *office in the 13th century. Four are for *hesperinos (intercalated with *verses from Ps 141) and 4 for *orthros (intercalated with verses from Pss 148–50). Eight sets of these exist, 1 for each of the *octoechos. DMP

Aneinu <Anenu> [Hebrew]. "Answer us." (1) A petitionary prayer added to the *Amidah on fast days, asking God to answer prayers during great distress. Recited at *shacharit as a separate *blessing while the reader repeats the *Amidah;* recited at *minchah by each individual and the reader during the repetition of the *Amidah,* though not a separate blessing here but incorporated into the *Shema Koleinu.

(2) An aphabetical acrostic composed by several Geonim (including Rav Amram Gaon, *d* 875). It was incorporated into the *Selichot, *Yom Kippur *ma'ariv and fast days (including *Tisha B'av*). While generally recited in the traditional *Selicha *mode, there are several cantorial compositions setting this text in other modes. IAG

Anerio, Felice (*b* Rome *c* 1560; *d* there 1614). Composer for the papal chapel, who succeeded *Palestrina. The brother of G. F. *Anerio, he wrote madrigals, *masses, *Magnificats, *motets, *laude, etc. His style bridged the late *Renaissance and early *Baroque periods. Anerio worked with *Soriano on the *Medicean edition of *chant. LFH

Anerio, Giovanni Francesco (*b* Rome *c* 1567; *d* Graz 1630). Prolific composer and RC priest; the brother of F. *Anerio. Active in Rome, Verona and Poland, he composed *c* 83 *motets, *masses, *psalm settings, dramatic dialogues (important for the development of the *oratorio) and secular vocal works. LFH

Angelic hymn [Latin *hymnus angelicus*]. An alternate name for *Gloria in excelsis.

Angel of peace litany. See *aitesis.

Angelus [Latin]. "Angel." (1) A prayer composed of *versicles, *responses and the *Hail Mary, honoring Christ's incarnation. Recited morning, noon and evening, it was often announced by church *bells.

(2) An opera by E. Naylor (1867–1934), awarded the Ricordi prize for English opera.   MSD

Anglican chant. A term first used in the 19th century to describe short melodies harmonized in 4 parts for chanting *psalms and *canticles in Anglican worship in which textual units were divided into 2 roughly equal parts. Closely related to the singing of *plainsong in parts in pre-Reformation worship.

Presently the term refers to a harmonized 10-note melody, the first half of which consists of a reciting chord (on which most of the text's first phrase is sung) and 3 ending chords. The second half consists of a reciting chord followed by 5 ending chords. This structure is closely related to that of the *Gregorian *psalm tones. *Pointing indicates the syllable at which singers are to leave the *reciting tone beginning each half-verse and move through the ending chords, as well as groupings of syllables to be sung on each ending chord so that musical and textual stresses coincide. Instrumental accompaniment is appropriate and useful.

Bibl: P. Scholes, "Anglican Chant," *New Oxford Companion to Music* (Oxford, 1983) I:77–80; A. Wyton, ed., *The Anglican Chant Psalter* (New York, 1987).   CAD

Anglican worship music. For 250 years following its establishment under *Henry VIII the Anglican Church consisted of the Churches of England, Ireland and Wales. Its music was predominantly British in tradition and in texts sung. Beginning in 1784, however, the following churches have entered the Anglican Communion: Aotearoa-New Zealand-Polynesia, Australia, Brazil, Burma (Myanmar), Burundi, Canada, C Africa, Ceylon (Sri Lanka), Churches of East Asia, Province of the Indian Ocean, Japan, Jerusalem and the Middle East, Kenya, Korea, Melanesia, Nigeria, Papua New Guinea, Philippines, Portugal, Rwanda, Southern Africa, Southern Cone of America, Spain, Sudan, Tanzania, Uganda, US, West Africa, West Indies, Zaire, The United Churches (in communion) of South India, North India, Pakistan and Bangladesh as well as various churches (extra provincial) under the jurisdiction of various Anglican primates. Therefore, Anglican worship music includes music appropriate for use in any of these churches: a vast range of styles and forms of musical composition and presentation, *instruments and languages.

Until recently, however, Anglican worship music ordinarily designated that which was appropriate for cathedral and parish churches within the British Isles, and often used in Anglican churches throughout the world. During the 1500s a reformed version of vernacular W *liturgy encouraged a tradition of liturgical *responses and *hymns sung by congregations and *choirs which continues today. Harmonized or *Anglican chant developed and *anthems were composed. The monastic *offices were collected into 2 daily *services (*morning and *evening prayer) for which much music for choirs and congregations has been written. Choirs of robed men and boys, pipe organs and dignified liturgical texts have been characteristic of Anglican worship music. During the 1960s and 70s English Anglicans were leaders in experimenting with *guitar masses and popular religious song.

Bibl: N. Temperley, *The Music of the English Parish Church,* 2 vols. (New York, 1979); C. Doran and W. Petersen, *A History of Music in the Episcopal Church* (Little Rock, 1990), 39–45; E. Routley, *A Short History of English Church Music,* rev. ed. (Carol Stream, 1997). CAD

Anhel'skij sobor [Slavonic]. See *anastasima eulogetaria.*

Animuccia, Giovanni (*b* Florence *c* 1500; *d* Rome 1571). Composer. He succeeded *Palestrina at St. Peter's Cappella Giulia in 1555. Animuccia composed 2 books of *laudi spirituali* for the Oratory of Filippo Neri in Rome (see *oratorio); other works include *masses and *Magnificat*s. MJK

Anim zemirot <*An'im zemiroth*> [Hebrew]. "I sing hymns." A liturgical poem ascribed to Rabbi Jehudah he-Hasid of Regensburg (12th century) sung at the end of *shacharit* on the *Sabbath and *Three Festivals. SJW

Antecommunion. A non-eucharistic *liturgy (including *Kyrie, *Gloria, *psalms, readings, sermon, prayers and a *blessing) used by some Lutherans as the Sunday liturgy. See *mass of the catechumens. RDH

Anthem [from Greek *antíphonon,* originally "something sung alternately by two choirs"]. (1) An English term for a choral *motet, designating a *polyphonic setting of the *plainsong melody of an *antiphon. In the 16th century the anthem became a distinctive genre of *Anglican worship music: a freely-composed setting of a biblical text, usually taken from the *psalms. By the 17th century the accompaniment, usually *organ, was frequently independent of the voice parts. Two primary forms developed: the *full anthem, a through-composed choral piece; and *verse anthem, a sectional composition in which solo voice(s) alternated with the choir.

(2) In England, America and elsewhere anthem has become the general term for any choral composition used in worship.

Bibl: E. Wienandt and R. Young, *The Anthem in England and America* (New York, 1970). RAL

Anthropology of music. An approach to *ethnomusicology which emphasizes its social science orientation; the study of music in culture, especially music as a mode of human social behavior. The methodological framework involves 3 interrelated levels of investigation: concepts about music, modes of human behavior employed in music making and the organization of musical sound. This approach assumes the integral role of field research which attends to the aural aspects of music as well as its social, psychological, aesthetic and cultural dimensions.

Bibl: A. Merriam, *The Anthropology of Music* (Evanston, 1964). MEM

Antiphon [Greek; Latin *antiphona*]. An ancient Greek musical term for "octave," the interval produced when a *choir is divided according to age (children/adults) or gender (women/men). As adapted in the W, the term came to mean 1) a brief *versicle sung before and after a *psalm (e.g., in the *divine office); 2) a phrase repeated in response to *verses of a psalm or *canticle sung by choir or *cantor (e.g., during a *procession); 3) a *chant accompanying a ritual action (e.g., the *communion rite at *mass); 4) a method of singing involving alternation between 2 choirs (see *antiphonal).

Attached to psalms, antiphons determined the psalm's musical *mode and performance method. Detached, antiphons became independent chants (e.g., *antiphons of the BVM).

Bibl: M. Huglo, "Antiphon," *NGDMM* I:471–81.   NDM

Antiphona ad communionem. See *communion antiphon.

Antiphonal. (1) Originally a form of *responsorial psalmody in which a *refrain or *antiphon is alternated between 2 choirs after psalm *verses sung by 1 or 2 soloists (e.g., soloist 1 - verse; choir 1 - refrain; soloist 2 - verse; choir 2 - refrain; etc).

(2) Later (and more commonly) a synonym for *alternating.

(3) *Antiphonary.   NDM

Antiphonale. See *antiphonary.

Antiphonary, antiphoner [Latin *antiphonale, antiphonarium, antiphonarius*]. A liturgical *book of the W church containing chants for the *divine office and/or *mass. Eventually the term is restricted to books containing only *office chants. See *gradual.   MSD

Antiphon of the Blessed Virgin Mary. A relatively long, independent *antiphon (not attached to *psalms) composed of non-biblical texts, asking for Mary's intercession. While special Marian antiphons appear in other contexts (e.g., *Adorna thalamum* for the *Candlemas procession), the term usually refers to 4 antiphons (*Alma redemptoris mater, *Ave regina caelorum, *Regina caeli,

Salve regina) sung at the end of *compline and other times in worship during various seasons of the year since the 13th century. Simple and solemn *chant settings as well as innumerable *polyphonic settings exist for these antiphons. See *Marian music.   RTR

Antiphony. (1) As related to *antiphon, it denotes the octave difference in the alternation of men's voices with women's and boys' voices.

(2) The deployment of two spatially separated performing groups that alternate or contrast material between them.

(3) *Alternating.   FCQ

Apodeipnon [Greek; Slavonic *povecherie*]. "After supper." Byzantine *compline; a monastic *service sung before the community retires for the night. Two traditional forms exist: *apodeipnon mikron* (Greek, "small compline"; Slavonic *maloe povercherie*) for ordinary days; and *apodeipnon to mega* (Greek, "great compline"; Slavonic *velikoje povecherie*) for solemn pentitential days. Great compline is sung on most days of the Great *Lent, and replaces *orthros* in the evening vigil service for *Christmas, *Epiphany and the Annunciation (March 25). In the later *Middle Ages, great compline developed into an elaborate service of 3 distinct parts: 1) small compline plus Isaiah's Canticle (Is 8:9-10, 12-13, 17-18; 9:1-6; *verse 10 serves as a *refrain), 2) an office of repentance, and 3) a short form of *orthros*.   DMP

Apodosis [Greek; Slavonic *otdanije*]. "Return." The final day of a feast in the Byzantine rite which has a post-festive period (*metheortia*). On this day the entire *office of the feast is repeated.   DMP

Apolysis [Greek; Slavonic *otpust*]. "Dismissal." In the Byzantine Church: (1) Originally the dismissal at any *office (corresponding to the Latin *missa*) consisting of the *aitesis, a concluding prayer and the "Prayer for the bowing of heads."

(2) The present liturgical dismissal, originating in monastic rites, which consists of a *blessing of Christ as "He-who-is," an *acclamation to strengthen the Orthodox faith, a *hymn to the Mother of God, the small *doxology and an invocation for Christ's blessing through the prayers of various saints. The *divine liturgy employs only the final 2 elements.   DMP

Apolytikion [Greek; Slavonic *tropar'*]. "Dismissal hymn." A *troparion in the Byzantine *liturgy, used as a dismissal *hymn at the end of *orthros and *hesperinos. In the Greek tradition, a *troparion* may be called an *apolytikion* even when used elsewhere in a *service. DMP

Aposticha [Greek; Slavonic *stihovne*]. "From *stichera*." A series of 3 or 4 *stichera in the Byzantine *office, sung according to the *octoechos and intercalated with selected *verses from the *psalms or (occasionally) Hebrew Bible *canticles. *Aposticha* originated in the Jerusalem office from *hymns sung at the end of a *service when the congregation processed from the Anastasis to Golgotha within the Church of the Holy Resurrection. Almost always sung today at the end of a service, particularly *hesperinos and daily *orthros, but not at festive *orthros* except the *Paschal *stichera* at *Easter.   DMP

Apostles, The. An *oratorio by *Elgar (op. 49) on biblical texts arranged by the composer, completed in 1903. *The *Kingdom,* a sequel, followed in 1905. KRH

Apostol [Slavonic] "Apostolic [reading]." In the Byzantine rite, a reading from the apostolic writings (Acts of the Apostles, *epistles of St. Paul, catholic epistles) or the book containing these readings. Greeks usually have the readings arranged as separate pericopes, while Slavs have a continuous text; asterisks and directions indicate the beginning and ending of a reading.   DMP

Apostolos [Greek; Slavonic *apostol*]. See *epistolary.

Aquinas, Thomas.   See   *Thomas Aquinas, St.

Arcadelt <Archadelt, Harcadelt, etc.>, **Jacques** (*b c* 1505; *d* Paris 1568). Prolific Flemish composer and pioneer in early 16th-century *polyphony. Active in Rome (the Julian and *Sistine choirs) and Paris (royal chapel), his works include madrigals (most significant), *chansons,* *masses, *motets, *psalms and *lamentations.   LFH

Aria [Italian]. "Air." A lyrical *strophic piece ordinarily for 1 voice with instrumental accompaniment. At first the aria stood by itself (*c* 1600) but since the 17th century it has become an integral part of opera, the *oratorio and the *cantata. *Da capo* (Italian, "at the head" or "back to the beginning") arias, which lose the strict strophic pattern and display various versions of the ABA form, were popular in the 18th century. J. S. *Bach and

*Handel established more equality between the voice and obbligato instruments in the aria. MPB

Arioso [Italian]. "Like an aria." A melodious vocal segment in regular rhythm inserted into a *recitative, often to offer devotional commentary. Shorter than an *aria, though with motivic imitation, the *arioso* (popular with J. S. *Bach and contemporaries) can be detected by title, and/or tempo markings, and/or other obvious musical changes. MPB

Armenian chant. *Monophonic music of the Armenian Christian Church. Divergent traditions exist, centered in Edjmiadsin, Jerusalem and Mechitarist monasteries in Vienna and Venice. Neumatic *khaz* notation, which appears by the 9th century, was reformed in 1813. Medieval melodies were categorized in an 8 *mode *(dzayn)* system and may have been diatonic, but by the 19th century chromatic intervals were used. The *sharaknotz*, developed by the 15th century, contains 1166 *hymns *(sharakan)* for the *divine office, including many by Nerses Shnorhali (*d* 1173). Other hymn types include the *gandz, tagh, erg* and *meghedi*. Percussive *instruments sometimes accompany the *chant.
Bibl: V. Nersessian, ed., *Essays on Armenian Music* (London, 1978). RGD

Armstrong, Anton (*b* New York 1956). Conductor of the *St. Olaf College Choir, teacher and editor. He studied at St. Olaf College, the University of Illinois and Michigan State. Armstrong frequently serves as a guest conductor in the US and abroad. PHW

Ars antiqua <*ars vetus*> [Latin]. "Ancient art." A term Philippe de Vitry (*d*

1361) applies in his treatise, *Ars nova* (1322–23), to music written in the late 13th century; music which contrasts considerably with the novelties of style in the *ars nova*.

The Parisian School dominated W music in the *ars antiqua*. Two of the first composers known by name, *Léonin and *Pérotin, made significant contributions to the early *polyphonic repertoire at *Notre Dame. The form of *organum* (usually taken from *chant) and the *conductus* (not based on chant) flourished from 1160 to 1240.

These forms were superseded by the *motet, the most important form in the 13th and 14th centuries. With this form *rhythmic modes were codified and mensural notation developed. Three-part writing became standard, though some 4-part writing occurred. Triple *meter was favored and sound was limited to a narrow vocal range. Few chromatic alterations were notated, but in performance *musica ficta* allowed other chromatic changes.
Bibl: J. Yudkin, *Music in Medieval Europe* (Englewood Cliffs NJ, 1989). DCI

Ars nova [Latin]. "New art." The title of a treatise (1322–23) by French theorist Philippe de Vitry (*d* 1361), whose work reflects the deep nature of the changes in music from the *ars antiqua*. The term was commonly applied to new compositional techniques of the 14th century. With *ars nova* duple divisions are on equal terms with triple. A method, called isorhythm, was developed as a means to increase the length of pieces. This is a special kind of structural organization used by 14th-century composers in the *tenor and sometimes other voices of their *motets in which a rhythmic pattern is established and reiterated 1 or more times throughout the piece. The same procedure is applied to the melodic pattern, but the two did not necessarily coincide.

The *ars nova* also presents the first efforts to collect various parts of the *ordinary into 1 unit. Many forms of secular music are cultivated. The most well-known composers in the *ars nova* are *Machaut and *Landini.

Bibl: J. McKinnon, ed., *Antiquity and the Middle Ages* (Englewood Cliffs NJ, 1991). DCI

Ars vetus. See *ars antiqua*.

Art music. A term referring to music thought to be written "for its own sake," that is, not for any programmatic or practical purpose, e.g., symphonic music, chamber music, opera. In contradistinction to *ritual music and, some think, *liturgical music. JBF

Ascension, L'. A 4-movement suite of symphonic meditations for orchestra by *Messiaen (1933); the work is more well known in the composer's arrangement of it for *organ, with a rewritten 3rd movement (1934). AJL

Ashamnu [Hebrew]. "We are guilty." A prayer in the form of an alphabetical acrostic, listing 24 moral trespasses, also known as the lesser confession (in comparison to the greater confession, *Al chet*). It is recited throughout *Yom Kippur *services, *Selichot,* during daily and afternoon prayers in many *Ashkenazic and *Sephardic congregations, during *shacharit and *minchah and on *Yom Kippur Katan* according to the Ashkenazic rite. IAG

Ashkenazic [Hebrew]. Jews from C and E Europe. The term is derived from the Hebrew word *Ashkenaz* (Gen 10.3) which was used to refer to Germany since *c* the 10th century. Jews living in other regions are called *Sephardic Jews. The rite of the Ashkenazic community is called *Minhag Ashkenaz*. A particular Hebrew accent is characteristic of Jews from this tradition. Attempts have been made to document Ashkenazic cantorial and synagogue music.

Bibl: E. Werner, *A Voice Still Heard* (University Park, 1976). MLK

Ashrei <*Ashré*> [Hebrew]. "Happy are they." An alphabetical *hymn consisting of Ps 145, prefixed by 2 psalm *verses (84:5, 144:15) in which the word *ashrei* appears 3 times. The prayer concludes with another psalm verse (115:18). It is recited twice at *shacharit* and before *minchah*. SIW

ASJM. See *American Society of Jewish Music.

Asmaticos office [Greek]. "Sung office." The Byzantine parochial *divine office that existed prior to the 13th century. DMP

Asperges [Latin]. "You sprinkle." A former Roman rite ceremony in which the priest sprinkled the assembly with holy water before the principal Sunday *mass, accompanied by an *antiphon and *verses drawn from Ps 51. In the current Roman rite it is replaced by an optional "Rite of Blessing and Sprinkling of Holy Water." GET

Association of Anglican Musicians <AAM>. Since 1966, an organization of musicians and clergy in the *Episcopal Church and throughout the Anglican *communion which works to elevate, stimulate and support music and the allied arts in the *liturgy of the Church. The annual national conference and the *AAM Journal* provide opportunities for collegial discussion and continuing education. CAD

Association of Lutheran Church Musicians. Founded in 1986, filling a void left by the demise of the *Lutheran Society for Worship, Music and the Arts. It sponsors biennial pan-Lutheran, national conventions; in alternate years there are 4 regional conventions. It publishes the newsletter *Grace Notes,* the journal *Cross Accent* and occasional papers, pamphlets and recordings. JLB

Association of Methodist Musicians. See *Fellowship of United Methodists in Music, Worship and Other Arts.

Athanasian Creed. See *Quicunque vult.*

Attwood, Thomas (*b* London 1765; *d* there 1838). Composer, organist at St. Paul's Cathedral (London) and composer to the *Chapel Royal. A student of *Mozart, he epitomized English classical style at its most refined. His intimate choral works (including 18 *anthems) best represent his substantial musical gifts. RDH

Audsley, George Ashdown (*b* 1838; *d* 1925). Architect and organ designer. He is best known for his writings, such as *The Art of Organ Building* (2 vols., 1905), which advocated a more scientific approach to organ design. JWK

Augustine of Hippo, St. (*b* Tagaste, N Africa 354; *d* Hippo 430). He was born Aurelius Augustinus to a devoted Christian mother, Monica, and a pagan father, Patricius. Educated in Tagaste, Madaura and Carthage. Although a catechumen from early childhood, he was not baptized until Easter of 387 in Milan by *Ambrose. Following his baptism he was ordained priest and later bishop of Hippo. He is one of the most influential theologians in the W church. His writings provide important though sporadic information about worship and music in the ancient church, especially his commentaries on the *psalms. It is possible that he first introduced *chant at the *offertory. He is known to have written a psalm against the Donatist party that was sung by the faithful, as well as a treatise on rhythm (*De Musica*). He never wrote a proposed treatise on melody. His most famous saying about music is "He who sings prays twice."
Bibl: W. Waite, "Augustine of Hippo," *NGDMM* I:695–96. PAB

Aulos. In ancient Greece, a double-reed *instrument of 2 even pipes. Associated with common people, it was used in the theater, at banquets, to celebrate the famous and victorious athletes, and was often linked with Dionysian revelry. DCI

Ault, Gary. See *Dameans.

Ausbund etlicher schöner Christlicher Geseng. . . [German]. "A Collection of beautiful Christian Songs . . ." A *hymnal published in 1583 by Swiss Anabaptists that has been in continuous use among the Amish for over 400 years. The second section of the hymnal contains 51 hymns written by Anabaptist martyrs imprisoned in Passau Castle from 1535–40, originally published in 1564. The first section (appended in the 1583 edition) contains hymns gathered from Dutch Anabaptist, Bohemian Brethren, Lutheran and Reformed sources. No music was included in the book, but tunes drawn from RC, Lutheran, *folk and *Meistersinger* sources were suggested. Currently the book, still in German, has 140 hymns (most with 15 or more stanzas), the confession of faith of Thomas von Imbroich (martyred 1558), an account of the suffering of Anabaptists in Zurich (1635–45) and 6 appended ballads.   RJS

Austin, John Turnell (*b* Podington, Bedfordshire 1869; *d* Hartford 1948). *Organ builder associated with the universal windchest system for providing a steady wind supply for organs. Austin began organ building in the US with *Ferrand and Votey in Detroit (1889); he established the Austin Organ Company in Boston (1898), soon relocating to Hartford (1899).   JWK

Austria <Austrian Hymn>. See *Emperor's Hymn.

Auto sacramental [Spanish]. "Sacramental play." In Spain, vernacular religious dramas, performed in the streets, dating from the 12th century. Their music and dance became secularized, leading to their prohibition in the 18th century. Missionaries introduced these musical dramas in the New World; the first was presented in El Paso in 1598. Based on Hebrew Bible or New Testament stories (e.g., *Comedia de Adan y Eva*) they served didactic and catechetical purposes. The *auto "Los Pastores"*

continues to be performed today during the *Advent and *Christmas seasons.   MFR

Aveinu Malkeinu <*Avinu Malkenu*> [Hebrew]. "Our Father our King." A *litany recited during the Ten Days of Repentance (the period between *Rosh Hashanah and *Yom Kippur) and on fast days. The ark is opened for its recitation. Petitions include: "inscribe us in the book of good life, inscribe us in the book of redemption and salvation, inscribe us in the book of prosperity and sustenance." Ten *verses are recited responsively. The number of verses differs by rite (from 25–53). In traditional synagogue *services the last verse is sung to a *folk melody. In the worship of *Reform Judaism a setting by *Janowski for *cantor, *choir and *organ is commonly sung.   MLK

Ave Maria. See *Hail Mary.

Ave maris stella [Latin]. "Hail star of the sea." A *Marian hymn, dating from at least the 9th century, traditionally sung at *vespers on Marian feasts. Many composers have written *polyphonic vocal and *keyboard settings based on its *chant melody. See *Marian music. RTR

Avenary, Hanoch <*b* Herbert Löwenstein> (*b* Danzig 1908; *d* Magen, Negev, Israel 1994). German born and trained musicologist who immigrated to Israel (1936) and changed his name. Avenary researched *chant and *cantillation among *Ashkenazic and *Sephardic Jews in both historic and modern contexts, e.g., *The Ashkenazic Tradition of Biblical Chant between 1500 and 1900* (1978).   MLK

Ave regina caelorum [Latin]. "Hail queen of the heavens." A *Marian antiphon, in use since the 12th century, traditionally sung at various hours of the *divine office between *Candlemas and Wednesday of *Holy Week. Frequently set *polyphonically in the *Renaissance era and used as the *cantus firmus of polyphonic *masses. See *Marian music. RTR

Ave verum corpus [Latin]. "Hail true body." A *plainsong eucharistic *hymn, often employed in *benediction or at *communion. Well known choral settings of the text are by *Byrd, *Mozart, *Elgar and others. AJL

Av Harachamim [Hebrew]. "Merciful Father." (1) A prayer composed by an unknown author in memory of Jewish martyrs massacred in Germany during the First Crusade; first appearing in a prayer book dated 1290. It emphasizes the merit of the martyrs who died "in the sanctity of God's name," quotes scriptural *verses (Deut 32:43; Joel 4:21; Pss 79:10, 9:13, 110:6-7) and asks God to remember the martyrs, avenge them and save their offspring. Originally recited in S Germany on *Sabbaths preceding *Shavuot and *Tisha B'av and at the end of the *Yizkor *service, it became part of every Sabbath *shacharit in the *Ashkenazic ritual. The Polish rite has varying traditions: in one, Av Harachamim is recited every Sabbath except those when a new moon occurs (see *Rosh Chodesh); in another, it is recited when Sabbath falls during a new moon or on a holiday. Some congregations say this prayer only on Sabbaths of the Omer (the period between *Pesach and *Shavuot) and Sab-

baths of the 3 weeks between the Fasts of Tammuz and Av (when it is recited after the *Torah reading before returning the scroll to the ark).

(2) A short prayer recited in many congregations before the Torah reading. A paragraph of the same name is part of the introduction to removing the Torah from the ark on Sabbaths and holidays, asking God to rebuild the walls of Jerusalem. Ashkenazic communities commonly sing this prayer to a melody written by Dunajewski. Many cantorial and choral compositions have been written for prayers bearing this name, but with no consistency regarding a particular mode. IAG

Avodah. See *Amidah.

Azusa Street Revival. A religious awakening which began in Los Angeles in April 1906 under the leadership of an African-American Holiness preacher, William J. Seymour. The revival continued for about 3 years, and was a major impetus for the spread of Pentecostalism. VAC

Az yashir Moshe [Hebrew]. "Moses [and the children of Israel] will sing." A poetic narrative *response by the children of Israel when God split the Red Sea and drowned the Egyptians (Ex 15:1-18). Also known as Shirah ("Song"), Shirat hayam ("Song of the Sea") or "The Song of Moses." In Temple days it was chanted by *Levites during *Sabbath worship. It became the closing paragraph of the *Pesukei dezimrah section of *shacharit; thus is recited every morning in Jewish *liturgy. Special musical settings can be found in each Jewish regional tradition. MLK

B

Ba'al tefilah <*baal tefillah*> [Hebrew]. "Master of prayer." The leader of prayers for a Jewish *service. See *chazzan.
MLK

Baccusi, Ippolito (*b* Mantua *c* 1550; *d* Verona 1609). Composer. He served as *maestro di cappella* at St. Mark's in Venice, later in Mantua and Verona (from 1592). His *masses, *motets and *psalms show influence of the Venetian school (e.g., *Willaert and the *Gabrielis). He was an early advocate of instrumental doubling of vocal parts.
MJK

Bach, Carl Philipp Emanuel (*b* Weimar 1714; *d* Hamburg 1788). The best known of J. S. *Bach's sons. A facile keyboardist and prolific composer, he studied music chiefly with his father, attended St. Thomas in Leipzig and studied law at the University of Leipzig and Frankfurt an der Oder. In 1738 he went to the court of *Frederick II in Berlin where he performed and composed for almost 30 years, producing *keyboard sonatas and *concertos, chamber music and symphonies. He then went to Hamburg (1768) where he directed music at 5 churches. Demands there led him to compose dozens of *passions, several hundred sacred *odes and songs, a popular *Magnificat, *oratorios (e.g., "Israel in Egypt"), orchestrated *psalm settings and a variety of *cantatas. His *Essay on the True Art of Playing Keyboard Instruments* (1753) is a major source for contemporary performance practice.

Bibl: H. G. Ottenberg, *Carl Philipp Emanuel Bach,* trans. P. J. Whitmore (New York, 1987).   MPB

Bach, Johann Christian (*b* Leipzig 1735; *d* London 1782). The youngest surviving son of J. S. *Bach. In 1750 he went to live with his brother C. P. E. *Bach, studied in Italy with *Martini and others, there converted to RC, and became 1 of 2 organists at Milan Cathedral. While in Italy he composed nearly all of his *church music, mostly pieces with liturgical texts (with *orchestra) in a variety of styles including *Palestrina-like techniques and accomplished fugal structures. In 1762 he moved to London where he

25

immersed himself in composing operas, chamber music and symphonies. MPB

Bach, Johann Sebastian (*b* Eisenach 1685; *d* Leipzig 1750). *Lutheran organist and one of the foremost composers of all time. Born as the youngest of 8 into an extended family (see *Bach family) whose musical gifts span 2 centuries. His early education included several years in his brother's home in Ohrdruf where he learned composing by copying works of others, and 2 years as a student in the Michaelisschule in Lüneberg.

He first worked as a court musician (string player) in Weimar; then organist in Arnstadt (1703–64) and Mühlhausen (1707). He returned to Weimar as court organist (1708); promoted to *Konzertmeister* (1714) he shifted focus from composing organ works to *cantatas, as he was required to write 1 a month. A failed bid as *Kappellmeister* in Weimar led him to accept that post in Cöthen's court of Prince Leopold (1716). There he concentrated on instrumental composition. The death of *Kuhnau led Bach to apply for the *Kantor* position at St. Thomas and director of music in Leipzig; he remained there from 1723 until his death.

As *Kantor* Bach was responsible for teaching music and Latin to the boarding school students. As director he supervised the music for 4 city churches and provided music for important civil functions. Liturgically St. Thomas was conservative: services of *holy communion every Sunday followed the liturgical *year, included Latin *prefaces, a Greek *Kyrie and Latin *Gloria. *Christmas, *Easter and *Pentecost were each observed for 3 days; liturgical and musical energy was expended on numerous special days, including 3 "Mary" observances.

In addition to a wide variety of instrumental music and various instruction books, Bach composed much music for worship: *c* 200 so-called sacred *cantatas in 5 cycles (another 100 perhaps which are lost), 5 *passions (*St. John and *St. Matthew survive with music, *St. Mark with text only), 3 *oratorios, 4 *Missae breves, 5 *Sanctus settings, the *B-minor Mass, at least 8 *motets and nearly 200 *keyboard pieces based on *chorales (e.g., *Orgelbüchlein).

A renowned keyboard improvisationalist, he privately taught *c* 80 students. Though unsuccessful in meeting *Handel, he had contacts with *Telemann, *Buxtehude and many others. As a Lutheran *Kantor* he understood himself as a musical preacher. Though influenced by contemporary *pietism, stronger orthodox theological leanings are reflected in his impressive theological library which at his death numbered 52 titles in *c* 112 volumes

Bibl: K. Geiringer, *Johann Sebastian Bach,* rev. ed. (New York, 1978); C. Wolff, "Johann Sebastian Bach," *The New Grove Bach* (New York, 1983) 44–237; G. Stiller, *Johann Sebastian Bach and Liturgical Life in Leipzig* (St. Louis, 1984). MPB

Bach, Wilhelm Friedemann (*b* Weimar 1710; *d* Berlin 1784). The oldest and favored son of J. S. *Bach; gifted keyboardist, and capable composer. Organist at Dresden's Sophienkirche (1733) then Halle's Liebfrauenkirche (1746–64). He remained in Halle until 1770; after a brief period in Brunswick he moved to Berlin (after 1774). Later years heightened his personal instabilities; he died in poverty. His *c* 25 church *cantatas show a dedication to older styles, often containing large sections lifted from his father's works. MPB

Bach (family). A large family of musicians which, according to a genealogy prepared by J. S. *Bach, begins with Viet (*d* 1578), his great, great grandfather, born in Moravia or Slovakia but who moved to Wechmar in Thuringia. The last notable member of the family was Wilhelm Freidrich Ernst (*d* 1845). Family members included musicians of all sorts, chiefly instrumentalists, who ordinarily were trained by relatives, rooted in the cultural traditions of C Germany and solidly committed to Thuringia's Lutheranism. One or another of the family reached every level and sphere of contemporary musical activity. Those remembered as composers include: Johann Sebastian; his brother Johann Christoph; a distant cousin, Johann Ludwig; and Johann Sebastian's sons, Wilhelm Friedemann *Bach, Carl Philipp Emmanuel *Bach and Johann Christian *Bach.
  Bibl: C. Wolff, *The New Grove Bach Family* (New York, 1983). MPB

Bach-Gesellschaft [German]. "Bach society." An organization founded in 1850 by O. Jahn, M. *Hauptmann, C. F. Becker and R. Schumann. The society took on a 50-year task of publishing all of J. S. *Bach's compositions in 46 volumes. MPB

Baek, Sven Erik. (*b* Stockholm 1919). Violinist and composer. He studied at Stockholm's Music Academy (1939–43), in Basel and Rome. Baek wrote string quartets, orchestral sinfonias, *oratorios, chamber operas and 13 choral *motets. JLB

Baer, Abraham (*b* Posen province of Prussia 1834; *d* Gothenburg 1894). *Cantor. One of the earliest collectors of Jewish liturgical melodies, collecting C and E European melodies from both oral and written traditions. In his monumental *Ba'al tefilah* (1877 [reprint 1953]) he cites musical examples for many liturgical texts, often citing variants between the 2 European traditions. As the earliest complete compilation of 19th-century cantorial practices, it is authoritative and has served as a textbook for training cantors for almost a century. MLK

Bairstow, Edward C(uthbert) (*b* Huddersfield 1874; *d* York 1946). Composer and organist of York Minster (from 1913). He was a major figure in English *church music in the first half of the 20th century. His compositions include a *communion service (1913) and organ sonata (1937). AJL

Bajoncillo [Spanish, diminutive of *bajón*, "bassoon"]. (1) A small *Dulzian* (German) or *bajón* (Spanish), an early bassoon constructed in 1 piece and often employed in sacred music.
  (2) An *organ stop found in late 17th-century Spanish *instruments at 4-foot pitch. JPM

Baker, Henry William (*b* London 1821; *d* Monkland 1877). *Hymn writer, translator and author of devotional prayer books. The vicar of Monkland, Herefordshire (1851–77), he chaired the editorial committee for *Hymns Ancient and Modern*. RJS

Baker, Robert Stevens (*b* Pontiac IL 1916). Organist and liturgical musician at New York's Fifth Ave. and First Presbyterian Churches, and Temple Emmanuel. He also served as the director of the *Union Seminary School of Sacred Music and *Yale Institute of Sacred Music. JBW

Bakkashah (pl. **bakkashot**) [Hebrew]. "Request." A liturgical poem chanted as a prayer of supplication before prayers on the *Sabbath. *Bakkashot* recitation begins late Friday night and continues until sunrise at which time *shacharit* begins. Moroccan and Syrian communities in particular have continued this practice.

Bibl: E. Seroussi, "Politics, Ethnic Identity and Music in Israel," *Asian Music* 17 (1985) 32–45. MLK

Balbi <Balbus>, **Ludovico** (*b* Venice *c* 1545; *d* there 1604). Composer. He served as *maestro di cappella* at the Franciscan monastery in Venice (1578), St. Antonio in Padua (1585–91), Feltre (1593–97) and Treviso (1597–98) Cathedrals. His works include *masses, *motets and sacred songs. He compiled collections of *graduals and *antiphons by Italian masters (1591). MJK

Balhoff, Michael. See *Dameans.

Banchieri, Adriano (*b* Bologna 1568; *d* there 1634). Benedictine monk and composer. He served as organist at the monastery of St. Michele in Bosco. He authored a series of treatises on performance practices and composed *masses, *psalm settings, *motets and other *sacred as well as secular music. DCI

Baptist worship music. The range of Baptist worship styles in N America is wide, governed by regional style more than theological or denominational distinctions. Some congregations are formal in style, nearly liturgical; others are quite informal. In the vast majority of Baptist churches, worship is the personal experience of worshipping God through Jesus Christ, proclaiming his gospel and seeking to persuade the non-believer to believe in him. Congregational music is shaped to meet these ends.

In their early history Baptists did not sing in worship. 17th-century congregations began singing *psalms. George Whitefield's revivals introduced American Baptists to the hymns of *Watts and others. *Camp meeting songs of the early 19th century, *singing schools and the publication of oblong *tune books (most notably *Sacred Harp) expanded Baptist hymnic repertoire particularly in the S. The growth of the Sunday school movement and the revivals of Charles Finney and *Moody in the N encouraged writers like *Bradbury and *Bliss to compose songs with *choruses expounding the need for redemption and the personal joy experienced from Christ's death for the believer's salvation.

Frontier and urban revivalism in the 19th and 20th centuries shaped Baptist worship and music practices. Many Baptist *services end with an invitation for believers to recommit or non-believers to commit themselves to Christ; appropriate *hymns or songs of invitation are sung by the congregation or *choir. Many African American Baptist congregations begin their worship with an extended song service. Baptist congregations have recently been influenced by *charismatic worship and musical styles.

*Organs have been used in Baptist worship since at least the 19th century. Southern Baptists, in particular, have encouraged the use of wind and string *instruments in forming *orchestras during much of the 20th century. Praise bands to accompany contemporary musical styles can be found across the spectrum.

Choirs were organized in larger churches of the N by the late 18th century; in the S by the 19th. Regularly providing *anthems, they may also sing more of the service music (e.g., *introit, *responses, *offertory, etc.) and lead the congregation in singing a *doxology following the offering. In some congregations "special" music may be sung by soloists or small groups in addition to or replacing the anthem. See *African American Baptist worship music.

Bibl: Baptist History and Heritage 19:1 (Jan 1984) 2–62; D. W. Music, "Baptist church, music of," *NGDAM* 1:140–41; D. P. Hustad, *Jubilate II* (Carol Stream, 1993). RJS

Barber, Samuel (*b* West Chester PA 1910; *d* New York 1981). Composer of works in all the principal genres, including choral works on religious texts (e.g., *Prayers of Kierkegaard,* op. 30, 1954). He was known for his conservative style, Romantic lyricism and sensitive text setting. KRH

Barbireau, Jacques <Jacobus> (*b* Mons? *c* 1420; *d* Antwerp 1491). Composer. He was choirmaster at Antwerp Cathedral (from 1448), where he was succeeded by *Obrecht. *Ockeghem was a pupil. His works include *masses, *antiphons and *psalms. MJK

Barechu <*Barekhu*> [Hebrew]. "Blessed is He." The first word of the call to worship (*"Barechu et Adonai hamevorach,"* "Praised be the Lord forever and ever") in Jewish prayer. This call to worship begins *shacharit* and *ma'ariv,* introducing the *Shema* section; it also begins the *blessing that precedes the *Torah reading. In each case, after the call to worship the congregation responds *"Baruch Adonai hamevorach le'olam va'ed"* ("Blessed is the Lord who is blessed forever and ever"). Its musical treatment is usually *chant-like, in the *mode of each particular *service (see *Jewish prayer modes). Some well known musical examples are the High Holiday *Ashkenazic tune, the Ashkenazic chant sung at the blessing before reading the Torah, and the 3-part choral setting by *Rossi. BES

Bärenreiter Verlag [German]. "Bärenreiter Publishing House." A major publisher of W European music and books about music; founded by Karl Vötterle in Kassel (1923). Has published many critical editions (e.g., *Schütz, J. S. *Bach, *Mozart); also published works from the German *church music revival. MPB

Barnard's collection. A significant collection of English *church music compiled by John Barnard; published as *The First Book of Selected Church Music* (1641). It includes works by *Tallis, *Byrd, *Gibbons, *Weelkes and others. DWM

Barnby, Joseph (*b* York 1838; *d* London 1896). Church organist and conductor. He composed *anthems, *chants, *hymn tunes and *oratorios in a Victorian style. He served as musical advisor to Novello and Company and edited 5 *hymnals including *The Hymnary* (1872). RJS

Baroque [French]. "Irregular, grotesque" [from the Portuguese for "rough or imperfect pearl"]. The period of music in the W from *c* 1600–1750. Its general boundaries are Giulio Caccini's collection *Le Nuove Musiche* (1602), or 20 to 30 years earlier, and J. S. *Bach's death (1750). Three approximate half-century subdivisions of the period are early (*Monteverdi, *Carissimi, *Schütz), middle (*Purcell, *Pachelbel) and late (Bach, *Handel, *Vivaldi); these subdivisions can vary from country to country. Baroque meant a rough or grotesque artistic style at the mid-18th century, and only in the 20th century was the term applied to this musical period, which moves from the *monody of Monteverdi to the *polyphony of Bach, with a *basso continuo* underlay.

Varied musical developments included *Nicolai's *chorales; Carissimi's *oratorios (e.g., *Jephte*); Monteverdi's sacred vocal music and *masses; *Frescobaldi's and *Sweelinck's *organ music; the works of *Hassler, *Schein, *Scheidt and *Scheidemann; M. *Praetorius' prolific composing plus his historical, liturgical and theoretical work in the *Syntagma musicum;* Schütz's *passions, *psalm settings and other choral works; Pachelbel's organ music, *motets and *Magnificat*s; Purcell's *anthems and *services; *Crüger's *hymn tunes and his collection *Praxis pietatis melica;* *Greene's anthems; *Kuhnau's vocal music; Handel's motets, organ *concertos and oratorios (e.g., *Messiah*); Corelli's *church sonatas*; *Vivaldi's masses, psalm settings, motets, oratorios, *cantatas and instrumental music; the *Schnitgers' and *Silbermanns' organ building; and J. S. Bach's passions, *B Minor Mass, Magnificat,* motets, *cantatas and organ works.

Liturgical expressions were equally varied. The development of opera pushed the mass in the direction of a sacred drama and stimulated cantata composition; Presbyterians and Independent Puritans produced the *Westminster Directory* (1645); the hymns of *Watts and C. *Wesley and a Wesleyan movement unfolded; *Pietism shaped public and private prayer, while the full practice of Bach's Leipzig continued.

Bibl: M. F. Bukofzer, *Music in the Baroque Era* (New York, 1947); C. Palisca, *Baroque Music,* 3rd ed. (Englewood Cliffs NJ, 1991); D. Grout, *A History of Western Music,* 5th ed. (New York, 1996), chps 9–11. PHW

Barraclough, Henry (*b* Windhill, England 1891; *d* Philadelphia 1983). Revival pianist, *gospel hymn composer and administrator for the United Presbyterian Church in the US. He succeeded R. *Harkness as pianist for C. *Alexander. Barraclough wrote "Ivory Palaces" and about 120 other *hymn tunes. DWM

Bartók, Béla (*b* Nagyszentmiklós, Hungary 1881; *d* New York 1945). Composer and pianist who extensively researched the *folk music of E Europe. With *Kodály he produced 12 volumes of folk songs. He wrote *Romanian Christmas Carols* (1915) for piano, based on materials collected in N Romania. Among his masterpieces are *Concerto for Orchestra* (1942–43, rev. 1945) and *String Quartets* 3–6 (1927–39). JBF

Baruch <*Barukh*> **she-amar** [Hebrew]. "Blessed be he who spoke." A prayer opening the *Pesukei dezimrah* section of *shacharit* in the *Ashkenazic tradition and employed in the middle of that section in the *Sephardic rite. The prayer lists several praises to God; *baruch* ("blessed") occurs 13 times in the prayer. Traditions differ concerning whether the *chazzan* (in whole or part) or the congregation recites the prayer. MLK

Basso continuo [Italian]. "Continuous bass." In *Baroque music, a type of accompaniment consisting of a bass line with numbers above it indicating harmonies, hence the almost synonymous "figured bass." When associated with vocal *church music, the *basso continuo* is understood to help proclaim and interpret a text rhetorically. VEG

Batastini, Robert J (*b* 1942 Chicago). Music editor, organist, choral director and *pastoral musician. Senior editor at *GIA Publications (from 1968), he has supervised various editions of the *Worship* *hymnal series, other hymnals and *liturgical music publications. FJM

Bateson, Thomas (*b* Cheshire County *c* 1570–75; *d* Dublin 1630). Composer. He served as organist at Chester Cathedral (from 1599), then *vicar choral and organist at Christ Church Cathedral, Dublin (from 1609). One of the earliest (first?) music graduates from Trinity College, Dublin. Noted for his madrigals. MJK

Batten, Adrian (*b* Salisbury 1591; *d* London 1637). Organist and composer who was active primarily in London. His surviving music (numerous *services, over 40 *anthems) is highly competent, although not particularly innovative. He is best remembered as the copyist of the "Batten Organbook,"

an extensive collection of English *church music. AJL

Battishill, Jonathan (*b* London 1738; *d* there 1801). Composer whose output was primarily secular, but includes some 10 *anthems (notably "O Lord look down" and "Call to Remembrance") and a handful of *chants. AJL

Bay Psalm Book. *The Whole Booke of Psalmes Faithfully Translated into English Metre* was the first book published in N America (Cambridge MA, 1640), designed to replace both the *Ainsworth and *Sternhold and Hopkins psalters. Revised editions, known as *The New England Psalm Book,* continued in use through the 18th century. Early editions contained no music: the first edition commended the tunes found in *Ravenscroft; the 9th edition (1698) included 13 tunes, the earliest printed music in N America. RAL

BCL. See *Bishops' Committee on the Liturgy.

Béatitudes, Les [French]. "The Beatitudes." An *oratorio by C. *Franck (1879) in 8 parts based on a gospel text from Matt 5:3-12. One of Franck's major works, it shows Wagnerian influences. RAD

Beatitudes, The. A text from Matt 5:3-12. Aside from its use as a *gospel reading, this text has no separate liturgical use in the Roman rite. In the *Lutheran Book of Worship* (1978) it appears as an optional *canticle for the "Service of the Word." In the Canadian *Book of Alternate Services* (1985) it appears among the canticles for use at *morning and *evening prayer. For use in E churches, see *Blazhenny.* JMT

Beck, Theodore A. (*b* Oak Park IL 1929). Teacher and composer. Awarded a Ph.D. from Northwestern University, he taught at *Concordia College, River Forest IL (1950–53) and Concordia Teachers' College, Seward NE (from 1953). He wrote and published *organ *preludes, *intonations and choral works. JLB

Becker, Cornelius (*b* Leipzig 1561; *d* there 1604). Lutheran theologian and pastor of St. Nicolai (Leipzig). His *psalter (1602), written to counter Lobwasser's *Reformed Psalter* (1573), was the source for *Schütz's book of *metrical psalms. RDH

Bédos de Celles, François (*b* Caux 1709; *d* St-Denis 1779). Benedictine *organ builder and writer. His important *The Art of the Organ Builder* (1766–78) describes the workings of the organ and gives directions for registration and ornamentation. PKG

Beethoven, Ludwig van (*b* Bonn 1770; *d* Vienna 1827). Composer whose enormous and influential output includes 9 symphonies, 1 violin and 5 piano *concertos, 17 string quartets, 32 piano sonatas, 10 sonatas for violin and piano, the opera *Fidelio,* *cantatas, the *oratorio *Christus am Ölberge* and 2 *masses. His works changed W Classical music, ushering in the *Romantic era. He likewise expanded traditional music forms of the RC Church, infusing them with the power of religious feeling and faith. His *Mass in C Major* (1807) and *Missa Solemnis* (1819–23), useful mainly for concert performance, provided symphonic scope and complexity to the *ordinary of the mass.
Bibl: W. Kinderman, *Beethoven* (Berkeley, 1995). JBF

Bell, John L. (*b* Kilmarnock, Scotland 1949). An ordained minister in the Church of Scotland, Bell composes *hymn tunes, texts and other worship materials that reflect the Celtic spirituality of the *Iona Community, of which he is a member. KRH

Bellavere <Bell'Haver>, **Vincenzo** (*b* Venice? *c* 1530; *d* there 1587). Organist and composer. He was a pupil of A. *Gabrieli, whom he succeeded as first organist of St. Mark's in 1586. Bellavere composed *toccatas and much *church music, though best-known for his madrigals. MJK

Belli, Guilio (*b* Longiano *c* 1560; *d* Imola *c* 1621). Composer and Franciscan friar. He served as *maestro di cappella* at Imola (1582–90, 1611–13, 1621), Ferrara, Ravenna, St. Anthony in Padua and St. Mark's in Venice. His works include *psalms, *masses, *motets and *church concertos. MJK

Bells. Hollow *instruments, usually metal (occasionally hard clay or glass), shaped like a cup (e.g., *handbells) or hollow sphere. They sound when struck externally or internally (by clapper). The widest range in size of any *instrument, bells are used extensively in religious rites throughout history and across cultures. In Christianity they are used to call people to worship, announce *hours of the *divine office, signal the *elevation and toll for the dead. See *change ringing. RKW

Belshazzar's Feast. A *cantata by *Walton for baritone, *choir and orchestra (1931) to a text by Osbert Sitwell drawn from the *psalms and the book of Daniel.   JBF

Bema [Greek]. "Platform." The raised space in E Christian churches containing the altar. Separated from the nave by the iconostasis, it corresponds to the sanctuary in the W. See *bimah.   EBF

Benda, Georg Anton <Jirí Antonín> (b Stare' Bena'tky 1722; d Köstritz 1795). A chamber musician in Berlin (1742–49), then *Kappellmeister in Saxe-Gotha (1750–88). He developed the novel idea of the music-drama with spoken words. His early works were chiefly *church cantatas.   JLB

Bender, Jan Oskar (b Haarlem, Netherlands 1909; d Hanerau 1994). Composer. The only student of *Distler. *Kantor in Lübeck and Lüneberg, he taught music at *Concordia (NE), Wittenberg University (OH), *Valparaiso and other Lutheran schools in the US. He retired to Germany. As a church composer, he published over 300 works for *organ, *choir and *instruments.   MPB

Benedicamus Domino [Latin]. "Let us bless the Lord." A *versicle sung as the conclusion to each *hour of the *divine office (the *response is Deo gratias, "Thanks be to God"). Before the reforms of *Vatican II it was also used at the close of *mass in place of *Ite missa est on all days when the *Gloria in excelsis was not sung. *Chant settings varied according to the degree of solemnity from simple syllabic or *neumatic to elaborate *melismatic ones.   CJK

Benedicite [Latin]. "Bless [the Lord]." A *canticle from Dan 3:52-90; also called the "Canticle of the Three Young Men." Widely employed in Christian worship, e.g., *Easter vigil, *lauds, *orthros and the morning office of the *BCP.   MJG

Benediction [from Latin bene, "well" and dicere, "to speak"]. (1) A *blessing, especially that imparted at the end of worship.

(2) A RC, Anglo-Catholic *service in which consecrated eucharistic bread is exposed to public view in a monstrance. Incense, *hymns (e.g., *Tantum ergo), *litanies and prayers accompany the exposition, which ends after the people are blessed with the *sacrament.   NDM

Benedict of Nursia, St. (b Norcia c 480; d Monte Cassino 550). Author of an influential monastic rule, rich with information about early monastic liturgical practice, especially the *divine office with its 1-week *psalmody cycle and *office hymns.   AWR

Benedictus (Dominus) [Latin]. "Blessed (be the Lord)." The *Canticle of Zachary (Luke 1:68-79). A traditional element in *lauds, it is now sung at *morning prayer in the RC, Lutheran and Anglican *divine office.   FCQ

Benedictus (qui venit) [Latin]. "Blessed is he (who comes)." Part of the fourth element of the *ordinary of the mass. The text is adopted from Matt 21:9, first appearing in Roman usage c 7th century. Sung as the closing part of the *Sanctus; by 1600 it was sung separately after the consecration.   PAJ

Beneventan chant. The *chant of S C Italian medieval use, centered in

Benevento and Monte Cassino. Sources date from the 10th to 13th centuries. After the influx of *Gregorian chant into the region, the 2 musical traditions coexisted for a time. Eventually submerged by the Gregorian, the full Beneventan repertoire is not recoverable; many individual chants have survived within sources that are principally Gregorian. Beneventan melodies show a preference for stepwise movement and repetition of phrases is common. Liturgically, the Beneventan tradition has similarities to the *Ambrosian; musically, it is nearer to the *Old Roman repertoire. Beneventan manuscripts have a characteristic elegant script and notational style.

Bibl: T. F. Kelly, *The Beneventan Chant* (Cambridge, 1989). JMH

Benevoli, Orazio (*b* Rome 1605; *d* there 1672). Composer. He served as *maestro di cappella* at St. Peter's Cappella Giulia and other Roman churches, then briefly *Kapellmeister* to Vienna's Archduke Leopold Wilhelm. His compositions, ranging from solo vocal pieces with *continuo* to large works for 24 voices, include *masses, *motets, *Magnificats, and *psalms. The famous 53-voice *Missa salisburgensis* once attributed to him is now thought to be by Biber or Hofer. DWM

Bennett, William Sterndale (*b* Sheffield 1816; *d* London 1875). Composer, pianist and conductor. He befriended F. *Mendelssohn and R. Schumann. The founder of the Bach Society (London, 1849), he taught at Cambridge. Besides orchestral compositions, he wrote an *oratorio, a *cantata and many *anthems. MJK

Berakah. See *blessing.

Berger, Jean (*b* Hamm 1909). Composer. He emigrated from Germany to work in Paris and Rio de Janeiro before moving to the US (1941). Berger is best known for his choral works, including *Brazilian Psalm* (1941) and *Vision of Peace* (1948). VAC

Berkeley, Lennox (Randall Francis) (*b* Boar's Hill 1903; *d* London 1989). Composer. On the music staff of the BBC (1942–45), he then taught composition at London's Royal Academy of Music (1946–68). His choral works include *Domini est terra* (1937), *Missa brevis* (1960), *Stabat Mater* (1947) and *Magnificat* (1968); he also wrote some *organ music. MJK

Berlinski, Herman (*b* Leipzig 1910). Composer. He studied at the Leipzig Conservatory (1928–32), then in Paris with Boulanger (1934–38). He emigrated to the US and became organist at New York's Temple Emanu-El (1954) and Washington DC's Hebrew Congregation (1963). He wrote sacred works for soloists, *chorus, *organ or *orchestra, e.g., *Avodat Shabbat: Sacred Service* (1958). JLB

Berlioz, (Louis-) Hector (*b* La Côte-St-André 1803; *d* Paris 1869). Composer, critic and orchestrator. He helped turn French *church music to symphonic forms. His sacred works include *Messe solennelle* (1824), *Grande messe des morts* (*Requiem) (1837), *Te Deum* (1849) and *L'*Enfance du Christ* (1850–54). He wrote the influential *Grand traité d'instrumentation* (1843; later published as *Treatise on Instrumentation*, 1855). JBF

Bernardi, Steffano (*b* Verona *c* 1585; *d* Salzburg? 1636). Composer and theorist.

He served as *maestro di cappella* in Verona (1611–22), then moved to Salzburg where he became *Kapellmeister* (by 1628). He composed *masses, *psalms, *motets, a *Te Deum* for 12 choirs and a *counterpoint manual (1615).   MJK

Bernard of Clairvaux, St. (*b* Fontaines-Dijon 1090/91; *d* Clairvaux 1153). Cistercian theologian, mystic, reformer and statesman. He preached the 2nd Crusade. He wrote an *office for St. Victor, a *hymn in honor of St. Malachy and the prologue to the Cistercian *antiphonary. Bernard promoted Cistercian liturgical reform involving both textual and musical revisions of traditional chants: modifying florid melodies, resolving modal ambiguities and excising *musica ficta*. He introduced newly composed pieces into the Cistercian repertoire.   JMJ

Bernhard, Christoph (*b* Kolberg, Pomerania 1628; *d* Dresden 1692). Composer and theorist. He was a pupil of *Schütz for whose funeral he composed a *motet. In *Tractatus compositionis* he classified styles of *Baroque music; *church music was *stylus gravis* or in the style of *Palestrina. He wrote sacred *concertos.   VEG

Bernstein, Leonard (*b* Lawrence MA 1918; *d* New York 1990). Composer, conductor, pianist and teacher. Bernstein was equally prolific in musical theater composition, symphonic composition and performance. His major religious works (all for voices and *instruments) are *Kaddish* (Symphony n. 3, 1963), *Chichester Psalms* (1965) and *Mass* (1971).   FJM

Berthier, Jacques (*b* Auxerre 1923; *d* Paris 1994). Composer, organist and teacher. His instrumental compositions (especially for *organ) use the harmonic/rhythmic language of 19th- and early 20th-century impressionism. Much of the music sung at *Taizé is his.   FJM

Bertoni, Ferdinando (Gasparo) (*b* Saló 1725; *d* Desenzano 1813). Organist and composer who studied with *Martini. He served at St. Mark's in Venice as first organist (1752), later *maestro di cappella* (1785). He wrote many operas, over 50 *oratorios and almost 200 other sacred works.   MJK

Bethel A(frican) M(ethodist) E(piscopal) <AME> worship music. Founded (1862) as an extension of the *AME Church, the music of this church includes Wesleyan *hymns, Negro *spirituals, *gospel hymns, African American *gospel music and independent *refrains. The congregation sings from the *AME Bicentennial Hymnal* (1984) accompanied by pipe *organ. The *choir features *anthems, Negro spirituals and gospel music.   HCB

Betsingmesse [German]. "Pray-sing-mass." 20th-century adaptation of the traditional *Singmesse* which included the communal recitation of vernacular texts (parallel to the priest's recitation of those texts in Latin) and singing vernacular *hymnody somewhat related to the liturgical action.   AWR

Bible, music of the. See *Temple music and *New Testament, music of the.

Bibelorgel. See *regal.

Bible Regal. See *regal.

Bidding prayer [from Anglo-Saxon *béodan,* "to offer"]. (1) A form of intercessory prayer, inserted after the sermon at *mass, developing by the 9th century. Commonly known as "bidding the bedes" (Anglo-Saxon for "offering the prayers"). It became part of *prone. Fixed and required by Anglican Canon 55 (1604), it is now optional in Anglican worship.
(2) *Prayer of the faithful.   EBF

Billings, William (*b* Boston 1746; *d* there 1800). Singing master and leader of the *First New England School. Eccentric, physically disabled and defiant in spirit, he epitomized rough-hewn New England ingenuity. Musically self-taught, he led *singing schools around Boston. His intensely patriotic *hymn tune CHESTER (to his own text) became a Revolutionary favorite.
He wrote *fuging tunes and *anthems, published in 6 major collections, from *The New-England Psalm Singer* (1770) to his last, *The Continental Harmony* (1794), always following his instincts or rules of "nature" rather than rules of composition. Billings uses vivid rhythms and spare harmonies thus helping define an emerging American sound in music.
Bibl: The Complete Works of William Billings, ed. K. Kroeger, H. Nathan (Charlottesville VA-Boston, 1977–).   VEG

Billups, Kenneth Brown (*b* St. Louis 1918; *d* there 1985). Educator, arranger, composer and conductor. A high school teacher, he organized and directed the first interracial *choir in St. Louis. Noted for compositions employing themes from *spirituals.   MWC

Bimah [Hebrew]. "Platform." The platform in the synagogue where the *Torah reading occurs. It is usually separate from the Ark. Part or all of the *service may be conducted from the *bimah.* See *bema.*   MLK

Binchois, Gilles de Bins <Binch, Binche> **dit** (*b* Mons? *c* 1400; *d* Soignies 1460). Composer and organist who served the Burgundian court in Dijon (1427–53). Famous for *chansons,* he also wrote *motets, *hymns, *mass parts (no complete cycle survives), **Magnificat*s and a **Te Deum.* Much of his *liturgical music employs simple melodies, balanced phrases, uncomplicated rhythm, often in *fauxbourdon.*   LFH

Binder, Abraham (*b* New York 1895; *d* there 1967). Composer, writer and organist. Influenced by Palestinian *folk songs (music in Israel prior to its formation as a state in 1948), he sought to incorporate traditional Jewish elements into compositions for Reform synagogues. He edited the *Union Hymnal* (3rd edition, 1946). His writings focused on *cantillation and a range of liturgical issues, e.g., his *Studies in Jewish Music* (1971).   MLK

Birkat hachodesh. See **Rosh Chodesh.*

Birkat hamazon <*hammazon*> [Hebrew]. "Grace after meals." A prayer recited after a meal at which bread has been eaten, in evidence by the 1st century BCE. Today it contains 4 *blessings: 1) praising God for providing food for all creatures, 2) thanking God for the land of Israel, 3) requesting the coming of the time of the Messiah and the rebuilding of Jerusalem, and 4) acknowledging God's goodness and one's desire for peace (added after the destruction of the Second Temple). Personal blessings follow. On *Sabbaths and festivals, Ps 126 (see *Shir hama'alot) is recited at the beginning. On holidays, weddings and circumcisions other blessings and petitions are inserted. Most frequently sung around the table to *folk-like melodies; one familiar example was composed by M. Nathanson.   BES

Birkat haschachar. See *shacharit.

Birkat kohanim <nesiat kappayim> [Hebrew]. "Blessing of the priests <raising the hands>." The priestly *blessing from Num 6:24-26; originally recited by priests (Hebrew, kohanim) during Temple times. Today it concludes the *Amidah and is recited publicly when the Amidah is repeated, with members of the priestly class coming to the *bimah. *Ashkenazic and *Sephardic traditions differ in this practice.

Ashkenazic Jews musically elaborate the prayer on the *Three Festivals and *High Holidays; Sephardic Jews and Ashkenazic Jews in Israel use musical elaboration everyday. Musical elaboration entails the *chazzan reciting 1 word of this blessing and kohanim repeating it. At the end of each of the 3 biblical sentences the congregation responds *amen. For Ashkenazic Jews kohanim sing a melody to extend the word at the conclusion of each of the 3 sentences prior to the congregation's amen. When Birkat kohanim is recited without musical elaboration members of the priestly class do not come forward, and the chazzan recites the biblical sentence in full without musical elaboration. The priestly class coming forward and the use of melodic elaboration is called duchanen ("those who come forward to the platform").

Birkat kohanim is recited during the wedding ceremony by the clergy and often recited privately on Friday night by the father or parents to children. In Reform synagogues an elaborate composition based on this text and practice may close a *service (usually called a *benediction). The setting by *Freed is widely used.   MLK

Bishops' Committee on the Liturgy <BCL>. A standing committee of the US National Conference of RC Bishops. Responsible in the bishops' conference for all matters liturgical, including the preparation and approval of liturgical *books, texts and a limited amount of music for the rites. The BCL includes a group of advisors and a secretariat in Washington DC to carry out its work.   JBF

Bizet, Georges (b Paris 1838; d Bougival 1875). Composer and pianist. Celebrated for his operas, he also wrote some choral music. Not seriously interested in religious music, only a few of his vocal solos and choral works have religious texts, such as his *Te Deum (1858).   VAC

Black National Anthem. A designation given to the *hymn "Lift Every Voice and Sing" (1921), composed by J. R. *Johnson. The text by J. W. *Johnson expresses faith born of the "dark past" of African American slavery and hope for future victory. It is performed across denominational lines.   MEM

Black spiritual. See *spiritual.

Blankenburg, Walter (b Emleben 1903; d there 1986). Theologian and musicologist. He edited the German Lutheran periodical on *church music *Musik und Kirche* from 1941–86. He also promoted scholarly theological research on the works of J. S. *Bach by founding (1976) the *Internationale Arbeitsgemeinschaft für theologische Bachforschung.* MPB

Blazhenny [Slavonic; Greek *makarismoi*]. "The Beatitudes." The Beatitudes, according to Matt 5:3-12, are frequently sung in the Slavonic tradition as the 3rd *antiphon in the *enarxis* of the Byzantine *divine liturgy. In monasteries they are intercalated with *stichera. *Blazhenny* are taken from the office of *typika* where they originated, and are still used in all branches of the Byzantine Church. DMP

Blessing. (1) For Jews, a blessing in everyday speech is a prayer said for the good of a person. The formal Hebrew blessing thanks, praises or petitions God. Common are blessings for the privilege of deriving enjoyment from God's creations or observing God's commandments. The recitation of blessings is central to Jewish worship and daily living. See entries beginning with *Baruch, *Birkat.

(2) For Christians, a blessing is ordinarily an invocation or declaration of divine favor, often trinitarian in form, addressed to people (e.g., "May almighty God bless you, the Father, the Son and the Holy Spirit"). Blessings commonly conclude worship. MLK

Bliss, Philip (*b* Rome PA 1836; *d* Ashtabula OH 1876). *Hymn writer and singer who often collaborated with *Sankey. His numerous *gospel hymns (e.g., "Hallelujah, what a Savior"), written with the encouragement of *Moody, were popular in mid-19th century revivals. FJM

Bloch, Ernest (*b* Geneva, Switzerland 1880; *d* Portland OR 1959). Composer and teacher. Bloch studied in Belgium, Germany and France. He taught at the Mannes School of Music in New York (1917–19) and the University of California-Berkeley (1940–52); also serving as director of the Cleveland Institute of Music (1920–25) and the San Francisco Conservatory (1925–30). His large catalogue of works (25 orchestral works as well as chamber, vocal and instrumental works) shows neo-classical, neo-romantic and expressionist influences. Bloch is most celebrated for expressing his commitment to Judaism through music, e.g., *Trois poèms juifs* (1913), *Prelude and 2 Psalms* (1914), *Israel Symphony* (1916), *Schelomo* (1916) and his sacred service *Avodah hakodesh* (1933).

Bibl: D. Kushner, *Ernest Bloch* (New York, 1988). RAD-SIW

Blow, John (*b* Newark, Nottinghamshire 1649; *d* Westminster 1708). Composer. After service as a chorister in the *Chapel Royal, he was named organist at Westminster Abbey (1668), and then became master of the children of the Chapel Royal (1674). Later posts included master of the choristers at St. Paul's Cathedral (1687–1703) and official composer of the Chapel Royal (first to hold that post in 1700). Blow's *church music includes 25 symphony *anthems, numerous *services and many non-orchestral anthems (both *full and *verse). His secular works include numerous *odes and the short opera *Venus and Adonis;* he also wrote a considerable amount of *keyboard music.

Bibl: B. W. Wood, "John Blow's Anthems with Orchestra" (Cambridge University: Ph.D. diss., 1977).   AJL

Blume, Friedrich (*b* Schlüchtern 1893; *d* there 1975). Musicologist who taught at the Universities of Berlin and Kiel, and Spandau's *church music school. He wrote significant articles on the German church music revival. Blume edited *Praetorius' work, a series on early choral works (*Das Chorwerk,* 1929–38) and the encyclopedia *Die Musik im Geschichte und Gegenwart* (1st edition 1949–68). He published *Geschichte der evangelischen Kirchenmusik* (1965; later published as *Protestant Church Music,* 1974).   MPB

B-minor Mass. A large-scale Latin work for *choir, soloists and *orchestra by J. S. *Bach. It was compiled/composed by Bach in 1748–49, making it one of his last compositions. The text is the 5-part Latin *mass with some variants. Music for the *Kyrie* and *Gloria* comes from a 1733 *missa brevis;* the *Sanctus* dates from 1724; the *Agnus Dei* derives from *cantata BWV 11; the *Gloria* and *Credo* were newly composed but also incorporated parodied sections from earlier works (e.g., *cantatas BWV 12 and BWV 120). Unlike his later cantatas, the mass contains no *da capo* *arias or *recitatives. While the *ordinary was employed during *services at Leipzig's St. Thomas, the B-minor Mass was impractical for use there. Bach never heard the work performed as a whole.   MPB

Boatner, Edward (*b* New Orleans 1898; *d* New York 1981). Educator, arranger, composer and conductor. Educated at New England and Boston Conservatories, he became dean of music at Wiley and Houston Colleges. A pioneer researcher in African-American studies, he was also renowned for arrangements of *spirituals sung by Paul Robeson and Marian Anderson (e.g., "Oh, What A Beautiful City").   MWC

Boccherini, Luigi (*b* Lucca 1743; *d* Madrid 1805). Violinist and composer known for his large output of chamber music, 20 symphonies and virtuoso *concertos. His vocal compositions are scant, but include an opera, 2 *oratorios, *Stabat Mater,* a *mass and Christmas *cantata (both lost), and other sacred pieces for *chorus. *Mozart was influenced by his graceful melodic style.   DCI

Boëllmann, Léon (*b* Ensisheim, Upper Alsace 1862; *d* Paris 1897). Composer and organist at Paris' St. Vincent-de-Paul (from 1881). A student of *Gigout, he wrote *organ and other instrumental pieces. His *Suite gothique* (1895) is a *tour de force* of 19th-century French organ music.   FJM

Boethius, Anicius Manlius Torquatus Severinus (*b* Rome *c* 480; *d c* 524). Philosopher and mathematician. Born of a patrician Roman family he held various government posts including that of consul under Emperor Theodoric, who executed him for treason. His treatise on music, *De institutione musica,* written in 5 books, divides music into 1) the harmony of the universe (Latin *musica mundana*), 2) the harmony of humans (Latin *musica humana*) and 3) practical music (Latin *musica instrumentalis*). He also applied Latin letters to tones of the scale, a system used by many after him. *De institutione musica* was a chief source for musical theorists through the *Middle Ages. His affirmation that "music is related not only to speculation but also to morality" was reiterated in works such as *Docta sanctorum patrum, which perpetuated the belief that music embodied the essence of virtue or vice. JLB

Bogoroditchen [Slavonic]. See *Theotokion.

Böhm, Georg (b Hohenkirchen 1661; d Lüneburg 1733). Organist and composer. He studied at the University of Vienna (1684). After work in Hamburg (1693–98) he became organist at Johanniskirche in Lüneburg. While he wrote *church cantatas, *motets and a *passion, he is best known for his *chorale partitas and other *organ and harpsichord pieces and their influence on J. S. *Bach. JLB

Boismortier, Joseph Bodin de (b Thionville 1689; d Roissy-en-Brie 1755). Prolific *Baroque composer known primarily for instrumental compositions, especially for flute. His now lost *motet Fugit nox, based on popular *noels, was performed at the *Concert spirituel for 20 years. Of his sacred works, only a solo motet and a grand motet on Ps 29 survive. RTR

Bonds, Margaret (b Chicago 1913; d Los Angeles 1972). Composer, author, conductor and pianist. Educated at Northwestern University and Juilliard, she received numerous awards from the *National Association of Negro Musicians, the Julius Rosenwald Foundation and others. An accomplished pianist, she concertized and accompanied vocalists frequently. Well-known for her skillful arrangements of *spirituals (e.g.,

"He's got the whole World in His Hands"), she utilized syncopation, *jazz and ragtime chords in many of her compositions, including The Negro Speaks of Rivers, Three Dream Portraits and Mass in D. MWC

Bonnemere, Edward Valentine (b New York 1921; d there 1996). *Jazz pianist and singer, teacher and composer of RC *liturgical music in an African American style. His Missa Hodierna (Latin, "Mass for Today," 1966) was the first mass in a jazz idiom celebrated in a RC *liturgy in the US; it incorporates jazz, *Gregorian chant, bossa nova, *gospel, and *spirituals. MEM

Bonnet, Joseph (b Bordeaux 1884; d St-Luce-sur-Mer, Quebec 1944). Organist, composer and historian. A student of *Guilmant. His 6-volume anthology of early organ music, Historical organ-recitals (1917), paved the way for subsequent organ scholarship. FJM

Bononcini, Giovanni (b Modena 1670; d Vienna, 1747). Composer and cellist who studied in Bologna, and then served as *maestro di cappella at S. Giovanni in Monte (1687–92). After successes in Rome and Vienna, he moved to London (1719) where 60 stage works, 250 solo *cantatas and his many sacred pieces were very popular; his operas were often more popular than *Handel's. His style was harmonically bold, with unusual dissonances and quick modulations; his *arias were graceful and very expressive. DCI

Books, liturgical. In a restricted sense, these are books intended for actual use during worship; in a more general sense, they are books containing texts of the rites and ceremonies intended for worship.

Major "pure" forms for the Roman rite include the *antiphonary, *evangelary, *lectionary, *ordo and *sacramentary. "Mixed" liturgical books include the *pontifical, *missal, ritual (containing prayer-texts for *occasional services), *breviary, *martyrology (containing lives of saints celebrated during the year) and ceremonial of bishops (recording particular variants in episcopal liturgies).

Books for E churches include the *apostol, archieratikon (roughly equivalent to the pontifical), *euchologion, evangelion (the gospel book), *hirmologion, *horologion, *liturgikon (containing priest's parts for the *divine liturgy and other ritual texts), *menaion, *octoechos, *psalterion, *triodion and *typikon.

Liturgical books vary across Protestant denominations. Some traditions employ only the bible and a *hymnal. Others, like the Anglicans, have particular genres of books like the *BCP which they employ in combination with lectionaries and other books. Recently many denominations have produced new service books, shared by assembly and ministry, containing *hymns, *psalters and orders of worship for *eucharist, occasional services, *morning and *evening prayer (e.g., Lutheran Book of Worship, 1978); companion minister's manuals are sometimes produced as well (e.g., Lutheran Book of Worship: Minister's Edition, 1978).

Bibl: C. Vogel, Medieval Liturgy, 2nd ed. (Washington, 1986); "Books, Liturgical" in The New Westminster Dictionary of Liturgy and Worship, ed. J. G. Davies (Philadelphia, 1986), 96–114; E. Palazzo, A History of Liturgical Books (Collegeville, 1998 [1993]).   JMJ

Bornefeld, Helmut (b Stuttgart 1906). Choirmaster and organist at Heidenheimer-Brenz (1937–71); a founder of the Heidenheimer Conference (1946–60) for new *church music. He wrote liturgical *motets, *hymn variations for *organ and 3 books about organs and organ music.   JLB

Bortnyansky <Bortniansky>, **Dmitry Stepanovich** (b Glukhov, Ukraine 1751; d St. Petersburg 1825). Composer of opera and *sacred music. He served as *Kapellmeister at St. Petersburg court (from 1779). Ten volumes of his *anthems, *concertos, *hymns and *liturgies were edited by *Tchaikovsky.   RJS

Bossi, Marco Enrico (b Saló, Lake Garda 1861; d at sea 1925). Organist, teacher and composer. He directed conservatories in Venice (1895–1902), Bologna (1902–11) and Rome (1916–23). A leader of *church music reform in Italy, his compositions include 3 religious choral works: Canticum Canticorum (1900), Il paradiso perduta (1903) and Giovanna d'Arco (1914).   FJM

Bourgeois, Loys <Louis> (b Paris c 1510–15; d c 1560). Composer and theorist. He was active in Geneva (1545–52?) where he is credited with playing a major role in developing the *Genevan Psalter, by adapting and amending previously composed tunes and writing new ones for *Marot's translation of the psalms (*OLD HUNDREDTH, RENDEZ À DIEU and others attributed to him). In 1547 his 2 collections of 4-part *psalm settings were published in Lyon: [50] Pseaulmes de David the more homophonic collection, and Le premier livres des [24] pseaulmes the more elaborate.   EBF

Bower, John Dykes (*b* Gloucester 1905; *d* Orpington 1981). Organist who served cathedrals at Truro, Durham and St. Paul's (London). He toured with the St. Paul's choir to the US (1953), performing for President Eisenhower at the White House and in Carnegie Hall. He was knighted in 1968. FKG

Bowman, Thea <Bertha> (*b* Yazoo City MS 1937; *d* Canton MS 1990). Singer, dancer, author, teacher, evangelist and theologian. A Franciscan Sister of LaCrosse WI, she received a Ph.D. from *Catholic University of America. Bowman was a major catalyst for the incorporation of African American sacred song in RC worship. MEM

Boyce, William (*b* London 1711; *d* Kensington 1799). Composer, organist and music editor. He was composer for the *Chapel Royal (from 1736), and organist there (from 1758). Increasing deafness ended his career as organist in 1769, though he continued composing. He also edited *Cathedral Music* (1760–78), a 3-volume collection of *church music by earlier English composers (e.g., *Gibbons, *Purcell). His compositions include *anthems, *service music for the church, secular songs and theatrical music. His instrumental music, especially the 8 symphonies, are recognized as innovative.
  Bibl: C. Dearnley, *English Church Music 1650–1750* (NY-London: 1970) 271–76. CAD

Boy choir. A traditional choral singing group typically consisting of boys on the highest voice part(s) and alto; men sometimes join on the alto, and/or supply tenor and bass parts. Evidence of choristers exists from the 4th century (*Egeria). The *Schola cantorum* frequently trained boys along with men. Monastic rules (e.g., *St. Benedict's) provided for the presence of boys, who were trained in *psalmody and *chant, sometimes joining the monastic choir. Because of proscriptions against *women singers, boys' voices were cultivated for worship (e.g., in the *Chapel Royal). Some traditions (e.g., Anglican) continue to emphasize boy choirs. LJC

Boyer, Horace Clarence (*b* Winter Park FL 1935). Educator, pianist, composer and arranger. Ph.D. from Eastman. Professor of music at the University of Massachusetts and United Negro College Fund Distinguished Scholar-at-large. Boyer edited the African American *hymnal *Lift Every Voice and Sing II* (1993) and authored *How Sweet the Sound: The Golden Age of Gospel* (1995). MWC

Bozhestvennaya Liturgia [Slavonic]. See *divine liturgy.

Bozhestvennaya Liturgia Prezhdeosvyashchennych [Slavonic]. See *presanctified divine liturgy.

Bradbury, William B. (*b* York Co ME 1816; *d* Montclair NJ 1868). Prolific New York publisher and composer of Sunday school songs and *hymns (e.g., "Jesus loves me"), whose work foreshadowed the *gospel hymn style. His major published collection was *The Jubilee* (1857). VEG

Brahms, Johannes (*b* Hamburg 1833; *d* Vienna 1897). Composer, pianist and conductor. His career was launched by an 1853 article by R. Schumann, and his stature fully recognized with the appearance of his *Ein *Deutsches Requiem* in 1868. Brahms lived in Vienna from 1869 until his death. He composed major works in all genres except opera.

Except for *Ein Deutsches Requiem,* whose biblical texts of consolation the composer chose himself, Brahms' *church music employs short forms. His 16 choral works reveal the influence of J. S. *Bach and other earlier composers in their use of *chorale, *canon and *fugue. Most of these are settings of biblical texts in German for mixed voices. A few are settings of Latin liturgical texts for women's voices. A set of 11 *chorale preludes for *organ was published posthumously.

Bibl: M. MacDonald, *Brahms* (New York, 1990).   KRH

Braunfels, Walter (*b* Frankfurt 1882; *d* Cologne 1954). Composer, founder and director of Cologne's Hochschule für Musik (1925); though he resigned from the Hochschule in 1933, he returned after the war to reorganize it. He wrote operas, an *organ *concerto and large choral/orchestral works including *Passionskantate* (1943).   MJK

Breviary [Latin *breviarium*]. "An abridgment." A 1 volume W liturgical *book for praying the *divine office. It appears by the 11th century as an abbreviated compilation of the several books used in the monastic *office. It allows those traveling (e.g., Franciscans) to pray the office individually. "Choir breviaries" with musical notation for communal performance were introduced in the 12th century.   CSP

Brewer, (Alfred) Herbert (*b* Gloucester 1865; *d* there 1928). Organist and composer. He studied with *Stanford at the Royal College of Music. He was organist at several churches, including Gloucester Cathedral (1896–1928). His compositions include sacred *cantatas, *organ pieces and songs.   MJK

Brewster, William Herbert (*b* Somerville TN 1899; *d* Memphis 1987). African American *gospel song writer and singer. A singing evangelist in Baptist churches in Memphis, he was a popular writer of religious songs, such as "How I got over" which sold over a million copies.   FKG

Bridge, John Frederick (*b* Oldbury 1844; *d* London 1924). Organist, composer (mainly of *oratorios) and professor at the University of London. Bridge was organist at Westminster Abbey for Queen Victoria's jubilees and the coronations of Edward VII and George V.   RDH

Brink, Emily R. (*b* Grand Rapids 1940). Music and worship editor of CRC Publications (Grand Rapids). Brink edited the *Psalter Hymnal* (1987), *Songs for Life* (1994) and the journal *Reformed Worship.* She was president (1990–92) of the *Hymn Society.   JDW

British Methodist worship music. The Methodist revival in Great Britain began with the conversions (1738) of C. and J. *Wesley, who formed and sustained it as an evangelical movement within the Anglican church. In addition to Anglican *cathedral music, British Methodist worship music consisted of standard German and English tunes, and others composed by amateur Methodist musicians based on *folk motifs. The interplay of preaching and song was a way to praise, teach, confess, remember doctrine and enhance preaching. Worship music developed in 4 genres: 1) indoor revival *services led by a *song leader or *precentor (which began at the Foundery in London, spreading throughout Great Britain and Ireland) featuring *hymns of C. Wesley and others; 2) open-air revivals or field preaching with singing usually led by a preacher or another strong voice aided by an oboe; 3) urban hospital chapels (e.g., Foundlings Hospital) where singing was led by *choirs supported by *keyboard and *instruments; 4) operatic-style solo settings of hymns with keyboard (e.g., J. F. Lampe, *Hymns on the Great Festivals and Other Occasions,* 1746), choir *anthems and *fuging tunes.

J. Wesley comments on worship music in his letters, sermons, instructions (e.g., "Thoughts on the Power of Music," 1779) and the prefaces to his tune collections *Sacred Melody* (1761) and *Sacred Harmony* (1780, containing "Directions for Singing").

Bibl: N. Temperley, *The Music of the English Parish Church* (Cambridge, 1979); C. Young, *Music of the Heart* (Carol Stream, 1995).   CRY

Britten, (Edward) Benjamin (*b* Lowestoft 1913; *d* Aldeburgh 1976). Prolific composer, pianist and conductor. He is distinguished for his choral works (*A Boy was Born,* 1933; *A *Ceremony of Carols,* 1942; *Hymn to St. Cecilia,* 1942; *St. Nicholas,* 1948), songs, operas (*Peter Grimes,* 1945; *The Turn of the Screw,* 1954) and instrumental works (*String Quartet in D,* 1931, rev. 1971; *Symphony for Cello and Orchestra,* 1963). His liturgical works include *Te Deums (1934, 1944) and a *Missa brevis (1959). The *War Requiem (1961) received worldwide acclaim following its first performance at Coventry Cathedral. In the 1960s he wrote a Latin setting of the parable of the Good Samaritan (*Cantata Misericordium,* 1963), then a trilogy of church parables: *Curlew River* (1964), *The Burning Fiery Furnace* (1966) and *The Prodigal Son* (1968). Despite an early venture into serialism, Britten never abandoned the principles of tonality which he employed with remarkable originality. He is particularly successful in his compositions for treble choirs that are so much a part of English choral music.

Bibl: H. Carpenter, *Benjamin Britten* (New York, 1992); P. J. Hodgson, *Benjamin Britten* (New York, 1996).   MSD

Brixi, František <Franz> **Xaver** (*bapt* Prague 1732; *d* there 1771). Composer and organist. He served as *Kapellmeister at Prague's St. Vitus Cathedral (1759). His many sacred works include 105 *masses, 263 *offertories and *anthems, and 6 *oratorios.   MJK

Brown, Grayson Warren (*b* Brooklyn NY 1948). Composer of numerous settings of RC liturgical texts and other worship music in an African American *gospel style. Brown is also a singer, pianist, author and recording artist. Several of his compositions appear in *Lead Me, Guide Me: The African American Catholic Hymnal.*   MEM

Brubeck, David (*b* Concord CA 1920). *Jazz pianist and composer, Brubeck was a major figure in the popularization of "cool jazz" in the 1950s. Beginning in the late 1960s he composed *cantatas and *oratorios on sacred themes; later he set the texts of the reformed RC *mass in his *Festival Mass to Hope* (1980). RTR

Bruck, Arnold von (*b* Bruges? *c* 1500; *d* Linz 1554). *Kapellmeister* to several courts, he wrote *church music in *Josquin's style, especially using *cantus firmus* techniques. Bruck was RC and not, as sometimes supposed, a Protestant church composer. VEG

Bruckner, (Joseph) Anton (*b* Ansfelder near Linz 1824; *d* Vienna 1896). Composer and organist. First a choirboy, he later became teacher and organist at St. Florian Augustinian monastery, his lifelong spiritual home (he is buried in the crypt beneath the St. Florian *organ). Appointments as court organist, conservatory professor and university lecturer in Vienna followed. He was acclaimed internationally for his organ playing and improvising.

A pious, somewhat eccentric RC (he knelt to pray the *angelus* during his lectures), his music is profound, even mystical: harmonically indebted to Wagner, with the lyricism of *Schubert and a certain *Baroque splendor. Besides 9 symphonies, he wrote much *liturgical music, including: 3 large *masses, other smaller or partial masses, *Requiem* (1849), *Te Deum* (1881–84), some *psalms, over 40 *motets (e.g., *Os justi*, 1879), but almost nothing for the organ. Although some of his choral writing recalls *Palestrina, the orchestral adventurousness of his music was condemned by some from the *Cecilian movement. Today his music finds wide use in his homeland in *liturgies and concerts.

Bibl: A.C. Howie, "The Sacred Music of Anton Bruckner" (University of Manchester: Ph.D. diss., 1969); D. Cooke et al., *The New Grove Late Romantic Masters: Bruckner, Brahms, Dvorak, Wolf* (New York, 1985). AWR

Bruhns, Nicolaus (*b* Schwabstedt 1665; *d* Husum 1697). Organist, violinist and composer. A student of *Buxtehude, he became organist in Husum (from 1689). Twelve *church cantatas and 5 *organ works are extant. JLB

Brumel, Antoine (*b* Brunelles? *c* 1460; *d* *c* 1515). Composer and priest who held various positions at Notre Dame (Chartres and Paris), St. Peter's in Geneva and was *maestro di cappella* at Ferrara (1506–10). In a period of musical change, his work integrates Franco-Netherland and Italian developments. Though he composed some secular works, his reputation rests on his *masses and *motets, characterized by contrapuntal complexity and tonal creativity. RAD

Brustwerk <*Brustpositiv*> [German]. "Breast-work." A division of a pipe *organ located directly above the keydesk, often containing regals, small-scaled flutes and principals, mutations and high-pitched mixtures, occasionally enclosed with shutters. MDJ

Bucchi, Valentino (*b* Florence 1916; *d* Rome 1976). Composer. He was director of the Perugia (1957–74), then Florence (from 1974) conservatories. His religious works include *Laudes Evangelli* (sacred *choruses for mixed voices and orchestra) and *Lettres de la Religieuse Portugaise* (sacred songs for unaccompanied high voice). MJK

Bucer, Martin (*b* Schieftstadt, Alsace 1491; *d* Cambridge 1551). Reformer of Strasbourg in the Reformed tradition who championed congregational singing. He began close to *Zwingli's eucharistic theology but moved in a catholic direction. Considered an ecumenical mediator, Bucer became Regius Professor of Divinity at Cambridge (1549). PHW

Buchner, Hans (*b* Ravensburg 1483; *d* Konstanz? 1538). Composer and organist at Konstanz Cathedral (from 1506). He wrote *Fundamentum* (*c* 1520), a manual for composition and improvisation on the *organ, illustrated with over 50 (mostly his) musical examples. MJK

Buck, Dudley (*b* Hartford 1839; *d* W Orange NJ 1909). Organist, teacher and composer. Trained in Hartford, Leipzig, Dresden and Paris, he taught at the New England Conservatory and served as a church musician in Brooklyn. Buck composed secular and *sacred music (*cantatas, *anthems, sacred songs), wielding great influence on 19th-century *church music in the US. FJM

Bull, John (*b* Old Radnor? *c* 1562; *d* Antwerp 1628). Composer and *keyboard virtuoso. He was organist at Hereford Cathedral (1582–86), then gentleman (1586) and organist (1592–1613) at the *Chapel Royal, finally serving as organist in Brussels (1613–14) and at Antwerp Cathedral (from 1617). He composed *In nomines, *motets, *verse and *full anthems, as well as teaching pieces for keyboard, including *canons and hexachord fantasias. RKW

Bullock, Ernest (*b* Wigan 1890; *d* Aylesbury 1979). Teacher and organist at Exeter Cathedral (1919–27) and Westminster Abbey (1928–41). He was professor of music at Glasgow University

(1941–52), then director of the Royal College of Music (1953–60). His compositions include 12 *anthems, 4 *canticles and *organ works. AJL

Bunjes, Paul (*b* Frankenmuth MI 1914; *d* Chicago 1998). Music editor of *hymnals and *service books for the Lutheran Church-Missouri Synod. He published *psalm tones and liturgical *chant settings. He was professor at *Concordia Teachers College, River Forest IL (from 1951). VEG

Bunyan, John (*b* Elstow, Bedfordshire 1628; *d* London 1688). Particular Baptist minister. He authored *The Pilgrim's Progress* from which Valiant's song was adapted as the *hymn "He who would valiant be." Bunyan supported congregational *psalm and hymn singing among English Baptists. RJS

Burgundian school. The Burgundian court under the Valois dukes (1364–1477) achieved great musical splendor. Secular music was particularly cultivated; *Dufay, *Binchois, van Ghizeghem and Busnois (all masters of the *chanson*) benefited from the dukes' patronage. The musical language established by these composers was an essential foundation for the rest of *Renaissance music. AJL

Burkhard, Willy (*b* Evilard-sur-Bienne 1900; *d* Zurich 1955). Composer who studied in Leipzig, Munich and Paris; then taught at Bern and Zurich conservatories. His *sacred music includes a *mass, *oratorios, *cantatas, *motets and *organ works. JLB

Burkhardt, Michael (*b* Sheboygan WI 1957). Choral conductor, organist and composer who has served as music director of churches in Anaheim, Minneapolis and on the music faculty of *Concordia University (Irvine CA, 1984–92). His compositions include *organ and choral settings of *hymns.   PKG

Burleigh, Glenn Edward (*b* Guthrie OK 1949). Pianist, composer, arranger and conductor. He has served as music director for the National Baptist Congress and composer-in-residence for Oklahoma City's Ambassador's Concert Choir. His *gospel songs, *anthems and arrangements of *spirituals are well known in the worship of African Americans. His 10 major symphonic choral works include "Alpha Mass" and "Lamentation and Celebration."   MWC

Burleigh, Harry <Henry> **T(hacker)** (*b* Erie PA 1866; *d* Stamford CT 1949). African American composer, arranger and concert artist. He studied with A. Dvořák at the National Conservatory in NY. He served as soloist at NY's St. George's Church (1892–95) and Temple Emanu-El (1900–25). Burleigh produced 187 vocal arrangements of African American *spirituals, and was the first to perform and publish them in the style of European art songs.   MEM

Burning Fiery Furnace, The. The second of 3 "Parables for Church Performance" by *Britten (op. 77, 1966). A stylized dramatic setting of the story of Nebuchadnezzar and the 3 young Israelites (based on Dan 3) for voices and chamber orchestra.   KRH

Buszin, Walter E. (*b* Milwaukee 1899; *d* Omaha 1973). Musician and scholar. He taught at Concordia Theological Seminary in Springfield IL (1925–33),

Bethany Lutheran College in Mankato MN (1933–39), *Concordia College in Fort Wayne IN (1939–46) and Concordia Seminary in St. Louis. He authored articles on worship and music and chaired the Lutheran Church-Missouri Synod's commission on worship. Buszin was also known for his editions of 4-part *Bach *chorales.   JLB

Buxtehude, Dietrich <Diderik> (*b* Oldesloe 1637?; *d* Lübeck 1707). Composer and organist. He was trained by his father, whom he succeeded as organist in Helsingor (*c* 1657) and Elsinore (1660). He was appointed organist and general manager *(Werkmeister)* of the Protestant Marienkirche in Lübeck (1668), one of the most important positions in N Germany, where he served until his death. Many musicians made the pilgrimage to Lübeck, including *Handel (1703) and J. S. *Bach, who walked 200 miles from Arnstadt (1706).

Buxtehude served as organist for the main morning *service, afternoon service and *vespers the afternoon before all Sundays and feast days. He composed a large quantity of vocal music for worship (128 pieces survive, only 8 of which are not liturgical), including *arias, *concertos and *chorales. Some of the texts he employed reveal the influence of *pietism. Approximately 90 *organ compositions are extant, almost evenly divided between various types of *chorale settings and freely composed works. Buxtehude is also remembered for reinstating *Abendmusik services on the 5 Sunday afternoons before Christmas.

Bibl: K. J. Snyder, *Dietrich Buxtehude, Organist in Lübeck* (New York, 1987); P. Walker, ed., *Church, Stage and Studio* (Ann Arbor, 1990).   EBF

Byrd, William (*b* Lincoln? 1543; *d* Stondon Massey, Essex 1623). Outstanding *Renaissance composer. He was a student and protégé of *Tallis. With him Byrd became an official royal publisher of music. A RC in the anti-Catholic English realm, Byrd's loyalty to the crown was never doubted. He published Latin *sacred music throughout his lifetime, still the most widely performed of his writings, including 3 Latin *masses and 2 books of *Gradualia* (1605, 1607), intended to supply mass *propers for every major feast. He also wrote a *Short *Service,* a *Great Service,* 2 books of *motets under the rubric of *Cantiones Sacrae* (1589, 1591) as well as *anthems and *psalms. Byrd wrote extensively for nearly every medium then available; his almost 100 pieces for virginal are particularly distinguished.

Bibl: A. Brown and R. Turbet, eds., *Byrd Studies* (New York 1992); J. Harley, *William Byrd* (Brookfield VT, 1997). JBF

Byzantine chant. *Monophonic Greek *liturgical music of the Orthodox Church in the Byzantine Empire (330–1453). Musical practice is obscure before the 9th century, but after this time neumatic notation is found in over 1200 manuscripts. Important types of chant books include the *akoluthia, *hirmologion, *octoechos and *sticherarion.* An 8-*mode system was used. Melodies are formulaic, sometimes with entire *chants *(prosomoia)* based on pre-existing melodies *(automela).* Musical style ranges from simple and syllabic (e.g., *kontakion, *sticheron, *troparion*) to very florid (e.g., *allelouiarion, *koinonikon, *prokeimenon*). Early *chants were composed anonymously, but beginning *c* 1300 melodies became more elaborate *(kalophonic)* and composers were identified, notably Johannes Koukouzeles, Johannes Glykes and Xenos Korones.

Byzantine chant influenced other Christian chant repertories including *Coptic, *Georgian and *Russian. For Greek Orthodox chant after 1453, see *Greco-Byzantine Chant. The series *Monumenta Musica Byzantinae* contains numerous facsimiles of Byzantine manuscripts and transcriptions of chants.

Bibl: E. Wellesz, *A History of Byzantine Music and Hymnography,* 3rd ed. (Oxford, 1963); O. Strunk, *Essays on Music in the Byzantine World* (New York, 1977). RGD

C

CAA. See *Cantors Assembly of America.

Cabanilles <Cavanilles>, **Juan Bautista José** <Josep> (*b* Algemesi 1644; *d* Valencia 1712). Organist, composer and priest working at Valencia Cathedral. Recognized as the greatest of the 17th-century Spanish *organ masters, he composed a *mass, *Magnificat, Spanish *motets and organ works (especially *tientos*).   JPM

Cabbala, music in. See *kabbalah, music in.

Caecilia, St. See *Cecilia, St.

Caecilian movement. See *Cecilian movement.

Caecilian Society. See *Cecilian Society.

Caldara, Antonio (*b* Venice 1670?; *d* there 1736). Composer. Once a chorister at St. Mark's in Venice, he became music director for a princely household in Rome and then Vice *Kapellmeister* of the imperial court in Vienna. Except for a few trio sonatas, all of his almost 3,000 works are vocal. A chapel musician most of his life, he composed a variety of liturgical works and some 50 *oratorios. His operas and oratorios made him a distinguished figure in the creation of music drama.   DCI

Calenda <*kalinda*> [Spanish]. Calends. An early dance form, popular in Santo Domingo, which originated in Africa, then spread throughout South America. *Calenda* became an important part of carnival celebrations by the mid-19th century.   LJC

Call and response. A musical form of alternation between 2 musical forces (e.g., a soloist and group), in which the call from 1 source (usually improvised) is answered in the response of the other. Common in African music and in African American *gospel music.   RDH

Calvin, John (*b* Noyon 1509; *d* Geneva 1564). The reformer of Geneva and a central figure for the Reformed tradition. Calvin studied theology and philosophy in Paris, then law at Orléans. As a humanist he wrote *De dementia* (1532). He fled Paris in 1533 after the negative response to it by his friend Nicholas Cop, rector at the University of Paris, which was sympathetic to a Lutheran view of justification. In 1535 Calvin wrote the first edition of the *Institutes of the Christian Religion* which included his view of spiritual real presence in the *Lord's Supper. The final edition of 1559 became the primary Reformed theological text. Called to Geneva in 1536, he sought to introduce his continuing concerns: weekly *communion and a system of discipline. Calvin proposed *psalm singing which led to the complete *Genevan Psalter of 1562. Expelled in 1538, he went to Strasbourg at *Bucer's beckoning. Called back to Geneva in 1541, he continued preaching *lectio continua* where he had left off in 1538 and remained (with conflicts) until his death.

Bibl: B. Thompson, *Liturgies of the Western Church* (Cleveland, 1961) 185–224; C. Garside, "The Origins of Calvin's Theology of Music: 1536–1543," *Transactions of the American Philosophical Society* 69 (Aug. 1979) 5–35.   PHW

Calvin Institute of Christian Worship.
An ecumenical, interdisciplinary study center for worship and the arts founded (1997) at Calvin College and Calvin Theological Seminary in Grand Rapids. JDW

Calvisius, Sethus (*b* Gorsleben 1556; *d* Leipzig 1615). Theorist, astronomer and *Kantor* in Leipzig. He transmitted *Zarlino's teaching to Germany in his *Melopoeia* (1592). Calvisius composed *hymns, *psalm settings and *motets. VEG

Cambridge Camden Society <Ecclesiological Society>. A group concerned with ecclesiastical art and architecture, founded by *Neale and B. Webb (1839) while they were attending Cambridge University. The name was soon changed to the Ecclesiological Society (1846). Members of the group applied the symbolic system of William Durandus (13th century) to the study of church buildings. The resulting Gothic Revival movement dominated church architecture into the 20th century. Members advocated separating the chancel from the nave, which provided a focal place for the choir and helped introduce the modern Anglican choral *service.   PAJ

Campbell, Lucie Eddie (*b* Duckbill MS 1885; *d* Nashville 1963). The first recognized woman composer of African American *gospel songs. Campbell was a dynamic music leader in the *National Baptist Convention of the USA and National Baptist Music Convention for which she composed numerous songs (e.g., "He Understands").   MEM

Camp meeting. A gathering associated with the revival movements of the 19th century, usually in E and S states. People gathered in a rural or wooded location, camping out in tents or wagons to hear revivalist preachers and experience conversion. Congregational singing was valued as an incentive to spiritual ecstasy and charismatic experience. Gathered around high platforms or great campfires, the assembly sang in response to the preacher, often combining memorized phrases or short *stanzas in highly repetitive fashion, even reaching a feverpitch of clapping and shouting, sometimes in nonsense syllables, until the people would experience the "jerks," sometimes falling trance-like to the ground. Camp meeting songs provided an early source for the *gospel song.

Bibl: G. Chase, *America's Music from the Pilgrims to the Present,* 3rd ed. (Urbana-Chicago, 1987) 194ff.   VEG

Campo aperto [Latin]. "Open field." A term for the earliest *neumes (9th century on) which are not written on a line or lines, and thus do not give exact pitches.   AWR

Campra, André (*b* Aix-en-Provence 1660; *d* Versailles 1744). RC priest and choirmaster at Paris' Notre Dame Cathedral until 1700. Later he became a successful composer of opera. *Concerto-like rhythms and *da capo* *arias occur in his many solo *cantatas and sacred *motets. DCI

Canción [Spanish]. "Song." A popular song form, whose texts cover a wide range of poetic themes, set to varying tempos. Religious festivals were important contexts for the development of certain forms of the "lyrical" *canción,* similar in structure to the *villancico* (ABBA form). Until the 15th century the term was interchangeable with *cantar, canson* and *cantiga.   MFR

Candlemas. A Christian feast, celebrated on February 2, commemorating the purification of Mary in the Temple; renamed the feast of the Presentation of the Lord by RCs. In evidence by the 4th century, the characteristic blessing of candles in this ritual was introduced by the 5th century. Though *Epiphany is presently the official end of the *Christmas season, this feast is traditionally celebrated as the close of the Christmas cycle; thus special settings of the *proper and *Marian antiphons have been written for this feast.   EBF

Canon. (1) A contrapuntal device in which a continuous melody in 1 voice is imitated strictly and entirely in another voice, at a temporal distance (e.g., 1 measure). Imitative voice(s) can begin at any interval from the original (e.g., at the 5th, 3rd, etc.). A canon utilizes any number of voices.

(2) *Canon of the mass.

(3) *Kanon.*   JBF

Canonical hours. See *divine office.

Canon of the mass. Former name for the *eucharistic prayer.

Cantata [Latin]. "Thing sung." A multi-sectioned vocal form which can include *recitatives, *arias, *ariosos, duets, *choruses, instrumental *ritornelli* and *strophes: all derived from narrative, dramatic or religious texts. It originated as a secular form in Italy *c* 1600 as a series of recitatives, arias or a mixture of both. By 1620 the form was used for religious texts and adopted by N Protestant composers in particular as a tool for addressing the popular desire for drama and mysticism in worship. The German cantata has roots in the biblical *concerto (*Schütz), *chorale motet (*Scheidt) and sacred madrigal-like *motet. Early examples (*Kuhnau, *Pachelbel) are distinguishable from the "reform" type. *Neumeister proposed the latter in the early 1700s through librettos (used by J. S. *Bach) merging operatic purposes with the current preaching style and a warmer spiritual expression proposed by the *pietists. The form received lavish attention: *Telemann wrote 1518 cantatas and *Graupner 1418. The form persisted through the 1800s (F. *Mendelssohn) into the 20th century (K. *Thomas, *Bartók) but became more broadly understood as a sectioned choral piece based on a compelling text.

Bibl: F. Blume, *Protestant Church Music* (New York, 1974) 269–302; F. Krummacher, "Cantata II: German to 1800," *NGDMM* 3:702–13.   MPB

Cantata da chiesa. See *church cantata.

Cantatorium [Latin]. "Of the singers." An early medieval liturgical *book containing the *chants sung between the readings during *mass (e.g., the *tract and *alleluia), often by a soloist or *cantor. This book was eventually subsumed into the *gradual and later into the *missal.   RTR

Cantica de tempore. See *de tempore hymns.

Canticle [from Latin *cantare,* "to sing"]. A biblical song of praise from the Hebrew Bible (not part of the Book of Psalms) or the New Testament. Canticles have a distinctive role in the *divine office.   MSD

Canticle of Simeon. See *Nunc dimittis.

Canticle of the Sun. A *hymn text written (c. 1225) by *Francis of Assisi, calling on all of creation to praise God, the maker of heaven and earth.   RDH

Canticum Sacrum ad honorem Sancti Marci nominis [Latin]. "Sacred song in honor of St. Mark's Name." A 5-movement work by *Stravinsky for *choir, soloists and *instruments on biblical texts. Written for St. Mark's in Venice. The 5th movement is a palindrome of the 1st; the middle 3 movements employ serial technique.   DWM

Cantiga [Galician]. "Song." A *monophonic medieval song of the Iberian peninsula. In musical style and form, the religious *cantigas* in **cantigas de Santa Maria* resemble the few surviving *cantigas de amor* (love songs); in both genres the primary influence is *folk song and dance, the secondary influence is French troubadour song. Collections of unnotated satirical and narrative *cantigas* suggest a stable repertoire of melodies to which texts were adapted as **contrafacta.*   RTR

Cantigas de Santa Maria [Galician]. "Songs about St. Mary." A collection of over 400 vernacular *monophonic songs about the Virgin Mary, assembled under the direction of King Alfonso (X) el Sabio between 1250–80. Every 10th song is a text praising Mary but most of the songs concern miracles attributed to Mary's power. Many *cantigas* are **contrafacta* of secular tunes in the form of the *virelai.* Most of the melodies are in *dorian or mixolydian *modes. Iconographic evidence indicates that they were often instrumentally accompanied, that dance was sometimes involved, and that they might have been sung in church as well as at devotional or social gatherings.

Bibl: C. C. Bouterse, "Literacy, Orality and the Cantigas" (University of Maryland Baltimore County: Ph.D. diss., 1996).   RTR

Cantillation [from Latin *cantillare,* "to sing low"]. A form of semi-improvisatory *recitative falling between speaking and song, most frequently employed in reference to the chanting of liturgical texts (especially the Bible) among Jews. Rhythmic and melodic elements are at the service of the proclaimed word in its semantic, syntactical and poetic structures. The shape of the cantillation is also determined by the intended hearer of the text (e.g., whether it is addressed to God or to the congregation), the ritual form of the text and its literary genre (e.g., prose or poetry). See *ta'amim.* GET

Cantio (pl. **cantiones**) [Latin]. "Song." A *monophonic, *strophic, medieval song (usually with *refrain) based on a Latin non-liturgical text. Stylistically, its regular rhythm and melodic leaps distinguish it from *chant *(cantus).* It sometimes exhibits characteristics associated with *tropes. RTR

Cantional [Latin *cantionale;* German *Kantionale;* Czech *kancionály*]. (1) A 16th–17th-century collection of *chant and choral music by German Lutherans for *eucharist and *divine office. Famous exemplars are J. Spangenberg's *Cantiones Ecclesiasticae* (1545) and L. Lossius' *Psalmodia Sacra* (1553).
(2) A style of musical setting (homophonic, 4-part, with the melody in the top voice) found in German *Kationale.* JMT

Cantiones sacrae [Latin]. "Sacred songs." A common title for 16th–17th-century *motet publications, e.g., collections by *Tallis and *Byrd (a joint work, 1575), Byrd (1589, 1591) and *Schütz (1625). AJL

Cantique [French]. "Canticle, hymn." A type of popular religious *hymn with a French text; found in the Calvinist tradition, then in the RC tradition from the 17th century. Used in worship and in catechesis. CSP

Cantor [Latin]. "Singer." (1) In Christianity, a 5th-century term for the *psalmist; later, the medieval singer (often cleric) who intoned and led the *chants; more recently a leader of congregational song who often sings the *verses to the congregation's *refrain.
(2) In Judaism, a synagogue official (*chazzan) who sings *liturgical music and chants prayer texts.
(3) Sometimes the English equivalent of *Kantor. See *precentor. VCF

Cantorei. See *Kantorei.

Cantorial Council of America <CCA>. A professional organization for Jewish *cantors, mainly serving Orthodox congregations. Many members are alumni of The Philip and Sarah Belz School of Jewish Music which originated as a music education program (1946) for prospective cantors, teachers and group leaders. The program developed into a Cantorial Workshop (1951), then the Cantorial Training Institute (1954), finally changing its name to the Belz School (1983). The Council publishes the *Journal of Jewish Music and Liturgy* (from 1976). MLK

Cantoris [Latin]. "Of the cantor." In the divided chancels of English churches and cathedrals, the *cantor's side (left side, when facing the altar), and also the singers on that side; contrasted with the *decani* or dean's side. AJL

Cantors Assembly of America <CAA>. Professional organization for Jewish *cantors, founded in 1947, primarily serving congregations in the US. Affiliated with the Conservative Movement, the Assembly serves as the official placement agency of member congregations of the United Synagogue of America. Many members are alumni of the H. L. Miller Cantorial School of the Jewish Theological Seminary of America. CAA helps cantors and congregations meet the changing needs of American Jewish worship. The Assembly publishes the *Journal of Synagogue Music.* MLK

Cantus [Latin]. "Song, melody." (1) An individual piece of *chant.

(2) A chant piece against which other voices were composed, i.e., the *tenor (a term which superseded it).

(3) Medieval and *Renaissance term for the melody, especially for the soprano part in 16th–17th-century *polyphonic compositions. In *Baroque *organ literature it was marked CF (*cantus firmus*). ACL

Cantus firmus [Latin]. "Existing (or fixed) melody." (1) Melody on which a *polyphonic composition is based, whose notes are sometimes in long duration (thus, the *tenor). Originally *chant was used as the *cantus firmus* for other compositions (*organa,* *motets, etc.).

(2) Later (e.g., in the *Renaissance) *cantus firmus* is any melody used as basis for a contrapuntal subject.

(3) In Protestant (especially Lutheran) traditions, either a chant melody or the *chorale (*hymn) tune used in a choral or *organ composition.

(4) In a derived sense, the term may refer to the sung chant or hymn melody standing alone.

(5) Metaphorically, *cantus firmus* may symbolize the enduring, fixed song of the church throughout the ages or even the voice of the congregation.

Bibl: L. Lockwood, "Cantus firmus," *NGDMM* 3:738-41. VEG

Cantus gregorianus. See *Gregorian chant.

Cantus in directum [Latin]. "Straightforward singing." A song performed straight through, without alternation or *response. FCQ

Cantus planus [Latin]. "Plainsong, plainchant." A term used since the 13th century to denote non-measured music. It is often used as a synonym for *Gregorian chant with the implication that the music is to be sung with equal note values. CJK

Cantus planus binatim [Latin]. "Double plainsong." An alternate form of *descant in which an improvised second voice is added to an existing *chant, forming non-parallel, 2-part *counterpoint; practiced in Italy from the 13th to 15th centuries. JPM

Canzona <*canzone*> (pl. **canzoni**) [Italian]. "Song." An Italian *keyboard or instrumental composition of the 16th–17th centuries. It originated in arrangements of French *chansons,* from which the name and form were derived. After 1570 the term often applied to newly-composed pieces. It generally featured 4 or 5 parts, dactylic opening, lively rhythms and several imitative sections based on different themes. Some works were monothematic or used *antiphonal technique.

The primary liturgical use was after the *epistle or *communion at *mass.

*Merulo, G. *Gabrieli and *Frescobaldi were important composers of keyboard *canzoni*. A. Raverii's *Canzoni per sonare* (1608) was an important collection of *canzoni* for instrumental ensemble.
Bibl: J. Caldwell, "Canzona," *NGDMM* 3:742–45. DWM

Capelle. See *Kapelle.

Capellmeister. See *Kapellmeister.

Cappella [Italian]. "Chapel." See *a cappella* and *Kapelle.

Caput mass. A *tenor mass in which the *cantus firmus* is taken from a *melisma on the word *caput* (Latin, "head") as found in the *Sarum chant *Holy Thursday *antiphon *Venit ad Petrum*. Examples by *Dufay, *Ockeghem and *Obrecht exist. MEC

Cardine, Eugène (*b* Courseulles-sur-mer 1905; *d* Solesmes 1989). Monk of *Solesmes and musicologist. He founded the semiological approach for studying the rhythm of *Gregorian chant and its intimate relationship to the spoken word. CJK

Cardoso, Manuel (*bapt* Fronteira 1566; *d* Lisbon 1650). Composer and Carmelite friar. While influenced by *Palestrina, his *masses are distinctive in their daring harmony. He published 3 books of masses, 2 sets of *motets and other sacred works; many were lost in the Lisbon earthquake of 1775. RAD

Carillon. Chromatic, stationary tower *bells on which compositions can be played; developed in Flanders. Originally controlled by a *keyboard and pedalboard or pegged barrel; later versions were controlled electronically. Important composers include *Gheyn and *Pinkham. RDH

Carissimi, Giacomo (*b* Marini 1605; *d* Rome 1674). Composer who pioneered the *oratorio and *cantata, adapting operatic innovations for the church. Among the several oratorios attributed to him, *Jepthe* (before 1650) is best known. Carissimi was *maestro di cappella* at the Jesuit German College (from 1629), preceded in that post several years before by *Victoria. His students there included *Charpentier, *Kerll and *Bernhard. He also composed *masses (e.g., *Missa L'*Homme armé*) and *motets. Suppression of the Jesuits (1773) meant the loss of his autographs, rendering the chronology and authenticity of his works problematic.
Bibl: T. Culley, *Jesuits and Music: A Study of the Musicians Connected with the German College in Rome* (St. Louis, 1970). JKW

Carlebach, Shlomo (*b* Berlin 1925; *d* New York 1994). Rabbi and composer of contemporary Jewish music (see *Jewish popular music), sometimes known as the "Rabbi with a guitar." The son of a rabbi, his family moved to Brooklyn in 1935. Exposed to *Hasidic music, he set out to reach Jews through devotion and music. It is estimated that he wrote thousands of melodies; he produced over 25 recordings (beginning in 1959). His melodies, effectively combining the repeated binary structure of Hasidic and *folk music, have become standard in synagogues, at weddings, camps and other celebrations in all Jewish denominations.
Bibl: M. Brandwine, *Reb Shlomele* (Israel, 1997). MLK

Carol. A medieval round or line dance with musical accompaniment, appearing in England by the 12th century; the term eventually referred to songs with an English or Latin text, especially those relating to *Christmas or the saints of that season. As a dance song, people stood while the leader sang the *stanzas, then all joined with dancing and singing on the *refrain or burden. Carols could have narrative, lyrical or dramatic content. Medieval carols were usually intended to inspire and engage ordinary Christians. Franciscans and other religious groups evangelized by using vernacular forms of these popular songs. *Polyphonic carols developed by the 15th century; some were *conductus-like and may have served as processional music; others in various forms were employed for wide-ranging religious and non-religious purposes. Carols declined in popularity during the *Reformation. The late 19th century saw a renewed interest in the carol, as well as a broadened definition. Today the term is applied to works of non-English origin (e.g., *noël, *Weihnachtslied) and a wide range of *hymnody. Christians have incorporated carols into worship for *Advent, *Lent, *Holy Week and *Easter as well as Christmas.
   Bibl: P. Dearmer, R. V. Williams, M. Shaw, *The Oxford Book of Carols,* rev. ed. (London, 1964); R. L. Greene, *The Early English Carols,* rev. ed. (Oxford, 1977).   MAK

Carr, Benjamin (*b* London 1768; *d* Philadelphia 1831). Composer, organist, editor and the first important American music publisher. Carr was central to the development of music in the RC church and secular society in Philadelphia in the early 1800s (known as the "father of Philadelphia music"). Of his almost 350 surviving works, *c* 85 are *sacred. CAD

Carter, Roland (*b* Chattanooga 1942). Educator, conductor, arranger and composer. He was professor of music and chapel musician at Hampton University (1965–89); then on the faculty at the University of Tennessee at Chattanooga. Carter has served as director of the *Hampton University Choir Directors' and Organists' Guild. His arrangements include *"Lift Every Voice and Sing." MWC

Carter, Sydney B. (*b* London 1915). Poet, *folk singer and composer of *c* 100 congregational songs in popular style. The best known of his songs is "Lord of the Dance" (1963).   CRY

Carver, Robert (*b c* 1490; *d* after 1546). Scottish composer who may have been associated with the Scottish *Chapel Royal. Five *masses and 2 *motets survive in an important manuscript collection of *sacred music, known as the "Carver Manuscript" or "Scone Antiphonary."   RKW

Cassiodorus, Flavius Magnus Aurelius (*b* Scylaciam *c* 485; *d* Vivarium *c* 580). Author and statesman. The member of a patrician Roman family, Cassiodorus became the spokesperson for the Ostrogothic rulers at Ravenna. He founded a monastery at Vivarium for translating and preserving ancient and Christian materials. His writings include *Expositio psalmorum* and *Institutiones divinarum et saecularium <humanarum> litterarum:* the latter the primary source for studying liberal arts in monasteries in the 7th to 9th centuries. His ideas on music theory therein are referenced through the 12th century. JPM

Castrato (pl. **castrati**) [Italian]. A male singer castrated as a boy to preserve the soprano or alto range with the chest and lungs of an adult. *Castrati* were employed in Italian churches and opera from the 16th century, and in the *Sistine Chapel until 1903. AWR

Caswall, Edward (*b* Yately 1814; *d* Edgbaston 1878). *Hymn translator. His activity in England's *Oxford Movement led him to the RC church. Many of his English translations of Latin *hymns are found in his *Lyra Catholica* (1849). Among his most popular is "Come Holy Ghost." FJM

Catechumens, mass of the. The former name for the first part of the *mass (from the opening rites to the *Creed), the only part of the *service which catechumens were allowed to attend. Now called the *liturgy of the word. GET

Cathedral hours. *Lauds and *vespers celebrated in a parochial setting (not necessarily a cathedral), distinguished from the parallel monastic *hours. Cathedral hours are characterized by structural simplicity, the repetition of elements, texts related to the time of day (e.g., Ps 141 for vespers) and rich ceremony (e.g., vesture, incense, processions). MJG

Cathedral music. English *church music is broadly divisible into parish and cathedral music; the latter, though not restricted to cathedrals, presupposes a highly trained *choir (divisible into 8 or more parts) and typically exhibits a rich and often conservative style. Its primary genres are the *anthem and *service. AJL

Catholic Choirmaster. The official bulletin of the Society of St. Gregory of America, devoted to *liturgy and *sacred music. Published from 1915–64, it then merged with *Caecilia* to form the new journal *Sacred Music*. MEC

Catholic University of America, The. A national university erected by RC bishops of the US in 1887. Founded to offer graduate studies in ecclesiastical disciplines for American clergy, it began accepting undergraduates in 1905. Its doctoral program in liturgical studies was established in 1971. The Benjamin T. Rome School of Music collaborates with the School of Religion and Religious Education in offering graduate degrees in *liturgical music. ADC

Cavaillé-Coll, Aristide (*b* Paris 1811; *d* there 1899). Builder or rebuilder of almost every important *organ in France. His *instruments inspired an organ revival throughout W Europe; notable for mechanical and tonal innovations, especially powerful *chorus reeds and solid foundation stops. Sonorities of his instruments deeply influenced French organ composers from C. *Franck to *Messiaen. JBW

Cavalieri, Emilio de' (*b* Rome *c* 1550; *d* there 1602). Organist, composer and singing teacher; also employed as an administrator by the Grand Duke of Tuscany. He is best known for *Rappresentatione di Anima et di Corpo* (1600), a *rappresentatione sacra;* Cavalieri also composed a set of 1- to 5-voice *lamentations and *responses for *Holy Week. DWM

Cavalli, (Pietro) Francesco (*b* Crema 1602; *d* Venice 1676). *Maestro di cappella* at St. Mark's in Venice. He composed mostly concerted works for church, as well as *Marian antiphons, 3 *Magnificats and instrumental pieces for worship. He was widely known for his 41 operas, indicating an increased acceptance of Italian opera in other countries. DCI

CCA. See *Cantorial Council of America.

CCT. See *Consultation on Common Texts.

Ceasar, Paul <Buddy>. See *Dameans.

Cecilia, St. Early Christian martyr. Legend has it that, at her wedding, she sang "in her heart to God alone." The first *antiphon of *lauds for her feast (November 22) repeats this text (minus the phrase "to God alone"). By the 15th century she is celebrated as the patroness of music and musicians. AWR

Cecilian movement. An influential 19th-century RC reform movement (named after St. *Cecilia), originating in *Regensburg; the *Society of St. Cecilia was founded in 1868. It sought to purify *liturgical music of perceived worldly (e.g., operatic) encroachment by propagating authentic *sacred music thought to be found in the music of the past, especially *Gregorian chant (but in its degenerate *Regensburg edition form) and *Roman school *polyphony (often through imitations of *Palestrina rather than the masters themselves). Cecilians opposed (with limited success) the *Deutsches Hochamt. Their numerous *hymnals, intended primarily for *low mass and devotions, revived much traditional Catholic *hymnody. Orchestral liturgical music was generally opposed (though not in Austria), causing tensions with leading composers (e.g., *Bruckner and *Liszt) and leading to criticism of the movement's narrowness. *Singenberger propagated the movement in the US. Cecilian ideals found substantial official affirmation in *Tra le sollecitudini.

Bibl: A. Hutchings, *Church Music in the Nineteenth Century* (London, 1967); R. Damian, "A Historical Study of the Caecilian Movement in the United States" (Catholic University of America: Ph.D. diss., 1984). AWR

Centonization [from Latin *cento,* "patchwork"]. The practice of constructing a *chant from preexisting formulas; *Gregorian *tracts, *graduals and *responsories are often described thus. Some argue that the existence of shared musical formulas is the result of improvisation: written melodies are merely examples of how a *cantor might have "centonized" a piece. The intimate relationship between text and melody in the earliest recorded repertoire, however, suggests intentional, text-driven composition in which the employment of a centonized text prompted the use of a musical phrase traditionally associated with it. AWR

Ceremony of Carols, A. A musical setting of *carols for *Christmas by *Britten (1942) for treble voices and harp in 11 movements. See *lessons and carols. MSD

Certon, Pierre (*d* Paris 1572). Clerk at Notre Dame in Paris, then choirmaster at Sainte-Chapelle. He composed *masses, *motets and *chansons spirituelles*. In longer works he used a variety of vocal combinations for increased interest. Certon experienced great success with his first published book of *chansons* (1552). DCI

Chaconne. See *passacaglia.

Chad <*Had*> **gadya** [Hebrew]. "One kid." The most famous *Pesach song, composed during the Middle Ages by an unknown author. An allegory, it describes the trials and tribulations of Israel's journey through history. Israel (the only kid) is purchased by the father (God) for a monetary value (The Ten Commandments) and then subjected to all its foes; each object described in the song symbolizes one of Israel's enemies. It is normally sung as part of the *Pesach* *seder*. SIW

Chair organ. See *choir organ.

Chaldean chant. The *monophonic *liturgical music of the Chaldean Church, the Mesopotamian (Iraqi) branch of the *E Syrian church, in union with Rome since the 16th century. This *chant was allegedly reformed in the 8th century by Babai of Gabilta. Today the *modes have names of Arabic *maqāmāt* and chromatic intervals are used. Melodies are predominately syllabic, with a narrow range. The types of chant books and genres of chant are similar to those of other E Syrian churches. "Dot" notation (perhaps a form of *ecphonetic notation) exists in some manuscripts. Percussive *instruments are used.

Bibl: H. Husmann, ed., *Die Melodien des chaldäischen Breviers-Commune nach den Traditionen Vorderasiens und der Malabarküste* (Rome, 1967). RGD

Chandos Anthems. Twelve *anthems on religious texts (one is the *Te Deum*) by G. F. *Handel (1717–18) for soloists, *chorus and orchestra for James Brydges, later the Duke of Chandos. JLB

Change ringing. The systematic sounding of hand-pulled tower *bells peculiar to England and N America based on mathematical permutations, several bearing names (e.g., Plain Bob, Grandshire Doubles, etc.). Each peal, or set of bells has a given number of possible combinations or changes. A bell's progress throughout the changes is called a plain hunt. RDH

Chanson spirituelle [French]. "Spiritual song." A 16th-century secular composition with moralistic or sacred words. A setting features new music or preexisting music with the substitution of doctrinally acceptable words for an original love poem. The genre rose from religious conflict in France. Both RCs and Protestants composed these, including Guéroult (texts), Waelrant, Pasquier and Goulart. *Le Jeune produced the masterpiece of the genre, "*Octonaires de la vanité et inconstances du monde*." LMT

Chant. Music for ritual, here confined to Christian *liturgy. Chant is *monophonic, without instrumental accompaniment (an exception being *Anglican chant), and is created for the delivery of sacred text in worship, apart from which the music cannot be properly understood. In essential characteristics, the style of chant in E and W is grounded in patristic thought which valued the human voice as preeminent over *instruments, unison singing as a symbol of unity, and the primacy of text over music. The main W families of chant are *Ambrosian, *Gallican, *Gregorian, *Old Roman and *Old Spanish; major E repertoires are *Armenian, *Byzantine, *Coptic and *Syrian. In each, the main corpus of music serves the principal liturgical *services: mass and the *divine office.

Chant texts are drawn largely from *psalms, as well as from other biblical books, traditional liturgical prayers, Christian poetry and prose and (especially in later medieval times) hagiography. Musical settings, shaped in form and character by requirements of text and liturgical function, range from simple *cantillation by a solo voice to elaborate musical styles and lengthy structures with interchange of solo and choral roles.

Across all repertoires, some features are common. Chant melodies tend to occur within a relatively circumscribed range, often moving stepwise or by small intervals. The text-melody relationship can be identified as syllabic (1 note per syllable), *neumatic (2 to 5 notes per syllable), or *melismatic (several notes over a single syllable). In the W and E (where notated sources are later) many chant manuscripts have rhythmic indications, though their interpretation continues to be a matter for further study.

Bibl: M. Velimirović, "Christian Chant of the Eastern Churches," in *The Early Middle Ages to 1300,* ed. R. Crocker and D. Hiley (Oxford, 1990), 3–66; D. Hiley, *Western Plainchant* (Oxford, 1993); P. Jeffery, "Liturgical Chant Bibliography," *Plainsong and Medieval Music* 1–5 (1992–96). JMH

Chanukkah <*Ḥanukkah*> [Hebrew]. "Dedication." An 8-day festival beginning on the 25th of the Hebrew month *Kislev* (typically mid-December) commemorating the Jewish victory of the Maccabees over the Greek army (165 BCE). One candle on a *menorah* ("candelabra") is lit for each night of the holiday. Three *blessings are recited the 1st night and 2 each of the remaining nights. In the *Ashkenazic tradition a traditional melody is used for the blessings. A declarative paragraph, *Hanerot halalu* ("These lights we kindle") follows, then the chanting of *Maoz tsur*. In the synagogue the *Hallel is recited and a paragraph beginning *Al hanisim* ("And for the miracles") is added to the *Amidah. Songs based on the Hebrew text used for this holiday as well as Hebrew and English songs associated with activities such as playing with a *dreydl* (a top that is spun) or eating *latkes* (fried potato pancakes) are sung at home or public celebrations for the holiday. MLK

Chapel master. See *Kapellmeister.*

Chapel Royal. The collective name for singers and instrumentalists who provide *church music for the English court in London and at its other residences. Historically, to be a gentleman (or member) of the Chapel Royal was both an honor and real work; though members might (and frequently did) hold other posts, they were at least nominally responsible for 2 daily sung *services. AJL

Charismatic worship music. "Charismatic" was first used *c* 1960 to refer to a particular style of worship. The 1950s saw a surge of neo-Pentecostalism within mainline Christian denominations, particularly Episcopalians, Lutherans and eventually RCs. This movement reclaimed the charisms of speaking and singing in *tongues, interpreting tongues, prophesying and healing. It emphasized personally claiming Jesus' Lordship and immediate experiences of the Holy Spirit through worship.

Music plays a significant role in *Pentecostal and charismatic worship. Charismatic worship patterns often begin with an extended song *service, move to preaching and conclude with extended prayer. Praise is often the focus of the opening song service, designed to prepare the worshiper emotionally and spiritually for meeting God. Music for the song service is energetic, often requiring bodily movement, e.g., waving hands, rhythmic swaying, clapping and stamping feet. Short *choruses or scripture songs may be repeated or fashioned into a medley. Traditional *hymns may be included in the medley, often modified in tempo, harmonization and accompaniment. A worship leader sets the pace of the song service, directs the instrumentalists and may intersperse comments, scripture or testimony. A team of singers sometimes lead the songs. Songs may be sung from memory or projected by an overhead or slide projector. *Organ, piano, synthesizer, guitars, drums, various wind and string *instruments may accompany the singing. Amplification is frequently employed.

In many charismatic congregations the end of the song service is given to "singing in the Spirit." In some gatherings a *keyboard provides a foundational tone or chord while members of the congregation freely improvise praise in the vernacular or in tongues. Layers of harmony and intricate rhythmic patterns emerge in the sound. This Spirit-singing may continue until the worship leader signals an end or until the singers reach a point of "holy hush." In some congregations "singing in the Spirit" is unaccompanied.

Bibl: The Hymn 38:1 (1987) 7–30; B. Liesch, *People in the Presence of God* (Grand Rapids, 1988); D. P. Hustad, *Jubilate II* (Carol Stream, 1993). RJS

Charlemagne [Latin, Carolus Magnus] (*b* Aachen 742; *d* there 814). King of the Franks (768–814) and Emperor of the Romans (800–14) who encouraged the standardization of liturgical practices in his realm. To that end, Charlemagne requested a "pure Roman *sacramentary" from Pope Hadrian I; the document eventually received was supplemented extensively (by Benedict of Aniane?), producing a fusion of Roman and Frankish elements. Charlemagne also issued capitularies enforcing initiatives begun by his father, Pepin, to replace local *chant traditions with *cantus Romanus;* the resulting Roman-Frankish fusion is thought by many to provide the core of the so-called *Gregorian chant repertoire. JMJ

Charpentier, Marc-Antoine (*b* Paris *c* 1645–50; *d* there 1704). Important *Baroque composer. He probably studied with *Carissimi in Rome. A collaborator with Molière, he wrote much music for the Comédie-Française in the 1670s. In the 1680s he directed music in the Jesuit church in Paris before being appointed (1698) to Sainte-Chapelle, a prestigious royal chapel. Most of his extant compositions are sacred (vocal and instrumental). Most of his 11 *mass settings are accompanied by *orchestra (strings, winds, *basso continuo); 3 use basso continuo only. He also wrote 84 *psalms, 10 *Magnificats, *antiphons, over 200 *motets and 4 *Te Deums.

Bibl: C. Cessac, Marc-Antoine Charpentier, trans E. T. Glasow (Portland, 1995).   MEC

Chasi [Slavonic]. See *chasy.

Chasoslov [Slavonic]. See *horologion.

Chassidic music. See *Hasidic music.

Chasy <chasi> [Slavonic, sing. chas]. See *horai.

Chatimah <ḥatimah> [Hebrew]. "Seal." The final portion of a prayer (ordinarily its last 2 or 3 lines) intoned by the *chazzan or prayer leader; after this final portion is chanted the congregation then moves on to the next passage. MLK

Chazak chazak venitchazeik <Ḥazak Ḥazak venitḥazeik> [Hebrew]. "Strong, strong, make us strong." A phrase recited at the conclusion of the recitation of each of the 5 books of Moses during the public *Torah reading. Traditionally the congregation chants these words in unison which are then repeated by the reader of the Torah.   MLK

Chazzan <ḥazzan> (pl. **chazzanim**) [Hebrew]. "Cantor." A term denoting one who leads prayer; also called *ba'al tefilah and *sheliach tsibbur. In modern times chazzan typically refers to a trained

expert who holds the clerical office of a religious officiant.

The term first appears in rabbinic literature, referring to a teacher of children (Mishna Shabbat 1:3), overseer of the synagogue (Mishna Yoma 7:1), or one who buries the dead (Babylonian Talmud Ketubot 8b). References to the chazzan as a prayer leader occur in the 6th century CE. Jewish prayer was not canonized until c 1000 CE; the role of the chazzan until then was to create the text in poetic form and recite it. After 1000 CE prayer books circulated and prayer texts became fixed; literacy waned and the chazzan's role was to recite the prayers for those who were unable to read Hebrew.

Clear musical practices were not recorded until the 18th century (see *Jewish music). Manuscripts of this period, as well as oral and iconographic evidence of earlier centuries, shows the practice of the *meshorerim (assistants of the chazzan). Prior to 1800 the music consisted of lengthy melodic elaboration from a variety of European secular influences. During the 19th century tremendous change occurred. C European composers sought to elevate synagogue music by composing music in a style that eliminated melodic elaboration. E European composers sought to incorporate artistically the *Jewish prayer modes into their writing. Solo singing of E European chazzanim developed into an artistic style characterized as the "golden age of the cantorate" (1880–1930). Legendary figures are immortalized through their recordings (e.g., *Rosenblatt and *Glantz).

In the 20th century US these musical trends continued (see *Reform Judaism). Schools devoted to the teaching of *cantors and professional societies were formed (see *ACC and *CCA). The first female cantor was invested in 1976 in *Reform Judaism; 1987 in the Conservative Movement.

Bibl: L. Landman, *The Cantor* (New York, 1972); M. Slobin, *Chosen Voices* (Urbana, 1989); V. Pasternak and N. Schall, eds., *The Golden Age of Hazzanut* (Cedarhurst, 1991). MLK

Chemin-Petit, Hans (*b* Potsdam 1902; *d* Berlin 1981). Composer and conductor. He studied at Berlin's Musikhochschule (1920–26) where he became professor (1929), then assistant director (1965–68). He directed the Magdeburg Cathedral choir (1939–44) and the Berlin Philharmonic choir (1944). He wrote chamber operas, many choral works and an *organ *concerto (1963). JLB

Cherubic hymn. See *Cherubikon.*

Cherubikon (pl. **cherubika**) [Greek; Slavonic *cheruvimskaya pesn'*]. "Cherubic hymn." An elaborate *hymn sung at the beginning of the *liturgy of the *eucharist in the Byzantine *divine liturgy as ministers transfer the bread and wine from the altar of preparation to the sanctuary altar in solemn procession (the *great entrance); it is said privately 3 times by the celebrants at the altar before the entrance. Introduced in the time of Emperor Justin II (d 574), it is probably the most magnificent expression of the symbolism of the divine liturgy as the earthly manifestation of eternal angelic worship. In modern use the hymn is interrupted so the celebrants can intone intercessions for church and state authorities, local founders, benefactors and all Orthodox Christians. Alternate

Cherubika exist for the *liturgy of presanctified gifts and *Holy Thursday. The *Cherubikon* for the Paschal Vigil divine liturgy comes from the W Syrian Liturgy of St. James.

Bibl: D. Conomos, *Byzantine Trisagia and Cheroubika of the Fourteenth and Fifteenth Centuries* (Thessaloniki, 1974); R. Taft, *The Great Entrance* (Rome, 1975). DMP

Cherubini, Luigi (Carlo Zanobi Salvadore Maria) (*b* Florence 1760; *d* Paris 1842). Composer, teacher and church musician. After concentrating on opera composition (he wrote over 30) and conducting early in his career, Cherubini turned increasingly to *sacred music. He wrote 13 *masses and 2 highly regarded *Requiems:* C minor (1816) and D minor (1836). He was appointed 1 of 2 superintendents of the king's music (1816–30) and director of the Paris Conservatory (1821). His sacred works avoid operatic vocal techniques and restrict the use of soloists, rendering the music more subordinate to the *liturgy.

Bibl: B. Deane, *Cherubini* (New York, 1965). MEC

Cheruvimskaya pesn' [Slavonic]. See *Cherubikon.*

Cherwien, David M. (*b* W Union IA 1957). Organist, composer and improviser. He is a graduate of Augsburg College (Minneapolis) and the University of Minnesota with study at Berlin's Kirchenmusikschule. Cherwien has served as a church musician in Seattle, Chicago, Berlin and Minneapolis-St. Paul. He is well-known for his musical leadership at *hymn festivals. PHW

Chichester Psalms. A choral work by *Bernstein (1965) in 3 movements, setting *Pss 108, 100, 23, 2, 131 and 133 in Hebrew for countertenor, *choir and orchestra. It was commissioned by the dean of Chichester Cathedral where it was first performed.   MSD

Child, William (*b* Bristol 1606; *d* Windsor 1697). Composer and church musician who served as organist at St. George's Chapel, Windsor and the *Chapel Royal (1630–45, 1660–97). Known for his innovative use of major/minor keys and scoring, he wrote *services, *motets, *psalms, *hymns and over 50 *anthems.   RKW

Chin [Slavonic]. See *akoluthia.

Chin nad kutijeju [Slavonic]. Alternative term for *panikhida.

Chironomy <cheironomy> [from Greek *cheir,* "hand"]. The use of hand movements to indicate melodic curves and rhythmic flow in the performance of a piece of music, widely used in ancient cultures (e.g., Egypt and Greece). Employed by Jews to transmit the *Ta'amim. Some believe that for Christians such hand movements were transformed (9th–10th centuries) into the earliest *neumatic notations for *Gregorian chant.   CJK

Choir, architectural. An early medieval designation (Latin *chorus*) for the space around the altar for clergy and singers, which became increasingly distinct from the nave. Defined by ever higher barriers, the choir eventually became self-enclosed and occupied the middle of the building. Protestant reformers either removed choirs entirely or placed the assembly there. RC churches of the *Baroque period were generally built without a choir, bringing the congregation closer to the altar. Singers were placed in side galleries or the rear loft which, though acoustically desirable, separated them from the liturgical action.

Bibl: P. G. Cobb, "The Architectural Setting of the Liturgy," C. Jones et al., *The Study of the Liturgy,* 2nd ed. (New York, 1992), 528–42.   AWR

Choir, deaf <sign choir, sign language choir>. A group of hearing impaired people with their leader, who rhythmically interpret the sung texts in worship through signs and gestures. A drum supplying coordinating vibrations and rhythm is sometimes employed as well. Such choirs emerged in the last third of the 20th century as part of the overall ministry to persons with impaired hearing.   CSP

Choir, musical. Organized groups of singers performing as part of worship date back to antiquity. Homer's *Iliad* (*c* 850 BCE) mentions a *chorus performing a paean to Apollo. The Hebrew Bible provides many references to groups of professional singers as part of the Temple personnel (e.g., 2 Chr 5:12-13). The first trained group of singers in the W church appears to have been the *schola cantorum;* earlier in the E there is evidence of *boy choirs and choirs of *women singers. Choirs became an important part of E and W Christian *liturgy, increasingly replacing congregational singing. In order to restore the assembly's song *Calvin sought to ban choirs altogether, but Lutheran and other Reformed traditions encouraged the use of choirs in addition to congregational *hymnody. Few examples of synagogal choirs are found before the 17th century. Since then choral music is performed as part of the liturgy in some Jewish Reformed, Conservative and Orthodox congregations.

Bibl: B. Isaacson, "Choirs," *EJ* 5:486–89; A. J. G. Smith and P. Young, "Chorus," *NGDMM* 4:341–57. JPM

Choirbook. A manuscript format in which all voice parts of a *polyphonic piece appear on the same opening (facing pages), rather than in separate *partbooks. Common in the *Renaissance, such books were often large enough to permit an entire *choir to sing from them. AJL

Choir organ. (1) The manual division of the *organ with a separate chest behind the organist usually provided with swell shutters; also called a chair organ.
(2) An independent organ used to accompany the *choir. PAJ

Choir stalls. Seats arranged in 1 or more rows facing each other across an aisle for celebration of the *divine office, often located within a separate choir area (see *choir, architectural). From the 12th century stalls were constructed with continuous backs and individual seats divided by partitions. The bottom of the seat, which could be raised, contained a bracket (*misericord* from Latin *misericordia,* "mercy") for the monks or clerics to lean against during the lengthy celebrations. Choir stalls offered woodworkers opportunities for fanciful decorations. FCQ

Choralbearbeitung [German]. "Hymn setting." A composition based on a *chorale or *chant melody. Examples include *motets, *cantatas and *chorale preludes for *organ. JLB

Chorale [from German *Choral,* "chant"]. A vernacular German Protestant congregational *hymn. The term can refer to both the text and tune, or just the tune. In the 16th century the term referred to hymns of the people. *Luther wrote bold hymn texts and tunes when he started to edit the *mass. His *Formula Missae* (1523) and *Deutsche Messe* (1526) used German metrical versions of parts of the *ordinary and *proper after the Latin *chants or as substitutes for them. Later, versions of the *Kyrie* and *Gloria* completed the ordinary in the vernacular. The *gradual hymn became the *hymn of the day. Chorales gave people an integral role in the *service. *Schaff suggests that up to 100,000 German hymns were written by the end of the 19th century. According to *Schalk, sources for chorales included *Gregorian chant, *Leise, *cantiones, *contrafacta* and newly created works, initially in the tradition of the Meistersingers using the barform (AAB).

Hymns of the Bohemian Brethren, exemplified in Michael Weisse's *Ein new Gesengbuchlen* (1531), entered the stream, as did the influence of Strasbourg. After the *Reformation *Nicolai created *WACHET AUF and *WIE SCHÖN LEUCHTET. Congregations originally sang in unison and unaccompanied, alternating *stanzas with the *choir in *polyphonic settings. Tunes then migrated to the soprano in simple 4-part settings so the choir could accompany the congregation; the first example of this is Osiander's *Fünffzig geistliche Lieder und Psalmen* (1586). In the 17th century

*Gerhardt and *Crüger created warmer, smoother texts and tunes, for the first time with *basso continuo. The Thirty Years' War stimulated devotional texts for home use. *Organ accompaniment became common. *Pietism produced Freylinghausen's massive collections (1704, 1714), with basso continuo and melodies containing leaps of a sixth. J. S. *Bach's harmonizations gave life to tunes which had moved from their rhythmic origins to isometric stasis. The Enlightenment modified texts to bend faith to reason, reduced the number of texts and tunes, used the *organ more, and slowed the pace to several seconds per note by the 19th century. A confessional movement sought to recover the chorales in their original rhythmic forms. In the 20th century *Franzmann, *Bender and others created anew in the chorale stream.

Bibl: J. Riedel, The Lutheran Chorale (Minneapolis, 1967); R. Marshall, "Chorale," NGDMM 4:312–321; C. Schalk, "German Church Song" in The Hymnal 1982 Companion, ed. R. F. Glover (New York, 1990), 1:288–309. PHW

Chorale cantata. A *cantata comprised of movements which are strictly or loosely based on the *strophes of a *chorale. In his second Leipzig cycle J. S. *Bach fully explored the form.   MPB

Chorale concerto. A 17th-century vocal piece built on a *chorale with 1 or more voices and *basso continuo. Important examples were written by M. *Praetorius, *Schein and *Scheidt.   PHW

Chorale fantasia. A large composition for *organ, built on a *chorale which is often employed freely in the work. *Scheidemann, *Buxtehude, *Lübeck, J. S. *Bach and others were important composers of this form.   PHW

Chorale fugue. A *fugue, usually for *organ, possibly improvised, built on the first phrase of a *chorale, employed to introduce the chorale for the congregation's singing. Important examples were composed by *Pachelbel and J. S. *Bach.   PHW

Chorale mass. A *mass or *missa brevis, based on *chorale settings of the *ordinary. *Pepping and *Distler provide important examples.   PHW

Chorale motet. A *polyphonic piece for 2 or more voices and *instruments based on a *chorale, which often is the *cantus firmus. In the 16th century the chorale motet was intended either as a freestanding composition or as a *stanza sung in alternation with the congregation's unison stanzas.   PHW

Chorale partita. See *chorale variations.

Chorale prelude. (1) A short *organ piece built on a *chorale, possibly improvised, often with the melody ornamented, used to introduce the chorale for congregational singing, e.g., J. S. *Bach's *Orgelbüchlein.

(2) A generic term for a piece built on a chorale, usually for organ. See *organ chorale.   PHW

Chorale variations. A set of pieces using a *chorale tune as the theme, employing different forms and compositional techniques, written for harpsichord or *organ; also called chorale partita. Important examples have been composed by *Sweelinck, *Scheidemann, *Buxtehude and J. S. *Bach.   PHW

Chorale Vorspiel [German]. "Hymn prelude." See *chorale prelude.

Choralis Constantinus. The first complete, *polyphonic collection of *mass *propers for the entire liturgical *year, by *Isaac in 3 volumes, commissioned by the Cathedral at Constance in 1508. VEG

Choraliter [Latin]. "In the manner of chant." (1) In the style of *plainsong, as contrasted with measured music.
(2) Monody in contradistinction to *figural, or *polyphonic music.   RAL

Choristers Guild. An organization founded in 1949 by Ruth Krehbiel Jacobs, dedicated to "nurturing the spiritual growth of children and youth through music." Its monthly publication *Letters* includes articles for directors, music for children's and youth *choirs and *handbells, study plans and curriculum. With local chapters throughout the US and Canada, Choristers Guild hosts national seminars and produces a variety of publications.   RKW

Chorus. (1) A general term for a body of singers with more than 1 singer on a part. The distinction between *choir (liturgical ensemble) and chorus (secular ensemble) is disappearing. The terms are now used interchangeably, especially in secular settings.
(2) The *refrain of a *strophic song. DCI

Chorus reed. Any reed *stop on an *organ designed to be part of the en-

semble of the *instrument as opposed to one with a distinctly solo color.   JBW

Christian Church <Disciples of Christ> **worship music.** Liberty in "nonessentials" has been a hallmark of the Christian Church since its beginnings in the 19th-century Stone-Campbell movement. Though prevalent in nearly all *services, music is often considered a nonessential, thus practiced with great freedom and diversity. Music styles range from classical to popular. Published *hymnals, including the *Hymnbook for Christian Worship* (1970) and *Chalice Hymnal* (1995), provide some clues to the repertoire of music in many congregations and to the general emphasis on congregational singing. Though the denomination does not have an official *liturgy or liturgical *books, *Thankful Praise: A Resource for Christian Worship* (1987) provides one published resource illustrating the liturgical framework for music in some congregations. Since 1962 the Association of Disciples Musicians has promoted greater professional development among the denomination's musical leaders. The centrality of the *Lord's Supper in Disciples' worship has led to a significant amount of *communion-centered *hymns and *anthems.
Bibl: F. B. Brown, "Styles and Substance in Christian Worship," in *Interpreting Disciples* (Fort Worth, 1987).   JDW

C(hristian) M(ethodist) E(piscopal) <CME> **worship music.** This Church was first organized as the Colored Methodist Episcopal Church (1876) following an 1870 withdrawal of African American members from the Methodist Episcopal Church South, in protest against the segregated and demeaning treatment they received. The name was changed to Christian Methodist Episcopal Church in 1954.

CME hymnological history is one of adapting and adopting. The inaugural *hymnal, *Hymn Book of the Colored Methodist Episcopal Church in America* (1891), was an adaptation of the 1889 Methodist Episcopal hymnal by L. Holsey, a founding bishop. The CME edition contained 595 of 929 hymns found in the Methodist Episcopal hymnal, 46 hymns from an earlier Methodist Episcopal hymnal and other hymnals, songs from a *Sankey collection of *gospel hymns, rituals of the newly formed Church and a preface by CME bishops. An additional hymnal, *Songs of Love and Mercy* (1904), also appeared. Its 198 hymns included some traditional Methodist hymns, compositions by Holsey and F. M. Hamilton (a prolific CME hymnist). The 1939 hymnal of the Methodist Church was adopted in 1950. *Songs of Love and Mercy* was reprinted for the Church's centennial commemoration in 1970.

The CME Church was originally influenced significantly by the texts of C. *Wesley. From the hymnal of 1891 through the adoption of the Methodist hymnal in 1950 little attention was paid to the music of African Americans. That changed with the publication of *The Hymnal of the Christian Methodist Episcopal Church* (1987): basically *The New National Baptist Hymnal* (1977) with the addition of a Holsey hymn. Traditional Methodist hymnody is absent, while there is an ample amount of Negro *spirituals and African American *gospel music by *Dorsey, *Akers and others. Congregational singing, some in the gospel style, is accompanied by *organ and *piano.

Bibl: J. Spencer, *Black Hymnody* (Knoxville, 1992) 44–58.   HCB-MWC

Christian Reformed worship music. Strong congregational singing has long been at the heart of worship in the Christian Reformed Church, founded in 1857. Succeeding editions of the *Psalter Hymnal* (1934, 1957, 1987) have been used by the majority of congregations for public worship. Each edition begins with metrical settings of all 150 biblical *psalms, includes a wide variety of *hymns and concludes with liturgical materials. Other worship resources include the children's *hymnal (*Songs for Life,* 1994) and a quarterly periodical (*Reformed Worship*). Recent changes have broadened the musical repertoire of most congregations to include a greater use of popular musical styles, music of the world church, praise and worship *choruses and a wide variety of instrumental music.

Bibl: Psalter Hymnal Handbook (Grand Rapids, 1998).   JDW

Christian rock <contemporary Christian music>. A broad genre of religious music employing Christian texts and rock music styles, ranging from pop-folk to rap. It began in the late 1960s when young Christians desired music communicating the Christian message in a popular style. Resulting "Jesus music" included songs by Christian artists (e.g., Larry Norman) and secular pieces on religious or semi-religious themes (e.g., Webber and Rice's *Jesus Christ, Superstar*). During the early 1970s Christian rock, though often popular with Christian youth, was generally frowned upon by church leadership and rejected by the rock industry. In 1975 the first all-Christian rock radio stations were founded and the Christian rock recording industry was growing significantly (see A. *Grant). Until the 1980s Christian rock was primarily an aspect of the concert/recording industry and not used in worship. During the 1980s and 1990s, many churches (especially those targeting young people) made Christian rock the standard musical style for worship.

Bibl: P. Baker, *Contemporary Christian Music* (Westchester, 1985). DWM

Christiansen, F(redrik) Melius (*b* Eidsvold, Norway 1871; *d* Northfield MN 1955). Composer and choral director who founded the choir of *St. Olaf College (1912). His arrangements and choral leadership (especially emphasizing *a cappella* singing) set a high standard for choral performance in the first half of the 20th century. FJM

Christiansen, Olaf C. (*b* Minneapolis 1901; *d* Northfield MN 1984). Choral conductor, composer and arranger. The son of F. Melius, from whom he assumed leadership of the *St. Olaf Choir in 1943, expanding their *a cappella* repertoire and widening their influence through numerous clinics and conferences. FJM

Christian year. See *year, liturgical.

Christmas. A Christian feast (December 25) and season of the liturgical *year commemorating the birth of Christ (the E parallel is *Epiphany or Theophany). Clear evidence for the feast of Christmas exists in the W by 336. The duration of the season varies among Christian communities; for some (e.g., RC) it extends to the feast of the Baptism of the Lord. Musically it is marked by *carols, the *Gloria in excelsis,* proper *antiphons (e.g., *Hodie*), traditional *chorales and *hymns (e.g., *Adeste fideles*). The feast has been the inspiration for innumerable larger *sacred and *liturgical works, e.g., J. S. *Bach's *Christmas Oratorio.* MJG

Christmas Concerto. (1) The *Concerto Grosso in G minor (op. 6, n. 8) by *Corelli, inscribed *fatto per la notte di Natale* (Italian, "made for Christmas night"). Composed as a *church concerto.

(2) G. Torelli's 12 *concertos for strings and *continuo* (op. 8, 1709), inscribed *con un pastorale per il Santissimo Natale* (Italian, "with a pastoral for the most holy night of Christmas"), the pastoral being n. 6 in G minor. JBF

Christmas Oratorio. A composite work by J. S. *Bach (BWV 248) comprising 6 *church cantatas for the first 3 days of *Christmas, New Year's Day, the following Sunday and *Epiphany. Composed in 1734–35, but not performed as a complete work until the 19th century. Many elements were borrowed from Bach's earlier secular *cantatas. JBW

Christological hymn. A New Testament song, *hymn or fragment which addresses, describes or praises Christ. There is no unanimity among scholars in identifying specific New Testament passages as christological hymns; commonly mentioned examples are Phil 2:6-11, Col 1:15-20, Eph 2:14-16, 1 Tim 3:16, 1 Pet 3:18-22, Heb 1:3, John 1:1-14. It is not clear to what extent such texts were (if ever) actually employed in early Christian worship. They do testify to the growing tendency within Christianity to honor Christ as God and indicate the lyrical way such testimony may have emerged in Christian worship.

Bibl: R. Karris, *A Symphony of New Testament Hymns* (Collegeville, 1996). CRY

Christus [Latin]. "Christ." (1) A German *oratorio by F. *Mendelssohn (op. 97), begun in 1844 and left unfinished at his death; text by C. Bunsen.

(2) A Latin oratorio by *Liszt on episodes from the life of Jesus drawn from the Bible and the RC *liturgy, completed in 1867.

(3) The part of Christ in a sung *passion. KRH

Christus am Ölberge [German]. "Christ on the Mount of Olives." An *oratorio by *Beethoven (op. 85, 1803) to a text by F. X. Huber, for soprano, tenor, bass, *choir and orchestra. PAB

Chrodegang (*b* 715?; *d* Metz 766). Chancellor to Charles Martel and Bishop of Metz (from 742). As leader of the Frankish church Chrodegang introduced Roman *chant and the Roman *liturgy into the church of Metz. MSD

Chrysander, (Karl Franz) Friedrich (*b* Lübtheen, Mecklenburg 1826; *d* Bergedorf 1901). Musical scholar. Originally self-taught, he eventually earned a doctorate from Rostock University (1855). He published works on numerous composers and *church music. A cofounder of the Händel-Gesellschaft (1856), he published an edition of *Handel's complete works (1856–94) and a multivolume biography of him. JLB

Chrysanthine notation. The revised notation for Greek *liturgical music devised by Chrysanthos of Madytos, Gregory the Protopsaltes and Chourmouzios the Chartophylax in 1814. At that time liturgical melodies were passed on orally in a complicated, sometimes chaotic system. Chrysanthos and co-workers attempted to simplify this system, adopting some of the principles of W notation.

Bibl: K. Romanou, "A New Approach to the Work of Chrysanthos of Madytos," in D. Conomos, ed., *Studies in Eastern Chant* V (Crestwood, NY 1990) 89–100. DMP

Chtets [Slavonic]. See *anagnostes.*

Church cadence <modal, plagal cadence>. The resolution of a musical phrase by the IV - I chord progression. Used in numerous *hymns and sacred compositions. See *amen cadence. JBF

Church cantata [Italian *cantata da chiesa*]. A *cantata for worship. Related to the *gospel motet, it is often placed after the *gospel and before the sermon: articulating the former and preparing for the latter. By the 18th century it had acquired orchestral accompaniment and consisted of an opening *chorus and concluding *chorale, interspersed with *recitatives and *arias. J. S. *Bach wrote over 200. JBW

Church concerto [Italian *concerto da chiesa*]. A term describing Italian and German *sacred music of the late 16th and early 17th centuries for voices and *instruments. It is used for *polychoral and other large-scale works (e.g., the *Concerti* of the *Gabrielis, 1587), as well as for more intimate works for soloists or small vocal ensembles with *continuo (e.g., *Viadana's *Cento concerti ecclesiastici,* 1602). DWM

Church drama. See *drama, liturgical.

Church Light Music Group. See *Twentieth Century Church Light Music Group.

Church modes. See *ecclesiastical modes.

Church music [Latin *musica ecclesiastica*]. (1) An encompassing term for all the types of music employed by the Christian churches. While the term includes music sung at worship, it embraces much more including Sunday school songs, devotional *hymns and a broad range of inspirational music.

(2) Commonly employed as a synonym for *liturgical music, *religious music or *sacred music.   EBF

Church Music Publishers Association <CMPA>. An organization founded (1926) by 10 *gospel music publishers. Headquartered in Nashville, CMPA currently has 42 members covering the broad range of *church music publishing. CMPA addresses issues such as copyright legislation, infringement and education. Publishers are elected to membership in CMPA.   RJB

Church of Christ (Holiness) USA worship music. C. P. *Jones founded this movement, which eventually became a denomination in 1898. Two years later he published its first *hymnal, *Jesus Only*. The present hymnal, *His Fullness Songs* (1977), contains many of Jones' compositions (e.g., "I'm Happy With Jesus Alone"). These and other songs are sung *a cappella* and at sight.   HCB

Church of God in Christ worship music. C. H. *Mason established this Holiness church in 1897; after attending the *Azusa Street revival he reestablished the church as *Pentecostal (1907). Mason encouraged African American *gospel music, which comprises 95 percent of all music in *services today. Such music has been the inspiration for the compositions of church members *Crouch, E. and W. *Hawkins and others. The official *hymnal, *Yes, Lord!* (1982) is one of the few hymnals including the *call and response form. Singing is accompanied by *piano, electronic *organ, synthesizer, horns and percussion.   HCB

Church of Jesus Christ of Latter-day Saints <Mormon> **worship music, The.** Music has been an important part of Latter-day Saints (Mormon) worship since the Church's foundation (1830). Worship *services include a simple pattern of *prelude and *postlude music, congregational singing (see *sacrament hymn), *choir music and special musical selections. *Hymns are the basic music for Church meetings; their use is encouraged for all musical elements. The first hymn collection was prepared by E. *Smith in 1835; many editions have followed. The current English edition, *Hymns of The Church of Jesus Christ of Latter-day Saints,* was published on the 150th anniversary (1985) of the first hymnbook's publication; subsequent editions exist in over 20 languages.

The General Music Committee was organized in 1920 to coordinate the Church's music program. Under the direction of a central administration the patterns of worship music in the Church are unified worldwide, including a standard collection of hymns and the use of *organ and piano for accompaniment. Variations on standard musical practices are made under the direction of local ecclesiastical leaders.

Bibl: K. L. Davidson, *Our Latter-day Hymns* (Salt Lake City, 1988). MFM

Church of the Living God worship music. The church was founded in 1889 at Wrightsville AR by W. Christian. Highly influenced by the music of the *Pentecostal *Church of God in Christ, the denomination uses no *hymnal but sings chiefly independent *refrains. Clapping, *keyboard and percussion accompaniment and body movement are characteristic of the worship music. HCB

Church sonata [Italian *sonata da chiesa*]. An instrumental work, often in 4 movements, prevalent from the mid-17th to mid-18th centuries, especially in Italy. It was often employed as a replacement for the *gradual or *communion at *mass, or in place of *psalm *antiphons at *vespers. AWR

Church year. See *year, liturgical.

Chvalitny [Slavonic]. See *Ainoi.

Ciconia, Johannes. This name is alternately applied to a single composer/theorist, and to an older and younger Ciconia (possibly father-son). (1) The elder may have been born in Liège *c* 1335, where he became canon at St. Jean l'évangéliste.

(2) The younger may have been born in Liège *c* 1373; *d* Padua 1411. It is probable that he is the composer, since no compositions ascribed to this name date from before *c* 1390. He worked at Padua Cathedral (from 1403). He wrote treatises *Nova musica* and *De proportionibus;* his music includes secular

vocal works, *c* 12 *mass movements and 11 *motets. JLB

Cipher. The sound which results from an *organ pipe speaking without a key having been struck, generally due to a faulty pallet or slider. Often used (inaccurately) to refer to a stuck key. PAJ

Cistercian chant. *Chant of the Cistercian Order, which was founded as a rigorous monastic observance in 1098. Chant was systematically revised in order to achieve modal purity, a limited range for melodies (ordinarily within a single octave), avoidance of the B-flat in notation and reduced *melismas. Around 1190, a compendium of *liturgical music was ready for use as a standard in all Cistercian houses (over 300 at the time). This chant constituted a major reform of the received medieval repertoire.

Bibl: C. Waddell, "The Origin and Early Evolution of the Cistercian Antiphonary," in *The Cistercian Spirit,* ed. M. Basil Pennington (Spencer MA, 1970), 190–223. JMH

Clark, Elbertina <Twinkie> (*b* Detroit ?). Composer and performer of contemporary African American *gospel music within the *Church of God in Christ. The founder of the singing group the Clark Sisters, she is also a well-known recording artist, organist, choir director and evangelist. MEM

Clarke, Jeremiah (*b* London *c* 1674; *d* there 1707). Composer of *cantatas, *anthems, *odes, harpsichord pieces and theater music. He served as organist at Winchester College, St. Paul's Cathedral and the *Chapel Royal (from 1704) with *Croft. He wrote "Trumpet Voluntary," originally for trumpet and wind ensemble. RJS

Classical period. The period from approximately 1750 to 1820. So called because much music of this period is characterized by such "classical" attributes as balance, proportion, elegance and clarity. This period's music typically differs from that of the *Baroque period that preceded it in its more frequent use of homophonic texture, lyrical melody, simpler harmony, balanced phrase structure and greater thematic contrast within movements.

Broadly speaking, *church music was in decline during this period, especially in Protestant countries. The greater importance of public concerts (and consequently of instrumental music), the general reduction of financial support for *choir schools and church music, and the desire of a growing middle class for music of more immediate appeal all contributed to decreased importance of church composition. Church music was written in the prevailing secular style of opera, sometimes tempered by more conservative stylistic features, or (especially in Austria) blended with the new orchestral style to produce the so-called *symphonic masses of *Mozart, F. J. *Haydn, *Cherubini and others.

Church music in England continued to be written in a more conservative style by such composers as *Boyce. Music in cathedrals continued to deteriorate, and *hymn singing remained unauthorized in the Church of England. However, Methodist and Evangelical revivals produced a flood of new hymns that sought to express the full range of Christian experience in lively, accessible tunes. Especially noteworthy are those by C. *Wesley, and J. Newton and W. Cowper's collection *Olney Hymns.

European Jewish worship music during the 18th century included *cantatas in various communities, as well as instrumental music (including *organ) in a few centers.

Notable developments in North America include the proliferation of *shape-note notation and its use in *singing schools, the popularity of the *fuging tune (especially those of *Billings), the influence of the *Moravians who introduced significant European sacred works to North America and the development of *Shaker hymnody.

Bibl: M. Bangert, "Church Music History, Classic and Romantic," *Key Words in Church Music,* ed. C. Schalk (St. Louis, 1978), 127–38; J. Rushton, *Classical Music* (London, 1986); P. Downs, *Classical Music* (New York, 1992). KRH

Clausula (pl. **clausulae**) [from Latin *claudere,* "to falter"]. (1) In medieval *polyphony (especially the *Notre Dame school), a musical section often set in the midst of simple *organum and based on the same *plainsong, which displays a more complex musical style, especially rhythmic *discant. It was the basis for the development of the *motet.

(2) Medieval term for a cadence. AJL

Claviorgan(um) [French *clavecin organisé;* Italian *claviorgano*]. A *keyboard instrument that combines harpsichord (or piano) and *organ; described already in the 15th century, and still built in the 18th century. JLB

Clemens (non Papa) <Clement, Jacob> (*b* Ypres? *c* 1510–15; *d* Dixmuide 1556). Composer. His works include 15 *parody masses, over 200 *motets, 159 *souter-liedekens* and *lofzangen* (Dutch, "praise songs") and 89 *chansons*. While there might have been some serious reason for his nickname *non Papa* (Latin, "not the Pope"), it probably was a joke.   LFH

Clement of Alexandria (*b c* 150; *d c* 215). Eminent theologian of the E church and leader of the catechetical school at Alexandria (*c* 190). His writings are rich in musical imagery (e.g., Christ as the "new song") and instructions about the role of music in worship. He wrote "A Hymn to Christ, the Savior," one of the earliest extant Christian *hymn texts; it is often sung today as "Shepherd of Tender Youth."   CFS

Clérambault, Louis Nicolas (*b* Paris 1676; *d* there 1749). Among the most illustrious of French Classical *organ composers. While he wrote for harpsichord and voices he is best known for his organ music. Notable are the 2 suites on the 1st and 2nd tones, dedicated to his teacher, A. Raison, whom he succeeded as organist at St. Sulpice.   JBW

Cleveland, J. Jefferson (*b* Elberton GA 1937; *d* Baltimore 1986). Composer and arranger of African American *spirituals and *gospel songs. He coedited *Songs of Zion* (UMC, 1981), the first collection combining all genres of African American religious songs in a single source. This set the standard for black denominational *hymnals.   MEM

Cleveland, James (*b* Chicago 1932; *d* Los Angeles 1991). African American *gospel singer, composer, pianist, recording artist and Baptist minister. A protégé of R. *Martin and *Dorsey, Cleveland

became a pivotal figure in gospel music both because of his prolific composition and influential performance style. He founded the Gospel Music Workshop of America (1968).   MEM

Codex Calixtinus. See *Santiago de Compostela, repertory of.

Coleridge-Taylor, Samuel (*b* London 1875; *d* Croydon 1912). Composer, conductor and educator. He studied with *Stanford at London's Royal Academy of Music, later becoming professor of composition at London's Trinity College. He wrote *anthems, songs, chamber music and *cantatas, especially the celebrated *Hiawatha's Wedding Feast* (1898). Conscious of his African roots (his father was from Sierra Leone), he often composed on black themes, e.g., *African Suite* (1901), *Twenty-Four Negro Melodies* (1905) and *Symphonic Variations on an African Air* (1906). He guest conducted on 3 trips to the US (1904, 1906, 1910).   MWC

Collect [from Latin *collectum*, "gathered"] <oration, from Latin *oratio*, "prayer">. (1) A short prayer in W Christian worship, ordinarily comprised of an invocation, petition and conclusion.

(2) The proper prayer of the day spoken or chanted by the priest at the end of the entrance rite at *mass.

(3) The name applied in some traditions to similar prayers for *morning and *evening prayer.   GET

Collect tone. A recitation formula used for chanting a *collect. The Latin *liturgy employed various collect tones whose use was dependent upon the nature of the feast and its degree of solemnity, as illustrated in the *Liber Usualis*.   GET

Collegeville. See *St. John's University.

Comes [Latin]. "Companion." (1) Originally a liturgical *book containing scriptural passages to be read at *mass.
(2) A list of readings (usually arranged by *incipit) for mass.   MJG

Common of saints. A sets of texts for saints who do not have a complete set of *propers for their memorial. Ordinarily it includes *collects and readings for *mass; *hymns, *antiphons, collects, readings and *psalms for the *divine office. Such commons exist for the BVM, apostles, martyrs, doctors of the church, virgins, holy men, etc.   GET

Common of the mass. Those parts of the *mass which are relatively unchanging, as opposed to the *proper. It includes some public and most private prayers prescribed for the presider and other ministers as well as congregational *responses and *acclamations and other ritual elements. A more comprehensive term than *ordinary of the mass.   GET

Communion [from Latin *communio,* "union with"]. (1) Part of the *eucharist during which ministers and assembly receive Christ under forms of bread and wine. Though varying among Christian traditions, ritual elements often include the *Lord's Prayer, sign of peace, fraction rite with accompanying *fraction litany, communion procession with accompanying *communion anthem and the prayer after communion.
(2) In some Protestant traditions, a synonym for the eucharistic *liturgy.
(3) RC *service, technically called Sunday Celebrations in the Absence of a Priest, in which communion is distributed, but no *mass is celebrated.

(4) The *communion antiphon, or *psalm sung during communion.
(5) The consecrated elements of bread and wine.
(6) A church or denomination, e.g., the Lutheran communion.   GET

Communion antiphon <anthem> [Latin *antiphona ad communionem*]. A W Christian *chant sung during *communion at the *eucharist. *Antiphons were originally sung between *verses of selected *psalms, especially Ps 34; psalm verses were dropped *c* 11th–12th centuries leaving only the antiphon. Anglicans sometimes set texts of communion antiphons in *anthem style. Texts are biblical, often chosen to reflect the *gospel of the day.   GET

Compère, Loyset (*b* Hainaut *c* 1445; *d* St. Quentin 1518). Composer. A singer at Milan's ducal chapel, he held subsequent positions at Cambrai's St. Géry, Douai's St. Pierre and St. Quentin (from 1404?). Compère wrote many *chansons,* *masses, *motets and 4 *Magnificat*s. JLB

Compline [Latin *completorium,* "completion"]. Night prayer in the *divine office, in evidence by the 5th century. Its current structure in the Roman rite is: opening dialogue and *doxology, examination of conscience or penitential rite (optional), night *hymn, *psalmody, scripture reading with *responsory, *Nunc Dimittis,* *collect, *blessing and *antiphon of the BVM or concluding hymn. Many variations exist across Christian denominations.   JMJ

Concentus [Latin]. "Harmonious music." A term used since the 16th century to refer to liturgical *chants with a distinctive melodic contour (ordinarily sung by soloists or *choir) such as *antiphons or *responsories; as opposed to *accentus. LJC

Concertato [Italian]. "Concerted." A term employed to describe 17th-century music with music making forces of contrasting size and textures. In choral literature the concept is reflected in Venetian *polychoral works, English *verse anthems, German *cantatas and more recently in 20th-century Anglo-American *hymn anthems. CRY

Concerto [from Italian concertare, "to join together"]. In the 17th century a mixed ensemble of *instruments and/or voices, or a composition (sacred or secular) for such a group. After the 17th century, a composition (ordinarily secular) for soloist(s) and orchestra. See *church concerto. VAL

Concerto da chiesa. See *church concerto.

Concert spirituel [French]. "Sacred concert." A concert series (1725–90) of sacred vocal and instrumental music founded in Paris by A. Philidor to fill the need for music during *Lent when concerts and opera were prohibited. Eventually secular music was also included. FJM

Concordia University. (1) The name of individual institutions of the Lutheran Church-Missouri Synod in Austin TX, Irvine CA, Mequon WI, Portland OR and River Forest IL.

(2) A designation for the "system" linking these with 5 other colleges in Ann Arbor MI, Bronxville NY, St. Paul MN, Selma AL and Seward NE. Many of these schools offer programs in *church music. JLB

Conductus (pl. **conducti** or **conductus**) [from Latin conducere, "to escort"]. A Latin *strophic song of the 12th–13th centuries, both *monophonic and *polyphonic, not based on a liturgical *chant but on a freely invented melody. The term variously meant a musical piece used as an "introduction" (to a lesson) or an "escorting" or processional song. The polyphonic conductus (usually 2- or 3-part and note against note in style) represents, along with *organum, *clausula and *motet, a chief type of 13th-century *polyphony. CFS

Confractorium [Latin]. "With the breaking." The *antiphon accompanying the breaking of the bread which occurs before the *Our Father in the *eucharist of the Ambrosian, Gallican and Mozarabic rites. CRY

Congregationalist worship music. Congregationalism arose in England from the Separatist and Puritan movements as a second wave of the English *Reformation. Showing their Calvinist influences, Congregationalists initially sang unaccompanied *psalms in unison, believing that *hymns of human composition were not allowed by scripture. The *Bay Psalm Book, the first book printed in the New World, was for Congregationalist worship. In the 17th century *singing schools were begun to bolster congregational singing. Hymns by *Watts were introduced in *hymnals and public worship. In the 1760s *choirs began to appear to support congregational singing and to provide *anthems. *Organs came into use in the 1770s. Congregationalist *hymnody was influenced by 18th- and 19th-century *revival songs. In 1957 the majority of Congregationalist Churches in the US joined the Evangelical and Reformed Church and the Christian Church to form the United Church of Christ.

Bibl: J. White, *Protestant Worship* (Louisville, 1989), especially 117–34; J. von Rohr, *The Shaping of American Congregationalism 1620–1957* (Cleveland, 1992). RJS

Console. The cabinet containing *keyboards (manuals and pedals), *draw stops and couplers of an *organ. Before the 20th century, keyboards were connected directly to windchests by strips called trackers. See *detached console. JBW

Constitution on the Sacred Liturgy. See *Sacrosanctum Concilium.*

Consultation on Common Texts <CCT>. An ecumenical organization founded in the mid-1960s, through which 20 churches and their agencies in Canada and the US developed liturgical texts, rites and other materials for worship. CCT was the N American member associate of the *International Consultation on English Texts (1969–75) and then the *English Language Liturgical Consultation (1985–). JBF

Contemporary Christian music. See *Christian rock.

Contrafactum (pl. **contrafacta**) [Latin]. "Made against." The practice of substituting a new text for an old one. Many examples exist in which new texts were provided for different liturgical *chants, sacred texts for secular music, or (in Protestantism) theologically acceptable texts for older music (e.g., *Marian hymns). VEG

Copland, Aaron (*b* Brooklyn 1900; *d* North Tarrytown NY 1990). Dean of American classical composers. In 1936 Copland began to concentrate on American *folk themes. *Appalachian Spring* (1944) is famous for its inclusion of the Shaker *hymn tune SIMPLE GIFTS. He also arranged this song for piano and voice in *Old American Songs,* Set 1, which he orchestrated in 1954–55. JBF

Coptic chant. The *monophonic *liturgical music of the Coptic Orthodox Church of Egypt. There is an ancient tradition of blind *cantors and performance by men only. The musical tradition is transmitted orally (no musical notation exists), but books of *hymn texts are used, including the *difnar* (for feasts of the saints) and *psalmodia* (for a choral *service of the same name connected with several *offices). Some melodies have been altered to accommodate the increasing use of Arabic in the *liturgy. Percussive *instruments accompany specific *chants. Many texts are common to Coptic and *Byzantine chant, but the musical relationship has not been adequately studied.

Bibl: M. Robertson, R. Moftah, M. Roy and M. Tóth, "Music, Coptic," in *The Coptic Encyclopedia* (1991) 6:1715–47. RGD

Corbin, Solange (*b* Vorly 1903; *d* Bourges 1973). Musicologist who specialized in medieval music, especially neumatic notation; she also studied liturgical *drama, *rhymed offices and secular medieval song. Educated at the *Schola Cantorum and Sorbonne, she authored *L'église à la conquête de sa musique* (1960).   RTR

Corelli, Arcangelo (*b* Fusignano 1653; *d* Rome 1713). Composer and violinist. He studied violin locally, then in Bologna (1666) with G. Benvenuti and L. Brugnoli, possibly studying *counterpoint under M. Simonelli. In Rome by 1675, he was employed as a violinist at the church of San Luigi (1675–85). He gave numerous public performances under the patronage of Swedish Queen Elizabeth, Cardinal Pamphili (for whom Corelli served as music director, 1687–90) and especially Cardinal Ottoboni (his music director from 1690). Corelli published 6 sets of 12 compositions each, mainly solo and trio sonatas (*sonate da chiesa* and *sonate da camera*) and concerti grossi (especially *Christmas Concerto,* 1712).
   Bibl: M. Pincherle, *Corelli: His Life, His Work* (New York, 1956).   LFH

Cori spezzati [Italian]. "Broken choirs." The practice, originating in 16th-century Italy (especially Venice), of 2 or more accompanied or unaccompanied *choirs performing a single composition, often from separate parts of a building. See *polychoral.   AWR

Cornysh(e) <Cornish>, **William** (*d* 1523). Composer and master of the children of the *Chapel Royal (1509–23). His often florid music is preserved in the *Eton and Lambeth Choirbooks and the Fayrfax Manuscript.   AJL

Coronach <*corrynogh, corinoch, corranach, cronach,* etc.> [Scottish, Irish]. "Outcry." A lament for the dead (often sung by women) in Scotland and Ireland.

The church attempted to suppress it in the 17th century as barbaric, objecting to its resemblance to howling; it survived, however, well into the 19th century.   LJC

Coronation anthems. *Anthems by *Handel for George II's coronation (1727): "Zadok the Priest," "The king shall rejoice," "My heart is inditing," "Let thy hand be strengthened." Also, the anthem by *Purcell for James II's coronation (1685): "My heart is inditing."   RKW

Coronation Mass. (1) A popular name for *Mozart's *Mass in C major* (German *Krönungsmesse;* K 317, 1779). Contrary to other legends, it was named for its performance on anniversaries of the crowning of members of the Austrian royal family.
   (2) A common name for F. J. *Haydn's *Mass in D major* (Hob XXII:11, 1798), also known as the *Nelson* or *Imperial Mass.*   AWR

Corps glorieux, Les [French]. "The glorious bodies." An *organ suite (1939) by *Messiaen, which he described as "7 short visions of the life of the resurrected." The various movements are meditations on selected New Testament and liturgical texts.   JBW

Corrette, Michel (*b* Rouen 1709; *d* Paris 1795). Organist, composer and author. The son of organist G. Corrette (*d* by 1733), Michel was a successful organist in Paris and composer of *sacred music, works for *organ, hurdy-gurdy, harpsichord and flute. He authored several method books for various *instruments.   FKG

Cotton, John (*b* Derby, England 1585; *d* Boston 1652). Anglican preacher who was ejected from the Church of England for his Puritanism. He immigrated to New England, ministering at Boston's First Church. One of the architects of the *Bay Psalm Book,* he also authored *Singing a Gospel Ordinance* (1647).   RAL

Council of Trent. See *Trent, Council of.

Counterpoint. The simultaneous sounding of multiple melodic lines whose horizontal motion can be perceived separately and yet at the same time provide coherence. Counterpoint has distinguished W music from that of other cultures for over 9 centuries (especially from *c* 1300–1800). It is characterized by forward motion, rhythmic differentiation and intervallic separation.   MDJ

Counter Reformation <Catholic Reformation>. A response to the challenges posed by 16th-century Protestant Reformers which sought to renew the RC Church at every level: liturgical, moral, spiritual, pastoral, theological and institutional. This renewal prompted activity on 3 fronts: clerical, scholarly and conciliar. In the 1520s, new or renewed religious orders (e.g., the Capuchins) confronted the issue of clerical corruption by seeking a return to gospel ideals of simplicity and poverty. At the level of scholarship, Catholic historians (e.g., C. Baronius) attacked their Protestant counterparts (e.g., M. Flacius) by defending traditional dogma against charges that it was unbiblical or lacked historical legitimacy. At the conciliar level, the Council of *Trent clarified basic church dogmas (e.g., regarding faith, justification and sacraments) and reformed both *liturgy and *liturgical music.

Trent thus set the RC church's course for the next 4 centuries until *Vatican II.
Bibl: A. G. Dickens, *The Counter Reformation* (London, 1968); L. Chatellier, *The Europe of the Devout* (New York, 1989).   NDM

Couperin, François <*le grand*> (*b* Paris 1668; *d* there 1733). Organist, harpsichordist, composer and teacher; the nephew of L. *Couperin. Proclaimed "the great" *(le grand),* he was considered the zenith of the French *Baroque style. Organist at St. Gervais in Paris (from 1685), he was also court organist and harpsichordist to Louis XIV (from 1693). Most famous for his harpsichord works (4 published collections) and an instructional thesis (*L'art de toucher le clavecin,* 1716), his only published organ compositions are 2 *organ masses (1690). Vocal works include *motets, *versets and 3 of a planned 9 *Leçons de ténèbres* (1703–05) with texts from *Lamentations to be sung during *Holy Thursday *matins.
Bibl: P. Beaussant, *François Couperin* (Portland, 1990).   PAJ

Couperin, Louis (*b* Chaumes *c* 1626; *d* Paris 1661). Composer, organist and harpsichordist; the uncle of F. *Couperin. Organist at St. Gervais in Paris (from 1653), he wrote *c* 130 works for harpsichord and *c* 75 for *organ. He was the first to designate specific tone colors or registration in his works.   PAJ

Courtois, Jean (*fl* 1530–45). Composer. He served as *maître de chapelle* at Cambrai Cathedral (1540), and wrote *c* 19 *chansons,* 14 *motets and 2 *masses.   JLB

Cranmer, Thomas (*b* Aslockton 1489; *d* Oxford 1556). Reformer and architect of the *BCP. Ordained priest by 1520, he became Archbishop of Canterbury in 1532. Cranmer began some reforms under *Henry VIII, which became more extensive under Edward VI. His views on *church music are not entirely clear: neither of the first 2 *Prayer Books* (1549, 1552) make much reference to music, though it is known that he favored simplified *plainsong (one note per syllable) for the vernacular *liturgy. RAL

Creation, The [German *Die Schöpfung*]. An *oratorio by F. J. *Haydn (Hob XXI:2, 1798) for soloists, *chorus and orchestra setting a German text translated from an early 18th-century English libretto based on Genesis 1 and Milton's *Paradise Lost*. AJL

Creation Mass [German *Schöpfungsmesse*]. A common name for the *Mass in B-flat by F. J. *Haydn (Hob XXII:13, 1801) for *choir, soloists and *orchestra. *"Qui tollis"* of the *Gloria* contains a musical quote from *The* *Creation* (part 3). AWR

Credo <Nicene Creed> [Latin]. "I believe." The third element of the *ordinary of the mass. Like other Christian creeds this is a concise, authorized summary of doctrine. Such creeds originally developed within baptismal liturgies, typically comprised of three sections (1 for each person of the Trinity). This *Nicene creed was based on a formula from the Council of Nicaea (325); it emerged as a complete text in the acts of the Council of Chalcedon (451). It first appears in the *mass in the W in 6th-century Spain where it was sung before the *Pater noster; *Charlemagne apparently introduced it into the mass after the *gospel; it was

not used at Rome until 1014. Sung to syllabic *plainsong for centuries, the earliest chant setting dates from the 11th century. Musical settings of the *Credo* underwent great musical development, especially in *oratorio-style masses of the *Baroque and *Classical eras.

Bibl: J. A. Jungmann, *The Mass of the Roman Rite* (Westminster MD, 1992 [1951]) 1:461–74. NDM

Creed. See *Credo* and *Nicene Creed.

Cremona. (1) A city in the Lombard region of Italy, noted for its musical life centering on its cathedral and for the manufacture of musical *instruments.

(2) An *organ stop found in English *Baroque instruments: a reed at 8-foot pitch with cylindrical resonators. JPM

Creston, Paul (*b* New York 1906; *d* San Diego 1985). Composer and organist. Self-taught in composition and harmony, he received a Guggenheim fellowship (1938) and the New York Critics' Circle Award for his Symphony n. 1 (1941). He served as organist at St. Malachy's Church, New York (1934–67). MSD

Croce, Giovanni (*b* Chioggia *c* 1557; *d* Venice 1609). Composer and RC priest. A pupil of *Zarlino, Croce was a chorister at St. Mark's in Venice; he succeeded Donato there in 1603 as *maestro di cappella*. Croce was widely known for his 4- to 7-voice caprices (humorous songs in Venetian dialect); he published sonatas for 5 voices, 3 volumes of 5- and 6-voice madrigals, and 4-voice *canzonettas*. His *sacred music was conservative, responding to the Council of *Trent's instruction on the intelligibility of texts. He wrote 2 volumes of 8-voice *motets, 2 volumes of 8-voice *cantiones sacrae, *masses for 8 voices, 4- and 6-voice *lamentations, *Magnificats for 6 voices and *vesper *psalms for 8 voices.

Bibl: J. Bettley, "The Office of Holy Week at St. Mark's, Venice, in the late 16th century, and the musical contributions of Giovanni Croce," *Early Music* 22:1 (1994) 45–62.   JLB

Croft, William (*b* Nether Eatington 1678; *d* Bath 1727). Composer. Onetime student of *Blow, he became organist at the *Chapel Royal (with *Clarke until 1707), then Westminster Abbey (1708–12). He composed *anthems, *hymn tunes (e.g., St. ANNE) and settings for *morning, *evening, *communion and burial *services. His published anthem collection *Musica Sacra* (2 vols., 1724) was the first such publication in full score rather than *partbooks.   RJS

Cromorne [French]. (1) An *organ pipe of the reed family, warmer than the German *Krummhorn.
(2) A French wind *instrument of uncertain identity; questionable whether it was equivalent to the crumhorn (Old English *crump;* German *Krummhorn*).   ACL

Crosby, Fanny (*b* Southeast NY 1820; *d* Bridgeport CT 1915). Prolific writer of texts (estimated at *c* 8,000) for *gospel and Sunday school songs, including "Blessed assurance."   VEG

Crotch, William (*b* Norwich, England 1775; *d* Taunton, England 1847). Composer and organist. A child prodigy, he performed at the *organ by age 3; by age 11 he was assisting at Trinity and King's

Colleges, Cambridge. Crotch produced his first *oratorio (*The Captivity of Judah*) by age 14. His prolific output in many genres included 10 *anthems and 3 organ *concertos.   FKG

Crouch, Andraé (Edward) (*b* Los Angeles 1942). Singer, pianist and composer of African American *gospel music. A recording artist, Crouch founded several gospel performing groups. His innovative compositional and performance style greatly influenced the emergence of "contemporary" gospel.   MEM

Crucifixion, The. An 1887 work by *Stainer for *choir, soloists and congregation with *organ accompaniment. It was described by Stainer as "a meditation on the sacred passion of the Holy Redeemer."   JBW

Crucifixus [Latin]. "He was crucified [for us under Pontius Pilate, he suffered death and was buried]." A text from the *Credo which is sometimes a separate movement in larger musical settings of the *ordinary, e.g., J. S. *Bach's *B Minor Mass.*   PAB

Crüger, Johannes (*b* Gross-Beesen 1598; *d* Berlin 1662). German church musician, composer and *hymnal editor. He was *Kantor* of Nicholaikirche in Berlin (1622 until his death) where his colleague was *Gerhardt. He published the influential hymnal *Praxis pietatis melica* (Berlin 1647), which was enlarged and reprinted numerous times. In this hymnal melodies were given with *figured bass accompaniment. Crüger's own *hymn tunes include HERZLIEBSTER JESU and JESU MEINE FREUDE.   RAL

Cum Sancto Spiritu [Latin]. "With the Holy Spirit." The final section of the *Gloria in excelsis,* acknowledging the 3rd person of the Trinity. It often marks a subdivision of musical settings of the *Gloria.*   ACL

Curlew River. The first of 3 "Parables for Church Performance" by *Britten (op. 71, 1964). A stylized dramatic setting for voices and chamber orchestra, it is about a madwoman crossing a river in search of her son. The text is by W. Plomer after a Japanese play (the Noh *Sumidagawa*) by Juro Motomasa (*d* 1431).   KRH

Curwen, John (*b* Heckmondwike, Yorkshire 1816; *d* Manchester 1880). Congregational minister and publisher who established Curwen & Sons in 1863. He was a proponent of the tonic sol-fa, an English method of solmization using "movable do" and manual signs to teach singing, originally used in Sunday school.   RKW

Cyclic mass. A genre of *mass writing originating in the compositional technique of 14th-century France, whereby various elements of the *ordinary are linked through unifying devices such as opening motifs and *cantus firmus.* LMT

Czerny, Carl (*b* Vienna 1791; *d* there 1857). Composer and pianist. A student and friend of *Beethoven, he became an important piano teacher; *Liszt was among his students. He wrote numerous pedagogical works and much *sacred music, including *graduals, *offertories and 11 *masses.   VAC

D

Daigle, Gary. See *Dameans.

Daily office. See *divine office.

Dallapiccola, Luigi (*b* Pisino d'Istria 1904; *d* Florence 1975). Composer who studied, then taught at Florence Conservatory. He blended Italianate lyricism with the Germanic formalism of 12-tone music. Writing in all major forms, his operas *Volo di notte* and *Ulisse* are most memorable. His religious works for solo voice and *instruments are: *Concerto per la notte di Natale dell'anno* (1956), *Preghiere* (1962), *Parole di San Paolo* (1964); choral works include *Requiescant* (1958) and *Tempus destruendi-Tempus aedificandi* (1971).   JKW

Dameans. A group of RC composers, founded in 1967, producing *folk-style *liturgical music. Members include Gary Ault, Michael Balhoff, Paul "Buddy" Ceasar, Darryl Ducote and (after 1977) Gary Daigle. They released numerous recordings and printed music collections. Their compositions are commonly included in current *hymnals and worship aids.   RJB

Damon <Daman> **William** (*b* Liège *c* 1540; *d* London 1591). Elizabethan composer, known for his editions (London, 1579 and 1591) of 4-part harmonizations of English *psalm tunes of the *Sternhold and Hopkins Psalter.   RAL

Dance, liturgical. Dance has marked the religious rituals of many cultures through the ages. According to the biblical tradition, Miriam (Ex 15:20) and David (2 Sam 16:4) danced; other texts indicate that dance was a way of worshipping God (Ps 149:3 and 150:4). Processional dances, circle dances and ecstatic dances existed. Early Christians employed dance metaphors when speaking of worship, and used dance in worship. Eusebius, Gregory of Nyssa, Basil, *Ambrose, John Chrysostom and other writers praise dance as a way to pray with one's whole self; they also warn against inappropriate or pagan dances. Increased liturgical legislation in the late patristic period included new restrictions on dance in worship. Unruly dance was unacceptable; the "sober" dance, however, seems to have been an appropriate form of participation in *services and festivals. Dance continues in some E Christian traditions (see *Ethiopic chant).

Dance associated with worship and devotions is mentioned fairly frequently until the 16th-century *Reformation. Dance enhanced the celebrations of major festivals such as *Easter and *Christmas as well as saints' days. Records document dances by clergy, nuns, special groups (such as *Los Seis* in Seville Cathedral) and congregational dances. In general, Protestant Reformers emphasized word over ritual action, simplified worship forms and eliminated innumerable devotions (e.g., *processions) which provided the context for many dances. A notable exception were the *Shakers, who regularly included dance in their worship. The *Counter Reformation addressed many abuses within RC worship, attempted to define appropriate sacred art, and virtually eliminated dance in official worship.

The 20th century has witnessed a revival of liturgical dance among W Christians. Dance can be used for praise, proclamation and meditation. Groups such as the *International Christian Dance Fellowship, the *International Liturgical Dance Association, *Omega Dancers, and the *Sacred Dance Guild have helped people to reclaim dance as a traditional and meaningful way to worship.

Bibl: J. G. Davies, *Liturgical Dance* (London, 1984); R. Gagne et al., *Introducing Dance in Christian Worship* (Washington DC, 1984); D. Adams and D. Apostolos-Cappadona, eds., *Dance as Religious Studies* (New York, 1990). MAK

Dance of death [French *danse macabre;* German *Totentanz*]. A theme associated with the plagues and wars of the 14th-15th centuries that was used in preaching,

literature, music and other arts. Death, personified as a dancer or musician, comes to take the living of all classes. Evidence exists for such ritual dances literally occurring in and around churches of the *Middle Ages. The image inspired compositions by *Liszt, *Saint-Saëns, *Distler and others.   MAK

Dandrieu, Jean-François (*b* Paris *c* 1682; *d* there 1738). Organist, harpsichordist and composer. He served as organist at St. Merry in Paris (from 1704) and the royal chapel (from 1721). Besides 6 harpsichord collections, he composed for *organ *Noëls* (*c* 1730, some of which may be the work of his uncle P. Dandrieu) and *Livre de pièces d'orgue* (1739).   PAJ

Daquin <D'Aquin>, **Louis-Claude** (*b* Paris 1694; *d* there 1772). Organist at the royal chapel (from 1739) and Notre Dame in Paris (from 1755). He composed 2 *masses, *motets, *cantatas and *organ works. His organ variations on 12 French *noëls* remain popular.   JBW

Darke, Harold Edwin (*b* London 1888; *d* Cambridge 1976). Composer and organist at St. Michael's, Cornhill (1916–66). He wrote several *cantatas (e.g., *The Sower,* 1929), 3 settings of the Anglican *communion service, other *sacred music and *organ works.   FKG

David, King (*d c* 970 BCE). King of ancient Israel. A noted musician in his youth (1 Sam 16:18), he may have invented some musical *instruments (Amos 6:5), and probably composed some elegies (e.g., 2 Sam 1:17-27). He is traditionally regarded as the author of the

Book of *Psalms; it is more likely that he wrote very few Psalms which underwent significant development in the succeeding centuries. While influential in the organization of early *Temple music, the biblical assertion that he established professional Temple music (1 Chr 15) and placed *Levites in charge (1 Chr 25) is improbable. EBF

David, Johann Nepomuk (*b* Efording 1895; *d* Stuttgart 1977). Composer. A master of *counterpoint, he taught in Leipzig (1934–45) and Stuttgart (1947–63), also serving as director of the Mozarteum in Salzburg (1945–48). His religious works include a *Stabat Mater,* *oratorio, many *motets and *organ works. JLB

Davidde Penitente [Italian]. "David the Penitent." An *oratorio by *Mozart (K 469, 1785) to a libretto perhaps by da Ponte. The music is largely a *contrafactum of the earlier *Mass in C minor.* DWM

Davidson, Charles (*b* Philadelphia 1929). *Cantor, teacher and prolific composer of *liturgical music. He serves on the faculty of the H. L. Miller Cantorial School at Jewish Theological Seminary. His compositions incorporate *Jewish prayer modes, *Hasidic and *Sephardic traditions into *Ashkenazic congregational worship. His works are used in Reform and Conservative synagogues. MLK

Davies, (Henry) Walford (*b* Oswestry 1869; *d* Wrington 1941). Composer and organist. He studied at the Royal College of Music with *Parry and *Stanford, then taught there. Associated with the BBC, he became music director of the Royal Air Force (1917) and master of the King's Music (1934). His *anthem "God be in my head" is a staple in choral repertory. FJM

Davison, Archibald T(hompson) (*b* Boston 1883; *d* Brant Rock MA 1961). Music educator, choral conductor and author. He championed *Renaissance *a cappella* music and its use in the 20th century. His views on *church music were expressed in *Church Music: Illusion and Reality* (1952); with W. Apel he edited the 2-volume *Historical Anthology of Music* (1946). FJM

Davisson, Ananias (*b* Shenandoah Co VA 1780; *d* Weirs Cave VA 1857). Compiler and publisher of *shape-note *tune books, most notably *Kentucky Harmony* and *A Supplement to Kentucky Harmony* (1820, 1825). A Presbyterian, he promoted *singing schools in the Shenandoah Valley. RJS

Daw, Carl P., Jr. (*b* Louisville 1944). *Hymn writer, author and Episcopal priest. His works include *To Sing God's Praise* (1992) and *New Psalms and Hymns and Spiritual Songs* (1996). Executive Director of the *Hymn Society (1997–). JDW

Dawson, William Levi (*b* Anniston AL 1899, *d* Tuskegee 1990). Composer, conductor, arranger and educator. He is remembered for conducting the Tuskegee College Choir, for whom he arranged many *spirituals (e.g., "There is a Balm in Gilead"). His *The Negro Folk Symphony* was premiered by the Philadelphia Orchestra (1934) under Stokowski. Among his many other works are *Trio for Piano* (1925) and *Out in the Fields* (soprano and orchestra, 1928). MWC

Day Psalter. A collection of 4-part harmonizations of the English *psalm tunes of the *Sternhold and Hopkins Psalter, published by John Day in 1563. It is also known as the "Parsons Psalter," after William Parsons who composed most of the settings.   RAL

Dead, mass of the <*Requiem*>. A funeral *mass, or mass celebrated on the anniversary (e.g., 30 days, 1 year) of death. In Latin known as a *Requiem* ["rest"] from the first word of the *introit traditionally employed at such masses. Masses for the dead were already occurring in the 4th century, and became especially common in monasteries from the 7th century. The *proper (including the *sequence *Dies irae*) was frequently set by composers, e.g., *Mozart.   MJG

Dead, office of <for> **the.** *Divine office for the dead. Besides *eucharist for the departed, the early church offered *psalms for the dead. A recognizable office of the dead emerged in the 8th century; one consisting of *vespers, *matins and *lauds appears by *c* 800, possibly introduced by Benedict of Aniane (*d* 821). This and other "votive" offices (such as that of the BVM) became an ordinary part of medieval monastic worship along with the standard divine office and eucharist. This office was rejected by Protestant reformers. The revised RC *liturgy of the hours (1971) contains a full office for the dead, and the revised RC Order of Christian Funerals includes an abbreviated one.

Bibl: E. Foley, *The First Ordinary of the Royal Abbey of St-Denis* (Fribourg, 1990) 93–98.   MJG

Dearmer, Percy (*b* London 1867; *d* there 1936). Author and editor. Educated at Oxford, he became a canon at Westminster Cathedral (1931). Dearmer wrote on theological and liturgical topics, and edited *hymn books, including *Songs of Praise* (1925, 1931) and *Oxford Book of Carols* (1928).   JLB

Decani [Latin]. "Of the dean." In English *church music, a term referring to the dean's side (right side, when facing the altar) and the singers on that side; contrasted with the *cantoris* on the cantor's side. *Psalms, *canticles and *hymns were usually sung in alternation between these 2 groups. Late 16th-century English composers (e.g., *Tallis and *Byrd) employed these 2 groups *antiphonally, separately or together for special tonal effects.   CFS

Deering, Richard. See *Dering, Richard.

Degree of the antiphon. See *anabathmoi.

Deiss, Lucien (*b* Alsace 1921). Scripture scholar, liturgist, composer and RC priest of the Congregation of the Holy Spirit. A leading figure in the liturgical reform, Deiss was cofounder of the Association St-Ambroise and the periodical *Assemblée nouvelle*. Besides his writings on scripture and *liturgy, he is best known for composing *liturgical music based on biblical texts.   CSP

Delande, Michel-Richard. See *Lalande, Michael-Richard.

Dello Joio, Norman (*b* New York 1913). Composer and educator. He was trained at Juilliard (1939–41) and Yale with *Hindemith (1941). His teaching positions included professor of music and dean of the School of Fine and Applied Arts (1972–78) at Boston University. He synthesized early influences of Italian opera, RC *church music and *jazz into highly accessible music marked by modal harmonies and supple rhythms; *Gregorian chant was a prominent feature of his best work, e.g., *Magnificat* (1942) and *The Triumph of St. Joan* symphony (1951). Other works include *Meditations on Ecclesiastes* (1956) for string orchestra (1957 Pulitzer Prize winner), 2 choral *masses (1968, 1976) and *Nativity* (1987) for soloists, *chorus and orchestra.

   Bibl: T. Bumbardner, *Norman Dello Joio* (Boston, 1986).   RAD

Demantius, (Johannes) Christoph (*b* Reichenberg 1567; *d* Freiberg 1643). Church musician and composer. *Kantor* of the Lutheran Cathedral in Freiberg (from 1604), he wrote *polyphonic settings of the *proper, the *ordinary and music for the *daily office. Most important are his *gospel motets (*Corona harmonica,* 1610) and *St. John Passion (1631).   CFS

Demessieux, Jeanne Marie-Madeleine (*b* Montpellier 1921; *d* Paris 1968). Organist and composer. A pupil of *Dupré, she became professor of organ at Liège (from 1952). She also served as organist in Paris at St. Esprit (1933–62) and the Madeleine (from 1962), where she was celebrated for her improvisatory skills. Her compositions include numerous organ works and a *Te Deum.*   PAJ

De Musica Sacra [Latin]. "Concerning sacred music." A 1958 RC instruction by the Sacred Congregation for Rites. It provides directives for Roman rite *liturgical music in light of the principles enunciated in Pope Pius XII's *Musicae sacrae disciplina* and *Mediator Dei* (1947).   JMJ

De profundis [Latin]. "Out of the depths." *Ps 130. One of the 7 *penitential psalms. Traditionally used in the *mass and the *office of the *dead.   ACL

Dering <Deering>, **Richard** (*b* Kent *c* 1580; *d* London 1630). Composer and organist. He wrote *church music for both Anglican and RC worship, having converted to the latter. His Latin music, especially *Cantiones sacrae* (1625), was influenced by Italian practices of the early *Baroque period.   CFS

Descant. (1) *Discant.
   (2) A countermelody written above the *cantus,* often featured in arrangements of congregational *hymns.   RDH

Desprez, Josquin. See *Josquin Desprez.

De tempore hymns [Latin]. Hymns "of the time." *Hymns employed for specific times, seasons or Sundays of the church *year. In early Lutheranism the *de tempore Graduallied* ("gradual hymn of the time") was sung between the *epistle and *gospel; subsequently the hymn was moved later in the liturgical order and now is termed the "hymn of the day/week."   RAL

Dett, R(obert) Nathaniel (*b* Drummondsville ON 1882; *d* Battle Creek 1943). Pianist, composer, educator and arranger. He studied at Eastman (M. Mus.) and then with Boulanger in Paris. His *The Ordering of Moses* was the first major *oratorio utilizing African and African American *folk motifs. Other works include piano suites, orchestral and chamber music, choral works and many arrangements of *spirituals; his SATB edition of *Religious Folk Songs of the Negro* is a classic.   MWC

Dettingen Te Deum and Anthem. *Handel's setting of the *Te Deum,* commemorating the British victory over the French at Dettingen (26 June 1743), first performed at the *Chapel Royal (27 November 1743). Some of its themes are apparently taken from Francesco Urio's *Te Deum* (c 1682) of which Handel owned a copy. The *anthem sets the text "The king shall rejoice."   CFS

Deutsche Messe [German]. "German Mass." (1) An order of *holy communion (1526) prepared by *Luther in response to local need for "the unlearned lay folk." Concerns for the vernacular led him to employ the talents of *Walter and C. Rupsch to reconfigure *chant better suited to German texts. Here German *hymns replaced parts of the *ordinary, providing another impetus for the development of German *hymnody.

(2) A large-scale setting of the ordinary (in E-flat major) by *Schubert (1828).   MPB

Deutsches Hochamt [German]. "German high mass." *High mass during which the congregation and *choir sang most texts in German (in some places Hungarian or Slavic) translation or paraphrase while the priest performed the texts in Latin. Shorter Latin parts were sung in alternation with the priest. This was in contrast to a style of celebrating *low mass in which continuous vernacular *hymn singing was permitted with pauses (not always observed) for the *gospel, consecration and final *blessing. The *Deutsches Hochamt* became fully developed and widespread in the late 18th century, survived *Cecilian opposition in many regions, and became a point of controversy between pastorally-minded liturgists and some musicians. Although never canonically permissible, it enjoyed episcopal support and in 1943 Rome declared it was to be tolerated.

Bibl: B. Fischer, "Das 'Deutsche Hochamt'," *Liturgisches Jahrbuch* 3 (1953) 41–53; *idem,* "La 'Grand' Messe allemande'," *Les Questions liturgiques et paroissiales* 25 (1954) 22–33.   AWR

Deutsches Requiem, Ein [German]. "A German *Requiem.*" *Brahms' 7-movement work (op. 45, 1866; 5th movement added in 1868) for soprano and baritone soloists, *chorus and orchestra. Shunning the traditional Latin text of the *Requiem,* Brahms compiled a text from *Luther's translation of the Bible, providing a magnificent meditation on mortality, despair and hope. It was not intended for liturgical use. JBW

Diabelli, Anton (*b* Mattsee near Salzburg 1781; *d* Vienna 1858). Composer and publisher. A choirboy at Salzburg Cathedral, he studied with M. *Haydn. Diabelli cofounded a publishing house in Vienna which published much of *Schubert's music. He wrote *masses and *cantatas. He is best remembered as the composer of a theme on which *Beethoven wrote 33 variations (op. 120, 1823).   MEC

Diak [Slavonic]. See *cantor.

Diakonika [Greek; Slavonic *diakonik*]. "Deacon's things." In the Byzantine *liturgy the term usually refers to the *litanies (see *aitesis, *eirenika, *ektene, *synapte) which are part of the deacon's *office. The liturgical *book containing the deacon's office is the *diakonikon*, rarely seen in modern use. DMP

Dialogue mass. See *missa recitata*.

Dickinson, Clarence (*b* Lafayette IN 1873; *d* New York 1969). Teacher and organist. He was cofounder of the *Union Seminary School of Sacred Music, where he taught *organ and composition. He edited choral and organ music as well as *The [Presbyterian] Hymnal* (1933). FJM

Dieffenbach family. Four generations of *organ builders in PA between 1776 and 1900. Opus 1 is in the Museum of the Historical Society in Reading PA. JWK

Dies irae [Latin]. "Day of wrath." Best known of all the *sequences; the text was probably written by Thomas of Celano (*d* 1256?). Formerly it was part of the *proper for a *Requiem. Its *chant melody is often quoted in symphonic literature. JBF

Dietrich <Dieterich>, **Sixt** <Sixtus> (*b* Augsburg *c* 1493; *d* St. Gall 1548). *Kapellmeister* in Constance (1517). He joined the reform movement (1527) and became an important early Protestant composer. Dietrich wrote a *Magnificat, *antiphons, sacred *motets and songs. JLB

Differentia (pl. **differentiae**) [Latin]. "Diversity." The melodic pattern used as the termination of a *Gregorian chant *psalm tone. Each psalm tone generally has a variety of *differentiae*. JPM

D'Indy, Vincent. See *Indy, Vincent d'.

Directaneus [Latin]. "Directly." The practice of singing a text straight through without alternation between forces or any addition of a *response or *antiphon. FCQ

Directory for the Public Worship of God <Westminster Directory>. Published in 1645 by the Westminster Assembly, which was appointed by Parliament to reform the English church. It abolished the use of the *BCP in the Reformed tradition of England, Scotland and Ireland and provided instruction on public prayer, scripture reading, preaching, the administration of sacraments and singing *psalms. It became the rubrical and theological foundation for future Presbyterian worship practices. RJS

Directory for Worship. Directions or instructions setting theological and rubrical parameters for common worship and other liturgical practices for the Presbyterian Church (USA). First published in 1961; a 1990 revision has constitutional authority for the denomination, yet does not mandate the use of particular forms or texts. It is an important resource for strengthening congregational and personal spirituality. RJS

Direct psalmody. A *psalm sung *directaneus*. FCQ

Dirge [from Latin *dirige*]. A song, *hymn or poem for burial or memorial rites. EBF

Dirige [Latin]. "Direct." The *incipit* of the first *antiphon of *matins for the dead; thus, the cognomen for that *hour. JMT

Dirksen, Richard W. (*b* Freeport IL 1921). Organist and composer. An Episcopalian, Dirksen was educated at Peabody Conservatory. He served as organist of the National Cathedral, Washington DC (1977–88). He wrote works for *organ, *hymn tunes, *anthems, *oratorios, a *cantata, and a setting for the *eucharist. RJS

Discant. A medieval improvisatory technique, eventually found in written sources. It starts as note against note *polyphony based on a *plainsong *tenor. In the later 12th century this style admitted *neume against neume writing. The result was a quasi non-syllabic polyphony, since not all neumes contain the same number of notes. DCI

Discant mass. A whole or partial setting of the *ordinary of the mass in the 14th and 15th centuries with a *cantus firmus (often paraphrased) in the *discant (top) voice rather than in the *tenor. DWM

Disciples of Christ worship music. See *Christian Church worship music.

Distler, Hugo (*b* Nuremberg 1908; *d* Berlin 1942). Composer and teacher. He studied at the Leipzig Conservatory (1927–31), then held positions at Lübeck's St. Jacobi (1931–37) and the Musikhochschule in Stuttgart (1937–40) and Berlin (1940–42). Distler wrote *organ works, many sacred choral pieces using 17th-century forms, free rhythms and bold harmonies. Nazi harassment led to his suicide. JLB

Dithyramb. A choral song in honor of Dionysius (or Bacchus), the Greek god of wine. The term first appears in the early 7th century BCE. These songs became the subject of contests by the 6th century BCE; many were composed by eminent poets (e.g., Pindar); the form survived into the Roman imperial age. LJC

Divine liturgy [Greek *Theia Leitourgia;* Slavonic *Bozhestvennaya Liturgia*]. The title for the eucharistic *liturgy in the Byzantine tradition indicating that eucharist is considered a divine activity, the mystical reenactment of Christ's work of salvation in the people's "sacrifice of praise." Structurally similar to other Christian *eucharists: an *enarxis* (rite of 3 *antiphons, which in Byzantine music is a series of *psalm *verses with a *troparion* as a *refrain), the liturgy of the word beginning with the "small entrance" with the *gospel book, the liturgy of the eucharist beginning with the *great entrance of bread and wine, *communion and thanksgiving. Liturgical actions are accompanied by antiphons (see *Blazhenny, *Cherubikon, *koinonikon and *Trisagion). *Litanies (see *aitesis, *eirenika, *ektene and *synapte) introduce the ordinarily silent prayers of the priest.

Bibl: H. J. Schulz, *The Byzantine Liturgy* (New York 1986). DMP

Divine office <canonical hours, liturgy of the hours> [Latin *officium divinum*]. The official daily public prayer of the church, comprised chiefly of *hymns, *psalms, *readings, *responsories and *collects. Influenced by ancient Jewish custom, Christians prayed at sunrise (*lauds) and sunset (*vespers). Under the influence of ascetic ideology and monastic practice other *hours were added.

In the Christian E, distinctive forms developed among Armenians, E Syrians, W Syrians, Maronites, Copts and Ethiopians. Most widely celebrated is the hybrid form of the Byzantine office (see *apodeipnon, *hesperinos, *mesonyktikon and *orthros).

In the pre-Reformation Christian W, distinctive forms of the office developed in Milan, N Africa, Gallican areas, Spain and among various monastic communities. The Roman office with 8 hours (as in the *Rule of Benedict) became dominant. It included: *vespers (sunset), *compline (bedtime), *matins (c midnight), *lauds (daybreak), *prime (c 6 AM) and the *little hours of *terce (c 9 AM), *sext (c noon) and *none (c 3 PM). Characteristic of daily Roman Office is singing the *Magnificat at vespers, *Nunc dimittis at compline, Ps 95 in *responsorial form as the *invitatory and the *Benedictus at lauds.

In early Christianity 2 styles evolved: "monastic" and "popular" (celebrated in cathedral or parish churches). Monastic celebrations were lengthy, frequent and featured great variability in texts and *psalmody. Parish or "cathedral" *services were shorter, repetitive and appealed to the senses (through the use of lights, incense, music, movement). By the *Middle Ages these styles were conflated and the office had become a duty performed mainly by clerics (see *breviary) and cloistered religious. *Plainsong was used for singing the office (found in the *antiphonal) though *polyphonic settings (e.g., *Monteverdi's 1610 Vespers) were also known.

New patterns emerged after the *Reformation. *Luther provided a form for *morning and *evening prayer in *Deutsche Messe, including scripture reading and preaching; these services survived more in family than congregational worship until the 20th century. *Cranmer established 2 daily offices in a monthly cycle in the 1549 *BCP. Anglican matins combined elements from matins, lauds and prime according to *Sarum use; Anglican *evensong similarly fused elements of vespers and compline. The basic structure of both offices consisted of psalmody, scripture reading (Hebrew Bible), a *canticle, scripture reading (New Testament) and a second canticle. Structures of the Anglican daily office have been modified in 20th-century reforms. A formally structured daily office is less in evidence for the Reformed churches. *Vatican II simplified and shortened the RC office, reducing the hours to an "Office of Readings" (not bound to a specific time), morning and evening prayer, and brief daytime and night prayer. The ecumenical office developed in the late 20th century by the *Taizé community is widely used among many Christian denominations. See *horologion.

Bibl: R. Taft, The Liturgy of the Hours in East and West (Collegeville, 1986); C. Vogel, Medieval Liturgy (Washington DC, 1986) 166–69, 214–16, 363–68; G. Guiver, Company of Voices (New York, 1988). JMJ-NDM

Djiak [Slavonic]. An alternate form of *Diak.

Docta sanctorum patrum [Latin]. "Teachings of the holy fathers." A decree (1324–25) of Pope *John XXII which sought to limit perceived abuses in the evolution of *polyphony (e.g., the obscuring of the Latin text) by reemphasizing *Gregorian chant and limiting simple *organum to feast days. Ultimately this document had little effect on the evolution of worship music. AWR

Dogmatikon (pl. **dogmatika**) [Greek; Slavonic *dogmatik*]. "Doctrinal hymn." A *sticheron sung to the Mother of God at the end of Ps 141 in Byzantine *hesperinos. Dogmatika for each of the *octoechos, composed on the theme of the incarnation, were once sung according to a very elaborate melody; now they usually follow the *idiomelon. The Slavonic tradition now uses the more general term *bogoroditchen* for this *hymn. See *Theotokion. DMP

Doles, Johann Friedrich (Sr.). (*b* Thuringia 1715; *d* Leipzig 1797). Composer. Once a student of J. S. *Bach, he worked as *Kantor in Freiburg, then at St. Thomas in Leipzig (1755–89). Considered a tradition-based progressive, he composed *passions, *oratorios, *cantatas, *psalms, *motets and some *organ works; nearly all are unpublished. MPB

Domestikos [Greek, from Latin *domesticus*]. "Domestic (servant)." A general title in the Byzantine empire for civil, military and ecclesiastical officials. With regard to music, it refers to the *choir leader. See *psaltes. DMP

Dominican chant. The *chant of the Dominican Order (founded 1220); its first revisions were modeled on *Cistercian chant, although alterations are generally less drastic. Patterns of Dominican *liturgy/chant were established in the latter half of the 13th century, and the key manuscripts are preserved. Sources are consistent and the repertoire verifiable due to the early codification of the chant and the strong central organization of the Order. JMH

Dominicus Mass <*Pater Dominicus* Mass>. *Mozart's Mass in C (K 66), premiered in Salzburg (1769) for the first *mass of a priest who had taken the religious name "Dominicus." RTR

Dona nobis pacem [Latin]. "Give us peace." (1) The final *refrain of the *Agnus Dei. This is a 10th-century adaptation of the original refrain (*miserere nobis,* "have mercy on us"), possibly as the *Agnus Dei* was increasingly employed to accompany the greeting of peace.

(2) A *cantata by *Vaughan Williams on biblical and other texts (1936). VCF

Donato, Baldassare (*b* Venice? *c* 1530; *d* there 1603). Composer, associated all his life with St. Mark's in Venice, first as a choir member (1550). Upon *Zarlino's death he assumed the position of *maestro di cappella.* He composed *sacred music (mostly *motets) for use at St. Mark's. DCI

Dorian (mode). An *ecclesiastical mode with its final on *D*. As an authentic mode (mode 1), it has an ambitus of *d-d'* with its dominant (*tenor) on *a*. The related plagal mode (Hypodorian, mode 2) has an ambitus of *A-a* with its dominant on *f*. CJK

Dorian Toccata and Fugue. A subtitle given by later editors to a *toccata and *fugue by J. S. *Bach (BWV 538). Following a convention of the time, Bach wrote the work without a flat in the signature suggesting its pure *Dorian provenance. MPB

Dorsey, Thomas A(ndrew) (*b* Villa Rica GA 1899; *d* Chicago 1993). African American *gospel songwriter, lyricist, arranger, publisher, *choir director and teacher. Honored as the "father" of gospel music and its most prolific composer, Dorsey studied at the Chicago College of Composing and Arranging and had an initial career as a *jazz and blues composer, singer and pianist. From the late 1920s he dedicated himself to fusing the Christian gospel message with blues-based melodies and harmonies and ragtime/stride piano style accompaniments. His best-known song is "Take My Hand, Precious Lord."

Dorsey cofounded with T. *Frye the first gospel *chorus in the US (Ebenezer Baptist Church, Chicago); he subsequently became choir director at Pilgrim Baptist Church in Chicago (1932–83). He collaborated and toured the US with gospel pioneers S. *Martin, R. *Martin and M. *Jackson. With S. Martin he cofounded the National Convention of Gospel Choirs and Choruses (1932) for organizing and training gospel choirs in metropolitan centers across the country.

Bibl: M. Harris, *The Rise of the Gospel Blues* (New York, 1992); H. C. Boyer, "Take My Hand, Precious Lord, Lead Me On," in *We'll Understand it Better By and By,* ed. B. J. Reagon (Washington, 1992) 141–163.   MEM

Double choir. Two independent choirs that alternate with each other in *polychoral music. Used in most eras of *church music but associated particularly with late 16th-century Venice.   DWM

Double fugue. A *fugue with 2 subjects. Often the second theme is freer than the first, sometimes serving as a countersubject, but recurring throughout.   JBF

Double organ. (1) In ancient times, an *organ of 2 manuals.

(2) The Spanish and Italian *Baroque practice of building 2 almost identical organs facing each other.

(3) A modern organ provided with an antiphonal or echo division located some distance from the main *instrument. JBW

Douglas, Charles Winfred (*b* Oswego NY 1867; *d* Santa Rosa 1944). Organist, choirmaster, editor and Episcopalian priest. The music director at prominent churches in New York and Denver, he is best known for his work in adapting *plainsong to English and as the editor of 2 Episcopal *hymnals (1916, 1940).   RJB

Douroux, Margaret Jean Pleasant (*b* Los Angeles 1941). Composer, arranger, choir director, educator and recording artist. She earned degrees in music and educational psychology (Ph.D., University of Beverly Hills). Douroux founded the Heritage Music Foundation for the preservation of Gospel music. She published African American *gospel music, *hymns, *anthems and *spirituals.   MEM

Dowland, John (*b* London? 1563; *d* there 1626). Composer and lutenist. After studies at Christ Church, Oxford, he became court lutenist at several European courts and for James I of England (from 1612). His works include at least 14 *psalms or sacred songs (most for 4 voices), many more for *instruments including *Lachrimae* ("Seven Tears"). His novel accompaniments and chromatic part-writing were important compositional advances. FKG

Doxastichon [Greek]. "Doxology verse." A *sticheron sung after the smaller doxology (see *doxologia) at the end of a series of proper *stichera in the Byzantine *office. It is usually independent from the stichera which precede it, written by a different author and sung in a different *echos. DMP

Doxologia [Greek; Slavonic *slavoslovije*]. "Words of glory." A *hymn of glorification (similar to the W *Gloria in excelsis) sung in the Byzantine *office at the end of *orthros. It is found in 2 forms: the great *doxology, solemnly sung on Sundays and feast days, and the lesser doxology, a different arrangement of the text chanted according to a simple melody. The "small doxology" (similar to the *lesser doxology in the W) is usually sung as the concluding intercalated *verse to a series of *stichera or *troparia (see *doxastichon). Priestly prayers also usually end with an *ekphonesis glorifying the Trinity called the doxology (of the prayer). DMP

Doxology [Greek]. "Words of glory." A liturgical formula of praise, ordinarily occurring at the close of a prayer. Doxologies already appear in the Hebrew Bible. Each of the 5 books of the *psalter ends with a doxology (Pss 41.13; 72.18-19; 89.52; 106.48; 150:6). The New Testament is filled with doxologies (e.g., Rom 16.27). Most early Christian doxologies concluded with *amen, a pattern that continues today.

While there is common agreement that doxologies exist in Judaism and Christianity there is no unanimity in defining the form. Some contend that a true doxology must include the Greek *doxa* ("glory") or its equivalent in another language; others include as a doxology any praise formula containing the idea of God's eternity.

In Christianity doxologies sealed orations and *eucharistic prayers, as well as homilies and letters. The *Gloria Patri or "lesser" doxology (in contrast to the *Gloria in excelsis or "greater" doxology) has been of particular importance in this regard; among other usages it traditionally concludes all *psalms and *canticles in the Anglican, Lutheran and Roman rite *office (for Byzantine usages see *doxologia). Doxologies occurred with such frequency in Christian worship that the full text was not always written out but simply abbreviated (see *euouae).

The musical setting of a doxology is generally determined by the music of the text with which it is associated. Occasionally a doxology will receive an independent musical setting (e.g., the chorus "Worthy is the Lamb" from *Handel's *Messiah). EBF

Drama, liturgical. A broad term denoting drama created by the church either for use in, or influenced by the *liturgy. While both Jewish and Christian liturgy contain elements that could be considered dramatic (e.g., the *dialogue in the *Pesach *haggadah or processing with palms on *Palm Sunday), liturgical drama is a phenomenon of the *Middle Ages and *Renaissance (10th–16th centuries). Ordinarily in Latin, such dramas were sung *monophonically; thus distinguishable from vernacular forms of medieval drama into which some music was introduced such as *mystery or miracle plays. Multiple traditions developed simultaneously in various liturgical centers of Europe (e.g., St. Gall, Winchester and Fleury).

Most liturgical dramas were written for *Easter or *Christmas. The dialogue between an angel and the Marys visiting the tomb (*Quem quaeritis) is central to the Easter drama Visitatio sepulchri which accounts for almost two-thirds of the c 600 extant dramas. Probably originating in the early 10th century, Visitatio appears with stage directions, costuming instructions and texts in the Regularis concordia (Winchester, c 970). While no music appears in this text, the rubrics indicate it was sung. Other liturgical dramas for Easter include the disciples' encounter with Christ on the road to Emmaus (Peregrinus) and the meeting between Mary Magdalene and Christ in the garden. Popular dramas for Christmas include the angelic nativity announcement to the shepherds (Officium Pastorum), the coming of the Magi (Officium Stellae) and the slaughter of the Innocents (Lamentatio Rachelis). Other liturgical dramas developed around major church festivals, biblical narratives, and important saints (e.g., St. Nicholas).

Originally such dramas were integrated into worship, often serving as postludes to *matins, preludes to *mass or interpolations into *vespers. Increasingly, this liturgical linkage weakened. The number of new liturgical dramas sharply declined after 1300, with creative energy increasingly focused on mystery and morality plays which developed outside of worship. The 20th century has witnessed a renewed interest in liturgical dramas, now ordinarily staged outside of worship. Some traditions have also reintroduced dramas into worship (e.g., Seeker Services); these vernacular, largely spoken works, however, have more in common with morality plays than liturgical dramas.

Bibl: T. McGee, "The Liturgical Placements of the 'Quem Quaeritis' Dialogue," JAMS 29 (1976) 1–29; W. Smolden, The Music of the Medieval Church Dramas (Oxford, 1980); L. Muir, The Biblical Drama of Medieval Europe (Cambridge, 1995).   MAK

Drawstop <stop>. (1) The knob or switch on an *organ *console by which the player blocks off certain ranks (rows) or pipes, or causes them to speak by unblocking them.

(2) Rank(s) of pipes controlled by means of the drawstop.   JBW

Dresden Amen. A 2-fold *amen based on a *polyphonic work by J. G. Naumann (d 1801) sung in the royal chapel in Dresden. It was quoted by F. *Mendelssohn in Reformation Symphony and Wagner in Parsifal.   VAC

Dressler, Gallus (b Nebra 1533; d Zerbst 1580–89). Composer and theorist who served as *Kantor at the Magdeburg school (1558). His works are chiefly *polyphonic settings of Latin texts in the Netherlands style. He also contributed to the development of the German language *motet; his settings of gospel texts are precursors of later collections by M. *Franck and others.   CFS

Drum Mass [German Paukenmesse]. The nickname for a *mass in C major by F. J. *Haydn (Hob XXII:9, 1796), who titled it Missa in tempore belli (Latin, "Mass in Time of War"). Scored for *choir, soloists and *orchestra, it was written for Princess Josepha Esterházy. Its nickname is based on the tympani solo in the *Agnus Dei.   AWR

Dubois, (François Clément) Théodore (*b* Rosnay, Marne 1837; *d* Paris 1924). Composer and teacher. He served as organist in Paris at Ste. Clotilde, then the Madeleine. Dubois wrote much *organ music; of his 80 sacred choral works (*oratorios, *masses, *motets) the *cantata, "The Seven Last Words of Christ" (1867) is the most familiar.   FJM

Duchanen. See *Birkat kohanim.*

Ducis, Benedictus (*b* near Konstanz *c* 1490; *d* Schalckstetten 1544). Protestant pastor and composer. Ducis was among the first to produce *polyphonic settings of German *chorales. Some of his compositions were included in *Rhau's well-known collection *Newe deudsche geistliche Gesenge* (1544).   PKG

Duck, Ruth (*b* Washington DC 1947). *Hymn writer, *hymnal editor, United Church of Christ pastor. She is professor of worship at Garrett-Evangelical Theological Seminary. An early pioneer of inclusive language, Duck coedited a hymn collection designed to eliminate sexist language (*Because We Are One People,* 1974). Her hymns are included in several recently published hymnals.   LJC

Ducote, Darryl. See *Dameans.

Dudley-Smith, Timothy (*b* Manchester 1926). English poet, *hymn writer and Anglican bishop of Thetford (from 1981). His hymn texts are collected in *Lift Every Heart* (1984) and *Songs of Deliverance* (1988).   RJS

Dufay <Du Fay>, **Guillaume** (*b* in or near Cambrai *c* 1400; *d* Cambrai 1474). The leading composer of the mid-15th century. Educated in Cambrai, he spent considerable time in Italy, including work as a singer in the papal choir (1428–33, 1435–7); he was also employed by the Malatesta and d'Este families and the Dukes of Savoy. Dufay composed during a period of musical stability and was not an innovator. Many of his compositions, for example, are harmonized chants with the melody in the upper voice. Nonetheless, he was noted for his skill as a composer, particularly for his melodic gifts and sense of proportion. His many works include 8 authentic *masses and over 30 individual movements of the *ordinary and *proper, 15 *antiphons, *c* 30 *hymns, over 30 *motets (many isorhythmic and polytextual), and *canticles as well as many secular works.

Bibl: D. Fallows, *Dufay* (New York, 1988); A. Planchart, "The Early Career of Guillaume Du Fay," *JAMS* 46 (1993) 341–68.   VAL

Dunstable <Dunstaple>, **John** (*b c* 1390; *d* 1453). English composer, mathematician and astronomer. His contemporaries, especially on the Continent, recognized him as an important musical figure; Le Franc hailed him as the model for *Dufay and other *Burgundian composers. His works (mostly preserved in Continental sources) include several *cyclic masses, *c* 12 individual *mass movements, *c* 20 *motets (mostly on Marian texts), and important sacred examples of the isorhythmic motet (especially *Veni Sancte Spiritus-Veni Creator,* combining 2 *Pentecost chants). He also composed *antiphons, *sequences and *Magnificat*s. His isorhythmic motets are generally for 4 voices, the other works generally for 3.

Bibl: M. Bent, *Dunstaple* (New York, 1981). AJL

Dunstan, Sylvia (*b* Toronto 1955; *d* there 1993). *Hymn writer and ordained minister in the United Church of Canada. A collection of her hymn texts is published under the title *In Search of Hope and Grace* (1991). RJS

Duparc, <Marie Eugène> **Henri** <Fouques> (*b* Paris 1848; *d* Mont-de-Marsan 1933). Composer and transcriber of J. S. *Bach's music for orchestra and 2 pianos. A student of C. *Franck, Wagnerian influence is detectable in some of his 13 songs. He composed 1 sacred *motet and is known to have destroyed much of his early work. Because of psychological problems, he stopped composing at age 36. DCI

Dupré, Marcel (*b* Rouen 1886; *d* Meudon 1971). Organist, composer and teacher. He studied with *Guilmant, then *Widor whom he succeeded as organist at St. Sulpice in Paris. Dupré was a world-renowned recitalist, master of the art of *improvisation and teacher; his students included *Langlais and *Messiaen. He composed primarily *organ music and edited much of the standard organ literature. JBW

Durante, Francesco (*b* Frattamaggiore 1684; *d* Naples 1755). Leading Italian composer of *church music and noted teacher, associated with Naples. Among his pupils were *Pergolesi and Jommelli. His works, almost exclusively sacred, include *masses, *motets, *psalm settings, *canticles, sacred dramas and works for *Holy Week. CFS

Duruflé, Maurice (*b* Louvier 1902; *d* Paris 1986). Liturgical composer and *organ virtuoso. In Paris he was assistant organist at Ste-Clotilde (1919–1929), and from 1930 organist at St. Etienne-du-Mont. Duruflé taught harmony at the Paris Conservatory (1943–67). He often employed *Gregorian themes in his compositions, e.g., his *Requiem* (1947) and 4 *motets (1960). MSD

Dwight, Timothy (*b* Northampton MA 1752; *d* New Haven 1817). *Hymn writer, Congregational minister and president of Yale (from 1795). He revised *Psalms and Hymns* as *Psalms of David by Isaac Watts* (1800). Dwight's "I Love Thy Kingdom, Lord" remains one of the oldest, continuously used hymn texts by an American. RJS

Dykes, John Bacchus (*b* Hull 1823; *d* Ticehurst 1876). Composer, organist and *precentor at Durham Cathedral. He wrote many *hymn tunes, 60 of which were included in *Hymns Ancient and Modern*; many (e.g., ST. AGNES, MELITA, NICAEA) are still in use. FJM

E

East <Easte, Este>, **Michael** (*b c* 1580; *d* Lichfield 1648). Composer who wrote Anglican *anthems and *service music. He is sometimes confused with Thomas East (*d* 1608), the music printer and publisher.   RAL

Easter. A 50-day season of the Christian liturgical *year concluding with *Pentecost, celebrating Christ's resurrection, ascension and sending of the Holy Spirit. It is possible that a special annual observance of the resurrection was celebrated from the birth of Christianity; there is clear evidence of a 50-day season in the early 3rd century. Easter is musically marked by a reintroduction of the *alleluia and *Gloria in excelsis, proper *antiphons (e.g., *Regina caeli), a *sequence (*Victimae paschali laudes), *hymns and *chorales (e.g., *Luther's *Christ lag in Todesbanden*), and wide ranging *sacred and *liturgical music celebrating Christ's resurrection (e.g., *Schütz's Easter *oratorio).   MJG

Easter vigil. The first *liturgy of *Easter, celebrated after dark on Holy Saturday. Its 4 main sections are: the service of light; the liturgy of the word (with an extended selection of readings and *psalms); the liturgy of baptism (including baptism-confirmation and the renewal of baptismal promises); and the liturgy of the eucharist. Special musical elements include the *Exsultet, a *melismatic 3-fold *alleluia before the *gospel and the *litany of the saints.   GET

East Syrian Churches' worship music. The *liturgical music of the E *Syrian churches, including Nestorian (Assyrian), *Chaldean and *Syro-Malabar. Texts for the *chants are found in the *Kitāba bayt daqdhām wadbāthar* ("before and after," which contains paired chants of the same genre which precede and follow sections of the *offices) and 3 books of proper texts: the *gazā* (for immovable feasts) attributed to Yaballaha II (*d* 1222); *hūdhrdā* (for Sundays and *Easter) whose arrangement is attributed to Ishu'Yabb III (*d* 658); and *kashkul* (for weekdays). Genres of chant for the *divine liturgy and offices of *ramshā* (*vespers), *lelyā* (*matins) and *ṣaprā* (*lauds) include the *kārūzuthā* (a *litany with choral *refrains), *lākhumārā* (comparable to the *Trisagion*), *teshboḥtā* (song of praise), *qālā, qānunā* and *madrāshā*. The *psalter *(dawīdha),* divided into 20 sections *(hullāle),* is intoned over a 2-week period by *alternating *choirs. Chants are organized in a weekly octoechal cycle, although the 8-*mode system has been supplemented by several Arabic scales *(maqāmāt).*

 Bibl: H. Husmann, ed., *Die Melodien des chaldäischen Breviers-Commune nach den Traditionen Vorderasiens und der Malabarküste* (Rome, 1967); H. Husmann, "Assyrisch-chaldäische Liturgie," in *Geschichte der katholische Kirchenmusik,* ed. K. G. Fellerer (Kassel, 1972) 1:69–84. RGD

Eberlin <Eberle>, **Johann Ernst** (*b* Jettingen 1702; *d* Salzburg 1762). Cathedral organist in Salzburg (1729), then *Kapellmeister* there (1749). A highly respected composer of *organ *toccatas and *fugues and choral pieces, including 70 *masses, 35 *psalms and 160 *offertories. JLB

Eccard, Johannes (*b* Mühlhausen 1553; *d* Berlin 1611). Composer in Königsberg and Berlin. He studied with *Lassus. Eccard is noted for his *hymn settings combining clear expression of texts with great musical freedom, exemplified in his collection *Geistliche Lieder auf den Choral* (1597). VEG

Ecclesiastical modes <church modes>. A system for classifying *Gregorian chant into 8 *modes, formulated *c* 1000 and described in Guido of Arezzo's *Micrologus.* All chants were grouped according to their final note: D, E, F or G. Each of these 4 groups (*Dorian, *Phrygian, *Lydian, *Mixolydian) were then subdivided into authentic or plagal (Hypo-) modes according to their ambitus and their respective dominants (*tenors). CJK

Ecclesiological Society. See *Cambridge Camden Society.

Echad <*Eḥad*> **mi yodea** [Hebrew]. "Who knows one?" A poem sung at the end of the *Pesach *seder. Only found in the *Ashkenazic text of the *seder* (see *haggadah*), it was first seen in the 16th century. Its text associates numbers 1–13 with important historic events in Judaism: 1) God, 2) the 2 tablets of the covenant, 3) the patriarchs, 4) the matriarchs, etc. It is sung to several melodies. MLK

Echos (pl. **echoi**) [Greek; Slavonic *glas*]. "Sound." A musical *mode in which *hymns and *psalms are sung in the Byzantine *liturgy. Eight different modes (*octoechos*) exist for *allelouiaria, *exapostolaria, *kathismata, *kontakia, *prokeimena, *stichera, *troparia and others. DMP

Ecphonetic notation. *Notation for the *cantillation of scriptural *lessons. It exists in Latin, Greek, Hebrew (see *ta'amim*), Syriac, Armenian and Coptic manuscripts. From the 8th century Byzantine manuscripts have *c* 20 signs which are paired, framing each phrase. By the late 15th century, the meanings of these signs are obscure and they cannot be transcribed with accuracy. Ecphonetic systems also exist in Judaism and other E churches. RGD

Editio Medicea. See *Medicean edition.

Editio Ratisbonensis. See *Regensburg edition.

Editio Vaticana. See *Vatican edition.

Egeria <Etheria, Silvia>. A pilgrim who visited the Holy Land c 381–4. Her Latin diary contains detailed descriptions of Jerusalem's churches and liturgies during *Epiphany, *Holy Week, *Easter and *Pentecost. It also provides early testimony for various musical-liturgical elements, e.g., *Kyrie eleison and *boy choirs. NDM

Eichah. See *Lamentations.

Ein Deutsches Requiem. See *Deutches Requiem, Ein.

Ein' feste Burg [German]. "A mighty fortress." A *chorale text and tune by *Luther, written in the 1520s; the first extant printed copy is in Kirchegesang (Nürnberg, 1531). Drawn from Ps 46, it is one of the best-known of all chorales. It was used by Protestants as a battle cry of the *Reformation and employed by composers from the 16th century to the present. PHW

Ein kelohenu <ke'loheinu> [Hebrew]. "None is like our God." A simple *hymn which functions as a closing song, either at the end of a *service (in Reform synagogues), or following the Torah service. J. Freudenthal composed the best known congregational tune; other familiar settings include those by *Freed and *Carlebach. BES

Eirenika [Greek]. "The peace [things]" [Slavonic velikaya ekteniya, "Great Litany"]. The opening *litany for an *office or the *divine liturgy in the Byzantine rite comprising 12 petitions and said by the deacon. People respond "Lord, have mercy" to each petition. Originally it was the prayer of the faithful, recited after the *gospel and before the entrance with the gifts. A remnant of this litany still exists in the Russian rescension of the Byzantine *liturgy at this same place. DMP

Eisodikon [Greek; Slavonic vkhodnoje]. "Entrance [hymn]." The entrance *hymn of the Byzantine *divine liturgy. It ordinarily consists of Ps 95:6 (the 4th *verse of the 3rd *antiphon) sung with the *troparion, "O Son of God, save us who sing to you, alleluia!" The great feasts of the Lord have proper entrance *hymns, consisting of a *psalm verse with the proper troparion. DMP

Ejaculation. (1) A spontaneous *acclamation, usually performed by members of the assembly, evident in Christian worship since the New Testament period (e.g., *amen, *halleluia, *hosanna, etc.).

(2) A short, often unvocalized prayer, also called an "aspiration" (e.g., "My God and my all"). CRY

Ekphonesis [Greek; Slavonic vozglas]. "Exclamation." An *acclamation in the Byzantine *liturgy chanted by the priest according to a simple melody to conclude a prayer. Since most priestly prayers are said in a low voice, the ekphonesis is all that is heard by the congregation, which sings *amen in response. DMP

Ektene [Greek; Slavonic ekteniya]. "Intense." A *litany in the Byzantine rite sung by the deacon at the end of the *liturgy of the word in the *divine liturgy and at the end of daily *orthros and *hesperinos. The ektene is unique insofar as the deacon prays directly to God rather than proposing petitions to the congregation. It is called "intense" because the people respond by thrice singing "Lord, have mercy." Originally it was sung at special *services in times of need (see *lite). The Slavonic ekteniya is a general term for all litanies (see *aitesis, *eirenika, *ektene, *synapte). The ektene is called suhubaja ekteniya (Slavonic, "redoubled litany") because "Lord, have mercy" is "redoubled" or sung 3 times.   DMP

El Adon [Hebrew]. "God the Master." A liturgical poem, in the form of an alphabetic acrostic of 22 phrases, praising God. It is only recited on *Sabbath morning in the *Yotser section. Originally recited responsively with the *cantor, now the prevailing custom is for cantor and congregation to sing El Adon together using a metrical tune in the *magen avot mode. Following this prayer, the mode switches to *ahavah rabbah; some congregations anticipate this switch when the cantor recites the last 2 phrases of El Adon in the ahavah rabbah mode.   IAG

Elbogen, Ismar (b Posen, Prussia 1874; d New York 1943). Scholar of Jewish history and *liturgy. Trained in Breslau, he served as Dozent at Berlin's Hochschule für die Wissenschaft des Judentums (1902–37) before immigrating to the US (1938). His Der jüdische Gottesdienst in seiner geschichtlichen Entwicklung (1913) has served as the basis for Jewish liturgical studies throughout the 20th century; a Hebrew

version, edited and supplemented by J. Heinemann, appeared in 1972; R. Scheindlin published a combined translation of the 2 previous editions as Jewish Liturgy: A Comprehensive History (1993).   MLK

Electronic organ. A musical *instrument introduced after World War I to imitate the sound of the pipe *organ. Musical sounds created from electronic vibrations are transmitted via amplifiers to loudspeakers. Early tone sources include tone wheels (Hammond), brass reeds (Wurlitzer) and radio tubes (Baldwin). Today digital sampling of pipe sounds are the state-of-the-art tone source. The electronic organ is an important accompaniment instrument in some genres of *gospel music.   PAJ

Elevation [Latin elevatio]. That moment in the *mass after the consecration when the bread and cup are lifted by the priest. Its importance grew during the *Middle Ages when people preferred "ocular" *communion to physical reception of the elements. In the past it was sometimes accompanied by a *motet or *organ piece under the same title (see *Frescobaldi's Fiori musicali, 1635 for examples). *Bells are another traditional accompaniment to the elevation.   MSD

Elgar, Edward (William) (b Broadheath near Worcester 1857; d Worcester 1934). Composer. Unlike his contemporaries, he did not study with German master teachers; aside from violin lessons in Worcester and London, Elgar was largely self-taught. His compositions were popular because of their lush harmonies and sense of form (e.g., Pomp *and Circumstance* n. 3). His religious works (mostly for voices or voices and orchestra) include *psalm settings, *anthems and *oratorios (notably *Dream of Gerontius,* 1899–1900).   FJM

El hahodaot [Hebrew]. "God of thanksgivings." A liturgical text, sung throughout the many *Sephardic traditions at the conclusion of *Pesukei dezimrah*. It lists various praises of God, concluding with a *blessing acknowledging God as the One "who chooses musical songs of praise." In the Middle E Jewish traditions the melody is sung in the *makam* of the day.   MLK

Elijah <Elias> F. *Mendelssohn's greatest *oratorio (op. 70, 1846; revised in 1847) and last major work, composed for the Birmingham Music Festival. The text is by J. Schubring after 1 Kings 17–19.   JBW

Eli Tsiyon <*Zion*> [Hebrew]. "Wail, Zion." An anonymously written acrostic elegy for *Tisha B'av*. It is comprised of 12 *stanzas which describe the iniquities suffered during the fall of Jerusalem and the Second Temple. It is also sung during memorial services and, in recent years, for *Yom Hashoah* commemorating victims of the Holocaust. Famous settings have been composed by J. Achron, *Baer and L. Zeitlin.   DMR

ELLC. See *English Language Liturgical Consultation.

Ellington, Duke (Edward Kennedy) (*b* Washington 1899; *d* New York 1974). African American composer, band leader and pianist. His compositions and orchestrations exerted a lasting influence on *jazz. He pioneered the use of symphonic formal procedures in jazz, and by voicing across sections generated new timbral possibilities for jazz composers and arrangers. From the early 1940s he wrote larger works in the jazz idiom (e.g., *Black, Brown and Beige*); by the late 1950s he produced full film scores (e.g., *Anatomy of a Murder*). He composed 3 significant sacred works: *In the beginning God* (1965), *Second Sacred Concert* (1968) and *Third Sacred Concert* (1973).
   Bibl: J. E. Hasse, *Beyond Category: The Life of Duke Ellington* (New York). RTR

El male rachamim <*El male' raḥamim*> [Hebrew]. "God full of compassion." A prayer recited for the deceased at a Jewish *funeral; it is the highlight of the funeral *service in the *Ashkenazic rite. It is also said on the yearly anniversary of death (Yiddish, *yahrtzeit*) or when visiting graves; some *Ashkenazic practices include it in memorial services. The text differs slightly in each of the Jewish denominations. It is recited in the *ahavah rabbah* *mode.   MLK

El Melech <*Melekh*> **ne'eman** [Hebrew]. "God, trustworthy King." These words are said before reciting the *Shema privately. When the *Shema* is recited publicly in worship the leader says a 3-word phrase (*Adonai Eloheihem emet,* "Adonai, your God is true") at the end of the *Shema*. In both cases, the addition of the 3 words raises the total number of words in the *Shema* to 248: a number ascribed by the sages as corresponding with both the number of organs in the human body and the number of positive commandments in the Torah. MLK

El Melech <*Melekh*> **yoshev** [Hebrew]. "God the King, sitting on a throne of mercy." A prayer serving as a preamble to the 13 attributes of mercy, which are the central elements in all *selichot. El Melech* is generally recited in the *selicha* *mode with the concluding cadence ending on a major 3rd, a musical treatment typical for this particular section of the *service. The best-known musical setting is by Z. Zilberts.   IAG

Elu devarim [Hebrew]. "These are the obligations." A text recited as part of *Birchot hashachar* ("the morning blessings"), the first part of *shacharit. It is derived from 2 rabbinic passages (*Mishnah Peiah* 1 and *Babylonian Talmud Shabbat* 127a). Chanted in the "study mode" (a version of *magein avot*), the best known cantorial setting of this text is by J. Rappaport.   BES

Emet ve'emunah [Hebrew]. "True and trustworthy." The first *benediction following the *Shema* in the *ma'ariv,* which refers back to the message of the *Shema.*   SJW

Emet veyatsiv [Hebrew]. "True and certain." The phrase which begins the *geulah* ("redemption") section of *shacharit* immediately following the *Shema* and its *blessings. The Talmud (*Mishnah Berachot* 2:2) mandates that there should be no interruption between the words "*Adonai Eloheichem*" ("Lord your God"), which end the *Shema,* and "*emet*" ("true") so that one recites the phrase "*Adonai Eloheichem emet*" ("The Lord your God is true").   DMR

Emperor's hymn. A *hymn tune also known as Austrian Hymn or Austria, written by F. J. *Haydn in 1797 as a birthday gift for Emperor Franz II for use as the Austrian national anthem; so used until 1918, and again from 1929–47. Haydn probably based his composition on a Croatian folksong.   VAC

Enchiriadis <*enchiridion*> [Greek, Latin]. "Handbook." A manual or concise reference treatise. The term appears in the title of small booklets in the *Renaissance (e.g., *Musica enchiriadis*) and *Reformation eras. It was also employed for early German Lutheran *hymnals, especially those published in Erfurt, Nuremberg and Wittenberg (1524–27).   RAL

Enfance du Christ, L' [French]. "The Infancy of Christ." An *oratorio (op. 25, 1850–54) by *Berlioz for soloists, *chorus and orchestra to his own text describing Herod's reaction to the news of Christ's birth and the flight of the Holy Family.   RAD

Enfant prodigue, L' [French]. "The Prodigal Child." (1) An early *cantata by *Debussy (1884) for soloists, *chorus and orchestra which won the *Prix de Rome.*
(2) An opera by D. Auber (1850).   RAD

Engelstimme [German; Latin *vox angelica*]. "Angel voice." (1) An *organ stop composed of thin-toned flue pipes or a single-rank stop with a dulciana quality.
(2) In reed organs, a soft 8-foot stop.   JLB

English Hymnal. An influential *hymnal, edited by *Dearmer (texts) and *Vaughan Williams (music), published in 1906; the music was revised in 1933.   RAL

English Language Liturgical Consultation <ELLC>. An organization established in 1985 as successor to the *International Consultation on English Texts, encouraging cooperative work in countries where English is spoken in all aspects of Christian *liturgy. Members include liturgical representatives from Australia (ACOL), Britain (JLG), Canada (CCC-GOW), Ireland (AIL), N America (*CCT), New Zealand (JLGNZ) and the *International Commission on English in the Liturgy. Forty English-speaking churches are represented in ELLC.   FKG

Enkomion (pl. **enkomia**) [Greek]. "Panegyric." A speech, either in prose or *verse, in praise of a saint, a feast, a special occasion or a particular person. It had a general use in Byzantine society; *enkomia* were also inserted into the *liturgy. DMP

Ephraim <Ephrem> **the Syrian** (*b* Nisibis *c* 306; *d* Edessa 373). Principle author of the Syriac Christian tradition and a deacon. His works were highly influential in later Syriac and Byzantine hymnography. Ephraim served as the "interpreter" (exegete) of Nisibis, producing poetic works and prose commentaries defending orthodox Christianity; later he taught in Edessa. He produced repertoire for female *choirs.

Over 300 *madrāshā* (instructions or didactic songs) and *sogitha* (acrostics) are ascribed to him. *Madrāshā* consist of long *stanzas (4 to 10 half-verses, usually in a pattern of 7 + 7 syllables) sung by a soloist; the choir responds with an *onita* (*refrain), ranging from a single line to a short stanza. *Sogitha* usually had 5 to 6 4-line stanzas whose initial letters ap-

peared in alphabetical order or sometimes spelled out the author's name. There is a tradition that *antiphonal liturgical singing began under Ephraim's guidance; corroborating evidence for this is lacking.

Bibl: K. E. McVey, *Ephrem the Syrian* (New York-Mahwah, 1989).   JMJ

Ephrata Cloister <Society of the Solitary Brethren>. A quasi-monastic community of men and women founded (1732–34) under J. Beissel in Lancaster County PA; forerunners of the Seventh-day Baptists. Ephrata was renowned for its rich musical life and printing press. The *hymns of Beissel published there were highly influential.   NDM

Ephros, Gershon (*b* Serotsk, Poland 1890; *d* New York 1978). *Cantor and composer. He immigrated to Israel (then Palestine) in 1909, where he studied with *Idelsohn; then to the US in 1911. He served congregations in VA, NJ and the Bronx and was on the faculty at Hebrew Union College's School of Sacred Music. His 6-volume *Cantorial Anthology* (1929-69) is an important collection of liturgical compositions.   MLK

Epiclesis. See *eucharistic prayer.

Epiphany. See *year, liturgical.

Episcopal Evergreen Conference. See *Evergreen Church Music Conference.

Episcopal worship music. Anglicans arrived in America in 1607. The Protestant Episcopal Church in the United States of America was founded in 1784. In 1789 the Church's first *BCP included an appendix containing 150

*metrical psalms and 27 *hymns (texts only). The popularity of psalm singing at the time is underscored by the rejection of an earlier proposal for an appendix containing only 84 metrical psalms, 51 *hymns and 8 pages of tunes. The Episcopal Church's authorized *hymnals (1789, 1826, 1871, 1892, 1916 [the first edition with music], 1940 and 1982) were produced by predecessors of the Church's present Standing Commission on Liturgy and Music, with the intention of offering appropriate texts and music for congregational song.

*Anglican chant was sung and pipe *organs played during *services in the colonies. *Choirs which developed from *singing schools (*c* 1775) sang 2- and 3-part arrangements of psalms and hymns. The 19th-century *Oxford and *Cambridge Society Movements encouraged the use of *plainsong. Simultaneously westward expansion established new congregations which did not have the resources to sustain such music. Communities of immigrants, African Americans and evangelical awakenings and revivals were offering forms of worship music which have finally entered the mainstream of congregational song in the Episcopal Church. *The Hymnal 1982* reflects a wide range of worship music and includes traditional, *folk, newly composed and culturally varied works. Its sizable "service music" section contains both new and old settings of liturgical texts. The *Hymnal Companion* (3 vols.) is a compilation of essays and information about the contents of *The Hymnal*. The *Association of Anglican Musicians is dedicated to the elevation, stimulation and support of *liturgical music and allied arts in the church.

Bibl: A. Wyton, "Episcopal Church, music of the," *NGDAM* 2:53–54; R. Glover, ed., *The Hymnal 1982 Companion I* (New York, 1990); C. Doran and W. Petersen, *A History of Music in the Episcopal Church* (Little Rock, 1991) 90–139.   CAD

Epistle [from Latin *epistula,* "letter"]. (1) The first reading at *eucharist when there were only 2 readings; so called because it ordinarily was taken from one of 21 New Testament books in letter form, though in fact it could be from any Hebrew Bible or New Testament book except the *psalms and *gospels. In the early church it was read by a *lector; at the medieval *high mass, it was chanted by a subdeacon.

(2) The liturgical reading from any of the 21 New Testament books in letter form.   MJG

Epistle sonata. A short instrumental piece, played between the *epistle and *gospel at *mass. *Mozart composed 17 such works for *organ and *instruments.   JBW

Epistolary [from Latin *epistula,* "letter"]. A liturgical *book containing non-gospel readings for the celebration of the *eucharist, arranged according to the liturgical *year; called *apostolos* in Byzantine usage. It originated as a simple list of texts; a complete epistolary containing full readings appears by the early 6th century.   ADC

Epithalamium [from Greek *thálamos,* "bridal chamber"]. (1) An ancient Greek or Latin poem for marriage.

(2) A marriage song or *organ piece for use at weddings.   ACL

Erbach, Christian (*b* Gaualgescheim near Mainz 1568–73; *d* Augsburg 1635). Famed teacher of both Protestant and RC musicians. The city organist at Augsburg, Erbach was principal organist at its cathedral (from 1625) and a colleague of *Hassler. He composed much sacred choral music.   MPB

Erben, Henry (*b* New York 1800; *d* there 1884). *Organ builder who constructed more than 1,200 organs between 1824–84. His firm was the largest organ company in the US during the 19th century, employing more than 100 workers in 1850.   JWK

Erlebach, Philipp Heinrich (*b* Esens 1657; *d* Rudolstadt 1714). *Kapellmeister* at the Rudolstadt court (from 1678). He composed comic operas and ballets, but centered his energies in 6 *cantata cycles full of variety in form and texture.   MPB

Esther. The first English *oratorio, composed by *Handel, originally as a masque to a text by Racine. Handel revised it with textual additions and revisions by Humphreys. It was first performed in 1732.   JMT

Et exspecto resurrectionem mortuorum [Latin]. "And I look for the resurrection of the dead." A text from the *Credo. Sometimes it is treated as a separate movement in larger musical settings of the *ordinary, e.g., J. S. *Bach's *B Minor Mass.   MJG

Et incarnatus est [Latin]. "And was incarnate [of the Holy Spirit and the Virgin Mary and became truly human]." A text from the *Credo. Sometimes it is treated as a separate movement in larger musical settings of the *ordinary, e.g., J. S. *Bach's *B Minor Mass.   PAB

Et in Spiritum sanctum [Latin]. "And [I believe] in the Holy Spirit." A text from the *Credo. Sometimes it is treated as a separate movement in larger musical settings of the *ordinary, e.g., J. S. *Bach's *B Minor Mass.   MJG

Et in unum Dominum [Latin]. "And [I believe] in one Lord." A text from the *Credo. Sometimes it is treated as a separate movement in larger musical settings of the *ordinary, e.g., J. S. *Bach's *B Minor Mass.   MJG

Et resurrexit [Latin]. "And [on the third day] he rose [again in accordance with the Scriptures]." A text from from the *Credo. Sometimes it is treated as a separate movement in larger musical settings of the *ordinary, e.g., J. S. *Bach's *B Minor Mass.   PAB

Ethiopic chant. The *liturgical music of the Ethiopian Orthodox Church sung in Ge'ez. During liturgical celebrations music is performed from memory, but notational signs denoting melodic formulas are found in manuscripts after the 15th century. *Cantors *(debtera)* are trained in vocal styles associated with 3 major monasteries (Bethlehem, Qoma and Achaber). Books containing hymns include the *deggwā* (for feasts of the year excluding *Lent), *mawāše'et* (funerals and some feasts) and *me-erāf* (common of the *divine office). Melodies are divided into 3 modal categories or *zēmā (ge'ez, erārāy* and *azl),* attributed by tradition to St. Yared (6th century). At times, instrumental music and *dance accompany the chant.

Bibl: K. Shelemay, P. Jeffery, *Ethiopian Christian Liturgical Chant: An Anthology,* 3 vols. (Madison, 1993–97). RGD

Ethnomusicology. An interdisciplinary approach to the study of music, inclusive of the music of all cultures, peoples, classes and repertoires (*folk, popular and classical) with emphasis on non-Western music. Ethnomusicologists view music as a dynamic aspect of culture and a means of social communication, contextualizing musical realities (forms, structures, genres, styles) in the social organization of music and in the processes of composition and performance. Music making in ritual contexts is an important focus. Theory and methods are drawn from anthropology, musicology, sociology, linguistics, semiotics, history, folklore and emerging cross-disciplinary fields. Field research and analysis are considered primary tools. The term was introduced *c* 1950; the discipline is rooted in 19th century comparative musicology.
Bibl: K. Shelemay, ed., *Ethnomusicology* (New York, 1990). MEM

Ethos. The ethical, moral or emotional character of music. The ancient Greeks believed that music shaped people's moral character and should be included in the general education and regulated by the state. Plato and Aristotle agreed that a good person could be produced through education which stressed gymnastics to discipline the body and music to discipline the mind. The belief that each *mode embodied certain qualities (e.g., strength, lasciviousness, etc.), and could produce those qualities in the listener influenced the *ritual music of various religions including Christianity, and shaped the criteria for evaluating

whether music was appropriate for worship. DCI

Eton Choirbook <College Manuscript>. One of the principal surviving English sources of 16th-century Latin *sacred music, containing *Magnificat* and Passion settings and 54 *motets. Compiled between 1490 and 1504 for use at Eton College, almost a third of its original contents are missing. RAD

Euangelion heothinon [Greek; Slavonic *utrenneje evangelije*]. "Morning gospel." The *gospel read at Byzantine *orthros* on Sundays and feasts after the variable *psalmody and before the *kanon. Each *orthros* gospel has a corresponding *exapostolarion* and *doxastichon* (see *idiomelon heothinon*) at Pss 148–50. DMP

Eucharist [from Greek *eucharistìa,* "thanksgiving"]. The sacramental rite that lies at the heart of Christian worship. Grounded in the table ministry of Jesus, it recalls the last supper he shared with his disciples on the night before his crucifixion. Its climax is the sharing of blessed bread and wine. See *holy communion, *Lord's supper and *mass. NDM

Eucharistic prayer. In a restricted sense, this term designates the central prayer of the celebration of the *eucharist; in a more general sense, it could be applied to any prayer whose primary theme is thanksgiving. Cognate terms include *anaphora (E Christianity), "Canon of the mass" (Roman rite) and "Great Prayer of Thanksgiving" (various Protestant traditions). Primitive eucharistic prayers (e.g., *Didache* 9–10 [disputed], *Addai and Mari, Apostolic*

Tradition) evidence influences from Jewish *blessing and thanksgiving prayers. Scholars group eucharistic prayers into "families" based on their structure. E families include E Syrian, Alexandrian, Antiochene, Byzantine; W families include Roman, Gallican, Mozarabic.

Historically these prayers consist of basic elements occurring in varying sequence and of diverse importance: thanksgiving (especially in a *preface); acclamation (*Sanctus*); Christ's words of institution of the *sacrament; memorial of the great acts of redemption *(anamnesis);* invocation of the Holy Spirit on community and bread and wine *(epiclesis);* offering; intercessions; final *doxology and *amen.

Musical elements may include *responses in an opening dialogue, *Sanctus,* *memorial acclamation and final amen. Some eucharistic prayers provide for additional congregational interventions. While the leader may chant the entire prayer, those presidential elements most often sung are: opening dialogue, preface, institution narrative, *epiclesis,* invitations to acclamations, *anamnesis*-offering (often linked) and doxology.

Bibl: E. Mazza, *The Eucharistic Prayers of the Roman Rite* (New York, 1986); F. Senn, ed. *New Eucharistic Prayers* (New York-Mahwah, 1987).   JMJ

Euche opistambonos [Greek; Slavonic *molitva zaambonnaya*]. "Prayer behind the ambon." The dismissal prayer of the Byzantine *divine liturgy. Originally it was recited by the priest as he processed from the sanctuary to the narthex. When he passed the ambon (see *ambo) he turned, faced E and recited this prayer. Today the priest returns to the sanctuary

for the dismissal (see *apolysis*). Two ambon prayers are in the contemporary official books: one for the divine liturgy, another for the *presanctified divine liturgy. Many more were previously used, serving as commentaries on the various feasts. The Greek *Hieratikon* (Rome, 1950), containing texts of the divine liturgy and divine office, restored ambon prayers for Feasts of our Lord and the Mother of God.

Bibl: D. Petras, *Ambon Prayers* (Parma OH, 1972).   DMP

Euchologion (pl. **euchologia**) [Greek]. "Book of prayers" [Slavonic *sluzhebnik,* "service book"]. The main liturgical *book of the Byzantine rite, containing the commons of the *divine liturgy, *orthros* and *hesperinos.* It may also contain texts for the sacramental mysteries, *blessings and *occasional services. The earliest *euchologion* dates to the 8th century. Great (Greek *mega) euchologia* contain a varied selection of all *services; small (Greek *mikra) euchologia* omit the divine liturgy and office. *Hieratika* (or *liturgika*) omit sacraments and *blessings but include the divine liturgy and office.

Bibl: I. Hapgood, ed., *Service Book* (Brooklyn, 1965 [1906]); N. M. Vaporis, *An Orthodox Prayer Book* (Brookline MA, 1977).   DMP

Eulogetaria. See *anastasima eulogetaria.*

Euouae <evovae> [Latin]. An abbreviation from the vowels of the last 6 syllables of the *Gloria patri: "seculorum. Amen."* It is used to indicate the proper ending (*differentia*) of the *psalm tone for the *psalm or *canticle to follow.   PAJ

Evangelary <gospel book> [from Latin *evangelium,* "gospel"]. A liturgical *book used by the deacon or priest for proclaiming the *gospel at *mass, carried to the accompaniment of the *gospel acclamation. The book virtually disappeared with the advent of the *missal, but has come back into limited usage in the Roman rite since the reforms of *Vatican II.   MSD

Evangelistic music. The music of evangelical Christians which complements and expresses the message of the evangelist (the bearer and proclaimer of Christ's gospel). Such music is marked by its accessibility; typically in the vernacular, it is easily taught, memorized and recalled. From the beginning of Christianity (see *New Testament, music in the) music has supported and extended the evangelist's message, drawn people to worship and assisted in their conversion and renewal. *Clement of Alexandria composed *hymns in classical meter, probably to counter evangelizing efforts of gnostics who earlier adopted this form; *Ambrosian hymns were apparently written for a similar purpose. *Luther's evangelistic music employed well known melodies (*folk tunes, Latin *chant, etc.) and scriptural paraphrases.   17th-century German *pietists extended Luther's repertory to include hymns affirming the individual's heart as the main contact with God. The *Wesleys, emphasizing salvation for all in Christ, featured hymns that could be sung by divergent people of varying theological sophistication in diverse religious, social and economic settings. 19th- and 20th-century English and US evangelistic meetings and crusades developed a unique repertory of evanglistic music: mostly *gospel hymns, *camp meeting songs and *choruses, a repertory widely exported by missionaries. Contemporary evanglistic crusades and broadcasts of televangelists often mix standard gospel and evangelical hymns with choruses and scripture songs cast in popular musical genres, led by soloists, vocal ensembles and rock-style backup groups. This genre is often mirrored in the worship of local churches.   CRY

Evening hymn. An English designation for *Phos hilaron.* Notable English translations are by R. S. Bridges ("O gladsome light of grace"), *Keble ("Hail gladdening light") and W. Storey ("O radiant light").   RJS

Evening prayer. See *evensong, *vespers and *ma'ariv.*

Evensong. (1) A medieval English term for *vespers.
   (2) A traditional Anglican rite, found in the 1549 *BCP, which combined *vespers* and *compline according to *Sarum use; sung primarily by the officiant and choir.
   (3) An evening *service in which the majority of the officiant's and people's parts are sung.   CAD

Evergreen Church Music Conference. A summer school of *liturgical music, established by *Douglas at Evergreen CO in 1907. This annual week-long program includes presentations (in both Winter Park and Denver) by musicians, preachers and spiritual leaders well-known in the Episcopal Church.   CAD

Evovae. See *euouae.*

Exapostolarion (pl. **exapostolaria**) [Greek; Slavonic *svetilen*]. "One who is sent forth." A *troparion* sung at Byzantine *orthros* after the *kanon;* also called *photogogikon* (Greek, "Hymn of Light"). Originally sung to very elaborate melodies in 8 tones (*octoechos*), now it is generally recited. Sundays have a series of 11 *exapostolaria;* feasts have their own *exapostolaria,* which may still be sung according to special elaborate melodies.   DMP

Exposition of the Blessed Sacrament. See *benediction.

Extension organ <unit organ>. An *organ in which some ranks of pipes are playable on more than 1 *keyboard or at more than 1 pitch.   PKG

Exultate, jubilate [Latin]. "Exult, shout joyfully." A 3-part solo *cantata for coloratura soprano and *orchestra (K 158a, 1773) by *Mozart which concludes with a popular *Alleluia, *a tour de force* of operatic vocal technique.   RDH

Exultet <*exsultet*> [Latin]. "Rejoice." Also known as the "Easter proclamation" (Latin *praeconium paschale*) and the "praise" or "*blessing of the candle" (Latin *laus cerei, benedictio cerei*). *Exultet* derives its name from the first word of the Latin text in the Roman rite ordinarily sung by a deacon at the solemn lighting of the paschal candle during the *Easter Vigil. The attribution of its authorship to *Ambrose is doubtful. Clear evidence exists only from 8th-century Gaul; later it was taken over into the Roman rite. Its distinctive melody bears a resemblance to *chant formulas used for the *preface of the *eucharistic prayer. In S Italy, between the 10th and 13th centuries, text and music were copied on finely written, illuminated rolls ("*Exultet* rolls").

Bibl: A. J. MacGregor, *Fire and Light in the Western Triduum* (Collegeville, 1992).   NDM

F

Faber, Frederick William (*b* Calverley 1814; *d* London 1864). Writer, preacher and member of the Oratory of St. Philip Neri who was deeply involved in the *Oxford Movement. Besides numerous books Faber wrote many *hymn texts for RC devotions, e.g., "Faith of our Fathers" and "There's a wideness in God's mercy." FJM

Faithful, mass of the. The former name for the second part of the *mass (*offertory to dismissal), to which only the baptized were allowed. It is now called the *liturgy of the eucharist. GET

Familiar style. For textual clarity *Renaissance composers often had all voices singing the same syllable simultaneously. This homorhythmic writing emphasized special portions of the text, providing contrast and increased comprehensibility. Some secular songs were set almost entirely in this style. DCI

Fanfare. (1) A short tune for trumpets or other brass *instruments, sometimes with percussion, used as an introductory flourish or ceremonial signal, traditionally constructed of the tones of a major triad.

(2) A French term for a brass band. VAC

Fantasia [Italian; French *fantaisie;* German *Fantasie, Phantasie*]. "Fantasy." A term adopted in the *Renaissance for an instrumental piece which was improvisatory in character. Later it was more loosely applied to a wider variety of musical works which stretched the conventions of composition, sometimes marked by exaggeration or distortion. VAL

Farmer, John (*b c* 1570; *fl* 1591–1601). Composer who served as organist and master of choristers at Christ Church Cathedral in Dublin (1596–99). Best-known for his madrigals, he contributed many harmonizations to *Este's *Psalter* (1592). RKW

Farrand, William (*b* 1854; *d* 1930). *Organ builder who acquired the *Roosevelt patents and business with his partner Edwin Scott Votey in 1893. Important *instruments include those in the Carnegie Library in Pittsburgh and St. Ignatius Church in San Francisco. JWK

Farse [from Latin *farsa,* "stuffed"]. A Latin or vernacular interpolation in a chant or reading. Vernacular farsing was especially common in *epistles.   RTR

Fasch, Carl (*b* Zerbst 1736; *d* Berlin 1800). Composer and the son of J. F. *Fasch. At age 20 he became the second harpsichordist (after C. P. E. *Bach) to *Frederick II. Later he conducted the royal opera (1774–76) and organized Berlin's *Singakademie.* He wrote *cantatas, *masses, *psalms and *hymn settings.   JLB

Fasch, Johann Friedrich (*b* Buttelstädt near Weimar 1688; *d* Zerbst 1758). Composer. A student of *Kuhnau and *Graupner, he served as **Kapellmeister* at Zerbst (from 1722). Fasch composed 12 cycles of *church cantatas, 12 *masses and various instrumental pieces.   JLB

Fasola. A method of solmization in use in English by the 16th century utilizing the 4 syllables fa-sol-la-mi to replace the traditional hexachordal system (ut-re-mi-fa-sol-la). In fasola a major scale is fa-so-la-fa-so-la-mi-fa. Four corresponding shape-notes were employed for notating this system. In America *Tuft used the fasola solmization pattern, but replaced note heads with the letters "F-S-L-M" in *Introduction to the Singing of Psalm Tunes* (1721). William Smith and William Little combined shape-note heads with fasola solmization in *The Easy Instructor* (1802). *Tune book compilers, particularly in the S and Midwest, utilized this combined system in books for use in *singing schools to teach sight singing and musicianship in congregations where the quality of *hymn singing had declined.

Bibl: G. P. Jackson, *White Spirituals in the Southern Uplands: The Story of the Fasola Folk, Their Songs, Singings and "Buckwheat Notes"* (New York, 1965 [1933]).   RJS

Fauré, Gabriel (*b* Pamiers 1845; *d* Paris 1924). Composer who served as organist and choir director at important churches in Paris, including the Madeleine (1896–1905). Fauré was composition professor and later director of the Paris Conservatory (1905–20). Master of the song cycle (*La bonne chanson,* 1891–92), he wrote chamber music, piano works and opera. His many religious compositions, mostly choral, including *O Salutaris* (1887), **Tantum ergo* (1890), **Salve Regina* (1895); best-known is his **Requiem* (mostly 1887–88).   MSD

Fayrfax <Fairfax> **Robert** (*b* Deeping Gate, Lincolnshire 1464; *d* St. Albans? 1521). Composer and gentleman of the *Chapel Royal (1497). He wrote *masses, 2 **Magnificat*s and 10 surviving *motets. Fayrfax was important for cultivating the *cyclic mass.   RKW

FEL. See *Friends of the English Liturgy.

Felgemaker, Abraham (*b* 1836; *d* 1905). *Organ builder in Buffalo before moving to Erie. In 1875 Felgemaker built a new organ for the *University of Notre Dame. Felgemaker's firm was bought by the Tellers Organ Co. in 1918.   JWK

Felix namque [Latin]. "Happy indeed." The *offertory *chant for certain Marian feasts. In *Sarum use and among early Anglican composers, its melody was often used as a *cantus firmus* for *keyboard works.   RTR

Fellerer, Karl Gustav (*b* Freising 1902; *d* Munich 1984). German musicologist and authority on *church music, representing neo-*Cecilian perspective. Fellerer chaired the musicology department at the University of Cologne (1939–70). Author of *The History of Catholic Church Music* (German, 1949; English 1961), he also edited *Geschichte der katholischen Kirchenmusik* (2 volumes, 1972).   AWR

Fellowship of United Methodists in Worship, Music and Other Arts. A membership organization, founded in 1956, which offers practical resources for pastors, worship leaders, church musicians and those involved in the visual arts, drama, *dance and architecture. It publishes the bimonthly *Worship Arts;* a biennial national convocation brings together members of local chapters.   CAD

Ferguson, John Allen (*b* Cleveland 1941). Organist, director, composer, improviser and teacher. A graduate of Oberlin College, Kent State University and Eastman School of Music, he has served on the faculty at Kent State and *St. Olaf. Ferguson is well-known for *hymn festivals, at which he often performs with his St. Olaf *Cantorei.   PHW

Feria <ferial>. In classical Latin the term means "feast day." In ecclesiastical Latin it is the name given to all days except Saturday and Sunday on which no feast is celebrated. Week days are indicated by Roman numerals, e.g., feria II (Monday), feria III (Tuesday), etc. Certain *chant settings are prescribed for fe-

rias, e.g., the *Graduale Romanum* (1970) designates setting XVI of the *ordinary "for ferias throughout the year."   JMT

Festa, Costanzo (*b c* 1490; *d* Rome 1545). Perhaps the most important Italian composer between *Josquin and *Palestrina. One of a few Italian members of the papal chapel in the early 16th century, and one of the first to compete with emigrants from the N. His music, based on pervasive imitation, rich sonorities, and sprightly rhythms, was widely appreciated and disseminated. His *motets, *masses and madrigals, along with works by *Arcadelt, *Verdelot and *Willaert marked a stage in Italy's rise to musical dominance.   DCI

Fiddle Fugue. The nickname for J. S. *Bach's organ Fugue in D minor (BWV 539b), transcribed by the composer from the fugue of his sonata for solo violin (BWV 1001).   PKG

Field holler <holler, cry>. A song extemporized by Southern blacks to accompany work. While closely allied with other slave music emerging from the ante-bellum South, it differs in that it was often a solo and less patterned.   LJC

Fielding, Quincy, Jr. (*b* E St. Louis 1957). Composer, text writer and publisher of contemporary African American *gospel music. He served as pastor of the Cornerstone Institutional Baptist Church (Los Angeles) founded by James *Cleveland.   MEM

Figural <figurate, figured> [Latin *figuratus;* French *figuré;* German *figuriert;* Italian *figurato;* Spanish *figurado*]. (1) In a broad sense, a term employed to distinguish *polyphony from *plain-song, or any florid style of writing from a simpler one.

(2) More specifically, the Latin *musica figurata* was used to denote the florid style of some early Femish composers (e.g., *Ockeghem and *Obrecht). Sometimes *musica figurata* is used in contrast with *musica reservata*.   EBF

Figured bass. See *basso continuo*.

Figured chorale. An *organ *chorale in which the accompaniment to the (usually unadorned) chorale melody is dominated by the frequent use of a single melodic and/or rhythmic motive. J. S. *Bach's *Orgelbüchlein* contains many examples.   PKG

Finck, Heinrich (*b* Bamberg? *c* 1445; *d* Vienna 1527). Composer. He served Polish kings, courts in Stuttgart (1510–13) and Augsburg, the Cathedral at Salzburg (1519) and Vienna's court as *Kapellmeister* (1525–26). His compositional style moved from contrapuntal to more harmonic textures. Among 113 extant works are found 4 *masses, 2 *Magnificats, 4 *motet cycles, 7 *responsories and 24 *hymns (22 published by *Rhau).   JLB

Fiori musicali [Italian]. "Musical flowers." A collection of *keyboard music by *Frescobaldi for liturgical use, published in Venice (1635). It contains 3 *organ masses each with *canzoni, *ricercari and *toccatas.   LMT

Fire Baptized Holiness Church of God (of the Americas) worship music. This *Pentecostal denomination was established from the Fire Baptized Holiness Church by African Americans on racial grounds in 1908 by Bishop and Sister W. E. Fuller. *Hymnal of the F. B. H. Church* (1966) is the official *hymnal of this 10,000 member denomination; Scrive, *Watts and C. *Wesley are among the contributors well-represented in the 79 unaccompanied *hymns included therein. The hymnal is little used, however, and the congregation sings chiefly independent *refrains in *gospel style.   HCB

First New England School. A group of composers from around the 1770s who provided music for *singing schools, often setting *psalms as *fuging tunes, including *Billings, *Read, S. Belcher and J. Morgan. While borrowing much from English sources, these composers mixed religion and patriotism in an emerging new American idiom.   VEG

Fischer, Johann Caspar Ferdinand (*b* *c* 1670; *d* Rastatt 1746). Composer and *Kapellmeister to the margrave of Baden (from 1695). He published choral works for *vespers and a *litany, but mostly suites, *preludes and *fugues for *organ (e.g., his collection *Ariadne musica*, 1702).   JLB

Fisk (Jubilee) Singers. The Fisk University student choral ensemble founded by G. L. White (1871). They toured North America and Europe introducing a concertized, choral transformation of African American *spirituals performed *a cappella*. Their repertory was published by White and Theodore F. Seward (1884), and later by J. J. *Work (1915). The Fisk Singers played a major role in establishing the spiritual as a permanent American art form.   MEM

Flagellant songs. See *Geisslerlieder.*

Flamenco mass [Spanish]. "Of the gypsies." An RC *eucharist with the style of song, dance and *guitar music originating in Andalusia, Spain. Gypsy and Arab influence contributed to its rhythmic, passionate style. MAK

Flat twenty-first. (1) The 7th harmonic (counting the fundamental as one) in the overtone series, occurring as the interval of a minor 21st.

(2) A rank of *organ pipes tuned to produce this harmonic. JBW

Flex [Latin]. "Bend." A melodic drop in the first half of the *verse of a *psalm tone (before the mediant) when the line is too long (e.g., when 2 sense lines occur before the mediant); it is indicated in pointed *psalmody by a dagger or cross. In tones 1, 3, 5, and 6 this drop is a half step; in tones 2, 4, 7, and 8 it is a minor 3rd. In the formulary tones for readings and collects, it indicates the first change in the *reciting tone. JMT

Foley, John B. (*b* Peoria 1939). Composer and Jesuit priest. He studied music at Toronto's Royal Conservatory, privately with D. Argento and R. Smith Brindle; Ph.D. in theology from the Graduate Theological Union in Berkeley. He is best-known for liturgical compositions (e.g., "One Bread, One Body"), some written while a member of the *St. Louis Jesuits. EBF

Folk mass. (1) A term applied to a style of worship music that developed in the late 1960s, borrowed from or derivative of the US *folk music revival. Usually accompanied by *guitar, sometimes bass, piano and other *instruments.

(2) The style of worship associated with this music: ritually relaxed, it is often characterized by a casual approach to rubrics and texts. GET

Folk music. Narrowly speaking, folk music exists in oral tradition, without written notation. Ordinarily a rural or peasant phenomenon, constantly subject to change, it is relatively simple, generally performed by nonprofessionals and closely associated with everyday activities. Because of its significance in work, family life and public ceremonies, it may be considered functional, as distinguished from *art music which may be thought to exist for its own sake. From this perspective, much *ritual music originated as folk music.

Developments in communications and music in 20th-century Europe and N America have altered the definition of folk music. It now includes newly composed works modeled on traditional music, performed by professionals. W. Guthrie, P. Seeger and J. Baez were important figures in the US folk music revival in the 1960s which contributed to this redefinition, and prepared for the introduction of such music into contemporary worship. Often employing *guitar accompaniment, folk music and the *folk mass were symbols of the liturgical renewal. *Repp was an early exponent of such music, some of which was published in *Hymnal for Young Christians* (1966).

Bibl: H. Hucke, "Jazz and Folk Music in the Liturgy," *The Crisis of Liturgical Reform,* Concilium 42 (New York, 1969), 138–72; P. Bohlman, *The Study of Folk Music in the Modern World* (Bloomington, 1988). EBF

Foote, Arthur William (*b* Salem MA 1853; *d* Boston 1937). Organist, composer and teacher. Harvard trained, he served as organist-choirmaster at Boston's First Unitarian Church (1878–1910). Foote was a founder and first president of the *AGO. Besides orchestral and *organ compositions he wrote *c* 35 *anthems and 2 harmony text books.   FJM

Formula Missae (et Communionis) [Latin]. "An Order of Mass (and Communion)." A detailed instruction by *Luther (1523), outlining his revision of the *mass. It was designed to assist evangelical pastors in editing the Latin *service currently in use. Luther's revisions were liturgically and musically conservative, providing support for continued usage of *monophonic and *polyphonic repertoires except most of the *sequences.   MPB

Forster, Georg (*b* Amberg *c* 1510; *d* Nuremberg 1568). Composer, editor and doctor of medicine. He has a chorister at the court in Heidelberg by *c* 1521, where he began to compose. *Luther encouraged him to set biblical texts. Forster is most noted for editing *Frische teutsche Liedlein* (1539–56), containing 382 mostly 4-voice songs by 50 composers; 16 of his 52 songs included in this collection were sacred.   JLB

Fortunatus, Venatius (Honorius Clementianus) (*b* Treviso, Italy *c* 530; *d* Poitiers *c* 609). Poet. He briefly served the court at Metz (566–7) before settling in Poitiers where he became bishop (*c* 599). He composed *hymns in classical *meter, including *Vexilla Regis* and *Pange Lingua*.   RJS

Forty hours (devotion). A form of devotion before the exposed *eucharist (see *exposition) to commemorate the time that Jesus' body lay in the tomb after the crucifixion, which *Augustine judged to be 40 hours. It includes public *services interspersed with time for private prayer, and is often marked by a procession with the eucharist. The modern form of 40 hours began in Milan in the 16th century.   GET

Four questions. See *May nishtanah.*

Fraction anthem. A choral *anthem or congregational song (e.g., *Agnus Dei,* "Christ our Passover," etc.) sung during the *eucharist as bread is broken and prepared for distribution at *communion.   RDH

Fraction litany. A 3-fold or expanded *litany sung or spoken during the breaking of the bread or at *communion in Anglican, Lutheran and RC *eucharist. It is composed of a series of invocations ("Lamb of God" or some variation) and *responses ("have mercy on us"; with "grant us peace" as the final response). See *Agnus Dei.*   CLV

Francis of Assisi, St. <*bapt* Giovanni Bernadone> (*b* Assisi 1182; *d* there 1226). Founder of the Franciscan order. Author of various *laude;* the most famous is *Laudato si, mi Signor* (Umbrian dialect, "Praise to you my Lord," 1225), commonly known as "The *Canticle of the Sun." William Draper's famous paraphrase is "All creatures of our God and King."   VAL

Franck, César (-Auguste-Jean-Guillaume-Hubert) (*b* Liège 1822; *d*

Paris 1890). Composer and organist. Trained at Liège and the Paris Conservatory, he became organist at Ste. Clotilde in Paris (from 1858) where he was celebrated for his *organ improvisations. While he wrote numerous orchestral and sacred/liturgical choral compositions (*oratorios, *masses, *offertories, etc.), Franck is remembered for organ works as masterpieces of harmonic complexity and form within the frame of non-programmatic music. The massive *Trois chorals* (1890) is a landmark in organ literature. Franck's influence continues, e.g., in the work of *Messiaen. FJM

Franck, Melchior (*b* Zittau *c* 1579; *d* Coburg 1639). Important Lutheran composer associated with the towns of Nuremberg and Coburg (served there as *Kapellmeister* from 1603). He published over 600 *motets in various collections; among the most significant was *Gemmulae evangeliorum musicae* (1623), a collection of German *gospel motets for the liturgical *year. CFS

Franzmann, Martin Hans (*b* Lake City MN 1907; *d* Cambridge, England 1976). Theologian and *hymn writer. He taught at Northwestern College, Watertown WI (1936–46), Concordia Seminary, St. Louis (1946–69) and Westfield House in Cambridge, England (1969–72). Franzmann wrote 13 hymns, including "Thy Strong Word." JLB

Frederick II <the Great>, King of Prussia (*b* Berlin 1712; *d* Potsdam 1786). Flutist and amateur composer. He ruled from 1740. J. Quantz taught him flute; C. P. E. *Bach was his harpsichordist, as was C. *Fasch. He established an orchestra and opera house in Berlin. He wrote flute sonatas, *concertos and *arias. JLB

Freed, Isadore (*b* Brest-Litovsk, Russia 1900; *d* New York 1960). Composer, conductor, organist and lecturer. He immigrated to Philadelphia when very young. After studies at the University of Pennsylvania and Philadelphia Conservatory of Music he studied composition with *Bloch, then moved to France (1928) for studies with *D'Indy and others. In 1946 he began working with synagogues. His Jewish liturgical compositions written in the last decade of his life were the most influential, especially as he harmonized melodies within the Jewish modal system (see *Jewish prayer modes), e.g., *Sacred Service for Sabbath Eve* (1953). His *Jewish Modes* (1958) formulates his modal approach to harmony and is still used as a text in cantorial schools. MLK

Freemasonry and music. See *Masonic music.

Frere, Walter Howard (*b* Cambridge 1863; *d* Mirfeld 1938). Liturgical scholar. An Anglican priest, he became superior of the Community of the Resurrection, then Bishop of Truro (1923–35). He revised *A Manual of Plainsong* (1902) and wrote the historical edition of *Hymns Ancient and Modern* (1909). RKW

Frescobaldi, Girolamo (*b* Ferrara 1583; *d* Rome 1643). Composer and organist. One of the most influential and renowned of the early 17th-century keyboardists; considered "the father of the modern *organ style." He was trained by Luzzaschi in Ferrara. In 1608 Frescobaldi became organist of St. Peter's

Cappella Giulia in Rome; except for a time as court organist in Florence (1628–34) he remained there until his death.

Frescobaldi composed numerous sacred vocal works, but is best known for his *canzoni,* capriccios, *partitas, *ricercari,* *toccatas and liturgical pieces. The latter are found in 2 sources: the second book of toccatas (Rome, 1627) contains pieces based on *Gregorian *hymns and the first *elevation toccatas; *Fiori musicali* (Venice, 1635) includes 3 *organ masses (for feasts of the Lord, Mary and the saints) each comprising *intonations for *mass parts (e.g., the *Kyrie* and *Credo)* or as accompaniment to liturgical action (e.g., the elevation or time after *communion). Adventurous chromatic harmonies and acrid dissonances are hallmarks of his style.

   Bibl: F. Hammond, *Girolamo Frescobaldi* (Cambridge, 1983); J. Moore, "The Liturgical Use of the Organ in Seventeenth-Century Italy," in *Frescobaldi Studies,* ed. A. Silbiger (Durham, 1987) 351–84.   MDJ

Friedman, Debbie (*b* Utica NY 1951). Songwriter and performer. She originally taught music to children, subsequently becoming popular in Reform Jewish summer camps and other Jewish organizations. Since the 1970s she has recorded 15 albums. Her straight forward, *folk-style melodies are influential vehicles for congregational participation in the worship of *Reform Judaism. MLK

Friends of the English Liturgy <FEL>. Publishing company founded in Chicago (1963) by D. Fitzpatrick to promote music for the *mass in English. Its major publication was the *Hymnal for Young Christians* (1966).   GET

Froberger, Johann Jacob (*b* Stuttgart 1616; *d* Héricourt 1667). Organist and composer. A student of *Frescobaldi, he served as organist to the Viennese court (1641–58). He is best-known for *organ and harpsichord compositions (*toccatas, *ricercari,* etc.). Only 2 of his sacred vocal works survive.   EBF

Fromm, Herbert (*b* Kitzingen am Main 1905; *d* Boston 1995). Composer and conductor. Trained in Munich he immigrated to the US (1937), serving as music director in synagogues in Buffalo and Boston. Fromm composed for Jewish and non-Jewish contexts. His compositions for Jewish worship are choral; best-known is his Friday evening *service *Adath Israel* (1943).   MLK

Fryson, Robert (*b* Raleigh 1944; *d* Washington DC 1994). Vocalist, composer, conductor and gospel musician. A life member of *National Association of Negro Musicians, he founded the male sacred music ensemble The Voices Supreme. His most familiar *hymn is "Glorious Is Thy Name, O Jesus." MWC

Fuga alla giga [Italian]. "Fugue in jig style." A *fugue in the form of a jig in 12/8 time.   ACL

Fughetta [Italian]. "Small fugue." A term used since the late *Baroque for a short or "light" *fugue. No constructional principles seem to distinguish fugue from *fughetta;* only length and weightiness.   LMT

Fuging tune. A manner of setting *psalms or *hymns popular in England and 18th-century American *singing schools. The first section of the psalm or *hymn tune is set homophonically, followed by imitative voice entries (*fugue) leading to a cadence.   VEG

Fugue. A *Baroque contrapuntal form, usually in 3 or 4 voices. The subject is stated in imitative succession by each voice while others continue with figures. Episodes are free *counterpoint, often marked with recurring motifs. The subject returns in counterpoint at intervals, sometimes finishing in stretto (entries in quick succession). The form was brought to perfection by J. S. *Bach. JBF

Fulbert of Chartres (*b c* 960; *d* 1028). Bishop of Chartres (from 1007) to whom are attributed glosses of *Boethius' *De institutione musica* and some liturgical texts, especially concerning Mary and her Nativity. He is also the reputed composer of a *mass to St. James of Campostella and the *conductus *"In hac dies laudes."* RTR

Full anthem. An Anglican choral composition for "full" choir, in contradistinction to a *verse anthem.   RAL

Full service. See *service.

Funeral march [French *marche funebre*]. A slow march, sometimes occurring as an independent piece of *ritual music, especially during military funerals for heads of state. Otherwise a slow, march section of a larger work, such as the slow movement of *Beethoven's Symphony n. 3 ("Eroica," 1803), or Siegfried's funeral march in *Wagner's *Götterdämmerung* (1876).   ADC

Funeral music, Jewish. Rabbinic texts document the practice of flute players and lamenters at Jewish funerals (*Mishna Baba Matzia* 6:1, *Ketubot* 4:4), though such is no longer the practice in Jewish communities today. Several texts are commonly chanted or read at Jewish funerals, including **El male rachamim*, *Kaddish* and Ps 23.   MLK

Funk, Virgil (*b* LaCrosse WI 1937). A RC priest of the Richmond diocese, he is the founder (1976) and president of the *National Association of Pastoral Musicians.   JBF

Fux, Johann Joseph (*b* Styria 1660; *d* Vienna 1741). Theorist and composer. *Kapellmeister* at St. Stephen's Cathedral in Vienna, then at the imperial court (from 1715), he is best-known for his treatise *Gradus ad Parnassum* ("Steps to Parnassus") of 1725, which codified the contrapuntal compositional practice of *Palestrina and remained a standard textbook for centuries. His compositions include *c* 80 *masses, 3 *Requiems, 57 *vespers, *psalms and 10 *oratorios.
Bibl: H. White, ed., *Johann Joseph Fux and the Music of the Austro-Italian Baroque* (Brookfield VT, 1992).   AWR

G

Gabriel, Charles H(utchinson) <Charlotte G. Homer> (*b* Wilton IA 1856; *d* Los Angeles 1932). *Gospel song writer, composer and editor. Best-known of his estimated 7,000 songs is "I stand amazed in the presence" (1905). CRY

Gabriel-Burrow, Marjorie A. (*b* Detroit 1955). *Jazz musician who has served as a church musician since age 15. She founded and directs the Detroit Metro Catholic Gospel Choir (1982). She was a principal editor of the African American RC *hymnal, *Lead Me, Guide Me* (1987). RJB

Gabrieli, Andrea (*b* Venice *c* 1510; *d* there 1586). Organist and composer. He may have studied with *Willaert, also with *Lassus with whom he developed a lasting friendship. He was a chorister at St. Mark's in Venice (1536). After travel to Germany and Bohemia, he returned to Venice and became second organist at St. Mark's (1566), then succeeding *Merulo as first organist (1885). His compositions include 6 complete *masses, *c* 130 *motets, *c* 260 madri-

gals, *organ *intonazioni, *canzoni* and *ricercari*. Weekly 2-organ concerts with Merulo brought him widespread recognition. Outstanding masterworks, especially *polychoral and multi-voiced, brought enduring renown. His students included his nephew G. *Gabrieli, *Hassler and *Sweelinck.

Bibl: D. Arnold, *Giovanni Gabrieli and the Music of the Venetian High Renaissance* (London, 1979). LFH

Gabrieli, Giovanni (*b* Venice *c* 1553–56; *d* there 1612). Organist and foremost Venetian composer of his time. He studied with his uncle A. *Gabrieli, probably also with *Lassus. He served as court musician in Munich (late 1570s), second organist to his uncle at St. Mark's in Venice (1585) and organist for the confraternity of the Scuola di S. Rocco (1585). His partially preserved liturgical compositions include *Sacrae symphoniae* (1597) containing a *mass, *motets (e.g., *O magnum Mysterium*) and instrumental works; similar is *Symphoniae sacrae* (1615). He also wrote madrigals and a wide range of instrumental works including *intonazioni, *canzoni, *ricercari and *toccatas. He was famous for *cori spezzati technique in both his choral and instrumental music. *Schütz was among his students.

Bibl: D. Arnold, *Giovanni Gabrieli* (London, 1974).   LFH

Gallican chant. A repertoire indigenous to Gaul, used from the 5th century until its suppression under Pepin and *Charlemagne during the 8th–9th centuries. Liturgically there was no unified Gallican rite with a standardized repertoire, and no cycle of *chants can be reconstructed. Most Gallican chants survived within *Gregorian sources, and it is often difficult to distinguish original Gallican material on purely musical grounds; however, Gallican texts tend to be more colorful and descriptive than those of the Roman tradition. Certain Gallican chants have liturgical usage without parallels in Roman *liturgy, e.g., chants for votive masses, or *litanies for the beginning of Mass; there are also elaborate *offertory pieces which are possibly Gallican.

Bibl: W. S. Porter, *The Gallican Rite* (London, 1958); M. Huglo, "Gallican rite, music of the," *NGDMM* 7:113–25.   JMH

Gallican Psalter [Latin *Psalterium Gallicanum*]. The second translation of *psalms into Latin by St. Jerome made *c* 392, based on the Greek Septuagint text found in the Hexapla. First adopted for liturgical use by Gallican churches, it eventually replaced the Hebrew *psalter in all manuscripts of the Vulgate. It displaced the *Roman psalter under Pius V (*d* 1572), and remained as the *breviary psalter in the Roman rite until the revision of Pius XII (*d* 1958).   JMT

Gallus, Joannes [Jehan le Cocq] (*fl* mid-16th century). Composer. It is possible that he was *maestro di cappella to the Duke of Ferrara (1534-41?). His works were published after 1542. Twenty-two *chansons* and 9 *motets are attributed to him.   JLB

Galuppi, Baldasarre (*b* Burano 1706; *d* Venice 1785). Composer of operas, dramatic and instrumental works. *Vice-maestro* (1748–62) then *maestro di cappella* (1762–5) at St. Mark's in Venice; later he served as music director of Catherine the Great's chapel in St. Petersburg (1765–8). Galuppi wrote *cantatas, *oratorios, *masses and other sacred works, some in Russian.   VAL

Gardner, John Linton (*b* Manchester 1917). Composer. He studied composition and piano at Oxford. He subsequently held positions at Covent Garden, Morley College and the Royal Academy of Music (1956–75). His works include *Mass in C* (1965), *Sonata da chiesa* (1976–77) and *cantatas for *Christmas (1966) and *Easter (1970).   FKG

Gastoldi, Giovanni Giacomo (*b* Caravaggio 1550s?; *d* Mantua *c* 1622). Composer and long time *maestro di cappella* in Mantua (1572–1608). Famous for his 5-part *ballettos,* he also wrote *masses, *psalm settings and other *liturgical music in a wide variety of styles.   RJS

Gathering note. (1) A note sounded on the *organ to establish pitch.

(2) An elongated note at the beginning of a *hymn or *psalm tune, a feature of English psalm tunes and some German *chorales.   RAL

Geisslerlieder [German]. "Songs of the flagellants." Vernacular songs, often based on 4-line rhymed *strophes like the later German *chorale. They were sung by penitential confraternities, especially at the time of the Black Plague (mid-14th century). Some might be modeled on the more sophisticated *laudesi spirituali* (see *lauda*) of Italian confraternities; some are derived from earlier pilgrim songs. A collection of *Geisslerlieder* transcribed by Hugo von Reutlingen in 1349 is among the earliest written witnesses to religious *folk songs. Like secular folk songs of the period, *Geisslerlieder* often had a simple *refrain and expandable music for *verses. The 2 main categories are processional songs and songs for the flagellation ceremony. Processional *Geisslerlieder* sometimes show a *litany-like performance practice, and are often Marian in character, the most famous being *Maria, muoter reinû maît* ("Mary, mother and pure maiden"). Examples exist of songs for the flagellation ceremony in which the refrain recurs each time the penitent prostrated himself in the form of a cross.

Bibl: W. Wiora, "The Origins of German Spiritual Folk Song," *Ethnomusicology* 8 (1964) 1–13; R. H. Hoppin, *Medieval Music* (New York, 1978) 315–18.   RTR

Geistliches Konzert [German]. "Spiritual concerto." A piece for voice(s) and *instruments with a religious text. Protestant composers (e.g., *Schütz, *Kleine geistliche Konzerte,* 1636), building on Italian models from *Viadana, *Monteverdi and others, found the form suited to their own exegetical and dramatic purposes. By 1730 the term is interchangeable with *cantata (as in J. S. *Bach) and has been applied today to works of contemporary composers (e.g., *Raphael, *Micheelsen).   MPB

Gelineau, Joseph (*b* Champ sur Layon 1920). Liturgist, composer, author and Jesuit priest. He completed doctoral work at Institut Catholique in Paris, where he eventually joined the faculty as professor of liturgical musicology and pastoral *liturgy. Cofounder and a principal participant in *Universa Laus, he served as a member of the study group (1967–69) for the reform of the Roman *mass according to the decrees of *Vatican II. Famed for his versified settings of the *psalms, popularly known as the "Gelineau Psalms" (French edition, 1955; English edition prepared by The Grail, 1963), he has composed *liturgical music in many other forms, e.g., *antiphons, *cantatas, *eucharistic prayers and *motets. As a composer Gelineau has a special concern for music of the liturgical assembly. Among his influential writings are *Chant et musique dans le culte chrétien* (1962; trans., *Voices and Instruments in Christian Worship,* 1964), and his many contributions to the journals *La Maison-Dieu* and *Église qui chante.*

Bibl: C. Pottie, *A More Profound Alleluia* (Washington DC, 1984).   CSP

Gellert, Christian Fürchtegott (*b* Hainichen, Saxony 1715; *d* Leipzig? 1769). Lutheran classicist and poet who served as professor of philosophy at Leipzig (from 1751) where Goethe and Lessing were among his students. Best-known for his *hymns, popular among Lutheran and RCs alike; 54 of them appeared in *Geistliche Oden und Lieder* (1757).   CFS

Gemeindelied [German]. "Congregational song, chorale." A common term for congregational song or *hymnody in German-speaking churches, particularly the Lutheran Church.   RDH

General menaion. See *menaion.

Genevan <Geneva> **Psalter.** A French *metrical psalter compiled in Geneva under the guidance of *Calvin between 1542–62 (not to be confused with Anglo-Genevan *psalters, the English psalters published in Geneva 1556–61). The authors were *Marot and Beza; successive musical editors were *Bourgeois and *Goudimel. Reprinted numerous times, this was the model for later metrical psalmody across Europe and N America.   RAL

Georgian chant. The *liturgical music of the Georgian Orthodox Church, developed under the influence of Georgian monasteries at Jerusalem (St. Sabas), Mount Sinai and Mount Athos (Iviron). The Georgian *iadgari* (containing *troparia for the evening *office, morning office and the *divine liturgy), translated from a 6th-century Jerusalem chantbook with modal indications, is important for the study of the lost Jerusalem repertory. *Neumatic musical notation (still undeciphered) existed around 980. *Hymns translated from Greek are supplemented by indigenous *chants by medieval composers, notably Mikael Modrekili (11th century) and John Minchkhi (11th century). The modal system and types of chant manuscripts correspond generally to those of *Byzantine chant. An oral tradition of 3-voice *polyphony has existed since at least the 12th century.

Bibl: P. Jeffery, "The Earliest Christian Chant Repertory Recovered," *JAMS* 47 (1994) 1–38.   RGD

Gerhardt, Paul (*b* Gräfenhainichen 1607; *d* Lübben 1676). *Hymn writer and pastor in Mittenwalde, Berlin and Lübben. Next to *Luther, Gerhardt was the greatest of German hymn writers. More than 100 texts (e.g., "O Sacred Head Now Wounded," "Now rest beneath night's shadow") combine powerful imagery with deep personal trust in God in spite of personal suffering during the Thirty Years War and bitter church controversies. Many of his hymns (known in English translations by *Winkworth) are widely used in American *hymnals. A staunch adherent of Luther's teachings, he skillfully combined the expression of personal sentiment with orthodox Lutheran theology. His *verse appears not only as hymns but occasionally in *Lieder (e.g., by *Pepping).
Bibl: T. B. Hewitt, *Paul Gerhardt as a Hymn Writer,* 2nd ed. (St. Louis, 1976). VEG

German Mass. See *Deutsche Messe.

German Requiem. See *Deutsches Requiem, Ein.

Gerovitch, Elieser <Eliezar> (**Mordechai Ben Isaac**) (*b* Kiev 1844; *d* Rostov-on-Don 1913). *Cantor and composer of synagogue music. A fine *tenor, he began as a *chazzan. At 18 he went to Berditchev to study, eventually becoming assistant *chazzan* at the Choral Synagogue there; later he studied cantorial music in Odessa under N. Blumenthal; then he became one of the first Jewish cantors to study at the St. Petersburg

Conservatory. In 1887 Gerovitch became chief cantor at the Choral Synagogue in Rostov-on-Don, remaining there until his death. Well-known for compositions which reflect traditional synagogue motifs, he published a 2-volume set of music (*Shirei Tefillah* and *Schirei Zimra,* 1897); most famous is his setting of *Adon Olam,* often sung at the conclusion of *Sabbath *ma'ariv.   DMR

Geshem [Hebrew]. "Rain." An alphabetical acrostic prayer for rain, asking God to remember the merits of Abraham, Isaac, Jacob, Moses and Aaron, and the 12 tribes of Israel. Written by Rabbi Eliezar HaKallir (*c* 7th–9th centuries), it is recited on *Shemini Atzeret during *musaf. It introduces the formula *"mashiv haruach umorid hagashem"* ("return the wind and bring down the rain") which is inserted into the *Gevurot* section of the *Amidah, and recited between *Shemini Atzeret* and *Pesach.

The musical leitmotifs of the *Geshem* are introduced in the *Chatzi *Kaddish* preceding *musaf and continue in the *Avot* section of the *Amidah* through *"Af beri."* The melody belongs to the *Misinnai* corpus of tunes. Many W European synagogue composers incorporated the leitmotif into *verses. E European *cantors were not as stringent in the employment of the leitmotif, nor did they restrict the 6 verses to a particular mode.

Bibl: M. Nulman, *Concepts of Jewish Music and Prayer* (New York, 1985), pp. 29, 49, 73, 76, 85, 96.   IAG

Gesius, Bartholomaeus (*b* Müncheberg 1555–62; *d* Frankfurt an der Oder 1613). Composer and church musician who served as *Kantor* of Marienkirche in Frankfurt (from 1593). A prolific *hymn writer, his important works include a *St. John Passion (1588), *Psalmodia choralis* (1600), *Geistliche deutsche Lieder* (1601) and a *Magnificat* (1607).   CFS

Gesualdo, Carlo (Prince of Venosa) (*b* Naples? *c* 1561; *d* Gesualdo 1613). Composer and lutenist. Gesualdo is famous for arranging the murder of his first wife, her lover and a son whose paternity he questioned. Primarily a madrigalist, he was interested in conveying emotional expression in his music. Influenced by the chromaticism of *Luzzaschi, he employed chromaticism well by restricting its abundant use to passages that were not rhythmically complicated. Successions of unrelated chords and unusual dissonances, such as augmented triads, are most uncommon for his time. He composed 3 books of sacred works including *motets and *responsories in a style only slightly more restrained than his madrigals. His passion for music combined with advancing melancholia explain his rather aberrant compositional procedures.

Bibl: G. Watkins, *Gesualdo* (London, 1973).   DCI

Gheyn, Matthias van den (*b* Tirlemont 1721; *d* Louvain 1785). Organist at St. Peter's in Louvain (from 1741) and town carilloneur (from 1745). Renowned as an improvisor, his important compositions are for *carillon.   JLB

Ghost dance. A ritual developed by Native Americans under the influence of the Piute prophet Wovoka (or Jack Wilson) in the late 1880s. This dance supposedly allowed them to recover their land, unite with ancestors and live in peace. Sioux Indians who developed the dance as political protest were repressed by the government, some being massacred at Wounded Knee (1890).   MAK

Giant fugue. Nickname for J. S. *Bach's *chorale prelude on *Wir glauben all'* (BWV 680, from *Klavierübung*, part 3, 1739), presumably derived from the striding motion of its pedal ostinato figure.   AJL

GIA Publications. Publishing house founded by Clifford Bennett in Pittsburgh (1941) as The Gregorian Institute of America, an RC educational effort in *Gregorian chant. It was moved to Toledo (1942), then Chicago (1967). The name "GIA Publications" was introduced in 1968 and the original name phased out. It publishes *hymnals, choral, *organ and contemporary *liturgical music, and music education materials.   FJM

Gibbons, Orlando (*b* Oxford 1583; *d* Canterbury 1625). Composer and 1 of the finest English organists of the day. He joined the *Chapel Royal *choir in 1603, becoming organist there by 1615 and senior organist in 1625. Gibbons was also organist at Westminster Abbey in 1623. His compositions for Anglican *services exhibited the English Protestant *Reformation principles of clarity and ease of understanding in all sung texts. Gibbons set the standard for *verse anthems in the Chapel Royal style. He created full melodic lines and controlled *counterpoint within a well-planned structure with great skill. His works include 8 unaccompanied *full anthems, 21 verse anthems with instrumental accompaniment, short service music, verse service music, *motets, madrigals and numerous *keyboard pieces.

Bibl: P. Phillips, *English Sacred Music: 1549–1649* (Oxford, 1991).   RJS

Gigout, Eugène (*b* Nancy 1844; *d* Paris 1925). Organist, composer and teacher. A student of *Saint-Saëns at École Niedermeyer, Gigout later taught there (1863–85, 1900–05), then at the Paris Conservatory (from 1911). Organist at St-Augustin in Paris (1863–1925), he was renowned for his improvisational skills. Important *organ compositions include the collections *Album grégorien* (1895) and *L'orgue d'église* (1904).   FJM

Glagolitic Mass [Czech *Glagolská mše*]. A *cantata for *choir, soloists, orchestra and *organ by L. Janácek (1926, 3 later revisions). The Old Slavonic text is by M. Weingart, adapted from the *ordinary. The organ has an important role in the work. "Glagolitic" is a technical term for the Old Slavonic script and alphabet.   FJM

Glanz, Leib (*b* Kiev 1898; *d* Tel Aviv 1964). *Cantor and composer. The son of a cantor, Glanz led congregational prayer at age 8. *Chazzan in Kishinev and Rumanin, he immigrated to the US (1926) where he held positions in Brooklyn and Los Angeles. Later he immigrated to Israel (1954) and served as a cantor in Tel Aviv until his death. His musical style was graceful and devotional; he did not favor the excessive use of the minor scale as did other cantors (see *Jewish prayer modes). Glanz wrote over 100 unpublished compositions and made numerous recordings.   MLK

Glarean, Heinrich (*b* Mollis 1488; *d* Freiburg 1563). Theorist, humanist and poet. His *Dodechachordon* (1547), based to some extent on the work of *Boethius and Gaffurio, established the theoretical basis for 2 new *modes: aeolian (the modern natural minor tonality) and ionian (major tonality) and their *plagals, adding them to the existing medieval system of 8 modes. Despite Glarean's vigorous defense of *chant, this work hastened the process of replacing modality with major-minor tonality.   RTR

Glas [Slavonic]. See *echos*.

Gloria in excelsis (Deo) <angelic hymn, great(er) doxology> [Latin]. "Glory (to God) in the highest." A *hymn of praise and *psalmus idioticus*. An early Greek version from the late 4th century indicates that it was widely employed in the E as part of *morning prayer (see *orthros, *doxologia*). The prose text begins with the angels' song to the shepherds (Luke 2:14), followed by later elaborations. It became the second element of the Roman rite *ordinary (by the early 6th century?) sung after the *Kyrie,* though not in *Advent and *Lent. The current Latin text developed by the 9th century. Over 50 medieval melodies survive; 19 are preserved in the *Liber Usualis*. In the *BCP (from 1552–1982) this was the hymn of thanks concluding the *communion service.
   Bibl: D. Hiley, *Western Plainchant* (Oxford, 1993), especially pp. 156–161. PAJ

Gloria Patri <lesser doxology> [Latin]. "Glory to the Father." The *incipit* of the *doxology derived from Matt 28:19. Of Syrian origin, it is an affirmation of orthodox trinitarian theology. Used by Christians to conclude *psalms since the 4th century, it was subsequently employed in metrical form at the end of *office hymns. In many Protestant traditions, it serves as a congregational *response to scripture readings.   PAJ

Glory to God in the highest. See *Gloria in excelsis*.

Glossolalia. See *tongues, singing in.

Gluck, Christoph Willibald (Ritter von) (*b* Erasbach 1714; *d* Vienna 1787). Composer of operas, ballets, secular and sacred vocal works. Gluck is best-known for his operas (e.g., *Orfeo ed Euridice,* 1762), characterized by energy, simplicity, memorable melodies and a vivid dramatic quality. His work symbolizes the reform of opera from *Baroque excesses to *Classical simplicity. His sacred works include Latin *arias that are parodies of operatic arias and *motets for *choir and orchestra, including a *De profundis* which *Salieri conducted at Gluck's funeral.   JDW

Goemanne, Noël (*b* Poperinge, Belgium 1926). Composer and organist. A student of *Peeters, he immigrated to the US in 1952, settling in Dallas in 1972. His many published *mass settings and *anthems have provided effective music for RC post-*Vatican II worship.   FJM

Golden sequence. See *Veni Sancte Spiritus*.

Gombert <Gunbert, Gomberth>, **Nicolas** (*b* 1495?; *d* 1565?). Franco-Flemish composer. Gombert was employed at the court of Charles V until he was ex-

pelled in 1540 for personal impropri-
eties. His *masses, *motets, *chansons*
and *Magnificat*s exhibit a densely imitative contrapuntal idiom.   AJL

Good Friday. See *year, liturgical.

Goodrich, William Marcellus (*b* Tem-
pleton MA 1777; *d* East Cambridge MA
1833). *Organ builder who taught at
various *singing schools at Harvard and
Groton. Most Boston organ builders of
the mid-19th century were trained in his
workshop.   JWK

Goodson, Albert A. (*b* Los Angeles
1933). Composer of African American
*gospel music, pianist, choir director,
and minister of music at various churches
in Los Angeles and Chicago. His most
celebrated composition is "We've Come
This Far by Faith."   MEM

Gospel. (1) That part of worship devoted to the reading or chanting of some
section from one of the New Testament
gospels. In some worship traditions, this
reading is preceded by *responsorial
psalmody, an *alleluia, *gospel acclamation and/or a sometimes elaborate
procession by clergy and laity.
  (2) *Gospel music.   LJC

Gospel acclamation. An *acclamation
accompanying the procession of the
gospel book (see *evangeliary) before
the reading of the *gospel during *mass,
by which the assembly acknowledges
and honors Christ's presence in the
word. The classic form of this acclamation is *alleluia-*verse-alleluia, with the
verse drawn from the gospel reading.
The alleluia is replaced by another text
during *Lent.   VCF

Gospeler <gospeller>. (1) The minister
who reads or chants the *gospel; the
term is often applied to the deacon.
  (2) The minister who preaches the
gospel.   ADC

Gospel motet. A *polyphonic setting of
a *gospel text which 16th- and 17th-
century Lutheran composers intended to
be part of, or a replacement for, the gospel
selection appointed for public worship
according to the liturgical *year.   MPB

Gospel music, African American. A
form and style of vocal music originating
in the late 19th and early 20th centuries
as music for worship. It has its origin in
African American *spirituals, white
*gospel songs, blues, ragtime, *jazz and
the sanctified "shout" of early storefront
Pentecostal churches. It is characterized
by a freedom of vocal and instrumental
improvisation. The sacred/secular interconnection of this music has deeply influenced performance practices (e.g., its
driving rhythms, intricate harmonic
changes, etc.) that have rendered this
music admissible in worship, concert
halls and night clubs. Under the influence
of *Dorsey and *Tindley, gospel music
was published and made available for use
by African American congregations and
others.   MWC

Gospel music, White American. Originally a popular style of late 19th-century
*hymnody; *Bliss was the first to use
the term this way. This music can be
traced to *camp meetings, Sunday school
*hymns and popular music which, in
turn, it has influenced; it also shows a
mutual influence with *shape note music
of the S and Midwest and African
American gospel performance practices.

An early example of White American gospel music is W. Fischer's "I love to tell the story" (1869). Texts, especially those of *Crosby, often deal with salvation and conversion. Its popularity in Evangelical Protestant worship has extended to more liturgically oriented Protestant and RC worship.   MWC

Gospel Music Association <GMS>. An organization founded in 1964 by D. Butler, J. Blackwood and J. D. Sumner to set professional standards for artists, managers, retailers and booking agents in the *gospel music business, encompassing traditional gospel quartets and soloists, rap, heavy metal and contemporary Christian musicians. GMS annually presents Dove Awards for best gospel albums and vocalists.   RSJ

Gospel song <gospel>. A generic name for songs created and sung at 19th-century *camp meetings, or *hymns growing out of the revival movements of C. Finney and *Moody. The name gospels was given by *Sankey and *Bliss in their *Gospel Hymns* (1875). Texts of these songs generally express themes of personal conversion and salvation. Tunes usually have *refrains, are harmonically simple, in major keys and frequently use dotted rhythms.   RJS

Goss, John (*b* Fareham 1800; *d* London 1880). Cathedral organist, director and composer. He studied with *Attwood whom he succeeded as organist at St. Paul's Cathedral in London (1838–72). Goss wrote Anglican *psalm tones, *service music and *hymns. His tune LAUDA ANIMA is still widely used.   FJM

Gossec, François-Joseph (*b* Vergnies 1734; *d* Passy 1829). Composer. A cho-

rister at Antwerp Cathedral (1742), he studied violin and *organ in his youth. In Paris (by 1751) he composed operas, symphonies, vocal works, *masses (*Messe des morts,* 1760), *noëls,* *oratorios (*La nativité,* 1774) and *motets. Gossec directed the *Concert spirituel* from 1773–77.   JLB

Gothic motet. A *motet of the Gothic period (mid-12th to mid-15th centuries), but primarily of the *ars antiqua* or *ars nova* in which a *chant *tenor serves as the foundation for more rhythmically active upper voices that usually sing differing vernacular secular texts.   RTR

Goudimel, Claude (*b* Besançon 1500–14; *d* Lyons 1572). Composer and publisher. He wrote *chansons,* *motets and *masses. Goudimel provided *psalm tunes and harmonizations for *Bourgeois' *psalm tunes in the *Genevan Psalter for which he was musical editor. He died with the Protestant Huguenots in the St. Bartholomew's Day massacre.   RJS

Gounod, Charles (François) (*b* Paris 1818; *d* St. Cloud, France 1893). Composer best known for his Romantic *sacred music and operas. A devout RC who considered joining the priesthood, he admired the works of *Palestrina. His sentimental lyricism and mild romanticism was respected by many composers including *Saint-Saens, *Bizet and *Fauré. One of his greatest triumphs of sacred music was his *Messe solennelle de Ste. Cécile* (1855), which continues to be performed regularly.   DCI

Gradual [Latin *graduale*]. (1) The *chant of the *proper of the mass which occurs after the *epistle. Clearly established in the E by the 4th century and the W by the 5th century, it was originally sung from the "step" (Latin *gradus*) below the *ambo in the sanctuary. The text was a *psalm, performed in *responsorial style by *cantor and assembly. By the 6th century the assembly's role was taken over by trained singers. The resulting form was a *respond intoned by a soloist and completed by singers, a solo *verse and repetition of the last part of the respond by singers. *Gregorian graduals tend to be highly *melismatic. Today it is replaced by the *responsorial psalm.

(2) The liturgical *book which contains chants for the *mass. See *Graduale Romanum*.

Bibl: D. Hiley, *Western Plainchant* (Oxford, 1993).   EBF

Graduale Romanum [Latin]. "Roman gradual." The liturgical *book containing the *ordinary and *proper *chants of the Roman *mass.   VCF

Gradual hymn. See *de tempore* hymns.

Gradualia. A collection of 109 choral settings of liturgical material composed by *Byrd in 2 volumes. Volume 1 (1605) contains *Marian antiphons, Marian *office *hymns and miscellaneous pieces for *Easter. The remainder of this and the next volume (1607) contain settings of *propers (mostly for *mass but some for *vespers) for various feasts. Non-liturgical *motets are also included in the work.   JMT

Gradual psalm(s). (1) The "psalms of ascent" (Pss 120–134), thought to be sung by pilgrims journeying to Jerusalem. See *Shir hama'alot*.

(2) That section of *psalmody sung from the *gradus* (Latin, "step") of the

lectern by a *cantor, with or without a *refrain, as a *response to the first reading at *mass.   CJK

Grail, The. A secular society of single RC women living in community near London. In the late 1950s they commissioned a singable English translation (from the Hebrew) of the *psalms for their daily *office. Sanctioned for liturgical use in 1960, it rapidly gained widespread use.   RJB

Grande messe des morts [French]. "Solemn high mass for the dead." A *Requiem* mass, particularly associated with *Berlioz (op. 5, 1837) and other 19th-century *Romantic composers.   MSD

Grandi, Alessandro (*b c* 1575; *d* Bergamo 1630). Composer and singer. He probably studied with G. *Gabrieli. Grandi served as *maestro di cappella* for confraternities in Ferrara, was a singer and deputy to *Monteverdi at St. Mark's in Venice, and *maestro* at Bergamo. He composed *masses, *psalms, *litanies and over 200 *motets.   DWM

Grant, Amy (*b* Augusta 1962). Singer and composer. Grant began her musical career in contemporary Christian music (see *Christian rock) winning a series of "Dove awards" (see *Gospel Music Association) for albums as a teenager. She then successfully crossed over into the popular recording and concert industry.   FJM

Graun, Karl Heinrich (*b* Wahrenbrück *c* 1704; *d* Berlin 1759). Singer, conductor and composer. A *tenor at the Brunswick Opera (1725) he subsequently became music director (1735) for *Frederick II. Graun composed 26 Italian operas, also the *passion *Der Tod Jesu* (1755) and a *Te Deum* (1756).   JLB

Graupner, Johann Christoph (*b* Kirchberg 1683; *d* Darmstadt 1760). Keyboardist and composer who worked in Leipzig, Hamburg and finally as *Kapellmeister* in Darmstadt. Chosen over J. S. *Bach for the Leipzig post, he was prevented from accepting it, occasioning Bach's employment there. Graupner wrote over 1,400 *church cantatas.   MPB

Great antiphons. See *O Antiphons.

Great Canon of St. Andrew. A Byzantine penitential *hymn by Andrew of Crete (*d* 740), comprising 250 *troparia (9 *odes), sung at *orthros on Thursday in the fifth week of *Lent. RGD

Great <grand> **compline.** See *apodeipnon to mega*.

Great(er) doxology. See *Gloria in excelsis*.

Great entrance. See *megale eisodos*.

Great Fast. See *Lent.

Great Lent. See *Lent.

Great litany. See *eirenika*.

Great organ [French *grand orgue*; German *Hauptwerk*]. The primary manual division of a pipe *organ, usually unenclosed.   JBW

Great responsory [Latin *responsorium prolixum*]. The *response to the readings at *matins in the Roman *divine office. There existed a large body of these with very elaborate melodies. Their structure was: response - *verse - *repetendum - *lesser doxology - *repetendum*. Many were set chorally, especially those of *Christmas and *Tenebrae (e.g., *Byrd, *Tallis, *Victoria). In Lutheran *hymnals of N America these were assigned to *morning and *evening prayer.   JMT

Great service. See *service.

Great synapte. See *synapte*.

Great vespers. See *hesperinos*.

Grechaninov, Alexander (*b* Moscow 1864; *d* New York 1956). Composer. A student of *Rimsky-Korsakov, his works include settings of the Byzantine *liturgy and other liturgical compositions as well as chamber, orchestral and instrumental pieces.   VAL

Greco-Byzantine chant. The *liturgical music of the Greek Orthodox church, also called Neo-Byzantine chant. The relationship of this repertory to *Byzantine chant is not fully understood, but texts and genres are the same and some continuity of melodic formulas exists. Beginning in the 15th century, Byzantine chant became less formulaic and increasingly virtuosic *(kalophonic),* with long *melismata *(teretismata).* The 8 *modes, previously divided into authentic and *plagal forms, were supplemented by *mesoi* (mediant modes) and *phthorae* (modulation signs). Evidence for use of the *ison (drone) exists by the late 16th century. In 1821 Chrysanthos Madytos reformed late Byzantine *(koukouzelian)* notation, simplifying the system for printed books, and introducing a solmization system *(parallage)* and new signs for modulation and chromatic alteration. *Chrysanthine notation, now called the "New Method," is used in modern Greek Orthodox churches. Important composers include P. Bereketis (*d c* 1720), P. Peloponnesios (*d* 1778) and L. Protopsaltis (*fl* 18th century).

Bibl: M. Dragoumis, "The survival of Byzantine Chant in the Monophonic Music of the Modern Greek Church," *Studies in Eastern Chant 1* (1966) 9–36; F. Desby, "The Modes and Tuning in Neo-Byzantine Chant" (University of Southern California: Ph.D. diss., 1974). RGD

Green, Fred(erick) Pratt (*b* Roby near Liverpool 1903). Methodist minister, *hymn writer and poet. Having published 3 collections of *verse, Green turned his attention to writing hymn texts in the 1960s. His over 300 hymns have gained him recognition as a leader in the English hymn revival of the late 20th century.   CAD

Greene, Maurice (*b* London 1696; *d* there 1755). Composer. Organist at St. Paul's Cathedral in London and the *Chapel Royal, and professor of music at Cambridge. Greene produced *anthems (e.g., *Forty Select Anthems,* 1743), *oratorios and *organ pieces. *Boyce completed and published his *Cathedral Music* (first in 1760).   FKG

Gregorian chant. The principal *chant repertoire for the Latin Church of the Roman rite. It is preserved in manuscripts with *neumes from the 9th century, later with staff notation. The standard view is that the core of the repertoire was trans-

mitted from Rome to Frankish regions where it interacted with indigenous musical practice; codified in the *modal system, this chant was recorded first in Frankish manuscripts. After the 9th century it was attributed to *Gregory the Great, giving it the aura of authority but a misleading historical association; some consider "Frankish-Roman" a more suitable name. Largely displacing other repertoires, this chant came into use across a wide geographical area, yet maintained a remarkable degree of consistency from source to source.

It provided music for all *services of the medieval church: *mass, *divine office, various *occasional services and devotions. Stylistically, the repertoire lacks homogeneity, as it was composed over several centuries. Numerous forms evolved, from simple recitation types with much repetition to large formal structures consisting of complex melodic lines, some for alternation among solo and choral voices.

After the Council of *Trent, there were efforts to "revise" Gregorian chant according to humanistic ideals (see *Medicean edition); later a critical reexamination of the medieval manuscripts established the basis for the 19th-century "restoration" by *Solesmes (see *Vatican edition). The reforms of *Vatican II fully opened the *liturgy to vernacular language, in effect marginalizing the use of Latin chant in the RC church.

Bibl: H. Hucke, "Toward a New Historical View of Gregorian Chant," *JAMS* 33 (1980) 437–67; R. Crocker, "Liturgical Materials of Roman Chant," in *The Early Middle Ages to 1300,* ed. R. Crocker and D. Hiley (Oxford 1990) 111–45; D. Hiley, *Western Plainchant* (Oxford, 1993).   JMH

Gregorian Institute of America. See *GIA.

Gregory the Great, St. (*b* Rome *c* 540; *d* there 604). Pope (from 590) and last of the W "church fathers." He established a Roman monastery which followed the Rule of St. *Benedict, served as papal representative at Constantinople (579–86), and was adviser to Pope Pelagius whom he succeeded. His theological and spiritual writings were influential during the *Middle Ages. Since the 8th century he has been mistakenly associated with the compilation and editing of a *sacramentary and *antiphonary which bear his name, and with the composition of *Gregorian chant. The earliest mention of *Gregoriana carmina* (Latin, "Gregorian melodies") is a letter from Leo IV (*d* 855); the main source for the *chant legend is the life of Gregory compiled by John the Deacon of Montecassino in the 870s.

Gregory did decree that deacons should sing only the *gospel; all other *psalms and lessons were to be sung by those in lower orders. He probably organized a *schola cantorum* to train *cantors for worship. Other reforms during his pontificate included the incorporation of the 9-fold *Kyrie* and singing the *alleluia beyond the *Easter season.

Bibl: S.J.P. van Dijk, "St. Gregory Founder of the Urban Schola Cantorum," *Ephemerides Liturgicae* 77 (1963) 335–56; H. Hucke "Gregory the Great," *NGDMM* 8:699.   JKL

Grigny, Nicolas de (*b* Rheims 1672; *d* there 1703). Composer who served as organist at St. Denis Abbey (1693–95) outside of Paris and Rheims Cathedral (from *c* 1696). Grigny is considered the culmination of the French *Classical *organ school. He wrote *Premier livre d'orgue* (1699) containing organ settings of parts of the *ordinary of the mass *(Cunctipotens genitor)* and 5 Latin *hymns in *alternatim* style; J. S. *Bach copied the volume. Grigny's music is marked by complexity of *counterpoint and texture, the vivid use of contrasting colors and ornamentation, and greater use of pedal than his predecessors. He developed traditional forms, especially the *fugue, half of which have 5 parts.   MDJ

Grindel, Gracia (*b* Powers Lake ND 1943). *Hymn writer, poet and member of the *hymnal text committee of the Inter-Lutheran Commission on Worship (1973–78). Professor of pastoral theology at Luther Northwestern Theological Seminary since 1984, she is an advocate for the broadening of the musical literature among Lutheran churches.   LJC

Grosse Orgelmesse [German]. "Great Organ Mass." Common name for the *mass in E-flat (1766?) by F. J. *Haydn (Hob XII:4) for *choir, soloists and *orchestra, in which the *organ has an important part; contrasted with his *Kleine Orgelmesse.*   AWR

Gruber, Franz (*b* Upper Austria 1787; *d* Salzburg 1863). Organist and choir director. Gruber is thought to have composed the melody for *Stille Nacht* (German, "Silent Night"), on *Christmas eve 1818 at St. Nicholas church, Oberndorf; set for 2 soloists and *guitar. The melody is perhaps of earlier origin.   AWR

Grundtvig, Nicolai Frederik Severin (*b* Udby 1783; *d* Vartov 1872). Theologian, pastor and prolific *hymn writer. He published his hymnal *Sang-Värk til den Danske Kirke* in 1837.   RJS

Guéranger, Prosper (*b* Sablé-sur-Sarthe 1805; *d* Solesmes 1875). Diocesan then Benedictine priest who reestablished Benedictine life at *Solesmes. An ardent supporter of the Roman rite and its *chant, he was a significant contributor to the development of the modern liturgical renewal. He authored *Institutions Liturgiques* (3 vols., 1840–51), a call for a simple, uniform *liturgy and *L'année liturgique* (9 vols., 1841–66), meditations on the liturgical *year. See *Neo-Gallican chant.   VCF

Guilmant, Felix Alexandre (*b* Boulogne-sur-mer 1837; *d* Meudon 1911). Organist, composer and teacher. Organist at Ste. Trinité in Paris (1870–1901), he taught at the Paris Conservatory. With *Widor he established the French "*organ symphony." Guilmant also edited *Archives des maîtres de l'orgue des 16e–18e siècles.*   RDH

Guitar. A 6-stringed *instrument with fretted neck and resonating body; often considered a member of the lute family. It can be plucked or strummed. The classical 6-string guitar appeared in late-18th-century France or Italy; *Renaissance predecessors had 4 and 5 courses (sets) of strings. In wide use as a *folk music instrument, it was established as an instrument for art music by Tárrega (*d* 1909) and Segovia (*d* 1987). In the 1960s acoustic guitars with nylon or steel strings appeared in both RC and Protestant worship as part of the *folk mass phenomenon; electric guitars became more common with the emergence of *Christian rock music. Meanwhile, Mexican *mariachi* music, with guitars and brass, was adapted for liturgical use in many parts of the US.   MEC

Guitar mass. See *folk mass.

H

Ḥad gadya. See *Chad gadya.

Haftorah <haftarah> (reading) [Hebrew]. "Conclusion." A reading from one of the prophetic books of the Hebrew Bible which follows the *Torah reading in the synagogue service. The content of the reading relates to the weekly Torah reading. The melodic intonation follows the same system of *cantillation as the Torah reading, but with a different melodic formula.   DMR-SDC

Haggadah [Hebrew]. "Telling." In a narrow sense, the text which retells the Passover story recited at the *Pesach *seder (see *Mah nishtanah). By extension, the collection of *blessings, prayers, rabbinic commentary, *liturgy, *psalms and songs which provides the setting for this remembrance and serves as the basis for the home ritual that takes place on the first night of Pesach or the first 2 nights for those living outside of the land of Israel. The rabbinic commentary is taken from the Talmud and other sources. The psalm portion is the *Hallel. The songs are based on allegorical stories that tell the story of the holiday or other parts of biblical Jewish history (see *Addir Bimluchah, *Addir Hu, *Chad gadya, *Echad mi yodea). Jews of various regions in *Ashkenazic and *Sephardic traditions have different melodies for these songs. The text retelling the Passover story is often recited with a *chant that also varies by region. For some Ashkenazic Jews a particular *mode may be used (see *Jewish prayer modes).

Bibl: H. Coopersmith and M. Levin, *Haggadah* (New York, 1968).   MLK

Hagiasmatarion [Greek]. "Book of consecrations" [Slavonic trebnik <molitvenik>, "book of needs"]. The Byzantine liturgical *book containing the sacramental mysteries, consecrations and *blessings, prayers and *services for various occasions. Equivalent to a small *euchologion.   DMP

Hagios ho Theos [Greek; Slavonic Svjatyj Bozhe]. "Holy is God." The *incipit of the Byzantine *Trisagion.   DMP

Hail holy queen. An English *hymn text paraphrasing the *Marian antiphon *Salve regina*. See *Marian music.   RTR

Hail Mary [Latin *Ave Maria*]. A Christian prayer based on Luke 1:28, 42 combined with a non-biblical appeal for Mary's intercession. The present prayer form dates from the 15th century. It has been set in many *chant genres and by innumerable composers from *Josquin to *Stravinsky. See *Marian music. RTR

Hakkafot (sing. **hakkafa**) [Hebrew]. "Processions." The tradition of removing the Torah scrolls from the ark and processing through the synagogue. This ritual is performed 7 times on *Simchat Torah. Each *hakkafa* is accompanied by the chanting of prescribed *psalms. To these are added songs and *hymns of a joyous nature.   DMR-SDC

Ha-levi, Judah. See *Judah Ha-levi.

Hall, Thomas (*b* 1791; *d* 1875). *Organ builder primarily associated with Philadelphia and New York. In 1820 he built the organ for the RC Cathedral in Baltimore, described at the time as the largest organ in the US.   JWK

Hallel [Hebrew]. "Praise." (1) Pss 113–118. In Jewish usage these are said immediately following the *Amidah on *Pesach, *Shavuot, *Sukkot and *Chanukkah. A shortened version of *Hallel* (or "Half-Hallel," which omits the first parts of Pss 115 and 116) is recited on *Rosh Chodesh and on the intermediate and last days of *Pesach*. The recitation of *Hallel* by Jews is preceded by a *blessing. Jewish congregations stand while saying *Hallel* because it is a testimony to God's wondrous deeds and powers. *Hallel* is not recited in the evening except for the first night of *Pesach* because the climax of the Passover miracle took place at night and Ps 114 makes specific reference to the Exodus from Egypt; thus, Pss 113–118 are called the "Egyptian *Hallel*." The *Hallel* is part of the *haggadah* text and recited at the *seder. In Christian worship, these psalms were traditionally prominent at Sunday *lauds and *vespers, and Monday vespers.

(2) Ps 136 is alternately known as the "Great *Hallel*," as it is a *hymn of praise in the form of a *litany. In Jewish worship it is featured during the *Pesach* *seder.

(3) Pss 145–150 are alternately known as the "Daily *Hallel*," as they are a standard part of *shacharit. In Christian worship Pss 148–150 are a traditional part of lauds.   MLK

Halleluyah <*halleluiah, hallelujah*> [Hebrew]. "Praise to God." An *acclamation appearing 23 times in the book of Psalms. Rabbinic literature mentions it as the most exalted form in praise of God (*Jerusalem Talmud Sukkot* iii, 54a). According to Talmudic tradition *halleluyah* is used as a *refrain after each verse of *Hallel. The most popular musical setting is the "Hallelujah chorus" from *Handel's *Messiah*. *Lewandowski's *"Halleluyah"* based on Ps 150 is reminiscent of Handel's setting. See *alleluia.   MLK

Hallock, Peter (*b* Kent WA 1924). Organist and choirmaster at St. Mark's Cathedral in Seattle (1951–91). In addition to many choral and instrumental compositions, his liturgical works include the *Ionian Psalter,* widely used by Episcopalians and Lutherans.   AJL

Hammerschmidt, Andreas (*b* Brüx 1611–12; *d* Zittau 1675). Popular Protestant organist and composer. He worked nearly his entire professional life (from 1639) at St. John Church in Zittau, where he sought to improve the music of the church and city after the Thirty Years War. He wrote several *hymn tunes and produced 14 collections of music, mostly spiritual *concertos for the liturgical *year, including his noted *Dialogi* (1645).   MPB

Hampton, Calvin (*b* Kittanning PA 1938; *d* Port Charlotte FL 1984). Organist and composer. He was trained at Oberlin Conservatory and Syracuse University. Hampton served as organist and choirmaster at Calvary Episcopal Church in New York (1963–83). His compositions often fuse classical and popular elements.   AJL

Hampton University Ministers Conference and Choir Directors and Organist Guild Worship. Organized by African Americans in 1914 for ministers, in 1934 choir directors and organists joined in this annual 1-week event. Held at Hampton University (VA) the conference has a nondenominational, ecumenical focus, offering workshops on all facets of *church music and pastor-musician relationships, culminating with a *sacred music concert.   MWC

Handbells. A tuned *bell, cup-shaped with flared end, clapper and handle, held in the hand for ringing. Handbells are often played by a group or *choir with each ringer responsible for 2 diatonic notes plus sharps and flats, in octave sets from 2 to 5 octaves. Playing involves a stroke to sound the bell and then damping, or stopping, the sound.

Handbells are used in many religious traditions. In Christian worship they are particularly associated with festive *occasional services (e.g., weddings), seasons of the liturgical *year (e.g., *Christmas), and feasts (e.g., *Easter). Employed alone or in combination with voices and/or other *instruments, they may be used for sustaining *plainsong *intonations, playing melodies and *descants, accompanying *hymns, articulating *acclamations, or providing *preludes.

Bibl: J. Folkening, *Handbells in the Liturgical Service* (St. Louis, 1984). RKW

Handel, George Frideric (*b* Halle 1685; *d* London 1759). Composer. He studied oboe, harpsichord, *organ and *counterpoint with *Zachow in Halle. After a year at Halle's University he became violinist in Hamburg's German opera where he wrote his first operas. In 1706 Handel went to Florence, Venice, Rome and Naples to learn the Italian style of composition first hand. There he composed *church music including the *psalm setting *Dixit Dominus* (1707) and *oratorio *La resurrezione* (1708). He became *Kapellmeister* in Hanover (1710). When England liked his opera *Rinaldo* (1711), he returned there in 1712 and stayed, gaining royal favor with works like the *Utrecht Te Deum* (1713). From 1720–41 he composed and managed operas for London. His lasting legacy for England were oratorios on biblical material, particularly the *Messiah* (1741). A naturalized English citizen, he was buried in Westminster Abbey.

Handel's secular works include 46 operas, 100 solo *cantatas, 20 duets and numerous instrumental *concertos, sonatas and suites, the most famous of which is his *Water Music* (1717?). His *religious music includes 32 oratorios, 3 psalms, 5 *Te Deum*s and 20 *anthems.
Bibl: P. H. Lang, *George Frideric Handel* (New York, 1966); C. Hogwood, *Handel* (London, 1984).   JLB

Handl <Händl>, **Jakob** <Gallus, Jacobus> (*b* Ribniča? 1550; *d* Prague 1591). Composer and Cisterican monk. Handl was *Kapellmeister* at Olmütz and *Kantor* in Prague. He composed 20 *masses and 445 *motets (most published in the 4-volume *Opus musicum,* 1586–91).   FKG

Handy, W(illiam) C(hristopher) (*b* Florence AL 1873; *d* New York 1958). Composer, conductor and publisher. He gained fame for his '"Memphis Blues" and "St. Louis Blues." Besides popularizing the blues, Handy also wrote *spirituals. Important publications include his *Collection of Negro Spirituals* (1938) and autobiography, *Father of the Blues* (1941).   RKW

Hanff, Johann Nikolaus (*b* Wechmar 1665; *d* Schleswig winter 1711–12). Composer. Organist in Hamburg, then at Schleswig Cathedral. A master composer of *chorale preludes (wrote 6), he influenced J. S. *Bach's composing of the same. Hanff also wrote 3 *cantatas. FKG

Hanson, Howard (Harold) (*b* Wahoo NE 1896; *d* Rochester NY 1981). Neo-Romantic composer of Swedish ancestry, teacher and advocate of American music. He served as director of Eastman

School of Music (1924–64) which he developed into one of finest US conservatories. Influenced by Sibelius, Grieg and Respighi (his teacher), he frequently employed *chorale melodies and *Gregorian chant in works, among which is a 5th symphony (*Sinfonia Sacra,* 1954) on the crucifixion and resurrection according to St. John.   CFS

Ḥanukkah. See *Chanukkah.*

Harbor, Rawn (*b* Greensville SC 1947). Composer and arranger of RC *liturgical music in African American *gospel style, pianist, vocalist and choral director. A primary innovator for integrating African American music, spirituality and RC *liturgy, he served as a consultant and composer for the *hymnal *Lead Me, Guide Me* (1987).   MEM

Harkness, Robert (*b* Bendigo, Australia 1880; *d* London 1961). Revival pianist and *gospel *hymn composer. The accompanist for C. *Alexander for 12 years, Harkness established the gospel hymn piano accompaniment style that is still standard. He also composed over 2,000 gospel hymns.   DWM

Harmonia Sacra [Latin]. "Sacred harmony." (1) A 2-vol. English *hymn and *anthem collection, published by H. Playford (1688 and 1693 respectively); the last edition was published in 1726. It contains settings by *Blow, *Clarke, *Croft, *Humfrey and *Purcell.
(2) An American oblong *shape-note *tune book using *fasola solmization, published by J. Funk (Shenandoah Valley VA, 1851). Originally titled *Genuine Church Music* (1832), it was changed to *Harmonia Sacra* with the 5th edition

and *New Harmonia Sacra* with the 14th edition. It is the oldest shape-note collection in continuous use.   RJS

Harmoniemesse [German]. "Harmony Mass." Common name for *Hadyn's last *mass (Hob XXII:14, 1802) in B-flat for *choir, soloists and *orchestra. Written for Princess Maria's nameday, the name is based on the rich use of wind *instruments in the mass.   AWR

Harmonium <reed organ>. A free-reed *keyboard instrument invented 1810–20. Metal tongues vibrate on pitch as air is forced across them either by compression or suction. It gained popularity as a substitute for the pipe *organ in churches and homes (especially for *hymn accompaniment). Some composers wrote directly for it (e.g., Dvořák, R. Strauss).   MDJ

Harris, Renatus [René] (*b* France *c* 1652; *d* Bristol? 1724). The most prominent member of an English *organ building family, which included his father (Thomas) and sons (Renatus and John). A youthful experience in France significantly influenced his later work in England, some examples of which survive (e.g., Bristol Cathedral, 1685).   PKG

Harris, William Henry (*b* London 1883; *d* there 1973). English organist and composer who served New College and Christ Church in Oxford, then St. George's Chapel in Windsor. A professor of *organ at London's Royal College of Music (1921–53) he wrote *church music and organ works. Harris was knighted in 1954.   FKG

Harrison, George Donald (*b* Huddersfield, Yorkshire 1889; *d* New York 1956).

*Organ builder with *Willis in England and *Aeolian-Skinner in Boston. He was the most prominent leader of the organ reform movement which reintroduced historic tonal concepts into the modern organ.   JBW

Harwood, Basil (*b* Woodhouse, Gloucestershire 1859; *d* London 1949). Organist and composer who served Ely Cathedral and Christ Church Oxford. He wrote *organ sonatas and many *anthems.   FKG

Hashkiveinu <*Hashkivenu*> [Hebrew]. "Cause us to lie down." A prayer for protection through the night which serves as the second *benediction before the *Shema* at *ma'ariv*. Many cantorial and choral settings have been composed for this prayer; these are not consistent with regard to any particular *mode. The mode of this prayer reflects the occasion of the *ma'ariv* being chanted: weeknight, *Sabbath eve, festival or *High Holidays. This emphasizes that a designated *nusach* does not depend on the prayer text itself, but rather the occasion on which the prayer is chanted.   IAG

Hasidic <Chassidic> **music.** *Hasidim* (Hebrew, "pious ones") are members of a religious movement within Judaism that emerged in mid-18th century Poland around Rabbi Yisra'el Ba'al Shem Tov (*d* 1760). Rooted in the mystical tradition (see *Kabbalah), *Hasidim* are led by charismatic leaders *(rebbes)* who shape the group in their devotion to God through joy. Music plays an important role in Hasidic rituals.

Hasidic *rebbes* give music a higher status than words because a tune can alter one's mood. Since music can be used for holy or idolatrous practices, intention is important to achieve the desired elevated state (e.g., a non-Jewish melody can be used for Jewish purposes with the proper intention). Music is awarded a significant status because of its effect on the soul; thus Rebbe Nachman of Bratslav teaches that music has the capacity to elevate one to prophetic inspiration.

Since the music (not text) is significant, a wordless tune (see *niggun) conveys the essential emotional ingredient. Nonsense syllables ("ay-yai-yai" or "bum-bum-bum") are used in the singing. Melodies are typically in 2 to 4 sections with the highest and most intense portions in the 2nd or 3rd sections; the first section may be repeated at the end. Often sections may be contrasted by the use of different *Jewish prayer modes.

During the second half of the 20th century *Hasidim* follow European practices in the synagogue; but for home or individual use during the week, contemporary popular styles of music are increasingly employed (see *Jewish popular music).
Bibl: V. Pasternak, *Songs of Chasidim,* 2 vols. (Cedarhurst, 1968); A. Hadju and Y. Mazur, "Hasidism: The Musical Tradition of Hasidism," *EJ* 7:1421–32. MLK

Hassler, Hans Leo (*b* Nuremberg 1562; *d* Frankfurt 1612). Church musician. After studying with A. *Gabrieli, he served as *Kapellmeister* to the Saxon court in Dresden (from 1608). His early works were written for RC worship; later works for Lutheran use include *Psalmen und christliche Gesange* (1607) in fugal style and the *Kirchengesange . . . simpliciter gesetzt* (1608) in *cantional style. His secular love song *"Mein G'müt ist mir verwirret"* ultimately was associated with the passion text "O sacred head now wounded." CFS

Hastings, Frank. See *Hook & Hastings.

Hatikvah [Hebrew]. "The Hope." A *hymn which serves as the national anthem for the State of Israel. Written in 1878 by N. H. Imber; the 9-stanza poem was adopted by the First Zionist Congress in Basel (1897). *Idelsohn collected numerous occurrences of the melody showing how it was adapted in various *folk traditions and in *Sephardic *liturgy. Many note the strong similarity of the *Hatikvah* melody to Smetana's "The Moldau" from *Má vlast* (1874–79). Some have adapted this melody for use in parts of Jewish *liturgy (e.g., *Yigdal*).
Bibl: M. Nulman, *Concise Encyclopedia of Jewish Music* (New York, 1975) 100. MLK

Ḥatimah. See *Chatimah.

Haugen, Marty (*b* Zumbrota MN 1950). Liturgical composer who writes especially for Lutheran and RC worship. His works include *hymn tunes, *psalm settings, concert pieces and *masses, including the widely employed *Mass of Creation* (1985). VCF

Hauptmann, Moritz (*b* Dresden 1792; *d* Leipzig 1868). Composer, theorist and educator. He worked in Dresden, Vienna, Kassel and as *Kantor* in Leipzig. With others he founded the *Bach-Gesellschaft* (1850), editing the first 3 vols. of J. S. *Bach's works for that society. MPB

Hauptwerk. See *great organ.

Havdalah [Hebrew]. "Separation, distinction." The Jewish ceremony of *blessings recited at the end of a holiday, *Sabbath or festival. Conducted after sundown, it usually consists of 4 blessings: of wine, spices, light and separation. The blessing of separation mentions 4 separations: between the holy and the profane, light and darkness, Israel and the nations, and the 7th day of rest and the 6 working days. ISK

Hawkins, Edwin R. (*b* Oakland CA 1943). African American *gospel composer, arranger, singer, pianist and recording artist. His compositional style, inspired by *jazz and popular music, helped define contemporary gospel style. He introduced a multiracial audience to African American gospel music with his recording of "O Happy Day." MEM

Hawkins, Walter (*b* Oakland CA 1949). Composer, arranger of African American *gospel music, recording artist and minister (*Church of God in Christ). The brother of E. *Hawkins, he founded the Love Center Church and Choir. Walter is a leading composer/performer in the "contemporary" gospel style. MEM

Haydn, Franz Joseph (*b* Rohrau 1732; *d* Vienna 1809). Composer. His life spanned the *Classical era; with *Mozart he was one of the chief architects of the Classical style. Although his primary achievement lies in the genres of symphonic and chamber music, he also composed some of the most important *sacred music of the late 18th century.

Haydn's first surviving compositions, including a diminutive *Missa brevis* in F (1749?), date from near the end of his decade as a choirboy at St. Stephen's in Vienna. After leaving the *choir he worked as a freelance musician while studying composition; a *Salve Regina* in E (1756) demonstrates his growing accomplishment. In 1760 or 1761, he was engaged as Vice *Kapellmeister* to Prince Anton Esterházy; the Esterházy family remained his patron past the turn of the century. The enormous *Mariazellermesse* dates from 1766, the year he was promoted to full *Kapellmeister*. A *Stabat mater* (1767), 4 further *masses and *c* 12 *motets followed in the years up to 1782.

In the 1780s Haydn's intense activity as a composer, arranger and director of opera at the Esterházy court (and his increasing international reputation as a composer of symphonies and chamber-music) intervened in this productivity; there are no further sacred works until the 1790s. In 1790 his duties for the Esterházy family significantly decreased; he moved to Vienna and was free to make 2 highly successful tours to London. Every year from 1796 to 1802 (except 1800) he produced a large-scale *mass for the Esterházy court (including the *Nelson* and *Creation* masses): works which define the late classical sacred style. Also from these years came his famous *EMPEROR's HYMN (1797), The *Creation* (1798), the choral adaptation of his own *Seven Last Words* (originally an orchestral work from the mid-1780s) and the *Te Deum* in C (1800).

Bibl: K. Geiringer, "The Small Sacred Works by Haydn in the Esterházy Archives at Eisenstadt," *MQ* 45 (1959) 460–72; M. Chusid, "Some Observations on the Liturgy, Text and Structure in Haydn's Late Masses," *Studies in Eighteenth-century Music,* ed. H. C. Robbins Landon

(New York, 1970) 125–35; H. C. Robbins Landon, *Haydn,* 5 vols. (London, 1976–80).   AJL

Haydn, (Johann) Michael (*b* Lower Austria 1737; *d* Salzburg 1806). Composer and younger brother of F. J. *Haydn. A choirboy at St. Stephen's in Vienna, he spent his life in the service of Salzburg's archbishop (from 1763). A prolific liturgical composer, his Latin works include over 36 *masses, *graduals for the entire year, *offertories for most of the year, several settings of the *Te Deum, *litanies and *vespers. His *antiphonary (1792) is an example of simplified, reformed *Gregorian chant. Vernacular *liturgical music for *choir includes masses, offertories, *motets, vespers, *psalms and 8 *Singmesse settings (that with a text by Kohlbrenner was widely translated and remains in use today). He also edited a congregational *hymnal (1790).

Bibl: C. H. Sherman and T. D. Thomas, *Johann Michael Haydn* (Stuyvesant, 1993).   AWR

Hayom harat olam [Hebrew]. "This is the day of the world's birth." A prayer recited on *Rosh Hashanah after the blowing of the *shofar for each of the 3 sections of *musaf. It petitions God for compassion, likening God's mercy to a parent's love on this "birthday of the world." There are numerous cantorial and choral settings, as well as *folk tunes for this prayer. BES

Ḥazak ḥazak venithazeik. See *Chazak chazak venitchazeik.*

Ḥazzan. See *chazzan.*

Healing. See *Mi sheberach.*

Heiligmesse [German]. "Holy Mass." F. J. *Haydn's *mass in B-flat (Hob XXII:10, 1796) for *choir, soloists and *orchestra. Named either for quoting the song *"Heilig, heilig"* (German, "Holy, holy") at the beginning of the *Sanctus, or for its dedication to recently beatified Capuchin Blessed (German *Heilig*) Bernard of Offida.   AWR

Heiratikon [Greek]. "Priestly book." Byzantine liturgical *book for the priest containing the *divine liturgy and the *office. See *eucbologion.*   DMP

Helfman, Max (*b* Radzin, Poland 1901; *d* Dallas 1963). Composer, conductor and teacher. After studies at Philadelphia's Curtis Institute he conducted many Jewish and non-Jewish *choirs. From 1952 he worked in Los Angeles at Sinai Temple, the Brandeis Arts Institute and the University of Judaism. His output of Jewish music included writing and arranging liturgical, Israeli and Yiddish works. His settings of *Shema Koleinu* and *Haskeiveinu* are commonly heard in US synagogues. These and other pieces integrate *Jewish prayer modes and other *modes with 20th-century techniques (e.g., quartal harmonies, the use of motives) in well-crafted compositions.   MLK

Helmore, Thomas (*b* Kidderminster 1811; *d* London 1890). Anglican *precentor, teacher and priest. He introduced St. Mark's College in Chelsea to unaccompanied *chant and *anthems, and English parishes to choral *services. He edited *Psalter Noted* (1849) and *Hymnal Noted* (1851–54), the latter with *Neale. PHW

Henrici, Christian Friedrich <Picander> (*b* Stolpen 1700; *d* Leipzig 1764). Postal administrator, poet and librettist (under the pen name of Picander). He collaborated with J. S. *Bach for 20 years as librettist for *cantatas and the texts of the *St. Matthew and *St. Mark Passions.   MPB

Henry VIII (*b* Greenwich 1491; *d* Windsor 1547). King of England who sang, played lute, *organ and virginal. His 34 compositions were mostly homophonic and dance-like; he also wrote a *motet and a now lost *mass. An important patron of the arts, the *Chapel Royal flourished under him. His break with Rome (1533) eventually gave rise to the Anglican Church and a vast new arena for composers of *sacred music. In 1543 he formally authorized the *Sarum use for England.   DCI

Heothinon. See *Euangelion heothinon* and *Idiomelon heothinon*.

Herzogenberg, (Leopold) Heinrich (Pico de Peccaduc) <Freiherr von> (*b* Graz 1843; *d* Wiesbaden 1900). Composer and RC church musician. He led (1875) the *Bach Gesellschaft*. A lifelong friend of *Brahms, he was particularly interested in the music of J. S. *Bach and *Schütz. Herzogenberg wrote much *sacred music, including *oratorios and *cantatas.   CFS

Hesperinos [Greek; Slavonic *vechernya*]. "Vespers." The principal evening *service of the Byzantine Church; also called *lychnikon* ("lamp-lighting service"). Its basic order is: opening rite, Ps 104, variable *psalmody, Pss 141, 142, 130 and 117 (the *lamp-lighting psalms; the last 6 to 10

*verses intercalated with *stichera), processional entrance with the censer, *Phos hilaron*, daily *prokeimenon*, on feast days the *ektene*, *hymn "Vouchsafe, O Lord," second part of the *great doxology (see *doxologia*), *aitesis*, *aposticha*, *Canticle of Simeon, *Trisagion* and *Our Father, *apolytikion*, at daily *hesperinos* the *ektene*, and dismissal (*apolysis*).

On major feasts a series of *stichera* (*lite stichera*) are inserted after the *aitesis* with a solemn *ektene* invoking the saints. Bread, wheat, wine and oil are blessed at the end of feast day *hesperinos* and distributed to the people the next morning at *orthros*. At feast day *hesperinos* readings from the Hebrew Bible (*paremia*), usually 3 in number, are inserted after the *prokeimenon* and before the *ektene*. On *Christmas, *Epiphany, the Annunciation (March 25) and *Easter *hesperinos* is celebrated up to the *prokeimenon;* then the *divine liturgy is immediately joined to the service. In Great *Lent *hesperinos* is joined to the *presanctified divine liturgy.

Bibl: N. Uspensky, *Evening Worship* (Crestwood NY, 1985); R. Taft, *The Liturgy of the Hours in East and West* (Collegeville, 1986) 273–91.   DMP

Hessenberg, Kurt (*b* Frankfurt 1908; *d* there 1994). Composer and professor of music theory and composition at Frankfurt's Musikhochschule. His works, which encompass almost all forms except opera, include many choral and *organ compositions.   PKG

Hexapsalmos [Greek; Slavonic *shestopsalmie*]. "The 6 psalms." The fixed *psalmody at the beginning of Byzantine *orthros which introduces the variable psalmody. Currently it is comprised of

Pss 3, 38, 63, 88, 103 and 143; there are ancient references to Pss 3 and 63 as morning psalms. A *hexapsalmos* also exists for *apodeipnon,* comprised of Pss 4, 6, 13, 25, 31 and 91.   DMP

High Holidays. See *Yamim Noraim.*

High mass. A popular term used prior to *Vatican II to describe *mass in which the *proper and *ordinary of the mass were chanted or sung, but which required no subdeacon or deacon. See *Missa cantata.*   VCF

Hilary of Poitiers, St. (*b* Poitiers *c* 315; *d* there *c* 367). Bishop, theologian and *hymn writer. A collection of hymns is ascribed to him; only 3 fragmentary hymn texts are extant (*Ante saecula qui manes, Fefellit saevam* and *Adae carnis gloriosa*). It is unclear how these were to be used in the *liturgy, if at all. While rhetorically and theologically sophisticated, his hymns never achieved the popularity of those by *Ambrose.   JMJ

Hildegard of Bingen (*b* Bermersheim near Mainz 1098; *d* Rupertsberg near Bingen 1179). Abbess, author and composer. Born of nobility, she entered a convent when she was 8, becoming superior there in 1136, later founding a new convent at Rupertsberg (*c* 1147–50), then a daughter house (*c* 1165). In 1141 Hildegard had her first vision. She recorded her visions, wrote lives of saints, homilies, exegetical works and a 2-part encyclopedia on medicine. Between 1150–60 she composed and edited *Symphonia armonie celestium revelationum* (Latin, "Symphony of the Harmony of Celestial Revelations"). These 77 poems with *monophonic music, intended for liturgi-

cal use, included 34 *antiphons, 14 *responsories, 3 *hymns, 5 *sequences and a *Kyrie. Her poetry is marked by its unpredictability and daring imagery; her music is characterized by recurring melodic formulas, wide leaps, *melismas and modal irregularities.   EBF

Hiller <Hüller>, **Johann Adam** (*b* Wendisch-Ossig 1728; *d* Leipzig 1804). Composer. He studied with *Homilius. In Leipzig (by 1758) he brought orchestral concerts to a new level of excellence. There he was director of the *Gewandhaus* (1781–85), then *Kantor at St. Thomas (1789–1801). He originated the *Singspiel,* composing 14; he also wrote *Lieder,* instrumental music, sacred songs and *hymns.   JLB

Hillert, Richard (*b* Granton WI 1923). Composer and teacher. He studied at *Concordia College in River Forest IL (1951), later professor of music there (from 1959). Hillert received a doctorate in composition from Northwestern (1968). His compositions include chamber and orchestral works, sacred *cantatas, choral pieces, *holy communion setting and *hymn tunes.   JLB

Hindemith, Paul (*b* Hanau 1895; *d* Frankfurt 1963). Composer, conductor, teacher and author. A violinist in Frankfurt's opera orchestra he was also violist in the Amar String Quartet. Hindemith taught composition in Berlin (1927–35), fleeing when the Nazis banned his music, eventually accepting a professorship at Yale (1940). After the war he conducted and taught in Europe, settling in Zurich (1953). A prolific composer across the range of vocal and instrumental forms (including *Gebrauchsmusik*), his few religious works include a *mass (1963) and 13 Latin *motets.   JLB

Hineni <*Hinneni*> [Hebrew]. "Here I am." The *incipit of several prayers. Best known is *Hineni he ani mi ma'as* ("Behold here I am, meager in deeds") recited by the *chazzan before *musaf on *Rosh Hashanah and *Yom Kippur. In Reform congregations, it is recited on *Rosh Hashanah* evening before *Barechu. A personal prayer of supplication of unknown authorship, it asks that despite the unworthiness of the *chazzan,* God will accept the prayers on behalf of the congregation. Not restricted to any musical *mode or motif, many cantorial *recitatives have been written to this prayer; the majority begin in the *ahavah rabba mode.   IAG

Hirmologion <*heirmologion*> [Greek; Slavonic *irmolog*]. "Book of Irmosi." Byzantine liturgical *book containing the *hirmosi (initial *hymns of the *kanon odes) grouped according to the *octoechos. This arrangement is for the convenience of the *cantor since the *hirmos* serves as the melodic model for the *troparia of the *kanon* and usually only the *incipit of the *hirmos* is given in the text.   DMP

Hirmos <*heirmos*> (pl. **hirmosi**) [Greek; Slavonic *irmos*]. "Chain." The first *stanza of an *ode (a series of *troparia intercalated with the scriptural *canticles of the *kanon) in Byzantine *orthros. Thus it serves as the link or "chain" between the canticle and the *troparia* that follow. The theme of the *hirmos* is always the text of the canticle, while the *troparia* are about the feast or the saint being cele-

brated. An *hirmos* sung at the end of an ode is called a *katabasia.   DMP

Hispanic chant. See *Old Spanish chant.

Hispanic worship music. A broad category of music, used by Spanish-speaking people of various backgrounds, employed in the worship of N American churches. Represented in this category is music from Spain, Latin-America, Mexico, the Caribbean, N and S America.

The liturgical reforms of *Vatican II fueled the use of the vernacular and popular musical idioms among Hispanics, a traditionally RC population. Spanish-speaking composers of N America tapped into folkloric resources creating *Misas de *Mariachi, Misas Rancheras, Misa del Cante *Flamenco* and so forth. Melodies combined with the traditional forms and rhythms of *boleros, *canción, huapangos, merengue,* etc. were utilized to set liturgical, scriptural and religious texts. Hispanic Pentecostal congregations often sing short, popular *choruses called *coritos.* These are sometimes collected into books, but more often committed to memory and passed on orally. What Pentecostals call *coritos* are often referred to as *estribillos* by other Protestant Hispanics (e.g., Methodists).

These musical forms were influenced by the socio-political history and artistic expression of the many countries of Spanish speaking people in the W hemisphere. In the 16th–17th centuries, a fusion took place between indigenous, African and Iberian elements, creating a cultural and musical *mestizaje* (Spanish/Indian, "mixture"). The introduction of European instruments spawned new regional varieties. African rhythms wed to traditional Spanish melodies were accentuated and defined by the use of the marimba, bongos, maracas, claves and other percussion instruments. This fusion, accomplished in a myriad of different ways among diverse groups, has contributed to what could be considered a transnational musical identity, often defined in the popular culture as "Latin" or *Latino*.

The phenomenon of cultural transformation continues. Some musical elements are borrowed, others lost, changes are made and new idioms arise. Hispanic music has gone through a process of enculturation, hybridization and symbiosis. Some styles can be identified as specific to particular peoples, while others have been adopted across national boundaries. Thus liturgical music in the style of the *huapango, merengue* and *son* can be claimed by the peoples of Argentina, Brazil, Chile, Colombia, Cuba, the Dominican Republic, Mexico, Panama and others.

One of the first Spanish-language RC *hymnals published in the US was *Cánticos de Gracias y Alabanza* (1982), soon to be superceded by the hymnal *Flor y Canto* (1989); more recently *Cantos del Pueblo de Dios* (1998) appeared. The Lutherans, who published a Spanish translation of parts of the *Lutheran Book of Worship* (1978) as *Liturgia Luterana* (1983), later published *El Pueblo de Dios Canta* (1989), then *Libro de Liturgia y Cántico* (1998). Methodists published 2 collections entitled *Celebremos* (1979, 1983) and more recently published *Mil voces para celebrar* (1996). The Episcopalians, Presbyterians and the United Church of Christ jointly published *El Himnario* (1998). This burgeoning of Spanish-language

worship resources will only increase as this segment of the community continues to grow and their various cultural expressions are embraced by the Christian churches.

Bibl: G. Behague, *Music in Latin America* (Englewood Cliffs NJ, 1979); Y. Moreno Rivas, *Historia de la música popular mexicana* (Mexico, DF 1989); E. Aponte, "*Coritos* as Active Symbol in Latino Protestant Popular Religion," *Journal of Hispanic/Latino Theology* 2 (1995) 57–66; J. González, ed., *¡Alabadle!: Hispanic Christian Worship* (Nashville, 1996).   MFR

Historia (pl. **historiae**) [Latin]. "History." (1) The musical setting of a biblical story, particularly in Protestant Germany in the 16th–18th centuries. Popular subjects were Jesus' birth, *passion and resurrection (e.g., *Schütz's resurrection and Christmas *historiae*).

(2) A term for a reading from the Hebrew Bible or biographies of saints chanted during the *office.

(3) An office *responsory.

(4) A *rhymed office.   DWM

Historicus [Latin]. "Historian." The narrator's part in a 17th–18th century Latin *oratorio, usually sung by a soloist. DWM

Hodaah. See *Modim.

Hodie [Latin]. "Today." (1) The *incipit of the *Magnificat *antiphon for *Christmas day. The text has been set by many composers, including *Palestrina and *Sweelinck.

(2) A Christmas *cantata by *Vaughan Williams for voices and orchestra, first performed in 1954.   MSD

Hoelty-Nickel, Theodore (*b* Güstrow, Germany 1894; *d* Valparaiso IN 1986). Lutheran pastor and musician. Educated in Australia and Europe, he served on the faculty at Iowa's Luther College (1928–43) then *Valparaiso University (from 1943). He was the founder of the Valparaiso University Church Music Seminar. VEG

Hoffman, Elisha Albright (*b* Orwigsburg PA 1839; *d* Chicago 1929). *Hymn writer, pastor, publisher and music editor. He wrote *c* 2,000 *gospel hymns and Sunday school songs, including "Are you washed in the blood" and "Leaning on the everlasting arms." RJS

Hofhaimer, Paul (*b* Radstadt 1459; *d* Salzburg 1537). Leading court organist (at Salzburg Cathedral from 1519) and *Renaissance composer in Austria and Germany. He wrote numerous *polyphonic settings of vernacular *hymns. AWR

Holden, Oliver (*b* Shirley MA 1765; *d* Charlestown MA 1844). Composer, Puritan pastor and *singing school teacher. He wrote 235 compositions including *hymn tunes; his CORONATION is one of the oldest hymn tunes by an American in continuous use. Holden also compiled and edited *tune books. RJS

Holst, Gustav Theodore (*b* Cheltenham 1874; *d* London 1934). Pianist, trombonist, composer and teacher. A student of *Stanford at the Royal College of Music, Holst eventually joined the same faculty; previous to that he held various teaching positions including one at Morley College where he conducted the first modern performance of *Purcell's *Fairie Queen.* Like friend *Vaughan Williams, Holst was influenced by English *folk songs. Besides operas and orchestral works he wrote vocal *sacred music including an *Ave Maria,* choral *hymns (e.g., *Hymn of Jesus*), *psalms and *motets. FKG

Holtkamp, Walter Henry (*b* St. Marys OH 1894; *d* Cleveland 1962). *Organ builder, president of Holtkamp Organ Co. (from 1931), and leader of the organ reform movement in the US. JBW

Holy Communion. Name for both the eucharistic rite and consecrated elements used in that rite. The term is especially common among Lutherans. See *communion, *eucharist, *Lord's supper and *mass. RDH

Holy, holy. See *Kedushah, *Sanctus and *Trisagion.*

Holy Rollers. A pejorative term for members of *Pentecostal congregations which focuses on their physical movement in worship, especially their rolling on the floor when under the influence of the Holy Spirit. HCB

Holy Thursday. See *year, liturgical.

Holy Week. The last week in *Lent, immediately preceding *Easter. Because it encompasses the most important days of the Christian liturgical *year (see *Triduum) celebrating the passion and death of Christ, it is a week of solemn and unique *liturgies and worship music. EBF

Homer, Charlotte G. See *Gabriel, Charles H.

Homilius, Gottfried August (*b* Rosenthal 1714; *d* Dresden 1785). Composer and organist who studied both *organ and composition with J. S. *Bach. He was *Kantor of the Dresden Kreuzkirche (1755) and music director of Dresden's 3 principal churches. With *Doles, Homilius was the most important Lutheran church composer of his day, writing over 200 *cantatas, 60 *motets and many *organ works. CFS

Homme armé, L' [French]. "The armed man." A popular 15th-century secular song, used from the mid-15th to the early 17th centuries by many composers (e.g., *Ockeghem, *Dufay, *Morales, *Palestrina, *Carissimi) as a *cantus firmus for over 30 *polyphonic *masses. RTR

Homoion [Greek; Slavonic *podoben*]. "Like." A musical direction in the Byzantine *office attached to *stichera, *kontakia and other types of *hymns, indicating that the *stichera* are to be sung according to the melody of another model whose *incipit is given. Each of the *octoechos has 1 proper melody for each type of hymn (see *idiomelon) and variant melodies represented by a number of model *stichera*. *Homoion* is sometimes used as the name of the hymn itself in place of *sticheron*. DMP

Honegger, Arthur (b Le Havre 1892; d Paris 1955). Composer of operas, ballets, radio and film scores, orchestral works, chamber music and *chansons*. His music reflects the influence of the *chorales of J. S. *Bach. Honegger's sacred works include the *oratorio *Le roi David* (1926) and *Une cantate de Noël* (1941/1953). JDW

Hook & Hastings. US *organ building firm founded in 1827 by Elias Hook (d

1881) and George Greenleaf Hook (d 1880), both former apprentices of *Goodrich. In 1855 Frank H. Hastings (d 1916) came to the firm, becoming president after the death of both founders. Notable organs include Boston's RC Immaculate Conception Church (1863) and Holy Cross Cathedral (1875). JWK

Hope-Jones, Robert (b Cheshire 1859; d Rochester NY 1914). *Organ builder who emigrated to the US in 1903 where he founded the Hope-Jones Electric Organ Co. in Elmira NY (1907–10). He is credited with the application of the "unit" principle, in which a single rank of pipes serves several divisions at different pitches. JWK

Hopson, Hal H(arold) (b Mound TX 1933). Prolific composer and arranger with hundreds of published *anthems, mostly for the church. Hopson is also a leading composer of congregational song, especially *responsorial psalmody. JBW

Horai (sing. **hora**) [Greek; Slavonic *chasy,* sing. *chas*]. "Hours." The collective name given to the Byzantine *hours of *prime, *terce, *sext and *none. These are monastic *services (parochial versions once existed) usually read by a *cantor. Each hour begins with a *blessing, *Trisagion, *Our Father and select *verses from Ps 95. Three *psalms follow (prime: 5, 90, 101; terce: 17, 25, 51; sext: 54, 55, 91; none: 84, 85, 86), *troparion of the day (Great *Lent has a *troparion* proper to the hour with psalm verses), *Theotokion proper to the hour, select psalm verses, *Trisagion, Our Father, *kontakion of the day, prayer (common to all 4 hours), prayer (proper to each hour) and *apolysis.

Prime is commonly said at the end of *orthros, often reduced to its proper prayer. Terce is said before and sext after the *divine liturgy. None is said before *hesperinos. The day before certain great feasts, when no divine liturgy is prescribed, the hours are said together and conclude with the service of *typika (see *megalai horai).

Bibl: R. Taft, *The Liturgy of the Hours in East and West* (Collegeville, 1986). DMP

Horologion [Greek; Slavonic *chasoslov*]. Liturgical *book for the *divine office of the Byzantine rite, including texts to celebrate *mesonyktikon, *orthros, prote, trite, hekte, typika, enate, *hesperinos and *apodeipnon; it corresponds to the Latin *breviary. The *horologion* contains ordinary texts (*psalms and *preces), readings from saints' lives, some proper *Byzantine *chant texts (*apolytikia, *hypakoe, *kontakia, *stichera and *Theotokia) for the yearly cycle of feasts, *antiphons for the *divine liturgy, the *akathistos hymn and miscellaneous *kanons. It does not ordinarily include prayers of the clergy, which are found in the *euchologion. The earliest manuscripts date from the 9th century. Forms of the *horologion* are also used in the Coptic and Melkite rites.

Bibl: A Prayer Book (New Skete, 1976).   RGD

Hoshanot [from Hebrew *hoshana,* "please save"]. An extensive set of *piyyutim, all beginning with the word *hoshana,* recited through the week of *Sukkot while circling the *bimah with the *lulav* ("palm branch") and *etrog* ("citrus fruit"). They are recited in an order which varies each year according to the day on which the festival commences.   SIW

Hosmer, Frederick Lucian (*b* Framington MA 1840; *d* Berkeley 1929). Unitarian minister who was a leader in *hymn and liturgical renewal among Unitarians. Hosmer authored 40 hymns.   ACL

Hours. See *divine office.

House of God Church worship music. Mother (Bishop) Mary Lena Lewis Tate founded this denomination in 1903 and published its first *hymnal (1944). Though including *hymns in its worship (similar to those of *Tindley), the congregation principally sings the sanctified *refrains of the *Church of God in Christ.   HCB

Hovhaness <Hovaness>, **Alan** <Chakmakjian, Alan Hovhaness> (*b* Somerville MA 1911). Composer of symphonies, operas, ballets, instrumental, chamber, choral, vocal, band and piano works; over 400 in all. He was heavily influenced by E mysticism and by his studies of Armenian, Japanese and Korean music. Many works feature avant garde elements (e.g., complex polyrhythms, "rhythmless" blurs of sound) as well as traditional elements from W music (especially highly developed *counterpoint). *Sacred compositions include vocal and choral works on sacred texts (including *anthems for liturgical use), although he described nearly all his works as religious in nature. Hovhaness served as the organist of the Armenian Church of St. James in Boston in the 1940s.   JDW

Hovland, Egil (*b* Mysen near Oslo 1924). Organist and composer. He studied with *Copland (awarded the Koussevitzky prize in 1957) and *Dallapiccola. Best known for his *organ and choral compositions, e.g., *Missa vigilate* (1967) and *All Saints Mass* (1970). Hovland has been influential in the revival of Norwegian *church music and *liturgy.   PAJ

Huber, Jane Parker (*b* Jinan, China 1926). Presbyterian author of numerous *hymn texts which appear in many *hymnals published in the 1980s and 1990s. She has published 4 collections of her hymns, including *A Singing Faith* (1987) and *Singing in Celebration* (1996).   JBW

Hucbald (*b* Tournai *c* 840; *d* St. Amand 930). Monk and theorist. He studied with his uncle Milo, who then was director of Tournai's singing school. Hucbald became the singing school director at Nevers (860) and later succeeded his uncle in a similar position at St. Amand. Hucbald's main treatise *De harmonica institutione* was an instruction for *choirs about *chant, especially its notation and scales. He also composed several *offices for saints' days.   JLB

Hughes, Howard (*b* Baltimore 1930). Organist, teacher, prolific composer of *liturgical music and member of the RC Marianist community. Hughes studied *organ with R. Twynham prior to graduate music studies at *Catholic University of America. While Hughes has written in almost every liturgical form, he is especially well-known for his *responsorial psalms and *ritual music for *eucharist.   RJB

Humfrey, Pelham (*b* London? 1647; *d* Windsor 1674). Composer who successively served the *Chapel Royal as one of the children, gentleman and finally master of the children. He wrote *c* 20 *verse anthems, most with string accompaniment.   DWM

Hurd, David James (*b* Brooklyn 1950). Prize winning organist, especially celebrated for his improvisatory skills. Hurd is also a composer of much music for the Church and many of his *hymn tunes appear in contemporary *hymnals. He has served on the faculty of General Theological Seminary (Episcopal) in New York City since 1976.   JBW

Hutchings, George Sherburn (*b* Salem MA 1835; *d* Cambridge 1913). *Organ builder. He entered the *Hook firm of Boston in 1857 and established his own firm in 1869. Hutchings was a leader in the growing trend towards the Romantic style of organ building in the US.   JWK

Hydraulis [from Greek *hydrō*, "water" and *aulós*, "pipe"]. The earliest known form of the *organ, invented in Egypt *c* 250 BCE, which became popular in classical Greek and Roman civilizations. The name reflects the use of water in the organ's design as a weight to steady the air pressure in the instrument.   JBW

Hymn [Greek *hymnos*, "song (praising gods or heroes)"]. (1) A free poetic form set to music and sung liturgically.

(2) *Strophic poetry set to music and sung liturgically and extra-liturgically. Hymns in the E church are in free poetic forms. *Phos hilaron*, the 3rd-century lamp-lighting hymn, still forms part of *hesperinos*. Important Greek hymn writers include *Ephraim the Syrian, Gregory Nazianzus (*d* 389), *Romanos,

John Damascene (*d* 749) and *Joseph the Hymnographer.

In the W church strophic hymnody has predominated. *Ambrose of Milan wrote orthodox hymns to counteract the heterodox hymns of Arius, creating a model for the Latin *office hymn. Primary authors of Latin hymns include *Prudentius, Sedulius (5th century), *Fortunatus and *Abelard. In the early 11th century the *sequence, a new form of hymn, developed. During the medieval period various traditions of extraliturgical vernacular hymns were created: the *lauda spirituale* in Italy, *Leise* in Germany, *carol in England and, somewhat later, *noël* in France.

At the *Reformation hymnody was reintroduced for the congregation. *Luther and his Wittenberg colleagues not only wrote new hymns but also translated Latin office hymns, as well as adapting previously composed *Leisen.* Modern hymn singing in public worship thus has its roots in the Lutheran *Reformation. Calvinist traditions only allowed the singing of *metrical psalms, a genre that dominated the English speaking world until the 19th century. Hymnody in the 18th century was strongly affected by the evangelical revival, especially the hymns of *Watts and C. *Wesley, and in the 19th century by the *Oxford movement and American revivalism. The 20th century has seen a unprecedented period of hymn writing. Post-1960s iconoclasm and the reforms of *Vatican II have prompted the creation of hymns in a wide variety of poetic forms and musical styles.

Bibl: E. Routley, *The Music of Christian Hymns* (Chicago, 1981); R. F. Glover, ed., *The Hymnal 1982 Companion* 1 (New York, 1990); R. A. Leaver and J.

A. Zimmerman, eds., *Liturgy & Music* (Collegeville, 1998) 281–307.   RAL

Hymnal. An anthology of *hymns for practical use. Latin *hymnaria* provided the model for early Lutheran hymnals in the 16th century. In the same way that these Latin anthologies presented their hymns according to their usage throughout the liturgical *year, these Lutheran hymnals structured their first main section around the liturgical year. In the English-speaking world most congregations sang from words-only *metrical psalters rather than hymnals until approximately the mid-19th century. Then, with the expansion of hymnody, congregations enriched their repertoire beyond metrical psalmody. Thus from the 1870s, largely following the model of *Hymns Ancient and Modern,* the modern denominational hymnal was created. In America this meant the inclusion of both words and music.

Bibl: J. R. Sydnor, "The Structure and Use of Hymnals," *The Hymn and Congregational Singing* (Richmond, 1960) 7–86.   RAL

Hymn anthem. A short choral work in *concertato style based on a *hymn or scripture, frequently employing *hymn tunes or traditional melodies. The form originated in the early *anthems of C. Wood, *Vaughan Williams and *Holst. It was developed by E. Thiman as easy music for parish *choirs and imitated in North America by *Willan, C. *Dickinson and *Titcomb. In the later 20th century *Lovelace and others have made it a standard choral form and staple of music publishers.   CRY

Hymnary [Latin *hymnarium,* pl. *hymnaria*]. (1) W medieval liturgical *book, or part of a book, containing *hymns to be used in the *divine office in evidence by the 8th century.

(2) A book of hymns and possibly *psalms for public worship or private devotion; it sometimes includes tunes for singing. See *hymnal.   RJS

Hymn of Jesus. A major work for multiple *choirs and orchestra by *Holst (op. 37, 1917) to a text from the apocryphal Acts of St. John.   DWM

Hymn of light. See *photogogikon.

Hymn of the day. See *de tempore hymn.

Hymn of the week. See *de tempore hymn.

Hymnology. The historical and analytical study of *hymnody.   RAL

Hymns Ancient and Modern. An English *hymnal jointly edited by H. *Baker and W. Monk, published in 1861; numerous revisions and supplements have subsequently appeared. A musical companion to the *BCP, it was the first hymnal to append a musical *amen to *hymn tunes.   RJS

Hymn Society in the United States and Canada. Founded as the Hymn Society (1922) by Emily S. Perkins, its name was changed to the Hymn Society of the United States and Canada in 1991. Its purposes include the cultivation of congregational singing, encouraging the writing and publication of hymns, as well as research, discussion and the dis-

semination of scholarly work to improve modes of congregation prayer and praise. The society's quarterly publication is *The Hymn;* it also sponsors the *Dictionary of American Hymnology,* an index to hymn texts.   RJS

Hymn tune. (1) The unadorned melody of a *hymn (e.g., *plainsong melodies), early Lutheran *chorales, *Genevan psalm tunes, or the melodies of *folk hymns, which all tend to be modal.

(2) A hymn's complete musical setting in a given *hymnal, encompassing both the melody and a particular harmonization.   RAL

Hymnus angelicus. See *Angelic hymn.

Hymnus Paradisi [Latin]. "Hymn of Paradise." *Requiem for choir, soloists and orchestra by *Howells (1938) to English and Latin texts from *psalms, the *mass of the dead, the *BCP and the Salisbury diurnal. It was never intended for liturgical use.   DWM

Hypakoe [Greek; Slavonic *ypakoi*]. "Obedience." A type of *sedalen in Byzantine *orthros sung according to the *troparion tones (see *echos). Originally introduced after the 3rd *ode of the *kanon,* it still is found on a few select days. One is sung after the *anastasima eulogetaria sung with Ps 119 according to the tone of the week (see *octoechos). DMP

Hytrek, Theophane (*b* Stuart NE 1915; *d* Milwaukee 1992). Organist, composer, teacher and member of the RC School Sisters of St. Francis. She earned a doctorate in composition from Eastman. A gifted pedagogue, most of her career was spent teaching at Milwaukee's Alverno College. While she composed award winning works for various *instruments, Hytrek is best remembered for her *organ works and many liturgical compositions for *choir and congregation.   RJB

I

ICDF. See *International Christian Dance Fellowship.

ICEL. See *International Committee on English in the Liturgy.

ICET. See *International Consultation on English Texts.

Ictus [Latin]. "Stroke, beat." (1) A term used in prosody to indicate the stress or accent implied on certain syllables.

(2) A term used by Dom *Mocquereau for a vertical episema used to mark off 2- or 3-note groups in *Gregorian chant. CJK

Idelsohn, Abraham Zvi (*b* Kurland 1882; *d* Johannesburg 1938). Musicologist and composer. Considered by many to be the father of Jewish musicology. He lived and studied in London and throughout Europe. Idelsohn went to Leipzig (1902) where he was a *chazzan* and studied music at the Leipzig Conservatory. After living in Bavaria and Johannesburg, he moved to Jerusalem (1906) to teach and learn about Jewish song. He notated hundreds of melodies of various Jewish communities. He then traveled (1921–24) through Europe and the US sharing his research, settling in Cincinnati as Professor of Hebrew *liturgy and Jewish music at Hebrew Union College (1924–34).

His 10-volume *Thesaurus of Hebrew-Oriental Melodies* (1914–32) publishes the many melodies he collected in Israel and Europe, the first time these oral traditions were documented. His *Jewish Music in its Historical Development* (1929) remains the only complete history of Jewish music; *Jewish Liturgy and its Development* (1932) is also important.

Idelsohn's theory of *cantillation (see *ta'amim*) held that although regional traditions exist in the 20th century, these traditions are similar and emanate from a common source he defined as Palestinian *folk song. While contemporary scholarship criticizes this theory (e.g., A. Shiloah, *Jewish Musical Traditions*, 1992), Idelsohn's work challenged and inspired musicologists who study music in Jewish contexts. He also composed the first Hebrew opera, *Yiftah* (1922).

Bibl: E. Schleifer, "Idelsohn's Scholarly and Literary Publications: an

Annotated Bibliography," *Yuval* 5 (1986) 53–180.   MLK

Idiomelon [Greek; Slavonic *samoglasen*]. "Its own melody." (1) In the Byzantine *office, the proper *sticheron* melody for each of the *octoechos* to which various types of *stichera* are sung. (2) A synonym for *sticheron*. (3) A *troparion* with its own special melody.   DMP

Idiomelon heothinon [Greek]. "Proper morning melody" [Slavonic *stikhira evangel'skaya*, "gospel verse"]. A series of 11 *stichera* in Byzantine *orthros* corresponding to the 11 resurrection *gospels (see *euangelion heothinon*) read in sequence over a period of 11 Sundays. These *stichera* are sung after the small *doxology (see *doxologia*) concluding the *stichera* at the *ainoi.   DMP

Ikos [Slavonic]. See *oikos*.

ILDA. See *International Liturgical Dance Association.

Imperial Mass. See *Nelson Mass*.

Improperia [Latin]. "Reproaches." Scripturally inspired *verses sung during the veneration of the cross on *Good Friday; the *refrains are from Micah 6:3 and the *Trisagion* (Greek and Latin). The setting in *Graduale Romanum* is in *mode 3; restructured versions are found in the Anglican *Book of Alternative Services* for Canada, and Presbyterian *Book of Common Worship*. Noted choral settings are by *Victoria and *Palestrina.   JMT

Incipit [Latin]. "It begins." The first word(s) or formulaic introduction to a *chant, prayer or reading. *Incipit*s were used to identify biblical readings before chapter divisions and *verse numbering were introduced in the 13th and 16th centuries respectively. See *initium*.   GET

In dulci jubilo [Latin] "In sweet rejoicing." The first line of a 13th-century macaronic *Christmas *cantio* that has become a well-loved *carol in a number of variant forms.   RAL

Indy, (Paul Marie Théodore) Vincent d' (*b* Paris 1851; *d* there 1931). Composer and teacher. He studied composition and *organ with C. *Franck. With *Bordes and *Guilmant, d'Indy founded the Schola Cantorum, originally dedicated to the study of *church music. Besides operas, orchestral and chamber music, he wrote the choral works *Sainte Marie-Magdaleine* (1885) and *Deus Israel* (1896).   CSP

Ingathering, Feast of. See *Sukkot*.

Ingressa [Latin]. "Entrance." The processional *antiphon at the beginning of *eucharist in the Milanese (Ambrosian), Gallican and Beneventan rites. It is analogous to the Roman *introit, but contains no *psalm.   PAJ

Initium [Latin]. "Beginning." The beginning of a *chant, especially a *psalm tone (in which case it refers only to the first *verse). It is sometimes distinguished from an *incipit which can refer only to the beginning of a text without its music.   RTR

In nomine [Latin]. "In the name." 16th–17th-century English instrumental form using the melody of the *Sarum chant *Gloria tibi Trinitas* as **cantus firmus*. Its name is derived from *Taverner's use of this melody at the *"In nomine"* section of the **Benedictus* in his *Gloria tibi Trinitas* *mass. DWM

In seculum [Latin]. "In eternity." The *melismatic portion of the *Easter *gradual *Haec dies*. It was most often used as a *cantus firmus for 12th–13th-century *organa, *clausulae and *motets. DWM

Institute of Worship Studies. Founded in Wheaton IL (1995) as an independent educational institute by Robert Webber. With Northern Baptist Seminary (Lombard IL) and Tyndale Theological Seminary (Toronto) it offers degrees and programs in worship studies based on *The Complete Library of Christian Worship* (Nashville, 1995). The Institute primarily serves a broad range of evangelical and free church Christians. JDW

Instruments in worship. Musical instruments have frequently played an important role in human ritual and worship. The Hebrew Bible, particularly the *psalms, include many descriptions of instruments in worship (e.g., *bells, cymbals, rattler-sistrum and gong; flute or pipe, horn, trumpet and **shofar;* lyre, lute and harp). Some of these instruments were used in *Temple worship; only the *shofar* carried over to synagogue worship. *Organs were introduced into Reform synagogues in the 19th century.

Instruments were not part of early Christian worship; instrumental music is condemned by many Christian writers. Records show that organs existed in W churches by the 8th century, though their ritual role is uncertain; by the 10th century they were clearly used as part of worship. Wind and string instruments often doubled or substituted for voices in worship during the *Middle Ages, *Renaissance and into the *Baroque era. Bells signalled worship's beginning, ending and high points. Percussive instruments sometimes accompany chants in many E churches (see *Armenian and *Chaldean chant).

Organs have been celebrated as both the ultimate instrument for worship and the antithesis of true worship (thus banned or destroyed by parts of the Protestant *Reformation). Some Protestant denominations have opposed the use of all instruments in worship, notably *Calvin, *Zwingli and, to the present day, Quakers. Others (e.g., *Baptist) have encouraged the use of praise bands and orchestras. The *Salvation Army and *Moravians have also used instrumental ensembles as part of their worship. RC decrees on *church music (e.g., **Sacrosanctum Concilium*) often address the acceptability of certain instruments in worship. In the 20th century, many Christian denominations struggle over the use of *guitars, percussion, synthesizers and recordings of instrumental music in worship.

Increased cross-cultural influences have resulted in more instruments in North American worship. Drums of various sizes are used with Native American and African (-American) *hymnody. Hispanic congregations often employ guitar, accordion, tambourine and drum in addition to piano and organ. Asian communities increasingly employ indigenous wind instruments, double reeds, bowed or plucked lutes, zither and drum.

Today instruments are used to accompany congregational singing, *choirs and soloists, to provide musicians an opportunity to praise God, and to enable congregations to meditate on God's blessings and presence.

Bibl: J. McKinnon, "The Meaning of the Patristic Polemic against Musical Instruments," *Current Musicology* 1 (1965) 69–82; C. Schalk, ed., *Key Words in Church Music* (St. Louis, 1978) 20–29, 245–50, 317–23; I. Jones, "Musical Instruments," *Anchor Bible Dictionary* (New York, 1992) 4:935–39.   RKW

Interdenominational Theological Center. A theological school in Atlanta, established (1958) through the consortium of 6 seminaries: Gammon Theological Seminary (United Methodist), Morehouse School of Religion (Baptist), Turner Theological Seminary (African Methodist Episcopal), Phillips School of Religion (Christian Methodist Episcopal), Johnson C. Smith Theological Seminary (Presbyterian USA) and Charles H. Mason (Church of God in Christ). It offers various graduate degrees, including an M.A. in *church music.   MWC

Intermediate chants. The chants at *eucharist between the first (and second) scripture reading and *gospel, e.g., *responsorial psalm, *gospel acclamation and *sequence.   FCQ

International Christian Dance Fellowship <ICDF>. An ecumenical organization founded out of the Christian Dance Fellowship of Australia led by Mary Jones in 1988, to support and link Christians involved in dance and movement ministries. It has inspired the founding of Christian Dance Fellowships in 12 countries.   MAK

International Commission on English in the Liturgy <ICEL>. An organization established in 1963 to provide common liturgical texts for English-speaking RCs in the world. ICEL consists of an episcopal Board (governing body) representing 11 English-speaking national conferences of RC bishops; an Advisory Committee, overseeing the work of the Commission; standing subcommittees; and, a Secretariat in Washington DC. The "first phase" of ICEL work (1963–76) produced translations of the Roman Canon (1967), the various sacraments (1969–75), the Roman Missal (1974) and the *liturgy of the hours (1975). A "second phase" includes production of original texts, music for the rites and a pastoral reordering of the Roman books.

Bibl: P. Finn and J. Schellman, eds., *Shaping English Liturgy* (Washington, 1990).   JBF

International Consultation on English Texts <ICET>. An ecumenical group of liturgists and musicians convened in London (1969) to provide English translations of common liturgical texts used in various churches. Thirteen texts appeared in *Prayers We have in Common* (1970, 1971, 1975) intended for musical setting. ICET's last revisions were completed in 1975. Since 1983 the work of this consultation has been continued by the *English Language Liturgical Consultation, whose *Praying Together* (1988, 1990) provides additional minor revisions.   RJS

International Liturgical Dance Association. An organization which developed as an outgrowth of dance presented at *NPM conventions, founded by *Weyman in the early 1990s. Its purpose is to provide education and information on dance in (especially RC) worship.   MAK

Intonation. (1) The initial phrase of an *antiphon or *psalm sung by a *cantor to set the pitch for the *choir or congregation. In *plainsong books the intonation of the antiphon is often indicated by the use of an asterisk.

(2) An *intonazione.* JMT

Intonazione <intonatione> [Italian]. "Intonation." A short *keyboard piece that gives the pitch for a following vocal work. It was probably often improvised by 16th–17th century organists; significant examples were published by the *Gabrielis. DWM

Introit [Latin *introitus*]. (1) The first chant of the *proper of the mass, accompanying the entrance of the ministers. It appears by the early 7th century in Rome. The general structure that later develops is: introit *antiphon, *psalm, *verse, antiphon, *Gloria Patri, antiphon and *repetendum. Antiphon texts are almost all biblical; some make reference to the feast (e.g., *Puer natus* ["A child is born"] at Christmas). Antiphon melodies are highly individual and difficult to classify; verse and *Gloria Patri* are sung to simple formulas.

(2) In many Protestant traditions, any short choral piece or sentence at the beginning of the *service.

Bibl: D. Hiley, *Western Plainchant* (Oxford, 1993), especially 109–16. PAJ

Invitation hymn. A *hymn sung at the close of evangelical worship inviting individuals to come forward and make a commitment to Christ and the church. ACL

Invitatory [from Latin *invitare*, "to invite"]. (1) An invitation to prayer.

(2) The first major element in *matins, consisting of Ps 95 (*Venite*)

with an *antiphon. After the 1971 revision of the Roman *breviary, the invitatory was moved to the beginning of the first hour of the day, whether that was the office of readings or *lauds. The 1549 BCP retained the invitatory without any antiphon. EBF

Invocation. (1) A calling upon God or the saints in prayer.

(2) A particular kind of Christian prayer invoking the Holy Spirit's presence and/or activity in the worshipping community (Greek *epiclesis*), e.g., for consecrating bread and wine for *eucharist. RJS

Inwood, Paul (*b* Beckenham, Kent 1947). RC liturgical composer. Inwood is a graduate of London's Royal Academy of Music. He has served as part of the leadership for *Universa Laus. His works include *psalm settings, *mass parts, *anthems and other *ritual music. VCF

Iona Community. A Scottish ecumenical community whose worship reflects the traditions of the Celtic Church. Iona has published various worship materials, including the *hymns of *Bell. KRH

Irmolog [Slavonic]. See *hirmologion.

Irmos [Slavonic]. See *hirmos.

Isaac <Isaak, Izak, Yzac, etc.>, **Heinrich** <Arrigo Tedesco> (*b* Flanders 1450; *d* Florence 1517). Composer of vocal music. He served Lorenzo de' Medici in Florence (1485–92), was court composer to Emperor Maximilian I at Vienna (from 1497) and resettled in Florence when the Medicis regained power

(1514). His 3-volume *Choralis Constantinus* (1550), edited by his pupil *Senfl, containing the first complete *polyphonic setting of mass *propers for the liturgical *year (plus 5 settings of the *ordinary), influenced the development of German *liturgical music. He also composed *parody masses, *motets and a celebrated setting (his second) for *Isbruck, ich muss dich lassen* (1539).

Bibl: M. Picker, *Henricus Isaac* (New York, 1991). CRY

Isaacson, Michael (*b* Brooklyn 1946). A prolific composer of liturgical and non-liturgical Jewish music. He earned a DMA in composition from Eastman under *Adler. Isaacson employs classical, modern, popular and *folk styles in his composition. He has written many liturgical works including *Bayom Hahu, Psalm 23* and *Aveinu Malkeinu*. MLK

Isele, David Clark (*b* Harrisburg PA 1946). Professor of music and composer in residence at the University of Tampa; RC *pastoral musician. Isele holds a DMA from Eastman. The recipient of many commissions, he has numerous published works. Many of his compositions are liturgical (e.g., *mass and *psalm settings) or sacred (e.g., a *Requiem*). LMT

Isidore of Seville, St. (*b* Cartegena? *c* 560; *d* Seville 636). Spanish archbishop, theologian and encyclopedist. He promoted doctrinal and liturgical uniformity, as fostered by the Fourth Council of Toledo (633). Isidore also transmitted in modified form earlier theoretical writings on music in his *Etymologiae* (3:15-24), e.g., those of *Augustine and *Cassiodorus. He also discussed music's role in the Old Spanish (Mozarabic) *divine office in his *De ecclesiasticis officiis.* JMJ

Ison. A sustained pitch in Byzantine liturgical chanting held by certain singers while the *cantor and others sing the *chant melody. Similar to a pedal point, the device is used by some choral composers, notably the 20th-century's John Tavener. JMT

Ite missa est [Latin]. "Go, it is the dismissal," popularly translated, "Go, the mass is ended." An ancient *versicle concluding the Roman rite *mass (for which the *response is *Deo gratias,* "Thanks be to God"), giving the mass its name *(missa).* From the 11th century until the reforms of *Vatican II, it was replaced in masses without the *Gloria in excelsis* with *Benedicamus Domino.* Sometimes considered part of the *ordinary, there are numerous chant settings for *Ite missa est;* it was seldom set *polyphonically. VCF

Ives, Charles Edward (*b* Danbury CT 1874; *d* New York 1954). Composer. He was trained by his band leader father, then H. *Parker at Yale. Ives worked in the insurance business (1898–1930), though he briefly served as organist at New York's Central Presbyterian Church (1899–1902). In his free time he composed orchestral, vocal and *keyboard works with experimental harmony and rhythm; among his few religious works are a series of choral *psalms, including *Psalm 67* (1893). JLB

Izobrazitelnaya [Slavonic]. See *typika.*

J

Jackson, Francis (Alan) (*b* Malton 1917). Organist, conductor and composer. The recipient of a D.Mus., he is a Fellow of the *Royal College of Organists. Master of music at York Minster (1946–82), Jackson wrote works for *choir and *organ as well as *hymn tunes.   RKW

Jackson, George Pullen (*b* Monsan ME 1874; *d* Nashville 1953). Musicologist who researched *spirituals (white and black). His *White Spirituals in the Southern Uplands* (1933) uncovered a large body of American religious *folk music, including the *Sacred Harp *tune book.   FJM

Jackson, Mahalia (*b* New Orleans 1911; *d* Chicago 1972). African American *gospel singer and recording artist. Jackson was a major catalyst for establishing gospel music as a powerful musical and worship idiom. Noted for her compelling blues-based *melismatic vocal style, she was a long time collaborator with *Dorsey and other Chicago gospel pioneers. Jackson captured moments of national celebration and mourning in song, e.g., the presidential inauguration of J. F.

Kennedy (1961) and the funeral of M. L. King, Jr. (1968). She performed in church and concert settings throughout the US (including Carnegie Hall and the Newport Jazz festival) and Europe. In 1949 she received the French Academy's *Grand Prix du Disque* (1949).

Bibl: J. Schwerin, *Got To Tell It* (New York, 1992).   MEM

James, Willis Laurence (*b* Montgomery 1900; *d* Atlanta 1966). Composer, arranger and musicologist. James was music professor and choral director at Morehouse, Spelman and other colleges. A consultant to the Institute of Jazz Studies, he also lectured at Tanglewood. He published numerous arrangements of *spirituals and original choral compositions.   MWC

Janowski, Max (*b* Berlin 1912; *d* Chicago 1991). Composer of Jewish *liturgical music. He immigrated to the US in 1937, the following year becoming music director of *Kehilath Anshe Maarav* (the oldest Reform synagogue in IL). His settings of *Aveinu Malkeinu* (1967) and *Sim shalom* (1953) are commonly heard in Reform synagogues, especially on *Yamim noraim.   MLK

Jardine, George (*b* Dartford, England 1801; *d* New York City 1883). *Organ builder. He immigrated to the US in 1837. His son, Edward (*d* 1896), joined the firm in 1860. Notable *instruments from the Jardine firm include those in New York City's Fifth Avenue Presbyterian (1856) and St. Michael's Church (1893).   JWK

Jazz. An African American musical form, and the US's most significant original musical expression, performed in many styles around the world. Its roots are the vocal, instrumental and dance traditions of African Americans: especially slave songs, shouts, *spirituals and worship song. Slides, blue notes, growls, wails and a wide range of vocal colorings are featured. Improvisation, *call and response patterns, syncopation, driving rhythms and complex rhythmic and melodic overlays are characteristic.

Following the Civil War blacks improvised on *hymns (some played in march tempo to and from burials) with banjo, discarded military *instruments and piano. Traditional songs and spirituals were improvised in blues and ragtime patterns. Early jazz featured conservative European harmonic vocabulary, as well as American and French quadrille dance rhythms.

Jazz flourished in New Orleans, usually performed by black groups. It spread up the Mississippi and Missouri rivers to Memphis, Kansas City and St. Louis where distinctive styles developed. Prohibition-era jazz flourished in Chicago and New York, performed by blacks and whites. Big swing bands performed in theaters, night clubs and dance halls through the 1920s and 30s. Under the guise of "swing," jazz became a recording industry mainstay. Jazz entered the symphonic repertory with Gershwin's *Rhapsody in Blue* (1924) and *Stravinsky's *Ebony Concerto* (1945).

After World War II a new intricate style, "be-bop" or "bop," was introduced by Dizzy Gillespie, Charlie Parker and others. In the 1950s and 60s *Brubeck, Paul Desmond and others joined jazz and symphonic music into a "third stream" synthesis of both styles. The combination of jazz and rock elements in the 1970s and 80s by Miles Davis and others was labeled "fusion."

Jazz has recently been employed as a medium for religious music, e.g., *Brubeck's *The Light in the Wilderness* (1960) and *Ellington's "Sacred Concerts" (1965, 1968, 1973). It has also been used in worship (see *jazz mass). Despite its roots in religious music, however, its performance practices, contrasting styles and improvisatory qualities have proven as problematic to maintain with integrity in worship as in symphonic settings.

Bibl: M. Stearns, *The Story of Jazz,* 2nd ed. (Oxford, 1970); L. Feather, *The Encyclopedia of Jazz* (New York, 1988); M. Gridley, *Jazz Styles,* 6th ed. (New York, 1996).   CRY

Jehan le Cocq. See *Johannes Gallus.

Jennings, Kenneth (*b* Bridgeport CT 1925). Conductor emeritus of the St. Olaf Choir and Tosdal Professor emeritus of Music at *St. Olaf College. A distinguished conductor and teacher in US and Japan, he has also composed, arranged and edited numerous choral works.   LMT

Jenny, Markus (*b* Stein, Switzerland 1924). Professor of theology at University of Zurich and pastor in the Swiss Reformed Church. Jenny has authored numerous works on *liturgy and music, and been involved in numerous *hymnal projects.   AWR

Jesu, dulcis memoria [Latin]. "Jesus, how sweet the thought." A 12th-century *hymn for the *divine office; of uncertain authorship it is often attributed to Bernard of Clairvaux. Originally it encompassed 42 *stanzas; others were later appended. English translations include *Caswall's "Jesus the very thought of thee."   RJS

Jesu, Joy of Man's Desiring. A popular extended *chorale setting by J. S. *Bach. The music is from *cantata BWV 147 written for the Visitation of Mary (July 2); the text is the first *stanza of a 16-stanza *hymn by M. Jahn (1661). Bach used only stanzas 6 and 16 in his cantata. MPB

Jewish music. Jewish music is neither homogeneous nor easily definable. Due to the complex history of the Jewish people, their music reflects various contacts with local cultures throughout time. Musical traits in Jewish music are characterized as adaptations of music from local cultures within a Jewish context. Yet Jewish music is not only adapted from other sources; many musical genres are uniquely Jewish (e.g., cantorial *recitatives, *Hasidic music, "Judeo-Spanish" songs, *piyyutim). Jewish music needs to be considered within the context of the culture in which it is found, and situated within its place in history.

Ancient Jewish music was the concern of scholars like A. Sendrey and B. Bayer. *Werner focused on questions of the interconnection between the music of church and synagogue; his conclusions have been refined by *Avenary ("Contacts between Church and Synagogue Music," *Proceedings of the World Congress on Jewish Music,* Tel Aviv, 1978). *Cantillation of the *Torah is based upon the *ta'amim, a particular interest of *Idelsohn.

The 2 major regional groups identifiable in the second millennium are *Ashkenazic and *Sephardic Jews. Liturgical-musical practices are not necessarily common to both groups, though some have tried to find common practices as evidence of enduring ancient traditions (e.g., *Idelsohn). Ashkenazic Jews use *Jewish prayer modes whereas Sephardic Jews from the Middle E use the Arabic modal tradition (*makam). Diversity not only exists between these 2 traditions, however, but also within each tradition.

Prior to the 1700s few documents of musical notation exist. The early history of Jewish music is taken from the Bible, rabbinic literature and iconographic evidence. Some medieval rabbis were influential in their statements concerning music (e.g., *Maharil and *Maimonides). More manuscripts of European *liturgical music appear in the 1800s and regional practices can be discerned. Nineteenth-century European Jewish communities are influenced by W *Classical music. The C European tradition at this time is more syllabic and rhythmic; E European tradition is more *melismatic and free (see *chazzan); Hasidic music is more ecstatic. The 19th and 20th centuries were times of tremendous change in Jewish musical practices, especially within *Reform Judaism.

Musical practices shape the *liturgy of the entire year. Music for the *Sabbath makes use of particular *modes and melodies different from those used for *High Holidays and the *Three Festivals (see *Misinai tunes).

Bibl: H. Avenary, "Music," EJ 12:554–678; J. Walton and L. Hoffman, eds., Sacred Sound and Social Change (Notre Dame-London, 1992) pp. 13–83, 187–212; A. Shiloah, Jewish Musical Traditions (Detroit, 1992).   MLK

Jewish popular music. *Jewish music throughout history has been influenced by the music of its environs. Sometimes *art music is the influence, other times *folk and popular styles. Jewish wedding music in E Europe, for example, included various folk styles; the musicians were called klezmorim (Hebrew, "instruments of song"); the rebirth of that music today is termed klezmer music (e.g., that performed by the Andy Statman Ensemble, Brave Old World and the Klezmer Conservatory Band). Singing in Yiddish became prevalent c 1880 with E European immigrants to the US including New York's Yiddish theater (operative until 1950).

During the second half of the 20th century popular music styles in the US have steadily grown among Jews, with each religious denomination (Orthodox, Conservative, Reform) developing a range of popular music to fit its needs. Particularly after Israel's military victory in 1967 a renewed ethnic pride developed among US Jews. Israeli folk and popular songs increased in popularity and influenced the *liturgy. Melodies for the *Lechah dodi and other portions of the liturgy were shaped from Israeli and *Hasidic melodies in all denominations.

*Carlebach was among the first to create new US Jewish folk music. Others make use of various pop, rock and *jazz styles. Prominent representatives include Avraham Fried, *Friedman, Mordecai Ben David, Kol B'Seder and Safam.

Bibl: M. Slobin, Tenement Songs (Urbana, 1982); M. Kligman, "On the Creators and Consumers of Orthodox Popular Music in Brooklyn, New York," Yivo Annual 23 (1996) 259–93.   MLK

Jewish prayer modes [Hebrew nusach hat'fillah; Yiddish steiger, stayger, shtejger; Latin used in French gust; Slavic scarbove, skarbove]. A collection of musical motives that forms the basis for cantorial improvisation while chanting a particular prayer on a specific occasion. Some motives help to identify the syntax of the prayer text, though not as strictly and thoroughly as biblical tropes identify syntax in the Torah (see *ta'amim). Opening, concluding, preconcluding and pausal motives are used routinely in liturgical *chant.

Until the mid-19th century, Jewish prayer modes were transmitted orally. Thus both nomenclature (the modes were generally identified by the name of the particular prayer representative of the mode's use) and liturgical practice varied widely. As Jewish liturgical chant has been analyzed and notated more frequently, certain traditions have gained widespread acceptance.

Since these modes are motive- rather than scale-based they share important characteristics with oriental music, particularly the Arabic *makam and Indian raga. Distinctive characteristics of Jewish modes include stacked tetrachords, melodic intervals of an augmented 2nd, a leading tone a whole step below the modal tonic, and chromatically altered pitches in adjacent octaves.

Different prayer modes often share common characteristics, e.g., the similarity between the beginning and end of motives from the *Avot* prayer for *Sabbath morning and *Adonai malach* from *shofar* of *Rosh Hashanah *musaf.* Jewish prayer modes can be grouped into modal families of which there are 3 principal ones: *magein avot, ahavah rabbah* and *Adonai malach* (also see *Selicha* and *Ukrainian-Dorian mode). Each has a unique scale and set of motives, and is often categorized according to the scale that can be derived from the mode's motives.

Bibl: B. Cohon, "Structure of Synagogue Prayer Chant," *JAMS* 3 (1950) 17–32; H. Avenary, "The Concept of Mode in European Synagogue Chant," *Yuval* 2 (1971) 11–21.   AJB

John XXII (*b* Cahors 1249; *d* Avignon 1334). Pope (from 1316) who issued the decree *Docta sanctorum patrum* in reaction to growing complaints about abuses in worship music.   AWR

Johnson, (Francis) Hall (*b* Athens GA 1888; *d* New York, 1970). Composer, arranger and author. He was educated at the universities of Atlanta, Pennsylvania and the New York Institute of Musical Art. He performed in all-African American professional theater productions and was musical director for Broadway's *The Green Pastures.* Johnson established and conducted the professional "Hall Johnson Choir," dedicated to preserving African American *spirituals. He arranged spirituals, including the anthology *Thirty Negro Spirituals Arranged for Voice and Piano* (1949). His compositions include *Take My Mother Home* (1941, based on St. John's gospel), the *cantata *Son of Man,* and *Ain't Got Time To Die* (1956, for choir).

Bibl: E. Southern, *The Music of Black Americans,* 3rd ed. (New York, 1997) 420–22.   MWC

Johnson, James Weldon (*b* Jacksonville FL 1871; *d* Wiscasset ME 1938). Poet and Secretary of the NAACP. His publications include *The Book of American Negro Spirituals* (1925) and *The Second Book of American Negro Spirituals* (1926). He wrote *"Lift every voice and sing" with his brother J. R. *Johnson.   RJS

Johnson, J(ohn) Rosamond (*b* Jacksonville FL 1873; *d* New York 1954). Composer, author and singer. He arranged *spirituals in 2 collections produced with his brother J. W. *Johnson (1925, 1926). He also authored *Shout Songs* (1936), *Rolling Along in Song* (1937) and with his brother jointly wrote *"Lift every voice and sing."   RJS

Johnson, William Allen (*b* Nassau NY 1816; *d* Westfield MA 1901). *Organ builder. First associated with the *Hook firm, he began building his own *instruments in 1847, establishing a firm that would last until 1898 and produce 860 organs.   JWK

Joncas, J(an) Michael (*b* Minneapolis 1951). Liturgist, composer and teacher. A RC priest, he holds a doctorate in *liturgy from Rome's San Anselmo and serves on the faculty of the University of St. Thomas (St. Paul). Recognized in the post-*Vatican II era as a leader in compositions of *ritual music (e.g., "On eagle's wings"), his writings include *From Sacred Song to Ritual Music* (1997).   FJM

Jones, Charles Price (*b* Texas Valley GA 1865; *d* Los Angeles 1949). Minister, founder and first bishop of the Church of Christ (Holiness) USA. A *gospel and *hymn writer, Jones composed some 1,000 gospel hymns.   DWM

Joseph II (*b* 1741 Vienna; *d* there 1790). Holy Roman Emperor (from 1765). In the spirit of the Enlightenment he decreed simplicity and intelligibility in worship, i.e., increased congregational vernacular singing, less ceremony and brevity in instrumental and choral music. "Josephinism" is the name given to the effort to subordinate the church to national interests underlying these reforms.   AWR

Josephinism. See *Joseph II.

Joseph the Hymnographer, St. (*b* Syracuse, Sicily *c* 816; *d* Constantinople 886). Prolific Greek *hymn writer. He lived a monastic life at Thessalonica. Later at Constantinople he was associated with the Studium Monastery and sided with the "orthodox" party in the iconoclastic controversy, resulting in his exile. *c* 850 he founded a monastery in Constantinople. Of the 2,000 *canons in the *menaion, more than 1,000 of them are credited to Joseph.   CFS

Josquin Desprez <Josquin des Prèz> (*b* *c* 1440; *d* Condé-sur-l'Escaut, 1521). One of the greatest composers of the *Renaissance; certainly the most important before the latter half of the 16th century. Little of his early life and schooling is known. He was likely a singer at the collegiate church at St. Quentin, certainly a singer at the Milan Cathedral (1459–72). It is probable that he was a pupil of *Ockeghem. At various times he served in Milan, in Rome at the papal chapel, in France and Ferrara, where he was followed by *Obrecht. Highly esteemed by contemporaries, Josquin was the subject of 3 publications by Petrucci. He was *Luther's favorite composer of whom he said, "Josquin is a master of the notes, which must express what he desires; on the other hand, other choral composers must do what the notes dictate." His compositions include *c* 20 *masses, at least 110 *motets (many more of questionable authenticity) and a variety of secular works. Among his works worthy of special note are the *Missa pange lingua, Missa sine nomine, Missa de beata virgine* and that based on *L'*Homme armé.

Bibl: H. Osthoff, *Josquin Desprez* (Tutzing, 1962–65); F. Blume, *Josquin des Prez* (New York, 1971); S. R. Charles, *Josquin des Pres* (New York, 1983).   CFS

Jubilate (Deo) [Latin]. "Be joyful (in the Lord)." Ps 100. The *BCP (since 1551) indicates that it may be sung as an alternative to the *Benedictus* at *morning prayer. There exist innumerable festal settings of this psalm, e.g., by *Purcell.   KRH

Jubilee Singers. See *Fisk Jubilee Singers.

Jubilus [from Latin *jubilare,* "to shout"]. A *melisma on the final syllable of the *chant *allelu*ia* in the Latin *mass. Associated with the alleluia as early as the 4th century.   MSD

Judah Ha-levi <Judah Halevi, Yehuda ben Shemuel ha-Levi> (*b* Tuldea, Spain before 1075; *d* Egypt? 1141). Poet and philosopher. He wrote over 800 poems in Hebrew including secular and religious poetry; *Diwan* is his noted collection of both types of poetry. Ha-levi was an important creator of **piyyutim*. The themes in these texts range from biblical history to events during his life time. Many of his poems are found in *Ashkenazic and *Sephardic manuscripts and prayer books. One of the best-known is *Yom Shabbaton* (Hebrew, "Day of rest") traditionally sung at the Saturday morning *Sabbath meal. MLK

Judas Maccabeaus. *Oratorio by *Handel (1746) celebrating the Jewish hero who led the rebellion against Syria (2nd century BCE), recounted in 1 Macc 3:1–9:22. CRY

Julian, John (*b* St. Agnes, Cornwall 1839; *d* Topcliffe, Yorkshire 1913). Hymnologist. An ordained (1866) Anglican clergyman, he worked in parish ministry in the N of England. Julian published *Concerning Hymns* (1874), a number of pamphlets, and edited and contributed major articles to the monumental *Dictionary of Hymnology* (1892; rev. 1907; various reprints). It remains the standard reference work on *hymnology. RAL

K

Kaan, Fred (*b* Haarlem, Netherlands 1929). *Hymn text writer and minister for the United Reformed Church of England. He received a doctorate from Geneva Theological College for his dissertation "Emerging Language in Hymnody." His hymns appear in almost every late-20th-century, English-language *hymnal. PAB

Kabbalah <cabbala>, **music in**. *Kabbalah* (Hebrew, "reception") is a generic term for Jewish mysticism. More specifically, it is the esoteric theosophy that developed in 12th–13th century Spain and Provence concerned about the hidden connections between an unknowable God and the created world. The resulting symbolic cosmology posits the existence of 7 to 10 *sefirot* (Hebrew, "divine spheres") through which God's power emanates. To perfect the world all spheres have to be aligned in a proper portion. Keeping the biblical commandments activates the proper sequence of the spheres; music also serves to activate these spheres.

A central text is the *Zohar,* a mystical commentary on the Torah, mostly writ-ten by M. de León (*d* 1305). Musical considerations are prominent in the *Zohar.* One teaching is that new melodies are created everyday and these melodies stem from the holiness of God; thus music emanates from God. Singing *"Kadosh, kadosh, kadosh"* from the *Kedusha* section of *shacharit* is said to mirror the angels' activity. Singing these words in the earthly world provides a connection to the heavenly world and the *sefirot*. Other symbols such as the *shofar* play a significant role. When God gave the Ten Commandments a *shofar* was heard (Ex 19:13-16, 20:15). Its use on *Yamim Noraim* relates to the capacity of the *shofar's* sound to call the heart to repent.

Bibl: A. Shiloah, *Jewish Mystical Traditions* (Detroit, 1992) 131–56.   MLK

Kabbalat Shabbat [Hebrew, "meeting the Sabbath"]. The liturgical unit which begins Friday *ma'ariv. It contains Pss 95–99 and 29, continues with *Lechah dodi,* followed by Pss 92 and 93. It was introduced by Kabbalists in 16th-century Safed, Palestine. They would go out into the fields and literally "meet the *Sabbath."

The first 6 *psalms and *Lechah dodi* are recited in the *Adonai malach* *mode (though *Lechah dodi*'s 2 *stanzas *"Mikdash melech"* and *"Lo tevoshi"* revert to minor with a *Ukranian-Dorian inflection reverting back to *Adonai malach* before the *refrain). The many choral settings of *Lechah dodi* do not always adhere to any particular mode. Pss 92 and 93 are generally recited in the *Magein avot* mode. Nineteenth-century European composers often set Pss 92 and 93 chorally for synagogue worship, but not necessarily according to any particular mode or modal pattern. IAG

Kaddish <*Qaddish*> [Aramaic]. "Holy." A responsive prayer of consecration and praise; technically a *doxology, recited only with a *minyan* (Hebrew, "quorum"). There are 4 different forms of *Kaddish,* all in Aramaic and beginning with the same text *"Yitgadal v'yitkadash shmei rabbah"* ("May His great Name be magnified and sanctified"). The full version *Kaddish shalem* is recited by the *sheliach tsibbur* at the conclusion of a *service before the *Aleinu. The half-*Kaddish (or *Chatzi Kaddish*) is said after each sub-section of the service. In Middle E *Sephardic traditions the *Chatzi Kaddish* of *shacharit* is highlighted musically according to the *makam* of the day. A longer form is *Kaddish de'rabbanan,* recited in synagogue or classroom after the study of rabbinical literature, which includes a paragraph invoking God's blessings on all sages, teachers and students of Torah. *Kaddish yatom* is recited during a period of mourning. This "mourner's prayer" proclaims the supremacy of God and the immortality of Israel rather than the death of a relative or faith in the afterlife.

Bibl: EJ 10:660-62; I. Elbogen, *Jewish Liturgy,* trans. R. Scheindlin (Philadelphia, 1993 [1913]). SIW

Kaminski, Heinrich (*b* Tiengen 1886; *d* Ried 1946). Composer. His works combined *Bach-like *counterpoint, late German romanticism and mystical tendencies. In addition to an opera, symphonies and chamber music, compositions include a number of *organ and sacred choral compositions including a *Magnificat* (1925). PKG

Kanon [Greek; Slavonic]. "Rule, order." The central part of Byzantine *orthros sung after Ps 51 and before the *exapostolarion. Originally the *kanon* were the 9 scriptural *odes sung to conclude the *psalter, which was chanted in its entirety on all-night vigils (*pannychis) before Sundays and feast days. The 9 odes are: Ex 15:1-19; Deut 32:1-43; 1 Sam 2:1-10; Hab 3:2-19; Isa 26:9-20; Jonah 2:3-10; Dan 3:26-56; 3:57-88; Luke 1:46-55, 68-79. While singing ode 9, the deacon incenses the sanctuary, icons and church interior.

Ecclesiastical compositions (from 6 to 14 in number) are intercalated into the final *verses of the odes. They are sung according to the *octoechos with particular melodies that may be among the most ancient surviving *chants. The first to be intercalated is the *hirmos, on the theme of the ode. Then follow a series of *troparia, on the theme of the liturgical day, usually concluding with a *Theotokion. On feast days another *hirmos (*katabasia) follows, varying according to the season of the liturgical *year. Today the scriptural odes (except for Luke 1:46-55) are rarely sung; only the ecclesiastical compositions remain, intercalated with special *versicles written for the day.   DMP

Kantionale. See *cantional.

Kantor [German]. In Germany, a *church music leader and high-ranking school teacher responsible for instruction in music, and often Latin and rhetoric. See *precentor and *cantor.   VEG

Kantorei [German]. In the medieval period, a cathedral or court music ensemble. Later, a German church ensemble, often with students.   VEG

Kapelle [German]. "Chapel." By the 17th century the term refers to the group of instrumentalists and/or singers employed in a particular church or court. By the 19th century *Kapelle* had no necessary ecclesial referent and could connote any group of musicians.   VAC

Kapellmeister [German]. "Chapel master." (1) A leader of musicians in a court chapel or any court ensemble.
   (2) More recently, the term is interchangeable with "conductor."   VEG

Katabasia [Greek; Slavonic *katavasia*]. "The descents." The last in the series of *troparia sung at the scriptural *odes at Byzantine *orthros on Sundays and feast days. It is one of the *hirmosi of the *kanon, varying according to the season of the liturgical *year.   DMP

Katanyktikon [Greek; Slavonic *stikhir umitel'nyi,* also *pokajannyi*]. "Pentitential verse." A term applied to various penitential *stichera in the Byzantine *office,

particularly sung during *Lent at Sunday *hesperinos.   DMP

Katchko, Adolph (*b* Varta, Kaliscz Russia 1886; *d* New York 1958). *Cantor, composer and teacher. He served as cantor at Ansche Chesed in New York. A noted teacher, he also arranged many musical works; his archives are in the library of the Jewish Theological Seminary of America. His 3-volume *Thesaurus of Cantorial Liturgy* (1952) is an important collection of cantorial chanting.   MLK

Kathisma (pl. **kathismata**) [Greek]. "A sitting." (1) In the Byzantine rite, one of 20 sections into which the *psalter is divided. If chanted as a complete unit, each *kathismata* is followed by *katanyktikon and a prayer. One *kathisma* is sung at *hesperinos and 2 or 3 at *orthros, so that the whole psalter is sung during a week.
   (2) A *hymn sung at the end of a *kathisma* according to one of the *troparion tones of the *octoechos. In Slavonic this hymn is called *sedalen,* often translated as "Sessional hymn."   DMP

Keach, Benjamin (*b* Stoke Hammond, N Buckinghamshire 1640; *d* London 1704). Particular Baptist minister. Keach introduced congregational singing into his church at Horselydown which split the congregation and led to a pamphlet war including his *The Breach Repair'd* (1691).   PHW

Keble, John (*b* Fairford 1792; *d* Bournemouth 1866). Anglican clergyman whose sermon at Oxford University ("The English Apostasy," 1833) is widely regarded as the beginning of the *Oxford Movement. His *hymn texts and writings (e.g., collected poems *The*

Christian Year, 1827) gave direction to the movement's reforms.   FJM

Kedushah <*Qedushah*> [Hebrew]. "Sanctification." A prayer inserted into the third *benediction of the *Amidah* whenever the *Amidah* is recited publicly, deriving its name from the congregation's *response *"Kadosh, kadosh, kadosh"* ("Holy, holy, holy," Is 6:3). When the *Amidah* is recited individually the *Kedushah* is replaced by a blessing that sanctifies God. Besides *"Kadosh,"* the *Kedushah* contains 2 other congregational responses: *"Baruch k'vod"* ('Blessed be his honor," Ez 3:12) and *"Yimloch"* ("God will reign," Ps 146:10). These 3 congregational responses are common to the varying versions of the *Kedushah.* The version of the *Kedushah* employed depends on the type of day (whether *Sabbath, festival or holiday) and type of *service (whether *shacharit, *musaf or *minchah). Likewise the musical mode utilized by *chazzan or reader depends on the day and service. Since the *Kedushah* is a poignant demonstration of homage to God, many dramatic settings for *cantor, and especially cantor and *choir have been written.   IAG

Kelly, Columba <John> (*b* Williamsburg IA 1930). Benedictine monk and priest of *St. Meinrad Archabbey. He studied with *Cardine for a doctorate in Rome. As a musicologist, Kelly specializes in the manuscript history of *Gregorian chant. He is also a composer of contemporary *liturgical music in the *chant idiom.   NDM

Kemp, Helen (*b* Bucks County PA 1918). Children's choral specialist, com-poser and teacher who served on the faculty at *Westminster Choir College (1944–49, 1972–83). Kemp authored *Of Primary Importance,* 2 vols., (1989 and 1991).   JDW

Kemp, John (*b* Watsontown PA 1916; *d* Perkasie PA 1997). Church musician, choral conductor and educator. He taught at *Westminster Choir College (1944–49) and later headed its *church music department (1972–83). Kemp served as executive director of the *Choristers Guild (1968–72).   JDW

Kentucky Harmony. A collection of 143 *psalm tunes, *hymns and *anthems, first published by *Davisson in 1816. The tunes are mostly drawn from previously compiled *tune books, although 17 are new, including 7 by Davisson. The music is printed for 4 voices in *shape-note notation. A landmark in American hymnody, 5 editions appeared between 1816 and 1826.   EBF

Kerle, Jacobus de (*b* Ypres 1532?; *d* Prague 1591). Composer, organist and RC priest. Kerle held various church and court appointments in the Netherlands, Germany and Italy. He was commissioned by Cardinal Otto von Waldburg to compose *Preces speciales* (Latin, "special prayers"), sung at the Council of *Trent. Their restrained style and textual clarity probably influenced that council's decision to allow *polyphony.   LFH

Kerll <Kerl, Kherl, Cherl, Gherl>, **Johann Kaspar** (*b* Adorf, Saxony 1627; *d* Munich 1693). Organist and composer. He studied in Rome with *Carissimi, and then served royal courts in Munich and Vienna. Kerll was organist at St.

Stephen's Cathedral in Vienna, where he was assisted by *Pachelbel. Kerll wrote 18 *masses, 16 Latin sacred works, *keyboard pieces and dramatic works (most of which are lost).   FKG

Kerovah <*Qerovah*> (pl. **kerovot**) [Hebrew]. "To approach." A form of *piyyut* said during the repetition of the *Amidah* on 4 special *Sabbaths (Parashat Shekalim, Parashat Zachor, Parashat Parah and Parashat HaChodesh),* the *Three Festivals, *Purim* and fast days. SIW

Keyboard. A set of keys or levers which actuate the mechanism of musical *instruments such as the *organ, piano, harpsichord, clavichord, etc. The Greek *hydraulis is the most likely origin for keyboard instruments. Keyboards were diatonic (with an added B-flat) up to the 13th century, but by the early 14th century the continued development of *polyphony created the need for increased compass and more chromatic notes. By the 15th century the keyboard took on the general appearance it has today: 2 rows of keys with the sharp/flats grouped by 2 and 3 in the upper row. Organs, depending on the size of instrument, may have multiple keyboards as well as a pedal board (a keyboard played with the feet).   DCI

Kiddush <*Qiddush*> [Hebrew]. "Sanctification." A prayer sanctifying a *Sabbath or festival, said at home before a meal, over a cup of wine. For the Sabbath it states, "Remember the Sabbath day and keep it holy" (Ex 20:8), thus consecrating the Sabbath. In the *Ashkenazic tradition *Kiddush* is also recited at the synagogue on Sabbaths and festivals. It is usually chanted in the *Adonai malach* mode, although there are different motifs for each of the holidays. *Lewandowski's setting is the best-known, popular throughout the world.   BES

Kilgen, George & Sons. *Organ building firm. Founded by George Kilgen (*b* Durlach, Germany 1821; *d* St. Louis 1902) who immigrated to the US in 1848, first worked with the *Jardine firm, eventually established his own company in New York (1851) and finally moved it to St. Louis (1873). While son Charles Christian Kilgen (1859–1932) was the firm's president, an organ was built for New York's St. Patrick's Cathedral (1928).   JWK

Kimball, William Wallace (*b* near Rumford ME 1828; *d* Chicago 1904). *Organ builder. Kimball opened a reed organ factory (1880) near Chicago. There he developed a portable pipe organ, easily shipped to churches and small towns throughout the Midwest. Two of the firm's large installations are at Denver's RC Immaculate Conception Cathedral and Episcopal St. John's Cathedral. Enormous municipal organs were built for St. Paul, Memphis and Worcester.   JWK

Kindermann, Johann (*b* Nuremberg 1616; *d* there 1655). Composer and organist. He studied with *Staden, then pursued studies in Italy. Kindermann served as organist at Nuremberg's Egidienkirche (from 1640). He wrote instrumental and *organ compositions, but mostly sacred vocal works (*motets, *cantatas, etc.).   JLB

Kingdom, The. An *oratorio by *Elgar (op. 51, 1906) employing biblical texts.

It was a sequel to *The *Apostles*. A third oratorio in a projected trilogy, *The Last Judgment,* was left incomplete.   DWM

Kinnor [Hebrew]. A type of lyre played by King *David, used in the *Temple and mentioned elsewhere in the Hebrew Bible. It was played "by hand" (1 Sam 16:23) or with a plectrum.   DWM

Kinot [Hebrew]. "Dirges." Laments recited in the synagogue on *Tisha B'av. Most *kinot* were composed in the *Middle Ages and are recited to commemorate various disasters. The use of rhyme and acrostics (incorporating the author's name) are common features.   SIW

Kirleise. See *Leise*.

Kirnberger, Johann Philipp (*b* Saalfeld 1721; *d* Berlin 1783). Theorist, violinist and composer. He studied composition with J. S. *Bach, and wrote *sacred, chamber and *keyboard music. Kirnberger developed a system of tuning still used for neo-Baroque *organs. He is known chiefly for his theoretical writings, especially the 4-volume *Die Kunst des reinen Satzes in der Musik* (1771–79) in which he espoused Bach's compositional method.   MEC

Kleine Orgelmesse [German]. "Little Organ Mass." Nickname for F. J. *Haydn's *Missa brevis Sancti Joannis de Deo* (1775?) in B-flat major. The *organ has an extended solo in the *Benedictus*.   RDH

Koch, Johannes (*b* Börnecke 1918). Organist, composer and teacher who served on the faculty of the Landeskirchenmusikschule in Herford. His works include choral and instrumental music for church use.   PKG

Kodály, Zoltán (*b* Kecskemét 1882; *d* Budapest 1967). Composer. With *Bartók he collected and transcribed *folk songs. Folk elements occur in his music, but folk melodies are not directly quoted. The comic opera *Háry János* (1925) is his most popular work; among his sacred compositions are *Psalmus Hungaricus* (1923), *Te Deum* (1936) and *Missa brevis* (1944). His strong desire to advance musical literacy among young persons resulted in the "Kodály Method," which employs a "moveable do" solfege system as well as songs, games and graded exercises.   DCI

Koinonikon [Greek; Slavonic *prichasten*]. "Hymn of Communion." The *psalm sung at the distribution of *communion in the Byzantine *divine liturgy. Each *verse is sung with the *refrain of the triple *alleluia. The most ancient *koinonikon* was Ps 34:9, still sung at the *presanctified divine liturgy. The *koinonikon* is variable today, and reduced to 1 psalm verse. Ps 150 is sung on Sunday. Occasionally there are verses from *epistles (Titus 3:4 on *Epiphany), *gospels (John 6:56 for mid-Pentecost, the 25th day of the *Pentecostarion,* half-way between *Easter and *Pentecost) or purely ecclesiastical compositions, all sung with the triple alleluia. *Bibl:* D. Conomos, *The Late Byzantine and Slavonic Communion Cycle* (Washington, 1985). DMP

Koleda <kolenda, colenda> (pl. **kolędy**) [Polish]. "Carol." A *Christmas *carol.

Such songs were known from the 12th century; an especially large repertoire exists from the 17th–18th centuries. Many were brought by immigrants to the US; some have crossed over into common English usage (e.g., *"W zlobie lezy"* as "Infant Holy, Infant Lowly"). JMT

Kol nidre <*nidrei*> [Aramaic]. "All vows." A text recited on *Yom Kippur* evening to nullify all vows and oaths. The text probably originated in the 8th–11th centuries; the deeply expressive melody associated with the text most likely originated between the mid-15th and mid-16th centuries and is found only in *Ashkenazic communities (see *Misinnai* tunes). Since the first appearance of the *Kol nidre* melody in a manuscript by A. Beer (1765), cantors and composers have created numerous versions and arrangements.

Since its inception, rabbis have tried to minimize or eliminate its use, concerned that people will sin and use this prayer to nullify that sin. Congregations, however, insisted on its use in the *liturgy, claiming that the stirring melody set a spiritual tone for the holidays that they would not be without. M. Bruch's *Kol Nidrei* (1881) for cello and orchestra is based on the traditional melody.

Bibl: A. Z. Idelsohn, "The Kol Nidre Tune," *Hebrew Union College Annual* 8–9 (1931–32) 493–509. MLK

Kondak [Slavonic]. See *Kontakion*.

Kontakion (pl. **kontakia**) [Greek; Slavonic *kondak*]. "Scroll." (1) A configuration of *hymns in the Byzantine *office consisting of a *prooimion* ("preface"; also called *koukoulion*, "cowl") and ordinarily 24 *oikoi*. Composition of *kontakia* followed strict poetic rules. The *prooimion* is sung as a *refrain after each of the *oikoi*, which are usually *akrostichis* or *alphabetos*. Often described as a "sung sermon," *kontakia* were thematic, often dramatic presentations of the feast being celebrated. The most renowned writer of *kontakia* was St. *Romanos, though the genre is older. Each *kontakion* was written on a separate "scroll," hence the name. *Kontakia* were originally sung at *orthros, but after the 9th century were replaced by the *kanon. Today the *prooimion* is sung only once according to 1 of the *octoechos, and only 1 *oikos* is read (the original melodies having fallen into disuse) after *ode 6 of the *kanon. The complete *kontakion* for the deceased with all 24 *oikoi* is still sung at a priest's funeral. *Kontakia* have also entered the *divine liturgy and are sung as a *perissos* to the *troparia of the third *antiphon (see *mikra eisodos, also *akathistos) of the *enarxis*.

(2) The name of the priest's liturgical *book, containing the prayers of the *divine liturgy (see *liturgikon), presented to him as a scroll at ordination.

Bibl: M. Carpenter, trans., *Kontakia of Romanos, Byzantine Melodist*, 2 vols. (Columbia MO, 1970 & 1973); E. Lash, trans., *Kontakia on the Life of Christ* (New York, 1995). DMP

Krestobogoroditchen [Slavonic]. See *Staurotheotokion*.

Kreutz, Robert E. (*b* LaCrosse WI 1922; *d* Denver 1996). RC liturgical composer who studied composition at Chicago's American Conservatory and at UCLA. His works include *psalm settings, *masses, *motets, *anthems and *hymns including "Gift of Finest Wheat." VCF

Krieger, Johann Philipp (*b* Nuremberg 1649; *d* Weissenfels 1725). Composer, organist and *keyboard player, associated chiefly with the court at Weissenfels. He wrote over 2,000 *cantatas (of which 74 are extant). Kreiger was considered the "father of the new cantata" which introduced operatic *secco* *recitatives, *da capo* *arias and employed free texts (e.g., those written by E. Neumeister) beyond those from scripture or *hymns. CFS

Kuhnau, Johann (*b* Geising 1660; *d* Leipzig 1722). J. S. *Bach's predecessor as *Kantor* at St. Thomas in Leipzig. One of the most erudite men of his time, he composed *motets on *chorales and other sacred pieces. He was perhaps the greatest clavier composer before Bach. DCI

Kümmerle, Salomon (*b* Malmsheim near Stuttgart 1832; *d* Samaden 1896). Editor, writer, collector and publisher. He compiled the first modern encyclopedia of Protestant *church music, the 4-volume *Enzyklopädie der evangelischen Kirchenmusik* (1888–95). MPB

Kyriale [from Greek *Kyrios,* "Lord"]. A term used from the late 15th century for a collection of chants for the *ordinary of the mass. The modern edition is the *Kyriale Vaticanum,* with a supplement *Kyriale simplex.* FCQ

Kyrie eleison [Greek]. "Lord, have mercy." (1) The first chant of the *ordinary of the mass since at least the 8th century. Textually it is comprised of *Kyrie eleison* (3 times), *Christe eleison* (Greek, "Christ have mercy," 3 times), *Kyrie eleison* (3 times); today RCs and others reduce this 9-fold structure to *Kyrie-Christe-Kyrie.*

(2) A congregational *acclamation borrowed from pagan worship, appearing in Christian *litanies by the 4th century. PAJ

Kyrieleis <*kyrioleis, kirleis*>. A shortened form of *Kyrie eleison,* serving as a popular *refrain in *hymns and spiritual *folk songs in northern Europe. See *Leise.* PAJ

L

Lachan [Hebrew, Aramaic]. "Melody." The melody used to recite a Jewish liturgical text such as a *piyyut. The term is most commonly found in the Middle E *Sephardic Jewish communities where a prevalent practice has been to set Hebrew texts to existing Spanish, Turkish or Arabic melodies. The originating melody is known as the *lachan*. MLK

Ladies of the Grail. See *Grail, The.

Laetare Sunday. See *year, liturgical.

Lalande <Delalande>, **Michel-Richard de** (*b* Paris 1657; *d* Versailles 1726). Composer. He served as a singer at St. Germain d'Auxerrois in Paris and as organist for various churches there. From 1683 he held different positions at the royal chapel, becoming master in 1714. Lalande wrote ballets, symphonies and incidental music; especially notable are his over 70 *motets. JLB

Lallouette <Lalouette>, **Jean François** (*b* Paris 1651; *d* there 1728). Composer of popular and *sacred music, teacher and violinist. He studied composition with *Lully. Choirmaster of Paris' Notre Dame (1709–27), he wrote *masses, *motets and a *Miserere. RJB

Lamb of God. See *Agnus Dei.

Lamentations (of Jeremiah). (1) One of the 5 *megilot in the Hebrew Bible; its title is taken from the first Hebrew word of the opening chapter *("Eicha")*. Mourning the destruction of Jerusalem in 587 BCE, each of its 5 sections describe the lowly state to which Jerusalem had been reduced. A distinctively mournful melody is used to chant this text.

(2) A setting of some or all of the *Lamentations of Jeremiah* for use in Christian *liturgy, especially during *Holy Week. DMR

Lamp-lighting psalms. The *psalms for the *lucenarium. While *psalmody varies for this *service, Ps 141 is relatively constant. See *hesperinos. EBF

Landini <Landino>, **Francesco** (*b* Fiesole? or Florence? *c* 1325; *d* Florence 1397). Composer and instrumentalist. After being blinded by smallpox when young he turned to music, mastering several *instruments and earning renown as an organist, *organ builder and tuner, and poet. From 1365 until his death he served as musician at San Lorenzo in Florence. The most famous 14th-century Florentine *ars nova composer, he wrote over 150 extant works, all secular (primarily *ballate*). Perhaps he composed *sacred music, but none survives. While Landini did not invent it, he used what is now called the *Landini cadence.

Bibl: L. Ellinwood, "Francesco Landini and His Music," *MQ* 22 (1936) 190–216; K. von Fischer, "Landini, Francesco," *NGDMM* 10:428–34.   MEC

Landini cadence. Cadence in which the 6th degree of the scale is inserted between the leading tone and its resolution at the octave. It occurs often in the compositions of *Landini and was widely used throughout the *Renaissance.   JBF

Langlais, Jean (*b* Fontenelle 1907; *d* Paris 1991). Composer and organist at Ste. Clotilde in Paris (from 1945). Blind from birth, he studied at the Institut National des Jeunes Aveugles, then the Paris Conservatory with *Dupré and P. Dukas; at the latter he won first prize for *organ (1930) and composition (1932); eventually Langlais joined both faculties. He was renowned for his improvisational skills. His large output of organ music includes 2 organ symphonies (1942, 1977) and *American Suite* (1959); he also wrote many liturgical choral works. Much of his music is based upon *Gregorian themes.   MSD

La Rue, Pierre de (*b* Tournai? *c* 1460; *d* Courtrai 1518). One of the leading composers of his time. He was a singer at the Siena Cathedral (1482?–85), 's Hertogenbosch Cathedral (1489–92), the Burgundian *Hofkapelle* of Maximilian and son Philip (1492–1503?), the court of Marguerite of Austria in Mechelen and the private *Kapelle* of Archduke Karl (1514–16). His over 30 *masses and *motets feature canonic writing, use of *ostinato, sequences, frequent cadences and imitation. He also wrote *Magnificat*s, *lamentations and *chansons*. He preferred *plainsong to secular songs as the source of the *cantus firmus*.   JDW

Lassus, Orlande <Roland> **de** <Orlando di Lasso> (*b* Mons 1532?; *d* Munich 1594). Among the most significant of *Renaissance composers. He briefly served as choirmaster at St. John Lateran in Rome (1553–4); most of his career (from 1556) was in the service of Duke Albrecht V of Bavaria, becoming his *Kapellmeister in 1563. In that capacity he came to know both *Gabrelis.

Lassus produced over 2,000 vocal works, including secular pieces in Italian, French and German. His *liturgical music included *c* 70 *masses; *c* 50 of these are *parody masses, often employing material from his own sacred or secular compositions. He also wrote over 500 *motets (many in 5 parts), *c* 30 *hymns, more than 100 *Magnificat*s, 4 *passions and various *offertories, *antiphons, *psalms (e.g., *Psalmi . . . poenitentiales,* 1584) and private devotional pieces. Lassus published 5 large volumes of his religious music (*Patrocinium musices,* 1573–6); another was posthumously published by his sons (*Magnum opus musicum,* 1604). His writing demonstrates a wide versatility and expressive range. Some pieces exhibit highly chromatic writing, while still maintaining voice-leading. His contrapuntal technique was strongly influenced by the writing of *Willaert.

Bibl: J. Erb, *Orlando di Lasso* (New York, 1990); R. G. Gust, *Music, Mode and Words in Orlando di Lasso's Last Works* (Princeton, 1994).   JBF

Lauda, Sion [Latin]. "Praise, Sion." The *incipit* of a *sequence written (c 1264) by *Thomas Aquinas for the *mass on the feast of *Corpus Christi*. Its use is now optional.   NDM

Lauda (pl. **laude**) **(spirituale)** [Italian]. "Spiritual praise." Italian religious song from the *Middle Ages and *Renaissance. Originating in the mid-13th century, these songs were first associated with penitential groups, early Franciscan missionaries and other lay organizations. The earliest *laude* were *monophonic, usually in the vernacular; a notable example is the "*Canticle of the Sun" by *Francis of Assisi. Later *laude* were generally *polyphonic, often elaborations on the earlier monophonic works. For subject matter, these songs often spoke in praise of the Virgin or of the nativity, passion and resurrection of Christ. In spirit and form they were closely related to the early English *carol. They were employed in various settings: *processions of flagellants (see *Geisslerlieder*) or other penitents, sacred plays, preaching *services and the devotions of confraternities known as *laudesi* companies. During the *Counter-Reformation *laude* grew in popularity throughout Italy, and the song form remained part of the popular Italian musical tradition well into the 19th century.

Bibl: C. Barr, *The Monophic Lauda and the Lay Religious Confraternities* (Kalamazoo, 1988); B. Wilson, *Music and Merchants* (NY, 1992).   VAL

Laudes **(regiae)** [Latin]. "(Royal) praises." *Acclamations sung to honor a monarch or high-ranking prelate; an early medieval example (c 796–800) contains the *refrain *"Christus vincit, Christus regnat, Christus imperat"* (Latin, "Christ conquers, Christ reigns, Christ commands"). Often *laudes* were incorporated into *litanies in medieval worship.   NDM

Lauds [from Latin *laudo,* "I praise"]. (1) Dawn/morning prayer in the Roman rite *divine office. The fundamental structure in the present Roman rite comprises: opening dialogue and *doxology; morning *hymn; *psalmody (2 *psalms and a Hebrew Bible *canticle); scripture reading with (optional) short *response; *Benedictus;* intercessions; *Our Father; *collect; *blessing and dismissal. Ps 63 is frequently assigned to lauds.
(2) Pss 148–150.   JMJ

Law, Andrew (*b* Milford CT 1749; *d* Cheshire CT 1821). *Singing school teacher, *tune book compiler, *church music reformer and ordained Congregational minister. Law taught in singing schools in New England and the Middle Atlantic states. He published numerous tune books; in some he espoused the superiority of European over American *sacred music. He also invented a form of staffless *shape-note notation.   DWM

Lechah <*Lekhah*> **dodi** [Hebrew]. "Come my beloved." A *hymn recited during *Kabbalat Shabbat,* at the beginning of Friday *ma'ariv*. Written by Rabbi Sh'lomoh Halevi Alkavetz of

Safed in 1529, the author included his name in the first 8 of the poem's 9 *stanzas in an acrostic. The poem's title is from Song of Songs 7:12.

It opens with the *refrain "Come my friend to meet the bride, let us welcome the presence of the Sabbath." The idea of going out to greet the *Sabbath bride comes from rabbinic accounts that describes scholars going out to the fields to welcome the Sabbath Queen (*Babylonian Talmud Shabbat* 119a).

It is recited responsively. At the last stanza, *"Boi veshalom"* (Hebrew, "Come in peace") all rise and face the entrance of the synagogue to greet both the Sabbath bride and those mourning in the community. Immediately preceded by 6 *psalms, (*Kabbat Shabbat), Lechah dodi* is the 7th hymn parallel to the 7th day of creation. According to *Midrash Breishit Rabbah* 11, God told the newly created Sabbath, "Israel shall be your mate." Therefore, every week Israel waits for the approaching Sabbath as a groom awaits his bride. On the Sabbath, God and Israel are joined in holy union, symbolized in the *Lechah dodi.*

There are many musical settings of this text that are often elaborate; most notable is that by *Lewandowski. Since the 1960s *Lechah dodi* is sung to a range of *folk and popular melodies.

Bibl: M. Nulman, *The Encyclopedia of Jewish Prayer* (New Jersey, 1993). ISK

Lechner, Leonhard (*b* Adige Valley, S Tyrol 1553?; *d* Stuttgart 1606). Composer. A chorister under *Lassus in Munich, Lechner eventually became *Kapellmeister* at the RC court of Hechingen (1584) where his Lutheranism was problematic; later he became *Kapellmeister* at Stuttgart

(1587). He wrote a *Magnificat, *motets, *psalms, *masses and a celebrated *passion. JLB

Lectionary [from Latin *lectio,* "a reading"]. (1) A schema of selected (ordinarily scriptural) readings for liturgical use on specific days through the year. The synagogue provides the earliest examples of lectionaries in this sense.

(2) A liturgical *book containing scripture texts read at worship; it often includes *responsorial psalms and *gospel acclamations. See *epistolary and *evangelary. EBF

Lector [from Latin *legere,* "to read"]. (1) The reader of scripture at worship

(2) Formerly a minor order in the RC church, preparatory for priesthood. Today it is formally considered a "ministry," and open to the laity. RDH

Ledor vador [Hebrew]. "From generation to generation." The last paragraph of the *Kedushah, except on the *High Holidays when the prayer *Kadosh Atah* ("Holy are You") is the final paragraph. It is recited in the *Jewish prayer mode appropriate to the *service. However, on some occasions (e.g., *Rosh Chodesh) the *mode changes after the *Kedushah. At such times the new mode for the remainder of the *Amidah* repetition will be introduced immediately before *Ledor vador* (beginning with *Yimloch,* "God will reign forever") and continue through *Ledor vador.* IAG

Leise (pl. **Leisen**) [from Greek *eléison,* "have mercy"]. A German *folk *hymn from the *Middle Ages that developed as an expansion of the *acclamation *Kyrie eleison;* *stanzas are always concluded with *Kyrieleis or some variant. It was sung by the congregation in processions and at special religious occasions. One of the best-known is *Christ ist erstanden,* a gloss on *Victimae paschali* and a favorite *cantus firmus* (like many other *Leisen*) for *motets authored by several generations of Lutheran composers.   MPB

Le Jeune, Claude <Claudin> (*b* Valenciennes 1528–30; *d* Paris 1600). Composer whose application of theories of musical and textual relationships had a lasting influence on French secular and *sacred music. His sacred compositions were rooted in his Protestant faith, especially his many *psalms; he also wrote *motets, a *mass and *chansons spirituelles.*   LMT

Lent. The penitential season of the Christian liturgical *year preceding *Easter. In the W it begins on Ash Wednesday and lasts 40 days. The origins of the season are obscure; it was clearly a period of baptismal preparation by the 4th century. Musically Lent is marked by the absence of the *alleluia and *Gloria in excelsis,* and the inclusion of various musical forms focused on the suffering and death of Christ (e.g., the *spiritual "Were you there?"), especially *passions. In the E this season is called Great Lent or Great Fast. There it begins on the Monday before the W Ash Wednesday and ends before *Holy Week.   MJG

Léonin <Leoninus> (*b* Paris *c* 1135; *d* there? *c* 1201). Composer and poet. He was probably educated in the cathedral schools of Notre Dame. His title *Magister* (Latin, "master") suggests that he received the master's degree. He was canon at St. Benoît in Paris, and by the 1180s at Notre Dame where he achieved prominence in numerous fields. His poetry was highly regarded through the *Middle Ages.

His exact musical contributions are a matter of controversy. He appears to be among the first named composers of liturgical *polyphony, writing an impressive amount of music, and possibly was a key figure in the introduction of *rhythmic modes. The 13th-century English theorist Anonymous IV observed that Léonin made a "great book of *organum*" (Latin, *Magnus liber organi*). No single extant manuscript contains the entire *Magnus liber,* but many musical compositions in 13th-century sources have been traced to this collection. Based on Anonymous IV's description, it is likely that *c* 100 of the 2-voice works in florid *organum* in these sources were by Léonin, though these might not be original but revised versions by Léonin or others.

Bibl: C. Wright, "Leoninus, Poet and Musician," *JAMS* 39 (1986) 1–35; J. Yudkin, *Music in Medieval Europe* (Prentice Hall NJ, 1989), 363–376.   DWM

Lesser doxology. See *Gloria Patri.*

Lesser hours. See *little hours.

Lesser litany. See *Kyrie.*

Lesson. A reading from scriptural or patristic sources at *eucharist or the *divine office; the term is more commonly used by Protestants than RCs.   MJG

Lessons and carols. A *Christmas eve *service, developed in the late 19th century by Bishop E. W. Benson for Truro Cathedral; adapted by E. Milner-White (1918) for King's College, Cambridge. It consists of 9 lessons and Christmas *carols; sometimes it is celebrated in

*Advent, substituting Advent *hymns. This service was the inspiration for *Britten's *Ceremony of Carols.   VCF

Levite [Hebrew]. A descendant of Levi, the third son of Jacob and Leah (Gen 29:34). Levites served as attendants and musicians in the second *Temple (1 Chr 15:18, 20, 16:15); their role in the Temple of Solomon is less clear. Some evidence suggests that Levites needed to be 30 years old to serve in the Temple (1 Chr 23:3), and concluded service at age 50 (Num 4:3). Their musical activity in the Temple consisted of singing *psalms and possibly other religious texts, and the playing of *instruments (e.g., the *kinnor, *nevel and occasionally the flute). Their service was signaled by priests playing trumpets and a cymbal crash. These are not practices in synagogue worship today.
   Bibl: A. Z. Idelsohn, *Jewish Music in its Historical Development* (New York, 1929) pp. 3–23.   MLK

Lewandowski, Louis (*b* Posen 1821; *d* Berlin 1894). Composer and choral director. He sang in Berlin (1834) under *chazzan A. Lion, who introduced him to the music of *Weintraub. In Berlin a relative of F. *Mendelssohn supported Lewandowski's formal musical training, though a serious nervous disorder forced him to discontinue his studies. In 1840 he aided Lion in introducing *Sulzer's music to Berlin's Jewish community. In 1864 he became choir director at the Oranienburgerstrasse Temple, equipped with an organ, enabling Lewandowski to be the first to create a Jewish *service with organ accompaniment. This was also the home of an important reformer of the synagogue service, A. Geiger, strengthening Lewandowski's link with the *Reform Movement.

His compositions bear the mark of the German choral style. There are traces of the *ahavah rabbah *mode in certain of his works as well as the traditional interplay between *cantor and *choir. He published 2 collections: *Kol Rinah* (1871) and *Todah V'Zimrah* (1876–82); better-known works include *Lechah dodi, Enosh K'chotzir Yomov* and a setting of Ps 150.
   Bibl: A. Z. Idelsohn, *Jewish Music in its Historical Development* (New York, 1929) 273–79.   MLK

Liber Usualis [Latin]. "Book for ordinary use." A Roman rite book of *chants, prayers and readings mostly for *mass and the *divine office for Sunday and major feasts. It was published by the monks of *Solesmes (1896) with various revisions (1903, 1934, 1955, 1963) reflecting changes in the ritual.   VCF

Lied (pl. **Lieder**) [German]. "Song, poem." A song in the German vernacular, originally a *folk song. There existed both *monophonic and *polyphonic *Lieder, setting both secular and sacred texts. H. *Isaac's *"Isbruck ich muss dich lassen"* is one of the oldest and most beautiful songs in German. *Marienlieder* were simple songs addressed to Mary. Various forms of *Lieder* developed in the late *Middle Ages and *Baroque period; in English the term is most often associated with German art songs of the late 18th and 19th century, of which *Schubert composed over 600.   ACL

Lift Every Voice and Sing. See *Black National Anthem.

Lining out. The practice of singing *psalms or *hymns, begun in 16th-century England and brought to the US, in which each line of every *stanza is read or sung by an individual, then repreated by the whole congregation.   RAL

Liszt, Franz <Ferencz, Franciscus> (*b* Raiding 1811; *d* Bayreuth 1886). The foremost pianist of the 19th century and a prolific, innovative composer. After retiring from the concert stage, Liszt took minor orders in the RC church, devoting much of his time to teaching. A life-long interest in *church music resulted in the composition of *oratorios (e.g., *Christus*), *masses (including a *Requiem, 1867–68), *psalm settings, *motets and other shorter liturgical choral works (e.g., his *Salve Regina, 1885), as well as works for *organ.   KRH

Litany [from Latin, *litania, letania*]. A prayer form, ordinarily characterized by the announcement of varying invocations (e.g., names of deities or saints) or supplications by a leader, each of which is followed by a fixed congregational *response. This genre may be distinguished from other *responsorial forms by the relative brevity, sometimes parity of the *call and response elements, giving it something of an insistent quality. Often quite rhythmic, litanies frequently accompany processions. Thus the term can signify the procession or the day upon which the procession occurs.

Litanic patterns are discernible in the Hebrew Bible (e.g., Ps 136, Dan 3.52-90). Notable extra-biblical Jewish litanies include the *hoshanot and *selichot. In Christianity, St. Polycarp (*d c* 155) provided a litany-like instruction about whom to remember in prayer (*Letter to Philippi* 12.3), but it is not clear whether the prayer itself took a litany form. The *Acts of Thomas* (3rd century) contains 2 sets of invocations (27, 50) which are litanic in structure, but without any set response. Clear evidence for a litany in Christian worship only appears at the end of the 4th century: *Apostolic Constitutions* (8.6.4, 9) provides evidence for such at *eucharist where the response is *Kyrie eleison. Various litanic forms continue to punctuate Christian worship, e.g., the *fraction litany. Also see *aitesis, *ektene and *synapte.

Bibl: H. Huglo: "Litany," *NGDMM* 11 (1980) 75–77; P. Jeffery: "Litany," *Dictionary of the Middle Ages* 7 (1986) 588–94.   EBF

Litany of all Saints. A complex *litany, ordinarily beginning with *Kyrie eleison followed by invocations to the Trinity with the response *miserere nobis* (Latin, "have mercy on us"), invocation of various saints with the *response *ora pro nobis* ("pray for us"), other supplications with response (e.g., *libera nos, Domine,* "deliver us, Lord") and an optional *collect. Based on Greek antecedents, it appeared in England by the 8th century, from which it spread through the W. This litany is traditionally employed in baptisms, ordinations, blessings and consecrations of persons, the dedication of a church and the commendation of the dying.   CLV

Lite [Greek; Slavonic *litiya*]. "Entreaty." In the Byzantine rite, a procession of clergy and people to a designated church in celebration of a feast, for intercession, or in thanksgiving. *Lite* included *stichera appropriate to the occasion (sung without *psalm *versicles), a *litany, concluding prayer and a prayer of the bowing of the heads. The term *lite* may refer to the *stichera* themselves *(stichera litia)*, the litany, or the whole *service. Today *lite* are sung in **hesperi-nos* after the **aitesis*, while the congregation processes to the narthex, returning to the nave during the **aposticha*. The singing of *lite* is connected with the blessing of bread, wheat, wine and oil at the end of *hesperinos*, to be distributed during **orthros*.   DMP

Little, William (*fl* Philadelphia *c* 1798–1801). Composer and *tune book compiler. With W. Smith he compiled *The Easy Instructor* (1801), the first tune book in 4-shape *shape-note notation.   DWM

Little <small> **entrance.** See **mikra eisodos*.

Little <lesser, minor> **hours.** The 3 brief daytime *hours of the *divine office: *terce, *sext and *none. Sometimes *prime is counted among the little hours as well, although it does not share the antiquity of the original 3 little hours. MJG

Liturgia horarum. See *divine office.

Liturgical books. See *books, liturgical.

Liturgical dance. See *dance, liturgical.

Liturgical drama. See *drama, liturgical.

Liturgical music [Latin *musica liturgica*]. (1) Music which unites with the liturgical action, serves to reveal the full significance of the rite and, in turn, derives its full meaning from the liturgical event and not simply from its liturgical setting. Infrequently employed in the literature before the 20th century, this term came to prominence in the 1960s as a designation of music integral to the RC *liturgy reformed after *Vatican II.

(2) Commonly employed as a synonym for *church music or *sacred music.   EBF

Liturgical Music Today. 1982 statement of the RC *Bishops' Committee on the Liturgy, supplementing **Music in Catholic Worship*. The statement discusses the musical implications of liturgical structure, the function and form of liturgical song, miscellaneous pastoral concerns, language and musical idioms. It provides directives for use of music in sacramental worship, funerals, *liturgy of the hours and the liturgical *year. It also offers guidelines for the use of past music in contemporary worship and considers music as a cultural expression.   JMJ

Liturgical year. See *year, liturgical.

Liturgikon (pl. **liturgika**) [Greek]. "Book of liturgies" [Slavonic *sluzhebnik*, "service book"]. The Byzantine liturgical *book containing the priest's texts of the *divine liturgy. It may also contain texts of **hesperinos* or **orthros*. Originally only the priest's prayers were included; by the time of the printing press it also contained the deacon's *litanies and most of the congregational *hymns. See **euchologion*, **hieratikon* and **kontakion*.   DMP

Liturgy [from Greek *laós*, "people" and *ergon*, "work"]. (1) Official corporate public worship. Its etymology signifies "service done on behalf of a people" as well as "service done by a people."

(2) In E Christian usage, the celebration of the *eucharist.

(3) In RC usage, the celebration of the sacraments, sacramentals and the

*divine office; sometimes liturgy is distinguished from "para-liturgy" or other popular devotions lacking formal and official approbation.   JMJ

Liturgy of the hours. See *divine office.

Lity [Greek]. See *lite.

LLA. See *Lutheran Liturgical Association.

Löhe, Wilhelm (b Neuendettelsau 1808; d there 1872). Bavarian pastor who led an important Lutheran liturgical reform. Löhe sponsored missionaries to N America and founded various charitable institutions. Notable among his 60 writings is *Agende für christliche Gemeinden* (1844) and a number of prayer books.   VEG

London [Ontario] **School of Church Music.** Founded in 1949 by G. Jeffery and E. *White. Its library began with the extensive music collection of R. Nold, and now includes Jeffery's collection, as well as many rare books and manuscripts now at the music faculty of the University of W Ontario. The school has regularly sponsored *organ recitals, choral concerts, symposia and national radio broadcasts in Canada.   PAB

Long service. See *service.

Lord, have mercy. See *Kyrie.

Lord's Prayer. See *Our Father.

Lord's Supper. A synonym for *eucharist. This biblical term (1 Cor 11:20), was employed by 16th-century Protestant reformers who rejected RC eucharistic teaching and the term *mass which symbolized such teaching.   CRY

Lossius <Lotze>, **Lucas** (b Vacha 1508; d Lüneberg 1582). Theologian, teacher and music theorist. He compiled *Psalmodia* (1553 and later editions), an influential anthology of *Gregorian chant adapted for Lutheran liturgical use.   RAL

Lotti, Antonio (b Venice or Hanover 1667?: d Venice 1740). Composer. He served as a chorister with *Caldara at St. Mark's in Venice; later he was appointed organist, then *maestro di cappella there. He composed operas, most of which were serious. Lotti's largest output was *sacred music, including *masses, *motets, *psalms and *oratorios. He bridges the late *Baroque and early *Classical styles, tending toward fragile texture, balanced phrasing, lyric and sentimental tone and skillful counterpoint. Much of his sacred music is *a cappella and popular with many choral directors.   DCI

Lovelace, Austin (b Rutherfordton NC 1919). Composer and choir director. Lovelace earned a *sacred music degree from *Union and served as the first president of the *Fellowship of Methodist Musicians (1955–57). He has composed over 800 works for choir, *organ and voice, contributing to the elevation of choral repertory and the development of *hymnody in the major Christian churches. He authored *Anatomy of Hymnody* (1965).   FJM

Loveless, Wendell (b Wheaton IL 1892; d Honolulu 1987). Radio broadcaster and *gospel *hymn writer. Loveless led IL radio station WMBI for 21 years. He also has served as pastor in IL, FL and HI. His many songs, including "Every Day with Jesus," were published in 5 volumes of *Radio Songs and Choruses*. DWM

Low mass. A term used prior to *Vatican II to describe *mass celebrated by a priest with a server in which all the texts were recited in a low voice (Italian *sotto voce*). Sometimes it included quiet *organ music. Permission was granted in the mid-20th century to include congregational *hymns at specified intervals. VCF

Lübeck, Vincent (*b* Paddingbüttel 1654; *d* Hamburg 1740). Organist, composer and teacher. His 9 extant *organ works, mostly *preludes and *fugues, are similar to *Buxtehude's but more technically demanding. He also composed 3 vocal *cantatas. RDH

Lucenarium [Latin]. "Lamp-lighting service." (1) An ancient term for *evening prayer which occurred at the lamplight hour, celebrating Christ as light of the world (see *vespers).

(2) The opening portion of evening prayer, sometimes including a procession with a lit paschal candle and the *hymn *Phos hilaron*.

(3) *Hesperinos*. RDH

Lully <Lulli>, Jean-Baptiste <Giovanni Battista> (*b* Florence 1632; *d* Paris 1687). Leading French composer of his day. He wrote numerous operas, ballets and instrumental works. His *sacred music consists primarily of 14 *petits* and 11 *grands* *motets; also a *Miserere, *Te Deum* and *De Profundis*. RJB

Luther, Martin (*b* Eisleben 1483; *d* there 1546). Augustinian monk turned reformer, theology professor, author, translator and poet. An amateur musician, he challenged and primed Protestant and RC church musicians through his writings.

Luther was a lutenist, singer and the likely composer of a Latin *motet. He is noted more for his writings on music, consisting of prefaces to printed collections of *hymns and motets, references in biblical commentaries, offhand comments in his *Table Talk* and a short sketch lauding music. As a poet he wrote at least 36 hymns; it is also likely that he shaped some of their tunes. His unflagging support of the vernacular led him to introduce German hymns into his revisions of the *eucharist (*Formula Missae,* 1523 and *Deutsche Messe,* 1526); thus he is credited with establishing the hymn as a constituent part of the eucharistic *liturgy.

Luther studied medieval manuals on music. They provided a foundation on which he could develop his theological beliefs concerning music. He renewed the observation that music is both part of God's creation and a gracious gift from God. His fidelity to the word of God as "sounded act" led him to understand music as partner in the oral/aural process. He recognized certain therapeutic qualities in music which (because of music's divine origin) were to be received positively. Finally, his commitment to the vernacular provided folk song with a new profile which begged for attention from subsequent generations of Lutheran musicians. That was balanced by Luther's admiration for the art music of the day, provision for which was made possible in liturgies modeled after his *Formula Missae*.

Among contemporary musicians, Luther courted *Walter, K. Rupff, *Senfl and the publisher *Rhau. Often he wrote to encourage public support of such people. He was also not shy about his liking the music of *Josquin. Yet his desire that everyone be involved in the musical act prompted him to advocate strongly for the training of children in music and for developing musical skills in all ordained ministers.

Bibl: M. Luther, *Liturgy and Hymns,* Luther's Works, vol. 53 (Philadelphia-St. Louis, 1955); F. Blume, *Protestant Church Music* (New York, 1974); C Schalk, *Luther on Music* (St. Louis, 1988).   MPB

Lutheran chant. Since *Choral* (German, "chant") means unaccompanied liturgical *monody, Lutherans originally understood their unison congregational *hymns as evangelical *chorales. This did not deter them from continued usage of their inherited *chant repertoires. Church orders favoring *Luther's *Formula Missae* provided choral renditions of Latin chants; those following his *Deutsche Messe* prompted musicians to translate received materials into German or compose new chants. Well into the 1700s Lutheran liturgies included chants from the *ordinary in Latin or translation together with chants for *introits, *alleluias, *psalms, *canticles, prayers, lessons, *prefaces, *Lord's Prayer and (somewhat uniquely) the words of institution; Luther suggested that the latter be sung in tone 8, the tone for the *gospel. Anti-liturgical movements within Lutheranism beginning in the early 1700s turned popular taste against chant. Revival energies soon countered. In the late 1800s Lutherans in North America seeking English rather than German versions of the liturgy borrowed both text and chant from the Anglicans (see *Anglican chant). This helped establish chant in a wide variety of forms as a feature of most contemporary Lutheran liturgies.

Bibl: E. T. Horn, "Singing (Liturgical)," in *The Encyclopedia of Lutheranism,* ed. J. Bodensieck, 3 (1965) 2180–82.   MPB

Lutheran Society for Worship, Music and the Arts. An inter-Lutheran agency founded after 1950 to recover and renew worship and the arts. It published the journal *Response.* Eventually it merged with the Liturgical Conference (1979).   VEG

Lutheran worship music. In the first half of the 16th century differences between RC and Lutheran church musical practices were nearly non-existent. By 1550 Lutheran worship music began to take on distinct characteristics. These were the result of ever-changing understandings of the Lutheran liturgical project and of untiring loyalty to Luther's observation that all music is a gift from God.

Repertoires inherited by Lutheran musicians included *chant which first- and second-generation Lutheran musicians arranged to accommodate parallel vernacular texts or which they transformed into rhythmic *hymns (e.g., NUN KOMM, DER HEIDEN HEILAND). Some of these served as substitutes for the *ordinary of the mass, but Lutheran musicians have always been equally interested in providing non-hymnic materials for the ordinary.

Commitment to congregational participation ignited a flurry of hymns. At first these were modeled on preexisting chants, *pilgrimage songs, *psalms and useable *folk songs. In subsequent years new hymn styles arose to respond to changing worship styles and devotional needs.

At first *organs either supported the *choir or provided instrumental alternation for choral pieces (see *alternatim). New styles of *hymnody in the early 17th century called for the organ as the principal instrument for accompanying the congregation. For years to come this practice attracted the skill and imagination of notable keyboardists such as *Buxtehude and J. S. *Bach.

Lutheran musicians continued to explore the use of *choirs and *instruments in worship. The repertoires are expansive: *mass settings (many, because of liturgical practices, consist only of the *Kyrie and *Gloria), *polyphonic Latin and vernacular *motets (in which the hymn, more often than not, serves as *cantus firmus), *cantatas, *passions and the *historiae of *Christmas, *Easter, Annunciation (March 25) and *Ascension.

Changing musical and theological interests have invited varying degrees of attention to these different worship music forms. National contexts, particularly those of Scandinavia and the US, provide further nuances. Lutherans have had a strong interest in *de tempore hymn texts, with a parallel interest in musical rhetoric notable in the works of *Schütz and J. S. Bach.

Bibl: F. Blume, *Protestant Church Music* (New York, 1974); C. Schalk, ed., *Key Words in Church Music* (St. Louis, 1978); P. Westermeyer, *Te Deum* (Minneapolis, 1998).   MPB

Lychnikon. See *hesperinos.

Lydian (mode). An *ecclesiastical mode with its final on F. As an authentic mode (mode 5), it has an ambitus of *f-f'* and its dominant (*tenor) on *c'*. The related plagal mode (Hypolydian, mode 6) has an ambitus of *c-c'* and its dominant on *a*.   CJK

M

Ma'ariv <*'arvit*> [Hebrew]. "Evening." The daily Jewish *service recited after nightfall. It is often immediately preceded by *minchah. Ma'ariv consists of *Barechu, *Shema and its *blessings and the *Amidah. On holidays (including the *Sabbath) ma'ariv is expanded with other blessings and melodies appropriate to the time of year. BES

Machaut <Machault>, **Guilliaume de** (*b* Rheims? *c* 1300; *d* there? 1377). Outstanding composer of the *ars nova, principally remembered for composing the *Messe de Nostre Dame. In 1323 he became secretary to John of Luxembourg, King of Bohemia, quickly gaining recognition as poet, composer and musician. Following John's death (1346), he served various other members of the nobility; patrons included the King of Navarre, the Duke of Berry and the Count of Savoy. Machaut had a lifelong association with Rheims, an important center of French Catholicism and traditional site for crowning kings and queens. His poetic output was enormous and included 14 narrative poems and *c* 400 lyric poems. He left more music than any other composer of his time. In addition to the *Messe* his musical compositions include 24 *motets (almost all polytextual), many *ballades, rondeaux, virelais* and other vocal works.

Bibl: G. Reaney, *Guillaume de Machaut* (London, 1971); D. Leech-Wilkinson, *Machaut's Mass* (Oxford, 1990). VAL

Machzor <*maḥzor*> [Hebrew]. "Yearly cycle." The prayer book that contains the *liturgy used on *Rosh Hashanah, *Yom Kippur and the *Three Festivals. SJW

Madrigale spirituale [Italian]. "Spiritual madrigal." Sixteenth- and 17th-century *polyphonic settings of Italian or Latin *Counter Reformation devotional texts for non-liturgical use. Jesuits and Oratorians seem to have encouraged their use. Texts were sometimes parodied secular poetry, more often vernacular paraphrases of scriptural or liturgical texts (e.g., *Monteverdi's 1583 collection) or of current religious poetry. RAD

186

Magein <*Magen*> **avot** [Hebrew]. "Shield of our fathers." (1) A family of *Jewish prayer modes that takes its name from the central prayer near the end of the *Sabbath *Me'ain sheva*. It is the most simply rendered of the *modes, with few modulations, often declaiming the liturgical text on a single note. The pitches used for the *magein avot* family resemble those of the natural minor scale; however, the Jewish prayer mode is distinguished by the inclusion of a phrase in the relative major and the occasional use of a flat 2nd in concluding phrases.

(2) The central prayer of the *Me'ein sheva*, recited by the congregation after the *Amidah* in the Friday evening *ma'ariv*. AJB-IAG

Magnificat [Latin]. "[My soul] praises." *Hymn of Mary (Luke 1:46-55) praising God for overthrowing the mighty and vindicating the humble. Employed as the *canticle at *vespers in the W from at least the Rule of *St. Benedict; subsequently employed at *evensong in the *BCP and other Protestant traditions; sung as part of daily *orthros in the E. In the W musically set for congregation and *choir in various *chant arrangements; set *polyphonically since the 14th century by *Dufay, *Lassus, *Palestrina, *Schütz, *Monteverdi, J. S. *Bach and others to the present day. Anglican composers have used it with the *Nunc dimittis* in choral settings of the full *service. CRY

Magnus liber organi (de graduali et antifonario) [Latin]. "The great book of *organum* (for the gradual and antiphoner)." A 12th-century collection of 2-part *organa* for the entire liturgical *year, containing 59 pieces for the *mass and 34 for the *office. It was attributed to *Léonin

by the 13th-century theorist known as Anonymous IV; additions and modifications were thought to have been made by *Pérotin. CFS

Maharil <Mahari Siegel; Morenu Harav Yaaokov Levi; Jacob Molin, Moellin, Mölln, etc.> (*b* Mainz *c* 1360–65; *d* there 1427). A prominent rabbi who significantly shaped Jewish musical practice. He is said to have composed many synagogue melodies particularly for the *High Holidays. He standardized portions of the *liturgy that are sung on High Holidays (see *Misinnai* tunes). Many of his practices are recorded in the *Shulchan Aruch* (the code of Jewish law). MLK

Mahler, Gustav (*b* Kaliště 1860; *d* Vienna 1911). Composer of symphonic works and orchestral *Lieder*. A talented conductor (Vienna Opera, Metropolitan Opera, etc.), he was known for his accurate interpretations and attention to details. Soul-searching reflection resounds through many of his works. *Kindertotenlieder* (1904) tells of the love of a father for his child, a tragic loss, the serenity of God's protection and the promise of eternal life. The first part of "Symphony of a Thousand" (n. 8) is an affirmation of Christian faith and belief in the power of the Holy Spirit. DCI

Mah nishtanah <*nishtannah*> **(halailah hazeh)** [Hebrew]. "Why is this night different (from all other nights)?" The opening phrase of a passage from the *haggadah* that is recited at the *Pesach *seder*. Four questions follow: Why on this night is *matzah* ("unleavened bread") eaten? is *maror* ("bitter herbs") eaten? do we dip twice? do we eat reclining? These questions are asked by the youngest at the beginning of the seder; the answers to these questions encompass the text of the *haggadah*. Musical settings of this text vary with local custom. Some communities recite the *Mah nishtanah* in the vernacular; settings in Yiddish, English, Arabic and Ladino ("Judeo-Spanish") are also common.   MLK

Mahrenholz, Christhard (*b* Göttingen 1900; *d* Hanover 1980). Church administrator, theologian and musicologist who championed the Protestant *church music revival in Germany. He chaired the *Neue Bach-Gesellschaft* (1949–74). He also coedited various journals and series (e.g., *Musik und Kirche, Jahrbuch für Liturgik und Hymnologie*), books (e.g., *Handbuch der deutschen evangelischen Kirchenmusik*) and was the general editor of the critical edition of *Scheidt's compositions.   MPB

Mah tovu (ohalekka) [Hebrew]. "How lovely (are your tents)." The opening prayer of *shacharit taken from Num 24:5 which expresses praise and reverence for the synagogue as a tent of learning and prayer. This text is musically set to *Jewish prayer modes, *folk melodies and in more elaborate cantorial and choral genres. Well-known settings are by *Lewandowski (for *choir, *cantor and *organ) and *Bloch's *Sacred Service* (for cantor, choir and orchestra).   BES

Maître de chapelle. See *Kapellmeister.*

Makam <*maqam*> (pl. **makamat**) [Arabic]. "Modal system." The parallel Arabic term to *Jewish prayer modes. The number of *makamat* varies by region, numbering to 121 separate scales. A family of *modes is associated with a

central genus type (Arabic *fawasil*). Most regional practices employ a limited number of *fawasil* (between 8 and 12). Some *makamat* may include a quarter-tone not found on W instruments (e.g., what W musicians call "B quarter-flat" or "E quarter-flat"). Each note of a *makam* has a separate name.

The names of the main *makamat* used by Arabic musicians in the Levant are: *Rast, Bayat, Sikah, Saba, Hijaz, Nahawand* and *Ajam*. The names of these modes differ slightly in Turkish music. The last 2 have the same intervallic structure as the W natural minor and major scales respectively; the others include the use of 1 or more quarter-tones with the exception of *Hijaz* which contains an augmented 2nd between the 2nd and 3rd scale degrees (see *ahavah rabbah*). Melodic phrases and gestures are associated with each *makam*.

The *makamat* shape the *liturgy of Turkish, Syrian, Egyptian and Lebanese Jews, especially *shacharit for *Sabbath. An affect is associated with some modes (e.g., *Ajam* as happy or *Hilaz* as sad), and thus equated to the meaning of the *Torah reading for a given Sabbath. *Shacharit* would be sung in *Hijaz* one week and according to a different *makam* the next. The *chazzan selects melodies to sing in the chosen *makam*. Seven portions of *shacharit* (*El hahodaot, *Kaddish, *Mimits'rayim gealtanu, *Nak'dishach, *Nishmat kol chai, *Semechim beseitam* and *Shavat aniyim*) are initiated by the prayer leader and sung by the congregation in the *makam* of the day; the *chazzan* improvises the other sections.

Bibl: E. Seroussi, "Turkish *Maqam* in the Musical Culture of the Ottoman Jews," *Israel Studies in Musicology* 5 (1990) 43–68.   MLK

Makarismoi. See *Blazhenny.*

Malabar rite worship music. See *Syro-Malabar rite worship music.

Malaya verchernya [Slavonic]. "Small vespers." A monastic form of *vespers, abridged from great vespers (see *hesperinos*), containing its own *propers. It is celebrated on the eve of feast days before great vespers.   DMP

Malchuyot. See *Shofar.*

Malij vchod [Slavonic]. See *Mikra eisodos.*

Maloe povecherie [Slavonic]. See *Apodeipnon mikron.*

Manhattanville School. See *Pius X School of Liturgical Music.

Manz, Paul O. (*b* Cleveland 1919). Organist, composer and educator who led a revival of *hymn improvisation and the liturgical use of the *organ in the US. Manz studied organ with *Jennings, *Walcha and *Peeters (awarded first prize at the Antwerp Conservatory). He served as *cantor at Mount Olive Lutheran Church in Minneapolis and on the faculties of *Concordia College in St. Paul and the Lutheran School of Theology in Chicago.   VEG

Manzoni Requiem. A Latin *mass of the dead by *Verdi in memory of the Italian author Alessandro Manzoni (*d* 1873). Verdi emphasized dramatic aspects of the text through operatic techniques and styles. It was never intended for liturgical use.   DWM

Maoz tsur [Hebrew]. "Rock of ages." A song for *Chanukkah* which describes several events in Jewish history through which Israel was sustained by God's intervention. It was written by an unknown author between the 11th and 13th centuries. Today's melody, popular since the 15th century, was adapted from a German *folk song.   SJW

Marche funebre. See *funeral march.

Mariachi mass. A *mass performed by and in the musical style of a *mariachi conjunto* (Spanish, "group"), a traditional ensemble of W Mexico. Besides vocalists, *mariachi* ensembles originally included violins, harp, *vihuela, tololoche* and *tambora;* 6-string *guitars and trumpets were later added. The first *Misa de Mariachi* was celebrated in the cathedral of Cuernavaca in Mexico (1966). The introduction of *mariachis* into the Roman *liturgy has influenced the configuration of *instruments for such groups, and contributed to the popularity of the *canción* and *hymns composed in *bolero* style. MFR

Maria Laach. A Benedictine monastery in the German Rhineland founded in 1093 which became a center for the 20th-century liturgical movement under I. Herwegen (abbot 1913–46). It was the site of renewed liturgical worship (e.g., the *dialogue mass in 1921), study weeks, popular publications and scholarly research (e.g., *Jahrbuch für Liturgiewissenschaft* since 1921, and *Liturgiegeschichtliche Quellen und Forschungen* since 1928). CLV

Marian antiphon. See *Antiphon of the BVM.

Marian hymns. *Hymns celebrating the Virgin Mary, the most famous being *Ave maris stella*. The earliest were used for the *divine office. Later examples (Latin and vernacular) were used in various settings (*processions, evening devotions, novenas, etc.). In the 19th century, partly under the influence of Alphonsus Liguouri and led by *Faber in the English speaking world, Marian hymnody became sentimental. *Musicae sacrae disciplina* marks a trend towards more solid biblical and theological texts and less romantic music.   RTR

Mariazellermesse [German, Latin *Missa Cellensis*]. "Mass for Mariazell." F. J. *Haydn composed 2 *masses (1766 and 1782) for the shrine of Mariazell in Austria. The first is in the *cantata mass style; the second, commissioned by A. Liebe, shows elements of the emerging *symphonic mass style.   RTR

Marier, Theodore (*b* Fall River MA 1917). Church musician and teacher who served on the faculty at *Pius X School of Liturgical Music and *Catholic University of America. An advocate of quality *hymns, *service music and *chant for use in the RC *liturgy, he was one of the compilers of the *Pius X Hymnal* (1953); later he edited *Hymns, Psalms and Spiritual Canticles* (1972).   FJM

Maronite chant. *Monophonic music of the Maronite Christian Church, what was once the Monophysite branch (now united with Rome) of the Syrian Antiochean church (see *Syrian Churches). Although sung primarily in Syriac, Arabic has been used for *benedictions and *canticles since the 17th century. Simple formulaic melodies, including model melodies *(riš-qolō),* are based on chromatic Arabic scales (see *makam*). Some *chants for clergy belong to an improvisatory tradition. Chant books without notation include the *šḥīmtō* (daily office), *fanquiṭo* (festal office) and *ḥašō* (holy week office). *Strophic *hymns include *qāle* (interpolated into *psalms), *madrāshe* and *sughiāthā* (characterized by acrostics). Percussive *instruments are played during processions and on major feasts.
   Bibl: L. Hage, *Maronite Music* (London, 1978).   RGD

Maronite worship music. *Liturgical music of the Maronite Christian Church in Lebanon. The musical tradition is diverse. Approximately 150 Syro-Maronite (see *Maronite) *chants are supplemented by Syro-Maronite-Arabic melodies and an improvisatory tradition for some chants sung by the clergy. Arabic and W melodies have been adapted, especially for *canticles. New music is composed in Syrian, Arabic and W styles, or combinations of these. Traditionally only percussive *instruments were used, but recently the *organ, harmonium, violin and accordion have been used in some churches. Paul Ashkar (*d* 1962) was a leading figure in the reform of Maronite church music.
   Bibl: L. Hage, "Music of the Maronite Church," *Parole de l'Orient* 2 (1971) 197–206.   RGD

Marot, Clément (*b* Cahors 1496?; *d* Turin 1544). Court poet. His isometric *psalm translations were set by numerous Protestant and RC composers (Marot remained RC), including *Bourgeois for the *Genevan Psalter. His suave facility with language and poetic forms made him a favorite poet of Flemish *polyphonic composers, including *Arcadelt, *Gombert, *Lassus, *Sweelinck and *Willaert.   RDH

Martin, Roberta (*b* Helena AR 1907; *d* Chicago 1969). African American *gospel singer, pianist, composer, arranger, choral director and publisher. She studied with Boulanger and collaborated with *Dorsey. Her innovative choral sound and distinctive piano accompaniments defined classic gospel sound.   MEM

Martin, Sallie (*b* Pittfield GA 1896; *d* Chicago 1988). African American *gospel singer, music publisher and, with *Dorsey, cofounded the National Convention of Gospel Choirs and Choruses (1933). She performed internationally with the Sallie Martin Singers. MEM

Martini, Giovanni Battista <Padre> (*b* Bologna 1706; *d* there 1784). Composer, writer, educator and Franciscan friar. Martini composed a large body of sacred vocal music, including at least 32 *masses, several *oratorios, some secular vocal settings, 96 *keyboard sonatas and 24 sinfonias. His compositional style was conservative and did not reflect the musical developments of the late 18th century. Martini enjoyed great influence as a teacher; J. C. *Bach, *Mozart, Naumann and other distinguished composers studied with him. This influence was extended through his pedagogical writings on counterpoint and the history of music. He also collected an important library of *c* 17,000 volumes.
   Bibl: P. V. Zaccaria, *Padre Giambattista Martini* (Padua, 1970).   RAD

Martyrikon [Greek; Slavonic *muchenichen*]. "Martyr's hymn." *Sticheron or *sedalen sung in the Byzantine *office in honor of the martyrs, often as the penultimate of a series of *stichera* (see *Theotokia*).   DMP

Martyrology. A catalog of martyrs commemorated during the year, listed according to the day of their death (their feast day). It eventually includes all saints and feasts for each day of the liturgical *year. Monastic communities read or chanted these each day, often as part of the *divine office.   GET

Mary, music of (the blessed virgin). The *Magnificat and *Ave Maria are the Marian biblical texts most often set to music, the former achieving liturgical prominence because of its place in *vespers. The *Sub tuum and Marian references in both prose texts and *hymns of the patristic era received *chant settings. The cult of Mary began in the E; by the 6th century Rome celebrated 4 E feasts (*Candlemas, Annunciation, Dormition/Assumption and Nativity of Mary) as well as its original commemoration of Mary (January 1). During the medieval era many other feasts developed along with numerous *tropes, *prosulae and *sequences, of which only the *Stabat mater remains in use today. *Marian hymns became important elements of the *divine office, as did *Marian antiphons. In the late *Middle Ages and *Renaissance many *polyphonic *masses (e.g., *Messe de Nostre Dame*) and *motets were composed either in Mary's honor or based on Marian chants. *Monteverdi's *Vespro della Beata Vergine* ushered in the *Baroque era. With the *Counter Reformation, popular Marian hymnody, sometimes of an uneven character, became an important part of RC devotions. Marian motets and masses (e.g., *Mariazeller-messe*) continued to be composed, and elaborate settings of the *Stabat mater* became prominent. Present trends reveal simpler, more biblically-based Marian *ritual music, sometimes combining traditional and contemporary elements.

Bibl: J. Selner, "Our Lady in Music," *Mariology* 3, ed. J. Carol (Milwaukee, 1961) 398–41; R. T. Ridder, "Musical and Theological Patterns Involved in the Transmission of Mass Chants for the Five Oldest Marian Feasts" (Catholic University of America: Ph.D. diss., 1993); T. Thompson, "The Popular Marian Hymn in Devotion and Liturgy," *Marian Studies* 45 (1994) 121–51.   RTR

Mason, Lowell (*b* Medfield MA 1792; *d* Orange NJ 1872). Editor, music educator and composer. He first learned music from his father, a *singing school master. Later he studied European music theory with F. Abel, which he espoused against the singing school practices. An accomplished musician, Mason played the *organ and various instruments. He was an organist in Savannah, and later choirmaster in Boston.

Mason's career changed with the publication of his *Boston Handel and Haydn Society Collection of Church Music* (1822), running 22 editions. It embodied the ideals of "better music," a movement to bring *church music beyond the "crude" *fuging tunes of the singing schools by emulating European music. Trained choirs and "correct" compositions were preferred to the older *psalm tradition. Mason strengthened his views on church music during trips through England and Germany. He borrowed from German masters, adding his own compositions and hymns (e.g., MERIBAH). He published much music and music instruction, including *The New Carmina Sacra* (1850). Mason also pioneered music education in public schools.

Bibl: M. Broyles, "Lowell Mason on European Church Music and Transatlantic Cultural Identification," *JAMS* 38:2 (1985) 316–48; C. Pemberton, *Lowell Mason* (Ann Arbor, 1985).   VEG

Masonic music. Music connected with the rituals and socializing of Freemasonry, an allegory of morality in which initiates are taught virtue through the symbolism of stone masonry. Adherents work at constructing a temple of humanity (an analogue to Solomon's temple) supported by nature, reason and wisdom. *Hymns, *cantatas, processional music and songs play an important part in Freemasonry. Many important composers were freemasons (e.g., F. J. *Haydn); *Mozart's masonic music is particularly important. Besides cantatas, funeral music and *choruses, Mozart's opera *The Magic Flute* is the most famous exemplar of this philosophy of life (1791).   LJC

Masoretic accents. See *ta'amim*.

Mass. RC term for *eucharist. See *missa*.

Mass in D. See *Missa solemnis* (2).

Mass of the dead. See *dead, mass of the.

Matachines [from Arabic *mutawajjihin,* "mute spirits, masked dancers"]. A type of 15th–century morality play presented as an *auto sacramental*, depicting the struggle between good and evil personified by Christians and Moors. They were presented on special feast days, often accompanied by violin, *guitar and gourd rattles. Through the centuries different groups have altered the symbolism and staged variations on the basic theme of good versus evil.   MFR

Mathias, William (*b* Whitland, Wales 1934; *d* Menai Bridge 1992). Prolific composer. He was considered the unofficial "Master of the Queen's Music" for his music for church and state occasions. He composed a wide range of liturgical choral music as well as significant works for *organ.   RAL

Matins <mattins>. First of the 7 canonical *hours of the *divine office; also called *nocturns. This night office developed from an ancient monastic tradition of gathering for prayer around cockcrow (*c* 2:30 a.m.), consisting of the recitation of *psalms in sequence by a soloist with each psalm followed by prayer and prostration. *Cathedral hours also included a *morning prayer, sometimes called matins, but it occurred at daybreak and more properly corresponds to *lauds. The 1549 *BCP calls its lauds-like morning prayer "Mattyns." Matins traditionally consists of 2 *versicles and *responses, an *invitatory, 2 (*ferial days) or 3 (Sundays and feastdays) nocturns (each containing a set number of psalms and *antiphons, *lessons, *responsories and *collects) and the *Te Deum*. Musical settings for these elements are collected in the *antiphonal.

The Roman rite *breviary of 1971 replaced matins with the *office of readings; though official instructions suggest it is to be celebrated in common, it is designed for private recitation.

Bibl: R. Taft, *The Liturgy of the Hours in East and West* (Collegeville, 1986); G. Guiver, *Company of Voices* (New York, 1988).   EBF

Mattheson, Johann (*b* Hamburg 1681; *d* there 1764). Composer, critic and theorist. *Kappellmeister* at Hamburg Cathedral (1715–28). His writings include *Critica musica* (the first German music periodical, 1722–55), *Der vollkommene Capellmeister* (an encyclopedia for training a *Kappellmeister*, 1739) and *Grundlage einer Ehren-Pforte* (a lexicon of musicians, 1740).   LMT

Maundy Thursday. See *year, liturgical.

McKie, William Neil (*b* Melbourne, Australia 1901; *d* Ottawa, Canada 1984). Organist and conductor. He served as organist for the city of Melbourne, at Oxford's Magdalen College, and later at Westminster Abbey (1941–63). McKie directed the music for the coronation of Elizabeth II (1953) and was knighted the same year.   FKG

McLin, Lena Johnson (*b* Atlanta 1928). Composer, arranger, conductor and educator. She was educated at Spelman College, The American Conservatory and Roosevelt University, and taught at Chicago's Kenwood High School. She founded the McLin Ensemble for operatic productions. A prolific *church music composer, McLin blended traditional forms with contemporary idioms in her *anthems and *spirituals.   MWC

MCW. See *Music in Catholic Worship.*

Me'ein *<Me'en>* **sheva** [Hebrew]. "Seven-faceted blessing." A synopsis of the 7 *blessings that constitute *Sabbath evening *Amidah. It is recited after the *Amidah* (see *magein avot*) from Talmudic times in order to prolong the *service so that those who prayed at a slower pace, and those who arrived late could finish in time to return home with everyone else, as walking home alone after dark was dangerous. It is recited in the *magein avot* mode.   IAG

Medicean edition [Latin *Editio Medicea*]. The *gradual of 1614–15 in which the melodies were extensively "reformed," based on a misunderstanding of *chant's text-melody relationship. Named for the Medici-owned printing press which produced it, *Palestrina did not prepare it, as was later claimed. See *Regensburg edition.   AWR

Medieval period. See *Middle Ages.

Megalai horai [Greek]. "Great hours" [Slavonic *tsarskije chasy,* "royal <imperial> hours"]. A solemn form of the *horai* in the Byzantine rite formed by inserting a series of *stichera, a Hebrew Bible reading, *epistle and *gospel after the *troparion of the *hour. Sung on aliturgical days preceding a great feast, today they are celebrated only on the eves of *Christmas and Theophany, and on Good Friday.   DMP

Megale eisodos [Greek; Slavonic *velikij vchod*]. "Great entrance." The solemn entrance with gifts of bread and wine in the Byzantine *divine liturgy. In Constantinople's Hagia Sophia and elsewhere, they were brought into the church from a separate building used for their prepara-

tion. Since most churches could not afford a separate building, this procession now moves from an altar of preparation within the sanctuary, outside the icon screen, then back into the sanctuary. The gifts are carried by deacons and priests, preceded by lamp-bearers and acolytes while the *Cherubikon is repeatedly sung.

Bibl: R. Taft, *The Great Entrance* (Rome, 1975).   DMP

Megalynarion [Greek; Slavonic *velichanije*]. "Magnification." A *hymn in the Byzantine rite "magnifying" the feast or saint of the day. In the *divine liturgy it usually begins with the first words from the *Magnificat,* followed by a short description of the feast. It is sung during the *anaphora in place of the usual hymn honoring the Mother of God. In *orthros it usually begins "We extol," then a short description of the feast; it is sung as a *refrain to a catena of selected *psalm *verses. The priest sings at least the first *megalynarion* to an elaborate melody; *choir or *cantor sing the subsequent ones and the psalm verses (to a simpler melody). Today the *orthros megalynarion* is mostly found in the Slavonic tradition, accompanying the transference of an icon of the feast or saint from the altar to a place in the nave for later congregational veneration.   DMP

Megilot *<Megillot>* [Hebrew]. "Scrolls." Any of the 5 scrolls read in the synagogue on prescribed festivals: *Shir Hashirim* (Song of Songs) on *Pesach; Rut* (Ruth) on *Shavuot; Eichah* (*Lamentations) on the evening of *Tisha B'av; Kohelet* (Ecclesiastes) on *Sukkot; Ester* (Esther) on the evening and morning of *Purim. Like the Torah, Megilot are written on parchment and are chanted according to special sets of *ta'amim. Ester* is the only scroll which must be read publicly from a parchment scroll and over which an introductory *benediction must be recited.   SIW

Méhul, Étienne-Nicolas (*b* Givet 1763; *d* Paris 1817). Composer. In Paris by 1778, his early compositions were presented at the *Concert spirituel* in 1782. A celebrated composer of operas (most famous opera on a religious theme was *Joseph,* 1807), ballets, symphonies, he also wrote a *mass and accompanied vocal works.   JLB

Melanchthon, Philipp (*b* Bretten 1497; *d* Wittenberg 1560). Reformer, friend and coworker of *Luther. Melanchthon taught at the University of Wittenberg. He wrote prefaces for several *Rhau music collections and took on the task of redefining pedagogy in evangelical circles. In this connection he wrote about theology and music and was one of the first to use the term *musica poetica* (Latin, "musical poetic") to describe the rhetorical components of the compositional process.   MPB

Melaveh <*Melavveh*> **Malkah** [Hebrew]. "Escorting the Queen." The ritual of escorting the Sabbath ("Queen") out, symbolizing the departure of the Sabbath on Saturday night after sundown. *Zemirot* are sung to prolong the joy and sweetness of the Sabbath into the next day.   SDC

Melisma [Greek]. "Song." A *neume of more than 5 or 6 notes sung to a single syllable. When used on the last syllable of an *alleluia it is called a *jubilus*. It is also used as a form of musical punctua-

tion at the end of a phrase and to emphasize an important word accent (e.g., *jubiLAte*).   CJK

Melismatic. (1) Marked by the presence of *melismas.

(2) A passage of *chant where multiple notes (a melisma) are sung on a single syllable. Melismatic chant is used liturgically for purposes of ritual elaboration or as an expression of festivity.   CLV

Melkite chant. The *monophonic *liturgical music of the Melkite Christian church, the Antiochene branch which supported the emperor in the 5th century Monophysite controversy (compare *Maronite chant), today predominantly in union with Rome. The texts, *chant genres and 8-*mode system are closely related to those of *Byzantine chant. Until the 10th century Greek and Syriac were used, and Arabic has been used for some chants since the 17th century. Arabic musical influence can be heard in the use of chromaticism and drones. Forms of Byzantine neumatic notation are found in early Melkite manuscripts. *Chrysanthine notation is now used (see *Greco-Byzantine chant).

Bibl: A. Hebby, *Short Course in Byzantine Ecclesiastical Music* (Newton MA, 1988).   RGD

Melody choral. In *organ music, a composition based on a *hymn tune where the complete melody is presented in the highest voice with little ornamentation or interruption.   JPM

Memorial acclamation. A congregational *acclamation found in *eucharistic prayers of various Christian denominations. It follows the institution narrative and recalls the saving events of Christ's life and death. The most commonly employed text for a memorial acclamation is "Christ has died, Christ is risen, Christ will come again." VCF

Menaion (pl. **menaia**) [Greek; Slavonic *mineya*]. "Book of the Month." A Byzantine liturgical *book, containing the *propers of the immovable feasts of the liturgical *year for the *divine office. Since propers are so extensive, they are now in 12 volumes: 1 for each month. The first volume is September, the beginning of the Byzantine liturgical *year. Greek *menaia* have a *synaxarion* (the life of the day's saint or history of the feast) after the 6th *ode of the *kanon.

Bibl: Mother Mary and K. Ware, trans., *The Festal Menaion* (London, 1969); *Menaion: December, March* (Newton Centre MA, 1985), *September, October* (1988); *November, January* (1992), *August* (1994), *June* (1995). DMP

Mendelssohn, Arnold (*b* Racibórz 1855; *d* Darmstadt 1933). Church musician, conservatory professor at Frankfurt and *hymnal editor. He led the rediscovery of historic music, and emphasized the liturgical in *church music renewal. VEG

Mendelssohn (-Bartholdy), Felix (Jakob Ludwig) (*b* Hamburg 1809; *d* Leipzig 1847). Composer, pianist and conductor of Jewish background and Christian upbringing. Born into a wealthy family, he associated from an early age with prominent artists and intellectuals who frequented the Mendelssohn home in Berlin. Educated privately, he studied composition with *Zelter. In 1829 Mendelssohn conducted the first public performance of J. S. *Bach's *St. Matthew Passion* in over 70 years, thus contributing to the Bach revival of the following decades. Music director at Düsseldorf (1833–35) and of Leipzig's Gewandhaus Orchestra (1835–45), he founded the Leipzig Conservatory in 1843.

Mendelssohn composed important works in all genres except opera. Though regarded as a *Romantic composer, he was conservative by temperament and training; his style was influenced primarily by composers of earlier generations.

Foremost among his *sacred music are the *oratorios *St. Paul* (1836) and *Elijah* (1846). Sacred choral works include music for Lutheran, RC and Anglican *liturgies: 4 *chorale cantatas, *psalm settings (for solo voices, chorus, *orchestra), over 40 shorter *motets, *anthems and other works in German, Latin and English. He also wrote 6 sonatas, 3 *preludes and *fugues, and numerous other short pieces for *organ.

Bibl: E. Werner, *Mendelssohn* (London, 1963); P. Radcliffe, *Mendelssohn* (London, 1976). KRH

Mennonite worship music. Congregational singing is at the heart of Mennonite worship, though other musical mediums may be used. Anabaptists of the 16th-century wrote and borrowed *hymns for personal devotion and communal worship. Their unison singing was unaccompanied. Music was seldom printed in their *hymnals; a *Vorsänger* (German, "precentor"; Dutch *voorzanger*) *lined out the melody. The role of the *Vorsänger* continues to be important in congregations which still sing *a cappella. Mennonites of Holland and N Germany were influenced by *pietism and the cultural climate of Dutch life. By 1770 many Dutch churches had pipe *organs to support congregational singing. The *voorzanger* disappeared; most congregations sang in unison. By the 19th century Dutch Mennonites were singing in 4 parts.

Pietism of the 17th century and later Methodist revivalism greatly affected Mennonites. Preferred hymn texts were more personal in nature, and new hymn tunes were faster and lighter in character. Through 19th century *singing schools, Mennonites of Swiss-German descent began singing 4-part harmony.

*Choirs or special music groups are not ordinarily employed, so as not to weaken the congregation's musical participation. Such special groups may be organized for particular occasions. Russian Mennonites developed a choir tradition in the 19th century and brought their choral practices to N America.

Mennonites have not developed *service music outside of the hymn tradition. Settings of T. Ken's *doxology to the *OLD HUNDREDTH (often used with offering) or to DEDICATION ANTHEM (frequently used as a *benediction) are the only elements that can be characterized as service music broadly speaking.

Currently 4-part singing is strong among N American Mennonites. Musical styles for worship range across *Gregorian chant, German *chorales, *Genevan Psalter tunes, English hymn tunes, early American *folk hymns, African American *spirituals, *gospel songs, scripture songs, international songs and contemporary gospel music. In congregations of Swiss-German influence, *a cappella* singing is still practiced, though instrumental accompaniment may be used. Organ, piano, *guitar, wind or string *instruments and praise bands exist in various congregations. Song leadership may be assumed by instrumentalists, a song leader or a worship team. Christian hymns remain a significant repository for Mennonite congregations, though other sources of music and texts are used.

Bibl: H. S. Bender, "Music, Church," *The Mennonite Encyclopedia* 3 (1955–59) 791–95; M. K. Oyer, "Amish and Mennonite Music," *NGDAM* 1:42–43; R. J. Slough, "Public Worship (North America)," *The Mennonite Encyclopedia* 5 (1990) 945–47.   RJS

Merbecke <Marbeck>, **John** (*b* Windsor? *c* 1505–10; *d* 1585?). Church musician, composer and organist at St. George's Chapel, Windsor Castle (from 1531). He composed *polyphonic music for *Sarum use. Espousing Protestant views he was arrested for heresy (1543) but reprieved. He is best remembered for the *Booke of Common Praier Noted* (1550): quasi-plainsong settings of the 1549 prayer book *services (see *BCP). These were rediscovered in the mid-19th century and still sung today.   RAL

Mertvennyi [Slavonic]. See *nekrosimon*.

Merulo, Claudio (*b* Correggio 1533; *d* Parma 1604). Composer and organist. He served at Brescia Cathedral, at St. Mark's in Venice with A. *Gabrieli, and the ducal chapel in Parma. Merulo wrote *motets and *masses. He developed a distinctive idiom, especially in his *toccatas which were often in 5 sections, combining free and contrapuntal writing; they anticipate the duality of the form found in later toccatas or the *prelude and *fugue.   DCI

Meshorerim [Hebrew]. "Singers." Assistants to the *cantor during the cantorial flourishing in *Ashkenazic synagogues (16th–18th centuries), providing support to the cantorial melodic line. *Meshorerim* hummed or sang chords or sequential figures in an improvised style as an elaborate vocal accompaniment. The 2 primary parts were the "singer" (high boy's voice) and the "bass" (low male voice); other parts (e.g., falsetto) were later added. The term was later (19th–20th centuries) applied to those in the chorus.   BES

Mesochoros [Greek]. "Mid-choir." The leader or conductor of the *choir in the Greek Byzantine liturgy. The title derives from his position, standing in the middle of the choir.   DMP

Mesonyktikon [Greek; Slavonic *polunoshchnitsa*]. "Midnight office." A monastic *service of the Byzantine rite, celebrated in the middle of the night. The basic daily *office consists of Ps 51, Ps 119, the prayer "Look upon me and have mercy on me," *Nicene Creed, *troparion* "Behold, the Bridegroom comes in the middle of the night," common prayer of the hours, dismissal and service of mutual forgiveness. Longer forms of the *mesonyktikon* exist for Saturday and Sunday. This office replaced the monastic variable *psalmody when the latter was attached to *orthros*.   DMP

Mesoria [Greek; Slavonic *mezhdochasije*]. "Intermediate hours." A monastic *service in the Byzantine rite, celebrated after each of the *horai* during the fasts of *Christmas (November 15 to December 24) and the Apostles (from the Monday after All Saints' Sunday or the Sunday after Pentecost to June 29, the feast Sts. Peter and Paul).

They consist of 3 psalms (*prime: 46, 92, 93; *terce: 30, 32, 61; *sext: 56, 57, 70; *none: 113, 138, 140), *troparia* and a prayer attributed to St. Basil (*d* 379) proper to each hour.   DMP

Messe. See *mass.

Messe des morts [French]. "Mass of the dead." The *Requiem* composed either for an actual funeral, or for concert performance. Among the latter are those by *Berlioz, *Fauré and Duruflé.   ACL

Messe de Nostre Dame [French]. "Mass of Our Lady." *Machaut's *polyphonic setting of the *ordinary, the first unified work in this genre.   RTR

Messiaen, Olivier (Eugène Prosper Charles) (*b* Avignon 1908; *d* Clichy 1992). Influential 20th-century composer, teacher and organist. He studied with Dukas and *Dupré at the Paris Conservatory, eventually joining that faculty (1947) where Boulez and Stockhausen were among his students. For over 40 years he was the principal organist at Ste. Trinité in Paris (from 1931). His compositions reflect a deep RC faith through explicit doctrinal references, e.g., the instrumental *Hymne au Saint Sacrément* (1932) and *Et expecto resurrectionem mortuorum* (1964), and *O sacrum convivium* (1937) for voices and *organ. His compositions also include implicit doctrinal references, e.g., numeric references to the Trinity. His love of nature is illustrated through his use of birdsong in his compositions. He composed for organ, e.g., *L'*Ascension* and *La *Nativité du Seigneur;* he also wrote for piano, e.g., *Vingt regards sur l'enfant Jésus* (1944); his opera is *Saint François d'Assise* (1983).

Bibl: P. Hill, ed., *The Messiaen Companion* (Portland, 1995 [1994]).   JBF

Messiah [Hebrew]. "Anointed." A celebrated *oratorio by *Handel (1741); the text was drawn from scripture by C. Jennens. It has a 3-part structure: 1) prophesy and realization of the promised Messiah, 2) redemption through Christ's sacrifice, and 3) the promise of eternal life accomplished in Christ's resurrection, concluding with *hymns of praise and thanksgiving.   CRY

Meter. (1) The pattern of rhythmic pulses or beats in poetry and music. In poetry, meter is ordinarily determined by the number and type "feet" or groups of accented and unaccented syllables comprising a typical line. In music, meter is ordinarily determined by the number and grouping of beats per bar or measure and signaled by the time signature.

(2) In *hymnody, a numbering system indicating the poetic meter of a text. Ordinarily rendered in numerals (e.g., 8.6.8.6 = 8 pulses in the 1st and 3rd lines, 6 pulses in the 2nd and 4th), sometimes meter is given in letters (e.g., CM = Common Meter = 8.6.8.6). Periods often indicate which lines comprise a rhyme scheme or carry a single theme (e.g., 888.888 for the *hymn tune OLD 113TH). These metrical guides were an indispensable tool when *hymnals included only words, and song leaders searched the metric indexes of *tune books for a tune appropriate to the spirit and meter of a text.

Bibl: A. Lovelace, *The Anatomy of Hymnody* (Chicago, 1982 [1965]).   CRY

Metheortia [Greek; Slavonic *poprazdnstvo*]. "After the Feast." The extension of a celebration of a feast (usually of Christ or Mary). *Propers exist for each day on the theme of the feast. The longest *metheortia* period is that of *Easter extending from Easter Sunday to the day before Ascension Thursday; some feasts have only 1 day of *metheortia*. On the final day of the *metheortia* (*apodosis*), the *office of the feast is repeated. See *proeortia*.   DMP

Methodist Episcopal worship music. The Methodist Episcopal Church was founded in 1784 from several Methodist societies in the NE US. Its worship music developed in 2 contexts. First were the urban seaboard cities and other settled places where clergy selected and led *hymns from collections authorized by the church. Mirroring J. *Wesley's role in *British Methodist music, bishops were the music authorities (e.g., condemning *fuging tunes as vanity). A second important context was the interracial *camp meeting which mixed preaching, song and dance. Here music evolved from non-sacramental rural revivalism. In the late 19th century Methodists worship music was largely formed from privately published song books and *hymnals which featured *folk hymns, Sunday school songs and *gospel hymns (some composed by Methodists, e.g., *Crosby).

At the turn of the century *Tindley created the urban African American *gospel hymn. Written and arranged in quaint style, the harmonies, melodies and rhythms were reminiscent of the Reconstruction Days gospel hymn; performance practice, however, was distinctively urban black. African American Methodist hymnals did not include *spirituals until the mid-20th century.

In the urban N and E during Reconstruction new worship spaces were built with pulpit and *choir loft at the center. Choirs, often augmented by professional quartets, supported congregational song accompanied by pipe *organs. E. Tourjée provided the most comprehensive statement on urban Methodist worship in the preface to the hymnal *The Tribute of Praise* (1882).

The *Methodist Hymnal* (1878) was the first "full music edition" for congregation, choir and accompanist. The 1896 printing included the official order for worship, recommending *chants, *doxologies, *creeds and readings from the Hebrew Bible and New Testament. Folk hymnody, gospel hymns (in time supplanted by mission hymns) and repertory from *Hymns Ancient and Modern* were included.

The Church's General Conference created a commission on music (1924), the first established by a non-liturgical church. The commission greatly influenced *The Methodist Hymnal* (1935), featuring selections from *The English Hymnal,* 8 *Anglican chant settings for *canticles and *psalms, and music for the order of worship and *holy communion.

Bibl: R. Deschner, "Methodist Church, music of the," *NGDAM* 3:217–20; J. White, *Protestant Worship* (Louisville, 1989) 150–70; C. Young, *Companion to the United Methodist Hymnal* (Nashville, 1993). CRY

Methodist worship music. The Methodist Church was formed (1939) from the *Methodist Episcopal Church, Methodist Episcopal Church, South and Methodist Protestant Church. The worship song of these precursor urban churches had been influenced by Presbyterian and Episcopal musicians such as C. *Dickinson, *Williamson and P. Lutkin of Northwestern University. Issues and standards in worship music were often reduced to matters of taste, creating a tension between the prevailing theology of W. Rauschenbusch's social gospel of freedom and inclusivity and *Vaughan Williams' view that performing good music is "a moral rather than a musical issue" (preface to music, *The English Hymnal,* 1906).

After World War II Methodist worship music was profoundly changed by the establishment of graded *choir programs in local churches, and the founding of the *Fellowship of Methodist Musicians. The latter influenced *The Methodist Hymnal* (1966), the denomination's first to include selections for the full liturgical *year, *service music for the order of worship, *Merbecke's and new settings for *holy communion, a *psalter, and African American, Native American and Asian *hymns. Because of its perceived musical and linguistic conservatism, however, this *hymnal was largely set aside after 1970.

Bibl: R. Deschner, "Methodist Church, Music of the," *NGDAM* 3:217–20; C. Young, *Companion to the United Methodist Hymnal* (Nashville, 1993). Also, see *British Methodist worship music and *United Methodist worship music. CRY

Methuen Organ Company. See *Treat, James.

Metrical psalms <psalter>. The biblical *psalms rendered into *strophic verse and sung as *hymns. *Luther invented the genre in Wittenberg 1523–24. The Wittenberg metrical psalms were reprinted in Strasbourg where they were supplied with different tunes and augmented by new metrical psalms from Strasbourg authors. In 1539 Calvin produced French metrical psalms, based on German Strasbourg models, with texts by himself and *Marot. In Geneva Calvin continued to work with Marot, then T. Beza, producing a succession of metrical psalters, notably in 1542, 1551 and 1562, the latter being a complete *psalter of all 150 psalms. This *Genevan Psalter led to the creation of other collections of metrical psalms in many European languages. Vernacular metrical psalters existed both for Protestants and RCs alike (for the latter, e.g., Ulenberg's psalter published in Cologne, 1582). In the English speaking world the most influential metrical psalters were: *Sternhold and Hopkins (1562), *Ainsworth (1612), the *Bay Psalm Book (1640), the Scottish Psalter (1650), *Tate and Brady (1696–98) and that of Isaac *Watts (1719).

Bibl: R. Leaver, "English Metrical Psalmody," *The Hymnal 1982 Companion* 1, ed. R. F. Glover (New York, 1990) 321–64; *idem, "Goostly psalmes and Spirituall songes": English and Dutch Metrical Psalms from Coverdale to Utenhove 1535–1566* (Oxford, 1991).   RAL

Mezhdochasie [Slavonic]. See *mesoria.*

Mi Chamochah [Hebrew]. "Who is like You." The section of *shacharit* and *ma'ariv* that precedes the *Amidah;* taken from Ex 15:11. Various melodies highlight this portion of the *liturgy. On certain holidays (e.g., *Chanukkah* and *Three Festivals) melodies from songs for those holidays may be adapted to this liturgical text.   MLK

Micheelsen, Hans Friedrich (*b* Hennstedt 1902; *d* Glüsing 1973). Composer and teacher. He studied with *Hindemith in Berlin, then became organist there at St. Matthew's (1932–38). He taught in Hamburg (from 1938) and there became director of *church music at the Musikhochschule (1954–62). He composed *cantatas, a *mass, a *Requiem,* choral and *organ works.   JLB

Middle Ages. The period of W music from *c* 1100 to *c* 1400, bridging the *ars antiqua* through the *ars nova.* In architectural history this is the Gothic era, characterized by pointed arches, ribbed vaulting and flying buttresses. The term Gothic has sometimes been applied to this musical period as well. During the *ars antiqua,* the Parisian school with some of the first composers known to us by name (*Léonin and *Pérotin; *Hildegard was earlier), dominated W music. Though much *folk music was improvised, notated music was essentially sacred. *Organum* and *conductus* were developed well, but the *motet was favored by composers toward the mid–13th century. This new form sparked the codification of *rhythmic modes as well as a system of mensural notation, which found most favor with triple *meter.

Most compositions were based on rhythmically structured *chant, above which were added melodic lines of narrow vocal range. The emphasis was primarily linear. Except for *musica ficta* there were few chromatic alterations.

As time went on composers mixed sacred and secular, as well as Latin and vernacular texts. Eventually secular motets were composed, giving way to the new art of composition. Latin was used for settings of the *ordinary. *Machaut wrote the first through-composed *mass setting for 4 voices, as opposed to the usual 3-voice writing popular at the time.

Melodic and harmonic parameters were leading toward modal centers. More attention was given to what we now call cadences. What began earlier as separate schools (French, Italian and English) eventually coalesced. Suave English consonance, French structure and Italian zest combined, resulting in an international compositional style.

Important works on music theory appeared during this period, including those of Anonymous IV, Johannes de Garlandia, Franco of Cologne, Philippe de Vitry and Jacques de Liège. The growing tension between secular and sacred styles was noted in the first papal legislation on music in this period (*Docta sanctorum patrum*).

Bibl: R. Hoppin, *Medieval Music* (New York, 1978); J. Yudkin, *Music in Medieval Europe* (Englewood Cliffs, 1989); A. Seay, *Music in the Medieval World,* 2nd ed. (Englewood Cliffs NJ, 1991 [1975]). DCI

Midmer, Reuben (*b* 1824; *d* 1895). *Organ builder who worked primarily in Brooklyn. His firm merged (1920) becoming the Midmer-Losh Organ Co. In 1929 he received the contract to build the organ for the Atlantic City Convention Hall.   JWK

Mikra eisodos [Greek; Slavonic *malij vchod*]. "Small entrance." Entrance of the ministry and the *gospel book during the third *antiphon of the *enarxis in the Byzantine *divine liturgy. Originally this was the entrance procession of the whole congregation into church. In Constantinople this may have included stops at other churches, hence the "third" an-tiphon. This antiphon is usually Ps 95 with a short *troparion;* feasts of Christ have *proper third antiphons. Evidence for this procession exists from the 5th century, for the 3 antiphons from the 8th century.   DMP

Milanese chant. See *Ambrosian chant.

Milhaud, Darius (*b* Aix-en-Provence 1892; *d* Geneva 1974). Composer, pianist, conductor and teacher. He studied at the Paris Conservatory and *Schola cantorum. A leading figure in a prominent group of French composers known as *Les Six* ("the six"). He immigrated to the US (1940) teaching at Mills College; he returned to Europe (1947), but continued teaching at Mills until 1971. A prolific composer (441 op. numbers), he wrote several works based on Jewish liturgical texts including *Poèms juifs* (1916), *Chants populaires hébraïques* and *Service Sacré* (1947).   MLK

Mimits'rayim gealtanu [Hebrew]. "From Egypt You redeemed us." A section of the *liturgy describing one of God's mighty deeds in the history of Israel. It appears before the *Amidah and is musically highlighted among Jews from the Middle E (*Ashkenazic Jews highlight a similar section of the *Mi Chamochah*). Middle E Jews sing it in the *makam of the day to a rhythmic melody to facilitate congregational singing.   MLK

Minchah <*minḥah*> [Hebrew]. "Offering." Jewish afternoon prayer, recited anytime in the afternoon until sunset. It corresponds to the evening sacrifice in the Temple, receiving its name from the meal offering that was originally part of the sacrifice. It consists of *Ashrei, *Amidah, *Kaddish and *Aleinu.   MLK

Mineya [Slavonic]. See *menaion.

Minor hours. See *little hours.

Miracle play. See *mystery play.

Miserere [Latin]. "Have mercy." The *incipit of *Pss 51, 56 and 57. It usually refers to Ps 51, one of the *penitential psalms. Ps 51 is often employed in Lent, Friday *morning prayer in Anglican, Lutheran and RC use and in the *office of the dead. It has been set by *Allegri, G. *Gabrieli, *Josquin, *Palestrina and many others.   CLV

Mi sheberach [Hebrew]. "He who blessed." (1) That part of the Jewish *liturgy requesting a *blessing for good health, usually recited between sections of the *Torah reading.
(2) An alternate name for the *Ukrainian-Dorian mode.   MLK

Misinnai <Mi-Sinai> (**Aistet**) [Hebrew]. "(Melodies) from Sinai." Fixed melodies that, with the *Jewish prayer modes, have become inextricably linked to specific Jewish liturgical occasions. Their exact origin is unknown. Tradition says that they were given by God to Moses on Mt. Sinai; however, the oldest seem to have originated in the early second millennium CE in N Europe. There is considerable disagreement as to what exactly constitutes a *Misinnai* tune. For some they are the older layer of liturgical melodies in *Ashkenazic liturgy. Others use a broader definition that includes virtually any melody that is widely associated with a particular holi-

day (e.g., *Maoz tzur for *Chanukkah). Still others insist that it is the inclusion of a phrase of a biblical motif (see *ta'amim) that distinguishes a *Misinnai* tune. Widely recognized *Misinnai* tunes include the Great *Aleinu (for *High Holidays), *Chatzi* *Kaddish (for *Ne'ilah), *Kol nidrei and *Barechu (for *ma'ariv on *Yamim Noraim).

Bibl: H. Avenary, "The Cantorial Fantasia of the Eighteenth and Nineteenth Centuries," Yuval 1 (1968) 65–85; E. Werner, A Voice Still Heard (University Park, 1976) 26–45.   MLK

Missa [Latin]. Literally "sent"; more commonly, "mass." (1) A term for *eucharist, employed as early as *Ambrose.
(2) A common abbreviation for the *ordinary of the mass.
(3) In the Rule of St. *Benedict, the concluding blessings and prayers said before the end of any liturgical service (not necessarily eucharistic).   MJG

Missa brevis [Latin]. "Short mass." A musical setting of the *ordinary in which various movements are kept as concise as possible. Sixteenth-century usage referenced 5 main elements in the ordinary (*Kyrie, *Gloria in excelsis, *Credo, *Sanctus and *Agnus Dei). In and after the 17th century, the term could refer to settings of the Kyrie and Gloria only.   CSP

Missa cantata [Latin]. "Sung mass." (1) Before the reforms of *Vatican II, a RC celebration of the principal Sunday or feastday *mass with the singing of the *ordinary and *proper, without a deacon, sub-deacon and the full ceremonies of the *missa solemnis. Sometimes in the medieval period, however, a deacon was employed; furthermore, the absence of a *choir and extended processions often resulted in the elimination of some or all of the proper. Since singing and music are now possible in every celebration, the term is obsolete.

(2) In the Anglican tradition, sometimes a synonym for a choral *communion service.

(3) The term may also refer to a mass written in the style of a *cantata, e.g., J. S. *Bach's *B Minor Mass.   CSP

Missa Cellensis. See *Mariazellermesse.

Missa in cantu [Latin]. "Sung mass." Prior to the reforms of *Vatican II, a technical RC designation (see *De musica sacra n. 14a) for 1 of 2 general forms (other: *missa lecta) of the *mass in which official liturgical texts that could be sung, were to be sung in Latin.   CSP

Missal [Latin liber missalis, "mass book"; also, missale]. (1) A liturgical *book containing all prayers, readings, *chants and rubrics necessary for celebrating *mass. It appeared by the 10th century, combining elements from several other books. It was revised by the Council of *Trent (1570) and *Vatican II (1969), although the latter does not contain readings and all the chants, and is more a *sacramentary.

(2) A book ("hand missal") containing the same material for use by laity. GET

Missa lecta [Latin] "Read, low mass." Prior to the reforms of *Vatican II, a technical RC designation (see *De musica sacra n. 14b-c) for the second general form of the *mass (other: *missa in cantu) in which the official texts of the

*service must be said in Latin, though vernacular *hymns could be used, and the *epistle and *gospel could be repeated in the vernacular. These distinctions no longer hold.   CSP

Missa Papae Marcelli [Latin]. "Mass to Pope Marcellus." *Palestrina's *mass (1562–63?), dedicated to Pope Marcellus II (d 1555). Though it probably played no direct role at the Council of *Trent, it exemplifies the intelligibility of text desired by that council.   AWR

Missa recitata [Latin]. "Recited, dialogue mass." A variation of the *missa lecta, dating from the early 20th century in places like *Maria Laach, which encouraged the people's participation in words, actions and gestures of the Latin *mass. Vernacular *hymns were permitted in this form of celebration.   CSP

Missa salisburgensis [Latin]. "Salzburg Mass." A 54-part (*choirs and *instruments) *cori spezzati *mass. Long attributed to *Benevoli for the 1628 dedication of the Salzburg Cathedral, it possibly was written by Heinrich Biber (d 1704). It remains a colossal example of *Baroque exuberance.   AWR

Missa solemnis [Latin]. "Solemn mass." (1) The most elaborate form of *missa in cantu, celebrated with deacon and subdeacon, with all of the *ordinary and *proper sung. It developed from the bishop's solemn mass (pontifical *high mass), which was adapted for use by a simple priest.

(2) *Beethoven's *symphonic mass in D (op. 123, 1819–23), setting 5 main parts of the *ordinary for soprano, alto, tenor, bass, *choir, *organ and *orchestra.   CSP

Missouri Harmony. An early American *tune book in the oblong format containing the rudiments of music and *hymns in *fasola notation. Compiled by A. Carden, it was first printed in Cincinnati (1820) and reprinted in many editions. FJM

Mixolydian (mode). An *ecclesiastical mode with its final on *G*. As an authentic mode (mode 7), it has an ambitus of *g-g'* and its dominant (*tenor) on *d'*. The related plagal mode (Hypomixolydian or mode 8) has an ambitus of *d-d'* and its dominant on *c'*.   CJK

Mnogoletie [Slavonic]. See *Polychronion.

Mocquereau, André (*b* La Tessoualle, Marne-et-Loire 1849; *d* Solesmes 1930). Scholar, choirmaster and Benedictine monk. After Dom Pothier he became responsible for the scholarly work on *plainsong at *Solesmes. To support the Solesmes version of *chant in the *Liber gradualis* (1883), he inaugurated a search through European libraries for chant manuscripts, reproduced in *Paléographie musicale* (1889–1914). This collection of facsimiles permitted a comparative study of manuscript, variants of chants. His theoretical contribution rests on his study of Latin accent and chant rhythm in his 2-volume work, *Le nombre musical grégorien* (1908, 1927).
Bibl: P. Combe, *Histoire de la restauration du chant grégorien d'après des documents inédits* (Solesmes, 1969).   RAD

Mode [from Latin *modus,* "standard" or "'pattern"]. (1) A set of available pitches and a collection of melodic motives. Other names for a mode are *echos

(Greek), *rāga* (Indian), *makam* or *maqām* (Arabic), *pătet* (Javanese) and *chōshi* (Japanese); also, see *Jewish prayer modes. The basic features of a mode are: 1) a gapped scale (e.g., the pentatonic scale), 2) a hierarchy of structurally important pitches, 3) the use of ornamental pitches, and 4) some form of extra-musical association.

W medieval modal theory borrowed its terminology from the E Christian system of 8 modes, called the *octoechos. It was only partially successful in imposing that system on an already existing oral tradition. Two criteria were used to place a piece in a particular mode: 1) the final note and 2) the dominant, or recitation pitch of the piece. This organizational system produced the following categories: 8 modes based on the four finals D, E, F and G with the authentic modes (odd numbered) having their dominant on the 5th scale degree above the final, and the *plagal (even-numbered) modes having their dominant on either the 3rd or 4th degree above the final. Recent studies have shown that the W church modes developed from 3 basic source modes (French *modes mères*): C, D and E. Examples of these are to be found in the *Graduale Simplex* (Vaticana, 1988) and the *Psalterium Monasticum* (Solesmes, 1981).

(2) In mensural notation, a mode is a set of durational relationships between the long and the breve. See *rhythmic modes.
Bibl: A. Turco, *Il Canto Gregoriano: Toni e Modi* (Roma, 1991); D. Hiley, *Western Plainchant* (Oxford, 1993) 454–77.   CJK

Modim (anachnu lach) [Hebrew]. "(We) gratefully (thank You)." Part of the *Amidah,* thanking God for shielding Jews in every age, for God's presence, wondrous gifts and never ending mercies. When recited by the *chazzan* or *sheliach tsibbur,* the congregation recites the altered version *Modim derabanan* (*"Modim* of the rabbis"). MLK

Moleben [Slavonic]. "Prayer service." A popular prayer form in the Byzantine rite, derived from *orthros,* yet celebrated independently from the cycle of the liturgical *year. A *moleben* may be sung in honor of Christ, the saints, for blessing at the opening of a council, or in time of distress. It contains many of the sung elements from *orthros* and usually includes a *gospel, and prayers of kneeling; sometimes the *Te Deum* is included. DMP

Molin, Jacob. see *Maharil.

Molitva zaambonnaya [Slavonic]. See *euche opistambonos.*

Molitvenik [Slavonic]. Alternate term for *trebnik;* see *hagiasmatarion.*

Möller, Mathias Peter (*b* Bornholm, Denmark 1854; *d* Hagerstown MD 1937). *Organ builder. He immigrated to the US (1872) where he worked for Derrick & *Felgemaker. He founded the Möller Organ Co. in Warren PA (1875), then moved it to Hagerstown (1880). The company's earliest organs were mechanical action, but soon turned to pneumatic. Important installations by Möller include Baltimore's RC Mary Our Queen Church (1959) and Washington DC's RC National Shrine of the Immaculate Conception (1965). JWK

Monody. (1) A style of accompanied solo song, developed in the early 17th century in Italy, especially Florence. The voice part is often speech-like, akin to *recitative, and the accompaniment includes *basso continuo. Forerunners include 16th-century songs accompanied by lute.
(2) *Monophony. MEC

Monogenes [Greek]. "[Hymn of the] Only-Begotten." The *incipit of a celebrated *troparion, sung to its own melody as a *perissos to the second *antiphon of the *enarxis* of the Byzantine *divine liturgy. Introduced into the *liturgy in the time of the Emperor Justinian (*d* 536), it is also found in the Monophysite liturgies of Armenia, Syria and Egypt. DMP

Monophony <adj, monophonic> [from Greek *mónos,* "single" and *phōné,* "sound"]. Music which consists of a single melodic line without accompaniment, such as *chant, as opposed to *polyphony, homophony and heterophony. MEC

Monte, Philippe de (*b* Mechlin 1521; *d* Prague 1603). Composer. A singer in Naples and Rome (1542–68), with brief stints in Antwerp and England (1554–55), Monte eventually became *Kapellmeister* to the Hapsburg court in Vienna and Prague (from 1568). He wrote over 1,100 madrigals, many sacred madrigals, 40 *masses and over 250 *motets. JLB

Monteverdi <Monteverde>, **Claudio (Giovanni Antonio)** (*b* Cremona 1567; *d* Venice 1643). Composer who developed a *concertato style of *church music for voices and *instruments which rivaled the Roman *a cappella style of *Palestrina and *Victoria. As *maestro di cap-

pella in Mantua for Duke Vincenzo Gonzaga (1602–12) and at St. Mark's in Venice (from 1613), he influenced J. S. *Bach, *Handel, F. J. *Haydn and *Mozart in their practice of combined *choir, soloists (vocal and instrumental) and *orchestra as the staple idiom for expressing music for worship. His *Vespro della Beata Vergine* (written for Gonzaga) in mature style and of massive structure rivaling Handel's *Messiah,* incorporated all the resources used in his operas: orchestral interludes, *da capo* *arias, concertato style *choruses with instruments, duets, trios and nearly every imaginable kind of ensemble. He left a treasury of repertoire comparable to major composers who followed him; surviving sacred works (over 140) include 3 *masses, 2 *Magnificat*s, many *psalms and *motets. A widower, he was ordained a RC priest in 1632.

Bibl: D. Arnold, *Monteverdi Church Music* (London, 1982); *idem,* ed., *Monteverdi,* 3rd rev. ed. (London, 1990); L. Silke, *Monteverdi* (Oxford, 1991). JKW

Moody, Dwight Lyman (*b* Northfield MA 1837; *d* there 1899). Evangelist. He worked in revivals with many well-known *gospel musicians (e.g., *Bliss, J. McGranahan, *Stebbins) who often opened the revivals with a song *service. Moody made 2 tours (1873–75, 1881–83) in the British Isles with *Sankey from which he returned to the US as a popular revivalist. See *Moody Bible Institute. RJS

Moody Bible Institute. Founded in Chicago by *Moody as the Bible Institute for Home and Foreign Missions of the Chicago Evangelization Society (1886), it was renamed Moody Bible Institute (1900) in Moody's honor. Originally it trained missionaries for urban America, eventually becoming a school for training evangelists and revival musicians, a publishing house and pioneer of religious broadcasting. RJS

Moore, Undine Smith (*b* Jarratt VA 1904; *d* Petersburg VA 1989). Composer, arranger and educator. She taught at Virginia State College, where she co-founded the Black Music Center. Moore composed over 75 works for various media. Her published pieces include many choral works, e.g., *Scenes from the Life of a Martyr, The Lamb and Lord* and *Glory to God.* MWC

Morales, Cristóbal de (*b* Seville *c* 1500; *d* Málaga? 1553). Composer. He held numerous appointments at churches throughout Spain (Avila, Toledo, etc.). Morales sang in the papal choir (1535–54); during this period he composed most of his music. He wrote over 20 *masses, 16 *Magnificat*s and over 100 *motets. Widely published, his music appeared in Europe and the New World. Morales was attuned to texts, especially their various *chant associations which significantly influenced his settings. FMR

Moravian Brethren <Church> **worship music.** The Brethren (*Unitas Fratrum*) organized in Bohemia in 1457. Their worship was biblical and congregational, consisting of *hymn singing, *psalm recitation, Bible reading and a sermon. Their first *hymnal appeared in 1501. Linked with the Lutheran Church, they were strongly influenced by German *chorales and eventually included *Luther's "German litany" in their worship.

Suppressed in 1620 in Bohemia, a remnant reestablished the United Brethren *(Brüder-Unität)* in Saxony in 1722. During this stage they continued to emphasize *hymnody in worship and, especially because of the leanings of their patron, Count Zinzendorf, came under the influence of *pietism. It was during this phase that the "love feast" developed as an important ritual for the community. It consists of hymn singing and an informal instruction by the minister in the context of a simple meal.

Missionaries came to the US in 1735, establishing Bethlehem PA and other cities. Moravians in Europe and the US were famous for providing concerts of *Classical and pre-Classical music. Little distinguished the quality of this concertized music from their worship music. In the US hymnody (now in German and English) remained the basis of Moravian worship and culture: hymn memorization was a daily exercise for teaching spiritual discipline. Hymns in worship were often accompanied by *organ and other *instruments (e.g., strings). Many American Moravian composers wrote *anthems, especially for mixed *choirs; most important among these were J. F. Peter (*d* 1813) and J. Herbst (*d* 1812).

Instrumentalists were used in many different combinations. The "trombone choir," originally composed of a trombone quartet (SATB), announced the beginning of worship, especially *Easter Sunday and funerals. This choir is still a common feature of Moravian worship. A related tradition is the Moravian Band, composed of a larger group of instrumentalists. For various social and religious reasons the musical life of Moravian communities declined in the second half of the 19th century, although the late 20th

century has witnessed a revived interest in Moravian worship music.

Bibl: D. McCorckle, "Moravian Music in Salem" (Indiana University: Ph.D. diss., 1958); H. H. Hall, "The Moravian Wind Ensemble" (George Peabody College for Teachers: Ph.D. diss., 1967); L. W. Hatzell, *Ohio Moravian Music* (Winston-Salem, 1988).   LJC

Moravian Music Foundation. An organization founded in Winston-Salem NC (1956) to preserve, study, and publish modern editions drawn from the *c* 10,000 music manuscripts retained in the archives of the Moravian Church in America. Ranging from the 16th century to the present, these materials represent a rich musical heritage brought from Europe by Moravian missionaries beginning in the 18th century. See *Moravian Brethren worship music.   RJB

Morley, Thomas (*b* Norwich 1557–58; *d* London 1602). Composer, theorist and editor. A student of *Byrd, Moreley became organist at Norwich Cathedral (1583–87), then St. Paul's Cathedral (by 1589?). A gentleman of the *Chapel Royal (1598), he was master of the English madrigal. He also composed *verse and *full anthems, *service music, *motets, *psalm settings and *keyboard works. He wrote an important musical treatise, *A Plaine and Easie Introduction to Practicall Musicke* (1597).   RKW

Mormon Tabernacle Choir. The 300-plus voice mixed *choir that performs in the Tabernacle on Temple Square in Salt Lake City. Founded in 1847 (1 month after the first Mormons came to Salt Lake), it is sponsored by The Church of Jesus Christ of Latter-day Saints. Work on the Tabernacle began in 1863; this dome-shaped building is so acoustically sensitive, a pin dropped at one end can be heard at the other end (170 feet away). The choir is celebrated for its concert tours, recordings, and weekly radio and television program "Music and the Spoken Word" (the oldest continually broadcast program in the US). MFM

Mormon worship music. See *Church of Jesus Christ of Latter-day Saints, The.

Motet. A term used to describe various forms of music from the 13th–20th centuries. It is generally applied to short sacred choral works.

In the 13th–14th centuries it was a brief composition with part of a *chant melody as a *cantus firmus* in the *tenor voice and 2 to 4 upper-texted voices. The earliest motets were formed when words (French, *mots*) were added to upper voice(s) of preexistent *discant *clausulae*. Composers next wrote entirely new pieces in this form, ordinarily with secular vernacular texts in the upper parts. Very popular in the 13th century, its popularity diminished in the 14th century though it continued to be cultivated as a secular genre, with composers such as *Machaut applying isorhythmic technique to it.

In the late 14th and early 15th centuries secular texts were abandoned. The *Renaissance motet became a relatively brief choral setting for almost any sacred Latin text excluding the *ordinary and certain other liturgical items. Among the most important forms of Renaissance *church music, RCs of the era such as *Palestrina and *Lassus wrote hundreds of them, sometimes with, but often without *cantus firmi*. German Protestants (e.g., *Walter) wrote *chorale motets in essentially the same style but with *chorale *cantus firmi* and in the vernacular.

During the *Baroque period, motet was a generic term for sacred pieces rooted in the *a cappella Renaissance style. It also designated solo/small ensemble pieces (e.g., those of *Monteverdi) and large-scale vocal works (sometimes with *orchestra) that could approach the form and dimensions of the *cantata (e.g., J. S. *Bach's *Jesu, meine Freude*). The variety of diverse musical forms labeled motet continues to the present day.

Bibl: E. A. Wienandt, *Choral Music of the Church* (New York, 1965) chps. 3 and 10; E. H. Sanders, et al., "Motet," *NGDMM* 12:617–47.   DWM

Motet-chanson   <*cantilena*-motet, song-motet>. A *motet texture based on that of the late medieval *chanson* (most prevalent in the 15th century) in which a texted, relatively active treble part is supported by 2 untexted (instrumental?), slower-moving, relatively homorhythmic lower parts.   RTR

Motu proprio [Latin]. "Of his own accord." A papal statement issued without official consultation, e.g., *Tra le sollecitudini*.   CLV

Mount of Olives. See *Christus am Ölberge*.

Mouton, Jean (*b* Haut-Wignes 1459; *d* St. Quentin, 1522). Composer whose works include 15 *masses and over 100 *motets. His masses show the transition from *cantus firmus* technique to the newer *parody and paraphrase style of composing.   DCI

Movement prayer. Gesture, posture or simple dance used to deepen or enhance the words, song, or emotion of private or communal prayer. Sometimes this term is used interchangeably with congregational dance or liturgical *dance.   MAK

Mozarabic chant. See *Old Spanish chant.

Mozart, Wolfgang Amadeus (*b* Salzburg 1756; *d* Vienna 1791). Composer and principal figure in the *Classical period. Baptized Johannes Chrysostomus Wolfgangus Theophilus, he preferred the Latin form of Theophilus (i.e., Amadeus). A child prodigy, who played the clavier at 3 and composed at 5, his father Leopold showcased the young Mozart and his sister Maria Anna (1751–1829) at many European courts. Through this touring, Mozart was exposed to various styles of composition which he mastered and blended with his unique musical genius. He successfully composed in virtually every genre, with over 600 works ascribed to him including 41 symphonies, 27 piano *concertos, 25 string quartets and 16 operas.

Leopold Mozart served in the court of the Prince-Archbishop of Salzburg (first Schrattenbach, *d* 1772; then, von Colloredo) from 1743 until his death in 1787. The archbishops were also principal patrons of the young Mozart until the tension between von Colloredo and W. Mozart lead to his dismissal in 1871. W. Mozart composed most of his *liturgical music while at Salzburg.

He wrote over 60 works for the church, including 18 *masses. Nine are entitled

Missa brevis, highlighting the requirement that mass at Salzburg Cathedral was not to last more than 45 minutes. Both Archbishop von Colloredo and Emperor *Joseph II required the simplification of worship. The great *Mass in C Minor* (K 427, 1782–83), written to fulfill a vow at the time of his marriage, was never finished. Mozart also composed a *Te Deum* (K 141, 1768), almost 20 *motets including *Exultate, jubilate* (K 165, 1773) and *Ave verum corpus* (K 618, 1791), 4 *litanies, including *Litaniae de venerabili altaris sacramento* (K 125, 1772), 2 settings of *vespers including *Vesperae solennes de confessore* (K 339, 1780) and 17 *church sonatas. He died while writing the *Requiem* (K 626, 1791), completed by his student F. Süssmayr.

Besides properly liturgical works, Mozart also composed *sacred music, e.g., a passion *cantata (*Grabmusik,* K 42, 1767), *oratorios (e.g., *Davidde penitente,* K 469, 1785) and 3 *masonic cantatas. He was less a composer of sacred music, however, than a liturgical composer, at least until he left Salzburg.

Bibl: M. Kenyon, *Mozart in Salzburg* (London, 1952); K. Geiringer, "The Church Music," in *The Mozart Companion,* eds. H. C. Robbins Landon and D. Mitchell, 2nd ed. (London, 1965) 361–76; M. Solomon, *Mozart* (New York, 1995).   EBF

Muchenichen [Slavonic]. See *martyrikon.

Muffat, Georg (*b* Mègéve 1653; *d* Passau 1704). Composer, organist and father of Gottlieb *Muffat. Georg studied with *Lully in Paris and then Pasquini in Rome. He served as organist in Salzburg and *Kapellmeister to the bishop of Passau (from 1690). He was instrumental in bringing French and Italian styles into Germany. He composed *concerti grossi,* orchestra suites and *organ works. EBF

Muffat, Gottlieb <Theophil> (*b* Passau 1690; *d* Vienna 1770). Composer, organist and son of Georg *Muffat. He was director of the opera, chamber music and organist in the court at Vienna from 1717. He is best known for his *keyboard works. LMT

Multum ad commovendos animos [Latin]. "Much for moving souls." A document of Pope *Pius IX issued in 1870, confirming the German *Society of St. Cecilia in its promotion of *Gregorian chant, *polyphony and vernacular *hymnody (where the law allowed). AWR

Murray, A(nthony) Gregory <Joseph> (*b* Fulham 1905; *d* Downside Abbey 1992). Benedictine monk, priest, organist, teacher, composer, scholar and choirmaster at Downside Abbey. He wrote liturgical works for *organ, *choirs and many *hymn tunes. He also authored *Gregorian Chant, according to Manuscripts* (1963). RJS

Musaf [Hebrew]. "Addition." The additional Jewish *service added on the *Sabbath, *Rosh Chodesh,* the *Three Festivals and *Yamim Noraim;* it parallels the additional sacrifice that was offered at the Temple on similar days. Ordinarily recited immediately after *shacharit,* it consists of the *Amidah and various other prayers including the *Kaddish.* SJW

Musica ecclesiastica [Latin]. See *church music.

Musica enchiriadis [Latin]. "Musical handbook." An anonymous theoretical treatise from the W Frankish empire, *c* 900. It contains the earliest known written examples of parallel *organum. See *enchiridion. DWM

Musicae sacrae disciplina [Latin]. "The discipline of sacred music." The 1955 encyclical of Pope Pius XII. It provides historical and philosophical bases for RC worship music. It also expands on qualities demanded by and relaxes some prohibitions given in *Tra le sollecitudini.* JMJ

Musica liturgica [Latin]. See *liturgical music.

Musicam sacram [Latin]. "Sacred music." A 1967 instruction by the RC Sacred Congregation for Divine Worship. It applies the principles and directives found in *Sacrosanctum Concilium* for the Roman rite. Among other things, *Musicam sacram* distinguishes 5 functions of worship music: decorative, unifying, role differentiating, transcendental and eschatological. JMJ

Musica religiosa [Latin]. See *religious music.

Musica reservata <riservata> [Latin]. "Reserved music." A term which occurs in various writings from 1552 to 1625 with no single, agreed upon meaning. It can alternately mean: 1) a more text-oriented style of composition as in the writing of *Josquin; 2) a whole range of compositional techniques such as chromaticism which are employed for textual expression; and 3) chromatic and enharmonic music "reserved" for trained listeners.   EBF

Musica sacra. See *sacred music.

Music in Catholic Worship <MCW>. A 1972 statement of the *Bishops' Committee on the Liturgy (2nd ed. 1983) applying the principles of *Sacrosanctum Concilium* and *Musicam Sacram*. It provides a simple theology of *liturgy, encourages pastoral planning for liturgy and discusses how music serves faith. Most notably it directs that a 3-fold judgment needs to be made on every musical element: musical (is the music technically, aesthetically and expressively good?), liturgical (does it address the structural, textual and role requirements of worship?) and pastoral (does it help people express their faith in this place, age and culture?). Finally, it categorizes music for *eucharist as *acclamations, *processional songs, *responsorial psalms, *ordinary chants and *supplementary songs.   JMJ

Mystery (miracle) play. A vernacular religious drama of the *Middle Ages, flourishing after 1300. Modern terminology distinguishes plays which portray miracles and lives of saints (miracle) from those based on biblical narratives (mystery). Plays were episodic, often gathered into cycles of related scenes spanning salvation history; cycles were named after towns of important performances (e.g., Chester and York). Though performed away from the church, the debt to liturgical *drama is evidenced by the inclusion of some liturgical *chants within, and the *Te Deum* at the end of these plays. They were distinct from their dramatic ancestor insofar as they were spoken dramas that included some music.   MAK

N

Nak'dishach [Hebrew]. "We will sanctify." A variant form of the *Kedushah used in *Sephardic liturgy. In Middle E Sephardic traditions *Nak'dishach* is sung in the *makam* of the day.   MLK

National Association of Negro Musicians <NANM>. An organization founded (1916) by and for African Americans to "raise the musical standards of the teaching profession of the African American race throughout the country." Its first scheduled meeting (1916) was canceled after the onset of World War I; the meeting eventually occurred in Chicago (1919). NANM provides occasions for the performance of compositions by African Americans, encourages and provides financial support for artists and provides church music workshops. NANM gave its first scholarship for talented youth to Marian Anderson (1921).   MWC

National Association of Pastoral Musicians <NPM>. A membership organization founded by *Funk (1976) to serve the Church by fostering the art of musical *liturgy in RC communities in the US. Besides a biannual national convention and regional conventions on alternating years it sponsors a number of summer programs for cantors, choir directors, composers, etc. Its official publication is *Pastoral Music*.   VCF

National Fellowship of Methodist Musicians. See *Fellowship of United Methodists in Music.

Nativité du Seigneur, La [French]. "The Nativity of the Lord." A series of 9 meditations divided into 4 books composed for *organ by *Messiaen (1935). The compositional style is motival repetition, and each meditation represents a particular aspect of the nativity story.   PAB

Naumbourg, Samuel (*b* Dennolohe near Ansbach 1815; *d* Paris 1880).

213

*Cantor and composer. Trained as a cantor in Munich, he served a congregation in Strasbourg, then moved to Paris where he met J. Halévy (1843). Parisian grand opera influenced Naumbourg's synagogue music. By the mid-19th century his *liturgical music (along with *Sulzer's) was popular throughout Europe. His 3-volume *Zemirot Yisrael* (1847–57) included his own compositions and those of others including Halévy and Meyerbeer.   MLK

Nauvoo Brass Band. Leaders of The Church of Jesus Christ of Latter-day Saints established the city of Nauvoo IL in 1839 as a place of refuge for church members driven from their homes in MO. A band was organized in 1841 consisting of 9 drums, 5 fifes, 2 cymbals, bugle, clarinet, tambourine and triangle. This evolved into the Nauvoo Brass Band, whose purpose was to enhance community life in early pioneer settlements.   MFM

Neale, John Mason (*b* London 1818; *d* East Grimstead 1866). Author and hymnologist. With B. Webb he founded the *Cambridge Camden Society. Neale is best known for his English translations of Greek and Latin *hymns, his own original texts and innovative work in including *carols in *hymnals (*Carols for Christmastide,* 1853). His extensive knowledge of languages was combined with unusually fine literary gifts, enabling him to produce translations responsive to the *Oxford Movement's desire to reexamine the Church of England's historical and spiritual origins. His first collection of Latin *hymnody (*Hymnal Noted,* 2 parts: 1852 and 1854)

consisted of his and others' translations which followed the meters of the original Latin texts so carefully they could be sung to their *plainsong melodies. His *Hymns of the Eastern Church* (1862) opened the treasury of Greek hymns to the W. *Hymns Ancient and Modern* was deeply influenced by him. Many of his translations continue in use today.

Bibl: A. G. Lough, *The Influence of John Mason Neale* (London, 1962); M. Chandler, *The Life and Work of John Mason Neale 1818–1868* (Leominster, 1995).   CAD

Neander, Joachim (*b* Bremen 1650; *d* there 1680). The first significant *hymn writer of German *pietism. Neander is credited with 60 hymns, including *"Lobe den Herren den mächtigen König"* (German, "Praise to the Lord the Almighty"). He published his music as *Alpha und Omega, Glaub- und Liebesübung* (1680). RJS

Nebel <*nevel*> [Hebrew]. A stringed instrument mentioned frequently in the Hebrew Bible (e.g., Amos 5:23). Though often translated as "harp," its precise form is uncertain.   DWM

Ne'ilah [Hebrew]. "Closing." Originally a *service conducted on fast days at the Temple before its gates were closed in the evening. Today it is the final *service at the end of *Yom Kippur;* this is an added service special for the holiday. The *Kaddish* at the beginning of the service is a *Misinnai* tune. The service continues with the *Amidah* and concludes with climatic statements by the *chazzan* and the congregation (including the opening *verse of the *Shema) culminating in the sounding of the *shofar.   MLK

Nekrosimon (pl. **nekrosima**) [Greek; Slavonic *mertvennyi*]. "Hymn for the deceased." An intercessory *sticheron for the dead in the Byzantine *divine office. *Nekrosima* are usually sung in Saturday's office which is dedicated to the memory of the departed, since Christ lay in the tomb on that day.   DMP

Nelson Mass <*Imperial, *Coronation Mass;* German *Nelsonmesse*>. Nickname for F. J. *Haydn's mass in D minor (*Missa in angustiis,* "Mass in time of danger," 1798), possibly because it celebrated Nelson's victory at Aboukir, or because Nelson heard it at Eisenstadt.   JLB

Neo-Gallican chant. *Plainsong composed in France from the later 17th into the 19th century to replace traditional *chant in RC worship. Factors contributing to its creation were the neo-Gallican liturgical movement, a spirit of independence from Roman authority, and continuing disdain for "barbarisms" in medieval chant. The body of Neo-Gallican chant is comprised of: old chants that have been revised, particularly for tonal coherence; new compositions; and chants given "modern" stylistic elements such as solos, choral/instrumental sections, and rhythmic or improvisational features. By the late 18th century, this music (most based on Parisian models) was used widely in France. Its use was challenged by *Guéranger and his followers.

Bibl: D. Hiley, "Neo-Gallican Chant," *NGDMM* 3 (1980) 105–7.   JMH

Neporochnyi [Slavonic]. See *Anastasima eulogitaria.*

Nesiat kappayim. See *Birkat kohanim.*

Neue Bach-Gesellschaft [German]. "New Bach Society." With the completion of the *Bach-Gesellschaft* edition in 1900 this society was founded the same year to promote J. S. *Bach's music and attending scholarship, in part by publishing the *Bach Jahrbuch.* The American Bach Society, now independent, was founded as one of its branch organizations.   MPB

Neumatic. Related to *neume. An earlier term for *chant segments with moderate-length neumes over each syllable, in distinction to syllabic or *melismatic chant. Since, however, all chant can be considered neumatic (see neume), some prefer the term "oligotonic" for this type of chant.   JKL-AWR

Neume <neum> [Greek]. "Sign, gesture." A graphic design representing all the notes (whether one, few or many) over a single syllable. A neume can be composed of a number of individual graphic elements. According to Hucbald of St. Amand (*d* 930), these designs indicate the rhythmic and expressive qualities needed for the correct performance of a *chant.   CJK

Neumeister, Erdmann (*b* Uichteritz 1671; *d* Hamburg 1756). Theologian and poet who served as pastor at Hamburg's St. James Church. He wrote 9 cycles of *cantata texts (1695–1742) in which (*c* 1700) he expanded the cantata form to include poetic interpretations and applications of scripture in the form of secco *recitatives and *da capo* *arias. *Erlebach, J. S. *Bach and *Telemann set these texts to music. MPB

Nevin, John Williamson (*b* Franklin Co PA 1803; *d* Lancaster PA 1886). Reformed theologian at Mercersburg Seminary with *Schaff. Nevin was concerned with a broad range of ecumenical, sacramental, liturgical and musical issues. He authored *Address on Sacred Music* (1827), *The Anxious Bench* (1843) and *The Mystical Presence* (1846). PHW

New Bach Society. See *Neue Bach-Gesellschaft*.

New England School. See *First New England School.

New Testament, music in the. The New Testament does not address the issue of music in any comprehensive way. The various authors of the books comprising the New Testament (4 gospels, Acts of the Apostles, Pauline and "Catholic" epistles and the Book of Revelation) treat issues of cult only insofar as these contribute to their larger purposes of teaching and evangelizing. Christianity emerged in an auditory environment very different from that of modern North America. Contemporary W definitions of "music" do not necessarily apply to the New Testament. The boundaries between speaking and singing were quite fluid; communication was cued on the spoken rather than the seen or read. The spontaneous word-event was characteristic of the ministry of Jesus. Announcing the immediacy of the good news in a manner which some scholars have typified as "reckless of posterity" marked his ministry and that of his followers. Despite the development of written forms like the gospel, a primacy of audition characterized emerging Christianity. For them, hearing was believing.

The New Testament does contain numerous "musical" allusions. As Jesus and his early followers were Jews, there is plentiful evidence that they frequented the *Temple and synagogues in Palestine. In the former they would have heard the playing of *instruments and singing of the *Levites; in the latter the *cantillation that marked the public reading of the *Torah and other scriptural books (Luke 4:16-20 even depicts Jesus publicly declaiming a text from Isaiah). A distinctive Christian cult especially emerged in the homes of believers. Common elements there included meal rituals, public narrations of the Jesus story, preaching, readings from letters, prayers and songs. The idealized image of an early community in Acts 2:42 presumes some of these elements. While difficult to make clear distinctions between musical and non-musical elements in early Christian worship, to the extent that any worship element included public vocalization so to the same extent did it presume a certain degree of "musicality."

Aside from the general lyricism of this emerging cult, there are some passages where a marked degree of musicality is identifiable. The New Testament contains many remnants of short praise-passages (e.g., Rom 16:27), God-*hymns (e.g., 1 Pet 1:3-5) and *Christological hymns. It is also punctuated by a variety of lyric fragments (e.g., Matt 21:9), *acclamations (e.g., Rev 22:20), *ejaculations (e.g., Rev 22:20), *doxologies and other musical allusions (e.g., Rev 4).

The music-prayer style of the synagogue more than that of the Temple influenced emerging Christian worship. Given what is known about music-prayer leadership in the synagogue at the time, as well as Paul's instruction on public prayer (e.g., 1 Cor 14:13-19), it is probable that early Christian "music" served the proclamation of the word and engaged the community in a relatively democratic form of lyric worship. Musical elements were vocal not instrumental, amateur not professional, and integrated not separate parts of the worship. Though some solo and even professional musical contributions occurred within this worship, they did not dominate the musical landscape of primitive Christian prayer. This lyricism—even though quite ecstatic at times—was shaped for the common good.

*Psalms is the Hebrew Bible book most frequently cited in the New Testament, yet their use in Christian worship is not explicitly noted before the *Apocryphal Acts of Paul* (c 190 CE); the references to "psalms" in Eph 5:19 and Col 3:16 cannot be linked with surety to Davidic psalmody. As in the synagogues of the era, it is possible that psalms served as a book of readings for the early Christian community. It is also possible that some psalms—especially those like the *Hallel,* traditional for *Pesach* (Mark 14:26)—found a place in the home rituals of Jesus' followers. Fragments from the psalms could have found their way into preaching or proclamation. Given the wide diversity of first-century CE practice, however, it would be hazardous to suggest that there was any set pattern for employing psalms within New Testament worship.

Bibl: W. S. Smith, *Musical Aspects of the New Testament* (Amsterdam, 1962); J. McKinnon, ed. *Antiquity and the Middle Ages* (Englewood Cliffs, 1991); E. Foley, *Foundations of Christian Music* (Collegeville, 1996).   EBF

Nicene Creed. The profession of faith from the Council of Nicaea (325), amended at the Council of Constantinople (381), after which it was properly known as the Nicene-Constantinopolitan creed. Its tripartite structure is organized around the 3 persons in the Trinity. This creed was a source of division between the Latin W and Orthodox E due to the inclusion of a phrase indicating that the Holy Spirit proceeds from the Father *and* the Son (the Orthodox E held that the Spirit proceeds only from the Father). A post-381 version of this creed supplies the text for the *Credo.*   MSD

Nicolai, Philipp (*b* Mengeringhausen 1556; *d* Hamburg 1608). Lutheran pastor, poet and composer. His *Frewden-Spiegel dess ewigen Lebens* (1599) contains his 2 best-known *hymn texts and tunes, *WIE SCHÖN LEUCHTET DER MORGENSTERN and *WACHET AUF. PKG

Niggun (pl. **niggunim**) [Hebrew]. "Melody." This reference to melody stems from the *Hasidic practice of singing a wordless melody. Rooted in the *Kabbalah,* music is given a high status and deemed more important than the words. Singing a wordless melody is said to elevate the soul to ecstasy. The process of reaching this state is understood by each Hasidic sect uniquely. In general 3 types of *niggunim* are distinguished: *stam* ("plain") or *Tisch* ("table") *niggunim,* sung at the tables of the spiritual leaders *(rebbe)* of the sect, weddings or other celebrations usually in a fast tempo; *Deveykus* ("achieving the divine state of ecstasy") *niggunim,* emotional melodies sung freely with feeling; *Rebbes niggunim,* special melodies initiated by a *rebbe* or for a special occasion such as the procession of a bride at a wedding.   MLK

Night office. See *matins.

Nishmat kol chai <*Birkat ha-shir*> [Hebrew]. "The Soul of every living thing" <"Blessing of the song">. A prayer blessing God for countless favors, added to *shacharit for *Sabbath, *Three Festivals and *Yamim Noraim. It concludes the *Pesuke dezimrah section of the *liturgy, followed by *Chatzi *Kaddish*. The text contains *Shochen ad and *Yistabach,* sections musically highlighted in the *Ashkenazic tradition; also, *Shavat anivim and *El Ha-hodaot,* sections musically highlighted in the *Sephardic tradition. The Ashkenazic *cantor begins Sabbath *shacharit* with *Shochen ad,* the Sephardic cantor with *Nishmat kol chai*. Within Middle E Sephardic traditions this text is sung in the *makam of the day.   MLK

Nix, Verolga (*b* Cleveland 1933). Editor, arranger and church musician. She studied at the New England and Oberlin Conservatories. She coedited *Songs of Zion* with J. J. *Cleveland (1981). Nix also founded Intermezzo Choir Ministries, and the Foundation for the Preservation of African American Music, based in Philadelphia.   RKW

Nocturns [Latin *nocturni* from *nox,* "night"; also, *nocturnae orationes, vigiliae*]. (1) An alternate name for *matins.
(2) A division of matins. Each of 2 or 3 nocturns included a set number of *psalms (or *canticles) sung with *antiphons followed by a set number of *lessons interspersed by *responsories.   JKL

Noël [French; English nowell; Burgundian *noé;* from Latin *natalis,* "of birth"]. (1) Since the 15th century a term for a non-liturgical, *strophic verse of a popular character often sung to *chant tunes, popular songs and dances, especially during Christmastide.
(2) An instrumental (usually *organ) work, ordinarily intended for *Christmas worship.
(3) A *carol.   LMT

None [from Latin *hora nona,* "ninth hour"]. Mid-afternoon prayer in the Roman rite *divine office. The third of the *little hours. Its basic structure in the present Roman rite is: opening *dialogue and *doxology, midday *hymn, *psalmody, scripture reading, collect and concluding *acclamation.   JMJ

North American Liturgy Resources (NALR). A pioneer publisher of new *liturgical music of the so-called *folk or contemporary variety. It was founded by R. Bruno in 1969, then purchased by and incorporated into *Oregon Catholic Press in 1994.   JBF

Notker (Balbulus) (*b* near St. Gall *c* 840; *d* there 912). A monk of St. Gall, sometimes called *Balbulus* (Latin, "the stammerer"); the most famous author of *sequence texts of the early *Middle Ages. The preface of his *Liber hymnorum* (884), his chief collection of sequence texts, contains valuable information regarding the origin and development of the early sequence. His full output includes 32 large and 8 smaller sequences. CFS

Notre Dame, repertory of. Broadly defined, this refers to the *liturgical music of Paris' Notre Dame Cathedral and its surrounding churches. More specifically, it refers to the late 12th and early 13th century *polyphonic part of that repertory, especially as found in *Magnus liber organi*. Among these are 2-voice compositions attributed to *Léonin. His works show an alternation of *discant and *organum styles similar to *St. Martial polyphony, but with even longer *melismas and the application of modal rhythm to the *duplum*. In later compositions such as those attributed to *Perotin, one finds 2 and 3 contrapuntal voices added to the *plainsong *tenor as well as the application of modal rhythms to the tenor in discant sections. Later substitute *clausulae* were composed for these discant sections, and then texts (often commenting upon or amplifying the chant tenor) were added to the melismatic upper parts, giving us the first *motets. The repertory also included *conducti*.

Bibl: G. Anderson, ed., *Notre-Dame and Related Conductus* (Henryville PA, 1979).   JPM-RTR

Notre Dame University. See *University of Notre Dame.

Nowakowsky, David (*b* Kiev 1848; *d* Odessa 1921). Composer. He began his formal training in Berditchev; by age 21 he was choirmaster of the Brody Synagogue in Odessa where he served for 50 years. He created grandiose choral arrangements, fusing the conventions of W European choral composition with the traditional modes of the *Ashkenazic synagogue (see *Jewish prayer modes). During his life he published various collections including *(Shrei David) Kabalat Shabat: Gebete und Gesänge* . . . for Sabbath eve and evening *services (1901).   DMR

NPM. See *National Association of Pastoral Musicians.

Nulman, Macy (*b* Newark 1923). Composer and scholar. Nulman taught in the cantorial training program at Yeshivah University and cofounded the *Cantorial Council of America. He was the first editor of the *Journal of Jewish Music and Liturgy*. Nulamn also authored valuable reference works including *Concise Encyclopedia of Jewish Music* (1975) and *The Encyclopedia of Jewish Prayer* (1993).   MLK

Nunc dimittis [Latin]. "Now you dismiss [your servant]." The *Canticle of Simeon (Lk 2:29-32). It is sung at *vespers in the E rites, *compline in the Roman rite, *evensong in the *BCP and *evening prayer in contemporary Anglican worship.   LMT

Nusach <*nusaḥ*> [Hebrew]. "Removal, copying." (1) A term employed to designate varying liturgical rites within Judaism, especially either *Ashkenazic or *Sephardic.

(2) *Jewish prayer modes.   MLK

O

O <great(er)> Antiphons. Seven *antiphons for the *Magnificat* at *vespers, each of which begins with the exclamation "O" (e.g., *"O Sapientia"*). They are sung on each of the 7 days preceding *Christmas Eve. Each antiphon uses the same set of 2nd-mode melodic formulas carefully adapted to its specific text. Already mentioned by Amalarius of Metz (*c* 850), their texts and music may date from the 7th or 8th century. They are best known in English through the *hymn version, "O come, O come Emmanuel." CJK-NDM

Obednitsa [Slavonic]. See *typika*.

Oberwerk [German]. "Upper work." A manual division of the German *organ located above the *Brustwerk*. Since the mid-19th century it is often equipped with swell shutters. PAJ

Obrecht <Hobrect, Obertus> **Jacob** (*b* 1450–51 Bergen op Zoom?; *d* 1505 Ferrara). One of the outstanding composers of the late 15th century; also a RC priest. Little is known of his early life and education. He held several positions as choirmaster in Utrecht, Cambrai, Bruges and Antwerp but was never appointed to a court position, perhaps because he did not have the expected vocal ability.

His music is noted for its large structures capable of sustaining complex and lengthy sections. Rather than develop a borrowed melody (*cantus firmus*) simply by lengthening or shortening it in other voices (a common practice by 15th-century composers), Obrecht preferred to ornament or embellish the borrowed melody by quoting it in different voices, fragmenting it into short motifs and simultaneously employing several such melodies. This extraordinary inventiveness in holding together melody and counter-melodies by contrapuntal strategies was greatly admired by his contemporaries. Extant works include 29 *masses, 27 sacred *motets and 27 secular vocal pieces.

Bibl: R. C. Wegman, *The Life and Masses of Jacob Obrecht* (Oxford, 1994). RAD

Obschaya mineya [Slavonic]. See *menaion*.

Occasional offices <services>. In distinction from the regular cycle of *eucharist and the *divine office, these are worship events in response to specific needs or occasions, e.g., baptisms, weddings, funerals, ordinations, installations, blessings and dedications.   RDH

Ockeghem <Okeghem, Okchem, Ogkeguam>, **Johannes** <Jean, Jehan> (*b c* 1410; *d* Tours? 1497). Composer who was a contemporary and musical peer to *Dufay and *Josquin. Details of his early life are uncertain: it is thought that *Binchois was his mentor. Ockeghem was briefly in service to the Duke of Bourbon (mid-1440s to 1448). He then served prominently as first singer-chaplain and composer at the French court (from 1451 until after the death of Louis XI, 1483). During that time he was also treasurer of St. Martin-de-Tours Abbey and canon at Notre Dame Cathedral.

He enjoyed an enviable reputation as singer and master composer (primarily celebrated for his contrapuntal achievements). Works attributed to him are surprisingly few. Most substantial are his *mass settings: a *Requiem, 13 settings of the *ordinary and a *Credo. He also wrote a few *motets and more secular *chansons*.

Bibl: D. Plamenac, ed., *Collected Works of Johannes Ockeghem* (Philadelphia, 1947–92); P. Martin, *Johannes Ockeghem and Jacob Obrecht* (New York, 1988).   RJB

OCP. See *Oregon Catholic Press.

Octoechos [Greek; Slavonic *oktoikh*]. "Eight tones, modes." (1) The Byzantine musical system for singing *hirmosi, *stichera (see *idiomelon), *troparia and other types of *hymns. In each case, a model melody serves for various texts from the repertoire of hymns. Variant melodies also exist within each tone (e.g., *omoia* in the Slavonic tradition). The system is of ancient origin, probably Semitic through Syria; it antedates many of the Greek hymns composed in poetic *meter to fit the melodies. Originally there may have been a 7-tone system, corresponding to the days of the week. The development of 8 tones was possibly influenced by a theology of Sunday as the "eighth day," the beginning of a new creation. The *octoechos* was first used in Byzantine monasteries, entering parochial churches by the 11th century. Greeks number the tones: 1, 2, 3, 4, *plagal 1, plagal 2, barus ("deep') and plagal 4; Slavs number them from 1 to 8.

(2) The liturgical *book (in Greek *parakletike*) containing the texts of *kathismata, *stichera, *troparia, etc., which are sung daily apart from the immovable cycle found in the *menaion*. Beginning with tone 1 on Monday following All Saints Sunday (Sunday after *Pentecost) it follows a strict, uninterrupted cycle until Palm Sunday. The *typikon* is the liturgical book that contains the rules governing the order of texts from the *octoechos* and *menaion*.

Bibl: C. Hannick, "Le Texte de l'Oktoechos," *Dimanche* (Chevetogne, 1970) 37–60; A. Cody, "The Early History of the Octoechos in Syria," in *East of Byzantium* (Washington, 1982) 89–113. DMP

Ode. (1) In classical antiquity a lyric poem intended to be sung, often in honor of a special occasion, as those of Pindar.

(2) A text celebrating the monarchy or in honor of St. *Cecilia's Day in

17th–19th century England, set by *Purcell and others.

(3) An extended *cantata-like composition.

(4) In Byzantine practice, one of the 9 segments of the *kanon.   VAL

Ode for St. Cecilia's Day. A choral work, usually large scale, written for the feast of St. *Cecilia (November 22). Composers include *Purcell, *Blow, *Clarke, *Handel, *Greene, *Parry and *Britten.   RKW

Odell, J. H. & C. S. An *organ building firm founded (1859) in New York by John Henry Odell (1830–99) and Caleb Sherwood Odell (1827–93). The firm is credited with important inventions such as reversible coupler action, combination action and the crescendo pedal.   JWK

Odes of Solomon. See *Solomon, Odes of.

Offerenda [Latin]. "Offering." (1) The *offertory *chant of the Milanese (Ambrosian) rite (called *sacrificium* in the *Old Spanish rite). It is closely related to its Roman counterpart in both textual choice and musical style. It generally consists of 1 or a few *verses sung in a highly florid style.

(2) The elements "offered" at *mass, e.g., bread, wine, etc.   PAJ

Offertory [Latin *offertorium*]. (1) The process of receiving the offerings and preparing the altar for *eucharist and the *chant of the *proper of the mass accompanying these actions. The history of the offertory chant before the 9th century is unclear. It is possible that *Augustine introduced a chant here; a practice which

then may have spread to Rome. Offertories are the most elaborate chants of the *Gregorian repertoire. The *antiphon is ordinarily followed by 2 or more *verses, each of which is followed by all or some portion of the antiphon (usually the end). Texts are primarily from the *psalms, with occasional references to feasts (e.g., *"Ascendit Deus"* for *Ascension), but rarely mention "offering." Most striking textually is the repetition of words and phrases, an unusual Gregorian practice.

(2) That period of a *service when the collection is taken.

Bibl: D. Hiley, *Western Plainchant* (Oxford, 1993) especially 121–30.   PAJ

Offertory sentences. Scriptural verses in the *BCP spoken by the priest (occasionally sung by the *choir) at the beginning of the collection. These were set by *Merbecke in his *Booke of Common Praier Noted;* several composers (e.g., *Tallis and *Purcell) made settings of certain of them.   JMT

Office. (1) Abbreviation for the *divine office.

(2) A ministry or recurring ministerial service, e.g., the office of *cantor.   EBF

Office hymn. A *hymn of the *divine office, specific to the time of day, season or commemoration. Such are often patterned after the *Ambrosian hymns.   RDH

Office of readings. An hour of the RC *divine office, devised after *Vatican II. A radical revision of *matins, it may be prayed at any time of the day; it is possible to adapt it as an extended vigil. Its main elements are: *hymnody, 3 *psalms, readings (scriptural, patristic and writings from or about the saints), *responsories and a final *collect.   CSP

Office of the dead. See *dead, office of the.

Oikos (pl. **oikoi**) [Greek; Slavonic *ikos*]. "House, stanza." A variable poetic *response to a sung *kontakion. *Oikoi* are usually found in a series of 24, alphabetically arranged. Originally free-standing, *oikoi* are now part of Byzantine *orthros, specifically part of the *kanon and said after the 6th *ode.   DMP

Oktoikh [Slavonic]. See *octoechos.

Old hundred(th). The *hymn tune of Ps 100 ("All people that on earth do dwell") in the "old" *metrical psalter of *Sternhold and Hopkins. Also the hymn tune for Ps 134 in the French *Genevan Psalter of 1551.   RAL

Old Roman chant. The repertoire for the Roman rite; preserved in 5 principal manuscripts of the 11th to 12th or 13th centuries, produced in Rome. Textual sources allow these *chants to be traced back to the 8th century. The standard theory is that the Old Roman repertoire or its precursor was transmitted from Rome to N Europe where it was modified by Frankish musical practices; the resulting chant was eventually called *Gregorian. The repertoire which continued in Rome, possibly with some development, is thus called Old Roman (or Urban-Roman). Soon after being fully recorded in manuscript, it was superseded by the Gregorian repertoire. In liturgical usage, text and melodies it is similar to the Gregorian tradition, though there are often variants in Old Roman melodies. Generally, Old Roman melodies are more conjunct in motion and yet more ornate than the Gregorian counterparts.

Bibl: H. Hucke, "Gregorian and Old Roman chant," *NGDMM* 7 (1980) 693–97; E. Nowacki, "Studies on the Office antiphons of the Old Roman manuscripts" (Brandeis University: Ph.D. diss., 1980).   JMH

Old Spanish chant. The repertoire from what is now C and N Spain and Portugal; it includes what elsewhere is called "Visigothic" (from the Visigothic domination of Spain, 6th to early 8th centuries), "Mozarabic" (from the period of Arabic rule, 711 to the late 1000s) and "Hispanic." Old Spanish chant comprises various subtraditions differing in melodic readings, liturgical use and notational styles. Sources for early Spanish liturgy are *Isidore of Seville, 2 *service books predating 711, and 10th–11th century manuscripts with notation. While numerous manuscripts transmit the full repertoire, much is in imprecisely heighted *neumes. Old Spanish chant does not have an 8-*mode system and is not overly elaborate in musical style. Replaced by *Gregorian chant in the late 11th century, a later version of the Old Spanish rite and music continued in limited use in Toledo. Since *Vatican II elements of the rite have been incorporated into a renewed liturgy and there are efforts to use it more widely in Spain.

Bibl: D. M. Randel, "Mozarabic rite, music of the," *NGDMM* 12 (1980) 667–75; K. Levy, "Hispanic, Old Spanish, or 'Mozarabic' Chant," in *The Early Middle Ages to 1300,* eds. R. Crocker and D. Hiley (Oxford, 1990) 101–110. JMH

Olney Hymns. A collection of 350 *hymn texts by John Newton ("Amazing grace!") and William Cowper ("God moves in a mysterious way") published in 1779. Olney is a village in Buckinghamshire where Newton served as curate (1764–80) and Cowper as a lay assistant (1767–94).   KRH

O magnum mysterium [Latin]. "O great mystery." The *great responsory found in Roman *matins for *Christmas Day. It is perhaps best known in the *polyphonic setting by *Victoria.   NDM

Omega Dancers. An organization founded by *DeSola in 1974 to express the spiritual-healing dimensions of dance and to develop liturgical *dance. The dancers minister at the Cathedral of St. John the Divine (New York). The Omega West Dance Company was created in 1989 at Old St. Mary's Cathedral (San Francisco) and the Graduate Theological Union in Berkeley where DeSola is on the faculty.   MAK

Open air meeting. A generic term for outdoor gatherings in rural (e.g., a *camp meeting) or urban areas (e.g., a *Salvation Army concert or Billy Graham crusade), consisting of singing, preaching and prayer for revivalist or evangelistic purposes.   RJS

Opitz, Martin (*b* Bunzlau 1597; *d* Danzig 1639). German poet and *hymn writer. His *Buch von der deutschen Poeterey* (1624) influenced the development of smoother texts and natural word-tone rhythms in German Protestant *hymnody.   VEG

Oration. See *collect.

Oratorio [from Latin *oratorium,* "place of prayer"]. A type of dramatic musical theater performed by soloists, *chorus and orchestra usually without staging, costumes or scenery. Various elements contributed to its complex development, including: 1) The Italian oratorio which emerged as dramatic presentations of sacred narratives performed in worship contexts in 17th-century prayer rooms (oratories) of religious groups such as the Congregation of the Oratory (Oratorians). Two forms emerged: the Latin *oratorio Latino,* represented by *Carissimi's *Jephtha,* and the Italian *oratorio volgare* (partially anticipated in the *lauda*), represented by Carissimi's *Daniele.* 2) Neapolitan (Italian) opera which *Handel mastered and its English counterpart, *Purcell's lyric stage pieces. 3) German *church music forms including the *passion and *cantata (for which the oratorio sometimes served as a liturgical substitute) and the English *verse anthem. 4) Handel's expansion of the German cantata into large-scale *anthems (e.g., *Chandos Anthems*) and his successful first performance of Esther (1732) without staging, scenery or costumes. 5) The performance of oratorios in the late 18th century (such as *Mozart's reorchestrated *Messiah* in 1788) in large spaces with huge choruses and orchestras, paving the way for F. J. *Haydn's *The Seasons* and The *Creation.*

Other notable contributions to the genre include F. *Mendelssohn's *Elijah* (1847), *Berlioz's L'*enfance du Christ* (1854), C. *Franck's Les *Béatitudes* (1879), *Elgar's *The Dream of Gerontius* (1900), *Walton's *Belshazzar's Feast* (1931) and *Tippett's *A Child of Our Time* (1939–41).

Bibl: H. Smither, *A History of the Oratorio,* 2 vols. (Chapel Hill, 1977); E.

Wienandt, *Choral Music of The Church* (New York, 1965).   CRY

Orchestra in worship, the. Although the orchestra in the W is a 17th-century phenomenon, groups of instrumentalists have been employed in worship since ancient times, in many different locales and across many cultures. Professional instrumentalists were employed in Solomon's *Temple. *Instruments were not employed in the *synagogue, and sparsely employed in Christian worship in the first millennium. While gradually employed in the *Renaissance, instruments were more widely accepted in the worship of the *Baroque era, and orchestras consistently emerged in the worship of the *Classical period. J. S. *Bach, *Handel, F. J. *Haydn and *Mozart wrote much liturgical music involving instrumental groups of various sizes including full orchestra. The *Moravian Brethren brought the tradition of extensive instrumental worship with them to the American colonies starting in 1744. Symphonic orchestras and smaller instrumental ensembles increasingly provide worship music in various churches (e.g., *Baptist) in the late 20th century.   VAC

Order of Christian Funerals, The. The US revised edition (1989) of the Roman rite *Order of Funerals* (1970) containing rubrics and texts for the 3 central parts of the funeral rite (*vigil, *mass and burial), as well as various ancillary rites and texts, including a revised *office for the dead. Music's role is described in the rite's general introduction (nn. 30–33); some editions contain sample music. VCF

Ordinal <ordinary> [from Latin *ordo,* "order"]. (1) A medieval liturgical *book,

appearing by the 12th century, supplying *incipits* (without music) and rubrics for the *divine office, *eucharist and other ordinary worship through the liturgical *year. See *ordo* and *ordines Romani.*

(2) An Anglican liturgical book for the consecration/ordination of bishops, priests and deacons.   ADC

Ordinary chants. The *Lord, have mercy, *Glory to God, *Lord's Prayer, *Lamb of God and *Profession of faith. This is 1 of 6 categories of musical elements in the reformed RC *mass according to *Music in Catholic Worship* (nn. 64–69).   CLV

Ordinary (of the mass). (1) Five invariable texts of the *mass, sung at a *high or *solemn high mass: *Kyrie, *Gloria in excelsis, *Credo, *Sanctus* (sometimes subdivided into *Sanctus* and *Benedictus* [*qui venit*]) and *Agnus Dei;* distinguished from the *proper of the mass.

(2) All unchanging parts of the mass; since 1969 these elements are subsumed under the designation "Order of Mass" (Latin *Ordo Missae*).   MJG

Ordinary time. That part of the liturgical *year not included in *Advent, *Christmas, *Lent or *Easter. Ordinary time falls into 2 sections: 1) from the end of the Christmas season to the beginning of Lent, and 2) from the end of the Easter season to the beginning of Advent. Aside from the *proper of the mass, there are few particular pieces of music associated with this expansive season: an exception is the *Salve Regina.*   MJG

Ordines Romani (sing. **Ordo Romanus**) [Latin]. "Roman ordos." A set of booklets dating from the 8th–10th centuries containing descriptions of the liturgies of the Roman church, such as *eucharist, baptism and ordination. These served as guides for ministers in preparing for such worship. Originating in Rome, they were copied, taken elsewhere and adapted to local needs. Gathered into extensive collections, they exercised strong influence outside Rome. They provide considerable information on musical practices. FCQ

Ordo [Latin]. "Order." (1) An alternative term for a liturgical rite (e.g., Latin *Ordo Baptismi,* "The Rite of Baptism").

(2) A group with a particular status or function in the church (e.g., Latin *ordo episcoporum,* "the order of bishops").

(3) A text indicating the structure, personnel and/or movements of a particular rite.

(4) A detailed liturgical calendar. JMJ

Oregon Catholic Press <OCP>. A RC publisher of *liturgical music, including the Spanish *hymnal *Flor y Canto.* OCP began by publishing the *Catholic Sentinel* newspaper in 1870, becoming the Catholic Truth Society of Oregon in 1922; it acquired its current name in 1980. JBF

Orff, Carl (*b* Munich 1895; *d* there 1982). Composer and music educator. His most notable composition is the *oratorio *Carmina burana* (1937) based on 24 Latin medieval, secular poems. Orff created a music education method for children which leads them through guided improvisation using easy-to-play percussion instruments he designed. Some have employed his insights in creating worship music for children, e.g.,

composers published by the *Choristers Guild. MEC

Organ. A musical instrument consisting of pipes set on a windchest containing compressed air. Air is admitted to the various pipes by valves controlled by the player from a *keyboard. Organs have existed from antiquity (see *hydraulis), where they were primarily associated with public rites both secular and religious. While reaching a high point of perfection and appreciation in the churches of 18th century W Europe, organs varied greatly from one nation to another. A truly modern instrument, due to its ability to adapt to the aesthetic of each new era, it continues to evolve to the present.

In the modern organ there are 2 types of pipes: flues and reeds. Each is constructed to sound 1 note, and are arranged in rows (or ranks) to create a complete scale. Flue pipes range in size from smaller than a pencil to lengths of 32 feet or more, providing both the highest and the lowest notes of any instrument. Flue pipes are like the common whistle, constructed of either wood or metal. A reed pipe has a brass reed in its boot which vibrates to the desired pitch. The pipe above it acts as a resonator to give the reed the desired tonal quality. Large organs have many thousands of pipes.

Typically the *console has more than 1 manual (keyboard) and an additional keyboard which is played by the feet. The organ has several distinct divisions (e.g., *great, *positive, *swell and pedal), each controlling its own separate ranks of pipes. Couplers allow the divisions to be combined onto different manuals. The pipes of the swell division are enclosed in a box with louvers on its facade enabling the increase or decrease in volume.

A vast quantity of music has been composed for the organ, most of it intended for church use.

Bibl: P. Williams, *The European Organ,* 2nd ed. (Bloomington, 1978); P. Williams, "Organ," *NGDMM* 13:710–79; "Organ," *New Harvard Dictionary of Music,* ed. D. Randel (Cambridge, 1986) 578–89.   JBW

Organ case. (1) The 3-sided enclosures built around the pipework of the classical *organ, with some of the pipes forming a facade on the fourth side.

(2) The facade of any pipe organ. JBW

Organ chorale. An *organ piece based on a *chorale or *hymn tune. It is employed to introduce a congregational chorale, serve as an interlude between the congregation's *verses, or stand as an independent piece in worship. J. S. *Bach wrote over 140 of them. See *chorale prelude.   JBW

Organ hymn. A setting for *organ of alternate *stanzas (usually odd-numbered) of a *hymn, intended for use in *alternatim performance with a *choir. An example is *Grigny's *"Veni Creator Spiritus"* from his *Livre d'orgue* (1699). PKG

Organ mass. (1) The European custom of using the *organ in alternation with the *choir at *mass, e.g., the choir might sing every other *verse of the *Kyrie* with the organist playing the others. It usually includes improvised music, often based on the appropriate *Gregorian chant, although much composed organ

music of the early Italian and French schools consisted of collections of these.

(2) The *chorale preludes in J. S. *Bach's *Clavierübung* (part 3) are sometimes called an organ mass as they are presented in the order of the Lutheran *liturgy.

(3) A mass at which the organ is the chief musical resource.   JBW

Organ renewal movement [German *Orgelbewegung*]. The 20th century trend in *organ design and construction which reached a zenith in the US in the 1970s. This movement was characterized by preferences for mechanical action (tracker) and *Werkprinzip* (stoplists built upon principal choruses rather than imitative, "orchestral" sounds). *Schweitzer was an early herald of the movement. PAJ

Organ solo mass. A subcategory of the late 18th century concerted *mass in which the *organ plays not merely a *basso continuo* with the *orchestra but also performs an obbligato part in 1 or more movements (especially the *Benedictus*).   AJL

Organum (pl. **organa**). Early (9th to 13th centuries) manifestation of *polyphony, in which a piece of *monophonic *chant is augmented by 1 or more additional voices. Early in its development, these additional voices parallel the original line chiefly in 4ths and 5ths; as the style matures, they became increasingly independent, as in the works of *Pérotin. AJL

Orgelbewegung. See *organ renewal movement.

Orgelbüchlein [German]. "Little Organ Book." An unfinished collection of 46 (164 intended) short *chorale preludes for *organ by J. S. *Bach, arranged according to the liturgical *year.   EBF

Orthros [Greek; Slavonic *utrenya*]. "Rising service." The principal morning *service of the Byzantine Church, parallel to *matins. Three forms exist: festive/Sunday, daily and penitential. It formerly began with a supplicatory service for the emperor. Today it consists of an incensation, blessing, *hexapsalmos, great *synapte, Theos Kurios (select *verses from Ps 118), variable *troparion, 3 (occasionally 2) *kathismata, Ps 51, *kanon, *exapostolarion, psalms of praise (Pss 148–50), lesser *doxology (see *doxologia), *aitesis, *aposticha, *Trisagion and prayers, variable *apolytikion and *apolysis.

On feasts/Sundays the "office of reading the gospel" is added: after 2 *kathismata, *polyelaios (Pss 135–36) is sung, then *anabathmoi, *prokeimenon, the *ekphonesis of a prayer that has been eliminated, verses from Ps 150 with incensation, and the gospel (see *euangelion heothinon). Also, *stichera are added after Ps 51 and the great doxology is sung.

On Sunday the *anastasima eulogetaria replace *polyelaios from *Easter to the Exaltation of the Holy Cross (September 14) and are sung in addition to it the rest of the year. On Sunday, the Exaltation of the Holy Cross and daily from Easter to the Ascension a special prayer is read, the great doxology is sung after psalms of praise with a variable *apolytikion and the *aposticha and *Trisagion are omitted.

Penitential *orthros* is like daily *orthros* except that verses from the *Ode of Isaiah are sung with an *alleluia *refrain in place of Theos Kurios, and an office of prostrations is added at the end.

Bibl: M. Arranz, "Les prières presbytérales des matines byzantines," *OCP* 37 (1971) 405–36; 38 (1972) 64–115; R. Taft, *The Liturgy of the Hours in East and West* (Collegeville, 1986) 273–91.   DMP

O Salutaris Hostia [Latin]. "O Saving Victim." The *incipit of the final 2 *stanzas of the *hymn Verbum supernum prodiens ("The heavenly Word proceeding") ascribed to *Thomas Aquinas for the feast of Corpus Christi. As a separate hymn it is used frequently at *benediction; the most popular musical setting is by D. Duguet (*d* 1767).   VCF

Otdanie [Slavonic]. See *apodosis.

Othmayr, Caspar (*b* Amberg 1515; *d* Nuremberg, 1553). Noted composer of secular choral works and choral settings of Lutheran *chorales.   CRY

Otpust. See *apolysis.

Our Father <Lord's Prayer, Latin *Pater noster*>. A New Testament prayer which Christ taught his disciples (Matt 6:9-13; Luke 11:2-4). Part of the *eucharist by the 4th century; according to *Augustine it followed the *fraction rite; since *Gregory the Great it has been placed at the end of the *eucharistic prayer in the W *mass; the *BCP (1552) placed it after *communion. Part of daily prayer of the church since earliest times, it ordinarily concludes *lauds and *vespers or their parallels in various traditions. It is often sung in worship to *chant or innumerable other settings.   MJG

Oxford Movement <Tractarianism>. A 19th-century reform within the Church of England emphasizing its catholic (i.e., apostolic, universal) origins. It was launched by a sermon of J. *Keble (14 July 1833). Other leaders included John Henry Newman and Edward Pusey, all connected with Oxford University. Some adherents became RC (e.g., *Caswall, *Faber and Newman); most remained Anglican, known as Anglo-Catholics. The movement inspired achievements in architecture and church music (e.g., the restoration of patristic *hymnody and the revival of *chant, often in English).   FJM

Oxyrhynchus hymn. The earliest surviving piece of notated Christian music. It appears on a 3rd-century papyrus fragment discovered in Oxyrhynchus, Egypt. It contains the conclusion of a Greek trinitarian *hymn in Greek poetic *meter marked by classical Greek musical notation. It is unclear whether or how it was employed in worship; the repeated *amen may indicate a congregational *response to a soloist's singing.   JMJ

P

Pachelbel, Johann (*b* Nuremberg 1653; *d* there 1706). Organist and composer of *keyboard and choral music. Although a Lutheran, he began his career as assistant organist at St. Stephen's Cathedral in Vienna. As court organist in Eisenach (1677) he knew the *Bach family. As organist at the Protestant Predigerkirche in Erfurt he composed (partly in response to liturgical directives) much keyboard music, including numerous *chorale preludes, 95 *Magnificat* fugues or *intonazione,* *toccatas and variations. Brief employment in Stuttgart, then in Gotha brought him to St. Sebald in Nuremberg (1695) where he produced numerous *chorale-based *motets, sacred *concertos and 11 *Magnificat* settings in concerto style. Pachelbel also wrote chamber music and suites for the harpsichord.

Bibl: E. Nolte, "Pachelbel, Johann," *NGDMM* 16:46–54.   MPB

Palestrina, Giovanni Pierluigi da (*b* Palestrina 1525?; *d* Rome 1594). Leading RC liturgical composer of the *Renaissance period. He mastered compositional technique inherited from Franco-Flemish composers and exemplified the functional and aesthetic aims of the Council of *Trent.

A choirboy at St. Mary Major in Rome, he became choirmaster/organist in Palestrina (1544–51), then choirmaster of the Cappella Giulia at St. Peter's in Rome (1551–55, 1571–94). Expelled from the *Sistine Chapel in 1555 because he was married, he served as choirmaster at St. John Lateran and St. Mary Major before returning to St. Peter's. His grave is in the Cappella nuova in St. Peter's.

Palestrina has been called the "Savior of church music" because of the report (probably unfounded) that his *Missa Papae Marcelli* convinced church leaders at the Council of Trent not to ban *polyphony from worship. In 1577 he was appointed to a papal commission to revise *Gregorian chant; although not involved in the resulting *Medicean edition, he was of the same revisionist philosophy. His entrepreneurial skill and widespread reputation enabled much of his music to be published in Rome and Venice during his lifetime. His music has enjoyed uninterrupted liturgical use since the 16th century. Identified as the epitome of a so-called *Roman school of polyphony, he was promoted in *Fux's writings as the model of classical *counterpoint. The *Cecilian movement considered him the compositional model for authentic *sacred music.

He wrote over 100 *masses; 68 *offertories covering the entire liturgical *year; 375 *motets; at least 65 polyphonic settings of *office hymns; 35 *Magnificats (in which polyphonic *verses alternate with Gregorian chant); 4 or 5 sets of *lamentations; 140 madrigals, both sacred (see *madrigale spirituale) and secular.

Bibl: K. Jeppesen, The Style of Palestrina and the Dissonance, 2nd ed. (New York, 1970); T. C. Day, "Palestrina in history" (Columbia University: Ph.D. diss., 1970); G. Reese et al., The New Grove High Renaissance Masters: Josquin, Palestrina, Lassus, Byrd, Victoria (New York, 1984). AWR

PAM. See *Presbyterian Association of Musicians.

Pange lingua [Latin]. "Sing [my] tongue." Two medieval *hymns: 1) Pange lingua gloriosi proelium certaminis by *Fortunatus, for Passiontide, Good Friday and feasts of the cross; 2) Pange lingua gloriosi corporis mysterium (see *Tantum ergo) ascribed to *Thomas Aquinas, for Corpus Christi and *processions of the blessed *sacrament. RDH

Panikhida [Slavonic, from Greek pannychis, "all-night vigil"]. A memorial *service for the deceased; it may be sung at a funeral, anniversary of a death, or other appropriate occasion. It consists of 3 *troparia for the deceased, a *litany with special petitions and prayer ("O God of spirits"), the *apolysis and a *hymn

("Eternal memory"). Panikhida is one of the shortest services in the Byzantine *office. In the Greek tradition this service is also called *trisagion. It functioned as the dismissal (see apolysis) of *orthros from which it is now detached. "Great panikhida" is identical to the *parastas. DMP

Pannychis [Greek]. "All-night vigil." An *occasional service in the ancient Byzantine *office. It was celebrated on the eves of certain great feasts or days of penance, particularly the *Great Fast. Pannychis was abandoned when the Sabbaite office of Palestine replaced the older Constantinopolitan office in the 13th century (see *hesperinos). It is described by J. Mateos in his edition of Le Typicon de la Grande Église (Rome, 1963) 2:311. DMP

Parakletike [Greek]. "Consolation." (1) A popular prayer *service to the Mother of God, based on *orthros.

(2) A liturgical *book containing the *propers of the 8 tones of the *divine office; see *octoechos. DMP

Paraphonista [Greek, Latin]. "Sounding beside." A member of the *schola cantorum mentioned in the *ordines Romani. It is uncertain whether he sang in parallel 4ths and 5ths (paraphonic intervals), sang in support of the boys' choir or was assistant to the *cantor. In the last instance the word would be synonymous with the Latin succentor ("sub-cantor"). ADC

Paraphrase mass. A setting of the *ordinary based on a *cantus firmus which is adapted ("paraphrased") and used in 1 or all voices; common in the 15th–16th centuries. The cantus firmus could be sacred (e.g., *Josquin's *Missa *Pange lingua*) or secular (e.g., *Palestrina's *Missa L'*Homme armé*).   MEC

Parastas [Slavonic, from Greek *parastásis*, "a standing-by, attendance"]. A version of *orthros* for the departed arranged for popular celebration. It is frequently celebrated on the vigil of funerals or as a memorial. Also known as the great *panikhida*.   DMP

Paremia [Slavonic, from Greek *paroimía*, "parable"]. In the Byzantine rite, any reading from the Hebrew Bible or book containing readings from the Hebrew Bible. In the Byzantine *office the Hebrew Bible is read at *sext during the *Great Fast and at *vespers. Sext includes a *troparion* of the *paremia*, sung in connection with the reading, dating from the ancient *asmaticos* office.   DMP

Parker, Alice (*b* Boston 1925). Composer, arranger and conductor, long associated with the Robert Shaw Chorale, with many published choral works for church use.   JBW

Parker, Horatio (*b* Auburndale MA 1863; *d* Cedarhurst NY 1919). Composer and educator. Parker served as organist and music director at Boston's Trinity Church. He was professor (1894) then dean (1904) of Yale's music school; *Ives was one of his students. Parker wrote much *organ and choral music for the church; also the celebrated *oratorio *Hora novissima* (1893).   FJM

Parody mass. A *mass in which each movement is based on substantial segments of a preexisting *polyphonic work, i.e., a secular *chanson* or *motet.

Also called "derived masses," parody masses were usually named after the tune from which the musical material was derived.   DCI

Parry, (Charles) Hubert (Hastings) (*b* Bournemouth 1848; *d* Rustington 1918). Composer, educator and author. He taught at London's Royal College of Music (from 1883; director from 1894) and Oxford (1900–08). His religious compositions include *anthems and *hymn tunes (e.g., JERUSALEM). He also produced scholarly publications on J. S. *Bach and the history of musical styles.   FJM

Parry, Joseph (*b* Merthyr Tydfil, Wales 1841; *d* Penarth, Wales 1903). Composer. He immigrated to the US (1854), moving between the 2 countries often. Parry wrote *oratorios, *cantatas, operas, choral and instrumental works and over 400 *hymn tunes including ABERYSWYTH.   RJS

Partbook. First a manuscript, then a printed format containing music for only 1 vocal or instrumental part, appearing in the late 15th century. Opposite of the *choirbook.   LJC

Partita [Italian]. "Part." (1) A set of variations on a secular tune or *hymn. Adapted for liturgical use on the *organ by 17th-century Dutch and German composers.
(2) A synonym in the *Baroque period for a suite.   MDJ

Paschal [Latin *Paschalis*]. A Christian term for designating the time of *Easter.   JMT

Paschal stichera [Greek; Slavonic *stichiri paschi*]. "Easter hymns." *Aposticha sung according to special melodies at the end of Easter *orthros* as the faithful come forward to kiss the cross, *gospel book and icons. It originated as a solemn reconciling kiss of peace at the end of *Lent. The text is from a sermon of St. Gregory Nazianzus. They are sung Sundays from Easter to the Ascension. DMP

Passacaglia. A genre of musical composition in which a ground bass, ordinarily in triple *meter, is repeated throughout the movement. The distinction between passacaglia and chaconne is ambiguous, and the terms are often used synonymously.   JBW

Passion (from Latin *passio*, "suffering"). A term applied to the narratives of the suffering and death of Christ in the 4 Gospels, sung liturgically during *Holy Week: traditionally the *St. Matthew Passion on *Palm Sunday and the *St. John Passion on *Good Friday. Passions were first sung monodically by a single voice; later the *dramatis personae* were assigned to different voices; by the 15th century *polyphonic choruses were inserted into the *plainsong narrative. From the 16th century musical settings were written by both RC and Lutheran composers, either in a plainsong style (*Walter, *Schütz and Peranda) or through-composed, though sometimes retaining much of the plainsong for the biblical narrative (*Lassus, *Byrd and *Lechner). By the end of the 17th century, poetic movements were interpolated into the biblical narrative and, in Lutheran settings, *chorales added. By the 18th century orchestral accompaniment became the norm for the larger "*oratorio" passion, exemplified in the 2 great passions of J. S. *Bach. The post-Bach

passion was generally an extra-liturgical oratorio. Two notable 20th-century settings are *Penderecki's *St. Luke Passion* and Pärt's *St. John Passion.*

Bibl: B. Smallman, *The Background of Passion Music,* 2nd rev ed. (New York, 1970); R. Leaver, "Passion Music," in *Passover and Easter: The Liturgical Structuring of a Sacred Season,* eds. P. Bradshaw and L. Hoffman (Notre Dame, 1999) 146–80.   RAL

Passion chorale. A popular designation for the *hymn *"O Haupt voll Blut und Wunden"* (German, "O Sacred Head, now wounded"), or its tune (HERZLICH TUT MICH VERLANGEN) since J. S. *Bach used 5 *stanzas of the hymn in his *St. Matthew Passion.   MPB

Passiontide. Formerly the last 2 weeks of *Lent, centered on the passion of Christ. Suppressed in the RC liturgy since 1970. MJG

Passover. See *Pesach.*

Pastoral music. (1) A popular term, especially among RCs, for Christian *ritual music.

(2) Any music employed in a church or synagogue context, e.g., for worship, evangelization, religious education, etc.

(3) The title of the official publication of the *National Association of Pastoral Musicians.   VCF

Pastoral musician. A term that received currency in the US after 1976 to describe musicians committed to the reforms of *Vatican II. It evolved to describe musicians as ministers committed to the 3-fold musical, liturgical and pastoral judgments outlined in *Music in Catholic Worship.*   VCF

Pater Dominicus Mass. See *Dominicus* Mass.

Pater Noster. See *Our Father.

Paukenmesse. See *Drum Mass.

Paul, St. See *New Testament Music.

Paul of Samosata (3rd century). Bishop of Antioch (260–68). He was deposed in 268 for heretical christological views. He encouraged the E Syrian practice of chanting the *psalms with *alternating *choirs of virgins and men. He was accused of banning *hymns in praise of Christ since he considered Christ to be "an ordinary man." JDW

Peeters, Flor (*b* Tielen near Antwerp 1903; *d* Antwerp 1986). Composer, organist and teacher. He studied at the Lemmens Institute; also with *Dupré and *Tournemire. Peeters taught at various conservatories, e.g., Ghent, Tilburg and Antwerp (where he became director, 1952–68). His compositions are influenced by *Gregorian chant, Flemish *polyphony and *folk music; they are characterized by moderate harmonic expansions and rhythms. FJM

Peloquin, Alexander (*b* Northbridge MA 1918; *d* Providence 1997). RC composer who served as music director at the Providence Cathedral (1960–91). The founder of the Peloquin Chorale, he composed many liturgical works and *masses, including *Mass of the Bells* (1972). VCF

Penderecki, Krzysztof (*b* Dębica 1933). Composer. He was trained, then taught at Kraków Conservatory; he also taught at Yale. His compositions draw on historic *sacred music, and yet are quite avant-garde, using new notational symbols for voices and instruments. His choral works include: *From the Psalms of David* (1958), *Stabat Mater* (1962), *St. Luke Passion* (1965), *Dies Irae* (1967), *Utrenia* (1970–71), *Canticum canticorum Salomonis* (1972), *Magnificat* (1974) and *Te Deum* (1979). RKW

Penitential psalms. The traditional designation for 7 *psalms (6, 32, 38, 51, 102, 130, 143) which are penitential in character. Together they were extensively used as a unit in the medieval *divine office, private devotions, penance and prayers for the dying. *Lassus used them for his *Septem psalmi poenitentiales.* VAL

Pennsylvania spiritual. A type of revival song emerging from bush-meetings in SE Pennsylvania, Maryland and N Virginia during the Second Great Awakening (early 19th century) among German speakers. The song was a fusion of Pennsylvania Dutch texts with Methodist tunes. Each song appended an independent *chorus or *refrain to the original texts similar to *camp meeting songs. RJS

Pentecost. See *Shavuot* and *year, liturgical.

Pentecostal Churches' worship music. From its beginnings in the late 19th and early 20th century, Pentecostal music has expanded from freely improvised *spiritual songs and *gospel songs to include traditional Protestant *hymns, contemporary *gospel and *jazz idioms. Denominations which formed from the *Azuza Street Revival (e.g., the 2

*Church of God denominations, *Church of God in Christ, Assemblies of God, Pentecostal Holiness and Foursquare Gospel Church) originally sang without musical *instruments or printed hymns. Singing in the Spirit (or *tongues), improvised *call and response melodies, and testimony songs released God's Spirit in the congregation giving rise to various physical responses like clapping, dancing or "holy rolling." The order of worship was very open with a mixture of singing, preaching, testimony and prayer.

In the 1930s many Pentecostal congregations introduced musical *instruments, especially tambourine, drums, various wind instruments, *guitar and eventually *organ and piano. *Choirs began to provide *anthems or support for congregational singing. Jazz and blues influences emerged in the improvised music of worship as well as in choral anthems. *Hymnal collections, including a wide range of hymnic styles, were printed for use in several Pentecostal denominations beginning in the 1960s, which influenced the *Charismatic movement. By the 1990s many congregations used praise and worship songs shared by various Christian groups.

Pentecostal music is spirited and energetic with the expressed desire to experience the Holy Spirit's presence and to use music as a means of evangelization. More predictable worship orders emerged over the decades in all Pentecostal denominations. This has tended to decrease the improvised spontaneous singing of the early days and increase singing from published musical sources and prepared anthems.

Bibl: L. Duncan, "Music Among Early Pentecostals," *The Hymn* 38 (1987) 11–15; D. L. Alford, "Pentecostal and Charismatic Music," in *Dictionary of Pentecostal and Charismatic Movements,* eds. S. M. Burgess and G. B. McGee (Grand Rapids, 1988) 688–95; Q. Booker, "Congregational Music in a Pentecostal Church," *Black Perspectives in Music* 16:1 (1988) 31–44. RJS

Pentekostarion [Greek]. "Fifty days" [Slavonic *tsvetnaya triod',* "flowery *triodion*"]. A liturgical *book of the Byzantine *divine office, containing the *propers for *hesperinos, *orthros, *apodeipnon* and the *minor hours from *Easter Sunday to the Sunday of All Saints (the Sunday following Pentecost). The main editors of the *Pentecostarion* were Sts. Theodore and Joseph, 9th-century brothers and Studite monks. See *triodion.* DMP

Pepping, Ernst (*b* Duisburg 1901; *d* Berlin 1981). Composer and teacher. He studied at Berlin's Musikhochschule, then taught composition there (1953–68) and at Berlin's Kirchenmusikschule (from 1934). He composed a *passion, *masses, *psalms, *motets and *organ works. JLB

Pergolesi, Giovanni Baptista (*b* Iesi 1710; *d* Pozzuoli 1736). Composer and leading figure in the rise of comic opera. Besides operas he also composed *oratorios, *masses, *psalms and other sacred vocal works, chamber *cantatas, *arias and various instrumental works. His most famous religious work is his setting of the *Stabat Mater* (1736) for 2 solo voices and strings. VAL

Perissos [Greek; Slavonic *peris*]. "Superabundance." (1) The last in a series of identical *troparia* or *stichera* sung as a *refrain to *psalm *verses (e.g., the second *antiphon of the *divine liturgy, where the *perissos* is the *Monogenes*). A new text is introduced for the sake of variety.

(2) A synonym for *katabasia*.   DMP

Perosi, Lorenzo (*b* Tortona 1872; *d* Rome 1956). Composer, church musician and RC priest. He was longtime choirmaster of the *Sistine Chapel (1898–1956), with an 8-year absence due to mental illness. His compositions include 20 *oratorios, 33 *masses, and some 350 other sacred works.   RJB

Pérotin <Perotinus Magnus, Magister Perotinus> (*fl* Paris *c* 1200). Composer of *organum,* *discant, *clausula* and *conductus;* with *Léonin, he was a major contributor to the *Notre Dame repertory. There are contrasting reconstructions of his life; most agree that his 4-voice *organa* were composed in the 1190s (decrees of Paris' Bishop Eudes from 1198 and 1199 mention triple or quadruple *organum* for various feasts; Pérotin's works include such *organa* for these feasts). He probably revised the *Magnus liber organi* attributed to Léonin. Pérotin and his contemporaries were apparently the first to expand *organum* from 2-voice to 3- or 4-voice. The *cantus firmus* upon which the *organum* was built was sometimes sung rhythmically though in longer notes than the second and third voices, resulting in strikingly new harmonies punctuated by dissonance as the upper voices sound against the unchanging *tenor. Pérotin's experiments with the *conductus* were an essential step to the development of the *motet.

Bibl: D. Bent, "Pérotin," *NGDMM* 11:540–43; H. Tischler, "Pérotin and the Creation of the Motet," *The Music Review* 44 (1983) 1–7.   JKL

Persichetti, Vincent (*b* Philadelphia 1915; *d* there 1987). Composer, conductor, teacher and pianist. He taught on several faculties including the Philadelphia Conservatory (1941) and almost 40 years at the Juilliard School of Music (from 1947). He received important commissions from the Philadelphia Orchestra and St. Louis Symphony Orchestra.

His musical style was eclectic and facile. His works which enjoyed wide popularity in the 1950s and 1960s include 8 symphonies, 12 sonatas and 6 sonatinas for piano, choral works such as *Hymns and Responses for the Church Year* (1955), *Mass (1967), *Stabat Mater* (1963) and *Te Deum* (1963). He wrote an influential text, *Twentieth Century Harmony* (1961).

Bibl: D. and J. Patterson, *Vincent Persichetti* (New York, 1988).   RAD

Perti, Giacomo Antonio (*b* Bologna 1661; *d* there 1756). *Maestro di cappella* at Bologna's Cathedral (1690–96), then for 60 years at San Petronio. He gained fame as a composer of *sacred music (e.g., *masses, *psalms, *motets), opera and *oratorio. He was also a noted teacher, e.g., of *Martini.   RJB

Pesach <*Pesaḥ*> [Hebrew]. "Passover." The Jewish festival commemorating the liberation of the Israelite people from Egyptian bondage and the exodus from Egypt. *Pesach* begins on the 15th of *Nissan* (the first month of the religious year) and lasts for 8 days. The festival is governed by many special laws and customs, chief of which is a total prohibition of leavened bread. The first and second nights of *Pesach* are celebrated with the *seder* at which the *haggadah* is read. The main features of the *Pesach* liturgy are the recital of *Tal, the recitation of *Hallel and the recitation of *Shir Hashirim on the intermediate *Sabbath.   SIW

Pesukei dezimrah <*Pesuqei de-zimra'*> [Hebrew]. "Verses of song." The preliminary section of *shacharit, recited after *Birkat hashachar and serving as the prelude to *Barechu. It is composed of an opening adoration (*Baruch she-amar), Pss 145–150, other biblical and liturgical passages and concludes with *Yishtabach.   SIW

Petite messe solennelle [French]. "Little Solemn Mass." An overtly operatic setting of the *mass by G. Rossini scored for soloists, chorus, *harmonium and 2 pianos (1863); later arranged for full orchestra (1867).   RDH

Petra. One of the first and most influential Christian hard rock bands in the US. Formed in 1972, the group reached the peak of its popularity in 1984.   VAC

Petrucci, Ottaviano (dei) (*b* Fossombrone 1466; *d* Venice 1539). Printer who developed a method for printing music from movable type by 1488, which became crucial in the dissemination of *polyphonic music during the early 16th century. His printing process originally required 3 impressions: 1 each for staves, notes and texts. He obtained from the Venetian government exclusive rights for printing music between 1500 and 1520.   DCI

Pevetz [Slavonic]. See *psaltes.

Phos hilaron [Greek]. "Joyful light" [Slavonic *Svete tichij,* "Tranquil light"]. The central *hymn of Byzantine *hesperinos. It may be the most ancient Christian hymn still used in the *office. Already found in the writings of St. Basil (*d* 379) who considered it ancient, the hymn could date to the 2nd century. It is often wrongly attributed to St. Sophronius, a 7th-century patriarch of Jerusalem.   DMP

Photogogikon [Greek]. "Hymn of light." A term usually reserved for the *hymn of light at *orthros during the *Great Fast, whose theme is Christ the giver of light. The text varies for each of the *octoechos. See *exapostolarion.   DMP

Phrygian (mode). An *ecclesiastical mode with its final on *E*. As an authentic mode (mode 3), it has an ambitus of *e-e'* and its dominant (*tenor) on *b* (ancient) or *c'* (modern). The related plagal mode (Hypophrygian, mode 4) has an ambitus of *B-b* and its dominant on *g* (ancient) or *a* (modern).   CJK

Picander. See *Henrici.

Pidoux, Pierre (*b* Neuchâtel 1905). Musicologist who made a lasting contribution concerning the music of the Calvinist *Reformation. He published a complete edition of the *Genevan Psalter (text and music, 1962); also, a complete edition of *Goudimel's music (1967). Commentaries accompany these editions.   LJC

Pietism. (1) A 17–18th-century German religious movement influenced by English Puritanism.

(2) A general term for the religious perspective which stresses personal piety and experiential religion over ecclesiology. This emphasis was initiated by the Lutheran P. J. Spener, who called for personal renewal in *Pia Desideria* (1675), advocating meetings for prayer and devotional Bible study *(collegia pietatis)*. A. H. Francke followed Spener as leader of the movement and moved its center to Halle. He advocated ecclesiastical as well as personal reform, engendering a sharp division between "orthodox" and "pietist" Lutherans. Halle pietism promoted simplified liturgical forms, e.g. the eradication of complex church music and much of the "heavy" *chorale tradition, and the adoption of subjective *hymnody with "lighter" melodic forms. Pietism thus created a new German style of hymnody that influenced poets (e.g., P. Gerhardt) and composers (e.g., J. R. Ahle) alike. The pietist *hymnal edited by J. A. Freylinghausen (1704, with later editions) was a major influence within Zinzendorf's Moravianism and *Wesley's Methodism.

Bibl: F. Stoeffler, *The Rise of Evangelical Pietism* (Leiden, 1965); R. Leaver, "Bach and Pietism," *Concordia Theological Quarterly* 55 (1991) 5–22. RAL

Pilcher, Henry & Sons. *Organ builders. Henry Pilcher, Sr. (1798–1880) built organs in England; he immigrated to the US (1856) where he built organs in NJ and St. Louis. Henry Pilcher, Jr. (1828–90) established a firm in Louisville (1874) which built approximately 2,000 organs; the firm was acquired and closed by *Möller in 1944. Henry Jr. and relatives also built several hundred organs independently in New Orleans, St. Louis and Chicago. JWK

Pilgrimage Festivals. See *Three Festivals.

Pinchik, Pierre <Pincus Segal> (*b* Zhivitov, Ukraine 1900; *d* New York 1971). *Cantor who first served as *chazzan in Leningrad, then immigrated to the US. He was best known for his deeply spiritual singing; 2 of his best-known recorded selections are *Rozo d'Shabbos* and *Eileh ezk'ron.* MLK

Pinkham, Daniel (Rogers Jr.) (*b* Lynn MA 1923). Composer, organist and teacher. He studied at Harvard University with A. T. *Davison and Piston; later with Boulanger, *Copland and *Honegger. Pinkham served for many years as the organist at King's Chapel, Boston and taught composition at the New England Conservatory. His compositional style is Neoclassic, influenced by his belief that musical truth resides in the instrumental art of the *Classical tradition. His sacred compositions include the solo *organ works *Blessings* (1977) and *Proverbs* (1980); the choral works *Requiem* (1963) and *Lauds* (1984); *cantatas for chorus and orchestra for *Christmas (1957), *Easter (1961) and Ascension (1970); also works for *carillon.

Bibl: N. Solnimsky, *Baker's Biographical Dictionary of Musicians* (New York, 1992). PAB

Pitoni, Giuseppe Ottavio (*b* Rieti 1657; *d* Rome 1743). Composer. An accomplished musician at an early age, he was *maestro di cappella* at Rieti Cathedral at 18. Pitoni held similar posts at important churches throughout Rome. He was a prolific and respected composer of *church music in the tradition of *Palestrina. RJB

Pius IX <*bapt* Giovanni Maria Mastai-Ferretti> (*b* Senigallia, Italy 1792; *d* Rome 1878). Pope (from 1846) who imposed the Roman-Tridentine *missal and *breviary on France, and ratified the *Cecilian Movement's efforts to reform liturgical music in *Multum ad commovendos animos.   CLV

Pius X <*bapt* Giuseppe Sarto> (*b* Riese, Italy 1835; *d* Rome 1914). Pope (from 1903) who opposed the Modernist movement in the RC church. He exerted great influence on the renewal of liturgy and music. Already as archbishop of Venice, he issued an important pastoral letter on *sacred music (1894). His *motu proprio *Tra le sollicitudini provided significant impetus for the 20th-century liturgical movement. Another motu proprio, Col nostro (1904), affirmed the work of *Solesmes, and paved the way for the publication of the *Vatican edition of *Gregorian chant which officially replaced the *Medicean edition for the RC church. He also initiated other reforms, e.g., frequent *communion, communion for children, reform of the *breviary, revision of the Code of Canon Law and reform of the Roman Curia.

Bibl. R. Hayburn, *Papal Legislation on Sacred Music* (Collegeville, 1979).   CSP

Pius X School of Liturgical Music (1916–69). Founded by J. *Ward and G. Stevens at Manhattanville College of the Sacred Heart, this school was dedicated to the reform of RC *liturgical music. As a center for the study and performance of *Gregorian chant (according to the *Solesmes interpretation), it offered degrees in *sacred music with an international, interdisciplinary faculty. Its faculty collaborated in the work of the liturgical movement in the US prior to *Vatican II, compiling and editing *The Pius X Hymnal* (1953); after the council they encouraged the composition and publication of vernacular music for the reformed *liturgy.   MEM

Piyyut (pl. **piyyutim**) [Hebrew]. "Poetry." A form of Jewish liturgical poetry, inserted into private or communal prayers. *Piyyutim* developed from the beginning of the Common Era through the 1800s; some of the earliest evidence for them is in the Talmud and the Cairo *Genizah*. When they first appeared, set orders of prayer were just developing in Jewish liturgical practice, and *piyyutim* often replaced standard prayers in worship; when the *liturgy became fixed, they were interspersed throughout the prayers, the most elaborate appearing on major holidays and celebrations.

Piyyutim creators were called *paytanim* (sing. *paytan*); the earliest known was Yose b. Yose (6th century?) from Israel. *Piyyutim* flourished in Israel until the Arab invasions (7th century). European *piyyutim* appeared in S Italy (late 9th century) and especially developed in Spain (10th century).

The 2 earliest types are the *Kerovah and *Yotser, with various subdivisions within these categories. Hebrew language usage differs in terms of style and dialect depending on the *paytanim* and the school of poetry they follow. During the early period, *piyyutim* employed biblical and prayer vocabulary, tending to be clear and concise. Later *paytanim* employed more rhetorical devices and used the Hebrew vocabulary to its fullest. Until the time of the *piyyutim* of Yannai (6th–7th centuries?) and Kallir (8th–9th centuries?), *piyyutim* did not rhyme. *Pay-

tanim after the 9th century developed clever rhyme and metric schemes.

Well-known *piyyutim* include **Adon olam*, **Ein Keloheinu* and **Yigdal*. Over 35,000 *piyyutim* have been discovered and catalogued.

Bibl: E. Fleischer, "Piyyut," *EJ* 13:573–602. DMR

Pizmon [Hebrew]. "Chorus." A synonym for **piyyut*. A *pizmon* is typically described as a poem in *strophic form with a repeating *chorus. For *Sephardic Jews from the Middle E a *pizmon* is normally an adaptation of a Hebrew text to a pre-existing melody (see **Lachan*). MLK

Plagal mode [from Greek *plágios,* "placed sideways"]. (1) A church *mode whose typical range extends from the 4th below to the 5th above its final. *Gregorian modes 2, 4, 6 and 8 are plagal while 1, 3, 5, and 7 are authentic.

(2) In Byzantine modal theory, *plagios* refers to the 4 lower-lying *echoi. JKL

Plainchant. See *cantus planus* and *chant.

Plainsong. See *cantus planus* and *chant.

Plainsong mass. (1) A *Gregorian chant *mass.

(2) A *polyphonic mass in which each movement is based on the corresponding liturgical *plainsong.

(3) The term was later expanded to include any mass based on plainsong. The majority of 15th- and 16th-century examples are *cantus firmus* type in which the same chant is used in each movement, unifying the *ordinary (e.g., *Josquin's *Missa *Pange Lingua*). LMT

Plenary mass. A unified musical setting of both the *proper and the *ordinary of a mass, e.g., the **Requiem. JKL

Podoben [Slavonic]. See **homoion.

Pointing. The use of markings in a prose text (usually *psalms, but also collects and lessons) to indicate the correct singing of them to formulary tones. A late development, many 20th-century books (e.g., the **Liber Usualis*) provide multiple examples of pointing. Elaborate systems have been developed by Anglicans for singing psalms and *canticles in *Anglican chant. JMT

Pokayannyi [Slavonic]. Alternate term for **stikhir umilitel'nyi.

Polielej [Slavonic]. See **Polyelaios.

Polka mass. RC *eucharist with music and sometimes dance in the lively 2/4 style of dance music originating in early 19th-century Bohemia and popular in areas with Middle European immigrant populations. MAK

Polman, Bert (*b* Rozenburg, South Holland 1945). Teacher and hymnologist. He is professor of music at Redeemer College in Ancaster ON. The director of research at the *Hymn Society (1989–93), he coedited the *Psalter Hymn Handbook* (1998). JDW

Polunoshchnitsa [Slavonic]. See **mesonyktikon.

Polychoral. A term for music written for 2 or more *choirs, sometimes *instruments and choirs (see *cori spezzati*). The technique was developed by 16th-century composers in Venice (*Willaert, A. and G. *Gabrieli), Rome (*Benevoli) and Germany (*Schütz).   LMT

Polychronion [Greek; Slavonic *mnogoletije*]. "Many years." A *hymn sung for the health and welfare of a community member, usually for ecclesiastical or civil authorities. It is ordinarily sung at the end of a *service; if the *divine liturgy or *office is celebrated by a hierarch, it is sung for him whenever he blesses the congregation.   DMP

Polyelaios [Greek]. "Full of mercy" [Slavonic *polielej,* "full of oil"]. Pss 135 and 136, sung according to a special melody at feast day *orthros as the third *kathisma just before the *gospel. This name ("full of mercy") derives from the biblical *refrain to each *verse of Ps 136 ("God's mercy endures forever"); it is sometimes misinterpreted in Slavonic as "full of oil" because of similarity between Greek *elaios* ("mercy") and Slavonic *jelej* ("oil").   DMP

Polyphony <adj, polyphonic> [from Greek *polyphonia,* "a variety of tones"]. A term which generally designates simultaneous, linear writing of 2 or more parts. Used in contrast to *monophony or music consisting of 1 line (as in *Gregorian chant). It is also distinguished from homophony, which implies primarily chordal writing, with melodic interest focused on a single line (as in much *hymnody). Some ethnomusicologists use the term for all instances of simultaneous parts (including homophony) except heterophony.

In early experiments with seriously composed polyphonic music there emerges the instinct to develop independence of parts. *Organum was an early polyphonic form in which, at its origins, a second line began with the first, then separated to establish itself at a perfect 4th or 5th until rejoining the first line. Eventually the second line and other lines that followed bore their own identities. Through the *Middle Ages and into the *Renaissance, composers (and apparently congregations and listeners in general) heard music linearly without much regard for chordal progression within phrases, except for stopping points which we regard as cadences.

A *cantus, *duplum and *triplum were often in different measure and had different texts, sometimes in different languages. As music developed there was an increasing penchant for homophony, hence the *familiar style in polyphony, which sounds like homophony. In view of this development, polyphony can still be regarded as music in which each individual line maintains its own identity when sounding with 1 or more other lines. This kind of music was a glorious achievement, and its development from the 11th century on was enhanced by the sumptuous acoustical properties of churches and cathedrals.

Polyphony should not be confused with counterpoint, though the 2 share similarities. Polyphony is a general term, while counterpoint is a system with rules or guidelines (as those derived from the music of J. S. *Bach). Counterpoint also takes into account implied harmonic progression with regard to consonances and dissonances. Polyphony presumes no such responsibility, unless one wishes to write a polyphonic piece using techniques of counterpoint.

Bibl: B. Nettl, *Notes on the Concept and Classification of Polyphony* (Kassel,

1963); D. Seaton, *Ideas and Styles in the Western Musical Tradition* (Mountain View, 1991); K. Stolba, *The Development of Western Music* (Boston, 1998).   DCI

Pontifical [Latin *pontificale, liber pontificalis*]. A liturgical *book of the W Church containing ceremonies restricted to the bishop. Its origins date to the 9th century, and it was standardized by the 15th. As a rule, pontificals seldom contain music.   MSD

Poprazdnstvo [Slavonic]. See *metheortia*.

Porrectus [Latin]. "Extended." A compound *chant *neume involving 3 pitches, the second of which is lower than its surrounding pitches (e.g., sol-fa-sol or sol-re-fa). The name is derived from the broad "extended" stroke that swoops down from the first to the second pitch, extending the melodic syllable.   RTR

Porta, Costanzo (*b* Cremona 1528–9; *d* Padua 1601). Composer and Franciscan friar. He studied with *Willaert. Porta became *maestro di cappella* in Osimo (1552), Padua (1564–67 and from 1589), Ravenna (1567) and Loreto (1575). Most of his compositions are sacred, including 15 *masses, over 200 *motets, *introits, and *hymns. Some of his works are in grand *polychoral Venetian style; others are more in line with the Council of *Trent's teaching.   JLB

Portative. A small portable pipe *organ popular in the 14th–15th centuries. Carried by the player by means of shoulder straps, it was pumped with 1 hand while the other played the keys. See *regal.   JBW

Positive [French *positif;* German *Positiv*]. (1) A small, portable 1-manual pipe *organ.

(2) The secondary manual division of a larger organ (see *great organ).   JBW

Postlude. (1) An *organ or other instrumental piece played at the end of a worship *service, or a musical work played at the conclusion of a public gathering.

(2) The closing section of a musical composition.   JBW

Postnaya triod' [Slavonic]. See *triod.

Poulenc, Francis (Jean Marcel) (*b* Paris 1899; *d* there 1963). Composer and pianist. Although his musical education was somewhat haphazard, Poulenc gradually shaped a unique musical style. Underlying his superb melodic lines he created simple but piquant modal harmonies; his chamber and orchestra works are marked by an enlivening rhythmic verve. In his late 30s Poulenc had a profound conversion experience which resulted in some extraordinary *religious music including *Mass (1937), *Quatre petites prières de Saint François d'Assise* (1948), *Stabat Mater (1950), *Gloria (1959) and his opera *Dialogues des carmélites* (1956).

Bibl: W. Mellers, *Francis Poulenc* (Oxford, 1993).   RAD

Povecherie [Slavonic]. See *apodeipnon.

Power <Powero, Polbero>, **Leonel** <Lionel, Lyonel, etc.> (*d* Canterbury 1445). Composer. His works, heavily represented in the *Old Hall manuscript, exhibit mastery of a wide range of musical styles. Power was one of the earliest composers of *cyclic masses.   AJL

Praeambulum [Latin]. "Walking before." A generic term for an improvisatory work composed primarily for solo performers and not meant for dancing. Other names given this kind of piece are *prelude, *fantasia, *toccata, etc. Most such works were written for *keyboard or lute. There is no particular form; textures vary and use of *meter is free.   DCI

Praeconium *(paschale).* See *Exultet.

Praeludium. See *prelude.

Praetorius. The Latin surname of *c* 20 N German musicians of the 16th and 17th centuries with family name of Schultheis, Schultz, Schultze, Shulz, Schulze, etc. All were active in church music, mostly as composers in and around Hamburg. Significant names include:

(1) **Jacob Praetorius** (*b* 1530?; *d* 1586), composer, organist, editor and father of Hieronymus Praetorius.

(2) **Christoph Praetorius** (*b* Bunzlau?; *d* Lüneburg 1609), composer, *Kantor at Lüneburg (1563–81), and uncle of M. *Praetorius.

(3) **Hieronymus Praetorius** (*b* Hamburg 1560; *d* there 1629), 1 of most important N German composers of the early 17th century; he wrote *polychoral music in Venetian tradition, *c* 100 *motets, 6 *masses, 9 *Magnificat*s*; the son of Jacob Praetorius, he was the father of Jacob Praetorius II.

(4) **Jacob Praetorius II** (*b* Hamburg 1586; *d* there 1651), composer, organist, student of *Sweelinck, organist at St. Petri, Hamburg (from 1603), and a renowned *organ teacher.   LFH

Praetorius, Michael (*b* Creuzburg 1571?; *d* Wolfenbüttel 1621). Composer, organist and theoretician. He studied at Torgau, Zerbst and the University of Frankfurt an der Oder; at the latter he became organist at St. Mary's (1587). He was organist for Duke Heinrich Julius of Brunswick-Wolfenbüttel (1591), then *Kapellmeister* (1604). After the duke's death, Praetorius served temporarily in Dresden (1613–16), Magdeburg (1614), Halle (1616), Sondershausen (1617) and Kassel (1617).

One volume of secular instrumental dances survives. Most of his 1,000-plus sacred works were based on German Protestant *hymns, often involving *alternatim* practice. Many others set Latin liturgical texts or *psalms. In traveling he encountered a vast array of musicians, techniques and styles. This knowledge was brought into his 3-volume encyclopedic work *Syntagma musicum* (1614–20), which addresses: 1) religious music (principles, liturgies); 2) musical instruments (with a section on the *organ with illustrative woodcuts); 3) musical forms and performance techniques.

Bibl: W. Blankenburg, "Praetorius, Michael," *NGDMM* 15:188–192; D. Crookes, trans. and ed., *Syntagma musicum II: De Organographia, Parts I and II* (Oxford, 1991).   JLB

Pratt, Henry (*b* 1771; *d* 1841). *Organ builder. Pratt built 23 church organs and 19 chamber organs (all 1 manual) throughout New England and New York.   JWK

Prayer meeting. An informal gathering, often held mid-week, that supplemented *Sunday worship. Usually led by nonordained in the church or home, it typically includes prayer, scriptural meditations, testimony and song. Begun by the Puritans, later the prayer meeting was used by pietists, Methodists and in *camp meetings. Prayer meetings took on prominence during the Finney revivals of the early 19th century. The "Prayer Meeting revival" (1857–59) included noon meetings for business people in urban America. Led by lay people, they brought together believers from various denominations for scriptural exposition (not preaching), singing and intercession. *Moody used the noon prayer meeting during his revivals in the US and the British Isles. In churches with more evangelical and revivalist influences, prayer meetings continue as a regular part of congregational life.

Bibl: A. R. George, "Prayer Meeting," *The Westminster Dictionary of Worship,* ed. J. G. Davies (Philadelphia 1972) 321–22. RJS

Precentor [from Latin *praecino,* "I sing before"]. (1) The leader of *chant in a *schola;* the precentor usually intoned chants on the side of the first choir, while the *succentor* ("subcantor") intoned for the second choir.

(2) Another title for the *cantor.

(3) In some reformation traditions, the liturgical master of ceremonies, with special responsibility for the choral *services.

(4) The leader of congregational song in a church having neither a *choir nor instrumental accompaniment. ADC

Preces [Latin]. "Prayers." A series of prayers consisting of a *Kyrie, *Pater noster* and *versicles and *responses from scripture. *Preces* formerly concluded all *hours of the *divine office; they still exist in the *BCP at the conclusion of *morning and *evening prayer. FCQ

Predprazdnstvo [Slavonic]. See *proeortia.*

Preface [from Latin *praefatio,* "proclamation"]. The thanksgiving section which opens the *eucharistic prayer. After a brief *dialogue between presider and people ("The Lord be with you," "And also with you;" "Lift up your hearts," "We lift them up to the Lord," etc.), the preface continues with praise for God's works (in creation, history, Christ) and leads into singing the *Sanctus.* W *sacramentaries contained numerous prefaces for use with the old Roman *Canon (342 in an 11th-century example from Moissac). These were sung either to a solemn or *ferial *recitative-like *chant. As many new eucharistic prayers are now being composed across Christian denominations, so are many new prefaces emerging. The 1970 RC sacramentary contained over 90 of them.

Bibl: J. A. Jungmann, *The Mass of the Roman Rite,* 2 vols. (Westminster MD, 1992 [1951]) 2:115–28. NDM

Preghiera [Italian]. "Prayer." In operas, especially those of *Verdi, the heroine or *chorus often sings a prayer (e.g., the *Ave Maria* sung by Desdemona in the final act of *Otello*). Such works were sometimes used in church. RTR

Prelude. (1) A musical piece which evolved from short improvisations made by players checking tuning, touch or tone of their instruments, and by church organists to set mode and pitch of music to be sung during worship. Though originally preceding another piece, the term is used generally for a variety of freely composed works.

(2) An *organ or other instrumental piece played before worship or other public gathering. DCI

Presanctified divine liturgy. The third of the Byzantine *divine liturgies, formed by combining *hesperinos with *communion. Originally celebrated on all weekdays in the *Great Fast; it now occurs on Wednesdays and Fridays. Byzantine liturgical tradition forbids celebrating the divine liturgy on Lenten weekdays (Trullo Council in 692, canon 52) to abstain from the joy of the Resurrection commemorated in the divine liturgy. However, there is no abstinence from *communion, considered necessary for Christian life.

The rite consists of Sabbaite *hesperinos,* elements of *asmaticos hesperinos, a blessing with a candle and the solemn chanting of Ps 141, and a divine liturgy with a variant *Cherubikon at the *great entrance and presbyteral prayers proper to this liturgy. The prayer of offertory and *anaphora are omitted. Eucharistic bread consecrated the previous Sunday is brought in during the great entrance and mixed with unconsecrated wine for communion.

A less solemn form of the presanctified liturgy was celebrated at marriages, imperial coronations and rites of fraternal adoption. The liturgy is variously attributed to Sts. *Gregory the Great, Gregory Nazianzus or Epiphanius; these attributions are not historical.

Bibl: M. Arranz, "La liturgie des Présanctifiés de l'ancien Eucologe byzantin," *OCP* 47 (1981) 332–88; N. Uspensky, *Evening Worship in the Orthodox Church* (Crestwood NY, 1985).   DMP

Presbyterian worship music. Presbyterian and Reformed churches trace their roots to *Zwingli and *Calvin. Although both had sophisticated musical tastes, they were suspicious of music's potential to distract worshippers and obscure the scriptural word. For some 200 years Presbyterians were permitted to sing only *psalms and a few other scriptural texts, using *metrical paraphrases in the vernacular, devoid of instrumental accompaniment.

*Psalters were soon produced in England, e.g., Day's Psalter (1562), Este's Psalter (1592), Playford's Psalter (1677) and *Ravenscroft's Psalter (1691). Calvin's student John Knox spread the movement to his native Scotland. Scottish psalters were often printed with split pages. Thus the top portion containing music could be turned independently of the bottom containing texts, enabling any psalm to be sung to any like-metered tune. The *Bay Psalm Book* (1640) was an important resource for the Americas.

Originally psalms were *lined-out in worship. Because of the success of *singing schools in teaching people to enjoy "regular singing" (see *singing by rule), the American Presbyterian General Assembly (1788) recommended abandoning this practice.

In the 18th and 19th centuries many new *hymn-like English, Scottish and American psalm tunes were introduced to Presbyterian congregations, including the psalm paraphrases and hymns of *Watts. The use of hymns other than biblical paraphrases achieved gradual acceptance in the 19th century, along with the use of *organs and other *instruments in worship.

Presbyterian *hymnals of the early 20th century included *service music as an appendix, primarily meant for the *choir. Choral calls to worship, calls to prayer, prayer *responses, *benedictions, *amens and other accretions became widespread in the liturgy. *The Worshipbook* (1971) brought the reforms of *Vatican II into Presbyterian worship, providing the churches with congregational settings of the *Lord, have mercy, *Glory to God in the highest, *Holy holy, *acclamations and the *Lord's Prayer. It also reminded Presbyterians that Calvin had urged the weekly celebration of *eucharist. The *Presbyterian Association of Musicians and the quarterly *Reformed Liturgy & Music* have promoted these reforms in North America.

Bibl: G. L. Dougherty, "The History and Development of Music in the United Presbyterian Church in the United States" (University of Iowa: Ph.D. diss., 1966); J. Melton, *Presbyterian Worship in America* (Richmond, 1967); J. R. Sydnor, "Presbyterian Church, music of the," *NGDAM* 3:621–23.   JBW

Prèz, Josquin des. See *Josquin Desprez.

Prichasten [Slavonic]. See *koinonikon.

Priestly blessing. See *Birkat kohanim.

Prime [from Latin *hora prima,* "first hour"]. The *hour after *lauds in the Roman rite *divine office. Prime was suppressed in 1963. It consisted of a *hymn, *psalms, scripture reading, *versicles and *responses, and a concluding *collect.   JMJ

Pripiv [Slavonic]. See *stichos.

Processional [Latin *liber processionalis, processionale, processionarium*]. A medieval liturgical *book containing *chants, rubrics and *collects for processions integral to the celebration of *eucharist and the *offices, ordinarily

arranged according to the liturgical *year. Some also contain materials for *occasional services (e.g., profession, burial rites) and votive processions.   ADC

Processional song. (1) Broadly, any *hymn, song, *litany or *chant accompanying the linear movement by ministers and/or the assembly such as the *introit, *offertory, *recessional, etc.

(2) More narrowly, according to *Music in Catholic Worship,* the entrance and communion song in the reformed RC *mass.   JKL

Proeortia [Greek; Slavonic *predprazdnstvo*]. "Before the feast." In the Byzantine rite, the anticipation of a festival celebration (usually of the Lord or Mother of God). It ordinarily lasts 1 day before the feast, but 5 days for *Christmas and 4 for Theophany (*Epiphany). *Propers exist for each day on the theme of the feast. See *metheortia.   DMP

Proeortion [Greek; Slavonic *tropar' predprazdnstva*]. "[Hymn] before the feast." A *troparion sung on a day of *proeortia in anticipation of a feast of the Lord or Mother of God.   DMP

Profession of faith. See *Credo.

Prokeimenon (pl. **prokeimena**) [Greek; Slavonic *prokimen*]. "Placed before." A *verse taken from a *psalm or biblical *canticle, sung as a *refrain in the Byzantine *liturgy with 1, 2 or 3 verses of the same psalm. It is equivalent to the Latin *gradual. At the *divine liturgy it always precedes the *epistle; at *orthros it precedes the *gospel; at *hesperinos it may or may not precede a reading from the Hebrew Bible. *Prokeimena* are sung according to the *octoechos. *Troparia of the *hours in the *horai of *Great Fast are also called prokeimena. While apt for the first hour whose troparion is a psalm verse with *versicles from the same psalm, this is misleading for the other hours whose troparia are non-biblical, ecclesiastical compositions.   DMP

Prone [from Latin praeconium, "announcement"]. A medieval *service of preaching or catechesis, intercessory prayers (French prières du prône) and announcements inserted before the *offertory at the principal Sunday *mass (see *bidding prayer). Intentions, announced in the vernacular, were followed by a *psalm, *versicles and oration all said in Latin while the faithful prayed a series of *Our Fathers and/or *Hail Marys. In some places it became customary to delay prone to the end of mass and to include Latin or vernacular *hymns.   JKL

Proper. (1) An element of any liturgical rite particular to a specific day or feast.
  (2) The *proper of the mass.   GET

Proper (of the mass) [Latin proprium (missae)]. (1) Elements of the *mass particular to a specific day or feast, e.g., processional *antiphons, *collects, readings, the preface and sometimes ritual elements (e.g., the blessing of ashes on Ash Wednesday).
  (2) A previously employed designation for the *introit, *gradual, *alleluia, *tract, *offertory and *communion antiphons of the Latin mass.   GET

Proper tune. A *hymn or song tune composed for a specific text. Often the tune has the same name as the text's first

words or reflects a key aspect of the text's meaning.   RJS

Proprium (missae). See *proper of the mass.

Prosa. See *sequence.

Prosula (pl. **prosulae**) [Latin diminutive of prosa]. "Little prose." A text created to fit a *melisma or melismatic *chant, usually in strict syllabic style. Prosulae were most often written for the *Kyrie, *alleluia (see *sequence) and dismissals (*Ite missa est or *Benedicamus Domino), and sometimes for the *verse of the *gradual and *offertory. See *trope.   JKL

Protopsaltes [Greek]. See *psaltes.

Proulx, Richard (b Minneapolis 1937). Composer, organist, arranger and conductor. He was trained at McPhail College of Music, the University of Minnesota, and the Royal School of Church Music in England. Proulx was director of music at the RC cathedral in Chicago (1980–94) and a founding member of the Conference of RC Cathedral Musicians. The recipient of numerous commissions, his compositions include *masses, *psalm settings, *hymn tunes, the liturgical opera The Pilgrim (1978), and The Beggars Christmas (1989).   VCF

Prudentius, Aurelius Clemens (b Spain 348; d c 410). Latin poet and *hymn writer. His early career was as a lawyer and judge. He joined a monastery c 395 and wrote sacred epic, didactic and lyric poems. Some of his many hymns were extracted from his collection *Cathemerinon* for the *divine office. Still well known is his "Of the Father's love begotten." RKW

Psalm [from Greek *psalmós*, "song accompanied by string music"]. (1) One of 150 biblical poems collected in the Hebrew Bible book of Psalms. They are no longer believed to have been composed by King *David. The biblical psalms were important to ancient Jewish worship: used to some extent in the *Temple; sung as part of domestic feasts such as *Pesach* (see Mk 14:26); and may have been *cantillated as *readings in the ancient synagogue. They became increasingly important in Jewish worship after the destruction of the Second Temple. To this day they play a significant role in synagogue worship.

Psalms influenced Christian worship substantially and inspired imitation (see *psalmus idioticus*). They assumed a regular place in *eucharist by *c* 200 CE and were a fundamental building block of the *divine office since its inception. Christians have interpreted the psalms Christologically, believing them to image Christ or his prayer; Christians have also affixed a Trinitarian *doxology to psalms (see *Gloria Patri*) since the 4th century. The *Reformation's emphasis on scripture renewed interest in the psalms, which became the inspiration for much Reformation *hymnody and the backbone of *Reformed worship music.

(2) Any sacred song or poem.

Bibl: S. Mowinckel, *The Psalms in Israel's Worship,* trans. D. R. Ap-Thomas, 2 vols. (New York, 1962); M. Shepherd, *The Psalms in Christian Worship* (Collegeville, 1976).   MJG

Psalmist [Greek, Latin *psalmista*]. (1) One who leads (or sings the *verses of) the *psalm, usually in *responsorial style. The term appears by the 4th century in some lists of ecclesiastical ministers.

(2) The author of a Hebrew Bible psalm.   JKL

Psalm motet. A *polyphonic choral form (*motet), composed from the 13th–16th centuries, employing *psalm texts. Psalm motets were used in worship at moments when psalms were required.   JLB

Psalmody. (1) The singing of *psalms.

(2) That part within each of the *hours when the psalms and non-gospel *canticles are sung.

(3) The psalm(s) assigned for a specific *service.   JKL

Psalm tone. A melodic formula centered on structural pitches of the various *modes, designed to be sung to a great variety of non-metrical *psalm verses. A final cadence and frequently a mediant cadence pattern are used to mark the phrasing of the text. Psalm tones vary from simple syllabic to highly ornate melodic settings. See *reciting tone.   CJK

Psalms, metrical. See *metrical psalms.

Psalms of Solomon. See *Solomon, Psalms of.

Psalmus idioticus [Latin]. "Imitation psalms." *Hymns for Christian worship modeled on the Hebrew Bible *psalms. Only a few remain in liturgical usage (e.g., the *Gloria in excelsis, *Te Deum and *Exsultet). Such non-biblical songs were proscribed by the 4th-century Council of Laodicea. FCQ

Psalmus in directum. See *directaneus.*

Psalter. (1) The 150 Hebrew Bible *psalms; ordinarily in translation, either in prose or metrical versions. The emphasis on the weekly recitation of the entire psalter (e.g., in the *Rule of St. Benedict) marked the growing importance of psalms in all forms of Christian worship.

(2) A book containing the biblical psalms for use in worship, though not necessarily all 150. FCQ

Psalterium Gallicanum. See *Gallican Psalter.

Psaltery [from Greek *psaltērion,* "stringed instrument"]. A medieval instrument like a zither, consisting of a flat sounding board over which strings are placed for plucking. It is sometimes mistakenly identified with the biblical *psalterium* or *nebel.* ACL

Psaltes (pl. **psaltai**) [Greek; Slavonic *pevetz*]. "Singer, cantor." In modern Byzantine usage when *plainsong is used a *psaltes* or *cantor ordinarily leads the congregation by intoning and carrying the melody. In the Byzantine era (6th–15th centuries) Hagia Sophia had 2 *choirs of *psaltai;* the leader *(protopsaltes)* stood between them. *Psaltai* were ordained clergy; their ordination was similar to that of a *lector. Some Byzantine churches today have revived the order of cantor. DMP

Puccini, Giacomo (*b* Lucca 1858; *d* Brussels 1924). A celebrated opera composer who also wrote a few sacred songs and choral works (including his *Missa di Gloria,* 1880) and several unpublished *organ pieces. VAC

Purcell, Henry (*b* London? 1659; *d* there 1695). Composer. As a choirboy in the Restoration era *Chapel Royal until 1673, Purcell heard the latest musical fashions. He succeeded *Blow as organist of Westminster Abbey in 1679 and joined the Chapel Royal in 1682, continuing in both posts until his death. A pioneer of English opera, Purcell also wrote important consort and ensemble music. For the church he composed nearly 70 *anthems (some now incomplete) and 3 *services; he contributed a number of solo songs and duets (with *continuo*) to *Harmonia Sacra.* Fully a third of the anthems (such as the well- known *verse anthem *Rejoice in the Lord alway,* 1685) include strings; the *Te Deum and Jubilate* (1694) adds trumpets. Though slightly old fashioned, the dozen or so *full anthems (in up to 8 parts) include some richly expressive *polyphony (perhaps best-known is the funeral anthem *Thou knowest, Lord*).

Bibl: F. B. Zimmerman, *Henry Purcell, 1659–1695,* 2nd ed. (Philadelphia, 1983); *idem, Henry Purcell: A Guide to Research* (New York, 1989). AJL

Purim [Hebrew]. "Lots." The Jewish festival on the 14th day of *Adar* in the Hebrew calendar, commemorating the deliverance of the Jews from the massacre plotted by Haman as related in the Book of Esther. One of the happiest holidays in the Jewish calendar, *Megillat Ester* (see *Megilot) is read in the synagogue amid much revelry, e.g., noisemakers are used to drown out the name of Haman each time it is mentioned. The prayer *Al hanisim* ("For our miracles") is added to the *Purim* *liturgy, acknowledging God's role in the survival of the Jewish people.   SIW

Pythagoras (*b* Samos *c* 580 BCE; *d* Metapontum *c* 500 BCE). Philosopher, mathematician and religious leader who left no written works. He is credited with the discovery of the numerical ratios of the musical scale. The "Pythagorean doctrine" of the harmony of the spheres states that each planet produces a musical note as it travels in its orbit; these notes together formed a scale, or *harmonia*. The followers of Pythagoras formed one of the principal schools of Greek musical theory.

Bibl: W. Burkert, *Lore and Science in Ancient Pythagoreanism* (Cambridge, 1972).   JPM

Q

Qaddish. See *Kaddish*.

Qedushah. See *Kedushah*

Qerovah. See *Kerovah*.

Qiddush. See *Kiddush*.

Quadruplum (pl. **quadrupla**) [Latin]. "Fourfold." A 13th-century term signifying either the fourth (topmost) voice in a 4-part *organum* or an *organum* for 4 voices. *Quadrupla* were rare during the 13th century, most *polyphonic works calling for no more than 3 voices. *Pérotin's *Viderunt* and *Sederunt* are the best known examples.   DWM

Quasten, Johannes (*b* Homberg-Niederrhein 1900; *d* Freiburg 1987). A noted patristic and archeological scholar who was concerned with issues of music in early Christian worship, e.g., his *Music and Worship in Pagan and Christian Antiquity* (1983 [1973]).   JBF

Quempas [from Latin *Quem pastores laudavere,* "He whom shepherds praised"]. A popular 16th-century Ger-

man *Christmas song often combined with *Nunc angelorum* and *Resonet in laudibus* in the "Quempas Celebration" sung in churches. *Quempas singen* referred to the practice of Latin school students singing *carols from house to house, a practice in which *Luther participated; *Quempasheft* was the collection of such songs.   CFS

Quem quaeritis [Latin]. "Whom do you seek?" The *incipit* of a 10th century *trope, used with the *Easter *introit, or as an addition either to Easter *matins or to an Easter procession. It is the kernel of the Easter play *Visitatio sepulchri* ("Visitation of the tomb"), which tells of the 3 women who visited the tomb Easter Sunday to anoint the body of Jesus. The variations (e.g., parts assigned to different singers) and expansions of this text contributed to the rise of liturgical *drama.   RTR

Quicumque <*quicunque*> **vult** [Latin]. "Whoever wishes [to be saved]." The so-called "Athanasian Creed" (erroneously ascribed to St. Athansius, *d* 373), composed in Gaul (late 4th or early 5th cen-

tury). It was formerly chanted during Sunday *prime, and occasionally replaces the Apostles' Creed at *morning prayer in the Anglican *BCP. It was dropped from the first US BCP and has had no liturgical use in the US Episcopal Church since, though in Canada it may replace the Apostles' Creed. It is found in some Lutheran *hymnals for Trinity Sunday, without musical setting. It is also found (without the *filioque*) in some Greek and Russian *horologia.*
RDH-JMT

Quinn, James (*b* Glasgow 1919). *Hymn writer, translator and Jesuit priest. He holds degrees in classics (University of Glasgow) and philosophy (Heythrop College). His hymn texts are widely employed. Some are published in his *New Hymns for all Seasons* (1969) and *Praise for All Seasons* (1994).   MEC

R

Rachmaninov <Rakhmaninov> **Sergei (Vasilyevich)** (*b* Semyonovo 1873; *d* Beverly Hills 1943). Pianist, composer and conductor. Born into a musical family, he was educated at the Moscow Conservatory, graduating as a pianist (1891) then composer (1892). Prior to the 1917 Revolution he lived in Moscow, but then left Russia never to return. In 1935 he immigrated to the US, becoming a citizen shortly before his death. A composer of symphonies, *concertos, operas, solo piano works, etc., he also wrote choral works including a setting of *Vespers* and the *Liturgy of St. John Chrysostom*.
Bibl: G. Norris, *Rachmaninoff* (New York, 1994).   VAL

Raphael, Günter (*b* Berlin 1903; *d* Herford 1960). Composer and teacher. He taught composition at Leipzig, Duisburg and Cologne. In addition to symphonic and chamber music, his works include choral *psalm settings, *motets for the church *year and a large body of *organ music.   PKG

Rappresentatione sacra [Italian]. "Sacred representation." A 15th–16th-century Italian religious play with music, which was the forerunner of both opera and *oratorio. A late example is *Cavalieri's *Rappresentatione di Anima et di Corpo* (1600).   DWM

Rau banim [Hebrew]. "And the children saw." A section of *ma'ariv* that praises God as an introduction to *Mi Chamochah*. In Middle E *Sephardic traditions it is highlighted through congregational singing.   MLK

Ravenscroft Psalter. A common name for *The Whole Booke of Psalmes,* a harmonized *psalter edited by John Ravenscroft (London 1621; reprint 1633), which provided musical settings for the texts of the *Sternhold and Hopkins Psalter.   RAL

Ray, Robert (*b* St. Louis 1946). A baptist composer of *gospel-influenced worship music with broad ecumenical appeal. His works include *Gospel Mass* (1981) and *He never failed me yet* (1982). MEC

Read, Daniel (*b* Rehoboth MA 1757; *d* New Haven 1836). Composer, teacher and publisher. His 6 collections of vocal music (e.g., *The American Singing Book*, 1785) were influential in the *singing school movement; his *hymn tunes (e.g., WINDHAM) were fixtures in the US *psalmody repertory. FJM

Recitative. A vocal structure with roots in *plainsong that gained prominence *c* 1600 for its ability to present text dramatically. Usually scored for a single voice and simple instrumentation, recitative follows natural speech rhythm and accentuation, and is not subject to regular tempo. MPB

Reciting note <tone>. The central element in the *psalm tone. It is ordinarily preceded by an intonation formula and followed by a cadence; this sequence of intonation-recitation-cadence is then repeated. LMT

Recto tono [Latin]. "With a straight tone." The non-inflected singing of a text on the same pitch. The practice is usually associated with the performance of the Latin *divine office, reducing the time it took to pray the *hours. FCQ

Reda, Siegfried (*b* Bochum 1916; *d* Mülheim 1968). Composer and organist. He introduced contemporary compositional techniques into Protestant *church music. Reda served as director of the church music institute in Essen (from 1946), then Mülheim (from 1953).

He was a master of timbre and serial style composition. FKG

Reed, Luther D. (*b* North Wales PA 1873; *d* Philadelphia 1972). Lutheran liturgical scholar and teacher at Philadelphia Seminary. He edited *Common Service Book* (1917) and *Service Book and Hymnal* (1958), and authored *The Lutheran Liturgy* (1947) and *Worship* (1959). PHW

Reed organ. See *harmonium.

Reformation. In the W, the term ordinarily refers to the movements to reform the RC Church during the 16th century centered in N and E Europe. The principal leaders (*Luther, *Zwingli, *Calvin) provided theological interpretations of how this reformation was to take place. Each sought reconsideration of current worship and musical practices. In the end their individual theological positions gave birth to quite contrasting practices, repertoires and valuations of music.

In common they maintained the importance of the scriptures; for Luther that meant both freedom of style and an assured place for music as partner with sounded word; for Calvin that meant a return to *psalmody as the core of worship music; Zwingli deduced that the scriptures, from their silence on the matter, advocated a spiritual worship free from musical form. They shared a common passion for the use of the vernacular in worship, either by addition or by substitution.

These leaders dealt theologically with the relationship between form and substance in music; for Luther the incarnation of Christ secured a place for the oral word (and thus the making of music) as the carrier of the Spirit (substance); Calvin took another route and looked to the power of music as the means by which the Spirit drives the word home to an individual's heart; Zwingli sought to deal with music as form by separating it from the Spirit's activities. Worshipping in silence, he thought, is far better than dealing with musical distractions.

These reformers were students of Humanism, and were schooled to embrace music as central to all knowledge. Zwingli was the most accomplished musician of the trio. While well-versed in music's historic rank among the sciences, Luther valued it practically, putting him in touch with the common people. Together with Calvin he championed the importance of music education among the young, seeking to use them as musical leaders in worship.

Bibl: P. Le Huray, *Music and the Reformation in England 1549–1660* (New York, 1967); F. Blume *Protestant Church Music* (New York, 1974); P. Westermeyer, *Te Deum* (Minneapolis, 1998).   MPB

Reformed <Christian> **worship music.** *Zwingli, *Bucer, *Calvin and John Knox prepared worship forms or worship books in the vernacular. The music associated with these has been characterized by a nervousness which Calvin expressed when he reasoned "we must be the more assiduous in so controlling music that it may be useful to us and in no manner harmful . . . as it has a secret and nearly incredible power to move our hearts." His congregations limited sacred *art music to household devotions while singing in the church was restricted to unaccompanied, uni-

son, vernacular *metrical psalms and scripture verses. At the same time, Calvin encouraged composers such as *Bourgeois, *Goudimel and *Marot.

Today the practice of presenting a complete versification of each *psalm set to a single melody continues in some churches, while others have introduced *psalters containing a variety of musical forms. Most Reformed churches have *hymnals which are ecumenical and global in scope, contain complete liturgies with *service music, and have more scriptural *hymns as a result of the liturgical movement and the common lectionary.

Bibl: J. White, *Protestant Worship* (Louisville, 1989) 58–78.   PAB

Reform <Liberal> **Judaism, worship music of.** Reform Judaism is a movement which emphasizes the autononomy of the individual, marked by a liberal approach to Jewish legal traditions. Beginning in the early 19th century in Austria and Germany, its musical reforms sought to bring dignity and a contemporary European aesthetic to Jewish worship. *Sulzer and *Lewandowski were important early figures. By the early 20th century E and W European immigration brought composers such as *Bloch, *Binder, *Freed, *Helfman and *Fromm to North America. They defined a style using sophisticated harmonic treatment, often blended with traditional *Ashkenazic prayer *modes and melodies for *cantor, *choir and *organ. Reform Judaism established the Hebrew Union College School of Sacred Music (1948) to train cantors. By the 1960s Reform congregations began singing Israeli songs; by the 1970s *services accompanied by *guitar gained popularity (see *Jewish popular music). By the late

1990s Reform music was an eclectic mix of these new elements as well as *Sephardic and Ashkenazic melodies and prayer modes. Representative of this eclecticism is the *folk music of *Friedman, folk and rock services by J. Klepper and the more classically oriented works of *Janowski and *Steinberg. Variously sung by cantors, professional ensembles, volunteer choirs and congregations, accompaniment ranges from organ, to synthesizer, piano and guitar.   BES

Refrain. A textual and musical repetition occurring at the end of each *stanza in, for example, a *hymn, providing a specific textual focus. The term is frequently interchangeable with *chorus or *antiphon.   PAB

Regal. A small portable *organ in use from the 16th–17th centuries. Its metal reeds received air from 2 bellows. A small version which folded in half, like a book, was called a bible regal (German *Bibelorgel, Bibel Regal*).   JLB

Regensburg [Latin *Ratisbon*]. A German city which, with Munich, was the center of the *Cecilian movement. Leading musical figures of the city in this movement included Bishop J. Sailer and K. Proske who published much *Renaissance *polyphony; F. X. Haberl, the cathedral choir director, who founded the influential Regensburg school of church music (1874); and F. Witt, the founder of the *Society of St. Cecilia. The *Regensburg edition was issued from this city.   AWR

Regensburg edition [Latin *Editio Ratisbonensis*]. The 1869 reissuing of the *Medicean edition of the *gradual in *Regensburg, championed by the *Cecilian movement against efforts of the *Solesmes monks to restore authentic *chant melodies. The Regensburg edition was superseded by the *Vatican edition.   AWR

Regentchora [Slavonic]. "Choir director." In the Byzantine Slavonic tradition, a *choir director or principal *cantor. See *psaltes*.   DMP

Reger, (Johann Baptist Joseph) Max(imilian) (*b* Brand, Upper Palatinate 1873; *d* Leipzig, 1916). Composer. A fiery talent ahead of his era, Reger drew inspiration from the music of J. S. *Bach, *Beethoven and *Brahms. Chopin, F. *Mendelssohn and *Liszt influenced his harmonic imagination, while Wagner's chromaticism shaped his harmonic style. Reger extends all possibilities of tonality without obliterating it. His proclivity for counterpoint remains in almost all his composing. His technique of variation and fugue are astounding. While also a composer of orchestral music, his enormous output for the *organ renders him the most important German organ composer since Bach. A devout RC, Reger based many works on Lutheran *chorales, including large *chorale fantasias and 3 volumes of *chorale preludes. His combination of chromaticism and counterpoint makes his large organ works technically very difficult.   DCI

Regina coeli laetare [Latin]. "Queen of Heaven rejoice." An *antiphon of the BVM; traditionally sung at the end of *compline from *Easter Sunday until the Friday after Pentecost. It is attributed to Hermannus Contractus (*d* 1054).   LMT

Regular vs. usual singing. See *singing by rule.

Reitseh [Hebrew]. "Be favorable." A prayer recited as part of the *Amidah on all occasions, beginning the final (Avo-dah) section. Reitseh is chanted aloud during *shacharit, *minchah and *musaf, typically in the *Jewish prayer mode of the particular occasion. The musical setting by S. Richards for *cantor, *choir and *keyboard is widely known.   BES

Renaissance period [French from Latin renasci, "to be reborn"]. The era of renewal in art, literature, architecture, scholarship and music in Europe that began around the mid-15th century and continued to the beginning of the 17th century, though opinions differ on the exact dating of this period. The Renaissance brought closure to the medieval world and prepared the way for the modern era.

Franco-Flemish *polyphony, with its roots in the music of *Dufay and *Binchois, became the predominant musical language in Europe, characterized by *canon, ostinato, paraphrase and especially *cantus firmus. Primary composers of *masses, *motets and other common forms of the period include *Ockeghem, *Obrecht, *Isaac and *Josquin, the acknowledged master of the period. *Parody masses based on secular melodies were common, and the soaring *polyphonic lines often obscured the liturgical text. Around 1500 Erasmus criticized such polyphony, and about the same time Josquin changed his compositional style to make the music more closely related to the liturgical text. *Luther, who favored Josquin's music, encouraged the composition and use of music that similarly served the text for the new evangelical liturgical orders. The cantus firmus technique was continued but in addition to *plainsong melodies, Lutheran composers (especially *Walter) also employed the melodies of the new congregational *chorale. Other composers associated with Lutheran liturgical reforms (although there was much confessional ambiguity during these transitional years) included *Dietrich, *Ducis, *Resinarius, *Senfl, *Stoltzer and the publisher *Rhau.

Calvinist churches sang only *metrical psalms but the *psalm melodies received polyphonic settings for domestic use by such composers as *Bourgeois, *Goudimel, *Clemens non Papa, *Le Jeune and *Sweelinck. Later these were admitted into Reformed worship.

The reforms of the Council of *Trent led to the promotion of restrained counterpoint subservient to the liturgical text, epitomized by the later style of *Palestrina, and exemplified in the music of *Morales and *Victoria. Towards the end of the 16th century, polychoralism was developed in Venice, first by the *Gabrielis, then by *Monteverdi, and also by such Lutheran composers such as *Schütz and M. *Praetorius.

Developments in Jewish music of the period are well-represented by the work of *Rossi.

Bibl: G. Reese, *Music in the Renaissance,* rev. ed. (New York, 1959); I. Fenlon, *The Renaissance* (Englewood Cliffs, 1989); T. Knighton and D. Fallows, *Companion to Medieval and Renaissance Music* (New York, 1997).   RAL

Repetendum [Latin]. "Repeating." The portion of a *responsory which is repeated following the *verse. In printed versions it is often indicated by an asterisk.   JMT

Répons [French]. "Response." (1) A *responsory.

(2) An innovative orchestra composition by P. Boulez (*b* 1925), employing instruments and live electronic music together (1981).   CSP

Repp, Ray (*b* St. Louis 1942). Pioneer composer in the RC liturgical *folk music movement of the 1960s. He wrote numerous songs (e.g., "I am the Resurrection," "Allelu!") and a first and second *Mass for Young Americans*.   MEC

Reproaches. See *improperia*.

Requiem. See *dead, mass of the.

Resinarius, Bathasar (*b* Tetschen *c* 1485; *d* Leipa 1544). Important Lutheran composer of the early *Reformation. A student of *Isaac, he wrote *responsories, *hymns, *chorale settings and a *passion; they are known from *Rhau's publications and reflect the Wittenberg theologians' understanding of the importance of the scriptural word.   CFS

Respond [Latin *responsum*]. (1) The first part of a musical unit in *responsorial form, whose second part is generally a *versicle or *verse. The *gradual, *responsorial psalm and *invitatory are examples of *chants with a respond. Also called a *response.

(2) A *responsory.   PAJ

Response [Latin *responsum*]. (1) The answer to a *versicle, ordinarily supplied by congregation or *choir.

(2) A *respond.

(3) The answer to a ritual/musical invitation. See *call and response.   MJG

Responsorial psalm. A segment from a *psalm sung or read after the first reading at *eucharist, arranged to be performed in responsorial style.   GET

Responsorial singing. A form of singing in which a soloist (e.g., *cantor) or group of soloists sing the *verses (e.g., of a *psalm) while the congregation or *choir supplies the *response or *refrain. In this form the verse is ordinarily longer and more complex than the refrain, thus distinguishing it from the *litany. Reformed RC worship especially emphasizes this form (e.g., in the *responsorial psalm). The opposite form is singing *directaneus. See *call and response.   MJG

Responsorium. See *responsory.

Responsorium breve. See *short responsory.

Responsorium prolixum. See *great responsory.

Responsory [Latin *responsorium*]. A type of *responsorial chant which involves the repetition of some or all of the opening text, often immediately after it has been intoned by the leader. It is commonly employed as a musical epilogue to readings in the *divine office. See *great and *short responsories.   PAJ

Reuter Organ Company. *Organ building firm founded (1917) by A. C. Reuter (1880–1971) and 5 others in Mattoon IL; it moved to Lawrence KS in 1920. Initially Reuter made electro-pneumatic organs; in 1969 Reuter affiliated with Emil Hammer of Hanover, Germany in order to build tracker organs.   JWK

Reutter, Georg von. (1) (*b* Vienna 1656; *d* there 1738). Organist at St. Stephen's in Vienna (1686), then at the imperial court chapel (1696), subsequently becoming *Kapellmeister at St. Stephen's (1715). He composed *organ *toccatas.
(2) His son, (**John Adam Joseph Karl) Georg (von) Reutter** (*b* 1708 Vienna; *d* there 1772). He succeeded his father as *Kapellmeister* (1738), engaging the young F. J. *Haydn as a chorister; the younger Reutter became second (1747), then first *Kapellmeister* (1769) at the imperial court. He wrote over 500 sacred works.   JLB

Revival songs. Songs used in or whose origins are in revival settings. The texts ordinarily express personal experiences of sin, forgiveness, the joy of salvation, peace of soul and assurance of heaven. There is no specific "revival music" style.
*Hymns of the Great Awakening (its zenith was in the early 1740s) were mostly *psalms and psalm tunes. Texts by *Watts and C. *Wesley, paired with livelier tunes and appended *choruses, were sung at *camp meetings during the Second Great Awakening (end of 18th, beginning of 19th century). Many of these appeared in the oblong *tune books of *singing school teachers. J. Leavitt compiled *The Christian Lyre* (1831) from popular secular songs, folk hymns, ballads and hymns for use in revival *services. Such collections, with the Sunday school songs by *Bradbury and others, became the musical backbone of the "Prayer Meeting Revival" (1857–1859). By the time of the *Moody and *Sankey revivals, many composers like *Stebbins were publishing *gospel songs in broad sheets and small collections. Sankey and *Bliss' *Gospel Hymns* presented upbeat music with texts of a personal nature that had wide appeal in revival meetings. Revivalist preachers joined with musicians who frequently composed music for revival settings, many of whom entered the publishing business. Revival songs and hymns encompass a wide range of musical styles.
Bibl: W. McLoughlin, *Modern Revivalism* (New York, 1959); D. P. Hustad, *Jubilate II* (Carol Stream IL, 1993).   RJS

Rhau, Georg (*b* Eisfeld 1488; *d* Wittenberg 1548). Publisher and church musician. He studied at Erfurt and Wittenberg. In 1518 he became *Kantor at St. Thomas in Leipzig. After embracing the *Reformation, he became a printer in Wittenberg (1523). Rhau published *Luther's writings and collections of music. His *Newe deudsche geistliche Gesenge* (1544) included Latin and German works of Protestants (e.g., *Dietrich, *Ducis and *Resinarius) and RCs (e.g., *Bruck, *Senfl and *Stoltzer).   JLB

Rhymed office. Texts for the *divine office for given feasts with *antiphons and *responsories (as well as *hymns) written in rhyme. Very popular in the late *Middle Ages, most rhymed offices disappeared from the Roman rite during the revision of the *breviary issued by Pius V in 1568.   JMT

Rhythmic modes. By the 13th century composers notated and classified rhythms according to patterns called *modes. Modal rhythm was based on long and short values arranged in patterns similar to the metrical patterns in poetry. The 3-fold unit of measure for each mode was called a *perfectio* (Latin, "perfection). All modes were in triple *meter. The perfection of the number 3 was symbolic of the Trinity.   DCI

Ricercar <*ricercare*> [French; Italian *ricercare;* Spanish *recercario, recercada*]. "To seek." In the 16th and 17th centuries the term referred to 1) an instrumental piece which had the character of a *prelude with a homophonic texture, and 2) a *motet-like, contrapuntal, imitative instrumental piece, not necessarily derived from the motet but conceived in the tradition of *polyphonic *church music. Later the term refers to *fugal compositions written in a learned or archaic manner.   LMT

Richter, Franz Xaver (*b* Holleschau? 1709; *d* Strasbourg 1789). Composer and singer. He was Vice *Kapellmeister* in Kempten, Allgäu (1740), a court musician in Mannheim (1747) and *Kapellmeister* at Strasbourg Cathedral (1769). Richter wrote instrumental works, 39 *masses, 3 *Requiems, 50 *cantatas and numerous *motets.   JLB

Rimsky-Korsakov, Nikolay (Andreyevich) (*b* Tikhvin, Novgorod 1844; *d* Lyubensk, St. Petersburg 1908). Nationalist composer, conductor and music editor of Mussorgsky's and Borodin's works. Rimsky-Korsakov was a musical assistant at the imperial chapel (1883–94). Religious works include 8 settings of the *divine liturgy of St. John Chrysostom, traditional Orthodox liturgical *chants and the *Easter Festival Overture* (1888) built on liturgical themes.   RJS

Ring shout. A form of communal ritual dance, of African origin, occurring in early African American worship. It involved circular group movement with shuffling step to continuous chanting and clapping as a means of Spirit-induced religious fervor.   MEM

Ritual music. (1) Music whose character is determined by and integral to some ritual action.

(2) Christian ritual music is employed by some as a synonym for *liturgical music.   EBF

Rivers, Clarence Rufus J. (*b* Selma 1931). RC priest, liturgist and composer of *liturgical music in an African American style. He holds a Ph.D. from Union Graduate School in Cincinnati, and studied at the Institut Catholique in Paris. Rivers was a major catalyst for creating a synthesis between black music, art, gesture, drama and contemporary RC worship.   MEM

Roberts, Leon C. (*b* Coatesville PA 1950; *d* Washington DC 1999). Singer, choral director and composer/arranger in the African American *gospel tradition. He studied at Howard University. Roberts was a consultant and composer for *Lead Me, Guide Me* and other *hymnals. He was music director/artist-in-residence in Baptist and RC churches, notably St. Augustine's in Washington DC (from 1977).   MEM

Rock of Ages. See *Maoz tsur.*

Rodeheaver, Homer A(lvan) (*b* Union Furnace OH 1880; *d* Winona IN 1955). Editor, composer and singer with Billy *Sunday. He edited and compiled *c* 80

collections of *gospel songs, which shaped the style of *refrain/verse *hymnody prevalent in Protestant revivals of the early 20th century.   FJM

Roman Catholic worship music. Until the early 4th century, this music is coterminous with that of the "Great Church" in opposition to various sectarian movements. It apparently consisted mostly of vocalized texts: solo *cantillation of prayers and readings, and communal chanting of *acclamations and *responses. Music graced Christian initiation, word *services, *eucharist, domestic meals and devotions.

From c the early 4th to the 8th centuries, this music is coterminous with that of Orthodox Christianity in opposition to heretical/sectarian movements. Ritual traditions emerged based on language (e.g., Greek and Latin) and geography (e.g., Jerusalem and Rome) with corresponding distinct *chant families. Music leadership developed into set ministries (e.g., *psaltes and *schola cantorum). Monastic influence added new ceremonies and texts, frequently demanding *hymns and *processionals. Besides solo cantillation, communal *litanies, hymns and acclamations, monastic *choirs chanted more ornate *antiphonal *psalmody and *responsories.

From c 9th–11th centuries RC worship music became a Latin, W European repertoire. After separating from Orthodox Christianity (1054), E Catholics united with Rome worshipped in various languages and styles; Latin rites and chant traditions (e.g., *Ambrosian) flourished in W. Europe. *Charlemagne ordered *Roman chant employed in Frankish regions; *Gregorian chant emerged. Simple chant-based *polyphony (*organum) offered an aural response to the new Gothic architecture. Popular vernacular devotional songs (e.g., *Leise) arose.

Music complexified from c 12th–14th centuries. Textual embellishments (e.g., *tropes) were inserted into liturgical texts; other developments (e.g., *conductus) provided new poetic forms for worship. Léonin and Pérotin produced polyphonic compositions emancipated from single-note *counterpoint. Later *ars nova composers broke from the constraints of *rhythmic modes and experimented with multi-lingual *motets. Pilgrimage and instructional songs (e.g., *laude spirituali) appeared.

Fewer new texts appeared from c 14th–16th centuries; certain older ones were suppressed. Unified polyphonic settings of the *ordinary, *Requiem and festival *vespers developed. RC music was very different from that promoted by 16th-century Reformers. *Renaissance composers largely wrote choral music without assembly participation. The Council of *Trent recognized chant and polyphony as appropriate for worship, but settings must be faithful to official liturgical texts, and avoid secular resonances. This led to the development of national "schools" and the *stile antico.

Seventeenth-century RC worship music split between the stile antico and stile moderno. Instrumental music for the first time played a major role in RC worship (e.g., the *sonata di chiesa).

Eighteenth-century RC worship music adopted Enlightenment ideals (e.g., clear formal structure) and *Baroque theatricality. Operatic and symphonic writing was applied to liturgical texts

Nineteenth-century Romantic emphases on individuality, subjectivity and emotion was influential. New music continued the concerted mass tradition, or was intended for the concert hall, or sought to produce individual religious sentiments rather than enable communal worship. "Restoration" movements of chant at *Solesmes and the *stile antico* in the *Cecilian Movement opposed these currents.

RC worship music profoundly changed in the 20th century. *Tra le sollecitudini* encouraged vocal participation of all in worship employing chant, polyphony and "more modern" music. *Musicae sacrae disciplina* recognized the value of religious singing in popular devotions and confirmed trends developing since *Tra le sollecitudini*. *Vatican II called for renewal through the revision of liturgical *books and the reform of liturgical practices; it also emphasized full, conscious and active participation through singing, granted permission for the vernacular, and encouraged the preservation of the *treasury of sacred music as well as new compositions. *Musicam Sacram* offered guidelines for music in post-Vatican II worship. In recent years various episcopal conferences and scholarly groups have generated documents, applying the Council's directives to different languages and cultures.

Bibl: K. G. Fellerer, *The History of Catholic Church Music* (Baltimore, 1961); L. Hoffman and J. Walton, eds., *Sacred Sound and Social Change* (Notre Dame-London, 1992); J. M. Joncas, *From Sacred Song to Ritual Music* (Collegeville, 1997).   JMJ

Roman chant. See *Old Roman chant.

Romanian Catholic/Orthodox worship music. The *liturgical music of Romania, formed in 1859 by the union of Moldavia and Wallachia, where Romanian Orthodox *chant was prevalent (see *Romanian chant), and by the addition in 1918 of Transylvania, where Romanian Orthodox and *Gregorian chant were used. While Orthodox churches continued singing *monophonic chant, *polyphony and instrumental music were cultivated in Catholic churches. Important organists in Transylvania included H. Ostermeier (*d* 1561), G. Reilich (*d* 1677), I. Căianu (*d* 1698) and D. Croner (*d* 1740). Choral music gained importance in the 18th century. D. Kiriac-Georgescu (*d* 1928) developed a choral style using *folk music in his *Liturgica psaltică*.

Bibl: V. Cosma, *A Concise History of Romanian Music* (Bucharest, 1982).   RGD

Romanian chant. The liturgical *chant of the Romanian Orthodox church. The musical tradition, derived from *Byzantine chant in the 9th century, was centered in the Moldavian monasteries of Neamțu (founded in the 14th century) and Putna (founded in 1466). Some 16th-century manuscripts are bilingual (Greek-Slavonic), but Romanian has been used since the 17th century. Notable composers include Evstatie of Putna (*fl* early 16th century) and Philotheus the Romanian, author of a manual for chanting in Romanian (*Psaltichia Romaneascu*, 1713). A 19th-century reform of Byzantine *chant notation (see *Greco-Byzantine chant) was paralleled in Bucharest under Protopsaltis Macarie the Hieromonk.

Bibl: A. E. Pennington, "Seven Akolouthiai from Putna," *Studies in Eastern Chant* 4 (1979) 112–33.   RGD

Romanos, St. (*b* Emesa, Syria 485?; *d* after 555). The foremost composer of Byzantine *kontakia*. Fifty-nine genuine texts are extant, with many more attributed to him. No music by Romanos survives.   RGD

Roman Psalter. A Latin translation of the *psalms usually attributed to St. Jerome, though this authorship cannot be proven. It was employed in all churches of Rome and throughout Italy until it was replaced by the *Gallican Psalter under Pius V (*d* 1772), except at St. Peter's Basilica (Rome) where it continues to be used. It provided text for *introits, *graduals, *tracts, *offertories, *communions and *responsories of the Roman rite reformed after *Vatican II.   JMT

Romantic period. The period from *c* 1820–1910. The term "romantic" connotes greater subjectivity, intensity of emotional expression and freedom from formal constraint. This period's music typically differs from that of the preceding *Classical period in its wider ranging, less symmetrically phrased melody; more chromatic harmony and coloristic use of dissonance; freer, more flexible rhythm; more frequent use of the minor *mode; freer modulation; sonority of greater fullness; and variety of timbres. As in Classical music, homophonic texture predominates; contrapuntal writing also plays an important role, especially in *church music modeled on older styles. Music was accorded a quasi-religious status during this period, viewed as a means to the transcendent and infinite. Paradoxically, *liturgical music of this period is generally inferior to non-liturgical *religious music, such as the *oratorio.

The 19th century saw a widespread reform of church music based on a return to older music both for repertoire and as models for new composition. For RCs, the *Cecilian movement advocated the (supposed) *a cappella style of *Palestrina; Lutherans revived the music of J. S. *Bach and *Schütz. The *Gregorian chant renewal, centered at *Solesmes, was official sanctioned in *Tra le sollecitudini. England's *Oxford movement stimulated translation of Greek, Latin and German *hymn texts into English by *Neale and *Winkworth, and the composition of new hymns. Many of these were gathered in the seminal *Hymns Ancient and Modern. In many countries, *choirs were revived and institutions supporting church music were founded or strengthened.

This was also a period of renewal for Jewish worship music. *Sulzer and *Lewandowski made the foremost contributions to choral and congregational music, respectively. The *organ was adopted in many European synagogues, though this was controversial; choirs excluded women until near the end of the 19th century.

For RCs, important *masses and *motets were composed by *Schubert, C. *Franck, *Gounod and *Bruckner. For Protestants, F. *Mendelssohn and *Brahms contributed significant choral *liturgical music. Much work of English composers of this period is not well-regarded today; superior examples can be found in the *anthems of S. *Wesley and *services of *Stanford. For the Russian Orthodox, a new, full-textured, non-metrical, *a cappella* choral style was developed by *Bortnyansky.

Important developments in congregational song in North America during this period included *camp meeting song, *spirituals, *gospel hymns and *folk-based hymns published in numerous collections in the S states (e.g., The *Sacred Harp). Mid-century also saw the emergence of the denominational *hymnal in North America.

Bibl: R. Longyear, *Nineteenth-Century Romanticism in Music,* 3rd ed. (Englewood Cliffs, 1988), especially 341–45; G. Goldberg, "Jewish liturgical music in the wake of nineteenth-century reform," *Sacred Sound and Social Change,* ed. L. Hoffman and J. Walton (Notre Dame, 1992) 59–83; A. Wilson-Dickson, *The Story of Christian Music* (Minneapolis, 1996). KRH

Roosevelt, Hilborne Lewis (*b* New York 1849; *d* there 1886). *Organ builder. He established the Roosevelt Organ Works in New York (1872) and was succeeded in business by his brother Frank (*b* 1861; *d* 1894). Roosevelt organs were influenced by the European Romantic tradition, including the use of reed stops imported from *Cavaillé-Coll. JWK

Rorate caeli [Latin]. "Drop down rain, heavens." (1) The *introit for the Fourth Sunday of *Advent, drawn from Is 45:8.
(2) A *plainsong *hymn, traditionally employed at RC *benediction during Advent (so listed in the *Liber Usualis*). JKW

Rorem, Ned (*b* Richmond IN 1923). Composer and author. After studies with *Sowerby, Rorem graduated from the Curtis Institute and Juilliard. He worked as a copyist for Virgil Thompson. A leading American composer of art songs, he has written numerous operas, symphonic and chamber works. Over 50 sacred vocal compositions include a *Missa brevis* (1964) and *Three Christmas Choruses* (1978). PAB

Rosenblatt, Yosef <Yossele> (*b* Belaya Tserkov 1882; *d* Tel Aviv, 1933). *Cantor, composer and preeminent figure of the golden age of the cantorate (see *chazzan*). The grandson of a Hassidic Rabbi, he was influenced by *Hassidic music. An itinerant child cantor, he was chief cantor of the synagogue in Hamburg (1906), then cantor of Ohab Zedek Congregation (1912) in New York. He turned down the Chicago Opera Association's offer (1918) of the starring role in Halevy's *La Juive* as it conflicted with his religious beliefs. Rosenblatt concertized widely, frequently recording his liturgical works (some published in *Tefiloth Joseph,* 1927) and other compositions.
Bibl: S. Rosenblatt, *Yossele Rosenblatt* (New York, 1954). IAG

Rosenmüller, Johann (*b* Oelsnitz 1619?; *d* Wolfenbüttel 1684). Composer and organist. He served as assistant to the *Kantor at St. Thomas in Leipzig (from 1642), then organist at Nicolaikirche (1651–55). He was employed in Venice (1658–82), finally becoming *Kapellmeister* in Wolfenbüttel. He composed *Magnificat*s, *masses and many sacred choral works. JLB

Rosh Chodesh <Ḥodesh> [Hebrew]. "Beginning of the month." The beginning of the Hebrew month, celebrated as a minor holy day: for 1 day if the preceding month had 29 days, for 2 if it had 30. *Rosh Chodesh* is announced in the synagogue service of the preceding *Sabbath. The prayer *Birkat hachodesh* functions as an announcement, naming the incoming month and the day(s) when *Rosh Chodesh* will be celebrated. This prayer is recited immediately after the reading of the *Haftorah. Rosh Chodesh* is celebrated in the synagogue with a shortened version of *Hallel* and *musaf*. It is traditionally regarded as a day to honor women for their piety through which the Jewish people are eternally recreated. SIW

Rosh Hashanah [Hebrew]. "Beginning of the year." A feast of the Jewish New Year, beginning on the first day of the seventh Hebrew month *(Tishri);* also the beginning of the 10-day period culminating on *Yom Kippur,* the most important period of the Jewish religious year. On the Sunday before *Rosh Hashanah* *selichot* are recited before *shacharit;* if *Rosh Hashanah* begins before Thursday, *selichot* are recited on the Sunday of the preceding week. *Rosh Hashanah* is heralded by the blowing of the *shofar* at the conclusion of the weekday (but not Sabbath) *shacharit*.

Liturgical-musical highlights of the feast include *Hineni,* *Unetane tokef,* several *piyyutim,* the Great *Aleinu* and *shofarot*. The *shofar* is sounded after the *Torah reading and throughout *musaf*. The Torah is chanted in a special *High Holiday *cantillation. Various *Jewish prayer modes pervade the *services. The majority of *Misinnai* tunes and leit motifs handed down by tradition are utilized. Many cantorial and choral settings have been written for the *Rosh Hashanah* liturgy, especially *musaf*. IAG

Rossi, Salomone <Solomon> (*b* Mantua? *c* 1570; *d* there? *c* 1630). Composer. He was employed at the court of the dukes of Gonzaga of Mantua (*c* 1587–1628). Little is known about his life. Besides his 7 books of madrigals, he wrote choral music to Hebrew texts from the *psalms and *liturgy. Thirty-three of

these Hebrew works are collected in *Hashirim asher lish'lomo* (1623). MLK

Rosy Sequence. Part of the *hymn *Jesu dulcis memoria,* formerly appointed as the *sequence for the feast of the Holy Name of Jesus in *Sarum use (August 7). A 50-*stanza form of the hymn was used as a type of "rosary" (hence the name of the sequence). *Neale's translation with its Sarum *plainsong (*mode 5) is in the *English Hymnal. JMT

Routley, Erik (*b* Brighton, England 1917; *d* Nashville 1982). Hymnologist, churchman, prolific author and composer of *hymn texts and tunes. Ordained a Congregational minister (1943), he served congregations in England and Scotland, becoming president of the Congregational Church in England and Wales (1970). Involved in the editing of 6 *hymnals, he also edited the *Bulletin* of the British Hymn Society (1948–74). After visits to the US he moved there permanently (1975) to teach, first at Princeton Seminary, then at *Westminster Choir College.

Bibl: R. Leaver and J. Litton, eds., *Duty and Delight: Routley Remembered* (Carol Stream IL, 1985). RAL

Royal Canadian College of Organists. Formed as The Canadian Guild of Organists (1909), then renamed The Canadian College of Organists (1920), the organization was eventually granted the prefix "Royal" (1959). With headquarters in Toronto, its purpose is to promote a high standard of *organ playing, choral directing, *church music and composition through examinations, workshops, recitals and publications. PAB

Royal College of Organists. A membership organization founded in London (1864) by R. Limpus, which received its royal charter in 1893. An educational charity, its first objective is to promote the art of *organ playing and *choir training, and to advance music education by means of lectures, recitals, master classes, etc. It offers examinations for associateship, fellowship and choir-training diplomas.   RJB

Royal hours. See *megalai horai.

Ruf [German]. "Call." A popular medieval litanic song, often used during *processions, consisting of 2-line *strophes, sung by a leader, followed by a *refrain by the people such as *Kyrie eleison or a repeated *alleluia.   AWR

Russian and Slavonic chant. The *liturgical music of E Orthodox Slavic churches. Byzantine melodies were imported and adapted when the *liturgy was translated into Old Church Slavonic at the time of the conversion of the Slavs (10th century). *Hymns for Slavic saints appear by the 12th century. The modal system, types of *chant books and genres of chants are similar to *Byzantine chant. Slavic *kondakarian* and *stolp* notation were derived from Byzantine neumatic systems, but by *c* 1500 meanings of the signs had changed. Several chant styles existed, including Znammeny, Demestvenny, Kievan, Bulgarian and Greek. *Polyphony was used by the 16th century.
   Bibl: V. Morosan, ed., *One Thousand Years of Russian Sacred Music, 988–1988* (Washington DC, 1991).   RGD

Ruthenian worship music. The *liturgical music of the Greek Catholic Church of the Ruthenians of Sub-Carpathian Rus'. The tradition developed from Znammeny and Kievan chant (see *Russian and Slavonic chant). Part singing, improvised and composed, began *c* the 16th century. In the 17th century, square (Kievan) notation replaced neumatic notation. Only 1 chant book (*irmologion*) is used; it is an anthology including model *stanzas *(irmosy)*. Important redactions were made to it in the 18th–19th centuries; in 1906 a version entitled *Tserkovnoje Prostopinije* was compiled using modern notation. An *irmologion* incorporating a corrected version of the *Prostopinije* was published by S. Papp and N. Petrasevic (1970).
   Bibl: J. Roccasalvo, *The Plainchant Tradition of Southwestern Rus'* (Boulder, 1986).   RGD

Rutter, John (*b* London 1945). Composer, arranger and conductor of the Cambridge Singers, who under his direction received a Gramophone award for their performance of the *Fauré Requiem.* Among Rutter's liturgical and sacred compositions are numerous *anthems and a much celebrated *Gloria in excelsis.* CRY

Ryder, Noah Francis (*b* Nashville 1914; *d* Norfolk 1964). Composer, arranger, educator and conductor. He studied at the Hampton Institute and University of Michigan and taught at the Hampton Institute and Virginia State College (Norfolk). The director of the Harry T. Burleigh Glee Club, he wrote many vocal works including "Run to Jesus."   MWC

S

Sabbath [from Hebrew *Shabbat*, "to rest"]. The seventh day of the week. Its observance is a biblical command with many references in the first 5 books of the Hebrew Bible (e.g., Gen 2:1-3; Ex 20:8, 31:16-17). Consistently observed by Jews, some Jewish Christians continued to observe the Sabbath until the end of the second century. During the following century it remained an ideal for Christians, though they gradually transferred many Sabbath customs and observances to Sunday. Currently a few Christian groups (e.g., Seventh-day Adventists) observe Saturday rather than Sunday as the central day of worship and rest.

For Jews, the Sabbath *liturgy consists of alterations to weekday liturgy. Sabbath observance begins at sundown on Friday, concluding at sunset on Saturday. *Kabbalat Shabbat begins Sabbath *services on Friday, followed by *ma'ariv (to which *Veshamru and *Yismechu are added; changes are made to the *Amidah; and *Adon olam or *Yigal are commonly sung as closing *hymns). Saturday *shacharit includes additions (e.g., more *psalms in *Pesukei dezim-

rah). The Sabbath *Torah reading is longer than that found on weekdays. The *musaf is added. Sabbath *minchah includes additions and changes (e.g., to the *Amidah*); the Torah is also read. Traditionally a meal follows *minchah*. Sabbath meals at home include the singing of *zemirot. The Sabbath concludes with the *Havdalah.

The music of the Sabbath is unique. Several sections of the Sabbath liturgy are musically highlighted in the *Ashkenazic tradition to express the meaning of the text or to give prominence to that text in the liturgy (i.e., *Adonai malach, *Ahavat olam, *Av Harachamim, *El Adon, *Kedushah, *Lecha dodi, *Magein avot, *Nishmat kol chai, *Reitseh, *Shalom rav, *Shochen ad and *Sim shalom). The *Sephardic tradition also musically emphasizes particular elements (i.e., *El hahodaot, *Kaddish, *Mimits'rayim gealtanu, *Nak'dishach, *Rau banim, Semechim beseitam and *Shavat aniyim).

Bibl: A. J. Heschel, *The Sabbath* (New York, 1951); I. Elbogen, *Jewish Liturgy,* trans. R. Scheindlin (Philadelphia, 1993 [1913]). MLK

Sachs, Hans (*b* Nuremberg 1494; *d* there 1576). The foremost poet of the *Meistersingers* with 4,275 poems, 1,700 tales, 208 dramatic poems and many melodies to his credit. A strong supporter of *Luther, he was instrumental in putting *Meistergesang* at the service of the *Reformation. He was a central figure in Wagner's opera *Die Meistersinger von Nürnberg* (1868).   JLB

Sacrament. (1) A Christian liturgical action believed to embody the reality it signifies, thus bringing participants into contact with God's presence and power revealed in Christ's death and resurrection. *Tertullian was one of the first to so employ the term; in the early Church the term was applied to many different rites and feasts. By the 11th–13th centuries the term was restricted to 7 rites: baptism, confirmation, *eucharist, marriage, holy orders, reconciliation and anointing of the sick. Today most Protestant communities posit 2 sacraments: baptism and eucharist.
(2) Eucharist.   NDM

Sacramentary. A book for the presiding minister (bishop, presbyter) containing prayer texts and *chants for *eucharist, possibly other sacraments and the *divine office. It evolved out of small booklets, gathered into larger collections (e.g., the 6th-century Leonine/Verona sacramentary). A real sacramentary, as distinguished from such booklets, appears by the 7th century (Old Gelasian).   JMJ

Sacrament hymn. A congregational *hymn sung in the worship of The Church of Jesus Christ of Latter-day Saints while the emblems (bread and water) of the *Lord's Supper are being prepared.   MFM

Sacra rappresentazione. See *Rappresentazione sacra*.

Sacred Dance Guild <SDG>. A pioneering interfaith group founded in 1958 in the US by those who had shared religious dance both on stage and within churches since the 1920s. SDG encouraged "dance choirs" and interest in dance as a religious art form. SDG newsletters, workshops and resources have been major stimuli for liturgical dance.   MAK

Sacred Harp. An American oblong *shape-note *tune book using *fasola, compiled by B. F. White and E. J. King (1844, numerous revisions followed). Popular in the *singing schools, it included *hymns, *anthems and 3-part *fuging tunes. The editions by M. W. Cooper (1902) and T. Denson (1936) are used at Sacred Harp conventions today. *The Colored Sacred Harp* (1934) by J. Jackson consists of 70 songs by black composers in the shape-note tradition.   RJS

Sacred music [Latin *musica sacra*]. (1) The preferred term in universal documents of the RC Church for music composed for "the celebration of divine worship."
(2) *Liturgical music.
(3) A general term for *religious music not necessarily intended for use in worship, especially that which is considered *art music, e.g. the *Manzoni Requiem* by *Verdi.   EBF

Sacrosanctum Concilium [Latin] "Most holy council." *Vatican II's *Constitution on the Sacred Liturgy* (1963), providing direction for the restoration and promotion of RC worship. Chapter 6, on *sacred music, decrees that: vernacular texts may be sung; the *treasury of sacred music should be preserved while new compositions are produced; full, conscious and active participation in the liturgy through song and music-making is required of *choirs and assembly; instruction in sacred music should be fostered in all Catholic institutions; *Gregorian chant is recognized as proper to the Roman rite; other styles/genres of music are permitted; *organ and other *instruments are allowed during *liturgy; native cultural elements may be adapted for worship; sung texts for worship must conform with Catholic doctrine and derive from liturgical and scriptural sources.   JMJ

St. Anne Fugue. A popular designation (mostly employed in English) for the *fugue from the *Prelude and Fugue in E-flat (BWV 552.2) from J. S. *Bach's Clavier Übung III. The fugue's theme coincidentally corresponds to a segment of the *hymn tune ST. ANNE.   MPB

St. Anthony Variations. A composition by *Brahms (op. 56a for orchestra, 1873; op. 56b for 2 pianos, 1873) based on a tune attributed to F. J. *Haydn. The tune's origins are unclear; it may have been adapted from a medieval *hymn for the feast of St. Antoninus.   RTR

St. Denis, Ruth (b Boontown NJ 1879; d Hollywood 1968). One of the mothers of modern dance who employed mystical, religious and biblical themes in her choreography. She cofounded with husband T. *Shawn the Denishawn School in Los Angeles (1917), later in New York; also the Denishawn Dancers with whom she toured. She created numerous works for performance in liturgical contexts by dance ensembles, significantly influencing the 20th-century revival of liturgical *dance.   MAK-RJS

St. James Society. An association of clergy and laity of the Lutheran Church-Missouri Synod devoted to the recovery of full liturgical observance for the Lutheran church. Formed c 1925, the Society published a journal (Pro Ecclesia Lutherana) and held conferences until it merged with the Institute of Liturgical Studies at *Valparaiso University in 1948.   PKG

St. John Passion. A common designation for J. S. *Bach's Johannespassion (BWV 245, 1723): a setting of the *passion according to St. John's gospel with interpolations. Other composers, such as *Schütz and Pärt, also have set this text which is traditionally read at the Good Friday *liturgy in the RC and some other traditions.   MPB

St. John's Abbey. A Benedictine monastery in Collegeville MN, founded in 1856. An important center of the *liturgical movement from the 1920s, and before *Vatican II a center for the study and promotion of *Gregorian chant. The abbey operates The Liturgical Press and publishes the journal Worship.   AWR

St. John's University. A liberal arts university in Collegeville MN, founded (1857) by the monks of *St. John's Abbey. It offers undergraduate and graduate programs in liturgy and music. The University library houses an extensive microfilm collection of medieval manuscripts.   AWR

St. Louis Jesuits. Composers of contemporary *liturgical music (B. Dufford, J. *Foley, J. Kavanagh, T. Mannion, D. *Schutte; later also R. O'Connor), all Jesuits at the groups' inception. While not stationed together, their individual compositions were published jointly as *Neither Silver nor Gold* (1974), effectively giving birth to the group. Over the next decade they provided scripturally based texts with accessible music eagerly embraced by RCs and others.   FJM

St. Luke Passion. The narrative of Christ's *passion and death in Luke's gospel (22–23). In RC rites before *Vatican II it was read on Wednesday of *Holy Week; the common lectionary assigns it to Passion or *Palm Sunday in Cycle C. *Penderecki's choral setting of this passion is a great contemporary masterpiece.   ACL

St. Mark Passion. The narrative of Christ's *passion and death in Mark's gospel (14–15). In RC rites before *Vatican II it was read on Tuesday of *Holy Week; the common lectionary assigns it to Passion or *Palm Sunday in Cycle B. It has not received famous large-scale settings such as the *St. John and *St. Matthew Passions by J. S. *Bach, though *Henrici did prepare a text which Bach left unset.   ACL

St. Martial, repertory of. Works of the late 11th and early 12th centuries written in the Limoges region of France, centered at the monastery of St. Martial. This repertoire includes liturgical *monody such as *tropes, *proses, *sequences and *prosulae. The c 30 manuscripts of this repertory are noted for their examples of early *counterpoint, particularly 2-voice pieces in *discant and florid *organum styles. The innovation of the St. Martial composers was the enrichment of the *duplum of *organum to include extended *melismas sung against each note of the *plainsong *tenor.

Bibl: J. Yudkin, *Music in Medieval Europe* (Englewood Cliffs, 1989).   JPM

St. Matthew Passion. A common designation for J. S. *Bach's *Matthäuspassion* (BWV 244, 1727–29): a setting of the *passion according to St. Matthew's gospel with interpolations. Other composers, such as *Schütz and *Pepping, also have set this text which is traditionally read on Passion or *Palm Sunday in the RC and some other traditions.   MPB

St. Olaf College. A Lutheran liberal arts college founded in Northfield MN (1874). Here F. Melius *Christiansen established the St. Olaf Choir (1912), beginning a tradition of high quality choral music. Currently almost half of the student body participates in choral and instrumental programs.   FJM

Salieri, Antonio (*b* Legnano 1750; *d* Vienna 1825). Imperial court composer and Italian opera director in Vienna. Later he was appointed and served as *Kapellmeister* for 36 years, composing a vast amount of *sacred music adhering to the Italian tradition. After his style fell out of public favor, he remained a central figure as the teacher of *Beethoven, *Czerny, *Schubert and *Liszt.   DCI

Saliers, Don E. (*b* Fostoria OH 1937). Teacher, scholar, musician and Methodist elder. A Graduate of Ohio Wesleyan and Yale University (Ph.D), he is professor of theology at Emory University. Among his influential liturgical writings is *Worship as Theology* (1994). PHW

Salvation Army worship music. The Salvationists began as a 19th-century evangelistic movement in Britain and spread to North America to convert the poor and dispossessed to Christ. One early means of evangelization was to form bands of local musicians to play in *open air meetings and in worship settings to draw people to hear the message of salvation. These bands were seen as a new generation of British waits (instrumentalists or singers employed by towns who played on the street for public ceremonies, entertainment or at *Christmas). *Hymns used in Salvation Army worship present the Holiness theology of founders William and Catherine Booth. Tunes reflect idioms and melodies of popular culture as well as standard church tunes and may be accompanied by piano, *organ or band. Salvationist musicians continue to produce singing brigades, train musicians and compose for bands and choirs.

Bibl: E. McKinley, *Marching to Glory* (Grand Rapids, 1995). RJS

Salve Regina [Latin]. "Hail, queen." A *Marian antiphon traditionally sung at the *divine office from Trinity Sunday through the Friday before the First Sunday of Advent. In the *Renaissance and early *Baroque eras its solemn *chant melody was employed as the basis for both *keyboard and *polyphonic vocal works. See *Marian music. RTR

Samoglasen [Slavonic]. See *idiomelon.

Sanctorale [Latin]. "(Pertaining to) the saints." That portion of a Christian liturgical *book organized by calendar date (rather than the moveable feasts of the *temporale). It primarily provides *propers for saints' feasts, feasts of the Lord on fixed dates excluding *Christmas (e.g., the Annunciation, March 25), and *commons of the saints (providing texts for feasts without their own propers according to various categories of saints, e.g., martyrs). Until the reforms of *Vatican II, the *sanctorale* began with November 28 (the earliest possible first Monday in *Advent); RC books issued after the Council begin with January 1. JMT

Sanctus [Latin]. "Holy." The fourth element in the *ordinary; it is now considered an *acclamation, sung after the *preface in the *eucharistic prayer. The opening text is from Is 6:3. It was a common part of *eucharist in the E by the mid-4th century, and in W a little later. It endured longer than any other part of the ordinary as a congregational song (in some places to the 12th century) and was the last element of the ordinary to be set polyphonically. In the late medieval mass the *Sanctus* was ordinarily divided: the opening section (ending with the *Hosanna*) was sung until the consecration; the *Benedictus qui venit* was sung after the consecration. It retained its traditional place in eucharist of the *BCP, while *Luther placed it after the consecration in his *Formula Missae* (1523); other reformers like *Zwingli elminated it. In the late 20th century, the *Sanctus* or "Holy, holy" has reemerged in newly composed eucharistic prayers of some Protestant denominations. MJG

Sankey, lra David (*b* Edinburgh PA 1840; *d* Brooklyn 1908). *Hymn tune writer and singer who collaborated with *Moody during the great revivals of the 19th century. Sankey composed c 1,200 songs and collected many more. His music, with that of *Bliss, produced the designation *gospel. FJM

Santiago de Compostela, repertory of. In a general sense this refers to the music used in and around the pilgrimage church of St. James in Compostela in NW Spain. In a more specific sense, it refers to a collection of *chant and 20 *polyphonic pieces written in honor of St. James the apostle and contained (along with homiletic, devotional, descriptive pilgrimage material and a letter falsely attributed to Pope Calixtus II, d 1124) in the *Codex Calixtinus* of the Cathedral library in Compostela. The manuscript originated in C France in the mid-12th century, arriving in Compostela c 1173.

Bibl: J. Williams & A. Stone, eds., *The Codex Calixtinus and the Shrine of St. James* (Tübingen, 1992). RTR

Sarum chant. *Chant for *Sarum use. In comparison with other regional W traditions, a relatively late development with the earliest chant books dating from the first half of the 13th century. The chants are essentially the same as those sung elsewhere for the Roman rite, with minor variants in melodic detail such as the tendency to filled-in 3rds. English composers of the late medieval and *Renaissance periods used Sarum chant in *polyphonic settings of *masses, *hymns, votive *antiphons, *Magnificat*s, etc. Sarum use and chant continued into the *Reformation until the English language replaced Latin in the *liturgy.

Bibl: F. L. Harrison, *Music in Medieval Britain,* 2nd ed. (London, 1963); W. H.

Frere, ed., *Antiphonale Sarisburiense,* 6 vols. (London, 1966 [1901–24]); W. H. Frere, *Graduale Sarisburiense* (Farnborough, 1966 [1894]). JMH

Sarum use <Use of Salisbury>. The liturgical tradition originating in the diocese of Salisbury, England. A variant of the Roman rite, it developed under the influence of Norman liturgical practices after the Conquest in 1066 and was subsequently adopted throughout much of the British Isles. Rubrics provide for intricate ceremonies with numerous ministers; 1 special emphasis is elaborate processions. Sarum use provided the basis for the first *BCP. Sarum *chant was the source of many *cantus firmi* for English *polyphony. Among surviving sources are complete manuscripts and printed books, many edited and published, particularly by the Henry Bradshaw Society.

Bibl: W. H. Frere, *The Use of Sarum,* 2 vols. (Farnborough, 1969 [1898-1901]). MSD-JMH

Saul. An *oratorio by *Handel (first performed in 1739) to a libretto by C. Jennens. The text is based on the Hebrew Bible story of King Saul as found in 1–2 Sam. DWM

Sbornik [Slavonic, Greek *anthologion*]. "Collection, anthology." An E rite liturgical *book containing *commons of the *divine office and the more important *propers of Sundays, the *menaion, *octoechos, *pentecostarion and *triodion*. More popular in the Byzantine Slavonic tradition, such books are also known in the Greek tradition. DMP

Scarlatti, (Pietro) Alessandro (Gaspare) (b Palermo 1660; d Naples 1725).

Composer and the father of D. Scarlatti. A leading representative of the late Italian *Baroque, his reputation as the founder of the 18th-century Neapolitan school of opera is probably exaggerated. His patrons included the leading aristocracy of Rome and Naples. A prolific composer, he wrote over 100 operas, more than 600 (mostly secular) *cantatas and much instrumental music. He was *maestro di cappella at a number of churches including St. Mary Major in Rome. His *sacred music includes at least 35 *oratorios on biblical stories and lives of saints, over 70 *motets and 10 *masses. Some of his liturgical works are in a *Palestrina-like *stile antico, some in the newer *concertato style. He also wrote a setting of the *St. John Passion, *lamentations, *Magnificats, a *Stabat Mater and *Te Deum.

Bibl: C. F. Vidali, Alessandro and Domenico Scarlatti (New York, 1993). JDW

Schaff, Philip (b Chur, Switzerland 1819; d New York 1893). Church historian, liturgical scholar and hymnologist. He taught at Mercersburg Seminary with *Nevin and later at Union Seminary. His main works include Principle of Protestantism (1845), The Liturgy (1857), Schaff-Herzog Encyclopedia (1882–1891) and "German Hymnology" in *Julian (1892). PHW

Schalk, Carl Flentge (b Des Plaines IL 1929). Lutheran hymnologist, composer and teacher. His work is closely associated with the Lutheran *chorale tradition. Schalk is also well-known for choral settings of the works of contemporary poets. Among his writings is Luther on Music (1988). RDH

Schantz, Abraham J. (b Kidron OH 1849; d Orrville OH 1921). *Organ builder. Schantz apprenticed as a cabinet maker, then began building reed organs in Kidron OH (1873) before moving to Orville OH (1874). His tracker organs date from 1885–1908. His 3 sons worked for him, assuming control of the company when he retired (1913). JWK

Scheidemann, Heinrich (b Wöhrden c 1595; d Hamburg 1663). Composer, organist and teacher. A pupil of *Sweelinck, he is considered the founder of the N. German *organ school. He was associated with Hamburg's Catharinenkirche from 1629. His contributions to organ music include *chorale settings, 4-movement *Magnificat settings and the development of the *praeambulum. CFS

Scheidt, Samuel (b Halle 1587; d there 1654). *Church music master of the early *Baroque. He studied *organ with *Sweelinck. Scheidt helped introduce church music in the new Italian style into Germany. His major organ works appeared in the 3-volume Tabulatura nova (1624) which presented music in open score rather than in standard organ tablature. His choral collections were in *polychoral style (Cantiones sacrae, 1620) or with innovative *basso continuo (Geistliche Konzerte, 1622). VEG

Schein, Johann Hermann (b Grünhain 1586; d Leipzig 1630). Church musician who served as *Kapellmeister at Weimar (1615), then *Kantor at St. Thomas in Leipzig (from 1616). He wrote expressive, small *concerto-like works for various voices and instruments (Opella nova, 2 vols., 1618, 1626), sacred *motets and a *cantional (1627). VEG

Schlicker Organ Company. *Organ building firm, established in Buffalo NY in 1930 on the organ-renewal principles of German born founder, Herman Schlicker (*d* 1974). The company has evolved to embrace what could be considered an "American eclectic" design philosophy. Schlicker has a major installation at *Valparaiso University. MDJ

Schmieder, Wolfgang (*b* Bromberg 1901; *d* Fürstenfeldbruck 1990). Teacher and librarian. The long-time director of archives at the publisher Breitkopf and Härtel, he founded the music division of the Frankfurt library. Schmieder compiled the *Bach-Werke-Verzeichniß* (BWV) which provides accepted catalog designations for the works of J. S. *Bach. MPB

Schnitger, Arp (*b* Schmalenfleth 1648; *d* Neuenfeld 1719). A prominent builder of some 150 *organs (including that at St. Nicolai, Hamburg) who brought the N German *Baroque organ to its pinnacle of perfection. JBW

Schoenstein, Felix (*b* 1849; *d* 1936). *Organ builder in the San Francisco area who patented a tubular-pneumatic action in 1890. At least 40 Schoenstein organs were destroyed by the 1906 San Francisco earthquake. JWK

Schola [Latin]. "School." (1) A *choir of singers who lead the *chant in worship; abbreviated from **schola cantorum,* but without any necessary reference to that historical institution.

(2) A small group of especially competent singers chosen to perform particularly difficult chants, e.g., the *verse(s) of the *gradual. ADC

Schola cantorum [Latin]. "School of singers." (1) A *choir of singers for the Roman *liturgy established as early as *Gregory the Great, reorganized by Pope Vitalian (*d* 672). The Roman *schola cantorum* included a prior *(primicerius),* 3 assistants *(secundus, tertius* and *quartus),* other adult singers (*parafonistae) and students *(infantes).* The *quartus* (or *archiparofonista*) was responsible for training and assigning *cantors and *lectors; he also served as liaison between the singers and the other ministers during papal masses and stational celebrations of the *divine office. Popes Sergius I (*d* 701) and Sergius II (*d* 847) were trained in the *schola cantorum;* many others from there were invited to teach the Roman chants north of the Alps.

(2) Any **schola.*

(3) A Parisian institution established in 1894 for instruction in chant and *church music; eventually it became a place for specialization in early music and counterpoint.

Bib: S. J. P. van Dijk, "St. Gregory, Founder of the Urban *Schola Cantorum,*" *Ephemerides Liturgicae* 77 (1963) 335–56; J. Leonard, "Easter Vespers in Early Medieval Rome" (University of Notre Dame: Ph.D. diss, 1988) 255–60. JKL

Schöpfungsmesse [German]. See *Creation Mass.

Schreiner, Alexander (*b* Nuremberg 1901; *d* Salt Lake City 1987). A celebrated organist (1924–77) at the Tabernacle on Temple Square in Salt Lake City for The Church of Jesus Christ of Latter-day Saints. MFM

Schubert, Franz (Peter) (*b* Vienna 1797; *d* there 1828). Composer. Beginning as a *choir boy in the imperial chapel, he worked almost entirely in Vienna. He is best-known for numerous songs (some on sacred themes), symphonic and chamber works and piano music. Schubert wrote in the tradition of *Mozart, but with a strong *folk and lyrical quality. His *liturgical music includes 5 large *masses for choir, soloists and *orchestra (in which the text "one, holy, catholic, apostolic church" and other articles of the *Credo are sometimes omitted); several settings of *Tantum ergo, *Salve Regina and *Stabat Mater; some *offertories; 6 choral *antiphons for Palm Sunday; and a *Magnificat. His *Deutsche Messe of 1827 is a *Singmesse, originally for choir. Its congregational arrangement remains popular and has been adopted to various languages, including English.

Bibl: M. J. E. Brown, The New Grove Schubert (New York, 1983); J. Reed, Schubert (London, 1987). AWR

Schübler chorales. Six *organ pieces by J. S. *Bach (BWV 645–650) for 2 manuals and pedal, published by J. G. Schübler (1746 or later) in Zella. Five of the works are transcriptions of *arias from Bach's Leipzig *cantatas. MPB

Schuelke, William (d 1902). *Organ builder who worked in the Milwaukee area. His early *instruments were tracker organs; by 1890 he began to use tubular-pneumatic action. JWK

Schulz, Johann Abraham Peter (b Lüneburg 1747; d Schwedt an der Oder 1800). Composer, conductor and author. He was a student of *Kirnberger, who authored 2 music theory works with him. Schulz was a court composer in Poland, Prussia and Denmark where he produced *cantatas, *oratorios and other sacred vocal works. RDH

Schutte, Dan (b 1947 Neenah WI). *Pastoral musician and composer of popular *liturgical music. He was an original member of the *St. Louis Jesuits. Among his well-known liturgical compositions is "Here I Am, Lord." JBF

Schütz, Heinrich (b Köstriz 1585; d Dresden 1672). Composer. He began as a choirboy at the court chapel in Kassel (1599). He entered Marburg University (1609), but was soon sent to Venice by a patron to study with G. *Gabrieli. He became court organist in Kassel (1612), then *Kapellmeister at the Dresden electoral court (1617). Schütz later visited Italy (1628–29) where he studied with *Monteverdi. Since the Thirty Years' War reduced Dresden's court life, he became court conductor in Copenhagen (1633–35, 37–38, 42–45). He continued to compose in his retirement (1656).

Opera and ballet works are lost. His sacred works continue the *polychoral tradition and introduce monody's dramatic style. Except for large works like 3 *passions, Christmas and Easter *oratorios and Seven Words, all were useful in worship, including 2 *Magnificats, 138 4-part *psalms, 40 Latin sacred songs, 61 small sacred *concertos, 20 Latin and 22 German concertos, 10 *hymn settings and 6 funeral *motets.

Bibl: H. J. Moser, Heinrich Schütz, trans. C. F. Pfatteicher (St. Louis, 1959); G. Spagnoli, Letters and Documents of Heinrich Schütz, 1656–72 (Rochester, 1992). JLB

Schwab, Mathias (d 1864). *Organ builder. He opened a factory in Cincinnati (1831); his most important installation was at the RC Cathedral in St. Louis (1838). In 1860 the firm became Koehnken & Sons.   JWK

Schweitzer, Albert (*b* Kaysersberg, Upper Alsace 1875; *d* Lambaréné, Gabon 1965). Organist, *Bach scholar, theologian, physician, humanitarian and Lutheran pastor. His *The Art of Organ Building and Organ Playing in Germany and France* (1906) helped launch a movement to reform *organ building. He edited *J. S. Bach, Complete Organ Works: A Critico-Practical Edition* with *Widor (vols. 1–5, 1912–14) and Nies-Berger (vols. 6–8, 1954–67). Schweitzer was awarded the Nobel Peace Prize in 1952.   RKW

SDG. See *Sacred Dance Guild.

Second Vatican Council. See *Vatican (Council) II.

Sedalen [Slavonic]. "Sessional hymn." In the Byzantine Slavonic *liturgy, a *hymn sung at the end of a section of the *psalter. See *kathisma.   DMP

Seder [Hebrew]. "Order." (1) The evening meal on *Pesach when the *haggadah is read; here *seder* refers to the "order" of events in the meal. The biblical command to remember the Exodus from Egypt (Deut 16:3) is fulfilled through the various activities of the *seder*. Retelling the Exodus story is the ritual focus accompanied by the drinking of 4 cups of wine, washing, eating of vegetables, *matzah* and bitter herbs.

(2) More generally a prayer book (usually called *siddur*) or the order for reciting prayers.   MLK

Selah [Hebrew]. "Forever." A term which frequently occurs in the book of Psalms where it appears as a proclamation at the end of many *psalms. It is thought to be a musical instruction, possibly to the *Levites who recited psalms in the *Temple (e.g., to lift up their voices?). Jews often leave the term untranslated when it appears in psalms.   MLK

Selicha <*seliha*> (pl. **selichot**) [Hebrew]. "Forgive." (1) A *Jewish prayer mode. A dramatic variant of the psalm *mode used for penitential prayers, it has both major and minor scalar characteristics.

(2) Prayers of forgiveness recited on *Yom Kippur;* the section of the *liturgy that includes these is called *selichot.* Traditionally these prayers are recited beginning at midnight of Saturday the week before *Rosh Hashanah* and everyday until *Yom Kippur,* except on the *Sabbath. In *Sephardic practices *selichot* are recited during the entire month *(Elul)* that precedes *Rosh Hashanah.* Most of the texts were written during the *Middle Ages and follow the poetic devices of the *piyyutim.*   AJB-MLK

Semantron [Greek]. "Gong" [Slavonic *bilo,* "something beat, struck"]. A wooden board or metal plate placed outside Byzantine churches that is struck, according to elaborate rubrics, to announce the beginning of various kinds of *services. It was introduced during the Muslim occupation of E Christian territories, when the use of bells was forbidden to Christians.   DMP-JMT

Semechim betseitam [Hebrew]. "Glad as they go forth." The final 5 lines of the *El Adon *piyyut added to the *liturgy for the *Sabbath. In the Middle E

*Sephardic tradition this text is highlighted musically in the *makam of the day.   MLK

Senfl <Senfelius>, **Ludwig** (b Basel? c 1486; d Munich 1542–43). Composer whose *liturgical music was used by RCs and Lutherans. He began as a choirboy in the imperial court of Maximilian I, succeeding *Isaac as Kapellmeister there by 1513. From 1523 he served Duke Wilhelm of Bavaria. Senfl sympathized with *Luther's reforms. His music reflects the older style of *Isaac and *Josquin and the newer styles of the early *Reformation.   RAL

Sephardic [Hebrew]. "From Spain." This term was originally used to refer to Jews of Spain; it has now come to refer to all non-*Ashkenazic Jews, including Jews of the Arab world. Since the expulsion of Jews from Spain (1492), Spanish Jewry has spread its influence to Jewish communities worldwide. Liturgical texts of the Sephardic tradition differ slightly from Ashkenazic practices. On Sephardic *liturgy see *El hahodaot, *Nishmat kol chai, *Rau banim, *Semechim betseitam and *Shavat aniyim; for musical practices, see *Bakkashah, *Lachan, *makam and *Pizmon.   MLK

Sepulchrum play [Latin]. "Tomb" play. A liturgical *drama enacting the burial and resurrection of Jesus, originating within medieval liturgical celebrations of the *Triduum. *Quem quaeritis is a well-known example.   ADC

Sequence [Latin sequentia]. (1) A liturgical text sung after the *alleluia or *tract in the Roman rite *eucharist. Hiley suggests that there are so many opinions about its origins that providing one is impractical. In general these were poetic texts, most with parallel *verse structure, providing an extended reflection on a feast or season. Appearing by the 9th century, one of their most famous authors was *Notker Babulus. Though ordinarily sung by the *choir or *schola, vernacular paraphrases developed which were sometimes interpolated, with the congregation singing 1 vernacular *strophe after each Latin strophe. By the *Reformation thousands of sequences existed. The 1570 Roman Missal retained only 4: *Victimae paschale laudes (*Easter), *Veni Sancte Spiritus (*Pentecost), Lauda Sion (Corpus Christi) and *Dies irae (*Requiem); a later revision added *Stabat Mater (The Seven Sorrows of Mary). The 1970 Roman Missal retained 4 (though Lauda Sion and Stabat Mater were made optional); Dies irae was transferred to various *hours of the *divine office for the 34th week of Ordinary Time.

(2) The repetition of a melodic phrase or harmonic progression at different pitches.

Bibl: R. Crocker, "Sequence," NGDMM 17:141–51; D. Hiley, Western Plainchant (Oxford, 1993).   JMT

Serbian Orthodox worship music. The *liturgical music of the Serbian Orthodox Church. Before the founding of monasteries of Studenica (in Serbia after 1183) and Chilandarion (on Mount Athos in 1198), Serbian *chant is indistinguishable from Slavonic chant (see *Russian and Slavonic chant). Chants in honor of Serbian saints are found as early as the 13th century, and Serbian composers known from the 14th century: notably Joachim, domestikos of Serbia (*fl* 1347–85) and Isaiah the Serb (15th century). Important anthologies containing bilingual Greek-Serbian chants date from the 15th century. *Polyphony appeared in some Serbian churches in the mid-19th century.

Bibl: D. Stefanovic, *Old Serbian Music*, 2 vols. (Belgrade, 1975). RGD

Service. (1) Any worship event or *liturgy (see *akoluthia, *ordo and *seder).

(2) A musical setting of the parts of the liturgy that are to be sung.

(3) A term referring to the musical setting of liturgical texts for *morning and *evening prayer and *holy communion in the Anglican Church. A service setting could include some or all of the following parts: [for morning prayer] *Venite, *Te Deum, *Benedicite, *Benedictus and *Jubilate; [for evening prayer] *Magnificat, Cantate Domino, *Nunc dimittis and Deus misereatur; [for holy communion] *Kyrie, *Gloria, *Credo, *Sanctus, *Benedictus and *Agnus Dei. A complete setting of the music for morning and evening prayer and holy communion is a "full" service. A "short" service is distinguished from a "long" or "great" service by the scale or grandeur of music rather than the number of texts set (e.g., *Byrd's *Short Service* and *Great Service* set the same 7 texts for morning prayer). EBF

Sessional hymn. See *kathisma.

Sessions, Roger H(untington) (*b* Brooklyn 1896; *d* Princeton 1985). Composer, teacher, critic, editor and author. He studied with H. *Parker and *Bloch. Sessions taught at various schools including Princeton (1933–44, 53–65) and Juilliard (1965–85). His religious compositions include *Mass for Unison Choir* (1955), *Psalm 140* (1963) and *Three Choruses on Biblical Texts* (1975). RJS

Seven Last Words. The sayings of Jesus from the cross, found in the 4 *gospels. Musical settings include those by *Schütz, F. J. *Haydn and *Gounod. RKW

Seventh-Day Adventist worship music. *Hymn singing, originally *a cappella, has been central to Adventist worship from their beginning (1844), though they have no prescribed worship form. *Organs were accepted for hymn accompaniment by the 1870s. *Choirs and singing evangelists were also utilized to support congregational singing. Adventists borrowed freely from the *hymnody of other Protestant denominations. RJS

Sext [from Latin *hora sexta,* "sixth hour"]. Midday prayer in the Roman rite *divine office. The second of the *little hours, its basic structure in the present Roman rite is: opening *dialogue and *doxology, midday *hymn, *psalmody, scripture reading, *collect and concluding *acclamation. JMJ

Shacharit <*shaharit*> [Hebrew]. "Morning." (1) Jewish morning prayer. Rabbinic literature attributes *shacharit* to Abraham; this prayer period is also identified with the morning offering made in the *Temple of Jerusalem. It may be recited any time during the first quarter of the daylight hours, and contains the *Birchot hashachar, *Pesukei dezimrah, *Shema and its *blessings, *Amidah, sometimes *Torah reading and may be followed by *musaf.

(2) Technically the core portion of Jewish morning prayer, i.e., the *Shema and its blessings and the *Amidah. SJW

Shaker worship music. The Shakers, or The United Society of Believers in Christ's Second Appearing, was an 18th-century English millenarian movement. Ann Lee (*d* 1784) established the movement in N America (near Albany) in 1774. Their worship consisted of spontaneous song, dancing, shaking (thus, their name), shouting, *tongues and prophesying. Under Joseph Meachem, a community leader after Lee's death, Shaker worship was reshaped. During much of the 19th century, worship consisted of silent prayer, exhortation, congregational song, laboring exercises (dances), testimonies and spontaneous gifts of the Spirit.

The Shakers used popular *folk tunes for their songs, and new tunes were created or "given" to mediums in the community. *Millennial Praises* (1813) was their first *hymnal. Nearly all texts were "gifts" from the spiritual realm or written for specific instruction, borrowing little textually from other sources. Shakers produced 8,000 to 10,000 *hymns, recorded in *c* 800 manuscripts. Researchers have classified these as: hymns, *anthems, dance (laboring) songs, wordless solemn songs, occasional songs (e.g., for funerals), and songs of departed leaders or others in the heavenly realms (often given in nonsense syllables or tongues). Singing was *monophonic, without accompaniment; in the late 19th century small *organs were permitted for teaching singing; organ accompaniment helped introduce 4-part singing. Shakers had little impact on religious music in N America. Best-known is the Shaker hymn "'Tis a gift to be simple," popularized by *Copland in *Appalachian Spring.*

Bibl: E. D. Andrews, *The People Called Shakers* (New York 1953, 1963); D. W. Patterson, *The Shaker Spiritual* (Princeton, 1979).   RJS

Shalom aleichem <'aleikhem> [Hebrew]. "Peace unto you." A *hymn designed to welcome and seek the blessings of angels believed to escort Jewish worshippers to and from the synagogue on the *Sabbath; described in the Talmud (*Shabbat* 119b). It was introduced by the Kabbalists (see *Kabbalah) of the 16th century.   SJW

Shalom rav [Hebrew]. "(Grant) abundant peace." The last *benediction of the *Amidah of *ma'ariv. Due to its brevity and universal theme of peace, its text and traditional melody have gained widespread appeal; well known settings are by J. Klepper, *Steinberg and others.   BES

Shalosh Regalim. See *Three Festivals.

Shape-note <buckwheat, character or patent notation>. A method of musical notation using distinctively shaped note heads for degrees of the movable "do" scale. This system appeared in English *psalm *tune books by the 16th century. In the US, 4 shapes were matched with the solmization syllables fa-so-la-mi in *The Easy Instructor* (1802) by W. *Little and W. H. *Smith. This method, increasing beginner's ability to read music at sight, became the standard for many tune books compiled in the early 19th century for use in S and Midwestern *singing schools. *The Christian Minstrel* (1846) by J. Aikin was the first popular tune book with 7 shapes to match more closely conventional notation.

Bibl: H. Eskew and J. Downey, "Shapenote Hymnody," *NGDAM* 4:201-5.   RJS

Shavat aniyim [Hebrew]. "Cry of the impoverished." A prayer of **shacharit* which acknowledges that God hears the weak and brings them joy. It is highlighted musically among *Sephardic Jews; Jews from the Middle E render it in the **makam* of the day. The parallel in *Ashkenazic worship is **Shochen ad.*   MLK

Shavuot <*Shabuot,* Feast of Weeks, Pentecost> [Hebrew]. "Weeks." The second of the *Three Festivals, celebrating the giving of the Torah, the most important event in Jewish history. In biblical times it was a festival of thanksgiving for the grain harvest. Tradition teaches that God gave the Commandments to the Jews on the sixth day of the Hebrew month of *Sivan,* celebrated as the first night of *Shavuot.* In commemoration, many Jews convene for a special all-night study session called *Tikkun l'eil Shavuot.* The *Shavuot* *liturgy includes the reading of the Commandments (Ex 19–20) and the recitation of *Hallel. The Book of Ruth is read because of its association with the harvest season and the birthday of King *David, a descendant of Ruth. During the Torah service, **Akdamut* is recited.   SIW

Shawn, Ted (*b* Kansas City MO 1891; *d* Eustis FL 1972). Dancer. With his wife *St. Denis he cofounded the Denishawn School in Los Angeles (1917), later in New York; also the Denishawn Dancers. His dances used many religious themes

and were performed both on stage and in churches.   MAK

Shea, George Beverly (*b* Winchester, Canada 1909). Evangelistic singer and *gospel *hymn writer. Shea was a featured soloist for various radio programs and Billy Graham evangelistic crusades. He popularized "How Great Thou Art" and wrote the music for "I'd Rather Have Jesus" and other songs.   DWM

Sheliach tsibbur <*sheliah tzibbur*> [Hebrew]. "Messenger of the congregation." The one who leads the synagogue *service. This role can be filled by a **chazzan* or anyone else properly trained.   SJW

Shema <*Sh'ma*> [Hebrew]. "Hear." The **incipit* of Deut 6:4 ("Hear O Israel: Adonai is our God, Adonai the One and Only"). This fundamental statement of Jewish faith in one God, which must be recited every morning and evening, is joined to 3 other biblical passages (Deut 6:5-9; 11:13-21; Num 15:37-41) which together comprise the *Shema* proper.

It is framed by a series of *blessings. During **shacharit* the *Shema* is placed after the **Barechu* and before the **Amidah.* Two blessings (**Yotser*) precede the *Shema* and 1 blessing (*Tsur Yisrael*) follows. During **ma'ariv,* the *Shema* is preceded by 2 similar blessings and followed by 2.

It is a general Jewish practice for the congregation to recite the opening line of the *Shema* (a melody by *Sulzer is commonly employed for this in many *Ashkenazic communities). In the Ashkenazic tradition the first of the 3 paragraphs is recited aloud, the other 2 silently. In the *Sephardic tradition all 3 paragraphs are recited aloud. In *Reform

Judaism a shortened version of the 3 paragraphs is found. In all traditions the recitation is done according to the *cantillation system following the *ta'amim.

The first sentence of the Shema is recited during the *liturgy in 2 other instances: when the Torah is taken out of the ark (during the *High Holidays a special melody is used), and during the *Kedushah of *musaf on the *Sabbath, High Holidays and the *Three Festivals.

In both Ashkenazic and Sephardic traditions the singing of the Shema is marked by a change in *mode: in the Ashkenazic tradition the change is from the *ahavah rabbah mode to a major mode for biblical cantillation; in Middle E Sephardic traditions the *makam of the day's liturgy changes to makam sikah which is used to recite the Torah.

Bibl: I. Elbogen, Jewish Liturgy, trans. R. Scheindlin (Philadelphia, 1993 [1913]); L. Hoffman, ed., The Sh'ma and its Blessings (Woodstock VT, 1997); N. Lamm, The Shema (Philadelphia, 1998). MLK

Shema koleinu [Hebrew]. "Hear our voice." (1) The sixteenth blessing of the daily version of the *Amidah. When the Amidah is repeated at *shacharit and *minchah this prayer is chanted in the weekday *mode. In some congregations the middle 13 paragraphs of the Amidah recited during minchah are chanted in minor mode with *Ukranian-Dorian inflections, a practice thought to be of *Hasidic origin.

(2) a prayer recited before the *Vidui of the *selichot and *Yom Kippur *services (except *Ne'ilah), chanted in the *selicha mode. IAG

Shemini atzeret <'atseret> [Hebrew]. "Eighth day of solemn assembly." The last day of *Sukkot. Its major liturgical feature is the recitation of *Geshem during *musaf. It is also traditional to recite *Yizkor on this day. See *Simchat Torah. SIW

Shemoneh Esrei <Esreh>. See *Amidah.

Shenker, Ben Zion (b Brooklyn 1925). Composer and *cantor. Raised in the Williamsburg section of Brooklyn, he sang with many great cantors of the Golden Age (see *chazzan). Immersed in the music of the Modzitz Hasidim (see *Hasidic music) he recorded albums of Modizitz and original melodies. Many of these melodies are heard frequently in the synagogue. MLK

Shestopsalmie [Slavonic]. See *hexapsalmos.

Shirah <Shirat hayam> [Hebrew]. "Singing, poetry." Though employed across a spectrum of usage, the term ordinarily refers to *Az yashir Moshe. MLK

Shir hama'alot [Hebrew]. "Song of ascents." The superscription on Pss 120–134, which probably indicates that these *psalms were sung while going up to Jerusalem (Christians call these *gradual psalms). From this group, Ps 126 is sung before the *Birkat hamazon on *Sabbaths and festivals. Well-known settings of Ps 126 are by P. Minkowsky and *Rosenblatt. BES

Shir Hashirim [Hebrew]. "Song of Songs." The first of the 5 *Megilot in the Hebrew Bible. Traditionally attributed to King Solomon, modern scholarship dates it after the Exile. It is an allegorical love story between the people of Israel and God. In the *Ashkenazic tradition it is recited publicly on the *Sabbath of the week of *Pesach; in the *Sephardic and *Hasidic traditions it is recited during *Kabbalat Shabbat. Parts of the text are the basis for songs commonly sung at wedding ceremonies (e.g., 6.3).   MLK

Shochen ad [Hebrew]. "Who abides forever." The first of 3 paragraphs in *Sabbath *shacharit that follow the *Pesukei dezimrah section and precede the *Barechu. It is customary for the *cantor to begin shacharit at this point. The section of shacharit from Shocken ad through *El Adon is recited in the *magein avot *mode.   IAG

Shofar [Hebrew]. "Ram's horn." An instrument mentioned throughout the Hebrew Bible for signaling important occasions, e.g., the giving of the Torah (Ex 19:16-19), announcing the jubilee year (Lev 25:9) or New Year (Lev 23:34), calling people to battle (Jer 4:5) and to fasting (Ps 81:4). After the destruction of the Temple (70 CE) it was used to announce a death and signal the end of work before the *Sabbath. It is an important symbol in mystical writings (see *Kabbalah) since it signals the call to repent.

Today it is sounded at the end of the *Yom Kippur *service. In the *Ashkenazic tradition it is sounded after *shacharit during the month of Elul preceding *Rosh Hashanah (except on Sabbaths). In the *Sephardic tradition it is sounded on Hoshanah Rabbah, the final day of *Sukkot.

The shofar is prominent on Rosh Hashanah, alternately called Yom hateruah ("a day of sounding [the shofar]"). Prior to *musaf on Rosh Hashanah the shofar is sounded with several blasts in what is commonly called the "Shofar Service" (several compositions have been written for this service in *Reform Judaism). Musaf is expanded with the addition of biblical verses grouped into 3 sections: kingship (malchuyot), remembrance (zichronot) and shofar blowing (shofarot). Each of these is concluded with a *blessing, a sounding of the shofar, and congregational singing of *Hayom harat olam.

Soundings are combinations of 3 different types of blasts: tekiah ("blast"), a sustained tone; shevarim ("breaks"), 3 disconnected sounds; teruah ("blare"), 9 staccato notes. On Rosh Hashanah the final sounding is an elongated tiekiah gedolah ("great blast"). The proper length, quality and amount of sounds are discussed at length in rabbinic literature.

Bibl: A. Lewis, "Shofar," EJ 14:1442–47; M. Nulman, Concise Encyclopedia of Jewish Music (New York, 1975) 229–33.   MLK

Shofarot. See *shofar.

Short responsory [Latin responsorium breve]. The *responsory which occurred in the Roman secular *office after readings at *little hours and compline, and in monastic office at *lauds and *vespers as well. Currently it occurs after the readings at morning, evening and night prayer. Its standard structure is: *respond–respond–*verse–*repetendum–*lesser doxology–response. In today's Roman rite *plainsong books there are 2 basic musical formulas for these: *mode 4 (for *Advent), and mode 6 (for other times, slightly elaborated during *Easter). JMT

Short service. See *service.

Shtyger. See *Jewish prayer modes.

Siddur. See *seder.

Silbermann, Andreas (b Kleinbobritzsch 1678; d Strasbourg 1734). The builder of many important *organs in the French classical style in the vicinity of Strasbourg, and the older brother of G. *Silbermann. JBW

Silbermann, Gottfried (b Kleinbobritzsch 1683; d Dresden 1753). An important builder of *organs and other *keyboard *instruments who brought the art of the S German *Baroque organ to its highest point. He was the younger brother of A. *Silbermann. JBW

Simchat <*Simḥat*> **Torah** [Hebrew]. "Rejoicing with the Torah." The holiday which comes at the end of *Sukkot (the day after *Shemini atzeret), marking the yearly completion of the reading of the Torah scroll (see *Torah reading). In Israel, *Simchat Torah* and *Shemini atzeret* are celebrated on the same day; this is also the practice in *Reform Judaism. The holiday is observed with singing and dancing during *ma'ariv and *shacharit. Seven *hakkafot celebrate the joy of Torah. In the *Ashkenazic and *Sephardic traditions special songs are sung. MLK

Simmons, William Benjamin Dearborn (b Cambridge 1823; d there 1867). *Organ builder. He was one of the first in the US to employ a full-compass

*swell division and advocate the use of tempered tuning. JWK

Sim shalom [Hebrew]. "Grant peace." A prayer from the last *benediction of the *Amidah* in *shacharit*, sung to many tunes (*Ashkenazic, *Sephardic and *Hassidic) by congregations. It has been set for *cantor and *choir by *Janowski and others. BES

Singenberger, John (b Kirchberg, Switzerland 1848; d Milwaukee 1924). Organist, choral director, composer and teacher. A proponent of the *Cecilian movement, he was trained in *Regensburg, then moved to Milwaukee (1872) where he became a national leader in RC *church music. He wrote much *liturgical music (*motets, *hymns, *masses, etc.), and frequently contributed to journals such as *The Caecilian* and *Review for Church Music*. EBF

Singing by rule <"regular vs. usual singing">. A controversy which erupted in Puritan New England in the early 18th century. The clergy objected to the way congregations sang *psalms in their jurisdiction and started a movement to teach people to read music. The people wished to maintain the highly decorated and idiosyncratic way of singing (a form of group improvisation) and resented efforts of learned clergy to eradicate their singing style. The resulting conflict divided clergy and laity, urban and rural cultures. The clergy's efforts toward general musical education fueled the establishment and maintenance of *singing schools throughout the region. LJC

Singing in the Spirit <tongues>. See *tongues, singing in.

Singing school. A month or more of music instruction (largely part-singing of *psalms) under an itinerant master during colonial times. The movement originated in 1722 to overcome musical illiteracy in congregations (see *singing by rule).   VEG

Singmesse [German] "Sing-mass." A set of several congregational *hymns sung during *mass, more or less related to the *ordinary and *proper. With roots in the 16th–17th centuries, the practice of the *Singmesse* became widespread in German speaking, Hungarian and Slavic lands, especially because of 18th-century RC efforts to increase vernacular singing and supplant Latin *chant.   AWR

Sistine Chapel [Latin *Cappella Sistina*]. The main papal chapel in the Vatican, built (1475–83) under Pope Sixtus IV, from whom it derives its name. Michelangelo's frescoes of the Creation (1508–12) and Last Judgment (1536–41) are artistic landmarks of the *Renaissance. The chapel's *choir traces its lineage to the *schola cantorum;* Pope Leo X (*d* 1521) expanded the number of the chapel choir to 32. The chapel does not have an *organ and by tradition the choir sings without instrumental accompaniment. The term *a cappella* is thought to derive from this practice. Chapel musicians have included *Josquin, *Festa, *Morales, *Arcadelt, *Palestrina and *Victoria.
   Bibl: C. Pietrangeli et al., *The Sistine Chapel* (New York, 1986).   MEC

Skinner, Ernest M. (*b* Clarion PA 1866; *d* Duxbury MA 1960). *Organ builder. Originally employed as a draftsman in the *Hutchings' firm, he left to found E. M. Skinner Co. in Boston

(1901). Skinner obtained the contract for New York's Cathedral of St. John the Divine in 1910. Donald Harrison (1889–1956) entered the firm in 1927; in 1932 the firm became Aeolian-Skinner Organ Co. Under Harrison's leadership, the company became renowned for its *instruments. It closed in 1971.   JWK

Slavoslovie [Slavonic]. See *doxologia.*

Sluzhebnik [Slavonic]. See *eucholo-gion.*

Small compline. See *apodeipnon mikron.*

Small litany. See *malaya ekteniya.*

Small synapte. See *synapte.*

Small vespers. See *malaya verchernya.*

Smallwood, Richard (*b* Atlanta 1948). Pianist, singer, composer and arranger of African American *gospel music and *spirituals. He studied at Howard University. A black gospel stylist, he combines black traditional music with European classical idioms. He founded and directed the Richard Smallwood Singers, then the group Vision.   MEM

Smith, Emma (*b* Harmony PA 1804; *d* Nauvoo IL 1879). Wife of Joseph Smith, the prophet who founded The Church of Jesus Christ of Latter-day Saints. She was commissioned to prepare the Church's first *hymn collection, *A Collection of Sacred Hymns for the Church of the Latter Day Saints* (1835).   MFM

Smith, Willie Mae Ford (*b* Rolling Fort MS 1904; *d* St. Louis 1994). Singer, composer of African American gospel music, evangelist, teacher and recording artist. A seminal force in shaping gospel singing styles, she is celebrated in the gospel documentary film *Say Amen, Somebody*. Smith received the National Heritage Award from the National Educational Association in 1988.   MEM

Snetzler, John (*b* Schaffhausen 1710; *d* there 1785). *Organ builder who settled in England in 1746 where he built organs for the Moravian Brethren; later he became the official organ builder to George III. Many of Snetzler's *instruments were exported to the colonies before the American Revolution.   JWK

Society of St. Cecilia [German *Cäcilien-Verein*]. An organization formed to advance the aims of the *Cecilian movement. Founded in Bamberg (1868) under F. Witt, it received papal confirmation in *Multum ad commovendos animos*. Similar societies were organized throughout Europe; in the US *Singenberger founded the American Cecilian Society (1873).   AWR

Society of the Solitary Brethren. See *Ephrata Cloister.

Sola, Carla de (*b* New York 1937). Dancer, choreographer, writer and teacher. A graduate of Juilliard, she teaches on the faculty at the Pacific School of Religion in Berkeley. She has been a leader in the development of liturgical *dance and *movement prayer in the 20th century. De Sola founded the *Omega Dancers.   JBF-MAK

Solemn high mass. See *missa solemnis*.

Solesmes. The Benedictine abbey of St. Peter; originally a priory from its founding (1010) until its suppression (1791). The abbey was refounded by *Guéranger (1833) and it became a center for monastic liturgical renewal; its name is synonymous with the reform of *Gregorian chant, especially under the leadership of J. Pothier and *Mocquereau, and through the publications of *Paléographie musicale* and *Études grégoriennes*. It was largely the work of *Solesmes that generated the *Vatican edition of chant, displacing the *Medicean edition as the official authorized version.   ADC

Solomon, Odes of. A pseudepigraphical work, probably late 2nd-century Syrian in origin, composed in either Greek or Syriac. It consists of 42 short *hymns possessing the same general character as the canonical *psalms. The Odes were probably Christian in origin, though some thoughts and expressions lend themselves to Gnostic interpretations. They contain many allusions to baptism, though it is questionable whether they were baptismal hymns.   CFS

Solomon, Psalms of. A Jewish pseudepigraphical collection of 18 *psalms. Though extant only in Greek, they were most likely written in Hebrew, probably between 70–40 BCE. The last 2 psalms are important in that they predict the coming of a Messiah of the house of David.   CFS

Son [Spanish]. "Sound." A generic term associated with various types of Spanish regional music. The term indicates a manner rather than a repertoire (e.g., *bolero-son, merengue-son*). The peculiarities in rhythmic patterns or *matriz* (Spanish, "beat") enable the listener to recognize the particular musical form or style of the *son*. MFR

Sonata da chiesa. See *church sonata.

Song of Moses. See *Az yashir Moshe.*

Song of Songs. See *Shir Hashirim.*

Song of the Sea. See *Az yashir Moshe.*

Sono [Latin]. "To sound." In *Visigothic and *Mozarabic liturgies, a *melismatic *hymn sung at *lauds or *vespers after the *psalmody. In the Gallican *eucharist the *sonus* (like the **Cherubikon*) was sung during the procession of gifts to the altar. JLK

Souterliedekens [Dutch]. "Little psalter songs." An early and complete *metrical psalter in Dutch published by S. Cock (Antwerp, 1540). The texts, betraying Lutheran influences, are set mostly to popular European *folk melodies. This *psalter was frequently reprinted until the early 17th century; *polyphonic settings of its melodies were composed by *Clemens non Papa, among others. RAL

Southern Harmony. An American *shape-note oblong *tune book using *fasola solmization. It was compiled and edited by W. "Billy" Walker (1835; 2nd ed. 1847; 3rd ed. 1854). It included *hymns, *anthems, and 3- and 4-part *fuging tunes for *singing school, church and social use. A source for other S tune books, it is still used at the yearly Big Singing Day in Benton KY. RJS

Sowerby, Leo (*b* Grand Rapids MI 1895; *d* Port Clinton OH 1968). Composer, organist and teacher. He studied in Chicago (beginning in 1909) and then in Italy (1921–24) as the first recipient of the American Prix de Rome fellowship for music. Sowerby taught composition at the American Conservatory in Chicago (1925–62) while serving as organist and choirmaster at St. James' Anglican Cathedral (1927–62). He founded the College of Church Musicians in Washington DC (1962).

Besides major orchestra works (5 symphonies, 2 piano *concertos, violin concerto, etc.), Sowerby composed 2 *organ concertos, *Symphonia Brevis* for *organ, *c* 120 *anthems, several *communion services and numerous *cantatas including the Pulitzer Prize winning *Canticle of the Sunday* (1944).

Bibl: R. Huntington, "A Study of the Musical Contributions of Leo Sowerby" (University of Southern California: Ph.D. diss., 1957). EBF

Spencer, Jon Michael (*b* Amherst 1957). African American musician, hymnologist and theologian. Spencer developed the concept of *theomusicology. The founding editor of the journal *Black Sacred Music,* he has also authored various works on black culture and music, e.g., *Protest and Praise* (1990) and *Blues and Evil* (1993). RJS

Spiritual. An abbreviated name for spiritual song (Eph 5:19, Col 3:16). Originally it was a spontaneous song improvised in moments of intense spiritual feeling that melds the social, cultural and religious influences of a people into a distinctive *folk idiom.

Black spirituals are the most prevalent type found in North America. Forged in the midst of slavery, Christian indoctrination and 19th-century revivalism, these songs express the dignity, hope, resistance and faith of an oppressed people. They are songs that create a deep sense of community solidarity and identity. Their origins are in the praise houses or brush arbor meetings of slave communities. Recurring features of these spirituals include: a *call and response form; complex rhythmic structure usually with syncopation; ornamented melodic lines; improvised harmonization; flatted 3rds, 5ths and 7ths; some type of bodily accompaniment (e.g., dancing, clapping, swaying, foot tapping, moaning); and freedom in modifying any element of the song. Words for spirituals were improvised or drawn from well-known *hymn texts, most notably those of *Watts and C. *Wesley. The words served various communicative purposes within the slave community and black church. They could be intended literally or metaphorically, or signal other alternative meanings known only to the members of the community. The body of black spirituals is a primary indigenous musical form kept alive in North America.

White spirituals arose out of 19th-century revivalist *camp meetings. Secular tunes or melodic fragments, often of Celtic influence, were sung with religious texts, either improvised or drawn from hymns (often, again, those of Watts and C. Wesley). These songs nearly always included a *refrain that could be separated and used with other songs. The tunes for these spirituals were simple, repetitive and frequently pentatonic. Many white spirituals were written down eventually and included in *shape-note *tune books.

Bibl: P. K. Maultsby, "The Use and Performance of Hymnody, Spirituals, and Gospels in the Black Church," *The Western Journal of Black Studies* 7:3 (1983) 161–71; J. Downey and P. Oliver, "Spiritual," in NGDAM 4:284–90; J. Cone, *The Spirituals and the Blues* (New York, 1991 [1972]).   RJS

Stabat mater dolorosa [Latin]. "The sorrowful mother stood." A 13th-century poem of disputed authorship (often ascribed to the Franciscan Jacopone da Todi) addressing the sorrows of Mary at Calvary. It was gradually employed in worship during the later *Middle Ages, and officially approved in 1727 as a *sequence for the 2 feasts of the Seven Sorrows of the BVM and as an *office *hymn for those days. Currently it serves as an optional sequence for the Feast of Our Lady of Sorrows (September 15).   VAL

Staden, Johann (*b* Nuremberg 1581; *d* there 1634). Composer and organist. His works encompass the evolving forms of the early *Baroque. His *Harmoniae sacrae* (1616) includes some of the earliest sacred *concertos in Germany.   RDH

Stainer, John (*b* London 1840; *d* Verona 1901). Composer, organist and scholar. Stainer was organist at London's St. Paul's Cathedral (1872–88), then professor of music at Oxford (from 1889) where he pursued research in medieval music. His numerous compositions for Anglican usage include *anthems, *hymns, *services and the *oratorio *The *Crucifixion* (1887).   FJM

Stanford, Charles Villiers (*b* Dublin 1852; *d* London 1924). Composer, conductor, organist and teacher. Professor at London's Royal College of Music (1885–92) and Cambridge (1887–1924), his students included *Davies, *Holst and *Vaughan Williams. Stanford composed for stage (10 operas), concert hall (7 symphonies) and church (*anthems and *services). His greatest achievements were operas, choral music and songs, providing him an important place in the late 19th-century renaissance of English music.   FJM

Stanley, John (*b* London 1712; *d* there 1786). Organist and composer who was blind from childhood. Notable are his solo *cantatas in the tradition of *Handel and *Corelli, and 3 sets of *organ voluntaries.   RDH

Stanza. Two or more lines of a poem or *hymn, usually with a recurring pattern of *meter and rhyme. See *strophe and *verse.   RKW

Staurosimon [Greek]. "Cross hymn." A rarely used term in the Byzantine *office for a *sticheron sung in honor of the holy cross.   DMP

Staurotheotokion [Greek; Slavonic *krestobogoroditchen*]. "Hymn to the Cross and God-bearer." A *sticheron in the Byzantine *office sung at the end of a series of *stichera* on Wednesday and Friday (days dedicated to the Holy Cross). The last *stichera* in any *service are usually addressed to the Mother of God; these are addressed to Mary standing at the foot of her son's cross.   DMP

Stebbins, George C. (Coles) (*b* East Carlton NY 1846; *d* Catskill NY 1945). Composer, editor, compiler of *gospel

songs, and song leader in revivals of *Moody and *Sankey. With Sankey and J. McGranahan, Stebbins compiled 3 editions of *Gospel Hymns* (1878-91). The music and musicians of the reconstruction-era urban revival are recalled in his *Reminiscences and Gospel Hymn Stories* (1924).   CRY

Steinberg, Ben (*b* Winnipeg 1930). Composer. He was educated at Toronto's Royal Conservatory of Music and the University of Toronto. The director of music at Toronto's Temple Sinai since 1970, he has composed several *services and *cantatas for synagogue including a popular setting of *Shalom rav*.   MLK

Stepenny [Slavonic]. See *anabathmoi*.

Sternhold, Thomas (*b* Awre ?; *d* Slackstead 1549). A royal courtier to *Henry VIII and Edward VI. Sternhold was a pioneering author of English *metrical psalms. See *Sternhold and Hopkins Psalter.   RAL

Sternhold and Hopkins Psalter. *Sternhold's *metrical psalm texts were first issued in London *c* 1547; an expanded edition, with 36 texts by Sternhold and 8 by John Hopkins, appeared in 1549. These 44 texts became the nucleus of the "Old Version" of the psalms, or the Sternhold and Hopkins Psalter, finally completed in 1562.   RAL

Stevens, George (*b* Norway ME 1803; *d* E Cambridge MA 1894). *Organ builder. He worked as a journeyman with *Goodrich, producing a number of small and medium-sized *instruments.   JWK

Sticheron (pl. **stichera**) [Greek; Slavonic *stikhira*]. "Verse." A generic term for ecclesiastical *hymns in the Byzantine *office sung intercalated with *psalm *verses (particularly Pss 141 at *hesperinos and Pss 148–150 at *orthros). From 4 to 10 *stichera* are sung at Ps 141, and from 4 to 8 at Pss 148–50. *Stichera* are also sung at the end of *hesperinos* and *orthros* with specially chosen psalm verses (see *aposticha). Sung according to the *octoechos, they are designated either *homoia or *idiomela.   DMP

Stichologia [Greek; Slavonic]. "Recitation." A system in the Byzantine *office for singing *psalms with *stichera, or biblical *canticles in the *kanon with *troparia. The scriptural text is chanted and from 4 to 14 *stichera* or *troparia* are intercalated with its final verses. One or 2 *stichera* or *troparia* are then added, concluded by the smaller doxology (see *doxologia), which is chanted as 1 *versicle or divided (at "now and forever") to make 2 versicles.   DMP

Stichos [Greek; Slavonic *stich, pripiv*]. "Versicle." (1) A *verse of a *psalm or biblical *canticle in the Byzantine *office.
(2) The verses of a psalm sung with an *allelouiarion or *prokeimenon. See *aposticha.   DMP

Stikhir umilitel'nyi [Slavonic]. See *katanyktikon.

Stikhira [Slavonic]. See *sticheron.

Stikhira evangel'skaya [Slavonic]. See *idiomelon heothinon.

Stikhiry voskresny [Slavonic]. See *anastasima.

Stikhiry vostochny [Slavonic]. See *anatolika.

Stikhoven [Slavonic]. See *aposticha.

Stile antico [Italian]. "Old style." A term that developed in the 17th century for the style of *church music written in imitation of *Palestrina: unaccompanied, *polyphonic vocal music in smooth flowing lines. As distinguished from *stile moderno*.   JBF

Still, William Grant (*b* Woodville MS 1895; *d* Los Angeles 1978). Composer, conductor and arranger. Sometimes called the "Dean of Afro-American composers," he was educated at Oberlin, then studied privately with E. Varèse. Still was the recipient of Guggenheim and Rosenwald fellowships. A prolific composer across musical forms, he arranged *spirituals, composed a choral setting of Ps 29, wrote works for stage, orchestral works including the *Afro-American Symphony* (1930), compositions for voices and orchestra, chamber music and *organ works.   MWC

Stoltzer, Thomas (*b* Schweidnitz *c* 1475–85; *d* near Znaim 1526). Composer, probably the most important in early 16th-century Germany after *Finck and *Hofhaimer. He wrote *masses, *hymns and especially *motets. His compositions were especially popular in Saxony, the center of the *Reformation; *Rhau published at least 70 of them.   CFS

Stop. See *drawstop.

Straube, Karl (*b* Berlin 1873; *d* Leipzig 1950). Organist and teacher. He served as organist in Wesel (1897), then at St. Thomas in Leipzig (1902), where he became **Kantor* after 1918. Professor of organ at Leipzig Conservatory (from 1907), Straube championed **Reger's *organ* music. He also edited sacred choral and organ works.   JLB

Stravinsky, Igor Fyodorovich <Feodorovitch> (*b* Oranienbau 1882; *d* New York 1971). One of the most significant 20th-century composers. He studied with **Rimsky-Korsakov, and early on wrote music for the Ballets Russes (1909–29). Stravinsky lived in Switzerland (1920–39), then the US where he concertized as a pianist and conductor. He composed mainly for ballet, opera, chamber ensembles and orchestra. A few of his works have sacred texts, including **Symphony of Psalms* (1930), *Canticum sacrum* (1955) and *Requiem Canticles* (1965–66). While most were not intended for liturgical use, the **Mass* (1944–48) was written for worship. JLB

Strophe <adj, strophic>. (1) Poetry or **hymnody composed of units (strophes) identical in rhyme, **meter and length.

(2) Music for such poetry or hymnody, repeated for each strophe, common to most **hymns and **folk songs. See **stanza and **verse.   RKW

Sweelinck <Swelinck, Zwelinck>, **Jan Pieterszoon** (*b* Deventer 1562; *d* Amsterdam 1621). Organist, teacher and composer. He studied music with his father and then the countertenor and shawm player J. W. Lossy. Sweelinck served for over 40 years as organist at Oude Kerk in Amsterdam. He taught many Dutch and German organists, including S. **Scheidt. Sweelinck composed some 70 **keyboard and over 250 vocal works. Among his keyboard pieces were **fantasias, **toccatas and variations on **metrical psalm tunes, **chorales and **chants. Sacred choral works included 4 books of **metrical psalm tune arrangements (153 settings in all) and a collection of 39 Latin **motets, the most often performed of which is *Hodie Christus natus est.*

Bibl: F. Noske, *Sweelinck* (Oxford, 1988).   DWM

Sub tuum [Latin]. "Under your [protection]." The oldest known non-biblical Marian prayer text, from the 3rd or 4th century. The prayer is noteworthy both for the intercessory role assigned to Mary and for its impact on subsequent Marian texts. The medieval **antiphon setting of this text became an important part of the devotion to the (Seven) Sorrows of Mary, promoted by the Servite friars.   RTR

Suffrages [Latin *suffragia*]. A series of **antiphons (each followed by **versicle, **response and **collect) recited after **ferial **lauds and **vespers in the medieval **office, honoring saints of local import. They probably developed from the **preces. In the **BCP suffrages were transformed into a series of versicles and responses (devoid of sanctoral references) following the **Lord's Prayer and preceding the collect of the day at **morning and **evening prayer. Many Anglican composers wrote elaborate settings, which required alternation between the officiant and the **choir.   JMT

Sugubaya ekteniya [Slavonic]. See **ektene.

Sukkot <*Sukkoth,* Feast of Ingathering, Feast of Tabernacles> [Hebrew]. "Booths." The last of the *Three Festivals, celebrated from the 15th to 21st (or 22nd) of the Hebrew month of *Tishrei.* Originating as a harvest festival, it came to commemorate the 40-year wandering of the Jews in the desert. Dwelling in the *sukkah* ("booth"), representing the tents in which the Jews lived during their wanderings, is the premier observance. During *Sukkot* special prayers are added to *shacharit* (see *Hoshanot*) and *Hallel* is recited following the Torah service. *Megilat Kohelet* is read on the *Sabbath morning during *Sukkot.* The eighth day of *Sukkot* is *Shemini atzeret.* SIW

Sullivan, Arthur Seymour (*b* Lambeth 1842; *d* London 1900). Composer, conductor, organist and *hymnal editor. He began as a chorister at the *Chapel Royal, and later worked as a church organist (1862–72). Besides his well-known operettas written with W. S. Gilbert, Sullivan wrote *cantatas, *oratorios and *hymn tunes including St. Gertrude. RJS

Sulzer, Salomon (*b* Hohenems 1804; *d* Vienna 1890). Composer and *cantor. An important figure in establishing liturgical music in the modern synagogue, he is often considered the "father of the modern cantorate." He refined synagogue *chant by eliminating melodic excesses through adapting the music to 18th- and 19th-century European styles; in the process he elevated the office of the *chazzan. He also incorporated a 4-part *choir into the synagogue service.

Trained by the cantor from his home town, Sulzer then studied in Switzerland (1817–20). From 1820–25 he created his own synagogue *service. In 1826 he moved to Vienna where, with Rabbi I. N. Mannheimer, he established *Reform Judaism. While in Vienna he studied with von Seyfried (a pupil of F. J. *Haydn) and J. Fischhof.

Sulzer's *Schir Zion* (published in 1840) included original compositions and works of others, including von Seyfried and *Schubert; a second volume was published in 1866. Compositions in these 2 volumes make use of traditional *Jewish prayer modes but the harmonizations are in standard W harmony; later composers (e.g., *Gerovitsh) harmonized Jewish chant according to the Jewish prayer modes.

Many important individuals in Vienna admired Sulzer and came to the synagogue to hear him sing, including *Liszt. Sulzer received many honors and his music was popular throughout Europe. Many of his works are sung today and considered "traditional," e.g., his settings of *Lechah dodi* and *Shema.* MLK

Supplementary songs. A category of musical elements in the reformed RC *mass according to *Music in Catholic Worship* (nn. 70–74) for which there are no specified texts nor any requirements that there be a spoken or sung text. These include the *offertory (later changed to "preparation") song, the *psalm or song after *communion, *recessional and *litanies.   JLK

Svete tichij [Slavonic]. See *Phos hilaron.*

Svetilen [Slavonic]. See *exapostolarion.*

Swell organ. The manual division of the *organ enclosed by a box with louvered shutters opened and closed by the organist via a foot pedal to control volume.   PAJ

Sydnor, James Rawlings (*b* Rome GA 1911). Presbyterian organist, choirmaster, professor of *church music, *hymnal editor and *hymn writer. His numerous books and articles have focused on the use of hymns in worship and improving congregational hymn and music literacy.   RJS

Symbolum [Latin]. "Symbol." A term used from the 4th and 5th centuries onward as a synonym for the Christian *creed or profession of faith.   NDM

Symmes, Thomas (*b* Bradford MA 1678; *d* there 1725). Minister and church music reformer. He published *The Reasonableness of Regular Singing* (1720) and *Utile dulci* (1723), both advocating the reform of Puritan congregational singing.   DWM

Symphonic mass. A setting of the *ordinary characterized by large choral and symphonic forces, movements organized on a symphonic basis, soloists used as ensemble, and the dramatic setting of texts. Such settings developed in the late masses of *Mozart and F. J. *Haydn, and are more fully developed in the works of *Beethoven (*Missa Solemnis*) and *Schubert (Masses in E-flat and in A-flat).   LMT

Symphony of Psalms. A concert piece by *Stravinsky for *chorus and orchestra (without violins or violas) in 3 movements (1930). It was written after the composer's spiritual crisis and a return to his religious tradition (Russian Orthodox). The work draws on Pss 40, 41 and 150.   JBF

Synapte [Greek]. "Joined together" [Slavonic *ekteniya* from Greek **ektene*]. A general term in the Byzantine *liturgy for a *litany, in which the deacon proposes petitions and the congregation responds "Lord, have mercy" or "Grant this, O Lord." The great *synapte* is another term for the **eirenika*. The small *synapte* is a litany of 3 petitions from the great *synapte:* the first (to which the words "again and again" are added at the beginning), and the final 2. The small *synapte* was originally the diaconal introduction to a prayer, expanded when it began to be recited silently. See **aitesis, *diakonika* and **ektene*.   DMP

Syrian churches' worship music. The *liturgical music of Syrian Christian churches, including the Syrian-Antiochene (*Maronite and *Melkite), W Syrian (*Syro-Jacobite) and *E Syrian (*Chaldean and *Syro-Malabar). The Arabic language has been used in addition to Syriac since the 17th century. Melkites are unique in using the Byzantine *liturgy and notation. Other Syrian *chant books generally lack notation. Chant genres differ between E and W Syrian rites, but among those common to both are the *qālā, unithā*, *Trisagion, qānunā* and *madrāshā* (a *strophic *hymn type invented by *Ephrem the Syrian). *Madrāshe* in E and W Syrian traditions share basic melodic features (suggesting a common origin) but vary in embellishment and tuning. Chants are organized in a weekly 8-*mode cycle, with 8 melodies for each chant, but the modal systems of the Syrian churches have been influenced by Arabic scales (*makamat*) and tuning. Simple improvised *polyphony is sung in some Syrian churches.

Bibl: E. Beck, ed., *Ephrem Syri: Hymni* (Louvain, 1955–73); A. Cody, "The Early History of the Octoechos in Syria," *East of Byzantium: Syria and Armenia in the Formative Period,* ed. N. Garsoian et al. (Washington DC, 1982) 88–113. RGD

Syro-Jacobite churches' worship music. The *liturgical music of the Syrian Orthodox (Jacobite) Church, a branch of the W *Syrian church. Each text has 8 musical settings, 1 in each *mode. Modern practice incorporates aspects of Arabic scales (*makamat*). Important *chant genres include the *qālā* (sung between *psalm *verses and followed by a *bā'uthā* or petition), *sedrā* and *prumion* (preceding the *qālā*), *enyānā* (troped psalms), *eqbā, ququlion* and *madrāshā* (*strophic *hymn with *refrain). Troped psalms called *mā'irāne* (vigil songs) are sung at *lelyā* (*matins). Chant books, without notation, include the *šḥīmtā* (daily office), *penqīthō* (Sundays, Lent and feasts) and *Bayth-gazā* (model *stanzas for Sundays and feasts).

Bibl: H. Husmann, *Die Melodien der Jakobitischen Kirche,* 2 vols. (Vienna 1969–71). RGD

Syro-Malabar churches' chant. The *monophonic *liturgical music of the Malabar Christian churches of S India. There are 3 branches: Orthodox, those united with Rome (since 1599), and the Mar Thomas Church (a 19th-century re-

formed branch). The *liturgy is of E Syrian origin, but much has been translated into Malayalam. The genres of *chant are similar to those of other *E Syrian churches. The chants are predominately syllabic, the melodies (generally simpler than those of *Chaldean chant) have a narrow range, often reciting on a single note. Chromatic intervals are used. Some chants sung by the clergy are improvised.

Bibl: H. Husmann, ed., *Die Melodien des chaldäischen Breviers Commune nach den Traditionen Vorderasiens und der Malabarküste* (Rome, 1967). RGD

Syro-Malabar rite worship music. The Christians of Kerala in SW India, who trace their origins to the Apostle Thomas (thus called "Thomas Christians"), adopted the Chaldean *liturgy in Syriac in the 4th century. Ancient Syriac melodies form the basis of *Syro-Malabar chant. The influence of W liturgy and music (including use of *instruments) appears after the 16th century, when Malabar Christians were colonized by the Portuguese, renounced Nestorius and allied with Rome.

The Syro-Malabar liturgy has been celebrated in the vernacular (Malayalam) since 1962. In recent years newly composed melodies have come into frequent use, although some vernacular texts are sung to traditional Syriac melodies, especially at funerals and celebrations of the *divine office.

Bibl: J. Palackal, "Puthen Pāna: A Musical Study" (Hunter College of the City University of New York: M.A. thesis, 1995). JPM

T

Ta'amim <*cantillation> [Hebrew]. "Accents." A system of *ecphonetic notation which Jews use for cantillating the Bible. The Talmud states that the Bible should be "read in public and made understood to the hearers in a musical, sweet tune. . . . He who reads the Torah without tune shows disregard for it" (*Babylonian Talmud Megillah* 32a). This echoes the belief that Torah must be sung in order to render a fuller understanding.

Jewish music was transmitted orally. Over time attempts were made to transmit the *ta'amim* visually through *chironomy; this is still done in some places (e.g., Yemen). It was not until the 10th century CE that the *ta'amim* were put into writing by the Ben Asher family; their codification is known as the Masoretic (from Hebrew *masar,* "to hand down") text.

In Jewish worship all biblical books are cantillated publicly, each to a different melody. In the *Ashkenazic tradition there are 6 different melodic interpretations of the *ta'amim:* 1) Torah for weekday and *Sabbath; 2) Torah for *High Holidays; 3) prophetic books (see *Haftorah*); 4) Esther (see *Megilot*); 5) *Lamentations; and 6) Ruth, Song of Songs, Ecclesiastes and Proverbs. It is generally accepted that 4 *Sephardic regional practices exist: 1) Yemenite; 2) Middle E and N African; 3) Jerusalem Sephardic; and 4) N Mediterranean. Some Sephardic traditions (especially those from the W, e.g., from Spain and Portugal) have a separate melodic formula for each accent sign. Other Sephardic groups use the strong accent signs in a psalmodic pattern (see *psalm tone) where each *verse rises to a *recitation tone and then descends to the starting pitch with limited embellishment.

Numerous contemporary composers have attempted to incorporate melodies of the *ta'amim* into their music, e.g., *Binder, *Freed and *Janowski.

Bibl: See the sources listed under *Idelsohn; A. Herzog, "Masoretic Accents," *EJ* 11:1098–1112; A. Shiloah, *Jewish Musical Traditions* (Detroit, 1992) 87–109. DMR

Tabernacles, feast of. See *Sukkot.*

Tachanun <*Taḥanun*> [Hebrew]. "Supplication." The section of **shacharit* and **minchah* immediately following the **Amidah,* containing *psalms and prayers praising God and asking for mercy; it is also a part of **selichot. Tachanum* concludes with the prayer *Shomer Yisrael* ("Guardian of Israel") which has several musical settings. DMR

Taizé, music of. The *liturgical music used and promoted by the ecumenical monastic community at Taizé near Cluny in France (founded 1944). Notable are the compositions of *Berthier who wrote simple, multi-lingual works, often in ostinato style, for use during youth retreats held at Taizé. VCF

Tal [Hebrew]. "Dew." A prayer in the form of a reverse alphabetical acrostic, asking God to provide the regular descent of dew for the flourishing of plants in the land of Israel. It is recited during **musaf* on the first day of **Pesach.* Its recitation marks the end of reciting *"Mashiv ha ruach umorid hagashem"* ("You cause the wind to blow and the rain to fall"), which was inserted into the **Amidah* on the previous **Shemini atzeret. Tal* and its introductory *verse were written by Rabbi E. HaKallir (*c* 7th–9th centuries). For musical references see **Geshem.* IAG

Tallis, Thomas (*b c* 1505; *d* Greenwich 1585). Composer. He served as organist in various monasteries (1532–40) before becoming a gentleman of the *Chapel Royal (1541) where he was one of the singers and composers for the monarch. With *Byrd and others, Tallis created the Chapel Royal style of *Anglican music following the introduction of the 1549 and 1552 *BCP. The liturgical reforms called for a compositional style that would give primacy to the texts. *Melismatic writing gave way to a syllabic, more homophonic style. Tallis' gifts for harmonization, melodic fullness, rhythm, and phrase imitation pressed beyond the constraints of textual clarity. In the shifting political climate of the day, he wrote for both English and Latin texts. He composed 12 English *anthems in 4 to 6 parts, a Dorian short *service, *motets, votive *antiphons, *masses, *canticles and *psalm settings for English and Latin texts. A collection of motets by Tallis and Byrd (*Cantiones Sacra*) appeared in 1575, the year that Elizabeth I awarded them a patent for printing music.

Bibl: P. Doe, *Tallis* (London, 1968); P. Phillips, *English Sacred Music 1549–1649* (Oxford, 1991). RJS

Tanneberg <Tannenberg>, **David** (*b* Berthelsdorf, Upper Lusatia 1728; *d* York PA 1804). *Organ builder. Raised on the estate of Count Zinzendorf, Tanneberg immigrated to America with Moravian colonists in 1749. He settled in Bethlehem PA and there assisted another organ builder. He set up his own shop in Lititz PA (1865) where he produced an organ per year for churches in PA, NY, MD, VA, etc. JWK

Tantum ergo. See **Pange Lingua.*

Tate and Brady Psalter. Nahum Tate and Nicholas Brady issued their *metrical psalter, *New Version of the Psalms* (London, 1696; rev. 1698), as an attempt to supplant the "Old Version" of *Sternhold and Hopkins. RAL

Taverner, John (*b* near Boston, Lincolnshire *c* 1490; *d* there 1545). Composer.

His career as a church musician, though illustrious, can be traced only from 1524 to c 1537 when he seems to have retired altogether, apparently in some comfort. His works are mostly large-scale Latin *polyphony: *masses, *motets and *Magnificats. They continue the development of the late medieval English style of *Fayrfax and *Cornish, while adding a degree of rhythmic momentum (sometimes imparted through sequence or ostinato) not often found there. A few works (e.g., the *Western Wynde Mass and Playn Song Mass) exhibit an elegant though much simpler style, perhaps an early response to *Reformation thought about music.

Bibl: D. S. Josephson, John Taverner, Studies in Musicology 5 (Ann Arbor, 1979). AJL

Taylor, Margaret Fisk (b Oakland 1908). Author, teacher and dancer. Taylor was a major influence on the development of dance in Christian worship and education and on the *Sacred Dance Guild. MAK

Tchaikovsky, Pyotr <Piotr> **Ilyich** (b Votkinsk 1840; d St. Petersburg 1893). Composer. An important orchestral and operatic composer, he also wrote *religious and *liturgical music. The latter includes a unified setting of the Liturgy of St. John Chrysostom (op. 41, 1878) and *Vesper Service (op. 52, 1881–82): originally unaccompanied choral works through which Tchaikovsky hoped to revitalize Russian Orthodox worship music. He also wrote a lost *oratorio, *cantatas, a *Hymn in honor of SS Cyril and Methodius (1885) and a series of 9 sacred works for mixed chorus (1884–85).

Bibl: P. Tchaikovsky, The Complete Sacred Choral Works, ed. V. Morosan, 3 vols. (Madison CT, 1996). JBF

Te Deum [Latin]. "(We praise) you God." A non-biblical *chant sung at the end of *matins on Sundays and feast days; also a processional chant and song of thanksgiving. The text is attributed to Nicetas of Remesiana (d after 414). Festal settings of this text begin with *Purcell and continue to the present. DCI

Tefilah <tefillah> [Hebrew]. "Prayer." (1) In Judaism the term refers to both the formalized times of prayer (*shacharit, *minchah and *ma'ariv) as well as to one's personal prayers.

(2) In rabbinic literature it refers to the *Amidah. MLK

Teka beshofar [Hebrew]. "Sound the shofar." (1) The 10th *benediction of the weekday *Amidah.

(2) The final paragraph of the *shofarot section of the *Rosh Hashanah Amidah. The best known musical setting of this text is by *Rosenblatt. IAG

Telemann, Georg Philipp (b Magdeburg 1681; d Hamburg 1767). Composer, theorist and publisher. An advocate for amateur music-making, he began his career at age 20 by founding a student performing group in Leipzig. Later he became *Kapellmeister at Sorau (1705), court chorus and orchestra leader in Eisenach (1708) where he probably met J. S. *Bach, then Kapellmeister in Frankfurt (1712). Telemann finally settled in Hamburg (1721) as *Kantor of the prestigious Hamburg Johanneum; there he was responsible for teaching and directing the music of Hamburg's 5 chief churches. While maneuvering for the additional directorship of the Hamburg Opera, he sought and was offered the post of *Kantor* at Leipzig but turned it down, leading to its assumption by his good friend, J. S. Bach. Telemann composed operas, over 1,500 *church cantatas, numerous *passions (many performed in concert, not in worship) and an astounding amount of chamber music: all in a style which encompasses the *Baroque and early classicism. He represents a new wave of Protestant church musicians whose energies were drawn to the musical world outside the *liturgy.

Bibl: M. Ruhnke, "Telemann, Georg Philipp," *NGDMM* 18:647–659; B. D. Stewart, "Georg Philipp Telemann in Hamburg" (Stanford: Ph.D. diss, 1985). MPB

Temple, music of the. Following instructions from his father *David, Solomon (*d* 922? BCE) built the First Temple in Jerusalem. This small, majestic structure, soon became the religious center of Israel. Destroyed by the Babylonians in 587 BCE, it was rebuilt *c* 515 BCE. In considerable disrepair by the 1st century BCE, Herod the Great (*d* 4 BCE) demolished this Second Temple and began building a replacement *c* 20 BCE. Completed by 64 CE, it was destroyed in 70 CE during the revolt against the Romans.

David is remembered as having established professional Temple music (1 Chr 15) and having placed *Levites in charge (1 Chr 25). However, the earliest accounts of the Temple (2 Sam 6) do not mention professional musicians, which may have been a post-Davidic development. Music of the First Temple included the singing of religious texts accompanied by *instruments (Amos 5.23) and possibly trumpet flourishes (Ps 98.6). Professional choral singing, possibly in *responsorial or *antiphonal styles, accompanied by string instruments, was the central element in Temple music. Trumpets were used for signaling, while percussion instruments were used sparingly. Musicians were usually male, adults, well-trained and (at least in post-exilic times) Levites. Ordinary people probably joined in some of the Temple music, adding brief *refrains or an *alleluia to the prayer.

While *psalms played an important role in Israel's cult, few can be clearly linked with Temple worship. Ps 15 may have been employed as part of an entrance liturgy in the Temple, and Ps 24 may have accompanied a liturgical procession to the Temple. Most psalms, however, were probably not used regularly in Temple worship. Other texts besides psalms were sung in Temple worship. While these cannot be identified with certainty, they may have included texts like the song of Deborah (Judg 5) and the song of Moses (Ex 15:1-18, see *Az yashir Moshe*). Singing religious texts appears to have followed the offering of sacrifices (2 Chr 29:20-30), while trumpet blasts often accompanied the sacrifices (Num 10:10).

Bibl: B. Bayer, "Music-biblical Period," in *EJ* 12:559–66; E. Werner, "Jewish Musical, 1. Liturgical," *NGDMM* 9:614–34; J. A. Smith, "Which Psalms were sung in the Temple?" *Music and Letters* 71 (1990) 167–86.   EBF

Temporale [Latin]. "Temporal." The section of various Christian liturgical *books providing *propers for Sundays and feasts which derive their date from *Easter; it also includes fixed feasts from *Christmas through *Epiphany. Its counterpart is the *sanctorale. Focused on Sunday, it is the first section of the *sacramentary, *lectionary, etc. It is organized according to the sequence of the liturgical *year: *Advent, Christmas, *Lent, *Triduum, *Easter, solemnities and feasts of the Lord, and Sundays and weekdays of Ordinary Time. Certain composers (e.g., *Isaac) wrote complete musical settings for the temporale. JMT

Tenebrae [Latin]. "Darkness." A popular term for *matins and *lauds sung on the evening before Holy Thursday, Good Friday and Holy Saturday with dramatic visual and musical elements, including the gradual extinguishing of candles with departure in "darkness." The practice was in use in the RC Church before the 1955 Holy Week reforms; it has been revived in modified form in some churches since the 1980s. GET

Tenor [from Latin tenere, "to hold"]. (1) The *reciting note in a *psalm tone.
(2) In medieval *polyphony before the 15th century, the voice that "holds" the *cantus firmus, against which other voice parts were composed (Latin contratenor).
(3) The highest naturally occurring male voice. EBF

Tenor mass. A *Renaissance *polyphonic setting of the *ordinary in which a *cantus firmus held in long note values is placed in the *tenor beneath faster-moving upper voices. The composition is *cyclic, with the same cantus firmus used in all sections of the ordinary. MEC

Terce [from Latin hora tertia, "third hour"]. Mid-morning prayer in the Roman rite *divine office, and the first of the *little hours. Its basic structure in the present Roman rite is: opening *dialogue and *doxology, mid-morning *hymn, *psalmody, scripture reading, *collect and concluding *acclamation. JMJ

Tersanctus [Latin]. "Triple holy." Alternative term for the *Sanctus and the *Trisagion. PAJ

Tertullian (b Carthage c 160; d ? after 220). N African Latin Christian writer. The details of his life remain sketchy; he probably practiced law in Rome and may have been ordained a presbyter. An uncompromising rigorist on moral matters, he used his brilliant literary gifts as an apologist for orthodox Christianity and later for Montanism. One of the first to introduce the language of *sacrament to Christianity, he could also provide the earliest evidence for *psalm singing after the reading in Christian *eucharist. NDM

Thanksgiving. See *Modim.

Theia leitourgia. See *divine liturgy.

Theia leitourgia ton proegiasmenon. See *presanctified divine liturgy.

Theomusicology. A musicological discipline that studies the ethnic, religious and mythical aspects of *sacred, secular and profane music using various social science principles. Conceived by *Spencer, the basic tenets of this discipline are set out in his Theological Music (1991). RJS

Theotokarion [Greek]. "Book for the Mother of God." A Byzantine liturgical *book containing texts of *proper *stichera and *troparia to Mary. *Hymns to Mary are numerous. They are usually sung according to the *octoechos and used to conclude a series of *stichera dedicated to another liturgical theme.   DMP

Theotokion [Greek; Slavonic *bogoroditchen*]. "Hymn to the Mother of God." A *sticheron or *troparion in the Byzantine *office in honor of Mary. See *dogmatikon.   DMP

Theresienmesse [Latin]. "Theresa Mass." A common name for the *mass in B-flat by F. J. *Haydn (Hob XXII:12, 1799) for *choir, soloists and *orchestra. It was misnamed in the mistaken belief that it was written for Empress Maria Theresa; it was actually written for Princess Josepha Esterházy.   AWR

Thesaurus musicae sacrae. See *Treasury of sacred music.

Thomas, Kurt (George Hugo) (*b* Tönning 1904; *d* Bad Oeynhausen 1973). Choral conductor, composer and teacher. He taught in Leipzig, Berlin and Frankfurt and directed music at St. Thomas in Leipzig. Thomas wrote a *mass, *passion, *Christmas *oratorio, *cantatas, *motets, *psalms, *organ pieces and *The Choral Conductor* (3 vols.).   FKG

Thomas Aquinas, St. (*b* Roccasecca 1224–25; *d* Fossanova 1274). Dominican philosopher and theologian. He rejected Pythagorean (see *Pythagoras) notions of music as the expression of cosmic harmony in number and Platonic ideas of music education as awakening preexistent knowledge and capacities of the soul. Aquinas favored Aristotle's concept of music as sensed "consonance

of sounds" marked by proper qualities of beauty: perfection, proper proportion and clarity. A *proper of the mass and *office for *Corpus Christ* (including the *hymn "*Adoro te devote") are traditionally ascribed to him, though this ascription is questioned by contemporary scholarship.   JMJ

Thompson, Randall (*b* New York 1899; *d* Boston 1984). Composer and educator. He studied at Harvard with *Davison, and privately with *Bloch. Thompson taught at a series of important schools before returning to Harvard (1948–65). Fluent in many media, he was an especially gifted choral composer of both secular and *sacred music including *Alleluia* (1940), *Requiem* (1958), The *Passion According to St. Luke* (1965) and The Place of the Blest* (1969).   JFM

Thoroughbass. See *basso continuo*.

Three Festivals [Hebrew *Shalosh Regalim*]. The Jewish festivals *Pesach, *Shavuot* and *Sukkot;* called "pilgrimage" feasts because male Israelites were required to celebrate these feasts where "the Lord will choose" (eventually defined as Jerusalem). The *liturgy on these holidays is similar to *Sabbath worship. Additions include a special text for the *Amidah* (including *Ya'aleh veyavo*), the recitation of *Hallel* and additions to *musaf.* A special *Jewish prayer mode is used by the *chazzan* for these holidays.   MLK

Threni [Latin, sing. *threnus*]. "Lamentations." (1) A *lamentation.

(2) A composition by *Stravinsky on biblical texts for 6 soloists, *choir and orchestra (1957–58).   JLB

Tinctoris, Johannes (*b* Braine d'Alleud *c* 1435; *d* ? 1511). Theorist and composer. Little is known about him with certainty until *c* 1472 when he was a tutor at the court of Naples. By his own account he was trained in law, was a singer and a teacher of music. His 12 extant treatises cover a wide range of topics including definitions of musical terms, the philosophical and aesthetic dimensions of music, questions of musical notation, composition and counterpoint. These writings are important for their musical examples, citations of contemporary composers and view of the state of music theory in the late 15th century. His compositions include 5 *masses and several *motets.

Bibl: W. E. Melin, "The Music of Johannes Tinctoris" (Ohio State University: Ph.D. diss., 1973). RAD

Tindley, Charles Albert (*b* Berlin MD 1851; *d* Philadelphia 1933). Methodist minister, preacher and *hymn writer. A forerunner of African American *gospel music composition, Tindley influenced the compositional style of *Dorsey. His hymns are included in the recent *hymnals of several major denominations. MEM

Tippett, Michael Kemp (*b* London 1905; *d* there 1998). Composer. Tippett was the music director at Morley College and director of the Bath Festival. His compositions include an *organ piece, an *oratorio which employs black *spirituals (*A Child of Our Time,* 1941), *cantatas, a *Magnificat* and a *Nunc Dimittis.* He was knighted in 1966. FKG

Tisha B'av <*Tish'ah Be-'Av*> [Hebrew]. "Ninth day of Av." The most melancholy day in the Jewish calendar, serving as the climax of 3 weeks of mourning beginning on the 17th of the Hebrew month of *Tammuz,* commemorating the destruction of both the First and Second Temples in Jerusalem. Observed as a public fast day, the Book of *Lamentations is recited on this day and several additions (e.g., *Aneinu* and *Av harachamim*) are made to the *liturgy. SJW

Titcomb, Everett (*b* Amesbury MA 1884; *d* Boston 1968). Organist and composer. He served as the organist at St. John the Evangelist in Boston. Titcomb wrote many *anthems and a large amount of *service music for the Episcopal *liturgy of which *Communion Service in G* and *Victory Te Deum* are characteristic. FJM

Titelouze, Jehan (*b* St. Omer 1562/63; *d* Rouen 1633). Organist, composer and RC priest. The organist at Rouen Cathedral (from 1588), he was the first significant composer of *organ music in France. Celebrated as an organ consultant and poet in his own day, he composed and published *polyphonic organ *versets based on *plainsong. LMT

Toccata [from Italian *toccare,* "to touch"]. In the late *Renaissance, G. *Gabrieli, *Merulo and others wrote improvisatory *keyboard pieces called toccatas, often employing arpeggiated flourishes against held chords. These pieces could be slow or fast and multipartite in form. During the *Baroque era, J. S. *Bach sometimes substituted the toccata for a *prelude as a lively, dramatic introduction to a *fugue. *Widor and his French contemporaries popularized the form in works demanding

virtuoso displays of *organ technique.
JKW

Tod Jesu, Der [German]. "The Death of Jesus." A popular *cantata libretto by K. W. Ramier. Its setting by *Graun (1755), with its appeal to sentiment and simplicity, became the model of German *church music until the revival of J. S. *Bach's *St. Matthew Passion* in 1829. MPB

Tomkins, Thomas (*b* St. Davids, Pembrokeshire 1572; *d* Martin Hussingtree, Worcester 1656). Composer and organist. Born into a family of church musicians, he studied with *Byrd. Tomkins became organist and choirmaster at Worcester Cathedral (from 1596); later he became a gentleman (1620) and organist (1621–45) at the *Chapel Royal. He composed the majority of the music for the coronation of Charles I (1625). After 1628 Tomkins seems to have lived permanently at Worcester.

One of the most prolific composers of his day, Tomkins composed *services and almost 100 *anthems (both *full and particularly memorable *verse anthems). His *keyboard music for worship includes *offertories, *voluntaries, sets of variations and contrapuntal elaborations of *plainsong. He was also known for secular compositions, madrigals and dance variations for keyboard.
Bibl: D. Stevens, *Thomas Tomkins,* 2nd ed. (London, 1967).   RKW

Tonary <tonal> [Latin *tonarium, tonarius, tonale*]. A medieval liturgical *book (often incorporated into other books such as the *gradual) listing the *psalm tones according to the 8 ecclesiastical *modes. The tonary was in existence by the 8th century. It provided various endings peculiar to each tone and also included forms of the tones that were not part of the 8 tone system (e.g., the *tonus peregrinus,* the irregular tones and *tonus ad directum*).   JMT

Tones. See *echos.*

Tongues, singing in <*glossolalia* [from Greek *glōssa,* "tongue" and *laliá,* "talking"]>. A Christian prayer form with spontaneous and improvised melodies sung with unintelligible syllables inspired by the Holy Spirit. Also known as "singing in the Spirit." It is practiced by Pentecostal and Charismatic Christians in private prayer, small groups or corporate worship; it is often experienced in conjunction with periods of praise singing or spoken prayer. The biblical warrant for this form of prayer is drawn from 1 Cor 14:15. Singing in tongues may take musical forms similar to *chant, be marked by long *melismas, improvisation within a harmonic structure given by *instruments or free form singing with no specific beginning or end.
Bibl: C. M. Johnasson, "Singing in the Spirit," *The Hymn* 38 (1987) 25–29.   RJS

Tono [Italian, Spanish]. "Tone." (1) A key, *mode or recitation formula; in this sense the term is often used to indicate the mode of a composition, as in *Tiento de sexto tono* (a *tiento* in the 6th mode).
(2) Any type of Spanish song, sacred or secular.   JPM

Tonus [Latin]. "Tone." (1) In *plainsong, one of the 8 ecclesiastical *modes (e.g., *primus tonus,* "1st mode").
(2) The *tonus peregrinus.*
(3) A *psalm tone.   JKW

Tonus peregrinus [Latin]. "Wandering tone." The medieval name for an irregular *psalm tone (in evidence by the late 9th century) which changes the pitch of the *reciting tone after the mediant. It is associated with Ps 113 and the *Magnificat. RDH

Toolan, Suzanne (b Lansing MI 1927). Composer, educator and member of the RC Sisters of Mercy in Burlingame since 1950. She studied music privately in Hollywood, including *organ with R. Keys and piano with F. Darvas, then completed a B.A. in music at Immaculate Heart College and M.A. at San Francisco State. She has written numerous *hymns, including "I am the Bread of Life." JBF

Torah reading. The first 5 books of the Hebrew Bible (the "Books of Moses") are *cantillated in Jewish worship as mandated in Deut 31:10. The Torah is divided for weekly reading, and the whole of the Torah is read every year (see *Simchat Torah), though some groups read smaller portions, completing the Torah within a 3-year period. An allotted portion is read on Monday, Thursday and *Sabbath. Torah is also read on *Rosh Chodesh, *Rosh Hashanah, *Yom Kippur, the *Three Festivals and fast days such as *Tisha B'Av. SJW

Torculus [Latin]. "Of or belonging to a (wine or oil) press." A compound *chant *neume involving 3 pitches the second of which is higher than its surrounding pitches (e.g., sol-la-sol or sol-la-fa). The name comes from its "press-like" appearance. RTR

Tract [Latin tractus]. A *chant of the *proper of the mass, sung before the *gospel on penitential days; 4 tracts (cantica) were also assigned to the ancient *Easter Vigil. Texts for tracts were generally taken from the *psalms; structurally texts have multiple *verses without repetition or *responds, thus it was a form of *cantus in directum. Tract melodies are *melismatic, set in either *modes 2 or 8. Tracts appeared in the Roman *liturgy by at least the 9th century and were eliminated in the RC *mass after *Vatican II. PAJ

Tractarianism. See *Oxford Movement.

Tra le sollecitudini [Italian]. "Among the concerns." The 1903 *motu proprio by Pope *Pius X which defined the purpose of *sacred music as the glorification of God, and the sanctification and edification of the faithful. It recognized *Gregorian chant, *Roman school *polyphony and "more modern music" as appropriate for worship. It demanded qualities of holiness, beauty and universality in *sacred music. The decree also forbade women to be part of the *choir and prohibited "noisy or irreverent" *instruments (e.g., piano, drums) from liturgical use. JMJ

Transitorium [Latin]. "Passageway." An *Ambrosian chant sung during *communion. A *proper *chant, it is parallel to the Roman *communion antiphon, except that additional *psalm *verses are not appended to the transitorium, whose text is usually from the psalms. JMT

Treasury of sacred music. A term expressing the concern that works of the past (especially choral compositions) continue to be employed in the reformed RC liturgy. The term was first officially employed in *Sacrosanctum Concilium (n. 114). AWR

Treat, James Elbert (*b* New Haven 1837; *d* Boston? 1915). *Organ builder. He apprenticed with various firms, including that of *Hutchings. Treat then established his own organ factory in Methuen MA (*c* 1886) which became the Methuen Organ Co. (1894–1910). The company is best-known for the renovation and installation (1905–9) of the Walcker Boston Music Hall organ in Methuen MA. JWK

Trebnik [Slavonic]. See *hagiasmatarion*.

Trecanum [from Greek *trikanon*?, "triple canon"]. A *Gallican chant for *communion, parallel to the Roman *communion antiphon. The structure of the *trecanum* is: *antiphon–*psalm verse–*lesser doxology–psalm verse–antiphon. It may have been Trinitarian in content; no texts survive. JMT

Trent, Council of. A RC council held intermittently (1545–63) in response to the Protestant *Reformation; music in worship was treated only briefly. *Tropes and all but 4 *sequences were eliminated from the liturgy as a result of this Council. It decreed that music not contain "anything lascivious or impure" and called for greater comprehensibility of the Latin liturgical text. The proposal to eliminate *polyphony from worship was rejected, in effect enabling the continuing evolution of *art music in RC worship. The report that *Palestrina saved polyphony with his *Missa Papae Marcelli* is doubtful; of more likely influence were the *Preces Speciales* of *Kerle.

Bibl: R. Hayburn, *Papal Legislation on Sacred Music* (Collegeville, 1979) 25–31. AWR

Trent codices. Seven manuscript volumes, considered the most important body of 15th-century *polyphonic music (especially that of *Dufay). They were discovered by F. X. Haberl in the library of Trent Cathedral. The first 6 volumes contain 1,585 compositions by about 75 French, English, Italian and German composers. Volume 7 is almost identical to volume 4. CFS

Triadikon (pl. **triadika**) [Greek; Slavonic *troichen*]. "Trinitarian hymn." (1) A *troparion sung at *orthros following the *allelouiarion on days of fast. *Triadika* are sung according to the *octoechos and follow the tone of the previous Sunday.

(2) A *sticheron sung in honor of the Trinity. DMP

Tridentine. Derived from or related to the Council of *Trent; the term is also used for the Roman rite *mass found in the Missal of Pius V (1570). NDM

Triduum [Latin]. "The space of 3 days." (1) The 3-day period (calculated according to Jewish reckoning of a day from sunset to sunset), that begins on *Holy Thursday evening and culminates on *Easter evening. This Paschal or Easter Triduum is the culmination of the Christian liturgical *year.

(2) Any 3-day period of special observance in the Christian liturgical year, e.g., *Pentecost Sunday and the following 2 days were sometimes observed as a triduum. EBF

Triodion [Greek; Slavonic *triod*]. "Three odes." A Byzantine liturgical *book containing *propers for *hesperinos, *orthros, *apodeipnon and the *minor hours from 4 Sundays before the *Great Fast to Saturday of *Holy Week. The Greek title derives from the practice of singing 3 biblical *canticles at orthros from Monday to Friday during the Great Fast. The present triodion dates from the 15th century. Significant editors were Sts. Theodore and Joseph, 9th-century Studite monks. They gathered preexisting Byzantine *hymns, hymns from the Sabbas monastery (Palestine) and composed new hymns to complete the format.

Bibl: The Lenten Triodion, trans. Mother Mary and K. Ware (London-Boston, 1978).   DMP

Triplum [Latin]. "Threefold, triple." In medieval theory a 3-voice *polyphonic work or a third independent voice added above the *tenor and *duplum. Later the term triplum was replaced by cantus, superius, or the English "treble," since it was the highest voice part.   DCI

Trisagion [Greek; Slavonic trisvyatoe]. "Thrice-holy." (1) A *hymn in the Byzantine *liturgy, constructed on the 3-fold cry of "holy" in Is 6:3 and a variant reading (Codex Alexandrinus) of Ps 42:3 ("My being thirsts for God, the strong, the living"): thus, "Holy God, Holy and Mighty, Holy and Immortal." Its first recorded use was at the Council of Chalcedon (451). In many E churches it is used as an entrance hymn for the *divine liturgy. In the Byzantine Church the office of 3 antiphons has been added before it. It is sung 3 times, usually to festive or elaborate melodies. It is also the main component of the ordinary beginning and ending prayers of the *hours of the *divine office.

(2) Trisagion in the Greek tradition has been extended to mean prayer *services, particularly those for the departed (see *panakhida).

(3) The term occasionally refers to the *Sanctus, which in the Byzantine tradition is called the "Hymn of Victory." DMP

Trisvyatoe [Slavonic]. See *Trisagion.

Troeger, Thomas H. (b Suffern NY 1945). Poet, *hymn writer and Episcopalian priest. He is professor of preaching and communication at Iliff School of Theology in Denver. His publications include poetry and books on preaching and worship. With C. Doran he has written New Hymns for the Lectionary (1985) and New Hymns for the Life of the Church (1992).   CAD

Troichen [Slavonic]. See *triadikon.

Tropar' [Slavonic]. See *apolytikon and *troparion.

Troparion (pl. **troparia**) [Greek; Slavonic tropar']. "Refrain." (1) The name given to various *proper *hymns in the Byzantine *divine office sung according to the *octoechos. Originally they were sung as a *refrain to a series of *psalm *verses. Troparia are considered the most important variable hymns of the liturgical day. They are sung at the end of *hesperinos (called an *apolytikion in the Greek tradition), at the beginning and end of *orthros and at the *small entrance of the *divine liturgy, concluding the third *antiphon.

(2) A common term for many propers, including the refrain for the antiphons at the divine liturgy, the hymns of the

kanon (sung between the *hirmos* and *katabasia*), the *triadika* and the hymns at the *paremia*. DMP

Tropari voskresny [Slavonic]. See *Anastasima eulogetaria*.

Tropar' predprazdnstva [Slavonic]. See *proeortion*.

Trope (from Greek *trópos,* "turn"). A phrase of original text and music (or music alone) introductory to, or interpolated between, sections of preexistent *chant. Most tropes date from the 9th–11th centuries; many are *neumatic settings of texts in dactylic hexameter. Manuscripts from *St. Martial, St. Gall and Winchester indicate these were important troping centers. As amplifications of the chant repertoire, tropes are related to *prosulae, *sequences and *farses. Many tropes, especially those of the *proper, rendered a given biblical text (e.g., the *introit) more event-specific; some lengthy tropes (e.g., *Quem quaeritis*) are foundational for the development of liturgical *drama. The introductory *verses of many call the *choir to sing. Some trope verses might underscore a particular doctrine (e.g., *Sanctus* tropes with Trinitarian verses added to each repetition of the word "*Sanctus*"). While few tropes remained to be eliminated by the Council of *Trent, recent developments (especially the recovery of the *Kyrie* and *Agnus Dei* as *litanies) could be seen as a return to troping.
Bibl: R. Steiner, "Trope," *NGDMM* 19:172–87; D. Hiley, *Western Plainchant* (Oxford, 1993) 196–238. RTR

Troper [Latin *troparium*]. A Latin supplemental liturgical *book containing collections of *tropes, *sequences and other *chants added to the *ordinary and/or *proper of the *mass or *divine office. Few survive from before 1000 CE; many were compiled during the 11th and 12th centuries. JKL

Tsarskie chasy [Slavonic]. See *megalai horai*.

Tschesnokoff, Paul <Chesnokov, Pavel Grigor'yevich> (*b* Vskresensk 1877; *d* Moscow 1944). Choral conductor, teacher and composer. He taught at the Moscow Synodal School (1895–1920) and Moscow Conservatory (1920–44). Tschesnokoff composed over 400 choral works, mostly for liturgical use; many are based on early Russian *plainsong. His works are still performed in Russian Orthodox circles, and many have been translated into English. JMT

Tsvetnaya triod' [Slavonic]. See *pentekostarion*.

Tudor church music. A general designation for sacred *polyphony (both Latin and English) in England under the Tudor monarchs, from Henry VII through Elizabeth I (i.e., 1485–1603). AJL

Tufts, John (*b* Medford MA 1688; *d* Amesbury MA 1732). Congregationalist minister whose *Singing by note . . .* (1714, with 11 further editions) advocated singing the *psalms by notation versus by rote learning, contributing to the development of *singing schools. FJM

Tunder, Franz (*b* Bannesdorf 1614; *d* Lübeck 1667). Organist for the Gottorp court (1632–41), then St. Mary's in Lübeck where he founded *Abendmusik,* which was later taken over by his son-in-law *Buxtehude. Tunder wrote *cantatas, *chorale preludes, *toccatas and *fugues.   JLB

Tune book. An oblong-shaped book of tunes, ordinarily with musical instructions for *psalm singing, printed in the US in the 18th and 19th centuries. They commonly employed *fasola notation and were widely used in *singing schools.   JFM

Turba [Latin]. "Crowd." A term used in *passions to designate the musical settings of the texts spoken by the crowd in the biblical narrative (e.g., "Crucify him").   RAL

Twentieth-Century Church Light Music Group. A London musical group, formed in 1957, which produced settings of selected traditional words in a manner they considered "natural and relevant" to 20th-century Christians. Works by members Patrick Appleford, Geoffrey Beaumont and others strongly influenced worship in English churches at the time.   CAD

Tye, Christopher (*b c* 1505; *d* 1572?). Composer. He served as organist (1542–61) and choirmaster (1543–48, 1558–61) at Ely Cathedral and as a gentleman of the *Chapel Royal (although he did not serve under Mary I).

Tye held a Mus.D. from Cambridge (1545). He wrote *polyphonic *masses (including one on *Western Wynde), Latin *motets, English *services and *anthems. He was also celebrated for *keyboard compositions and 21 **In nomines* for instrumental consort. His *Acts of the Apostles* (1553) with harmonized tunes in chordal, syllabic style, influenced English *psalmody for many years; the adaptation of several of its tunes are still in use today. Tye was ordained an Anglican priest in 1560.
Bibl: J. R. Satterfield, "The Latin Church Music of Christopher Tye," Ph.D. diss. (University of North Carolina, 1962).   RKW

Typika [Greek; Slavonic *izobrazitelnayan*]. "Selected (psalms)" [also Slavonic *obednitsa*, "Supper service"]. A Byzantine *service celebrated in place of the *divine liturgy which usually follows *none. Originally it was a monastic *communion service, but today communion is not distributed. *Typika* is celebrated when a priest is not available or on "aliturgical" days (when a divine liturgy is not prescribed). The service consists of Pss 103, 146 and **Blazhenny* (intercalated with *stichera*); this structure sometimes replaces the 3 *antiphons at the beginning of the divine liturgy, hence it is called the "typical psalms." After these, the *Creed, *Lord's Prayer and Ps 34 follow.   DMP

U

Ukrainian Catholic/Orthodox worship music. The first immigration to North America from Ukrainian territory (1870–1900) was by people from Galicia (W Ukraine). The majority of these were Ukrainian Catholics who followed the Byzantine rite, using Church Slavonic and singing Galician *chant. Strong congregational singers, they had many choral organizations. Some reverted to Orthodoxy, forming the nucleus of the Russian Orthodox Metropolia and the Ukrainian Orthodox Church. A whole different immigration to North America after World War II brought the customs of E Ukraine. These people sang Kievan chant in their worship, and were more influenced by composers of Kiev and Russia.

South Bound Book NJ became a center of Ukrainian Orthodox music. The Scientific Liturgical Press published translations and transcriptions by V. Zapydnevych. These adapted Kievan chant, and the works of Russian and Ukrainian composers (e.g., Stetsenko, Leontovych, Koshyts) to modern Ukrainian. Ukrainian Catholics arriving after World War II were strongly influenced by composers such as Hnyatyshyn. Because of Soviet oppression of Ukrainians, until 1993 Catholic and Orthodox Ukrainians in the US and Canada felt it necessary to foster worship in the Ukrainian language; thus very little work was done to adapt the traditional melodies to English usage. Since the early 1990s, however, several musicologists have been working to transcribe the traditional chant of Galicia into English.

Bibl: I. Wlasowsky, *Outline History of the Ukrainian Orthodox Church* (South Bound Brook NJ 1956); *Encyclopedia of Ukraine* (Toronto, 1984–93).   JMT

Ukrainian-Dorian (mode). Related to but not strictly a *Jewish prayer mode because it has no inherent musical motives. It is a hexachord used for free improvisation whose most salient feature is the interval of an augmented 2nd between the 3rd and 4th scale degrees. AJB

Unetaneh tokef <*U-netanneh toqef*> [Hebrew]. "Let us proclaim." A *piyyut often ascribed to Kalonymus b. Meshullam of Mayence (11th century), though it was probably written earlier. It enumerates the ways people will perish, showing one's tenuous fate on earth. It is recited before the *Kedushah of *musaf on *Rosh Hashanah and *Yom Kippur. Among its many musical settings is that of *Lewandowski.   DMR

Union Seminary School of Sacred Music. An institution founded in 1928 by C. *Dickinson and his wife Helen Snyder Dickinson as part of Union Theological Seminary (founded in 1836). With New York's resources and a wide ecumenical perspective, the school trained many prominent church musicians. The School of Sacred Music moved to *Yale in 1973.   PHW

United Church of Canada Association of Musicians. An organization founded in 1989 by A. Barthel through the work of The United Church's national worship committee to promote the cooperation of musicians, clergy and congregations to create worship that has integrity. It sponsors workshops providing support and training for church musicians.   PAB

United Church of Canada worship music. The United Church of Canada was formed in 1925 as a union of Methodists, Congregationalists and Presbyterians and later the Evangelical United Brethren. An "ordered liberty" debate characterized by a struggle between ritual and anti-ritual perspectives has been a constant source of dynamic tension influencing its worship and music. The first hymnbook, *The Hymnary 1935*, reflected several continuing controversies: a *hymnal for "church universal" versus a truly Canadian hymnal, and *hymnody for common people versus more classical hymnody. The

Hymn Book (1971) was designed for the merged Anglican and United Churches, but the merger did not occur and the book, heavily critiqued from its inception, satisfied neither denomination. Ongoing liturgical renewal gave rise to new ecumenical models of worship which balanced word and table. Additional influences, such as the common lectionary and a desire for inclusive language, led to the publication of *Voices United* (1996). Typical of late 20th-century hymnals it is ecumenical, biblical, global and contains a complete *lectionary *psalter.
Bibl: T. Harding and B. Harding, *Patterns of Worship in The United Church of Canada* (Toronto, 1995).   PAB

United Methodist Church <UMC>, **worship music of.** The UMC, formed in 1968, combines Methodist and Evangelical United Brethren traditions; both consider *hymn singing a central, distinctive worship component. Methodism (see J. *Wesley) came from England in the 1760s, soon adopting a less formal order of worship better suited to the New World. The United Brethren in Christ Church in the US grew out of the spiritual awakening in the US during the late 1700s, sharing a German language heritage with the *Evangelische Gemeinschaft,* also a forerunner of the UMC. Pioneers of the present UMC built simple meeting-houses to accommodate their rapid growth. As wealth increased buildings and worship grew more substantial and ornate, with raised central pulpits, pipe *organs, increasingly formal *liturgies and expanded *choir programs.
Worship song was reformed in the 1970s and 80s by the Section on Worship within the General Board of Discipleship,

promoting a wide variety of hymns and musical styles. *The United Methodist Hymnal* (1989) and *Book of Worship* (1992) reflect a return to earlier emphases on scripture reading and regular celebrations of the *Lord's Supper. The *Hymnal* includes hymns by the *Wesley's, praise *choruses, *spirituals, *gospel hymns and music from various ethnic sources; African Americans have especially contributed to shaping UMC worship and music in the US. Music sources include *psalm tones, *plainsong, *folk *carols, traditional melodies, *chorales, *psalter tunes, *Anglican chant and new compositions from English and US composers. The *Hymnal* features 113 psalms *pointed for chanting (with sung *responses when read) and 5 settings for "Word and Table." Pipe organs ordinarily accompany congregational song but pianos, *guitars, drums, *handbells and other *instruments also aid increased musical participation.

The *Fellowship of United Methodists in Worship, Music and Other Arts and 3 periodicals *(Church Music Worship, Quarternotes: For Leaders of Music with Children, Jubilate! Newsletter for United Methodist Musicians)* support and inform those who lead music in the UMC.

See *African Methodist Episcopal worship music, *African Methodist Episcopal Zion worship music, *Bethel African Methodist Episcopal worship music, *British Methodist worship music, *Christian Methodist Episcopal worship music and *Methodist Episcopal worship music.

Bibl: R. Deschner, "Methodist Church, music of the," *NGDAM* 3:217–20; C. Young, ed., *Companion to the United Methodist Hymnal* (Nashville, 1993); H. Hickman, *Worshipping with United Methodists* (Nashville, 1996).   CAD-CRY

Unit organ. See *extension organ.

Universa Laus [Latin]. "Universal praise." An international study group, founded in 1965 to explore the implications of vernacular song in RC worship. Under the inspiration of B. Huijbers, *Gelineau, H. Hucke and G. Stephani, the notion of *ritual music emerged from this group as a key for understanding what *Vatican II considered to be the ministerial function of music in worship.   VCF

University of Notre Dame. A RC university in South Bend IN. Founded in 1842 by Edward Sorin of the Community of the Holy Cross of Le Mans, France. The school is renowned for its graduate program in liturgical studies.   MSD

Utrecht Te Deum and Jubilate. *Service pieces by *Handel for *choir, soloists and *orchestra in celebration of the Peace of Utrecht ending the war of Spanish Succession. They were first performed in St. Paul's Cathedral in London (1713).   DWM

Utrennee evangelie [Slavonic]. See *euangelion heothinon.

Utrenya [Slavonic]. See *orthros.

Uva Lesiyyon <*Uva l'Tsiyyon*> [Hebrew]. "A redeemer shall come to Zion." One of the concluding prayers in daily *shacharit; it is moved to *minchah for *Sabbath and festivals, and to *ne'ilah for *Yom Kippur.   DMR

V

Va'ani tefilati [Hebrew]. "As for me, my prayer." A *psalm *verse (69:14) recited in synagogue worship before removing the Torah scroll from the ark. It is sung to a melody on *Rosh Hashanah, *Yom Kippur and the *Three Festivals when these are not a *Sabbath.   SJW

Vajda, Jaroslav (b Lorain OH 1919). Lutheran pastor and editor at Concordia Publishing House. Vajda is known for his translations of Slovak *hymnody as well as his own *hymn writing (e.g., "Now the Silence," 1987) and sacred poetry.   VEG

Valparaiso University. Founded in 1859 in Valparaiso IN, with ties to the Lutheran Church Missouri Synod since 1925. The university is celebrated for its strong *church music, liturgical studies and *organ performance programs. Beginning in 1944 the school offered an annual Church Music Conference (later the name changed to Church Music Seminar) to develop and strengthen leadership in Lutheran church music renewal. The university also began an Institute of Liturgical Studies in 1949, which took over the work of the Church Music Seminar in the 1980s.   RDH-VEG

Vasquez <Vásquez>, **Juan** (b Badajoz c 1510; d Seville? c 1560). Composer. He began as a singer at Badajoz Cathedral (1530) then Palencia Cathedral (1539). He became maestro de capilla at Badajoz Cathedral (1545–50) then moved to Seville (1551). Vasquez was well-known for his secular music, especially 96 villancicos; his *sacred music was published in a monumental collection of music for the dead, Agenda defunctorum (1556).   JLB

Vater unser [German]. "Our Father." (1) The *Lord's Prayer (Matt 6:9-13).

(2) *Luther's 9-stanza *hymn paraphrase of this prayer.

(3) The tune name for Luther's hymn paraphrase. This is rarely used in Lutheran worship today for the Lord's Prayer which, when sung, is ordinarily set to a *chant melody.   JLB

Vatican (Council) II. The 21st general (ecumenical) council of the RC church (1962–65). It was called by Pope John

XXIII (*d* 1963) to renew the life of the church. The first decree of that council was on the *liturgy (*Sacrosanctum Concilium*), providing the basis for future reforms in liturgy and music. The council and its first document had a broad impact on liturgical reforms beyond the RC church. MJG

Vatican edition [Latin *Editio Vaticana*]. The official *Gregorian chant edition (*Kyriale*, 1905; *gradual, 1907; *antiphonary, 1912), largely based on *Solesmes' restitution of the authentic melodies, but without the historically unfounded rhythmic signs of *Mocquereau that appear in the *Liber Usualis*. AWR

Vaughan Williams, Ralph (*b* Down Ampney 1872; *d* London 1958). Composer, conductor and teacher. He studied composition at London's Royal College of Music and Cambridge's Trinity College with *Parry, Wood and *Stanford; later, he studied briefly with Bruch and Ravel. A prolific composer primarily of symphonies, choral music and songs, he also wrote music for the stage, chamber music and incidental music for theater, film and radio. His rugged, frequently visionary musical style was influenced by English *folk song and *Tudor *polyphony. He was music editor of the influential *English Hymnal*.

In addition to a number of large-scale sacred works with orchestra, Vaughan Williams wrote choral music suitable for worship. This includes 5 *motets, 2 *anthems, *service music, an unaccompanied *mass for double *choir, numerous *hymn and *carol arrangements, and 14 original hymn tunes. Of the latter SINE NOMINE and DOWN AMPLNEY are regarded as among the finest of the 20th century.

Bibl: M. Kennedy, *The Works of Ralph Vaughan Williams,* 2nd ed. (Oxford, 1980); R. T. Gore, *Ralph Vaughan Williams and the Hymn* (Springfield OH, 1981). KRH

Vayakhulu <*Va-yekhullu*> [Hebrew]. "Thus they were finished." The *incipit of a biblical passage (Gen 2:1-3) recited by Jews 3 times on Friday evening: twice during *ma'ariv (during and after the *Amidah) and once in the *Kiddush*. It is also recited during the *Torah reading on *Simchat Torah*. SJW

Vechernya [Slavonic]. See *hesperinos*.

Vehe, Michael (*b* Biberach *c* 1480; *d* Halle 1539). A Dominican who issued the RC *hymnal *Ein new Gesangbuechlin* (German, "A New Hymnal"), which provided *hymns, many of Protestant origin, for use before and after the sermon (see *prone) and during *processions. AWR

Vehu Rachum <*Raḥum*> [Hebrew]. "He, being merciful." A prayer (also known as the long *Tachanun*) recited by Jews on Monday and Thursday after the *Amidah*. SJW

Velichanie [Slavonic]. See *megalynarion*.

Velikaya ekteniya [Slavonic]. See *eirenika*.

Velikij vchod [Slavonic]. See *megale eisodos*.

Velikoe povecherie [Slavonic]. See *apodeipnon to mega*.

Velirushalayim Ir'cha [Hebrew]. "And Jerusalem, Your city." The fourteenth *blessing of the *Amidah, asking for God's blessing on Jerusalem. This text is set to several cantorial and *folk melodies.   MLK

Velorio [Spanish]. "Wake, night watch." A prayer *service for the dead or in honor of a saint, popular in Latin America and Hispanic communities. It commonly consists of prayers, *alabados and a meal.   MFR

Venatius Fortunatus. See *Fortunatus, Venatius.

Veni Creator [Latin]. "Come, Creator [Spirit]." A *hymn to the Holy Spirit, sung for *Pentecost, ordinations, confirmations, etc., to an ancient *chant tune in *mode 8. The text is frequently attributed to Rabanus Maurus (d 856). The most popular English translation is by J. Cosin (d 1672), "Come, Holy Ghost." GET

Veni Sancte [Latin]. "Come, Holy [Spirit]." A 10-*stanza *sequence for *Pentecost, sometimes called the "Golden Sequence." A masterpiece of sacred Latin poetry. Its *chant setting (with a *mode 1 melody) arranges stanzas as 5 double *versicles. The text was previously attributed to Pope Innocent III (d 1216); now to Stephen Langton (d 1228). Numerous English translations exist, including one by *Neale.   GET-JMT

Venite (exsultemus) [Latin]. "Come, let us praise." The *incipit of Ps 95, the *invitatory *psalm in RC, Anglican, Lutheran and Methodist daily prayer. It is ordinarily performed as a *responsorial psalm (RC) or in *directaneus fashion.   FCQ

Verdelot, Philippe (b Verdelot c 1470–80; d before 1552). Composer. Little is known about his early life. He served as *maestro di cappella at the Baptistry of S. Giovanni (1523–25), then the Cathedral (1523–27) in Florence. Verdelot was a pioneer of madrigal composition; 2 of his *masses and almost 60 *motets also survive.   JLB

Verdi, Giuseppe (Fortunino Francesco) (b Le Roncole near Parma 1813; d Milan 1901). A renowned operatic composer, who wrote a significant amount of *sacred music. Most notable was his *Requiem, originally conceived as a collective work by 11 composers to honor operatic composer G. Rossini (d 1868). Verdi composed the Libera nos (1868–69), completing the work in 1874 to honor the poet A. Manzoni; thus the piece is sometimes called the *Manzoni Requiem. Most of Verdi's religious compositions were written in his last years, including: an unaccompanied choral *Pater Noster (1880); Laudi alla Vergine Maria for women's voices (1888–89), published in 1898 with an *Ave Maria (1889) as Quattro pezzi sacri; a monumental *Te Deum (1895–96) for soloists and chorus; and *Stabat Mater for chorus and orchestra (1896–97).   JBF

Verse [Latin versus, "turned towards"].
(1) A small unit into which chapters of the Bible are divided.
(2) A division of the *gradual, *alleluia and other *mass and *divine office texts (sometimes indicated with the symbol V).
(3) A *versicle.
(4) In some popular song forms, the music and text preceding a *refrain or *chorus.

(5) Poetry, a line of poetry, or a poetic unit similar in *meter and rhyme to other such units.   RKW

Verse anthem. An Anglican choral composition with alternating passages between soloists and *chorus; in contrast to the *full anthem.   RAL

Verset. A brief composition or improvisation for *organ, intended for use in the *alternatim performance of a liturgical *chant or *hymn.   PKG

Versicle [Latin versiculus, "short verse"]. In Christian *liturgy, a short sentence spoken by a leader (sometimes indicated with the symbol V) initiating a dialogue with the assembly or other minister who provides the *response. Many versicles and responses are taken from the *psalms. JKW

Versus [Latin]. "Verse." (1) In W *chant, the verse(s) of the *psalm sung with either a *refrain (e.g., the *alleluia), an *antiphon (e.g., the *introit, *offertory, *communion) or a *respond (e.g., the *responsory).
(2) A medieval Latin song, sometimes based on a liturgical text (e.g., *Benedicamus Domino), often rhymed, *strophic and sometimes with a refrain; also called *conductus or *cantio.   JLK

Versus ad repetendum [Latin]. "Verse for repetition." In the *introit and *communion chant, a *psalm *verse sung after the *Gloria Patri before the final reiteration of the *antiphon. It is found in early Frankish and Old Roman sources.   PAJ

Veshamru <Ve-shameru> [Hebrew]. "They shall keep." The *incipit of a bib-

lical passage (Ex 31:16-17) recited during Friday *ma'ariv before the *Amidah, and as part of the Amidah during *Sabbath *shacharit (except if a holiday or festival falls on Sabbath). On Friday evening it is chanted in the *magein avot *mode. Some of the many choral, congregational and cantorial settings of this text use this same mode; others use W minor keys. *Sulzer and *Naumbourg set it in major, *Lewandowski in the *Adonai malach mode and *Freed in the *ahavah rabbah mode.   IAG

Vesperae solennes de Confessore [Latin]. "Solemn Vespers of a Confessor." *Mozart's 1780 setting of *vespers (K 339), and last church composition for Salzburg Cathedral. It consists of 5 *psalms and a *Magnificat for 4 voices, bassoon, 2 trumpets, 3 trombones, strings and *organ.   PAB

Vesperal [Latin vesperale]. A liturgical *book providing texts and *chants for *vespers and often *compline. It became useful for parishes where the celebration of the *divine office was limited to vespers on Sundays and feasts. A smaller version (vesperale parvum), contained music and texts only for Sundays and first-class feasts.   JMT

Vespers [from Latin vesper, "evening star"]. *Evening prayer in the *divine office. Its basic structure in the present Roman rite is: opening *dialogue and *doxology, evening *hymn, *psalmody (2 psalms and a NT *canticle), scripture reading, (optional) short *response, *Magnificat, intercessions, *Our Father, *collect, *blessing and dismissal. Some traditions prescribe a *lucenarium at the beginning of Vespers. Ps 141 is frequently used and *Phos hilaron* often sung as the evening hymn.   JMJ

Vespro della Beata Vergine [Italian]. "Vespers of the Blessed Virgin." *Monteverdi's 1610 setting of the *psalms and *canticles used for *vespers of Marian feasts along with other liturgical and non-liturgical texts. While containing many examples of late *Renaissance style, this work is widely regarded as one of the first masterpieces of the *Baroque.   RTR

Viadana, Lodovico Grossi da (*b* Viadana *c* 1560; *d* Gualtieri 1627). Composer and friar. He was *maestro di cappella* at Mantua Cathedral. A prolific composer in many styles, Viadana was one of the first to write *church concertos for a few voices with 1, 2 or 3 voices accompanied by *keyboard *continuo*. These 100 works (*Cento concerti ecclesiastici,* 1602) represent the earliest sacred vocal publications with a *continuo*. His style is ingratiating, buoyant and expressive.   DCI

Vicar choral. A lay or ordained musician who has responsibilities for vocal leadership in an Anglican cathedral either as a *precentor or, more often, as an adult chorister.   CAD

Victimae paschale laudes [Latin]. "Praise the paschal victim." The *sequence for *Easter, ascribed to *Wipo of Burgundy, praising Christ as the paschal lamb. It is only 1 of 4 sequences not suppressed by the Council of *Trent. MSD

Victoria, Tomás Luis de (*b* Avila 1548; *d* Madrid 1611). Composer and organist. After serving as a choirboy at Avila

Cathedral he studied at the Jesuit Collegio Germanico in Rome, where he may have studied with *Palestrina. A singer and organist at S. Maria di Monserrato in Rome, he was later appointed *maestro di cappella* at the Collegio. Ordained a RC priest in 1575, he joined the Oratory of St. Philip Neri, then held a chaplaincy at S. Girolamo della Carità. He returned to Spain in 1583 to serve as chaplain to the king's sister at a monastery in Madrid where he remained until his death, except for a time in Rome (1592–95) to supervise the printing of his music; he attended *Palestrina's funeral. The greatest Spanish composer of the *Renaissance, he wrote 20 *masses, *Officium Defunctorum* (1605), 18 *Magnificat*s, *c* 50 *motets, over 30 *hymns as well as *sequences, *antiphons, *psalms and *responsories.

Bibl: H. Anglés, "Latin Church Music on the continent, 3: Spain and Portugal," in *New Oxford History of Music* (London, 1968) 4:398–405; G. Reese et al., *The New Grove High Renaissance Masters* (New York, 1984).   VAL

Vidui <*viddui, vidduy*> [Hebrew]. "Confession." A confessional section of Jewish *liturgy which occurs in the *Amidah* on *Yom Kippur,* during *selichot and on fast days. Its 2 major forms are *Ashamnu* and *Al chet*.   MLK

Vierne, Louis (*b* Poitiers 1870; *d* Paris 1937). Organist and composer. Blinded at age 6, he eventually studied with C. *Franck and *Widor. Vierne became organist at Notre Dame Cathedral in Paris (from 1900) and taught at the Paris Conservatory (1894–1911) and *Schola Cantorum (from 1912). Associated with the French Romantic *organ school, he composed in classical forms including 6 organ symphonies, 1 choral *mass, a (*low) *organ mass, and 6 volumes of smaller works for organ.   MDJ

Vigil. (1) The eve of a holy day (e.g., *Christmas) dedicated to preparation for the festival.

(2) A *service of the word with scripture reading(s), *hymns and *psalmody.

(3) A funeral wake.   NDM

Virga [Latin, also *virgula*]. "Rod, staff." A *neume signifying a single note, usually made by a vertical stroke, often with a small adjoining stroke *(episema).* Frequently it represents a note higher than those before and after.   JKL

Visigothic chant. See *Old Spanish chant.

Vivaldi, Antonio (*b* Venice 1678; *d* Vienna 1741). Composer. He studied music with his father, a professional violinist; he then studied for the priesthood and was ordained in 1703. He was appointed *maestro di violino* (1703) at Pio Ospedale della Pietà in Venice, an institution established for the care of orphaned and abandoned girls and which specialized in musical training; he later became *maestro de' concerti* (1716) there, then *maestro di cappella* (1735–38). Vivaldi spent time in Mantua and in Rome, and traveled widely, devoting much time to composing and promoting his music. Although he composed many sacred works, he never held a position which required him to compose such music. His *concertos were particularly influential; his style was widely imitated, and J. S. *Bach transcribed 5 concertos for *keyboard. His works include more than 500 concertos, solo sonatas, trio sonatas, *masses and mass sections, *hymns, *sequences, *oratorios and operas.

Bibl: H. C. Robbins Landon, *Vivaldi* (New York, 1993); M. Talbot, *The Sacred Vocal Music of Antonio Vivaldi* (Florence, 1995).   VAL

Vkhodnoe [Slavonic]. See *eisodikon.*

Vogler, <Abbé> **Georg Joseph** (*b* Pleichach 1749; *d* Darmstadt 1814). Composer and theorist. He studied law and theology in Germany, music in Italy with *Martini and others. Vogler became chaplain, then Vice *Kapellmeister* in Mannheim (1775); he subsequently held the position of *Kapellmeister* in Munich (1784), Stockholm (1786) and Darmstadt (1807). He wrote *masses, *cantatas, *psalms and accompanied *hymn settings. Vogler also wrote theoretical, pedagogical treatises including *Tonwissenschaft und Tonsetzkunst* (1776). JLB

Voluntary. In the English tradition, *organ music played before or after a worship *service. The term implies a work not based on any *cantus firmus* but in a free improvisatory style.   JBW

Votive antiphon. A commissioned composition, usually on a *Marian antiphon text and in elaborate musical style. In late medieval and early *Renaissance England endowments were established for the singing of these works during *compline at major churches. See*Eton Choirbook, The.   RTR

Votive mass. A *mass whose principal variable parts (e.g., *collects, readings, *preface, etc.) are not based on the calendar of the liturgical *year but on a special devotion (e.g., the Sacred Heart of Jesus), object (e.g., the Holy Cross), or occasion (a wedding), though the latter are now more properly classified as "ritual masses" or "masses for various needs and occasions."   NDM

Vox angelica. See *Engelstimme.

Vozglas [Slavonic]. See *ekphonesis.

Vsednevnaya vechernya [Slavonic]. See *vechernya.

Vsenochnaya bdenie [Slavonic]. "All-night vigil." A combination of *hesperinos and *orthros in the Byzantine rite (Slavonic recension), celebrated in the evening of Sundays and great feast days. Today it replaces the now obsolete *pannychis, and lasts between 2 and 4 hours depending on the mode of celebration.   DMP

W

Wachet auf [German]. "'Wake' (Awake)."
A *chorale for *Advent; sometimes
called the king of *chorales. The text
and music by *Nicolai were first published in his *Frewden-Spiegel dess ewigen
Lebens* (1599).   PHW

Walcha, Helmut (*b* Leipzig 1907; *d*
Frankfurt 1991). Organist, composer
and teacher. Blind from age 16, he became a leading interpreter of the music
of J. S. *Bach. Walcha also composed 3
sets of *chorale preludes and edited
*Handel's *organ *concertos.   RDH

Walker, Christopher (*b* 1947 London).
Composer, conductor and *pastoral musician. He directed music in England
for the RC Clifton diocese (1972–89)
and the Cathedral in Bristol (1980–89);
later he served as a pastoral musician in
Los Angeles. His liturgical compositions were first disseminated through
London's St. Thomas More Centre.
MEC

Walter <Walther> **Johann** (*b* Kahla
1496; *d* Torgau 1570). Singer, composer, director and poet. He became the

first Lutheran *Kantor* (at Torgau before
1529), and then served as *Kapellmeister* to the Elector of Saxony in Dresden
(1548–54). Walter published *polyphonic
settings of early Lutheran *chorales in
Geystliches gesangk Buchleyn (Wittenberg, 1524; expanded editions in 1528,
1544 and 1550–51). He was *Luther's
musical consultant for the Reformer's
Deutsche Messe (1526), and wrote
some of the first German *passions.
MPB-RAL

Walther, Johann Gottfried (*b* Erfurt
1684; *d* Weimar 1748). Organist, theorist, composer and lexicographer. A
cousin of J. S. *Bach, Walther served as
a musician to the Weimar court (from
1721). Besides composing vocal works
and *chorale preludes, he wrote the first
major German musical dictionary (*Mu-
sicalisches Lexicon oder Musicalische
Bibliothec,* 1732).   MPB

Walton, William (Turner) (*b* Oldham
1902; *d* Forio d'Ischia 1983). Composer. He produced numerous grand
scale works including symphonies, coronation marches, film scores, the *orato-

rio *Belshazzar's Feast* (1931) and *Coronation *Te Deum* (1951). Other vocal religious music includes his **Missa brevis* (1965–66).   FJM

Ward, Clara (*b* Philadelphia 1924; *d* Los Angeles 1973). African American *gospel composer, arranger, singer, pianist and recording artist. She was a member of the Ward Singers who popularized many compositions of W. H. *Brewster through performance and recording.   MEM

Ward, Justine (*b* Morristown NJ 1879; *d* Washington DC 1975). Teacher. She was a strong advocate of congregational singing of *Gregorian chant as called for in **Tra le sollecitudini*. She developed the popular *Solesmes based "Ward Method of School Music." In 1967 *Catholic University of America dedicated its music building to her and opened the Center for Ward Method Studies.   AWR

War Requiem. A setting by *Britten (op. 66, 1961) of the mass for the *dead juxtaposed with 9 war poems of W. Owen for soloists, *boys' choir, *chorus, *organ and orchestra. It was composed for the consecration of Coventry Cathedral (Anglican), built on the site of the medieval cathedral destroyed during World War II.   KRH

Watts, Isaac (*b* Southhampton 1674; *d* London 1748). *Hymn writer. He is called the "Father of English *hymnody" because he freed English congregational song from the boundaries of *metrical psalmody so popular in his day by "Christianizing" and expanding it beyond strict scriptural paraphrase.

Though brilliant and creative, Watts was denied a university education because his father was a nonconformist minister; later in life (1728) he was awarded honorary doctorates from the Universities of Edinburgh and Aberdeen. He served as pastor of several Congregational churches but suffered frail health throughout his life, spending the years from 1713 until his death as a guest in the home of a benefactor. He wrote books on theology, logic and astronomy as well as poetry.

Much of his hymnody was written to complement his Sunday sermons. His choice of the 3 *meters most commonly used in his time (common, long and short) easily allowed congregations to sing his new texts with well-known tunes. Publication of Watts' *c* 750 *psalms and hymns began in 1706. His most enduring compositions were published in *Psalms of David Imitated in the Language of the New Testament* (1719) which contained 138 "expanded" metrical psalms. His *A Short Essay toward the Improvement of Psalmody* contained 3 important principles for congregational song: 1) using scripture other than psalms to enrich congregational song, 2) direct reference to God's revelation in Christ and 3) creation of hymns for the various occasions of Christian life. He believed that congregational song should be evangelical in the sense of reflecting the singers' own beliefs in their own words rather than reciting scripture exclusively. Watts' Calvinist theology, with its focus on the depravity of human nature and Christ's complete atonement, made his hymns less popular during the late 19th century; considerable numbers of them have been included in contemporary *hymnals.

Bibl: H. Escott, *Isaac Watts Hymnographer* (London, 1962); E. Routley, *A Panorama of Christian Hymnody* (Collegeville, 1979) 16–21; J. R. Watson, *The English Hymn* (Oxford, 1997) 133–70.   CAD

Weakland, Rembert G. (*b* Patton PA 1927). Benedictine, bishop and musicologist. He studied at *Solesmes (*chant and paleography, 1949), Juilliard (M.S. in piano, 1954) and Columbia University (Ph.D. in musicology, 2000). He has served as archabbot of Latrobe Archabbey (1963–67), abbot primate of the Benedictine Order (1967–77), and archbishop of Milwaukee (from 1977). A leader in liturgical and musical reforms following *Vatican II, Weakland has also done important research in medieval music, especially on *Ambrosian chant and *The Play of Daniel.*   FJM

Weckmann, Matthias (*b* Niederdoria *c* 1619; *d* Hamburg 1674). Composer and organist. He studied with J. *Praetorius, *Scheidemann and *Schütz. Weckmann was organist at Jakobikirche in Hamburg. His compositions include 13 accompanied sacred vocal works and *chorale variations for *organ.   FKG

Wedding music. Music for the Jewish wedding ceremony often consists of a *cantor chanting the first lines of Ps 116, the medieval acrostic *Mi adir* (Hebrew, "He who is powerful") and the *Sheva berachot* ("7 wedding blessings"). *Chants are usually in *Adonai malach* *mode, interspersed with the cantillation of musical motives from *Shir Hashirim.* Processional music includes Israeli, *Hassidic or other *folk melodies, as well as art songs, accompanied by *keyboard, flute, *guitar or other *instruments.

In Christianity music for marriage did not develop in the *Middle Ages comparable to other Christian rituals, at least in part because marriage was not widely considered a *sacrament until the 12th century. In reform traditions *hymns ordinarily accompany the *service; numerous *anthems have been composed for (especially royal) weddings. More recently *organ *preludes, *postludes and *processionals have been introduced to frame the *service; since the 19th century Wagner's bridal chorus from *Lohengrin* has frequently accompanied the entrance of the bride. Often solo music is interspersed during the rite. In RC and some other traditions it is common to celebrate a wedding in the context of *eucharist. When such is done, the *ordinary (e.g., *acclamations, *ordinary chants, etc.) becomes the musical focus of the rite.   BES-LJC

Weeks, Feast of. See *Shavuot.*

Weelkes, Thomas (*b* Elsted? *c* 1575; *d* London 1623). Composer and organist. He served as organist at Winchester College (1598–*c* 1602); also, organist (*c* 1602–23) and master of the choristers at Chichester Cathedral (before 1617, when he was temporarily dismissed for his drinking). His 5 volumes of madrigals exhibit bold and effective use of harmony for expressive purposes; his sacred works are harmonically less daring. They include 10 *services (all at least partially incomplete in the surviving sources), 12 more or less complete *full anthems and 5 intact *verse anthems. Innovation here comes in formal structures: structural rounding (e.g., A-B-A) appears in some single movement works and other devices unify some multi-movement services, even creating some links between services and *anthems. *Bibl:* D. Brown, *Thomas Weelkes* (London, 1969). AJL

Weihnachtslied [German]. "Christmas carol." See*carol.

Weintraub, Hirsch (*b* Dubno 1811; *d* Königsberg 1881). *Cantor and composer. The son of the reknowned cantor Salomon Weintraub (*d* 1829), Hirsch first studied with his father; later he received formal music instruction in Vienna and Berlin. He was cantor in Königsberg (1838–79). In his composition he was influenced by the music of *Sulzer. The first 2 volumes of the collection of synagogue music entitled *Shire Beth Adonai* (1859) are works by Hirsch; the third volume contains settings by his father which Hirsch reworked. MLK

Weisser <Pilderwasser>, **Joshua Samuel** (b Nova-Ushitser, Ukraine 1888; *d* Brooklyn 1952). *Cantor, composer and teacher. A student of *Gerovitch, he immigrated to the US (1914) where he served as cantor at New York's Tiferet Israel, Nahlat Tzvi and Tremont Talmud Torah synagogues. His prolific output includes the 2-volume *Shirei Beth Haknesset* (1951, 1952), and several synagogue *recitatives, a form in which he is an acknowledged master. He taught a generation of US singers, including Richard Tucker. MLK

Wellesz, Egon (*b* Vienna 1885; *d* Oxford 1974). Composer, musicologist and teacher. He provided seminal research on *Byzantine chant and its underlying structure, some of which is published in his *A History of Byzantine Music and Hymnography* (2nd rev. ed., 1961). His compositions include operas, symphonies, piano and chamber music, 3 *masses and the *Christmas *cantata *Mirabile mysterium* (1967). RAD

Werner, Eric (*b* Vienna 1901; *d* New York 1988). Musicologist who devoted his efforts to understanding Jewish music history. He attended Universities in Vienna, Prague, Berlin and Strasbourg, immigrating to the US in 1938. From 1939 until his death he was on the faculty of the Hebrew Union College-Jewish Institute of Religion; in the 1940s he helped to develop the School of Sacred Music, *Reform Judaism's cantorial school. He composed music of both a Jewish and general nature.

Werner wrote hundreds of articles and was interested in many liturgical issues. His 2-volume *The Sacred Bridge* (1959, 1984) investigated the interconnection between music of the synagogue and church. While influential, contemporary scholars have difficulty verifying his conclusions. Werner was also interested in documenting and investigating aspects of the *Ashkenazic liturgical music history (e.g., his *A Voice still Heard,* 1976).
Bibl: P. Jeffery, "Werner's *Sacred Bridge,* vol. 2," *Jewish Quarterly Review* 77 (1987) 283–98. MLK

Wesley, Charles (*b* Epworth 1707; *d* 1788 London). Anglican priest and poet. He was part of the "holy club" at Oxford which evolved into Methodism, though he always considered himself part of the Church of England. With his brother

*John, he shared a ministry of itinerant preaching and teaching. Charles wrote over 6,000 *hymns following his evangelical conversion in 1738. His first collection, *Hymns and Sacred Poems* (1739), contains the original form of "Hark! The herald angels sing."
Bibl: "Charles Wesley," in *Companion to The United Methodist Hymnal*, ed. C. Young (Nashville, 1993) 852–4.   CAD

Wesley, John (*b* Epworth 1703; *d* London 1791). Anglican priest, founder of the Methodist movement. While not as great a poet as his brother C. *Wesley, John did compile and publish *hymn collections which contributed to the development of strong congregational singing within Methodism.   CAD

Wesley, Samuel. (1) (*b* Bristol 1766; *d* London 1837). Composer, the nephew of C. and J. *Wesley, and an outstanding organist of his day. He championed the music of J. S. *Bach. He composed *motets, *masses, *services, *anthems and *psalm-tunes.
(2) (*b* London 1810; *d* Gloucester 1876). Organist, composer and the illegitimate son of (1). He served as organist at Hereford (1832–35), Exeter (1835–41), Winchester (1849–65) and Gloucester (from 1865) Cathedrals. He composed anthems, services and *hymns.   JLB

Westendorf, Omer (*b* Cincinnati 1916; *d* there 1998). Publisher, composer and church musician. He served as organist and choirmaster at St. Bonaventure in Cincinnati. The founder (1950) and president of World Library of Sacred Music, he published *People's Mass Book* (1964, 1971), the first vernacular

RC *hymnal for the *Vatican II *liturgy. He also wrote many popular *hymn texts, including "You satisfy the hungry heart."   FJM

Westermeyer, Paul (*b* Cincinnati 1940). Educator, organist and church musician. Awarded the Ph.D. in theology from the University of Chicago, he is professor of church music at Luther Seminary (St. Paul). He has served as the chaplain of the *AGO (1991–98) and president of the *Hymn Society. He has produced many publications on worship music including *Te Deum: the Church and Music* (1998).   JFM

Western Wynde Mass. The title of 3 Tudor *masses (by *Taverner, *Sheppard and *Tye). They share a common *cantus firmus, thought to be derived from the love song, "Westron wynde, when wyll thow blow."   AJL

Westminster Choir College. Founded 1926 by *Williamson as the Westminster Choir School in Dayton OH; the school operated in Ithaca from 1929–36, then moved to Princeton in 1936. It became Westminster Choir College in 1939 and merged with Rider College (now University) in 1992. Though broader in scope than when founded, Westminster continues its mission of training ministers of music for service in the churches.   RAL

Westminster Directory. See *Directory for the Public Worship of God.

Weyman, Gloria (*b* Cincinnati 1929). A pioneer in liturgical *dance, author and choreographer. She has coauthored works with *Deiss on liturgical dance, and founded the *International Liturgical Dance Association.   MAK

Whalum, Wendell Phillips (*b* Memphis 1932; *d* Atlanta 1987). Conductor, educator and composer. Professor of music at Morehouse, he also founded and conducted the Atlanta University Center Community *chorus, and prepared choruses for performances with the Atlanta Symphony. Whalum also published choral compositions and arrangements. MWC

Whirling Dervish. A member of the Islamic Sufi order called Mawlaw or Mevlevi, founded in 1273 by followers of the Persian mystic and poet Jalal ad-Din Muhammad Din ar-Rumi. His followers are noted for a ritual dance of cosmic symbolism in which they spin around seeking ecstatic experiences. MAK

White, Ernest Franklin (*b* London ON 1901; *d* Fairfield CT 1980). Organist and music director at the Church of St. Mary the Virgin in New York (1937–62). A student of *Willan, he became tonal director for M. P. *Möller. He is known for editions of early *organ and choral music; among his recordings was the first issued of *Messiaen's *La *Nativité du Seigneur.* PAB

White spiritual. See *spiritual.

Whittier, John Greenleaf (*b* Haverhill MA 1807; *d* Hampton Fall NH 1892). Quaker poet, whose poems have been shaped by others into *c* 30 *hymns, e.g., "Dear Lord and Father of Mankind" (from his poem, "The Brewing of Soma"). RJS

Whyte, Robert (*b c* 1535; *d* London 1574). Composer. His finest works (including 4 settings of *Christe, qui lux es* and 2 sets of *lamentations), all in Latin, rank with the best of *Tudor *polyphony. AJL

Wicks family. *Organ builders. Brothers Louis J. (1869–1936), Adolf (1873–1945) and John F. (1881–1948) were Swiss watchmakers and cabinetmakers. They established the Wicks Organ Company in Highland IL (1906), which has built over 6,200 *instruments. JWK

Widor, Charles-Marie (Jean Albert) (*b* Lyons 1844; *d* Paris 1937). Organist and composer. He studied in Brussels. He served as organist at St. Sulpice in Paris (1870–1934), and succeeded *Franck as professor of *organ at the Paris Conservatory (from 1890; composition professor from 1896) where *Vierne, Dupré and *Schweitzer were among his students. Widor wrote a treatise on orchestration and composed for various media including opera. He is most remembered for brilliant organ music, especially the 10 organ symphonies which are milestones in organ literature. FJM

Wie schön leuchtet [German]. "'How lovely shines' (the morning star)." *Chorale for Epiphany; sometimes called the queen of chorales. Text and music are by *Nicolai, and were first published in his *Frewden-Spiegel dess ewigen Lebens* (1599). PHW

Willaert, Adrian (*b* Bruges? *c* 1490; *d* Venice 1562). Composer. He served as *maestro di cappella* at St. Mark's in Venice (1527–62). Willaert was the most prominent composer of *masses, *motets and *chansons* in the generation after *Josquin. AJL

Willan, (James) Healey (*b* 1880 Balham, England; *d* Toronto 1968). Composer and church musician. He was choirmaster and organist at the Anglo-Catholic St. Mary Magdalene church in Toronto where he included *Gregorian chant and *Renaissance *motets in the worship. Willan taught at Toronto Conservatory (1913–37) and University (1937–50). He wrote over 600 works for *choir, *organ and other *instruments. In 1956 he received the Lambeth Doctorate from Queen Elizabeth. CAD

Willcock, Christopher (*b* Sydney 1947). Composer, educator and Jesuit priest. He studied theory and composition at the University of Sydney, then completed a joint doctorate in theology from Paris' Institut Catholique and Sorbonne. He is professor at Melbourne's United Faculty of Theology. Willcock's liturgical compositions include *psalms, *eucharistic prayers, *hymns and *anthems; he has also written works for harpsichord, orchestra and other *instruments. EBF

Williams, David McKinley (*b* Carnarvonshire Wales 1887; *d* Oakland CA 1978). Organist, teacher and composer. He served as music director at New York's St. Bartholomew's Church (1920–46) and chaired the *organ department at Juilliard. RJB

Williams, Ralph Vaughan. See *Vaughan Williams, Ralph.

Williamson, John Finley (*b* Canton, OH 1887; *d* Toledo 1964). Church musician, conductor, music educator and founder of the *Westminster Choir College. Williamson also edited choral music for the church. RAL

Willis, Henry (*b* London 1821; *d* there 1901). Leading English *organ builder, influenced by *Cavaillé-Coll and Barker. He built over 2,000 organs, including those at St. Paul's in London and Canterbury Cathedral. Strong choruses, clarity of flue stops and pedal division, brilliant reeds and excellent workmanship are hallmarks of his work. RDH

Winkworth, Catherine (*b* London 1827; *d* Monnetier, Savoy 1878). *Hymn translator. At 18 she went to Dresden where she became fluent in German. About 10 years later she began translating German hymns into English, successively published in *Lyra Germanica* (1855), *Lyra Germanica: Second Series* (1858), *The Chorale Book for England* (1863) and *Christian Singers of Germany* (1869). In all she translated *c* 400 hymns into English, many of which still grace modern *hymnals (especially US Lutheran hymnals) including "Now thank we all our God."

Bibl: R. Leaver, *Catherine Winkworth* (St. Louis, 1978). RAL

Winter, Peter (von) (*b* Mannheim 1754; *d* Munich 1825). Composer. He studied with *Vogler. In 1798 he became Munich's court *Kapellmeister* (1798). He wrote over 40 ballets and operas; his *sacred music included *motets, *psalms, *hymns, *responsories and 26 *masses. JLB

Wipo of Burgundy (*b* Solothurn? *c* 955; *d c* 1050). Poet and priest who served as chaplain to Emperors Conrad II (*d* 1039) and Henry III (*d* 1056). The authorship of the *Easter *sequence, *Victimae*

paschali laudes, is ordinarily attributed to him, although there is no proof for this attribution. VAL

Wiregrass. Black *shape-note singing from *The Colored Sacred Harp* (1934) by J. Jackson, used primarily in southeastern Alabama. RJS

Women singers. Women played a central role in the music of many ancient cults. The Hebrew Bible portrays Miriam leading women in song after fleeing Egypt (Ex 15.20-21), and 3 daughters of Heman participating in First *Temple music (1 Chr 25:6). Philo (*d* 50 CE) testifies that women sang in the worship of the Therapeutae communities. The Hebrew Bible, however, increasingly erases women from musical roles in worship. Rabbis often considered the singing of women unacceptable and dangerous.

Early testimony about Christian worship suggests that women sang in worship. Later evidence shows that they formed *choirs under *Ephraim and sang *psalms in the *divine office. By the 4th century CE, there are prohibitions against women singing in church (often replaced by boys or male falsettos). Through the *Middle Ages and *Renaissance, women's singing in Christian worship was confined to convents, encouraged by leaders like *Hildegard of Bingen. Choirs of nuns, particularly in Italy and France, drew admiring crowds

The increase in congregational singing during the *Reformation included women. They performed as soloists in *oratorios as early as 1716. Participation in choirs followed gradually as women participated in *singing schools, community *choruses and oratorio choirs. RC decrees excluded women from the choir into the 20th century (see *Tra le sollecitudini*).

In the 1900s, the ordination of women and their acceptance as liturgical leaders encouraged women's participation and leadership in singing. Reformed Judaism ordained its first women *cantor in 1976.

Bibl: J. Quasten, "Liturgical Singing of Women," in his *Music and Worship in Pagan and Christian Antiquity* (Washington DC, 1983) 75–87; I. Heskes, "Miriam's Sisters: Jewish Women and Liturgical Music" *Notes* 48 (1992) 1193–1211; M. Ericson, *Women and Music* (New York, 1996). RKW

Work family. Three generations of composers, arrangers, editors and leaders of African American music.

(1) **John W. Work, Sr.** (places and dates of his birth and death are unknown). Apparently he was associated with the *Fisk Jubilee Singers and directed the *choir of Nelson Merry's Church (now First Baptist Church) in Nashville.

(2) **John Wesley Work** (*b* Nashville 1872; *d* there 1925). He was educated at Fisk University, where he eventually chaired the History and Latin departments, and directed the Jubilee Singers and the Fisk University Jubilee Quartette. A leader in the preservation, study and performance of African American *spirituals, he and his brother Frederick Jerome published collections of slave songs and spirituals (e.g., *New Jubilee Songs as Sung by the Fisk Jubilee Singers,* 1901); he also published the first serious study of African American music by an African American author, *Folk Songs of the American Negro* (1907; apparently begun by his father).

(3) **Frederick Jerome Work** (*b* Nashville 1879; *d* Bordentown NJ 1942). Composer and conductor. He was educated at Fisk University, Columbia University and Temple College. He taught music at Bordentown Manual Training School (NJ) and served as organist-choirmaster in several New York City churches. He compiled *New Jubilee Songs* with his brother *John.

(4) **John Wesley Work III** (*b* Tullahoma TN 1901; *d* Nashville 1967). Eldest son of John Wesley *Work II, he studied at Fisk, Yale and Columbia Universities. He directed the Fisk Jubilee Singers and the Fisk University Men's Glee Club. A prolific arranger of African American spirituals, he also authored *American Negro Songs and Spirituals* (1940). His address to the International Hymnological Conference ("The Negro Spiritual," New York City, 1961), continued his father's lifelong effort by debunking G. P. *Jackson's claim (in *White Spirituals in the Southern Uplands,* 1933) that Negro spirituals are derived from white spirituals and *gospel songs.   CRY

Wren, Brian (*b* Romford, Essex 1936). *Hymn writer, author and minister of the United Reform Church (England). He was awarded a D. Phil. from Oxford (1968). Since 1983 he has followed a freelance ministry focused on issues of worship, *hymnody and language; he is a permanent resident of the US. Over 150 of his hymns have been published by Hope Publishing in various collections (1983, 1986, 1989, 1995). In 1989 he authored *What Language shall I borrow?—God-talk in Worship* (1989). EBF

Wren, Christopher (*b* East Knoyle, Wiltshire 1632; *d* London 1723). The greatest English architect of his day. He designed many churches that were rebuilt after London's Great Fire (1666), including St. Paul's Cathedral. Audibility was an important goal for Wren; he noted that it was enough for RCs to "hear the murmur of the Mass and see the elevation . . . [but our churches] are to be fitted for Auditories."   MEC

Y

Ya'aleh veyavo <*Ya'aleh v'yavo*> [Hebrew]. "May there rise and come." A prayer added toward the end of the *Amidah* on *Rosh Chodesh, the *Three Festivals and *High Holidays. It praises God and asks for deliverance and happiness, kindness and mercy, life and peace. MLK

Yad [Hebrew]. "Hand." The pointer used in Jewish worship when *cantillating the Torah scroll so as not to touch the parchment with hand or finger. It is usually made out of silver and used as an adornment to decorate the Torah scroll. ISK

Yale Institute of Sacred Music. A unit of instruction and research for church musicians and others which links the resources of the Yale's School of Music and Divinity School. A reconstitution and continuation of the *Union Seminary's School of Sacred Music, it began in 1973 when R. *Baker and R. French came to Yale from Union. PHW

Yamim Noraim [Hebrew]. "Days of Awe." A term which refers both to *Rosh Hashanah* and *Yom Kippur* as well as the entire 10-day period (the "10 days of repentance") between and including these 2 holidays. SJW

Year, liturgical. The annual cycle of feasts and seasons that shapes the worship, customs, music and ritual practices of a faith community. The basic unit of the liturgical year in Judaism and Christianity is the week, with *Sabbath central for Judaism and Sunday central for Christianity.

The Jewish calendar encompasses biblical and post-biblical festivals. The former includes the *Three Festivals (*Pesach, *Shavuot and *Sukkot), the *High Holidays (*Rosh Hashanah and *Yom Kippur), the 8-day festival following the 7 days of *Sukkot (*Shemini Atseret) and the monthly celebration of the new moon (*Rosh Chodesh). The most important post-biblical festivals are *Chanukkah and *Purim. *Tisha B'Av is a widely observed fast day commemorating various calamities which fell on the ninth of the month of *Av*.

In Christianity, the year can be divided into a *temporale* cycle (also called seasonal cycle or proper of the time) and *sanctorale* cycle. The former, which is broadly based on the life of Christ, is organized around 2 major feasts and their surrounding seasons: *Easter (the more important) and *Christmas. The sanctoral cycle, which is not observed by all Christians, celebrates holy women and men whom particular churches deem worthy of remembrance.

The Christian liturgical year begins with *Advent, which leads to Christmas and Epiphany (Theophany in E). *Candlemas (February 2, now called the feast of the Presentation of the Lord) has sometimes been identified as the end of the Christmas season; for RCs the Christmas season officially ends with the feast of the Baptism of the Lord. After a variable number of weeks known as Ordinary Time or Time of the Year, in the W *Lent begins with *Ash Wednesday. The last week of Lent is *Holy Week, culminating in the *Triduum (Holy or Maundy Thursday, Good Friday, Holy Saturday and Easter Sunday). In the E the Great Fast or Great Lent begins the Monday before the W Ash Wednesday and ends before Holy Week, which is not considered part of Lent. The Easter season lasts for 50 days, during which Ascension occurs. The season ends with *Pentecost, followed by a resumption of Ordinary Time.

The liturgical year has significantly influenced worship music in a number of ways. Certain feasts (e.g., *Yom Kippur*) have inspired specific compositions. Sometimes various types of music become characteristic of a liturgical season (e.g., *carols at Christmas). Occasionally the type of music and its performance is strictly regulated according to the feast or season (e.g., in me-

dieval Christianity the *organ and *bells were silenced during Lent).

Bibl: A. Adam, *The Liturgical Year* (Collegeville: Liturgical Press, 1981); M. Strassfeld, *The Jewish Holidays* (New York, 1985); T. Talley, "Calendar, Liturgical," in *The New Dictionary of Sacramental Worship,* ed. P. Fink (Collegeville, 1990) 150–63.   EBF

Yedid nefesh [Hebrew]. "Beloved soul." An acrostic poem in the tradition of the *Kabbalah* by Eleazar Azikri of Safed (*d* 1600). It is primarily sung at the start of *Kabbalat Shabbat* and during the last meal of the *Sabbath *(Seudah shelishit).* The text is sensual and romantic, depicting the intimate reuniting on the Sabbath of God and humankind as lovers.   BES

Yehi ratson [Hebrew]. "May it be your will." The *incipit* of various Jewish liturgical passages including *Birkat hachodesh* (see *Rosh Chodesh). It also serves as an introduction to passages in *Birkat hashachar* (see *shacharit).   MLK

Yekum purkan [Hebrew]. "May salvation arise." (1) A prayer that immediately follows the *haftorah* reading on the *Sabbath, praising those who uphold the Torah through teaching, study and dedication to following its precepts. Two paragraphs with this *incipit* are recited, 1 after the other: the first for individuals and the other for the congregation.

(2) A *Jewish prayer mode used to *chant the prayer of the same name. It is considered a variant of *Adonai malach.* MLK

Yigdal [Hebrew]. "May God be magnified." A metrical, rhyming *hymn dating from the 14th century, attributed to Rabbi Daniel ben Judah of Rome. The text, based on *Maimonides' 13 Articles of Faith, is sung at the beginning of daily *shacharit; it also may be said at the conclusion of *Sabbath and *High Holiday *ma'ariv. Its various musical settings reflect the text's optimism (praising God and the promise of the messianic age). Many composers have set the text for congregational singing, e.g., M. Lyon and the E *Ashkenazic melody notated by F. L. Cohen (now traditional at the end of the *Rosh Hashanah *ma'ariv). In *Sephardic communities many melodies for Yigdal originated as *folk songs or military marches. BES

Yishtabach [Hebrew]. "May his name be blessed." A *benediction that concludes *Pesukei dezimra in daily, *Sabbath and festival *shacharit. On weekdays it is chanted in *ahavah rabbah *mode; on Sabbath and festivals, in the *magein avot mode. On *Yamim Noraim motifs associated with the holiday are utilized when chanting it.   IAG

Yismach Moshe [Hebrew]. "Moses rejoiced." The *incipit of a prayer that alludes to Moses receiving the Ten Commandments in which the commandment to observe the *Sabbath is given. This prayer is inserted in the *cantor's repetition of the *Amidah after the *Kedusha on the Sabbath; it is recited in *ahavah rabbah *mode.   IAG

Yismechu [Hebrew]. "They shall rejoice." A liturgical text in the *musaf for *Sabbaths and festivals. The neo-*Hassidic setting of this text by G. Hedaya is widely known.   BES

Yizkor [Hebrew]. "Remember." The *incipit of the first in a series of prayers that together comprise a memorial *service for the dead. This service is traditionally recited before *musaf on *Yom Kippur, *Shemini atzeret, the last day of *Pesach and the second day of *Shavuot. During the recitation of these prayers it is customary to mention the names of the deceased, and to promise to donate to charity in their memory. In closing the prayer, the leader ordinarily recites *El maleh rachamim for all the dead, including those remembered by the local congregation, victims of the Holocaust and all Jewish martyrs.   IAG

Yom Kippur [Hebrew]. "Day of atonement." The holiest day of the Jewish liturgical *year, which occurs on the tenth of the Hebrew month of Tishri. It is also the tenth and climactic day of the 10 days of penitence that begin on *Rosh Hashanah and together constitute the *High Holidays. A day of confession, repentance and prayers for forgiveness of sins committed during the previous year, it is observed by fasting from the previous evening (*Kol Nidre) until sundown of the next day.

*Ma'ariv begins with the recitation of Kol Nidre; after the regular ma'ariv there follow several well-known *piyyutim and *selichot including *Vidui. *Shacharit and *musaf are liturgically similar to those on Rosh Hashanah except selichot and Vidui are recited. During musaf there is no Malchuyot-Zichronot-*shofarot section after the Great *Aleinu; instead the *service continues with the *Avodah depicting the rites of expiation on this day as observed in the Jerusalem Temple. This is followed by the martyrology describing the murder of the 10 sages of

Israel at the hands of the Romans. *Minchah* is highlighted by a special *haftorah* from the Book of Jonah. The concluding service is the *ne'ilah,* climaxing in the affirmation of faith by reciting the *Shema* (once), *Baruch shem* ("Praised be the name," 3 times) and *Adonai hu Haelohim* ("The Eternal is the true God," 7 times). Sounding the *shofar* concludes *Yom Kippur.*

Like *Rosh Hashanah,* various *Jewish prayer modes pervade the different services, as well as leit motifs and *Misinnai* tunes.   IAG

Yotser <*Yotzer*> [Hebrew]. "Create." (1) The first of 2 *benedictions in *shacharit* immediately preceding the *Shema,* praising God as the creator especially of light and darkness.

(2) The name (sometimes appearing in the pl., *yotserot*) given to various *piyyutim* inserted into the *Shema* during *shacharit* of festivals.   DMR

Young, Carlton R. (*b* Hamilton OH 1926). Teacher, editor and composer. He studied at Cincinnati College-Conservatory of Music, Boston University and Union Theological Seminary, later serving on the faculties of Southern Methodist University, Scarritt College and Emory University. He edited *The Methodist Hymnal* (1966) and *The United Methodist Hymnal* (1989). Among his *c* 150 published works for worship are *anthems, instrumental *preludes and *intonations, and *hymn tunes.   EBF

Ypakoi [Slavonic]. See *hypakoe.*

Z

Zachow <Zachau>, **Friedrich Wilhelm** (*b* Leipzig 1663; *d* Halle 1712). Organist, composer and teacher who counted *Handel among his students. Zachow worked in Eilenburg. He then became organist at Marienkirche in Halle (from 1684) where he wrote over 40 *chorale-based *organ works, *masses and *c* 100 *cantatas.   MPB

Zarlino, Gioseffo (*b* Chioggia 1517; *d* Venice, 1590). Theorist and composer. He held various church positions before becoming *maestro di cappella* at St. Mark's in Venice (from 1565). He is well-known for his work *Le istitutioni harmoniche* (1558), a treatise in 4 books that includes rules of *counterpoint, intonation, treatment of text and the general excellence of music. Zarlino credits *Willaert with ushering in a new golden age of emotional expression in music, where the composer's main concern is the beauty of contrapuntal writing. He states, "It is agreeable to the almighty God that his infinite power, wisdom, and goodness be magnified and manifested to [all] through *hymns accompanied by gracious and sweet accents."   DCI

Zelenka, Jan <Johann> **Dismas** (*b* Lounovice 1679; *d* Dresden 1745). Composer. He was educated in Prague and did further study with *Fux and *Lotti. Zelenka worked in Dresden (from 1719) and was named court church composer there (1735). He wrote over 20 *masses, 3 *oratorios, 2 *Magnificat*s, *psalms and various instrumental works.   JLB

Zelter, Carl Friedrich (*b* Berlin 1758; *d* there 1832). Conductor, editor, composer and teacher who counted F. *Mendelssohn among his students. In 1800 he assumed the leadership of the Berlin *Singakademie* where he championed the performance of old *church music, including collaboration with F. Mendelssohn for the 1829 revival of J. S. *Bach's *St. Matthew Passion.*   MPB

Zemirot [Hebrew]. "Songs." Traditional Jewish table songs sung during meals on the *Sabbath, emphasizing that singing adds to the joy of Sabbath. They are usually sung on Friday night at the first Sabbath meal, on Saturday during the daytime meal and again at the last Sabbath meal *(Seudah shelishit)*. Each of these meals has its own set of *zemirot* specific to each time, although some may overlap. *Zemirot* are also sung at the *Melaveh malkah* at the conclusion of the Sabbath on Saturday evening.   ISK

Zichronot. See *shofar.

Znamenny chant [Slavonic]. "Signed chant." A system for annotating music in the Slavonic liturgical tradition, dating from the 11th century. Note values were designated by various, often elaborate, signs. Znamenny chant eventually became 1 musical system among others, and reached a complexity that needed reform. In the 17th century the patriarch of Moscow, Patriarch Nicon (*d* 1658), attempted to conform the Slavonic *liturgy to Greek models. Znamenny chant survived the reform, but in a greatly simplified form. By the 18th century, though the melodies remained, W notation was introduced. Znamenny chant still survives in some of the Slavonic *plainchant melodies.

Bibl: J. Roccasalvo, "The Znamenny Chant," *MQ* 74 (1990) 217–41.   DMP

Zochreinu [Hebrew]. "Remember us." (1) *Zochreinu l'chayim* ("Remember us for life"), a prayer inserted in the middle of the *Avot* section of the *Amidah* during the 10 days of penitence between *Rosh Hashanah* and *Yom Kippur;*

often set for choral or congregational singing.

(2) *Zochreinu b'zikaron tov* ("Remember us with a good remembrance"), the *incipit of the final paragraph of the *Zichronot* section of *Rosh Hashanah* *musaf,* often set as a cantorial solo or choral composition.   IAG

Zwingli, Ulrich (*b* Wildhaus 1484; *d* Kappel 1531). Reformer and preacher, the first in the *Reformed tradition. He studied at Basel, Berne and Vienna. While a RC priest at Zurich he abandoned the *lectionary and, beginning with Matthew, preached through the NT. A Swiss patriot, he died at the Battle of Kappel. Zwingli believed Christ's substance was not received in the *Lord's Supper; he abandoned the *mass, created a preaching service for 48 Sundays of the year and on the other 4 Sundays kept the Lord's Supper as a reminder of grace. Under his direction churches were whitewashed, relics and images removed and *organs closed up. The best musician of the reformers, Zwingli loved music but believed that singing in worship was not commanded in Scripture. According to Zwingli, the essence of worship was praying to God in secret. Realizing public worship was necessary, he solved the dilemma by the silence of the people who were "to have an ear for the [spoken] Word of God alone."

Bibl: B. Thompson, *Liturgies of the Western Church* (Cleveland, 1961) 141–56; C. Garside, *Zwingli and the Arts* (New Haven, 1966).   PHW